Chronicle
of the
CINEMA

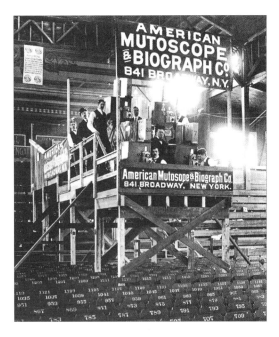

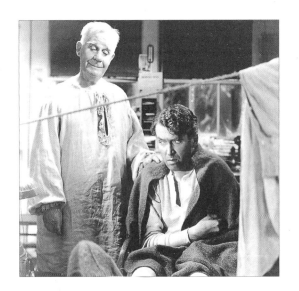

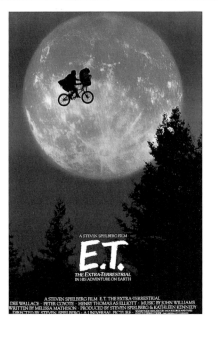

Chronicle
of the
CINEMA

DORLING KINDERSLEY

LONDON • NEW YORK • SYDNEY • MOSCOW

A DORLING KINDERSLEY BOOK

Production by Catherine Legrand

Editor in chief Robyn Karney
Associate editor Joel W. Finler
Contributors Ronald Bergan, Josephine Carter, Robin Cross,
Angie Errigo, Joel W. Finler, Clive Hirschhorn, Robyn Karney
Editorial assistant Ingrid Shohet
Editorial staff Josephine Carter, Nadège Guy, David Oppedisano,
Irina Zarb
Index Irina Zarb
Chief researcher David Oppedisano
Picture research Anne-Marie Ehrlich *(E.T. Archives, London)*,
Richard Allen *(USA)*, Simon Danger *(France)*
Designer Henri Marganne
E.D.P. Catherine Balouet
Software engineer Dominique Klutz

Editorial and design updated in 1997 by
Edel Brosnan, Sophy Friend and Colin Hawes,
Brown Packaging Books Ltd,
Bradley's Close, 74/77 White Lion Street,
London N1 9PF

First published in 1995 by Dorling Kindersley Limited,
9 Henrietta St, London WC2E 8PS

Visit us on the World Wide Web at http://www.dk.com

© Chronik Verlag
im Bertelsmann Lexikon Verlag GmbH
Gutersloh/Munchen, 1995

ISBN 0 7513 3018 3

Printed in Belgium by Brepols

Acknowledgments

Everybody who has contributed to this monumental project, not least
my writers, researchers and editorial assistants, deserves special thanks
for working under pressure and beyond the call of duty. Without the
cooperation and generosity of various film companies, agents
and public relations personnel, the task could not have been
accomplished. It is impossible to list the many individuals concerned,
but I would like to record my appreciation of the efforts of the
wonderful staff at the Kobal Collection and the British Film Institute
Stills Library, as well as those at Artificial Eye, CIBY Sales,
Consolidated Pictures, Electric Pictures, Entertainment
Film Distributors, ICA Projects, MacDonald and Rutter, Mainline
Pictures and Metro Tartan Pictures. A special mention is due to Sue
Hockey, to the British Film Institute Reference Library — particularly
Bob Phillips, Erinna Laffey, Luke McKernan, David Sharp and Olwen
Terris; to Philip Rose and Lucy Darwin at Columbia Pictures, and
Monda Meachin at Walt Disney. To Richard Allen in New Jersey, for
his immense hard work, enthusiasm and generosity in making
the Carson Collection of posters available. To Jim Watters in New
York, Jean-Louis Capitaine and Toby Rose in Paris, Jonathon Romney,
Howard Mandelbaum and his staff at Photofest, New York, the
same applies.
I must record my admiration of and gratitude to Catherine Legrand for
masterminding the assembly of my pages with taste and skill.

ROBYN KARNEY, 1995 (first edition)

Contents

BIRTH OF AN INDUSTRY
1900 to 1919
Page 78

MOVIES FIND A VOICE
1930 to 1939
Page 212

WAR AND AFTER
1940 to 1949
Page 306

THE SILENT ERA
1920 to 1929
Page 142

THE SWING OF THE PENDULUM
1950 to 1959
Page 394

THE NEW WAVE
1960 to 1969
Page 492

STRANGE BEDFELLOWS
1970 to 1979
Page 594

THE REAGAN YEARS
1980 to 1989
Page 694

Foreword

By Alexander Walker

This is a timely book. Cinema is 100 years old. It's the world's youngest, yet most influential entertainment and art form. Certainly, it is the most profitable ever invented: in the USA, the movie business ranks second only to the aeronautics industry. It is also the most controversial. Democrats as well as dictators regard movies with suspicion. They have been condemned, censored, suppressed and demonised. In addition, the blame for all society's ills has often been put squarely on the power of the moving image to seduce and, allegedly, corrupt. But when the worst has been said about them, and sometimes done to them, movies not only help us endure life, they even enhance it. Movies give us the myths we worship and the metaphors that simplify our existence. Stars' faces, fashions and life-styles assume an iconic hold over us on screen and off.

I could tell you more about a country's development — past and future — by watching its movies than I could by reading its statesmen's speeches. Television may be in everybody's home: but movies are in everyone's head, and they are vastly more influential in shaping our expectations of life. This is the social change you see as you turn the pages of this book. What makes this inventory so special is the emphasis it puts on the chronological connections that have shaped cinema. It arranges events in meaningful order. If there's one lesson to be learned, it is that cinema is an entertainment whose progress lies in the constant refinement of primitive emotions and techniques. If these raw emotions appear more sophisticated today, it's only because the technology that serves them has become so sophisticated.

Near panic was the emotion registered by the first filmgoers, for all their civilised veneer, who saw the train that the Lumière brothers had filmed apparently heading straight for them out of the screen at that historic premiere of the Cinematograph in Paris in 1895. But audiences soon discovered how enjoyable alarm could be in the cinema when mediated by suspense. Likewise, the first screen kiss to be seen in close-up shocked those accustomed to the public proprieties — and distancing perspective — of love scenes in the live theatre. But before long, they too were seeking hot tips from Rudolph Valentino on how to captivate a woman. And it wasn't long, either, before the dangers of big cities everywhere were rendered curiously exhilarating when presented on the screen. Thus, the basic pattern of cinema was established early and enduringly: as the first American film critic Pauline Kael said, it boiled down to "kiss, bang, bang," otherwise known as "sex and violence". The history of cinema, as many of this book's 3,000 illustrations show, is the story of the way that the inexhaustible demand for these staple commodities has been served down the decades and in all kinds of mutations, from the flagrantly erotic to the romantically escapist, from comic knockabout to sadistic overkill.

This book also illustrates how economics as well as emotions initiate change. The sensation of talking pictures, for instance, came along at the very moment the box-office was showing its first ominous dip as the novelty of silent pictures wore off. Inside three years — the fastest technological revolution in history — the movies were talking their heads off. Sound in turn ushered in a more realistic depiction of the world, if not exactly a truer one, and a more naturalistic style of acting. Hard times in 1930s America encouraged Hollywood to console the poor, the huddled masses, with upbeat musicals, escapist romances and screwball comedies that showed the way in which the movies could mediate between the haves and the have-nots and take the latter's minds off violence on the streets by offering them cheap and potent consolation in the comfort of picture palaces: in this way, movies can subvert revolutions as well as start them. CinemaScope (and all the letter-box formats) that suddenly appeared in the mid 1950s revolutionised aesthetics as well as reviving audiences, even though it was only intended as Hollywood's answer to the threat of television. And the busting of the Hollywood morality code in the late 1960s by movies like *Bonnie and Clyde,* which showed that although crime might still not pay in the end, it could be murderous fun along the way, began the current non-stop era of "anything goes" (or very nearly). The result is a contemporary cinema with the power to panic the moralists, bring out the censors, and summon the libertarians to man freedom barricades. What's more, it spills over out of the review columns into editorials that solemnly debate where we may all be headed, and conclude that movies like *Natural Born Killers* signify the end of "civilisation as we know it." Then along comes a *Four Weddings and a Funeral,* and suddenly the air is pure again.

Much of this *Chronicle* deals with Hollywood movies. That's inevitable, given the fascination that the American life-style, for good or ill or a bit of both, possesses for the rest of the world. But it is also a realistic acknowledgment of the muscle that Hollywood unsentimentally flexes at every foreign box-office its movies now colonise. Hollywood is America's overseas empire. This is another reason why this book is timely. For the truth is, we may be seeing the death of many a national cinema in countries where it's lost its economic basis, or its audiences, as Hollywood movies monopolise the screens and capture the young generations of Europe or the Far East, who have been suckled on television serials like *Dynasty* or blockbusters like *Jurassic Park.* The multitude of national cultures that the cinema once reflected is fighting a losing battle against the American take-over.

Soon, I fear, there will be only one cinema culture: Hollywood's. But for Hollywood, too, dangers lie ahead. The movie capital itself is undergoing change, far faster than maybe even it can control. New technologies are once more altering the balance of power in screen entertainment. In the future, there will still be films, but, as they say in that cliché beloved by the science fiction epics, they may not be films as we know them. "If Midas were a moviemaker out here," one of Hollywood's cynical young "instant moguls" told me recently, "he'd want everything he touched to turn into video." Movies are already mutating faster than you can watch them. The ever-shortening attention spans of audiences reared on pop videos and TV sound-bites means that films are cut to an impatient rhythm that's often hostile to any meditative rhythm of life. Box-office safety doesn't any longer lie in numbers — did it ever? — but in formula. Sequels are given priority over originals on the production roster. And while video games strive to achieve the look of movies, the plots of movies come to resemble video games: and who wins then, except the makers?

In such unsettled times, when we don't know what the future will bring, but have good reason to fear it won't favour creative people with the freedoms their predecessors pioneered, a book like this is more welcome than ever. It shows us the unbelievable diversity that cinema has achieved in little more than an average lifetime. It should also teach us (if it is not too late) to protect our cinematic heritage: there are plenty of forces around that would recycle it or junk it. *Chronicle of the Cinema* is a celebration: it would be a tragedy if it turned into a wake.

Alexander Walker has been the film critic for the London Evening Standard *since 1960, and is the author of more than 20 books on the cinema and filmmakers.*

The editorial team, l to r: Robin Cross, Angie Errigo, Robyn Karney, Joel W. Finler, David Oppedisano, Ronald Bergan, Clive Hirschhorn

Editor's Preface

Moving pictures, or movies, as we fondly call them, have been around for a very long time in one form or another. Indeed their origins can be traced to the first magic lantern and slide shows way back in the seventeenth century.

The cinema is, without a doubt, the major art form of the twentieth century. At its highest level of achievement it can be judged alongside great literature, great music and great painting, with filmmakers creating enduring masterpieces; at the lowest level it provokes disgust and encourages censorship.

Since the 1930s, with the coming of sound to the cinema, films have utilized an amalgam of all creative forms: words and music, light and colour, the drama of the theatre, the lure of adventure, the art of the actor, the animator. They have stretched the limits of the creative imagination, feeding our common need for escape into fantastical worlds.

The first fantastical worlds were created by Georges Méliès in France at the beginning of the century. The French Lumière brothers, and a dozen or so others in France, Germany, Britain and, to a lesser extent, the United States, were exploring technical possibilities as early as the 1890s, inventing cameras and projectors and screens that, crude though they may seem now, made it possible for Méliès and his successors to work the first movie magic.

The French were the major pioneers and the moving force behind the creation of the film industry as we know it today. They were soon joined, however, by the British, the Scandinavians, the Italians (who pioneered historical epics such as *Quo Vadis?*), the Russians, the Germans, the Indians and the Japanese and, of course, the Americans.

By the late 1920s, the Americans were beginning to lead the field: with the growth of Hollywood and the coming of the moguls and their studios, the development of sound and the birth of the American musical, the United States became, and has remained, the acknowledged leader in the field of popular film, exporting her products to the rest of the world. And with the films came the cult of the star personality, and the creation of styles and fashions inspired by these stars that have been slavishly copied by millions of men and women.

The history of the cinema is endlessly fascinating, and the films themselves are a record of our rapidly changing world. The movies have something for everyone — romance, comedy, thrills, adventure, horror, war, patriotism, dance, history, and the lure of the Old West. Films can delight or enchant; they can frighten, shock or appall. They transport us into fantasy worlds; they make us laugh and cry. They provide food for thought — educating and informing us — and teaching us about other cultures. Above all, though, a successful movie ENTERTAINS.

Literally thousands of books have been produced about the movies and the people who make them. Many are popular picture books with little to say; a number are comprehensive histories, or intellectual analyses — invaluable to the specialist, hard work for average fans.

Then, too, most books tend to deal in the films of only one country, thereby depriving us of any sense of a wider, richer world. And reference books are more often than not visually dull, while picture books are frequently short on facts.

With this book, in the format of the highly successful Chronicle series, we take a journey through one hundred years of cinema history and films, analysing events as they happen, in accessible journalistic style. *Chronicle of the Cinema* is, in fact, a lavishly illustrated and extended "newspaper", which aims both to inform and delight moviegoers and to provide a unique reference book for the buff or student. It is, we hope, a treasure trove into which you can dip at random, and find something fascinating on every page. While the major focus becomes the United States, in line with its premier place in the film industry, the reader will find entertaining and informative pieces about international cinema in every year.

ROBYN KARNEY

1894

New York, 5 February
Jean Acme LeRoy has organized the first projection of Thomas Edison's films with his Marvelous Cinematograph. The private session took place in the back room of the two Riley brothers' optics and magic lantern shop at 16 Beekman Street.

Paris, 14 May
Among those present at the Robert Houdin Theatre today were magicians Georges Méliès and Félicien Trewey, photographer Antoine Lumière and his assistant Clément-Maurice Gratioulet. The latter, who is more usually known as Clément Maurice, spoke at quite some length about the Kinetoscope, Edison's latest cinematic invention. Méliès and Lumière were particularly interested by the news.

Berlin, May
Max Skladanowsky has recorded a few scenes on film using his Bioskop.

Washington, 17 July
Senator Bradley has forbidden the projection of one of Edison's films made by W.K. Laurie Dickson in the West Orange studios. In the film, which is entitled *The Serpentine Dance*, the dancer Carmencita dares to show her undergarments. It is the first case of censorship in the moving picture industry.

France, 9 September
Charles Pathé has given a demonstration of the Edison-perfected phonograph at the Montéty fairground. He has just acquired the machine from the Werner brothers, Edison's agents in Paris. Pathé intends to take the machine, which is fitted with 12 acoustic tubes to allow 12 people to listen simultaneously, on a tour through France.

West Orange, 16 October
W.K. Laurie Dickson has used the Kinetograph to film an open air rodeo scene. This event was organized by Buffalo Bill's troupe of cowboys who happened to be in the region.

Paris, 22 October
Etienne Marey has projected a chronophotographic film for the Academy of Science. It shows pictures of a cat falling from a height of one-and-a-half metres. This gave rise to a polemic: the cat's fall was studied using Delaunay's calculations. As Alphonse Allais afterwards remarked: "Life at the Academy is never boring."

Paris, October
The Werner brothers have opened a Kinetoscope Parlor in their shop at 20 boulevard Poissonnière. Viewing tickets cost 25 cents. The machine itself sells for 6,000 francs.

London, October
The optician Robert William Paul has visited the Kinetoscope Parlor recently opened by the Greeks Georgiades and Tragedes Papastakyotenipoulos. He has decided to make and exploit the Kinetoscope.

Paris, 15 November
The German inventor Ottomar Anschütz has obtained a patent for his "stroboscopic projection procedure for images".

New York, 21 November
Herman Casler has invented the Mutoscope, a box for viewing a rotating reel of photographs.

Berlin, 25 November
Ottomar Anschütz has given a projection session with his Tachyscope. Derived from the Phenakistiscope, this machine has two lenses and can project 24 pictures.

Washington, 12 December
Charles Francis Jenkins has patented a camera with a rotating lens (a disc that has 14 lenses) and a mobile film, which will enable him to take approximately 215 images per second.

Paris, 14 December
The Lumière brothers have obtained a patent for a procedure which "synthesizes color by a rapid succession of monochrome images", using a type of Praxinoscope.

New York, 31 December
Burns have published the first book specifically about the techniques for taking moving pictures. The book, *History of the Kinetograph, Kinetoscope and Kineto Phonograph*, is written by Laurie Dickson and his daughter Antonia.

Paris, December
The editor Masson has published *le Mouvement* (*Movement*) by Etienne-Jules Marey, a synthesis of his research in chronophotography.

New York, December
Eugène Lauste, Jean Acme LeRoy's collaborator, has been hired by the brothers Otway and Grew Latham and their father, Major Woodville Latham, to turn the Kinetoscope into a projector.

Kinetoscope a success

New York, 7 November
First he gave us the Phonograph, and now he has come up with the Kinetoscope. Thomas Alva Edison's latest invention is all the rage, and not just in the States. In the main capital cities of the world, establishments called Kinetoscope Parlors built to showcase this machine are popping up like mushrooms. A constant stream of people arrives daily at the doors of these unusual places. Within the walls an even stranger sight greets the uninitiated visitor; dignified gentlemen, frequently elbow to elbow, solemnly await their turn to approach the coveted object – a very simple object to all outward appearances – a wooden case fitted with an eyepiece at easy viewing height. For the price of a small coin those interested can watch a short series of animated pictures mounted on an endless belt and lasting about a minute. Each Kinetoscope offers a completely different vision to the enthralled spectator. The subjects vary from fashionable dances, music-hall scenes, comic sketches and historical reconstructions to the highly popular boxing matches. The new Edison factories in West Orange are filming around the clock under the masterly supervision of Edison's young assistant William Kennedy Laurie Dickson to keep up with the exhibitors' demands for new material. A special film studio has been built for this purpose, nicknamed Black Maria by the employees due to its resemblance to a police lockup van. All the top stars of the moment are being filmed by Edison: Frederick Cody alias Buffalo Bill, Annie Oakley, Mae Lucas and the dancer Annabelle Whitford Moore. Some

The machine, with its endless strip.

One can buy this for $300.

of the films, such as the saucy *Fatima's Belly Dance*, are even shrouded with a hint of prurience; the censors insisted that the dancer cover the two "offensive parts" of her body.

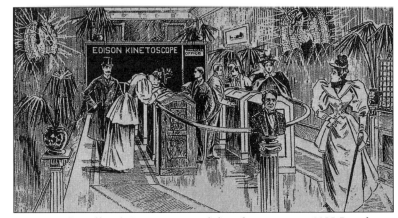
On 14 April, Raff and Gammon opened their first venue, at 1155 Broadway.

for the American inventor Thomas Alva Edison

Edison in his studio, as seen by his assistant W.K. Laurie Dickson.

loid film conceived by Eastman several years previously, had lateral perforations to ensure that the film moved smoothly on past the shutter. However, the quality of the picture obtained was not good enough to be projected on a screen, so Edison opted for the idea of individual viewing and arrived at the Kinetoscope. This machine's wooden exterior hid a fairly simple mechanism: a film approximately 17 metres in length attached to an endless belt which turned continuously, thanks to a dynamo. Right from the start the invention was a success, and the first Kinetoscope Parlor opened its doors on 14 April 1894, at 1155 Broadway in New York, with others soon following. For the spectator a whole new world of exciting images has now opened up – by simply looking through the eyepiece he can contemplate the world's most beautiful women or admire the prowess of the stars of the ring or music hall.

Edison's studio, affectionately called the Black Maria by his employees.

But how did the famous inventor of the microphone, the incandescent lamp and the Phonograph succeed in making animated pictures? The first research in this field took place in early 1887 in Edison's newly-founded Laboratorium situated in West Orange, New Jersey. It was an enormous structure teeming with activity, and inventions of all kinds were soon underway. Edison was already very taken with the idea of inventing a machine to produce moving pictures. He had in mind something that would be to the eye that which the Phonograph was to the ear, and he set up a special film laboratory to this end that is known as "Room 5". He gave his assistant Dickson free rein to develop the research. After a number of setbacks, the two men produced a prototype called the Kinetograph in 1889. This device, which used the flexible cellu-

A sneeze is registered for copyright

Washington, 9 January
The Edison laboratories are starting to produce their own films in readiness for the new projection equipment, which is soon to come on the market. One of the very first films, shot on 7 January and called *Edison Kinetoscope Record* *Of A Sneeze*, has just been lodged for copyright at the Library of Congress. In the film somebody named Fred Ott sneezes straight at the camera, to astonishingly realistic effect; the only thing missing is the sound. One almost wishes to call out, "Bless you!"

Boxing cats, an unexpected duo of actors for a Kinetoscope film.

1895

Paris, 1 January
Emile Reynaud is presenting two wonderful new illuminated pantomimes at the Grévin Museum, *A Dream Beside the Fire* and *Around a Hut*.

Paris, 14 January
Charles Pathé has opened a phonograph shop at 72 cours de Vincennes.

Paris, 13 February
The Lumière brothers, Auguste and Louis, have patented a machine "to film and view chronophotographic proofs." The machine comes fitted with a driving device, which was perfected in December, for rotating the negative film. The machine can also be used to record, develop and project films.

Paris, February
Charles Pathé has returned from London where he bought one of Robert William Paul's copies of the Edison Kinetoscope.

Lyon, 19 March
Louis Lumière has begun making his first film, *la Sortie des usines Lumière* (*Leaving the Lumière factory*), using the camera he patented last month.

Paris, 22 March
The Lumière brothers have held their first public film projection. They showed *la Sortie des usines Lumière* to a gathering at the National Society for Industrial Encouragement in rue de Rennes.

Washington, 25 March
Charles Francis Jenkins and Thomas Armat have formed a partnership to manufacture film projectors.

Paris, 30 March
The Lumière brothers have lodged a new addition to their registered patent N° 245032: a triangular cam-shaft to drive the film holder.

West Orange, 2 April
Laurie Dickson has left the West Orange laboratories after a difference of opinion with Edison.

Paris, 17 April
The Lumière brothers have held their second public projection. This time the film was shown at the Sorbonne for the Learned Society's National Conference.

New York, 21 April
Eugène Augustin Lauste has made the projector commissioned by the Latham brothers. He has called it the Pantoptikon.

New York, 20 May
The Latham brothers and Eugène Lauste have organized their first public projection with the Pantoptikon, now called the Eidoloscope.

Lyon, 10 June
The Lumière brothers showed eight films including *The Waterer Watered* and *Baby's Teatime* for the opening of the Photographic Society's Conference.

Lyon, 12 June
The Lumière brothers have projected 10 films for restaurant owners Berrier and Millet at their premises in Bellecour Square. One of the films showed the arrival of the members of the Photographic Society at the conference.

Paris, 11 July
Today marks the Lumières' fifth public projection, using a lamp designed by Alfred Molteni. The 500 guests who attended the session run by the French *Journal of Pure and Applied Science* were highly impressed by the films.

Paris, 12 August
The Photography Syndicate has now become Léon Gaumont and Co. It is a limited partnership in joint names, with its headquarters at 57 rue Saint-Roch. Léon Gaumont himself is the director of the new company.

Paris, 26 August
Charles Pathé and Henri Joly, who have been in partnership since 13 August, have lodged a patent for a chronophotographic machine. The camera will be used to make French films for the Edison Kinetoscope which Pathé intends to sell to fairground exhibitors.

Paris, 8 November
Henri Joly has perfected a new machine for Charles Pathé. The Photozootrope is a Kinetoscope with four lenses. It should bring fair exhibitors 36 francs per hour.

Paris, 16 November
On the occasion of the opening of Gabriel Lippman's lectures at the Sorbonne, the Lumière brothers held another projection session of their films.

Jersey City, 27 December
Laurie Dickson, Elias Koopman, Herman Casler and Harry Marvin have founded The American Mutoscope Company. The company has been set up to market the Mutoscope invented by Casler, who was formerly with Edison.

LeRoy improves on Edison's Kinetoscope

New York, 22 February
A hushed murmur of admiration rose from the audience at the Opera House as, before their very eyes, a fluttering dance of trembling images, produced by the Marvelous Cinematograph, filled the screen. Never before has such a wondrous event been seen in New York. The inventor of this incredible device is Jean Acme LeRoy, an American of French descent whose interest in the problems posed by animated pictures dates back to 1893; as early as that he tried converting an Edison Kinetoscope into a projector. His first public demonstration in 1894 was far from perfect: available images filed past in a jerky, irregular fashion. As a result, LeRoy decided to produce his own film material. He found a keen collaborator in Eugène-Augustin Lauste, and the two men soon came up with convincing results by reducing the speed to 20 images per second. He modeled his projector on the cam system developed by Frenchman Georges Demenÿ. There is a risk that Kinetoscope Parlors may be superseded by this novelty.

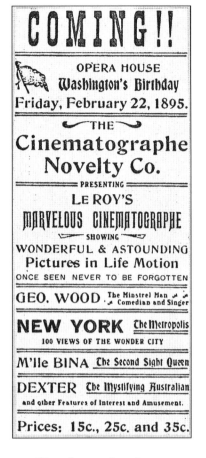

COMING!!
OPERA HOUSE
Washington's Birthday
Friday, February 22, 1895.
THE
**Cinematographe
Novelty Co.**
PRESENTING
LE ROY'S
MARVELOUS CINEMATOGRAPHE
SHOWING
**WONDERFUL & ASTOUNDING
Pictures in Life Motion**
ONCE SEEN NEVER TO BE FORGOTTEN

GEO. WOOD — The Minstrel Man
Comedian and Singer

NEW YORK — The Metropolis
100 VIEWS OF THE WONDER CITY

M'lle BINA — The Second Sight Queen

DEXTER — The Mystifying Australian
and other Features of Interest and Amusement.

Prices: 15c., 25c. and 35c.

Max Skladanowsky unveils the Bioskop

Berlin, 1 November
Today marked a crucial moment in the careers of two famous magic lantern operators, Max and Emil Skladanowsky. This morning Max applied for an inventor's patent in his name only for the Bioskop, his projection device for celluloid films with metal-reinforced perforations.

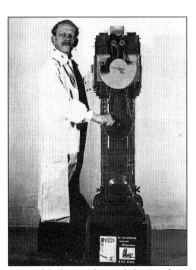
Max Skladanowsky and the Bioskop.

The Bioskop is designed to project two films simultaneously but with a slight discrepancy in the movements, thanks to a double objective fitted with a mobile disc. Max uses a chronophotograph he invented himself to film the scenes. This evening's session at the Wintergarten was the first time the public has paid to watch a show produced by the Bioskop. Included among the nine films projected were a sparring match between a kangaroo and a man named Delaware, *The Boxing Kangaroo*; a dance executed by Miss Ancion, *Dance Serpentine*; an *Italian Folk Dance*; and the brothers Tcherpanoff's *Kammarintsky Russian National Dance* to name but a few. The show is under contract to the Wintergarten until the end of November, and it appears to be set for a successful run judging by tonight's reaction. Apparently, the Parisian brothers Auguste and Louis Lumière, who have also been developing the animated picture business, were troubled by news of this unexpected competition.

The Lumières enter the Cinematograph market

Inventor Louis Lumière at age 31.

The first Lumière Cinematograph, manufactured by the engineer Carpentier.

License N° 245032 of 13 February.

Lyon, 20 December

The Lumière brothers are impatiently awaiting the arrival of their Lumière Cinematograph N° 1. The machine has just been sent off from Paris after undergoing two months of final adjustments by Jules Carpentier, the engineer contracted to develop a series of 25 of Lumière's machines. Negotiations took several months before an agreement was finally reached six months after their initial meeting on 22 March of this year. It was an important date for the Lumières as it marked Louis' very first public appearance in the capital, where he had agreed to speak in front of the Society For Industrial Advancement. The title of his lecture was "The Photography Industry," but Louis moved quickly and almost imperceptibly on to talk about the topic which had been up-permost in his mind for some time: the projection of animated pictures. Louis followed up his speech to the audience of 200 or so photographers, industrialists and researchers who had come to hear his ideas by showing a short film entitled *Leaving the Lumière Factory* (*Sortie des usines Lumière*), in which the dumbfounded gathering was able to watch the factory workers in action as they prepared to leave their workshops for the midday meal. This animated picture session, without precedent, left its mark on all those present, including the head of the Commercial Photography Syndicate Léon Gaumont. With the patent securely in hand, the inventors settled on the Cinematograph as a name for their projector – it seems they were totally unaware that the name had already been used in 1893 by one Léon Bouly. The brothers even went so far as to oppose their father who, influenced by a friend and no doubt Latinist, wanted to call the machine Domitor, in his opinion an easier name to protect legally than one so readily accessible, etymologically speaking. But, regardless, Auguste and Louis stood firm: it would be the Cinematograph.

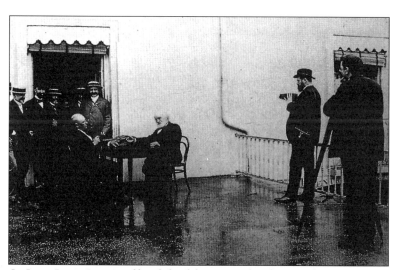

In June, Louis Lumière filmed the delegates at the photography congress.

*With **Leaving the Lumière Factory**, the Cinematograph came into being.*

On 28 December, in Paris, the Cinematograph

Paris, 28 December

Antoine Lumière, the industrial photographer from Lyon, has just opened a new show in the Indian Exhibition at the Grand Café at 14 boulevard des Capucines. The press and public were invited to attend tonight's inauguration. Antoine, who has every confidence in Louis' invention, obtained a year's lease on a basement room. However, the owner of the property Mr. Volpini has so little confidence in the undertaking that he refused an offer of 20 percent of the takings, preferring a fixed figure of 30 francs a day. A man has been standing outside the building all day handing out programs to passers-by. Unfortunately, today's cold weather prevented people from stopping, and most rushed past the entry of the Exhibition to the Grand Café next door, with only a distracted glance at the notice "Lumière's Cinematograph – Entry Fr 1." As a result only 33 tickets were sold for the first show, but luckily there were several invited guests. On arrival, spectators are shown to the lavish basement hall with its oriental decor, at the far end of which two turnstiles protect the entrance to the Exhibition. Here, Clément Maurice, a photographer hired by Antoine Lumière for the occasion, welcomes the audiences. To the right of the entrance there is a compressed air ventilator.

The room seats 100 people, and as soon as the audience has settled in comfortably, the lights go out. A hushed silence falls as the white backdrop lights up with a photo-

The historic showing was held in the Indian Salon, in the basement of the Grand Café. A seat costs one franc.

graphic projection depicting the doors of the Lumière factory in Lyon. At the first showing, a disappointed murmur went up: "Why, it's only the old magic lantern!" Then, without warning, the picture started to move. The factory doors were flung open letting out a stream of workers, dogs ran hither and thither, a carriage rolled by... Everything moved; it was an astonishing vision of reality – of life caught in full swing. Confronted for the first time

by these animated pictures, the audiences must have wondered if they were hallucinating. Ten different eventful scenes followed, each reel roughly 17 metres in length. *In The Photographical Congress Arrives in Lyon*, one recognized the inventor of the shoulder-held movie camera, Jules Janssen. *Cordeliers' Square in Lyon* was so realistic that a young woman in the audience leaped to her feet on seeing a horse-cab rushing toward her. *Baby's Dinner* shows

Auguste Lumière and his wife trying vainly to get their baby to eat his gruel. In the background trees sway gently in the wind, leaving the audience with the impression they can hear the rustling of the leaves. *The Sea* appears calm at first then slowly builds up. Towering waves come crashing around a young man who is swimming close to the shore. However, judging by the general hilarity, *The Waterer Watered* was no doubt the most comical film.

The rise of Auguste and Louis Lumière

In 1860 Antoine Lumière left his hometown in the Haute-Saône to set up a photography business in Besançon. His first son Auguste was born in 1862, and the second, Louis, arrived two years later. In 1870 Antoine moved to Lyon with his family and opened a new workshop. Over the next 10 years he gradually built up an industrial manufacturing plant for photographic plates. The factory was taken over by Auguste and Louis in 1893 and has since become a flourishing business, thanks to the

Lumière brothers' technical innovations; they had both trained as research scientists before becoming industrialists. As a rule, all patents are lodged in joint names, despite the fact that the individuals are not always involved in the same research. By 1894, when Edison's Kinetoscope arrived on the scene in France, the Lumière Company, with a capital of 3 million francs, already had a work force of 300 people and was producing 15 million photographic plates a year.

Life on the boulevard des Capucines, outside the Grand Café.

debuts in front of 33 paying spectators

The organizer Antoine Lumière.

The technician Clément Maurice.

toine Lumière the price of his new machine. The answer was quick and to the point: "The invention is not for sale. It would be the ruin of you. It can be exhibited for a while due to its scientific interest, but apart from that the machine has no future." However, Méliès and several other guests, unconvinced by his reply, were already wondering how they could make animated pictures without Lumière. Moreover, rumor has it that Antoine had brought forward the date for this evening's projection to avoid the possibility of someone else organizing the first paying projection. As early on as 2 November, Louis Lumière had asked Carpentier to speed up the production of the first Cinematographs because, in

his own words, "We are being hounded from all sides." Nevertheless, for the time being the Lumières have carried off a triumph: their rivals have been crushed. The small easy-to-handle Cinematograph produces excellent projections, even if the picture does jerk or oscillate from time to time. Those journalists with foresight, who took the trouble to attend the show, were delighted to notice the absence of their colleagues from the big dailies. For once, the first to go to print would not be *Figaro* or *Le Matin,* but *La Poste* and *Progrès.* Despite the small number of people who attended the show, Antoine Lumière is happy in the knowledge that he has won the invention race.

And lastly, in *The Blacksmith*, the rising swirl of smoke from the forge served as a fitting closing image. Each film lasted scarcely more than a minute.

When the lights came back on, the organizer of the evening's entertainment, Antoine Lumière, was given a well-deserved round of applause. Those who were interested in the Cinematograph managed to catch a glimpse of it hidden away in a velvet-lined box. The arc lamp for the lantern, made in Paris by Alfred Molteni, was adjusted by Jacques Ducom, an expert in photography. Strangely enough, the old magic lantern is still essential, even for such a modern invention. It is this bright light source that is projected through the small walnut box, with its seemingly complicated internal

machinery, known as the Cinematograph. Charles Moisson, who manufactured the first prototype from a registered patent dated 13 February, was given the job of turning the handle. The model used this evening had just come out of Jules Carpentier's workshops. It is fixed to a stand so that the film drops straight into a bag placed below the machine and is then rewound onto the reel by a small hand-driven spool designed by Louis Lumière. Lastly, on the wall there is an electricity board so that the intensity of the incandescent carbons for the arc lamp can be checked regularly. Some of the audience were openly envious of this brand-new projection equipment. One of the guests, the famous illusionist Georges Méliès, owner of the Robert Houdin Theatre, asked An-

Arrival of the Train in Ciotat station.

The Waterer Watered.

The Blacksmiths.

1896

New York, 15 January
Charles Raff and Frank Gammon have bought the Phantascope projector from Thomas Armat on behalf of Edison. It is to be called the Vitascope and is hailed by the press as Edison's latest invention.

Paris, 1 February
The Lumières' projections at the Indian Exhibition are proving highly successful; over 2,000 tickets are being sold daily. Sessions are almost continuous as the auditorium seats only 120 people.

Brussels, 1 March
The first paying session of the Lumière brothers' Cinématograph was held at 7 galerie du Roi. Tickets cost one franc.

Paris, 5 March
Raoul Grimoin-Sanson has taken out a patent for his Photo-tachygraph, a projector fitted with a mobile tetragonal cross.

London, 24 March
Robert William Paul has given his first public projections with his Theatrograph. He created this projector with Birt Acres.

Paris, 30 March
The Grévin Museum is advertising Emile Reynaud's animated pictures. The latter has given up his hand-painted magic lantern shows.

Paris, 4 April
Auguste Blaise Baron is patenting a new machine for "recording and reproducing sound and images simultaneously." However, the results obtained with this procedure, an electrical device connected to a phonograph, remain an approximate synchronization.

Paris, 6 April
Méliès is holding projection sessions in his Robert Houdin Theatre using Paul's Theatrograph (now known as the Animatograph) and moving pictures from Edison's Kinescope.

Paris, 30 April
Three establishments in the capital are holding projections of the Lumières' Cinématograph: the Eldorado, a cafe on the boulevard de Strasbourg, which has been holding afternoon viewing sessions on a daily basis since 16 April; the first floor of the Olympia, where projections started two days ago; and, lastly, in the Dufayel Stores on boulevard Barbès, the Cinematograph has been set up in what was previously the boardroom.

Berlin, 15 June
Oskar Messter has opened the city's first cinema at 21 Unter den Linden.

Russia, 4 July
Maxim Gorky has published an article about the recent demonstration of the Lumières' Cinématograph at Nijni Novgorod. According to him, "Everything went on in a ghostly silence... The greyness and silence of the images finishes by making one nervous and depressed."

St. Petersburg, 7 July
The French cameraman Eugène Promio gave the Czar and his family a private projection session of several films, using the Lumières' Cinématograph.

Paris, 2 September
Georges Méliès, Lucien Reulos and the technician Korsten have patented the Kinetograph, a small camera fitted with a helicoid screw which winds the film forward a notch after each shot. However, it is difficult to use.

Paris, 20 September
Henri Joly has stopped collaborating with Charles Pathé and is now working with Ernest Normandin on the commercialization of his reversible Chronophotograph. This very practical camera was patented on 17 March 1896.

Paris, 1 October
Charles and Emile Pathé have founded a company called Pathé Frères, with a capital of 40,000 francs.

Paris, 21 October
The photographer Eugène Pirou is holding projection sessions at the Café de la Paix in the boulevard des Capucines. The images are of the Czar Alexander III's recent visit to Paris. They were filmed with the camera perfected by Joly and Normandin.

Paris, 14 November
Victor Continsouza and René Bünzli have taken out a second patent (the first was registered on 28 April) for their system for feeding perforated film past the lens using a Maltese cross.

Nice, 30 December
In the winter garden at the casino, Eugène Pirou's projections of short scenes, such as *le Coucher de la mariée, Lever de Mlle Willy* and *Deshabillé d'un modèle*, are enjoying a certain success.

English pioneers make their presence felt

Acres, who created the Kineoptikon.

Paul, technician and industrialist.

London, 14 January
Birt Acres, a regular lanternist at The Royal Photographic Society, is back tonight with his first animated projections. The audience warmly applauded the lively series of moving pictures: *Three Burlesque Dancers, A Boxing Match, A Kangaroo Boxing its Master,* and *The German Emperor Reviews His Regiment.* The films are the end result of several months' work. Last summer Acres joined forces with Robert William Paul, a manufacturer of scientific devices who also specializes in animated pictures. In fact, Paul had himself been manufacturing and selling copies of Edison's Kinetoscope from his London shop since the end of 1894; a legal operation as Edison's invention is not patented in Great Britain. However, the main problem they faced was not how to produce the machine but how to find new films. Together with Acres, Paul perfected a type of camera that has the capability to produce quality shots. And seeing the queues outside his fairground Kinetoscopes, he then decided on animated projections – judging by today's show, they have a future.

When a kiss creates a major scandal!

New York, 15 June
Scandalous is the only word for the Edison Manufacturing Company's latest film *The Kiss Between May Irwin and John Rice.* The two stars of *Widow Jones* show a brazen lack of morality by kissing greedily in front of the camera. Reactions are strong. Today's issue of *The Chap Book,* has this to say: "The life-size view, bestial enough in itself, was nothing compared with this. Their unbridled kissing, magnified to gargantuan proportions and repeated thrice, is absolutely loathsome." In fact, from the very beginning the Kinetoscope has displayed very little delicacy: films include innumerable enticing dances, vulgar playlets and other lewd exhibitions. According to an increasing number of citizens, censorship could be the answer.

The Kiss between May Irvin and John C. Rice is the first of its kind ever seen on the screen.

Edison attempts to monopolize projections under French threat

Thomas Armat's invention is being developed by the West Orange firm.

New York, 29 June
The arrival of the French brothers Louis and Auguste Lumière in New York has dealt Thomas Alva Edison a hard blow. Their first show with the Cinematograph at Keith's Theater, the famous music hall in Union Square, has taken New York by storm. At the opening session, Félix Mesguich projected all the greatest successes from the Grand Café in Paris. For the first time the American public has been able to see the impressive *Arrival of a Train in Ciotat Station* and the comic gem *l'Arroseur arrosé* (*The Waterer*

Watered), both highly appreciated by the audience. Unfortunately for Edison, the French equipment is technically far superior and is better adapted to collective viewing than the American Vitascope. Until now Edison has enjoyed a position of relative supremacy in the field of animated pictures, but the quality of the pictures produced by the Cinematograph poses a serious threat to the future of the Vitascope. Naturally, Edison was well aware of his rivals' progress on the other side of the Atlantic.

It must be remembered that quite some time ago Edison, having been warned in advance of this serious competition, hastened to acquire the manufacturing and operating rights to the Phantascope, a projector designed in 1895 by Thomas Armat and Charles Francis Jenkins. The inventor renamed it the Vitascope, and mass production started last April. The first public projection took place on 23 April at Koster & Bial's New York Music Hall. On that auspicious occasion two beautiful hand-colored films were shown: *Annabelle Butterfly Dance* and *Annabelle Serpentine Dance*. The projection was an immense triumph, and, during the period of nationalist euphoria that followed, Edison was hailed by one and all as the inventor of animated projections. This was a rather exaggerated view, given that he had only bought up and manufactured an existing machine and that the Cinematograph was already in service in most major European

cities. It has now been exposed. Any honest comparison of the two machines is uncompromisingly damaging to the Vitascope. Not only do the pictures from this machine appear flat and dull, but the constant vibrations and oscillation are all the more irritating now that the public has proof that they can be largely overcome. And the Lumière brothers have certainly managed to alleviate most of these unsettling defects with the Cinematograph. Moreover, the French brothers' catalogue offers a far more interesting variety of material than does the American. The films range from comic sketches to panoramic views and aesthetically pleasing scenes. The audience at the opening show was particularly impressed with *The 96th Infantry Regiment on Parade* and cheered enthusiastically as the men went through their maneuvers. From now on Thomas Edison is going to have a serious competitor, and it looks as if it may be a tough struggle.

The first public showing on 23 April.

Successful launch of the Biograph

New York, 12 October
The closely packed audience in the Hammerstein Theater rose to its feet cheering the moment William McKinley, the Republican presidential candidate, appeared before them. However, the object of their enthusiasm had not even left his home in Ohio. His address for New York's Republican supporters had been filmed with a Biograph camera well before the show. American Mutoscope has reason to be proud of this new projector for animated pictures. The company was founded in 1895 by Herman Casler, Harry Marvin, Elias Koopman and W.K. Laurie Dickson. The New York Biograph program was exemplary. In addition to McKinley, the audience was able to admire Niagara Falls, a train – the Empire State Express at 60 mph – and a scene from *Trilby*. Mutoscope has passed its first test with flying colors.

Jehanne d'Alcy in *The Conjuring of a Woman at the House of Robert Houdin*, Georges Méliès' first film based on a trick of substitution.

The scope offered by the Cinematograph receives

Paris, 30 May

"A dazzling conquest! Never before has a new form of entertainment so rapidly become a vogue. Are you interested in the Cinematograph? Naturally! They are everywhere – in the basement of all the boulevard cafes, in music-hall outbuildings, in theaters where projections are often fitted into variety shows, even in private homes – guests are offered viewing sessions of this fashionable amusement." This distinctive journalistic style leaves little room for doubt: the success of the Cinematograph is assured. The above article from the pen of Dr. Félix Regnault appeared in today's issue of *L'Illustration*, a Parisian weekly. Not content to simply sing the praises of the

Cinematograph, he is distinguishing himself from his colleagues by offering readers a precise history from Joseph Plateau's Phenakistiscope to Lumière's latest invention. And a great deal has been written on the subject. Since the first projections in the Grand Café's Indian Exhibition last December, Lumière's invention has been examined from every angle: sometimes scientifically, sometimes amateurishly. Journalists have shamelessly copied each other without even bothering to cite the source, as seen by a great many repeated passages written by the polytechnician A. Ray and published in the scientific journal *la Revue générale des sciences pures et appliquées*. This work contained an ex-

tremely lucid explanation of how the Cinematograph works. All the articles are marked by the same feeling of surprise and emotion in the face of what seems to be the event of the century. One detects a vague uneasiness on reading in the *Courier de Champagne*: "All these scenes seem totally detached from the realities of life." Or elsewhere: "The whole thing is strangely silent. Life goes on before us, yet we are unable to hear the din of passing wheels or footfalls or even a few words. Not a sound; not a single note of the complex symphony of sound which always accompanies the crowds' movement." And Henri Parville adds: "What about colored moving projections? When that happens, the il-

lusion will be complete. We shall see objects in their true colors. How shall we distinguish illusion from reality?" The Cinematograph resembles the magic lantern but with an indefinable something extra. For Henri Béraud from *la Dépêche de l'Ouest*, the most extraordinary aspect is to find oneself looking into the eyes of these ghosts: "Suddenly, the magic backdrop lit up and moved, a striking image, singular because familiar to everyone: Cordeliers' Square in Lyon... A passerby stops, turns his head, and starts walking toward us, his eyes fixed on the darkness surrounding us. He could see us! He must have been able to see us." This wonderful film, *Cordeliers' Square in Lyon*,

an enthusiastic welcome from French journalists

has received special attention from the press. *L'Univers illustré* underlines the "breathtaking realism of a tram overtaking numerous vehicles, all racing by at top speed." The paper concludes with: "These experiences, which are simply too marvelous for words, can only hint at what the future has in store and are a credit to Messrs. Auguste and Louis Lumière, Mr. Clément Maurice and their ingenious collaborators." However, this well-meaning article drew a polite correction from Maurice: "Sir, I am afraid your article of 4 January was mistaken in saying I had a part in the invention of Messrs. Lumières' Cinematograph. We owe this marvelous invention exclusively to the efforts of these two gentlemen. For my part, I simply operate the machine."

Some writers grow lyrical when confronted by the possibilities of the machine: "What deeply poignant emotions we shall experience on seeing before us those we have loved speaking and moving. Departed parents or loved ones, suddenly brought back to life, reappearing with their familiar gestures, their soft voices, all those memories that, alas, without this new invention fade further and further into the misty corners of our minds. Why, if this continues we could almost overcome memory loss, almost put an end to separations, almost abolish death itself." This from *Le Courier de Paris*. In Marseille, *Le Bavard* has announced that the lively scenes taken in the rue de Noailles "are going to disappear to be replaced by a new series of marvels which will captivate, to the point of anguish, all those who decide to contemplate them. It is said to be a show of such extraordinary dimensions that it surpasses anything one could possibly imagine." But the Lumières are no longer the only ones to make the columns of the newspapers. For example, the *Intransigeant* published a long article in their 25 February issue about Raoul Grimoin-Sanson's Phototachygraphe: "This new machine appears to be superior to Lu-

mières' Cinematograph. Gone are those interruptions, so irritating and painful to the eye." Nevertheless, those who attended the very noisy demonstration of the Phototachy-

graphe remain in favor of Louis and Auguste Lumières' machine, which already has a great number of rivals. *La Science française* sums up the general opinion by stating that the

Cinematograph is a "hallucinatory phantasmagoria," and "the show borders on the most unbelievably wonderful sorcery that has ever been dreamed of."

*Two posters for the showings at the Grand Café, in 1896. The publicity used the success of **The Waterer Watered** to attract visitors.*

1897

Cuba, 7 February
The cameraman Gabriel Veyre, who is in Havana to demonstrate the Lumière Cinematograph, has made the first film to be actually filmed in Cuba, *Simulacre d'un incendie* (*Enactment of a Fire*).

Belgrade, 6 March
The French cameraman André Carré has shot the first film to be made in Yugoslavia, *Départ du roi Alexandre Obrenovic de la cour pour la cathédrale* (*King Alexander's Departure for the Cathedral*).

Paris, 12 March
The cafe-concert Bataclan is projecting Georges Méliès' films featuring Paulus. Paulus himself produces the sound by singing, behind the screen, songs such as *En revenant de la revue* (*Coming Home from the Theater*).

Paris, March
A Lumière Cinematograph has opened at 6 boulevard Saint Denis. The building was formerly a theater for magicians. Entry costs 50 cents. It is the fifth Lumière auditorium to open up since 28 December 1895, and the first establishment to specialize in projections.

New York, 31 March
The caricaturist J. Stuart Blackton and the ventriloquist Albert Smith have founded the Vitagraph Company. They intend to project Edison's films in theaters.

Paris, April
Léon Gaumont has started shooting films in his studios in rue des Alouettes near the Buttes Chaumont. Gaumont's secretary, Alice Guy, is in charge of production.

England, April
The Cinematograph is creating increasing interest here. While James Williamson and George Albert Smith have commenced making their first films, the inventor Robert William Paul has founded the Paul Animatograph Company.

Stockholm, 15 May
The cameraman Eugène Promio has filmed the jubilee celebrations of King Oscar II of Sweden. The King was able to watch the film on the same day.

France, May
The Lumière Establishment in Lyon has put the Cinematograph on the market. The machine complete with all its accessories sells for 1,650 francs. The projector alone costs 300 francs.

Brussels, May
A special exhibition of optics has opened for the World's Fair, which is being held in the parc du Cinquantenaire. The exhibition, which is run by the Belgian Optique company, a branch of the French Optique company directed by François Deloncle, is offering sessions of cinematographic projections.

Paris, 1 July
Berthon, Dussaud and Jaubert have patented a system which "combines a microphone with a camera to enable filmmakers to reproduce living scenes and sounds." The words are recorded then mimed by the actors in front of the camera.

Paris, 15 July
The film *Premier cigare* (*First Cigar*), made by Emile Reynaud for the Optic Theatre at the Grévin Museum, has just been projected for the public. The film took a year longer than expected to complete. The Museum has announced its intention to turn further toward the Cinematograph.

Shanghai, July
The American James Ricalton is projecting Edison films in tea rooms and amusement parks.

Paris, 1 August
After the accident at the Charity Bazaar, A. Delille has suggested using a water tank to protect films from the heat of the rayons produced by the condenser. It is to be hoped that this will help in avoiding further fires.

Washington, 5 August
Admiral Cigarette, produced by Edison, is the first advertising film to be lodged for copyright at the Congress Library.

Paris, 25 November
Raoul Grimoin-Sanson has obtained a patent for the Cinécosmorama. This innovative procedure can be used to film and project panoramic animated pictures on a circular screen, using 12 inter-connected projectors.

Paris, 30 November
Léon Gaumont has given up the Demenÿ 60mm "Chrono" format. He is increasing his production output using 35mm film. His films, which sell for 35 to 75 francs and cover a variety of subjects, including news items, street scenes and comic acts such as *Chez le barbier* (*At the Barber's*), *Une nuit agitée* (*A Disturbed Night*), are filmed by Alice Guy.

Cinematograph blamed

Paris, 4 May
A horrifying fire ravaged the Charity Bazaar last night, killing 121 people – 110 women and six men. A meticulous inquiry led by the Prefect of Police Mr. Lépine, has enabled the authorities to reconstruct events leading up to the disaster. The Charity Bazaar, founded in 1885 by members of Catholic high society and presided over by Baron de Mackau, opened yesterday and seemed set for success. The cream of Parisian society crowded in to the long wooden building in rue Jean-Goujon, where charity stalls divided by sheets of pasteboard lined the long hall, leaving a central passage six to seven metres wide. Overhead, an enormous canopy of white canvas, lined with a tarred material, formed a fake ceiling.

On this Tuesday, 4 May, 4,000 people were crowded into the building. At 3 p.m. Ernest Normandin, a concessionaire for the Cinematograph perfected by Henri Joli in 1895, decided to open the first session in the small nine-by-four projection room. The previous show had had to be canceled due to a technical hitch with the lamp. As a replacement, Albert Molteni, the magic-lantern manufacturer, had sent an oxyetheric lamp. A mixture of oxygen and ether fueled a flame which heated a small piece of lime to incandescence. Ironically, the lamp was called Securitas. At 10 minutes past 4 p.m., after the fourth session, the room was plunged into darkness, and the projectionist Bellac called for a pause to refuel the lamp. Brushing aside advice from the Baron's secretary to do it outside, he returned to his canvas projection box and started filling the reservoir with ether. His assistant, Grégoire Bagrachow, having asked where the matches were, proceeded to strike one – Bellac shouted in horror as soon as he realized his intention – too late... In a split second a flame spurted out of the lamp followed by a terrifying noise as the lamp and celluloid films exploded. In a few

The fire shocked France and caused attendances for film showings to drop.

for the loss of 121 lives at Charity Bazaar fire

At the moment of reckoning, survivors and the curious discovered the fragility of the building constructed for the occasion.

Legal consequences of the catastrophe

Paris, 24 August
Three people involved in the terrible fire at the Charity Bazaar appeared in court today on charges of negligence: Baron Mackau, the organizer; Bellac, Ernest Normandin's projectionist; and Bellac's friend and helper for the occasion, Grégoire Bagrachow. The verdict can only be described as controversial. Baron Mackau, who was in charge of the building and therefore the sole person in a position to ensure proper safety measures for the public, only received a 500-franc fine. Bellac, whose carelessness had inadvertently caused the fire, was given a one-year prison sentence as well as a 500-franc fine. But Bagrachow, who, though also responsible, had saved dozens of lives by his courage, has been condemned to eight months imprisonment and fined 200 francs. The public still find it difficult to understand why, once the fire had broken out, so few people were able to escape. On whom should responsibility for the disaster rest? Should the Cinematograph which, according to a deputy, "creates danger wherever it is used," be banned forever? No such decision has as yet been taken. Moreover, the Cinematograph has become so firmly established that nobody seriously believes it can be stopped.

seconds the fire had spread to the canopy, and a general panic seized the public, turning the Bazaar into a deadly trap. Burning tar from the roof ignited the fleeing women's billowing skirts, turning them into human torches. Bagrachow was able to save more than 100 people by smashing down one of the wooden walls. Dozens of women died trampled underfoot as men, all trace of chivalry forgotten, pushed and beat their way out through the ensuing melee. Two other emergency exits were opened: a fireman's ladder and a window into an adjacent hotel. Firemen and locals worked miracles, but by 6 p.m. it was over. All that remained was a mass of charred wood and ashes over which hung a pall of dreadful smelling smoke. The bodies were taken to the Palais de l'Industrie for identification. For many, this catastrophe was an act of God: a punishment for the proud, whose acts of charity required no real sacrifice. The Cinematograph has also come under attack, accused of being a scientific conquest that thought it could outshine God.

The Molteni ether lamp, considered directly responsible for the blaze.

How the decor for the occasion appeared before the conflagration.

An hour after the opening of the fete, the charity stalls were in ruins.

Georges Méliès opens a studio for moving pictures

Montreuil-sous-Bois, 22 March
Famous illusionist Georges Méliès, a recent Cinematograph convert, is thrilled. His first studio for animated pictures, built in the garden of his property in Montreuil, was inaugurated today. Since last October he has been recording films outside in his garden, in the streets nearby or in his laboratory right next to the Opéra in Paris, but bad weather and insufficient light have often prevented him from working. As a result, he decided to have a studio built. It was to be 17 metres long by seven metres wide, with an overall height of six metres. To ensure a maximum exposure to natural light he decided on a north-south orientation and to cover it entirely with glass like a photographic studio. Inside he planned a small set with a depth of five metres for actors to play out their scenes; the rest of the space was set aside for the camera and workshop. The studio floor is laid with parquet, and all sides and the roof are covered with frosted glass, except for the three spans in front of the set which are equipped with single-thickness clear panes to allow the sun's rays to light up the actors. Frames fitted with tracing-cloth are available to soften the sunlight if necessary. In fact it was Méliès himself who drew up the plans for the studio himself, but the glazier was far from impressed when he came to fit the glass roof. His first

reaction was, "Who is the idiot that designed this?" Somewhat put out, Méliès, nevertheless, was forced to admit that the middle supports were leaning over in a worrying fashion. The construction underwent urgent modifications for an overall cost of 90,000 francs! However, not even this could spoil Méliès' pleasure. Ideas for films are already taking flight in his imagination; the new studio is going to open up a whole new world. Méliès is intending to begin his first projects using reconstructed news films, and the recently started Greek-Turkish War should make an excellent subject.

Méliès' films shown in his own theater

Paris, 30 October
The Robert Houdin Theatre at 8 boulevard des Italiens, is presenting the latest animated pictures produced by its owner Georges Méliès in his studio in Montreuil. For the last six months the Cinematograph has been filling the house every evening. Sessions last three quarters of an hour. For 50 cents a seat, the audience is treated to wonderfully imaginative scenes. In *L'Auberge ensorcelée* (*The Bewitched Inn*), a man chases his boots, which walk unaided. A truly astonishing sight.

The building constructed on the Méliès property in Montreuil.

Georges Méliès and his associate Lucien Reulos inaugurate Star Film.

Pathé and Gaumont have begun production

Paris, 28 December
The brothers Charles and Emile Pathé have organized and founded the General Company of Cinematographs, Phonographs and Film, with strong financial backing from banker Jean Neyret and industrialist Claude Grivolas. The new company, with a capital of 1 million francs, takes over from the Pathé Brothers' establishment. Emile Pathé will deal with the phonography branch and run the factory in Chatou. Charles Pathé will be supervising both sections but intends to devote more time to the smaller cinematography branch with an eye to increasing film production. The head office and phonograph shop are situated at 98 rue de Richelieu. The same district is also home to the General

Photography Syndicate (Comptoir Générale de Photography) which was acquired by Léon Gaumont on 11 September 1895. The Syndicate started out with the modest capital of 300,000 francs at the beginning of this year. But this extremely active little company not only manufactures excellent quality cameras and projectors, made to Georges Demeny's patents, but has produced a few greatly appreciated films: *At The Barber, Transformation of a Hat, Negros Bathing, Arrival of a Train in Auteuil Station...* Gaumont offers over 80 different films and also sells the Lumière collection. Nonetheless, Charles Pathé looks set to take over the still-modest animated picture market, thanks largely to his backers' support.

*With **After the Ball, the Bath,** played by Jehanne d'Alcy and Jeanne Brady, Georges Méliès dared to present nudity on the screen!*

America embargoes Lumière material

Edison goes into battle over patents

New York, 28 July

It all happened at dawn off the Hudson Estuary. A dinghy rocked gently on the calm morning swell. On board were two Frenchmen – Monsieur Lafont, the representative in America for the French Lumière Company, and his favorite cameraman Félix Mesguich. After waiting a considerable time, a transatlantic ship flying the French flag approached, took Lafont on board and immediately set sail for France. Thus ended the Cinematograph's short-lived American epic. Congress had pulled the rug from underneath the French company four days earlier by voting in the Dingley Bill. This new law, aimed at protecting American manufacturers, hits foreign technical material with prohibitive import taxes, ranging from 25 to 65 percent of their value. American Mutoscope and the Biograph Company, whose links with the new President William McKinley are common knowledge, quickly took advantage of the situation by lodging a complaint against the Lumière Company for a supposed violation of customs regulations viz that its material, and in particular the Cinematographs, were brought into the United States without the necessary authorization. Perhaps, faced with the threat of arrest, Lafont preferred to leave the country. However, for him and a number of his colleagues the American dream is well and truly over.

Thomas Edison is happy to demonstrate the Vitascope, the machine invented by Thomas Armat.

New York, 7 December

A warning shot has been fired in the seething world of animated pictures. The International Film Company has just been ordered to cease all its business activities by Dyer & Dyer, the well-known legal firm in charge of Thomas Alva Edison's interests. The company, which was founded in November 1896 by Charles H. Webster and Edward Kuhn, specializes in the importation of foreign films and is marketing a projector, the Projectorscope, an exact copy of existent models. Charles Webster, no stranger to the world of images, was charged with the promotion of the Vitascope over in England. Impressed by the photographic superiority of European films, he worked to facilitate their arrival on the American market as soon as he returned. Kuhn was one of the filmmakers responsible for the first Kinetoscopic films. Like W.K. Laurie Dickson, he left his job, and, accompanied by his cameraman Edwin S. Porter, joined forces with Webster. In order to justify this move against his former collaborators, Edison put forward the definitive registration of his patent to August of this year. By this legal artifice, the Wizard from West Orange has become *de facto* the sole inventor of animated projections, and, therefore, has the right to bring proceedings against his rivals under the shadowy pretext of unauthorized imitations. Furthermore, the prosecutions look set to continue. Apparently, the Maguire and Baucus Company has also been summoned to appear before the courts, and other similar injunctions could be underway. Who will be the next to go? Biograph, Cinematograph, Magniscope, Polyscope and Projectorscope: could all these deliciously repetitive names be doomed to soon disappear from our vocabulary?

A Lumière cameraman in the United States, as seen by the American press.

A San Francisco Kinetoscope parlor, modeled on a West Orange hall.

1898

Naples, 18 January
The whimsical transformist Leopoldo Fregoli has presented several short films at the Gran Circo delle Varietà. The films were made with a camera called the Fregoligraph.

New York, 16 February
Theater producers Mark Klaw and Abraham Erlanger, who have imported the Lumières' film *Passion*, have received a visit from Edison's legal representatives, Dyer & Dyer. The lawyers warned them against exhibiting foreign films in America.

Spain, 28 February
Fructuoso Gelabert Badellia is in Barcelona to film the first Spanish newsreels.

France, 25 March
Clément Maurice has won the first cinematographic prize in the history of the cinema. The competition was organized by the Bain de Mer company in Monaco. The jury included well-known personalities such as Léon Gaumont, Frederic Dillaye and Georges Mareschal. Contestants were required to make a 15-minute film of "a subject with movement filmed in Monaco."

Paris, 25 March
The Pole Boleslaw Matuszewski has published a brochure entitled *Une nouvelle source d'histoire* (*A New Source of History*), where the idea of gathering, saving and stocking films is suggested for the first time.

Paris, 4 April
Auguste Baron has obtained a patent for a new sound system for the cinema. It consists of a phonograph driven by an electrical mechanism which in turn receives its impulse from the rotational movement of the camera. This results in a fairly satisfactory synchronization of sound and image. Baron has already started making sound films in a purpose-built studio.

Paris, 26 April
The first projection of Georges Méliès' new film, *Quais de La Havane et Explosion du cuirassé Le Maine* (*The Explosion of the Battleship Maine in Havana Harbor*), a reconstructed news film about the American intervention in Cuba. This is the first film in a series of five 20-metre reels dealing with the same subject. Méliès re-created the wreck in his studio in Montreuil and filmed the actors through an aquarium filled with fish.

London, 5 May
The American Charles Urban is in London to set up a branch for Edison. The new firm is called Warwick Trading Company.

New York, 19 May
Vitagraph has started making its own films. One of the first, *The Battle of Manila Bay*, about the American victory in Cuba on 1 May, was filmed using models and photographs.

Prague, 19 June
Jan Krizenecky has presented his footage of filmed news showing the river-boat which exploded on the Moldau yesterday.

Paris, 22 June
Emile Reynaud has suffered yet another disappointment. The Grévin Museum has insisted that he include in his show, Gaumont's "chronophotographic experiences", filmed with the Demenÿ camera.

New York, 13 July
J. Stuart Blackton, one of the founders of the Vitagraph Company, has settled out of court in the case brought against him by Edison. The director of the Edison Manufacturing Company, William Gilmore, dealt with the negotiations. From now on, Blackton and his associate Smith will be working under license to Edison.

Prague, 1 October
Jan Krizenecky has released three reels of fiction played by the actor Joseph Svab-Malostransky. One of them, *Smiles and Tears*, is made up of close-up shots of the actor's face.

Italy, 18 October
The cameraman Vittorio Calcina, the Lumière agent in Italy, is in Monza to present the Cinematograph to the royal family.

Paris, 18 October
The Lumière brothers and cameraman Félix Mesguich have set up an outdoor screen, at 5 boulevard Montmartre, to project a film on the merits of Ripolin's paintings.

Paris, 29 October
Lucien Reulos, Méliès' former associate, has patented his Mirograph. This machine is the first in France to use a film with the reduced width of 21mm.

Denmark, 31 December
Arnold Poulson has perfected a magnetic procedure for recording sound on bands of steel.

New developments in the patents war

New York, 13 May
There seems little chance of an end to Thomas Alva Edison's offensive, launched last December to protect his interests. Armed with the fact that he owns the first registered patent, the inventor continues to plague his rivals by instituting proceedings against them. Having attacked Webster and Kuhn, Maguire and Baucus, Sigmund Lubin, William S. Selig, Klaw and Erlanger and many others, his lawyers have now turned their attention to the American Mutoscope and Biograph Company. Biograph has received an order to cease all activity. The company's directors, especially William Kennedy Laurie Dickson who formerly worked on the Kinetoscope with Edison, are accused of fraudulent imitations and threatened with blacklisting. According to his lawyer, Edison hopes to settle out of court. The idea of a financial agreement has been mentioned, but it seems doubtful that Biograph will accept without a fight.

EDISON'S

Copyrighted Production of

All Moving Pictures.

True to Life.

THOS. A. EDISON, Inventor.

THE PASSION PLAY

The Passion inspires many filmmakers

New York, 30 January
The Cinematograph is at last reconciled with the Church, due to the popularity of Passion films. New versions are constantly appearing on the scene. Richard Hollaman's Eden Museum is presenting *The Oberammergau Passion Play*, by Henry C. Vincent. Though a huge success, the film was made on the roof of the Grand Central Palace in New York and not in Bavaria, as the bills lead one to believe. In France the Passion is also drawing in the crowds with Lumière's *Life and Passion of Christ* by Georges Hatot. Gaumont are planning their *Life of Christ*, and the Catholic *Maison de la bonne presse* is distributing Albert Kirchner's version of the story.

Medical science films are pioneered by Dr. Eugène-Louis Doyen

Pathé opens film studio at Vincennes

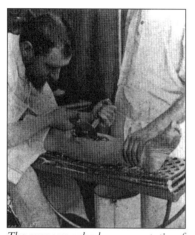 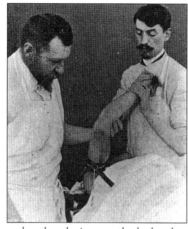 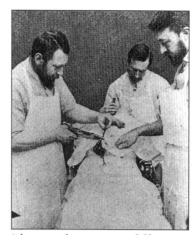

The surgeon, who has a reputation for novel and audacious methods, has been quick to use the resources of film.

Vincennes, June
Charles Pathé is constructing a film studio at 1 rue Polygone, though not as elaborate as Georges Méliès' Montreuil studio. It consists of a small room in a former bistro with several upstairs bedrooms which have been converted into a laboratory and workshops for developing films. Pathé leased the premises from a wine merchant, the widow Hervillard. Filming takes place, weather permitting, in the courtyard on a wooden stage measuring six by eight metres, with a naively-painted canvas as a backdrop. The wind often shakes the backcloth, and when it rains the scenery is ruined. A wooden hut serves as a storage space for the costumes, backcloths and accessories. Pathé has no real reason to invest too much money in making animated pictures, apart from a personal desire to increase film production. The powerful General Company of Cinematographs, Phonographs and Film, run jointly with his brother Emile and Claude Grivolas, makes its major profit from the sale of phonographs and cylinders. Meanwhile, Gaumont, Méliès and other artisans are taking over the market.

Paris, 21 October
The renowned surgeon Eugène-Louis Doyen has organized, at his own expense, a projection session of medical films at the Learned Societies building. Dr. Doyen's passion for photography goes back several years. In 1890 he built up a collection of glass plates to use in similar sessions for medical students. With the invention of the Cinematograph, Doyen immediately thought about making scientific films. In 1897 this became a reality, thanks to Clément Maurice's brilliant technical assistance; the cameraman from the Grand Café has a complete mastery of the Lumière Cinematograph. Finally, a third man joined the team, Ambroise-François Parnaland, the owner of an animated-picture camera with central perforations. The two experts first made a trial film of a craniectomy in Dr. Doyen's operating room on avenue d'Iéna. Then, at the beginning of this year they started filming again, this time in a new clinic on rue Piccini equipped with powerful electric reflectors. This time the results obtained were excellent. At this point, Dr. Doyen left for England, and on 28 July he projected the films of his operations, a hysterectomy and a craniectomy, for the English Medical Association. This first film demonstration was received with enthusiasm. But in France it has been a different story. Since Dr. Doyen's return he has had to face up to a veritable cabal of scientists who feel that the Cinematograph has no role to play in the operating theater. One after another, doors have shut in his face. The Medical Academy turned down a paper he was scheduled to give, and the Surgical Congress in Paris has refused to allow him to project his films. Luckily, Dr. Doyen's films are a great success at the Learned Society.

Lumière cameraman expelled from Russia

St. Petersburg, 27 September
Félix Mesguich, one of the Lumière brothers' best cameramen, has been escorted to the border by the Russian police. This unfortunate incident puts an end to his, until now, triumphantly-successful tour of this country with the Lumière Cinematograph. Everything had started out so well. Mesguich was first sent to Odessa on 13 November 1897 by Arthur Grunewald, the Lumière agent in Russia. After Odessa, he continued on to Yalta to show the Cinematograph to Czar Nicholas II who appeared to find the films most interesting. From there the "image hunter" journeyed throughout Russia. After a short stay in Moscow, he set up the projector in a large hall at the annual fair in Nijni-Novgorod. The audience was completely stupefied, looking behind the screen to find out how the diabolical mystery worked. The Coronation of Nicholas II was screened next. It was too much; some made the sign of the cross, others muttered angrily. A few nights later the Lumière Establishment was burned to the ground by a group of fanatics. In St. Petersburg, a final catastrophe awaited Mesguich. The Frenchman filmed the beautiful Caroline Otéro in an "explosive waltz" with stunning results. Unfortunately, her closely-held partner was a Russian officer. The following day when the film was projected at the Aquarium Theater in front of the Russian aristocracy, the entire audience rose to its feet, and in the ensuing uproar, Mesguich, himself at a complete loss, was brutally seized. The explanation given was that he had seriously offended the Russian army by turning one of its officers into a "music-hall dancer." Poor Mesguich! What an ignominious end to what had been such a wonderful journey.

Presented for the first time at the Casino de Paris, in September 1897, the films produced in New York by the American Biograph Company have been enjoying a great success there. The managers are continuing to capitalize on the exclusivity of these programs, which are presented by Eugène Lauste. The films have proved to be a choice addition to their own cabaret program. Each film lasts a quarter of an hour.

1899

Paris, 6 January
Léon Gaumont has demonstrated a Chronophotograph projector capable of screening over 600 metres of film, thanks to a system of spools, at a meeting of the French Photographic Society.

Paris, January
Young actor Ferdinand Zecca, originally from Corsica, has been taken on in the phonographic section of the Pathé brothers' establishment, directed by Emile Pathé. Zecca, who has a wonderful speaking voice, will be reading the official speeches given by politicians so that they can be engraved on sound cylinders.

Paris, 23 February
Georges Méliès was present with his camera to film President of the Republic Félix Faure's funeral. For once, Méliès has decided not to make a reconstructed news film.

Paris, 31 March
Léon Gaumont has brought out two new films in the Elgé Collection: *Panorama pris d'un train en marche* (*Scenery from a Passing Train*) and *Arrivée en gare d'un train* (*A Train Arriving at the Station*).

Vincennes, April
Ferdinand Zecca has taken part in the filmed fiction stories made by Pathé for the Galeries Dufayel. He supervised and acted alongside the comedian Charlus in *le Muet mélomane* (*The Mute Music-Lover*), a burlesque film directed by cameraman Maurice Caussade, with synchronized sound provided by a phonograph.

France, 4 May
A fire broke out at a fairground show in Cognac which was presenting the American Vitagraph. The film burst into flames and in eight terrifying minutes the entire fair was burned to the ground. The 40-metre long Vitagraph, run by fairground exhibitors Dane and Oger, is beyond repair. The damages are estimated at over 50,000 francs.

Paris, 24 May
Etienne Jules Marey has patented a device "to adjust the movement of positive film in the chrono-photographic projector."

Paris, 13 July
The Pathé brothers' General Cinematograph, Phonograph and Film Company is a thriving concern. At the annual general meeting, profits were estimated at nearly 360,000 francs.

Paris, 14 July
The shares in the Pathé brothers' General Cinematograph, Phonograph and Film Company have risen considerably in a very short time; they are now being negotiated by the bank for between 235 and 255 francs.

Prague, 30 August
Eduard Tichy, from the Variety Theater, asked the cameraman Otto Ditto to make a film for him on the Emperor François Joseph's recent visit to the capital.

France, August
Georges Méliès is in Granville to film footage of the sea. He intends to combine the views with studio scenes for his new fiction film, *le Christ marchant sur les eaux* (*Christ Walking over Water*).

Paris, 16 October
The Grévin Museum board has terminated Emile Reynaud's contract. The father of the Praxinoscope and the Optic Theatre is to be replaced by a puppeteer named Saint-Genois.

Paris, 1 November
A fight broke out today at the Lumière Cinematograph in the boulevard des Capucines. A certain Mrs. King, unable to see the screen, sat on the arm of her seat, but this obstructed the projection. When a policeman grabbed her arm to remove her, some of the audience sprung to her defense, causing a general upheaval. Seats were ripped apart and paintings were damaged... Mr. Lafont, the owner of the property has filed a complaint.

Paris, 21 November
Victor Continsouza and René Bünzli are registering their "stereoscopic animator" for patent.

Paris, 1 December
Charles Pathé has brought out a new series of animated scenes "particularly aimed at schools and youth movements."

Paris, 15 December
The Pathé productions rely heavily on dramatization but show very little artistic improvement. Charles Pathé has brought out three films all entitled *Un incendie* (*A Fire*), where one of the firemen is seriously hurt. The catalogue also lists *Arrivée d'un train* (*The Arrival of a Train*), a humorous sketch in which a cyclist falls off his bicycle, knocking over a station hand on the platform, and a host of other films very much in the same vein as the Lumières' films.

Clandestine filming of championship fight

Coney Island, 3 November
"Winner on points: Jim Jeffries!" At the referees' decision the spectators rose to give a standing ovation to the well-deserved champion and his unhappy rival Thomas Sharkey. The fight had been superb – no less than 33 brisk rounds. As the audience started to make its way out of the hall, the 400 arc lights suddenly went out, throwing the ring into shadow. However, a group of men busy with their cameras paid little heed to the general exodus; the camera crew from the American Mutoscope and Biograph Company still had work to do. During the match they had filmed almost 1,800 metres of footage equivalent to 30 minutes viewing time. It should be remembered that the enterprising company recently acquired film rights to the Jeffries-Sharkey boxing match from the impressario William Brady. However, it would appear that this completely new type of contract has been knowingly sabotaged by Thomas Alva Edison, who views the whole business with a very jaundiced eye. The facts are as follows: Albert E. Smith, the joint founder of Vitagraph, was caught in the act of filming the match with his camera, which was hidden under a tangle of umbrellas near the cloak-room. The deception discovered, Smith and his rival cameraman almost came to fisticuffs, just like the pugilists whose match was at stake in the conflict. In the end, Albert Smith packed up and ran, escaping with his precious negatives. When questioned later on, the daring offender confessed that his company's financial difficulties as well as pressure from the Edison Company were responsible. Smith claims that James White, the manager of the West Orange studios, had contacted Smith for the job, threatening him with legal action should he refuse. Resigned, Smith, in collusion with several people placed around the ring, had managed to elude the vigilance of Biograph's police contingent. The rival companies certainly seem set for an all-out fight between their leaders.

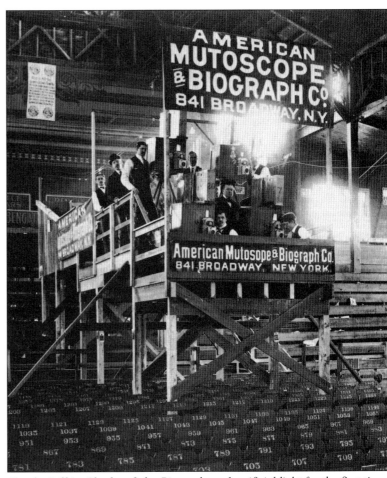

For the Jeffries-Sharkey fight, Biograph used artificial light for the first time.

The cinema takes on the scandalous Dreyfus affair

Paris, November

Everyone in France has been following the Dreyfus affair with passionate interest. The Cinematograph has taken up this sensational subject, and even fairground exhibitors are screening reconstructed newsreels (presented as genuine) showing the misfortunes of ex-officer Alfred Dreyfus. Moreover, the wave of pro-Dreyfus feeling, which has swept the country since the beginning of the year, was so strong that the new government led by Emile Loubet decided to re-open the trial. And not without reason: falsified documents were located in the dossier, and Colonel Henry, who was strongly suspected of having lied, killed himself. In August the new trial opened in Rennes amid feverish speculation from the public. On 9 September, Dreyfus was once more condemned but was immediately granted a pardon by President Loubet. This decision did little to calm the situation. In fairgrounds and cinemas Georges Méliès' series of films has met with incredible success and with feelings running so high that audiences often fight among themselves. Some regions have preferred to ban all pro-Dreyfus projections. Méliès filmed the whole affair in his Montreuil studio. The 11 films (10 20-metre films and one 40 metres in length) that he produced for sale are aston-

Journalists fighting over the Dreyfus affair, filmed by Méliès after the court verdict was delivered in Rennes.

ishingly realistic. The role of Laborie, the lawyer hired to defend Dreyfus, is interpreted by Méliès himself, and the owner of a local hardware store who bears an uncanny resemblance to the unfortunate defendant, plays Dreyfus. The films, which are also distributed in England by Charles Urban, the head of Warwick Trading Company, show Dreyfus' arrest, his imprisonment on Devil's Island, Colonel Henry's suicide, the trials in Rennes, the attempt on Laborie's life, Dreyfus leaving for prison after the trial... The copies sold so well that Charles Pathé decided to produce his own *Affaire Dreyfus*. The eight films, which have just been released for sale, also have a pro-Dreyfus slant. Jean Liezer, an actor from the Ambigue-Comique troupe, plays Dreyfus. This film series depicts Colonel Henry's arrest and avowal, his suicide, Dreyfus in his cell in Rennes, the court martial, General Mercier's deposition... Pathé's series is also sold overseas, but Méliès' films have achieved a far greater success. Who can forget the dramatic *Attempt on M. Laborie* or *A Brawl between Journalists* in which Méliès' actors battle it out with such conviction that one honestly believes the magician slipped his camera into the courtroom in Rennes?

Images of war from Cuba to Africa

New York, 1 November

The latest offer from the American Mutoscope and Biograph Company and W.K. Laurie Dickson: war from the comfort of your chair! Dickson, a British subject, and his cameraman William Cox, have just returned from covering their compatriots' war with the Boers in the Transvaal. The news footage from Pretoria is genuine. Because of this, the faraway conflict on African soil appears closer and more tangible, a far cry from the faked images produced of the Hispano-American Conflict. In 1898 Edward Hill Amet reconstructed a *Naval Battle in Cuba* in his garden for Magniscope. Built around a large pond representing Santiago Bay with numerous model ships controlled to move in front of the camera by an electric device, his creative decor completely duped the public. Reality or fiction? The cinema's power of persuasion is surely without equal.

*Pathé made their own **Dreyfus Affair** with the actor Liezer.*

British films build a studio

New Southgate, 1 September
Robert William Paul, the well-known manufacturer of movie cameras and projectors, has had his own film studio built on Sydney Road. The studio, which adjoins his Theatrograph and Animatograph factory, is available to clients for all types of films, from advertising to fiction. Paul has been producing films since 1895 and is the only filmmaker in the country with such a mastery of photographic techniques, thanks to his extensive collection of theatrical props. Nothing has been left to chance in the new studio: trapdoors, pulleys, a drawbridge, a painting workshop for sets and a stock of 50 painted backcloths ready to provide any imaginable background. The building itself, built to Paul's own plans, is raised approximately two metres from the ground to allow actors to disappear through the trapdoors when special effects are required. The camera is mounted outside on a raised platform set on rails. This ingenious idea allows Paul to move the camera quickly and smoothly to produce magnified or reduced images. The results speak for themselves: the spectator feels he is actually approaching the action in scenes with "close-ups". The set measures roughly 8.5 metres by 4.25 metres and is protected by an iron structure fitted with sliding walls and a glass roof that faces north. Preparations for filming sessions are simple; it is just a matter of sliding back the walls and placing the camera at the desired distance. Paul's studio is without a doubt the most modern in Europe. Even his friend Georges Méliès is overwhelmed by such amazingly advanced techniques, but Paul has had more experience than Méliès in animated pictures. Moreover, the cinematograph has become a lucrative business for him since April 1897 when he founded Paul's Animatograph Ltd., with an initial capital of 60,000 pounds. His ambitions are artistic as well as commercial: "The public has seen too many trains, trams and buses. We have not as yet explored the possibilities of animated pictures to make people laugh, cry or simply astonish." Paul intends to change that and has begun work on a series of both comic and dramatic films.

Auguste Baron makes the cinema talk

Paris, 16 November
Just how far can the cinema go? On learning of the latest developments in the animated picture business, one might well ask this question. The engineer Auguste Baron has just applied for a patent for an outstanding new invention: a system for producing circular panoramic animated projections, with both color and sound. The Talking Cinematorama – for such is the name given to this incredible machine – consists of 10 movie cameras fitted to a circular platform and all connected to phonographs. Each camera films a section of the chosen landscape or set and records all its corresponding sounds. For projections, 10 projectors connected to loudspeakers are used instead of the cameras. Baron envisages a circular panorama with a diameter of 32 metres and a 100-metre-long screen. He has been a specialist in the talking film field for a long time; his first patent dealing with this speciality was lodged in April 1896 – an electric commutator which resulted in a very approximate synchronization. Within two years, the inventor had perfected a much more innovative procedure. The phonograph was connected to the camera by a commutator which was synchronized by

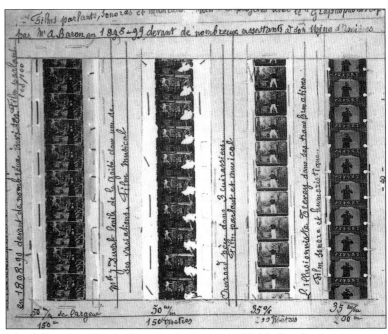

The different tests carried out by the inventor with his Graphonoscope.

the driving wheel on the camera and ensured that the two machines ran at the same speed. The principle has also been applied to projections. With this set-up, Baron is able to make talking films in a specially constructed studio in his garden in Asnières. There, inside the glass-paned studio, the camera, hooked up to the phonograph by cables, travels back and forth on rails. On the set, Guillier, a musician from the Lamoureux Concerts, poses in front of the objective, a cornet to his lips, the music flows out and is captured. The next act shows Lagrange from the Parisian Theatres – he takes a dramatic stance and declaims *The Dream of Athalie...* What more can one possibly ask for?

Twenty-six-year-old secretary heads production at Gaumont

Paris, 30 November
Her name is Alice Guy, she is only 26-years-old, and her latest film, *L'Angelus*, has just been released for sale. She is now head of production

Mademoiselle Alice Guy at home.

for the General Photography Syndicate. Initially, her director Léon Gaumont was hesitant about confiding such an important position to a woman... but Guy, who has a deep passion for the Cinematograph, showed herself such a capable and original filmmaker that the Gaumont film catalogue sales soon increased noticeably. It all started in 1895 when she turned up at 57 rue Saint-Roch and knocked timidly on the door to Gaumont's office. He was looking for a simple secretary, but when he caught sight of her he exclaimed, "I'm afraid that you are too young for the job." "Sir, that won't last for long," retorted the young girl, taking the rather stern Gaumont so thoroughly off guard that he hired her. In the beginning, Alice Guy often ran into Gustave Eiffel, a company stockholder, and Georges Demenÿ, who had sold his

patents to Gaumont. She became friends with them and also with the company's cameraman Anatole Thiberville, who initiated her in filming techniques. Early in 1897 Guy asked her employer's permission to try her hand at filming a few scenes. With Thiberville's help she directed several scenes at Belleville on a glassed-in terrace. Some were comic such as *le Planton du colonel* (*The Colonel's Orderly*) and *Une nuit agitée* (*An Agitated Night*), and some were light-hearted such as *le Coucher d'Yvette* (*Yvette's Bedtime*). The films sold quite well; fairground exhibitors appreciated the humor of "Mademoiselle Alice Guy." Since then her style has become more refined, and her last film, inspired by Millet's famous painting *The Angelus*, depicts an old farmer and his wife at prayer while the Angelus (on loudspeakers) rings out.

Cinema artists born in the pioneering days

Paris, 4 January 1857
Emile Cohl (Emile Courtet)

Germany, 17 January 1867
Carl Laemmle

Hungary, 11 January 1873
Adolph Zukor

France, 19 February 1873
Louis Feuillade

Kentucky, 22 January 1875
David Wark Griffith

Paris, 2 February 1878
Maurice Tourneur (M. Thomas)

Canada, 17 January 1880
Mack Sennett
(Michael Sinnott)

San Francisco, 13 September 1880
Jesse L. Lasky

Massachusetts, 12 August 1881
Cecil Blount DeMille

Poland, 12 December 1881
Harry M. Warner

Philadelphia, 15 February 1882
John Barrymore (John Blythe)

France, 18 November 1882
Germaine Dulac
(Germaine Saisset-Schneider)

Denver, 23 May 1883
Douglas Fairbanks
(Douglas Elton Ullman)

Bordeaux, 16 December 1883
Max Linder
(Gabriel-Maximilien Leuvielle)

France, 17 December 1883
Raimu (Jules Muraire)

Michigan, 16 February 1884
Robert Flaherty

Switzerland, 26 July 1884
Emil Jannings
(Theodor Emil Janenz)

Warsaw, 27 August 1884
Samuel Goldwyn (Goldfish)

St. Petersburg, 21 February 1885
Sacha Guitry
(Alexandre-Georges Guitry)

Minsk, 4 July 1885
Louis B. Mayer
(Eliezer Mayer)

Brussels, 21 July 1885
Jacques Feyder
(Jacques Frédérix)

Vienna, 22 September 1885
Erich von Stroheim
(Erich Oswald Stroheim)

France, 5 March 1886
Léon Mathot

France, 24 December 1887
Louis Jouvet

Paris, 23 April 1888
Marcel L'Herbier

Paris, 12 September 1888
Maurice Chevalier

Budapest, 14 December 1888
Michael Curtiz
(Mihaly Kertesz)

Germany, 28 December 1888
Friedrich Wilhelm Murnau
(F.W. Plumpe)

Copenhagen, 3 February 1889
Carl Theodor Dreyer

Paris, 23 February 1889
Musidora (Jeanne Roques)

Pennsylvania, 4 March 1889
Pearl White

London, 16 April 1889
Charles Chaplin

France, 5 July 1889
Jean Cocteau

Russia, 26 September 1889
Ivan Mosjoukine

Paris, 25 October 1889
Abel Gance

England, 16 June 1890
Stan Laurel
(Arthur Stanley Jefferson)

France, 14 October 1890
Louis Delluc

Vienna, 5 December 1890
Fritz Lang

Paris, 19 April 1891
Françoise Rosay
(Francoise Bandy de Nalèche)

Georgia, 18 January 1892
Oliver Hardy

Berlin, 28 January 1892
Ernst Lubitsch

New York, 11 March 1892
Raoul Walsh
(Albert Edward Walsh)

New York, 17 August 1892
Mae West

France, 21 August 1892
Charles Vanel

Russia, 16 February 1893
Vsevolod Pudovkin

Toronto, 8 April 1893
Mary Pickford (Gladys Smith)

Nebraska, 20 April 1893
Harold Lloyd

Vienna, 29 May 1894
Josef von Sternberg
(Jonas Sternberg)

Paris, 15 September 1894
Jean Renoir

Poland, 31 December 1894
Pola Negri
(Barbara Apolonia Chalupiec)

Maine, 1 February 1895
John Ford
(Sean Aloysius O'Feeney)

France, 28 February 1895
Marcel Pagnol

Geneva, 9 April 1895
Michel Simon

Italy, 6 May 1895
Rudolph Valentino
(Rodolfo Alphonso
Raffaelle Guglielmi)

Kansas, 4 October 1895
Buster Keaton
(Joseph Francis Keaton)

Los Angeles, 29 November 1895
Busby Berkeley
(William Berkeley Enos)

Poland, 12 January 1896
Dziga Vertov
(Denis Kaufman)

Texas, 8 February 1896(?)
King Vidor

Indiana, 30 May 1896
Howard Hawks

France, 8 October 1896
Julien Duvivier

Ohio, 14 October 1896
Lillian Gish
(Lillian de Guiche)

Warsaw, 26 March 1897
Jean Epstein

Sicily, 18 May 1897
Frank Capra

Latvia, 23 January 1898
Sergei Mikhailovitch
Eisenstein

France, 15 May 1898
Arletty
(Leonie Bathiat)

Tokyo, 16 May 1898
Kenji Mizoguchi

Paris, 11 November 1898
René Clair
(René Chomette)

Netherlands, 18 November 1898
Joris Ivens

Chicago, 27 March 1899
Gloria Swanson

Nebraska, 10 May 1899
Fred Astaire
(Frederick Austerlitz)

New York, 30 May 1899
Irving Thalberg

England, 1 July 1899
Charles Laughton

New York, 7 July 1899
Georges Cukor

London, 13 August 1899
Alfred Hitchcock

New York, 25 December 1899
Humphrey Bogart

1900

★ ★

Paris, 1 January
Pathé has released a reconstructed news film, *Episodes of the Transvaal War*, filmed by Lucien Nonguet in the bois de Vincennes.

New York, 20 January
Thomas Edison has terminated Vitagraph's license in reply to a lawsuit threat over Edison's alleged failure to acknowledge Vitagraph's royalties on print sales.

Paris, 15 February
Léon Gaumont has opened show rooms at 41 avenue de l'Opéra and is marketing the Kinora, a viewing machine invented by Louis Lumière in 1896 that can transform photos into moving pictures.

Paris, 15 March
The Dufayel stores at 24 rue de Clignancourt are organizing sessions of sound film, using Charles Pathé's phonograph.

Paris, 8 April
François Parnaland, inventor of the Photothéagraph, patented in 1896, is trying to compete with the two giants, Gaumont and Pathé. He is offering films in both historical and comic genres, which he prints in all sizes of perforation.

Paris, 13 May
The Hippodrome in rue Caulaincourt, a huge edifice planned by Louis Gaillot for the World's Fair and able to seat 3,945, has opened with an equestrian pantomime, *Vercingétorix*, produced by Victorin-Hippolyte Jasset, former theater wardrobe master.

Peking, 14 June
Japanese cameramen T. Shibata and K. Fukaya have made a film of the Boxer uprising against the Western powers in China.

Nîmes, 17 June
The newspaper *Torero* has published the first article by a young aficionado named Louis Feuillade.

Berlin, 30 June
Oskar Messter has formed his own production company, Messter Projections. Cameramen shot their first footage from an airship.

Paris, 10 September
Pathé has taken over Victor Continsouza and René Bünzli's precision camera factory. The new company (General Company of phonographs, cinematographs and precision machines) is making the Maltese Cross camera devised by Bünzli.

London, 28 September
According to the *British Journal*, the longest cinematographic footage to date was filmed here during the boxing match between Sharkey and Jeffries. Cameramen used four movie cameras and 400 arc lights to make the half-hour film.

Paris, 30 September
Léon Gaumont has launched a new machine, the pocket Chrono, which takes and projects films with central perforation.

Paris, 10 November
Clément Maurice and Henri Loiret's Phono-Cinéma-Théâtre, one of the central attractions at the World's Fair, has re-opened its doors on a permanent basis at 42 boulevard de Bonne-Nouvelle near the Gymnase. Overseas tours are also planned.

Montreuil, 1 December
Méliès' latest extravaganza, *Rêve de Noël*, a "full-length film" that is comprised of 160 metres with a running time of nine minutes, is selling for 435 francs.

BIRTHS

Paris, 7 January
Robert Le Vigan (R. Coquillaud)

France, 4 February
Jacques Prévert

Spain, 22 February
Luis Buñuel

Germany, 2 March
Kurt Weill

Paris, 6 March
Henri Jeanson

Milwaukee, 5 April
Spencer Tracy

Hamburg, 26 April
Douglas Sirk (H. Detlef Sierck)

Rome, 3 July
Alessandro Blasetti

Paris, 17 July
Marcel Dalio

Memphis, 8 August
Robert Siodmak

Montreal, 10 August
Norma Shearer

Paris, 14 September
Robert Florey

Switzerland, 22 December
Marc Allégret

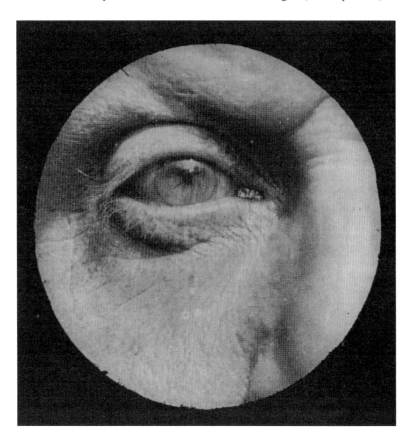

Grandma's eye as seen by her grandson through her magnifying glass. A striking image from G.A. Smith's **Grandma's Reading Glass***.*

Grimoin-Sanson's Cinéorama programs, cleverly filmed from a balloon, are attracting very large crowds at the World's Fair.

Vast audiences at the World's Fair are favorably

The Lumière Brothers provide one of the surprises of the fair

A serious crisis appears to be over

Louis Lumière personally directed the installation of this giant screen, 25 by 15 metres, visible to an audience of 25,000.

Paris, 12 November
The Universal Exhibition is over. The Cinematograph, which was unveiled five years ago, has been officially rehabilitated after the catastrophe at the Charity Bazaar on 4 May 1897. Since this fatal occurrence, moving images have been considered disreputable. Their purpose and even their morality were thought suspect. However, the Exhibition provided suitable space for a diversity of cinematographic experiments. Seventeen projection sites as well as 12 stands of cinematographic material were open to the public to mark one of the greatest inventions of the century. It's true that all the attractions devoted to moving pictures didn't enjoy as much good fortune. The panoramas attracted many more people than the Phonorama, Theatroscope and Phono-Cinema-Theatre as well as the Algerian Cinematograph. And it's better to forget the Cinéorama of Grimoin-Sanson, which was a disaster because the creator himself couldn't make it work. On the other hand, the Lumière brothers were wonderfully successful. Over one million spectators went to see their giant Cinematograph. The Lumière Company also received the Grand Prize from an international jury, who also awarded an equivalent prize to the firm of Léon Gaumont.

Paris, 15 May
One of the major events of the Exhibition was the first performance of the giant Lumière Cinematograph, which took place today in the vast Machine gallery. The overall supervisor Alfred Picard requested that Lumière undertake the projection on an enormous screen. They obviously didn't take the easy option in erecting an immense 400-square-metre white canvas in the center of the gallery that, nightly, has to be taken down to a large water storage tank. Just prior to the showing, the canvas is erected by a winch installed above the glass roof. Thus, the dampened material absorbs the light and remains sufficiently transparent to be seen from both sides. The program lasted 25 minutes and was comprised of 15 films. Originally, the Lumières wanted to use a film format in a 75-mm size. A camera was even manufactured to do this, but the projector failed to turn up on time, so they were forced to use the normal 35-mm one. Yet another Lumière project consisted of the projection of their films on a huge screen set up outside in front of the Eiffel Tower. However, the wind threatened to blow the screen down, and it was considered wiser to return to the safety of the Machine gallery. Despite these technical difficulties, the first showing was a triumph. The Lumière brothers had carried it off.

Brothers Auguste and Louis Lumière, close associates in all their ventures.

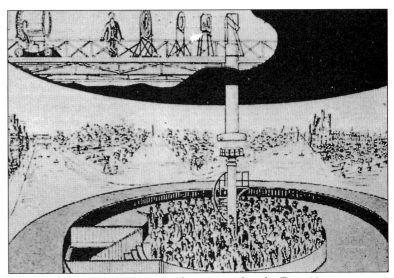

The new Photorama process was also presented at the Exposition.

impressed with the brilliance of the cinema

A risky undertaking by Grimoin-Sanson

The audience watches the screen from seats in the gondola of an air balloon.

Paris, 18 August

The French firm of Cinéorama, founded on 8 July 1899, has just been declared bankrupt. Eleven 70-mm cameras, 11 projectors and 119 spools of film – all the property of Raoul Grimoin-Sanson – had to be sold off at the famous Paris auction house, the Hôtel Drouot, in order to reimburse the shareholders. Grimoin-Sanson, who has claimed with self-assurance to have invented the cinematograph at the same time as the more celebrated Lumière brothers, really has had very little luck. He had triumphantly announced the opening of Cinéorama for May, when the Exhibition was in full swing. Having picked up an idea expounded in 1896 by Auguste Baron, Grimoin-Sanson patented a machine he called Cinécosmorama the following year, which later became known as Cosmorama. It consisted of moving projections across a panoramic screen. Ten cameras firmly mounted on a 2.5-metres-high wooden platform secured the steady taking of shots. The method of moving the cameras was synchronized with one large hand crank, operated by three assistants, that started the simultaneous unreeling of the films in the 10 cameras. With the financial backing of the company's shareholders, Grimoin-Sanson was able to shoot various films in many different European countries,

Device for a bank of ten cameras.

despite his odd working methods. He even shot one of these films from an air balloon he had installed in the Champs-de-Mars to mark the occasion of Cinéorama's christening. Why then this failure? At the moment, in the Cinéorama building constructed near the Eiffel Tower, there happen to be 10 projectors placed side by side which cannot operate because they release too much heat, thus putting the nitrate films in danger of catching fire. In other words, Cinéorama is just too risky to be used. Therefore, sadly, no showing took place.

Clément Maurice and Henri Lioret attract the crowds to their Phono-Cinema-Théatre with the Phonorama, developed by Berton, Dussaud and Jaubert, at the pavilion set aside for the first demonstrations of sound cinema. The films boast great names from the theater and music halls.

1901

★ ★

Trieste, January
Alexandre Lifka and his brother Karel, who came originally from Czechoslovakia, have fitted out the Electro-cinematographic Theatre for the Gaumont company. It is a large traveling cinema under a big top, with seating for 460.

Vincennes, January
Charles Pathé has decided he will increase production and plans to film one to two reels a day.

Montreuil, April
Georges Méliès has begun work on his new film, *Little Red Riding Hood*, described as a "full-length film" in 12 scenes.

Paris, 20 May
Claude Grivolas, one of Pathé's main shareholders, has invented a projector that produces three-dimensional pictures.

Paris, 27 July
Georges Mendel, the camera manufacturer, situated at 10 boulevard Bonne-Nouvelle, has launched a Parisian Cinematograph. He also produces comic and transformation scenes aimed at fairground shows.

London, 5 August
The Royal Animated and Singing Picture Co. today opens a cinema in the Mohawks' Hall, Upper Street, Islington. Admissions are the highest to date, with a top price of three shillings, but the inaugural program is packed with a variety of items.

Stockholm, 1 September
As part of his European tour, the talented French cameraman Clément Maurice is presenting a session of the Phono-Cinéma-Théâtre at the Olympia.

New York, 14 September
Edwin Stanton Porter has just been promoted to chief cameraman and film-director of the New York based Edison studios.

Paris, 21 September
Pathé has released *The Czar in France*, a newsreel about Nicholas II's recent visit to Paris, and the fairground shows are snapping it up. Meanwhile, the Lumière company's Paris agent H. Chevrier is trying to compete with Pathé and has brought out two new films: *les Fêtes franco-russes* and *Le tsar et le Président à Dunkerque*.

Belgium, 28 September
The fairground showman, Salsman, has put his Great Cinematograph up for sale. It consists of a 22-metre-long stall, "with gas and paraffin motors, a dynamo, lights, machinery, films and caravans."

London, October
Release of director James Williamson's *The Big Swallow*, *Stop Thief!* and *Fire*.

Paris, 15 November
Hugues Eugène Frey, the Opéra's décor designer, has just perfected a triple projector that is capable of producing still and moving projections specially intended for use in the theater or opera.

Washington, 16 December
Edison has lodged a copyright for *The Mysterious Cafe* from Edwin Porter at the Library of Congress.

Vincennes, 31 December
This year Pathé has produced 70 films (totaling 3,000 metres) in its rue du Polygone studio. Almost two-thirds of the films were directed by Ferdinand Zecca, Lucien Nonguet and Georges Hatot.

BIRTHS

Ohio, 1 February
Clark Gable

New York, 25 February
Zeppo Marx (Herbert Marx)

Georgia, 5 April
Melvyn Douglas (Hesselberg)

Montana, 7 May
Gary Cooper
(Frank James Cooper)

Philadelphia, 18 June
Jeanette MacDonald

Italy, 7 July
Vittorio De Sica

France, 3 October
Jean Grémillon

Paris, 3 November
André Malraux

Chicago, 5 December
Walt Disney

Berlin, 27 December
Marlene Dietrich
(Maria Magdalena von Losch)

*Drame au fond de la mer (Drama at the Bottom of the Sea), directed by Ferdinand Zecca, was inspired by **Cuirassé Maine** (Battleship Maine) of Georges Méliès.*

*Ferdinand Zecca in **The Conquest of the Air**, one of his first films as a director after joining the creative team at Charles Pathé's company.*

Law rules on licensing rights

New York, 12 January
The break between Edison and the Vitagraph company is complete. Vitagraph, controlled by Albert E. Smith and J. Stuart Blackton, has been notified of the cancellation of its film license. Its commercial operations have been placed under court supervision and its films sequestered, pending an appeal. This is the latest episode in the legal dispute which began on 12 July 1898 when Edison initiated his lawsuit against the newly formed Vitagraph Company in New York. The latter had made its own films dealing with the Spanish-American War which imitated those already produced by Edison, such as *Transport Whitney Leaving Dock*. Vitagraph was accused of having infringed on the rights of Edison's Kinematograph Company, and Blackton and Smith subsequently found themselves in serious trouble. It was necessary for them to come to some new arrangement to resolve the dispute, and Edison granted a special license to his rivals. This permission was subsequently withdrawn, and a new trial, not yet concluded, began in October 1900.

Cinematograph in city store

Paris, 6 July
Dufayel, the large department store situated near Barbès-Rochechouart, has announced that it has obtained the exclusive rights to the film of the Paris-Berlin automobile race, shot by Gaumont. The most spectacular images are those of the vehicles crossing the French/Belgian border. The film, almost 500 metres long, which represents 10 to 15 minutes of continuous projection, has already attracted a large audience. Dufayel, unhappy to be solely the marble temple of good taste, opened a hall of side shows in the spring of 1896. There, the department store offered alternating magic shows and cinematography. It brought happiness to children, as well as to people passing through. Today, the Cinematograph Dufayel is as famous as the facade of the store, which was designed by Falguière.

Film cameras document the final journey of a great monarch

Crowds follow the new King Edward VII and Queen Victoria's cortège.

London, 4 February
Film cameras are out to record the funeral of Queen Victoria. At Victoria Station Cecil Hepworth films the cortège and the principal mourners lining up. As the procession moves off, King Edward VII, the Kaiser and the Duke of Connaught pass right in front of the camera. The King reins up for a moment to allow Hepworth to get a better shot. Later Hepworth's camera obtains a spectacular shot of the procession from the vantage point of the Canadian arch on Whitehall. However, the noise of the cameras disturbs the solemn silence of the occasion, and an embarrassed Hepworth confesses that he wished that the earth could have swallowed both him and the camera up.

Clever tricks and unpleasant surprises from the house of Méliès

Paris, 22 September
Georges Méliès was present, on crutches, at the inauguration of his new theater the Robert Houdin. The old one was burned down last January. Méliès actually broke his femur during the shooting of his latest film *Bluebeard* in Montreuil. He was showing an extra how to die, when he fell backwards. *The Man of a Thousand Tricks*, also shot by Méliès this year, clearly revealed his creative ability. It's not for nothing that his films are imitated worldwide, particularly in the U.S. In his *The One-Man Orchestra*, made in 1900, Méliès himself audaciously portrays seven men, each with a different musical instrument, who form a whole orchestra. Then the seven musicians merge into a single person – the conductor. In *The Mysterious Dislocation*, a Pierrot's arms, legs and head get detached from his body. The creator of these weird spectacles also demonstrated several astonishing conjuring tricks.

*Made in the studio, the two-minute long **The Chrysalis and the Butterfly** is available in a color version.*

The irresistible rise of Monsieur Ferdinand Zecca

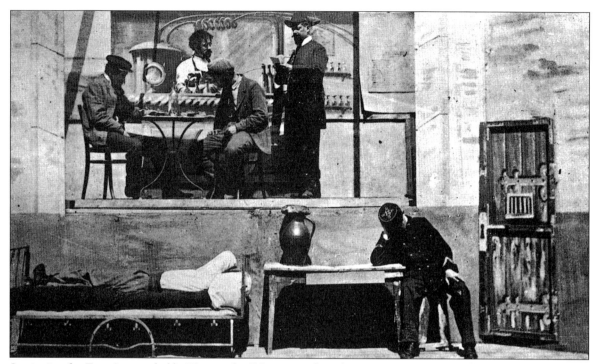

*Inspiration for Zecca's remarkable **History of a Crime** came from famous scenes on view at the Grevin Museum.*

Britain's James Williamson delivers a hat trick to audiences

Hove, 15 October
In the backyard of a spacious house in the southern coastal resort of Hove, Englishman James Williamson is running a flourishing film business. Williamson is a former chemist for whom photography was both a hobby and a sideline to his chemist's shop. In 1896 he took up cinematography to enliven his magic lantern shows. He did not start selling films until 1898. In the same year he wound up the chemist's side of his business in Church Road, Hove, and concentrated solely on the photographic side, moving to the premises in Western Road. With the help of his family Williamson writes, produces, develops, prints and often acts in his own films. His output includes *Two Naughty Boys Upsetting the Spoons*, which was made in 1898, and *Attack on a Chinese Mission Station* (1900), in which he employs parallel action and cross-cutting techniques which are advanced for the time. His latest offerings include three lively chase films: *Fire!*, *Stop Thief!* and *The Big Swallow*. The last has an ingenious climax. The film opens with a gentleman objecting to having his photograph taken. Seen from the point of view of a still photographer, the man bears down on the camera until his head fills the screen. At this point his mouth yawns open across almost the entire width of the screen. Then there is a cut to a shot of the photographer and his camera – invisible up until now – spinning around in a black void. Finally, we leave the hungry gentleman walking happily along munching his photographic snack. This imaginative work places Williamson in the front rank of technical innovators.

Paris, 19 October
Charles Pathé's *eminence grise*, a young man called Ferdinand Zecca, has doubled the takings of the Vincennes company since his arrival at the cinematographic workshop in the rue Polygone. The second son of a theater concierge, Zecca knows a lot about the entertainment world. Pathé noticed the young employee during the Universal Exhibition, where Zecca had been assigned to the Pathé stand. After a few days, Pathé asked Zecca if he would like to work in cinematography. Zecca immediately accepted the offer and has rapidly become Pathé's right-hand man and head of production. Under his management, production has increased and so have the profits. Theater managers appreciate his simple style, which corresponds to the expectations of the public. He clearly has no second thoughts when it comes to copying Méliès and Gaumont. For example, Pathé sold a large number of copies of *The Seven Castles of the Devil* because Zecca saw a great demand. This ambitious film, containing 40 tableaux, attempts to compete with that specialist of fantastic tales, Georges Méliès. However, Zecca's triumph is *The Story of a Crime*. The success of Grévin's waxwork museum has been transposed to the screen with unprecedented realism. In this tale, a bank clerk arrested for murder dreams about his past. When women and children are in attendance in the auditorium, the film is stopped before the last scene – the terrifying fall of the guillotine's blade.

*This close-up is from James Williamson's **The Big Swallow**.*

A former cafe-concert entertainer.

1902

★★★★★★★★ **1902** ★★★★★★★★★★★★★★★★★★★★★★★★★★★★

Paris, 15 January
The Lumière brothers have opened a Photorama at 18 rue de Clichy. The panoramic cinema has replaced the old Pole Nord cinema.

Poland, January
Kazimerz Proszynski has used his sophisticated Pleograph to shoot some short films.

Paris, 9 April
The Medical Tribune has expressed indignation at fairground showmen for their apparent commercialization of "sensational scenes" from films of surgeries performed by Dr. Eugène-Louis Doyen. On 9 April, Clément Maurice filmed him during an operation separating the Siamese twins Radica and Doodica.

Los Angeles, 16 April
The opening of the Electric Theater, the first venue in the city to be entirely dedicated to cinematographic projections (200 seats).

Vincennes, April
Charles Pathé has had a new film studio built. Situated in rue du Bois, the glass building includes a workshop for film sets.

New York, 2 May
Vitagraph has won its court case against Edison. Stuart Blackton and Albert Smith will now be able to recommence film production.

Paris, 31 May
Pathé has released two newsreels, *The President in Russia* and *The King of Spain's Coronation*, an animated film *la Poupée merveilleuse* (*The Marvellous Doll*) and a realistic drama by Ferdinand Zecca *les Victimes de l'alcoolisme* (*The Victims of Alcoholism*) based on the seventh of Zola's Rougon-Macquart novels, *L'Assommoir*.

Paris, 4 August
One of the Gaumont cameramen, Léo Lefèvre, has become the only holder of the royal warrant, filmmaker by appointment to the Royal Spanish household. He has made a series of films about King Alphonse XIII's visits to France.

London, August
The American-born Charles Urban has just resigned from the Warwick Trading Company to form his own production company, The Charles Urban Trading Company.

Paris, 16 October
Emile Reynaud has invented the Stereo-praxinoscope. With this machine a double series of photographs can be viewed, showing the different sequences of a movement and giving the illusion of three-dimensions.

Paris, 18 October
Georges Mendel has put a newsreel on the market, *les Obsèques de Zola* (*Zola's Funeral*), and two fiction films *The Magic Table or the Talking Heads*, a plagiary of a Méliès' film, and *les Mousquetaires au couvent* (*The Musketeers at the Convent*). The films are sold with a cylinder that allows synchronized sound.

Paris, October
Warned by the American corporate magazines that his films are being copied in the United States by both Edison and Sigmund Lubin, Méliès has decided to open a New York branch. His brother Gaston is to be the general manager.

Paris, 27 December
One week after Thérèse Humbert's arrest, Georges Mendel has edited *l'Affaire Humbert*, a film about the much publicized swindle.

Japan, 31 December
One of the first Japanese films, *Monijigari*, springs from the Kabuki theatrical tradition.

BIRTHS

Paris, 3 April
Henri Garat (H. Garascu)

Germany, 6 May
Max Ophuls (Max Oppenheimer)

Pittsburgh, 10 May
David O. Selznick

Moscow, 16 June
Boris Barnet

France, 1 July
William Wyler

Berlin, 22 August
Leni Riefenstahl

Nebraska, 5 September
Darryl Zanuck

Italy, 20 September
Cesare Zavattini

England, 19 December
Ralph Richardson

The refinement of Méliès' special effects is seen in **La danseuse microscopique (The Microscopic Dancer)**; *the dancer appears in place of an egg.*

*The imagination of Méliès goes even further with **Voyage to the Moon**, a 13-minute film with 30 sets, filmed between May and July.*

The new King of England is crowned in advance!

London, 9 August

At Westminster Abbey the coronation of King Edward VII unfolds without incident. The ceremony, originally set for 26 June, was postponed after the King fell ill. This evening at the Alhambra Theatre in Leicester Square, the British public is queuing to watch *The Coronation of King Edward VII,* a film directed in Montreuil by Georges Méliès and produced by the American Charles Urban, who is a London resident. It was impossible to film the ceremony in Westminster Abbey; the cameras make too much noise, and the lights are too weak. Méliès has, therefore, carefully re-staged the coronation in his own studio. Over 150 performers took part in the film, which does not last as long as the original five-and-a-half-hour ceremony. The interior of Westminster Abbey has been re-created using a painted backdrop and cardboard. Méliès' edited version of the coronation was ready by 26 June, the date originally set for the ceremony. The "magician" of Montreuil experienced great difficulty in finding a double to play Edward VII. Happily, he eventually located a man who fit the bill working in a laundry at Kremlin-Bicêtre. Edward's consort Queen Alexandra is portrayed by a dancer from the Châtelet Theatre. This ambitious reconstruction of one of the great

The Coronation of King Edward VII, produced by Charles Urban and made in a few days at Montreuil.

British occasions of state has been launched amid a blaze of publicity by Charles Urban, the owner of the Warwick Trading Company and Star Film's agent in Britain. With commendable honesty, the publicity makes it clear that the re-creation of the ceremony is not accurate in every detail. Nevertheless, in spite of Urban's frankness, many French journalists have accused the film-makers of deceiving the English public. But, in addition to crying "God Save the King," the British should give three cheers for Méliès.

Sound cinema according to Léon Gaumont

Paris, 7 November

The French Photographic Society welcomes the engineer and industrialist Léon Gaumont, who is delivering a lecture on sound cinema and his new Chronophone system. To the succesful manufacture of motion picture apparatus, Gaumont has added a flourishing film production business. The process that he and his technicians, Georges Laudet and René Decaux, have devised is similar to that of Auguste Baron. It uses an electric motor to synchronize a phonograph and cinematograph. Filming and recording are simultaneous; the actors' gestures are fixed on film at the same time as their words are inscribed on the wax of a phonographic cylinder. A signal engraved on the cylinder – a whistle or a bell which sounds a few seconds

before the beginning of the sound accompaniment to the film – alerts the projectionist to start the cinematograph running. The two devices then operate in tandem to the end of the film with the motor synchronizing sound and image. Three films are shown. In the first, Léon Gaumont himself introduces the Block Note photographic system. The two other films show a gypsy dance and a gavotte accompanied by appropriate music. The problem with the system remains the sound. The audience had great difficulty in hearing Gaumont's explanation of the process. Gaumont has a surprise in store for his audience at the end of the evening. He announces his intention to overcome the problem of sound amplification by using compressed air.

A little fairy found in a cabbage patch

Paris, 11 October

A new version of *The Cabbage Patch Fairy*, a film originally shot in 1900 by Alice Guy and Anatole Thiberville in a garden adjoining the Gaumont development laboratories in Belleville, has been put on sale. This 20-metre-long film, interpreted by the actress Yvonne Mugnier-Sérand and emanating from Alice Guy's imagination, tells the story of a fairy who emerges from a cabbage to present a childless, young married couple with a living baby. The copies of this film have sold so rapidly to the fairground public that Guy, at the request of Léon Gaumont, has since turned out *The First Class Midwife*, or *The Birth of Children*, which follows a

*A scene from **The Cabbage Fairy**.*

similar outline to the earlier film of 1900. However, the new version, which is 100 metres long and costs 200 francs, could be sold colorized.

A wonderful work from Méliès enriches the cinema

Paris, 1 September

George Méliès' latest film, *Voyage to the Moon*, is an unprecedented triumph. The public at the fairground where it was shown, unreservedly applauded this fantastic tale, which contains 30 tableaux and lasts 13 minutes. Méliès has again manipulated the marvels of science with impressive dexterity. One wonders whether the Cinematograph will take the place of the large shows at the Châtelet Theatre. With Méliès anything is possible.

Completed in July, the 260-metre film has broken all records. It required three months shooting, a large cast, and cost 10,000 francs. Méliès got his inspiration from two Jules Verne novels – *From the Earth to the Moon* and *Around the Moon*. But there are episodes in the film which Verne himself would never have dared depict. The fantastic tale begins at the Congress of Astronauts presided over by Professor Barbenfouillis, who is played by Méliès himself. He and five other boffins take off for the moon in a giant shell fired by a cannon. The shell lands in "the eye of the moon" as the title of the ninth tableau explains. Subsequent to the moon landing, the group of intellectuals explore the place and come across some strange creatures called the Sélénites, who scarcely appreciate such an intrusion, and take the explorers prisoner. Professor Barbenfouillis then organizes their es-

Méliès' most remarkable film to date, **Voyage to the Moon** *consists of 10 scenes played out on 30 sets.*

cape after finding out that the Sélénites have a fatal weakness – they explode when they are struck. When the shell returns to earth amidst panic, it falls into the sea, and the heroes are fished out. The last two tableaux show the public rejoicing and the inauguration of a

statue to Professor Barbenfouillis. This amazing film has earned Méliès international popularity. However, a sole shadow was cast over *Voyage to the Moon* when, unfortunately, it was systematically pirated in the United States by the Thomas Edison and Sigmund Lubin companies. As

it turned out, Edison's London representative Al Abadie secretly made a copy of the film to send to the U.S., and the result was that many counterfeits were made. These fakes deleted the Star Film trademark that Georges Méliès had taken great care to imprint on all of his films.

This extraordinary fantasy is already being imitated by others.

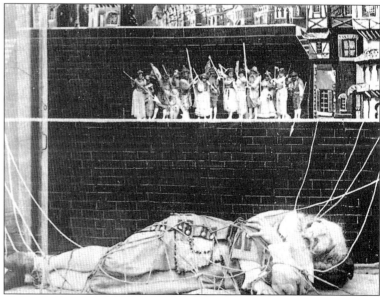

Gulliver's Travels, *based on Swift's novel, is another visual delight.*

★ ★

Lyon, 18 January
The Lumière firm has launched new footage of phantasmagorical, genre and transformation scenes.

Washington, 21 January
The Life of an American Fireman, Edwin Porter's first film using several different sets, has been lodged for copyright.

New York, January
Gaston Méliès has been sent to the United States by the Star Film production company to open offices at 204 East 38th Street. His son Paul is working with him.

Delhi, 8 February
Gaumont, Pathé, Georges Mendel and Warwick have all released films simultaneously about Edward VII's coronation.

New York, February
A Hungarian immigrant and furrier, Adolph Zukor, has opened a penny arcade called "The Bazaar".

Paris, 1 March
The first copy of *le Fascinateur*, a specialist publication for film lovers, is now available.

Vincennes, 5 April
Pathé has just released Ferdinand Zecca's *la Vie d'un Joueur*, a film in the same vein as *les Victimes de l'alcoolisme*.

London, May
Gaumont Ltd has been set up and is to be headed by Colonel Bromhead.

New York, 22 August
Gaston Méliès has made his producing debut with *Reliance - Shamrock III*, a film of a yacht race.

Berlin, 29 August
Oskar Messter is presenting the Biophon, his method of producing talking films, as the star attraction at the Apollo Theatre.

Paris, 12 September
The Lumière brothers have applied for a patent for Autochrome, their new trichromatic method to process color photographs.

Montreuil, October
Méliès has started shooting *Faust aux enfers*, adapted from the opera by Hector Berlioz. The film is to have 15 scenes and Méliès himself is to play the leading role.

Paris, 10 November
Léon Gaumont continues demonstrating his Chronophone to various photographic societies.

New York, November
Marcus Loew, the son of an immigrant family, has opened in New York and Cincinatti several penny arcades, which are also known as peep shows here.

Copenhagen, 31 December
Peter Elfelt has made Denmark's first fiction film, *Capital Execution* (*Henrettelson*).

Peking, 31 December
Lin Zhusan has returned to China from the U.S. with a projector and films. He is the first Chinese promoter of the cinematograph and has held several projections for his compatriots at the popular Tien Lo tea house.

BIRTHS

Alabama, 31 January
Tallulah Bankhead

Belgium, 12 February
Georges Simenon

Paris, 21 February
Madeleine Renaud

Marseilles, 8 May
Fernandel
(Fernand Contandin)

England, 12 May
Wilfrid Hyde White

Brussels, 25 May
Charles Spaak

England, 29 May
Bob Hope (Leslie Townes Hope)

Stockholm, 21 June
Alf Sjöberg

France, 23 June
Louis Seigner

France, 5 August
Claude Autant-Lara

France, 19 August
Claude Dauphin (C. Legrand)

Austria, 11 November
Sam Spiegel

Tokyo, 12 December
Yasujiro Ozu

This cinema, opened by Karl Knubbel on Germany's Frankfurter Allee (Station), is one of many such establishments that are springing up all over Europe.

One of many attempts to achieve sound on film, the Biophonograph has enjoyed some degree of success without managing to resolve all the problems.

The enterprising Charles Urban

London, 2 November

Charles Urban, the American producer and distributor, is personally in charge of his new firm, the Urban Trading Company. He has sent cameramen out all over the world to discover and to cover sensational events. Charles Rider Noble, his photographer in Macedonia, even shot the Ilindon uprising. Earlier this year Noble filmed the Moroccan revolution and the proclamation in Delhi, India of the coronation of Edward VII. Urban's films have been selling extremely well recently. Georges Méliès' output has been included in Urban's catalogue, some of which deals with other topical events, notably Edward VII's journey to Paris; a tremendous fire in London; the automobile race in Ireland for the Gordon Bennett cup, etc. Also well presented have been both comic and dramatic productions. *Burglary in Action* gave rise to enormous and enthusiastic applause as did *Attack on a Stage Coach Last Century*, comprising 11 tableaux. *Scientific Topics* was shot by Professor Martin G. Barker as part of a series concerning the way of life of bees, which has since been copied everywhere. In addition to his films, Urban also happens to be a manufacturer of cameras. His little Bioka, an apparatus that can be operated easily by amateurs, uses the 17.5-mm format, and the results are extraordinarily accurate.

The young American who wants to 'open all eyes to the universe'.

A new field of action for Ferdinand Zecca in Vincennes studios

*Filming of **William Tell** has just been completed at Pathé's second studio, opened at Vincennes in 1902.*

Vincennes, 10 October

The ill-equipped and tiny rue du Bois workshop and theater was unworthy of the large firm of Charles Pathé. Therefore, the latter destroyed it to build a far larger theater. As production could not be halted, Pathé rented a house located at 1 rue de Paris where Ferdinand Zecca, in charge of Pathé productions, works while waiting for the opening of yet another temporary workshop in Montreuil, at 52 rue du Sergent-Bobillot. Zecca – designer, scenarist, cinematographer and actor – has enjoyed so much success in a few months that he is credited with the reputation Pathé now enjoys in the fairground world. Today there were two films shown – *William Tell*, copied from the English picture by Robert William Paul, and also *Don Quixote*, a great comic piece which Zecca and his associate Lucien Nonguet had to cut down. Originally it was 430 metres, but the fairground stall-owners protested that it was far too long. The new version has been drastically reduced to 255 metres. In truth, this is not the first time that Zecca has plagiarized the films of his colleagues, particularly those of Robert William Paul, Charles Urban, James Williamson and even

Georges Méliès, all of whose work he has found useful as models. This is considered proof of his own good taste. After every success of a rival company, Zecca borrows the theme and special effects, and when he releases his own version, he adds a few details or variations of his own. Nobody can prevent him. But Zecca also possesses flair, imagination and know-how. The 1901 broad comedy

What Is Seen of My Sixth Sense, or *The Victims of Alcoholism*, a very realistic drama in five acts, were both instigated by Zecca. And sometimes his style reaches unequaled scatological heights, much to the joy of the fairground public. In *The Wrong Door*, shot this year, a peasant loses his way and sits himself down on a telephone seat, miming his satisfaction.

*With **The Victims of Alcoholism**, Ferdinand Zecca returns to the Zola-esque realism which marked his successful **History of a Crime**.*

Edwin S. Porter provides a model for the 'Western'

Washington, 1 December
The outlaw chief turns toward the camera, takes a bead with his Colt revolver and then fires repeatedly at the audience at point-blank range, whereupon the screen turns red! This is the major talking point of *The Great Train Robbery*, the latest film produced by the Edison Manufacturing Company, a copy of which has just been deposited in the Library of Congress. *The Great Train Robbery* has a Western setting, but most of its scenes were filmed on location at Paterson, New Jersey, in the fall of 1903. Director Edwin S. Porter, who is the head of production at the Edison Manufacturing Company, filmed much of the exciting action in the actual woods that surround the infamous Lackawanna ironworks, and the accent is on realism. In this story, a train is held up and the passengers are forced by the bandits to descend from their carriage and form a line by the track, their hands in the air. The robbers then make their getaway on horseback. In the meantime, the telegraph operator, who had been both bound and gagged, succeeds in raising the alarm at what the Edison catalogue describes as being a "typical Western dance hall." A posse is raised, and the outlaws are hunted down and killed. The 10-minute running time of *The Great Train Robbery* has been divided into 10 "tableaux" plus the dramatic medium close-up of the gun-toting outlaw, played by George

Filmed for Edison, Porter's **The Great Train Robbery** *creates an exciting new genre for the cinema.*

Barnes, which exhibitors can choose to place either at the beginning or end of the film. Action keeps briskly on the move; in addition to the robbery itself there are fisticuffs, horseback pursuit and gunplay. From a technical point of view there is an interesting use of double exposure plus a clever bit of jump-cutting when a dummy is substituted for

one of the trainmen and hurled off the engine after a frenzied fist fight. Porter, who not only directed but also photographed *The Great Train Robbery*, maintains a high degree of both suspense and action by intercutting between the outlaws and the posse. At times, however, the long shots used in the tableaux make it somewhat difficult to identify the

individual characters. Many Western vignettes have preceded *The Great Train Robbery*, and there have even been Western films with story lines of sorts, but Porter's film has established a formula which many producers are already rushing to imitate. Thus it is clear that the Western has well and truly arrived as a staple of cinema.

'A typical Western', according to the producer. The film opens new horizons.

Shooting at actual locations gives the film its realistic atmosphere.

1904

★ ★

New York, 13 January
Wallace McCutcheon has filmed *Photographing a Female Crook* for the American Mutoscope and Biograph Co. Included in the 40-second film is an interesting sequence of tracking in for a close-up of one of the characters.

Rome, 20 January
Filoteo Alberini has opened the Cinema Moderno, the first purpose-built cinema here. He had already opened a film theater in Florence in 1899. To date, the Italian cinema has only produced newsreels.

France, 6 February
The daisy stamped in the middle of the abbreviation "Elgé", the initials of Léon Gaumont, has appeared for the first time in the corporate newspaper *l'Industriel forain*.

Montreuil, 1 March
Charles Pathé has had a new studio built at 52 rue Sergent-Bobillot. Ferdinand Zecca is working there on a news reconstruction film called *l'Incendie du théâtre de Chicago* (*Fire in the Chicago Theater*) about the fire that destroyed the Chicago Theater on 1 January.

Paris, 24 March
Lucien Bull, director of the Marey Institute in the Bois de Boulogne, has photographed the path taken by a bullet through various objects, using an electrical procedure.

Paris, 2 April
Georges Mendel has opened the Cinéma-Grapho-Théâtre.

Helsinki, 4 April
Emil Stahlberg has inaugurated the town's first cinema with the film *Mailman Ympäri*.

Paris, 30 April
Léon Gaumont has released his film *l'Attaque d'une diligence*, shot in the open air by Alice Guy, a plagiarism of Charles Urban's *l'Attaque d'une diligence au siècle dernier*, which came out in Paris last November.

St. Louis, May
George Hale, head of the Kansas City fire brigade, is presenting a new attraction at the St. Louis Fair, Hale's Touring Car. The audience, seated in the replica of a train carriage, watches the passing scenery, supplied by films from all over the world, projected onto a screen.

Paris, 11 June
After the filming of *la Valse de Barnum* at Montreuil, Pathé has released a new Gaston Velle film for sale. The film, *Métamorphoses d'un papillon*, shows a woman turning into a butterfly. A former conjurer, Velle specializes in trick effects.

St. Louis, 10 July
For the occasion of the Olympic Games, German producer Oskar Messter used his Biophon to shoot his first films with synchronized soundtrack for the export market. *The Whistling Boy* is one of them.

Paris, 27 August
Léon Gaumont has released for sale *les Petits coupeurs de bois vert*, a realistic drama on the theme of poverty, produced by Alice Guy in collaboration with Henri Gallet.

Washington, 11 November
Biograph has lodged W. McCutcheon's *The Suburbanite* for copyright.

BIRTHS

England, 18 January
Cary Grant
(Alexander Archibald Leach)

Texas, 23 March
Joan Crawford
(Lucille Fay LeSueur)

London, 14 April
John Gielgud

Washington, 2 May
Bing Crosby
(Harry L. Crosby)

Paris, 17 May
Jean Gabin (Alexis Moncorgé)

Hungary, 26 June
Peter Lorre (Laszlo Löwenstein)

Paris, 4 August
Christian-Jaques (C. Maudet)

Algeria, 18 September
Orane Demazis

Paris, 12 November
Jacques Tourneur

DEATHS

England, 8 May
Eadweard J. Muybridge

Paris, 16 May
Etienne Jules Marey

The poster advertising the release of **The Strike***. Ferdinand Zecca was inspired by Emile Zola's title* **Germinal** *for this film about social conditions.*

A Love Story, directed by Lucien Nonguet for Pathé, is the first film with a sentimental theme to become a popular success with the public.

New initiatives in sound films

Paris, 2 April

Georges Mendel, the producer and distributor of many different kinds of films, has developed a new interest in sound and the talking films. He has published the first announcement about his experiments linking the phonograph with the cinema at his Cinema-Grapho-Theatre. It is apparent, however, that Mendel has not really invented anything himself. Henri Joly, another well-known pioneer and technical innovator who worked for Charles Pathé in 1895, has sold Mendel his original sound-film patents. The system utilizes a small electrical box to link the phonograph needle with the projector shutter and specially amplified sound. As George Mendel explains it, the bringing together of these two inventions "is designed to give the complete illusion of real life and a more satisfactory blending of gestures and words than has previously been achieved."

Cinema owner-exhibitors are now on the increase in the USA

New York, 19 June

This year has seen a rapid growth in the number of exhibition venues throughout the U.S., with new enterprises springing up almost daily. Clearly, a major stimulus has been the amazing success of *The Great Train Robbery* as well as *Hale's Tours and Scenes of the World*, which was one of the big attractions at the 1903 St. Louis Exposition. Typical of the new breed of entrepreneurs is the Warner family of Youngstown, Ohio. They have just opened the Cascade, their first small picture theater, in New Castle, Pa. However, the greatest activity can be seen in the larger cities such as New York where William Fox, who prospered in the garment trade, has just purchased the "Automat" on 14th Street. Similarly, the furrier Adolph Zukor joined Mitchell Mark earlier this year to form the Automatic Vaudeville Co. Business is so good at the Automatic One-Cent Vaudeville, they're planning more arcades in the coming months.

The Cascade cinema in Pennsylvania is owned by the Warner brothers.

Zecca the wanderer returns to Vincennes

Paris, 1 March

Ferdinand Zecca is well known at Pathé for his spontaneity and for the amusing ideas which augment his films. However, he also has a reputation for hypersensitivity. After a memorable quarrel with his superior, the eminent Charles Pathé, he slammed the door on the Vincennes offices and was employed by Léon Gaumont on Alice Guy's recommendation. He stayed two weeks at Gaumont and once again left discontented. Had he squabbled with Alice Guy? In the end, Pathé, who found he couldn't get by without his collaborator, re-employed him. Today, Zecca is shooting *The Chicago Theater Fire*, a reconstruction of a real event.

An actor-director's vision of himself as both the painter and the model.

An amorous chase in the heart of New York

New York, 8 August

A wild chase around the statue of General Grant on Riverside Drive: a man, clearly alarmed by the results of a personal advertisement he has placed for a bride, attempts to escape from a pursuing pack of women, all of whom are eager to marry him. This is the subject of a new picture, produced by the American Mutoscope and Biograph Company and entitled *Personal*. Besides its furious pace, the film is marked by its outdoor locations and an absence of painted backcloths. In their frantic rush the characters vault fences and hurdles, race across bridges, negotiate ditches and streams, causing chaos as they pass. As they leap over obstacles separating them and their prey, the young women lift their skirts and saucily reveal their ankles, to the great delight of audiences. Exhausted, the young man admits defeat and gives his heart to the first comer. Directed by Wallace McCutcheon, this is a new kind of comedy film, full of breezy visual flair and destined for success on both sides of the Atlantic.

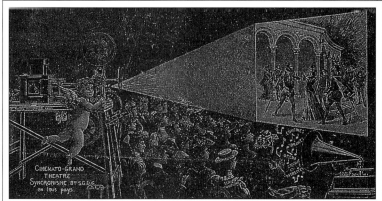

Henri Joly's Cinemato-Gramo-Theatre, demonstrated by Georges Mendel.

The international ambitions of M. Charles Pathé

New York, 31 July
The Pathé brothers are expanding abroad. They are opening a sales outlet for their phonographic and film equipment in New York, have established a factory in Bound Brook and set up a film studio in Jersey City. The brothers are bidding to create a worldwide empire. In February they opened a branch in Moscow. Pathé's aim is to control local production and to produce prints of their films on the spot. Charles Pathé wants to make his cockerel trademark an internationally-recognized symbol. Revenue from Pathé's films far outstrips that from phonographs, and the company is now the most important film production outfit in France. The most recent Pathé catalogue, published in August, contains over 1,000 titles of all kinds, some which can be enjoyed with sound provided by Pathé's Ciné-Phono. Among the company's specialities are bawdy scenes unsuitable for children.

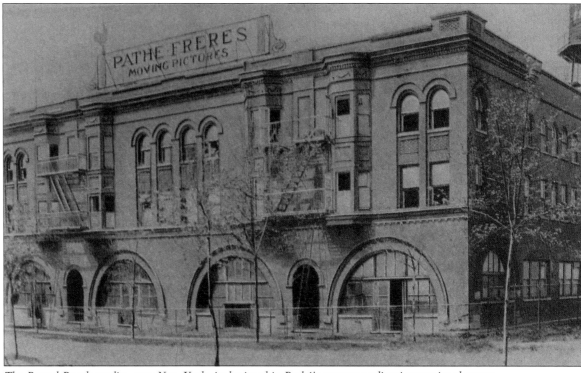

The Bound Brook studio, near New York, is the jewel in Pathé's ever-expanding international crown.

Georges Méliès surpasses his own best efforts

Montreuil, 31 December
After the international success of *Voyage to the Moon*, the creator Georges Méliès continues his astronomic fantasies. In his glass theater at Montreuil, he has shot *Voyage Beyond the Possible*, an exceptional film of 43 tableaux with a running time of about 20 minutes. Méliès once again takes the role of a slightly crazed professor. This time he is called Mabouloff, president of the Institute of Incoherent Geography, who maintains that he can reach the sun by means of the Automabouloff, a vehicle of his own invention. The journey fails at first, but with a steam-propelled locomotive which takes off from the summit of the Jungfrau, Mabouloff and his team arrive on the sun. A refrigerator keeps them alive in the 3,000-degree temperature. As in *Voyage to the Moon*, the film concludes with the descent to earth, this time by means of a sort of submarine. Crowds cheer as they return to the Institute. Méliès has taken great care with the decor and the special effects, and certain scenes are extremely poetic. A ravishing 18-year-old actress, May de Lavergne, plays the part of a nurse. Méliès is once more in love but has nonetheless remained faithful to former loves – Jehanne d'Alcy is also in the cast.

*The **Voyage Beyond the Possible** follows **Voyage to the Moon**.*

*A sketch by the prolific Méliès for a scene in **The Damnation of Faust**.*

★ ★ ★ ★ ★ ★ ★ **1905** ★

St. Petersburg, 6 January
Félix Mesguich, who has moved from the Urban Trading Co. to the Warwick, has filmed *The Attack Against the Czar.*

Paris, 7 January
The English firm, Warwick Trading Company, has edited four newsreels of the Russo-Japanese war. They are guaranteed genuine compared to the faked scenes in the films made by Méliès and Pathé.

London, January
Release of two action films: *The Life of Charles Peace* by the showman William Haggar, and *Rescued by Rover* by Cecil Hepworth.

Paris, 16 February
Charles Pathé has opened a display room at 31 boulevard des Italiens, to present his films to showmen and cinema owners.

Paris, 15 April
Pathé has released its first film with chase sequences, *Dix femmes pour un mari* (*Ten Women for One Husband*) by André Heuzé, a copy of the Gaumont Company's English film *Personal* by Alfred Collins.

Copenhagen, 23 April
Former circus impresario Ole Olsen has opened the city's first cinema, The Biograph Theatre.

New York, 1 June
Adolph Zukor has opened a Hale's Tour in Union Square.

Paris, 5 August
Pathé has released a film by Louis Gasnier, *A Schoolboy's First Day Out*, with Gabriel Leuvielle, an actor from the burlesque theater, now calling himself Max Linder.

Switzerland, 25 August
Félix Mesguich has filmed the traditional wine growers' festival using a long-focus lens. He sent the reel to Paris immediately, beating the cameraman for the Urban Trading Co. who had the exclusive rights.

Rome, 20 September
Release of the first Italian fiction film *La Presa di Roma*, made by Filoteo Alberini.

Paris, 1 October
The review *Phono-Gazette*, started by Edmond Benoît-Lévy, has become the *Phono-Ciné-Gazette.*

Rome, 31 October
Filoteo Alberini and Dante Santoni have set up a film studio, said to be Italy's first such establishment.

Paris, 15 December
Méliès has announced his new film, *la Légende de Rip Van Winkle*, to be filmed in 17 settings and played by himself and his son André.

Peking, December
The Feng Tai photographic studio is making its first Chinese film *The Tingchun Mountains*. Tan Xinpei, a popular singer from the Peking opera, is playing the leading role.

BIRTHS
France, 23 March
Paul Grimault

Paris, 26 April
Jean Vigo

Nebraska, 16 May
Henry Fonda

Paris, 29 July
Pierre Braunberger

Montana, 2 August
Myrna Loy

Mexico, 3 August
Dolores Del Rio
(Lolita D. Martinez Asunsolo Lopez Negrette)

Tokyo, 20 August
Mikio Naruse

New York, 25 August
Clara Bow

Paris, 17 September
Claudette Colbert
(Chauchoin)

Stockholm, 18 September
Greta Garbo (Gustafsson)

England, 30 September
Michael Powell

New York, 17 October
Jean Arthur
(Gladys Greene)

New York, 22 October
Constance Bennett

Paris, 22 December
Pierre Brasseur (Espinasse)

Brussels, 25 December
Fernand Gravey (Mertens)

A Pathé film, **The Apaches of Paris**, *continues the tradition of* **The History of a Crime***.*

A new success for Pathé, **The Moon Lover** *is directed by Gaston Velle who is a key member of Ferdinand Zecca's talented creative team.*

The cinema makes a court appearance

Narbonne, 4 March

To the all-round satisfaction of the professionals, the town court delivered a verdict exonerating the Cinematograph in a case which has been the talk of the town and in the news nationally. The Aerogyne Theatre, a fairground establishment run by the Dulaar family, had installed a cinematograph apparatus in front of the Church of Saint Just, at the time when people were coming out of mass. Jérôme Dulaar himself directed the cameraman, who had taken up a position on top of a stepladder. At the same time, a banner carrying the words "Cinematograph of the Aerogyne Theatre" was unfurled. Thus forewarned, the parishioners allowed themselves to be filmed without objection. Yet there were a few who, having seen themselves on the screen during the projection, believed they had been filmed without their consent and consequently took legal action. However, the judge decided that the filming had been done in a public place and the persons filmed had been informed. This decision came over a month after a judgment given by the civil court of the Seine. It concerned the renowned Dr. Doyen in his case against the cameraman François Parnaland. The latter, who had made educative films of the surgeon, was charged with profiting from them for commercial purposes without the physician's prior consent. The Parisian magistrates considered that the doctor could legitimately oppose all screenings.

Man's best friend is star of new film

*Cecil Hepworth, the producer of **Rescued by Rover**, also appears in the film which is directed by Lewis Fitzhamon.*

London, 3 July

The Hepworth Manufacturing Company Ltd. was registered just over one year ago, on 25 April 1904. As befits the head of a successful business, Cecil Hepworth has become currently more of a supervisor or producer and is less involved in the actual filmmaking process. The film most recently released by the Hepworth company is a truly delightful adventure story. Entitled *Rescued By Rover*, it is sure to be enormously popular with British audiences. In the case of this film, however, not only did Hepworth take charge of the production, but his entire family pitched in on the project. The story and scenario was written by Mrs. Hepworth, who also plays the role of the distressed mother in the film, Hepworth himself appears as the harassed father, and the couple's eight-month-old baby daughter has a cameo appearance as the infant abducted by gypsies in the story. And Rover, the faithful pet and undisputed star of the film, is the family's own collie. Two actors were hired for supporting roles. Each received a fee of half-a-guinea, which included the cost of fares from London to Walton-on-Thames, where the Hepworth company is based. According to Hepworth, the seven-minute long film cost exactly 7 pounds, 13 shillings and ninepence to make, but with prints on sale for 10 pounds, 13 shillings and sixpence, the producer expects to earn a good profit. Cecil Hepworth first became involved in the industry in 1897 when, at age 22, he began to put on his own film shows with a projector which he had adapted. The first film he made was of the Oxford and Cambridge boat race for the Warwick company in 1898. The following year he extended his interests from developing and printing to the actual production of films. He constructed a small studio in his garden and soon built up a catalogue of films for sale. His latest pictures are longer and more sophisticated, and include a version of *Alice in Wonderland* that is done in 16 scenes. His newest *Rover* seems to represent a fitting culmination to his recent efforts.

Notorious criminal makes gripping film subject in Great Britain

London, 1 October

One of Britain's most notorious criminals, the cat burglar and murderer Charles Peace, has now been immortalized on film by William Hagger in *The Life of Charles Peace*. The making of this film was something of a family affair. Hagger directs and takes the role of Peace, his four brothers appear in the film, and one of his daughters portrays Peace's mistress. Another daughter, age 12, has been dressed as a boy and cast as the burglar's assistant. Peace was executed in February 1879 after a 20-year career of crime. Stunted, gargoyle-faced and webfingered, Peace was a master of the silent art of cat burglary – strong and agile and the designer of a range of sophisticated housebreaking tools of the trade. His predilection for exotic disguises and his love of the violin, which he played incessantly and extremely badly, helped turn him into a criminal legend. Often the violin case served as the container for Peace's burglary implements as he went about his nocturnal business. Eventually, Peace was condemned to death for the murder of one Arthur Dyson, the husband of a woman with whom Peace had had an affair. While awaiting execution, Peace confessed to another killing for which an innocent man had been sentenced to life imprisonment. In *The Life of Charles Peace*, Hagger plays Peace posing as a clergyman to avoid capture by the police. The film reconstructs Peace's real-life leap from a train on his way to trial for the murder of Arthur Dyson and his execution. And for the final dose of realistic effect, Hagger returned to the scene of Dyson's murder, at Banner Cross in Sheffield, to film the fatal shooting.

Tinting of films is done by stencil

Paris, 31 August

Georges Méliès' new film *The Paris-Monte Carlo Rally in Two Hours*, which pokes gentle fun at the numerous automobile accidents suffered by the King of Belgium, is entirely in color. This kind of film is very popular with the public, reminding audiences of the magic lantern's colored slides. However, colored films remain a luxury as the images must be painted one at a time by hand. Since 1896 people have been preoccupied with painting film images. Artists in the Méliès studio used a very fine paintbrush to apply colors to clothing or countryside, but the results were inconsistent. During projection the colors seemed to run across the screen. Now, thanks to a stencil recently used by Pathé and Gaumont, the film images have been given dazzling colors. But the amount of work involved is daunting. First a master has to be cut out over a copy of positive film. Next each area of film to be colored is removed with a fine blade. The stripped film is then placed on a second positive copy, over the corresponding images. It remains only to superimpose the stencil using several different colors. There are four specialists in this field, all of them women. Mademoiselle Thullier is in charge of all the coloring for Méliès.

Nonguet tackles the Passion for Pathé

*Begun in 1902, Nonguet's **The Life and Passion of Jesus Christ** depicts the story of Jesus in 32 scenes.*

Vincennes, 28 July

Since 1902 Ferdinand Zecca has been supervizing the shooting of *The Life and Passion of Jesus Christ*, directed by Lucien Nonguet. Zecca and Nonguet set out to film 18 of the most well-known episodes in the life of Christ, but the success of the series prompted them to add additional tableaux. The colored prints make up an extremely attractive body of work, in spite of the disparity between the entries made in 1902 and those filmed three years later.

Organizations which cater especially to young people are keen customers of Nonguet's film, either in its entirety or in individual tableaux. Although the scenes can be purchased separately, Pathé insists that the 20 tableaux are "indispensable for a representation of the sacred drama," most notably *The Entry into Jerusalem*, *The Kiss of Judas*, *Jesus' Death on the Cross* and *The Ascension*. Pathé warns exhibitors that they will ignore this series at their own peril, emphasizing its novelty

"which has the power to touch the hearts of even the most profane." The exhibitors, however, are displaying a distinctly profane interest in other items in the catalogue, in which the religious scenes occupy a modest place near the back. Clearly, Pathé is reluctant to abandon the films which have been instrumental in the foundation of its fortune, for example, *Disheveled Woman* and *Love in All Its Stages,* both likely to horrify Catholic institutions seeking to buy religious films.

Pathé publishes its first catalogue

The Pathé Brothers' new summer catalogue of films available to customers gives ample evidence of the vitality of the company. According to founder Charles Pathé, the Pathé Brothers "suffused with the belief in themselves, necessary to every undertaking, possess a highly-educated personnel, consisting of the most competent people in every field. This has placed them in the top rank of cinematography in the world." Pathé believes in the wonderful possibilities of the Cinematograph, stating, "It's the theater, the school and the newspaper of tomorrow."

Harris and Davis open their first Nickelodeon in Pittsburgh

Pittsburgh, 6 November

"Nickelodeon" is the new name for the latest type of motion picture theater which John P. Harris and his brother-in-law Harry Davis have just opened at the storefront which they occupy on Smithfield Street. A variety of pictures, such as the Edison production of *The Great Train Robbery*, are shown each and every day for a full eight hours until midnight. This is the first purpose-built movie theater of its kind to be opened in the U.S., and, in order to gain admission, customers must pay an entrance fee of five cents – or a nickel – hence the name. Another innovation is that the screenings are accompanied by music from a pianist. It is a big success, with all 100 seats usually occupied.

The new Nickelodeon's takings for the first day was $23.

1906

★ ★

Germany, 21 February
The founding of the Union Theatre (UT) cinema chain. The first cinema to open is in Frankfurt-on-Main.

Chicago, 25 February
Carl Laemmle, a German immigrant who arrived in the U.S. in 1884 at the age of 14, has opened the city's first nickelodeon.

Paris, 24 February
Méliès has dropped the price of all films made before number 640 in his catalogue. Showmen are rushing in to buy up his greatest hits.

Paris, 1 March
The former lawyer Edmond Benoît-Lévy, who published *Phono-Gazette* last year, has founded a trade union for the cinema industry.

New York, March
Adolph Zukor is turning his Hale's Tours into nickelodeons. Marcus Loew is doing the same thing with his penny arcades.

New York, May
William Fox, the son of Hungarian immigrants, has opened a projection room at 700 Broadway.

Copenhagen, 11 July
Ole Olsen, owner of the Biograph Theater cinema, has recently founded a production company, Nordisk Film, in partnership with Arnold Nielsen. Film director Vigo Larsen has already started shooting footage on a variety subjects for the new venture.

Chicago, 23 July
Harry Aitken and John R. Freuler, former real estate agents, have just founded a distribution outlet, the Western Film Exchange.

Paris, 15 August
Pathé has released *la Course à la perruque*, a highly imaginative film full of comic scenes, which includes a wonderful chase sequence, from the producer Georges Hatot with a scenario by André Heuzé.

Paris, 30 August
Charles Urban, G.R. Roger and the financier Ernest May have created the Société générale des cinématographes Eclipse which takes over from the Urban Company in Paris. Two Gaumont producers, Georges Hatot and Victorin Jasset, have been taken on.

Paris, 4 October
Henri Joly, Leopold Lobel, Georges Akar and the financier Dubois de Niermont have founded the new Société des photographes et cinématographes Lux.

Chicago, October
Creation of the Carl Laemmle Film Service, a distribution company.

New York, October
James Stuart Blackton has perfected a single-frame technique which creates some interesting effects in two animated films he has completed: *Humorous Phases of a Funny Face* and *The Haunted Hotel*.

Paris, 2 November
Gaumont's latest innovation is the Elgéphone. It is an amplifier for phonographs which functions on compressed air. Sales are aimed at fairground showmen and cinemas.

BIRTHS

Japan, 3 January
Shiro Toyoda

Rome, 8 May
Roberto Rossellini

Paris, 26 May
Pierre Prévert

Vienna, 22 June
Billy Wilder (Samuel Wilder)

St. Petersburg, 5 July
George Sanders

Missouri, 5 August
John Huston

Budapest, 3 September
Alexander Trauner

Paris, 15 September
Jacques Becker

Philadelphia, 6 October
Janet Gaynor
(Laura Gainor)

Milan, 2 November
Luchino Visconti

Kansas, 10 November
Louise Brooks

Vienna, 5 December
Otto Preminger

Massachusetts, 6 December
Agnes Moorehead

*One of the gloriously extravagant scenes representing Georges Méliès' vision of how life looks **20,000 Leagues Under the Sea**.*

The Birth, the Life and the Death of Christ, *a popular subject this time from Gaumont, is the pinnacle of director Alice Guy's career to date.*

▷

Italians enter the production field

Rome, 2 May
The Italian film pioneer Filoteo Alberini has opened a small film theater here called the Cinema Moderno. It is the first in the capital. Having patented an original device, the Kinetografo Alberini, as long ago as 1895, Alberini finally formed his own production company last year and last September presented his first film, *La Presa di Roma* (also known as *La Brescia di Porta Pia*). Soon afterwards he opened his first production studio in the Via Appia Nuova. More recently, the firm of Alberini and Santoni has become a joint French-Italian stock company. Known as Cines, it is headed by Baron Alberto Frassini as secretary, the French engineer Pouchain as chairman and Alberini himself as technical director. With many ambitious projects planned for the near future, the company is set to spearhead a rapid advance in Italian production which has lagged behind until now.

Méliès the diabolical magician and his four hundred blows

The apocalyptic horse and astral carriage from Méliès magical spectacle.

The author (r) plays the title role.

Paris, 31 August
Georges Méliès has placed on sale *The 400 Blows of the Devil!!!*, a fantastic tale in 35 tableaux. It is, in fact, a lengthened version of the film that Méliès shot in 1905 for the Châtelet Theatre. Victor de Cottens, the author of the play of the same name, had actually requested the master of Montreuil to film a supernatural tale with the intention of screening the film during silent moments of the play. Méliès therefore prepared two films, one entitled *The Cyclone* and the other *Journey into Space*, which were well received during their 500 performances at Châtelet. The audience was amazed by the technical boldness of these pictures in which "an apocalyptic horse" and "an astral chariot" make their appearance. The new version lasts approximately 20 minutes, with Georges Méliès playing his favorite role, that of Satan. Here, he buys the soul of the English engineer William Crackford. In exchange, Satan must procure for him the pleasures of speed, because Crackford has a passion for breaking records. It is then that the famous apocalyptic horse appears, pulling a devilish coach carved in wood. There is a wonderfully effective descent into Hell, and the film ends with a diabolic ballet. Crackford is placed on a spit and roasted over a glowing fire, while demons and female devils dance around him. Méliès has really come to excel in the artistic expression of weird and wonderful images. As usual, he is credited with the scenario and the direction, as well as with all the special effects and decor of this incredible film.

New York becomes filmmaking center

New York, 25 August
According to the latest issue of *Views and Film Index*, the Vitagraph Company has opened a new film studio in the Flatbush area of Brooklyn, and has begun signing up a number of new players. In June, Biograph completed construction of a new stage for filming on East 14th Street, while Edison continues to make good use of his 21st Street studio. Filmmaking is flourishing in New York which, in recent months, has emerged more clearly than ever before as the undisputed center of filmmaking in the country.

Edison's new premises in the Bronx are designed to use natural light.

Jules Verne's imagination continues to influence Méliès' productions.

A love story in Provence for Alice Guy

The Birth, the Life and the Death of Christ by Alice Guy and Victorin Jasset.

The cinema has arrived on the boulevards

The attractive Omnia is the first cinema venue opened by Pathé.

Paris, 24 June
There was a sad return to Paris for Alice Guy's team after they finished shooting an adaptation of Frédéric Mistral's poem *Mireille* in the Carmargues. Louis Feuillade, a fairly new Gaumont employee and a great aficionado of the bullfight, had the idea of filming out of doors. After a few days at Nîmes where Alice was disgusted by the corrida, they had planned to show the film to Mistral, but catastrophe intervened: the negative was completely destroyed by electric discharges. Nevertheless, Alice got to know Herbert Blaché, a young employee of the Gaumont company in London. The failed expedition brought them together, and there is already talk of marriage.

Paris, 15 December
Since the beginning of the year cinemas have mushroomed on the main boulevards of the French capital. There is the Cinématographe Bonne-Nouvelle, the Select Saint-Denis and another on boulevard Poissonnière. Today sees the opening of Cinématographe Pathé at 5 boulevard Montmartre. On 2 November a new company was formed by Edmond Bénoît-Levy, Charles Dussaud, Maurice Guegan and Emile Maugras to launch this theater, which will show only Pathé films. Another luxurious, well-appointed cinema called the Kinéma-Théâtre, owned by Gabriel Kaizer, is opening its doors on the boulevard des Italiens. Grand cinemas are now truly with us.

Ned Kelly and his gang immortalized on celluloid

Melbourne, 24 December
Australian director Charles Tait has broken new ground with *The Story of Ned Kelly*, a biopic of Australia's most famous outlaw which, measuring 4,000 feet, has a running time of about 70 minutes. Premiered at the Athenaeum Hall last night, the film was shot over a period of about six months, much of it on location on Tait's farm. The body armor actually worn by Kelly, including a bullet-proof helmet and jerkin made from ploughshares, was borrowed from Victoria's state museum and worn by the actor playing Kelly. But the actor, a Canadian touring player, disappeared before filming was finished and had to be replaced by an extra who was filmed in long shot. Produced by the theatrical company J. & N. Tait of Melbourne, *The Story of Ned Kelly* recouped its cost within a week and looks set to earn a handsome profit at home and back in the United Kingdom.

A dramatic shoot-out from Charles Tait's ground-breaking Australian film about the notorious Ned Kelly.

1907

★ ★

Paris, 1 January
Pathé has released *Aladdin and his Magic Lamp*, Albert Capellani's 250-metre film and Méliès' 364-metre *Robert, Macaire et Bertrand*.

Paris 15 January
Georges Hatot's most recent film, *les Débuts d'un chauffeur*, starring André Deed, has been released for sale by Pathé.

Paris, 26 January
Pathé has just organized the Compagnie des cinématographes Théophile Pathé with a starting capital of 2 million francs. This new company intends to produce low-budget films for fairground shows.

Berlin, 1 February
The newspaper *Der Komet* has attributed the invention of the cinema to photographer Max Skladanowsky whose first sessions of Bioskop were held on 1 November 1895 in the Wintergarten. The claim has been refuted by French journalists, thus starting a controversy about who invented the cinema.

Sweden, 16 February
N.H. Nylander, a cycle repairman, sets up the AB Svenska Biografteatern cinema chain in Kristianstad.

London, 22 February
Former magic-lantern showman Joshua Duckworth has opened the first purpose-built cinema in Britain. Central Hall, in Colne, Lancashire, cost 2,000 pounds to build.

Copenhagen, 12 March
Following on the success of *The White Slave*, in which he starred with Gerda Jenson, Nordisk's accredited producer Vigo Larsen has filmed *Roverens Brud* with Robert Storm and Clara Nebelong.

Chicago, March
The creation of the Bell & Howell Company, the first manufacturer of cameras and lenses in America.

Turin, April
Arturo Ambrosio's production firm has become a stock company with backing from the Commercial Bank of Turin. Carlo Rossi, who founded his own firm, has taken on Charles Lépine, former director at Pathé, as well as an accountant named Giovanni Pastrone.

Paris, 1 April
Zecca's *The Life and Passion of Christ* has been released for sale by Pathé. This is a new version of the 1902 film.

Paris, 11 May
The magazine *Photo-Ciné-Gazette* is organizing a big festival at the Elysée-Montmartre. An audience of 2,000 will be treated to a session of "talking pictures with the Chronomegaphone." The projection of the films combined with the Elgéphone is going to produce a "powerful, new sound," according to the manufacturer Léon Gaumont.

Paris, 20 May
There are now 15 cinemas in the capital, and 15 new cinematographs have opened since last week.

Helsinki, 29 May
The first fiction film to be produced in Finland, *Salaviinan Polttajat*, by Louis Sparre and Teuvo Puro, is now showing.

Paris, 1 June
Pathé has released *La Lutte pour la Vie* (*Struggle for Life*), the story of a railwayman who makes good, written by André Herzé.

Paris, 16 June
The Variety Theatre is showing a filmed play, *The Prodigal Child*, by the director Michel Carré with performances from George Wague and Christiane Mendelys.

Paris, 1 July
Méliès has released a burlesque fantasy called *Le Tunnel sous la Manche ou le Cauchemar franco-anglais* (*The Tunnel under the English Channel or the Anglo-French Nightmare*).

Paris, 18 July
Creation of the French Union of Directors. Léon Brézillon has been elected president.

Paris, 1 August
As a follow-up to the comic, *Cul-de-jatte emballé*, Gaumont has released Roméo Bosetti's *L'homme aimanté*.

St. Petersburg, August
Alexander O. Drankov, who opened the first Russian film studio, has filmed extracts from Pushkin's play *Boris Godounov*, directed by Ivan Chouvalov.

Singapore, August
Charles Pathé has opened his eighteenth overseas branch. He began with subsidiaries in Moscow, New York and Brussels in 1904, added Berlin, Vienna and St. Petersburg in 1905, and in 1906, Amsterdam, Barcelona, Milan, Odessa and London. This year, offices have opened in Rostov, Kiev, Budapest, Calcutta and Warsaw.

Paris, 21 October
In his report on the cinema industry for the administration at Orsay, Edmond Benoît-Lévy stated: Gaumont employs 650 workmen in its 12,000-square-metre factory and turns out 15,000 metres of film a day. But Pathé, with factories in Vincennes, Joinville-le-Pont and in New York, turns out 100,000 metres of film a day, has studios in Vincennes and Montreuil and had a turnover of 4 million francs for 1906–1907.

New York, October
Jeremiah Kennedy, a consultant engineer, has taken over as director of Biograph. He will handle the reorganization of the company under the supervision of the Empire trust company, on whom Biograph is financially dependant.

Paris, 1 December
Gaumont's newest *Le Médecin de campagne* (*The Country Doctor*), directed by Etienne Arnaud, and the comic film *Le Lit à Roulette* (*The Bed on Wheels*), made by Roméo Bosetti are now on the market.

Paris, 15 December
Gaumont has released *Bluebeard*, produced by Etienne Arnaud. The film, judged too cruel, has undergone "a few changes." His other recent releases include *The Future Revealed by the Sole of the Foot*, *La Poudre Rigolo* (*Funny Powder*) and *The Sewer Worker's Fiancée*.

Paris, 24 December
A permanent cinematograph that was designed by the architect Malo was opened at the Winter Circus today in the presence of the owner Charles Pathé, Max Linder, Gaston Velle and Albert Capellani.

Paris, 31 December
The young German, Erich Pommer, has started a career in the cinema with Léon Gaumont.

Calcutta, 31 December
The cinema Elphinstone Palace has been opened here by J.F. Maden.

BIRTHS

England, 19 January
Lilian Harvey
(Helen L. Pape)

Sweden, 15 March
Zarah Leander
(Sarah Hedberg)

England, 22 May
Laurence Olivier

Iowa, 26 May
John Wayne
(Marion Michael Morrison)

London, 3 June
Paul Rotha

New York, 16 July
Barbara Stanwyck
(Ruby Stevens)

Ukraine, 11 August
George Wakhevitch

France, 25 September
Robert Bresson

France, 13 October
Yves Allégret

France, 29 October
Edwige Feuillère
(Caroline Cunati)

France, 7 November
Jean Mitry
(Jean René Goetgheluck)

Connecticut, 8 November
Katharine Hepburn

France, 16 November
Renée Saint-Cyr
(Raymonde Renée Vittore)

France, 20 November
Henri-Georges Clouzot

Italy, 10 December
Amedeo Nazzari
(Salvatore Amedeo Buffa)

Charles Pathé is the man of the year. In 10 years, he has built his business and his reputation from nothing, and now heads a filmmaking empire that is unique in the world.

Stuart Blackton is heir to Emile Reynaud

Paris, 1 March
Today the new Vitagraph film *The Haunted Hotel* is going on sale to French exhibitors. It's a novelty animated film in which furniture moves mysteriously about as if by its own agency. The man who dreamed this up is an Englishman, John Stuart Blackton, who went to America at the age of 10 in 1885. It was Blackton's good fortune as a young journalist to interview Thomas Edison in 1895 and to convince the great inventor of his own talent as a designer. Two years later, in conjunction with William T. Rock and Albert E.

Smith, Blackton founded the Vitagraph Company. In 1906 Blackton produced *Humorous Phases of Funny Faces*, which uses the technique of showing an artist drawing a still picture which then magically comes alive and moves. The effect was created using cardboard cutouts, but some genuinely animated sequences can be seen at the beginning of the film – notably a man sporting a bowler hat and umbrella seemingly drawing himself, and a man and a woman rolling their eyes. Blackton refers to this widely-used technique as the "American movement".

The Magic Pen is the third animated film made by J. Stuart Blackton.

Brussels won over by new art form

Brussels, 22 March
The Belgian capital has been swept up in the vogue of the Cinematograph, a trend coming mainly from Paris. Since 1905, Louis Van Goitsenhoven, the director of the Theatre of the Cinematograph, has also been running the Eden Theatre. He claims it is equipped for the presentation of "all the latest cinematographic productions from all over the world." In the autumn of 1900, the Pathé Brothers were the first to present animated films. The last few years have seen the rise of many competitors, but, on the other hand, the Molière Theatre has proudly made it known that it is "the only theater that the Cinematograph has not yet invaded."

World record beaten in Montreal

Montreal, 31 August
The largest luxury theater for the screening of animated pictures in North America, curiously named Ouimetoscope, has just opened its doors at the corner of Montcalm and Sainte-Catherine. Its 1,200 seats constitutes a world record. Léo-Ernest Ouimet, the owner, began his career as a stage electrician at the National Theatre and at the Sohmer Park, among others. In January 1906, he bought the former Poiré Hall and transformed it into a projection theater. Despite its success, the first Ouimetoscope was pulled down during the summer of 1907; since then an army of workers has rebuilt the hall of gigantic proportions on its ruins.

Louis Feuillade, new artistic director

Paris, 1 April
There have been quite a number of upheavals at Gaumont. Louis Feuillade, who came in as scenarist in 1905 under Alice Guy's direction, has replaced her as head of the department of theaters and production. Alice, who took charge of cinematographic production in 1899, got married a short while ago to the Belgian Herbert Blaché. Gaumont has appointed Blaché to the job of sales agent for the Chronophone, the projection apparatus of sound films, in Cleveland, Ohio in the U.S. Facing such a major relocation has been very sad for Alice. With great reluctance, she has been forced to quit the Buttes-Chaumont Theatre, which she managed with so much talent. In fact she herself had recommended Feuillade to the post when Gaumont made his decision known.

Feuillade and daughter Isabelle.

Vitagraph has a pretty new leading lady

New York, 7 June
The Vitagraph Company's most popular leading lady is diminutive, demure Florence Turner, star of *How to Cure a Cold*. The 20-year-old Turner, quite a successful stage performer, has been in the acting profession since the age of three. She was spotted in a crowd watching a Vitagraph production and was immediately taken on by the company as a wardrobe mistress at a salary of $18 a week with an extra five whenever she acted in a film. Like everyone in films, Turner is expected to combine several jobs in a production, but she is attracting more attention than other Vitagraph players. As yet her name has not been revealed to the public, and she is known simply as "The Vitagraph Girl." Film companies are still reluctant to name their most popular players. After all, these new stars might take the opportunity to ask for more money!

The former stage actress Florence Turner has switched to film.

Edmond Benoît-Lévy, the 'éminence grise'

Paris, 12 July
Who is Edmond Benoît-Lévy? He signed an exclusive contract today with Chares Pathé which will allow him the monopoly of Pathé films in nine French provinces as well as in Switzerland. Benoît-Lévy has gradually become the confidant of Pathé, being involved in every decision made by the Vincennes master. A former trial lawyer, he practiced law

for 20 years before branching out into other activities, one of which was a lecture position at the Popular Society of Fine Arts. In 1905 Benoît-Lévy published the *Phono-Gazette*, which at the end of the year became known as the *Phono-Ciné-Gazette*. After organizing the Union of Cinematograph Exhibitors, on 2 November 1906, he went on to found a company for the showing of the Pathé Cinematograph, at 5 boulevard Montmartre, the headquarters of his paper and of the Ciné Club founded in April this year. This newspaper supported Pathé invaluably at the time that it was decided to hire the films out. Benoît-Lévy, whose firm has just changed its name to Omnia, has Pathé's permission to establish a network of Cinematographs – permanent halls or traveling stalls – which would project only Pathé films. With a capital of up to 1.2 million francs, Benoît-Lévy has managed to consolidate the cinematographic industry, although remaining in the constant shadow of Charles Pathé.

Key developments in the Chicago cinema

Chicago, 4 November
Recent developments in the Windy City suggest that Chicago is set to rival New York as the leading film-making center in the U.S. In fact, this city is already ahead of New York in one respect: censorship. The authorities have passed the first local censorship ordinance in the country "prohibiting the exhibition of obscene and immoral pictures commonly shown in Mutoscopes, Kinetoscopes, Cinematographs and penny arcades." Earlier this year, projectionist Donald Bell and camera repairman Albert Howell founded the Bell & Howell Camera Co. which hopes to play an important role if the industry continues to grow at the same rapid pace as during recent years. But most important of all has been the formation of the Essanay Company in February by George K. Spoor and actor-producer G.M. Anderson, who is best-known for the Westerns he has made for Selig since 1904 (the company name is derived from the two founders' initials, "S" and "A"). Wasting no time, Essanay is already filming in its studio at 501 Wells

Street, having announced their first production, *An Awful Skate* or *The Hobo on Rollers*, on 27 July in *The Moving Picture World*. Not to be outdone, local entrepreneur Selig has just moved into his new plant on Western Avenue.

Essanay co-founder G.M. Anderson.

A secret meeting after a decisive ruling

Chicago, 30 November
The American film industry is once again in ferment. Some of the most important producers have just met in secret. Among them were George Kleine of Kalem Pictures, John Stuart Blackton and Albert E. Smith from Vitagraph, Essanay's George Spoor, and William N. Selig and Sigmund Lubin of, respectively, Selig and Lubin. A French presence is provided by Gaston Méliès, who represents Star Films, and Jacques-

uniting bitter rivals in agreement. What lies behind this sudden change of heart? Since its birth 10 years ago the motion picture business has been characterized by endless legal disputes. William Selig, founder in 1896 of the Selig Polyscope Company, has the dubious distinction of being on the receiving end of the largest number of writs. Only last October he was found guilty by a Chicago judge, Christian Kahlseat, of using cameras which infringed

Rescued from an Eagle's Nest, 'a fantastical vision' on a very popular theme, about small children captured and restored to their parents.

Emile Berst of Pathé. The meeting originally had been called to study a proposal put forth by the Edison Manufacturing Company. Edison has been proposing to award producers a license in return for a payment of a levy of half-a-cent for each foot of film printed or sold. The levy would be collected by the Eastman-Kodak foundation, which would then discount any excess profit in their accounts with the Edison company. In exchange for signing up with the scheme, Edison will undertake to protect the licensees and to take vigorous legal action on their behalf against any pirated prints, unauthorized screenings or other activities prejudicial to their interests. This is clearly an attempt to form a motion picture cartel. Edison's proposal was favorably received by the producers present,

upon patents taken out by Thomas Edison. This ruling had important consequences. It looked as if motion pictures would, by the same token, become the exclusive property of the wizard of West Orange. The possibility of this precedent being enforced sent a wave of alarm through the ranks of film producers. George Kleine was delegated to thrash out some common ground with the Edison Company. As a result, Kleine and Edison's business manager, Mr. Gilmore, met and agreed on the proposals which have just been considered in secret conclave by the most important figures in the industry. Observers are predicting that after several years of legal wrangling the end of the tunnel might be in sight. The resolution of these problems is welcome as an important financial shot in the arm.

1908

Paris, 1 January
The Ciné-voiture Omnia is on display at the Motor Show. Aimed at fairground exhibitions, it contains a generator which can be used either to run a car or project films.

France, 31 January
The Eclair Company has increased its capital from 150,000 to 500,000 francs and has purchased a 14-acre building site for a studio. Georges Hatot and Victorin Jasset have been hired as film directors.

France, 4 February
Louis Feuillade has started filming three historical stories for Gaumont: *le Retour du Croisé* (*The Return of the Crusader*), *le Serment des fiançailles* (*The Betrothal Pledge*) and *la Guitare enchantée* (*The Magic Guitar*).

New York, 5 February
In the ongoing struggle against Edison's monopoly, Biograph's Vice President Henry Marvin has bought up patents to which the Edison Co. claimed it held exclusive rights.

Paris, 8 February
Creation of the first cinematographic advertising business, the Publicité Animée.

New York, 20 February
Frank L. Dyer, Edison's lawyer, has replaced Stuart Gilmore as the company's vice president. On 15 February, he informed film distributors that they would be charged an annual license fee of $5,000.

Paris, 1 March
Gaumont has released *la Course aux potirons* (*The Pumpkin Race*), a film with trick effects by the newly recruited Emile Cohl.

Paris, 9 March
European producers gathered at the Continental hotel to unite against Edison's protectionism. But Charles Pathé refused to take part in the meeting, claiming that such an effort will "only defer the inevitable ruin of certain companies."

Turin, 15 March
Giovanni Pastrone and the engineer Sciamengo have bought up Carlo Rossi's production company, which was in liquidation, and have founded their own company, Itala Film.

Paris, 15 May
Photo-Ciné-Gazette has vaunted the benefits of the "Mallet protective case", which separates the reel of film from the arc light. It should be made compulsory for all projectors in order to prevent fires.

Buenos Aires, 24 May
Showing of Argentina's first fiction film *El Fusilamiento de Dorrego* (*The Execution of Dorrego*), directed by an Italian, Mario Gallo.

Rome, 31 May
Adapted from *Hamlet* and directed by Mario Caserini for Cines, the new film *Ameleto* has been shown.

New York, 18 June
D.W. Griffith, formerly the actor Laurence Griffith, has directed his first film, *The Adventures of Dollie*, for Biograph. His wife Linda Arvidson is in the cast.

Paris, 4 July
At the Fourth of July party held for Pathé's personnel at the Winter Circus, Max Linder caused a sensation – first on screen and then by leaping in person onto the stage. He made the burlesque film *les Débuts d'un patineur* (*A Skater's Debut*) last winter under Louis Gasnier's direction.

London, 4 July
The Gem in Great Yarmouth opens today under the management of C.B. Cochran. With its 1,200-seat auditorium, it is the first purpose-built cinema in Britain to hold over 1,000 people.

Chicago, 3 August
Gaston Méliès has set up a branch here of the Georges Méliès Manufacturing Company, with a capital of $75,000, to distribute Star films and to produce films under the supervision of Lincoln J. Carter.

Paris, 10 August
A police order has just been issued to control security in cinemas. It stipulates that the projection booth has to be fire proof and that the projectionist must have a five-litre fire extinguisher and two bottles of Seltzer water within reach.

Paris, 15 August
The weekly *Ciné-Journal*, run by George Dureau, has published its first number.

New York, 17 August
D.W. Griffith has signed a contract at $50 per week with the Biograph company and has become the firm's main director due to the departure of Wallace McCutcheon.

Paris, 25 August
Roméo Bosetti has created a relief fund for cinema actors.

Rome, August
Carlo Rossi has taken over as head of Cines. Mario Caserini and Enrico Guazzoni are to be his principal film directors.

Paris, 8 September
Eclair has released the first film in the "Nick Carter" series called *le Guet-apens* (*The Trap*), directed by Victorin Jasset.

New York, 9 September
Jeremiah Kennedy, the manager of Biograph, has threatened to obtain his own licenses if Edison refuses to allow him to use his movie cameras.

Paris, 9 September
Jean Durand, who was taken on by Pathé last June to film some trick effects with an unknown actor, Maurice Chevalier, has left for Lux.

Paris, 19 September
The technician André Debrie has submitted his camera, Le Parvo, for patent. It takes 120 metres of film.

St. Petersburg, 15 October
Stenka Razine, directed by Vladimir Romachkov and produced by A. Drankov, is the first significant film produced by the fledgling Russian cinema industry.

Fort Lee, New Jersey, 16 October
D.W. Griffith is filming *The Curtain Pole* with Linda Arvidson and a young actor named Mack Sennett.

Berlin, 13 November
The International Convention of Authors' Rights has extended the legal protection defined in Berne for artistic works to include films "having a personal and original form."

Paris, 15 November
Pathé has released, *Un Monsieur qui suit les Dames* (*A Man who Follows Women*), with the performance of an actor from the Charles Petit-Demange Variety Theatre.

Paris, 10 December
The first episode from the new Victorin Jasset series entitled *Riffle, le roi de la prairie* (*Riffle, the King of the Fields*) is now screening.

Pittsburgh, 31 December
The Warner brothers have opened a film distribution company called Duquesne Amusement.

Tokyo, 31 December
The first film studio has opened in the Meguro district.

BIRTHS

France, 12 January
Jean Delannoy

Texas, 26 February
Tex Avery
(Fred Avery)

England, 5 March
Rex Harrison

Alexandria, 7 March
Anna Magnani

Berlin, 17 March
Brigitte Helm
(Eva Gisela Schittenhelm)

England, 25 March
David Lean

Massachusetts, 5 April
Bette Davis
(Ruth Elisabeth Davis)

Pennsylvania, 20 May
James Stewart

England, 26 May
Robert Morley

Wisconsin, 31 May
Don Ameche (Dominic Amici)

France, 12 July
Alain Cuny

Indiana, 6 October
Carole Lombard

Portugal, 12 December
Manoel de Oliveira

The Assassination of the Duc de Guise, directed by André Calmettes of the Comédie Française has been filmed at least twice before. This version is the best and most successful.

Dumas' classic filmed in California

New York, 2 February
Southern California, with its sunshine and spectacular scenery, is beginning to attract filmmakers. The Selig Company, Edison's biggest rival, has recently filmed Alexander Dumas' *The Count of Monte Cristo* in Santa Monica. The film's interior scenes had been shot in Selig's Chicago studio, but director Francis Boggs felt that more authentic settings were required. Consequently, Boggs and another Selig employee, Thomas Persons, who leads a busy life as a cameraman, property manager, business manager and assistant director, settled on sunny California. The change of location then required a change of cast. A new Count of Monte Cristo was found in the form of an impoverished hypnotist who bore a passing resemblance to the actor who had played the role in Chicago. The hypnotist had never heard of the cinema but was only too happy to sign for Selig. Boggs set up a studio on a rooftop on Main Steet in downtown Los Angeles and also filmed on location on Santa Monica beach. Now on release, the one-reel version of Dumas' classic suggests that it will not be long before other companies follow Selig. California's benign climate, varied topography and availability of cheap labor are certain to encourage people to travel to Los Angeles, at present a sleepy town whose orange groves provide its citizens with their main source of income. And it definitely seems like the filmmakers are heading West.

The intransigent Pathé brothers make a few grand concessions

This advertisement bears witness to the growing popularity of cinema halls, such as this venue at Vincennes.

Paris, 15 April
Edmond Benoît-Lévy's *Phono-Ciné-Gazette* has published the list of concessionary firms who will have the monopoly of Pathé Brothers films. These firms, which have gradually been put in place since July 1907, have been permanently set up to hire out the films. Cinema-Omnia and Cinema-Theatre, both at boulevard Montmartre, are responsible for the Northwest, Central-West, Corsica, Switzerland and Algeria. Benoît-Lévy and Serge Sandberg, the director of the Cinema-Theatre, sit on the administrative council. The lending out of Pathé films for Paris is done by the intermediary of Cinema Exploitation, whose offices can be found at Pathé, 8 rue Saint-Augustin. The Central-East and the Southeast are represented by a firm called Cinema-Monopole located in Lyons at 6 rue Grôlée and presided over by Baron Gabet. In Bordeaux, Cinema National, situated at 5 Intendance Court, is in control of the Southwest. Finally, the Belgian cinema has its headquarters in Brussels at 40 place de Brouckère and covers Belgium, the Netherlands and Luxembourg. All in all, an extremely thorough job.

A typical fairground cinema of the kind in which Pathé has participated.

From now on a studio is reserved for the scientific films of Dr. Comandon.

The judicial spotlight is turned on Ben Hur

New York, 5 May
Ben Hur is condemned again! Not to the slave galley this time, but rather to pay damages totaling $25,000. The culprit is the Kalem Picture Company which was founded in Chicago in March 1907 by George Kleine, Samuel Long and Frank Marion (the company's name is derived from the initials of its three directors). One of Kalem's ambitious ideas has turned sour. In November 1907 the company made a one-reel version of Lew Wallace's best-selling novel of Ancient Rome, *Ben Hur*. Directors Sydney Olcott and Frank Oakes Rose rented background scenery left over from a summer exhibition staged by the well-known Pains Firework Company on the racetrack at Sheepshead Bay, New York and hired the Brooklyn Fire Department to stage the novel's climactic chariot race. Since Kalem had no indoor studios on any of its three lots, much of its output was shot on location. The script was written by Gene Gautier, Kalem's most popular leading lady dubbed the "Kalem Girl" and one of the busiest screenwriters in the business. The film's running time was about

15 minutes and the result, according to Kalem's publicity, was "16 magnificent scenes with illustrated titles." There was one small snag, however. Kalem had neglected to acquire any rights to the story, a not uncommon practice but one which incurred the wrath of Harper and Brothers, the book's publishers, Abraham Erlanger, the producer of the spectacular stage adaptation of *Ben Hur* and Henry Wallace, the administrator of the estate of Lew Wallace who died in 1905. Immediately after the first public showing of the Kalem version of *Ben Hur* in January, the aggrieved parties decided to take legal action, the first of its kind. The decision went against Kalem, thereby ensuring that film companies, which have previously played fast and loose with the law of copyright, will in the future have to respect the rights of authors. As a result, the posters for the Kalem version of *Ben Hur* disappeared overnight and the film was withdrawn. It was then seized by the court until Kalem came up with a surety. The film company is set to appeal the decision, and the battle might go to the Supreme Court.

Sound and color along the river Thames

London, 31 August
England is becoming the most audacious country as far as cinematography is concerned. Various pioneers are building on the work of Frenchman Eugène-Augustin Lauste who designed "a new method for the simultaneous reproduction of movement and sound." Lauste, who worked with William Kennedy Laurie Dickson some years ago, has been fascinated for a very long time by the problems of the synchronization of image and sound. Since 1904, he has dreamt of a system where the sound modulations would be etched directly onto the edge of the reel of film. One interesting experiment showed how sound managed to alter the intensity of a flame, the variations of which were subsequently recorded on film. The technique has been much improved upon since then, and the apparatus now seems to be completely satisfactory. The Englishman George Albert Smith, who made his reputation directing films in Brighton at the turn of the

century, has founded Kinemacolor Ltd. together with Charles Urban. Although the company was established five months previously, the first films, which are documentary rather than fiction, have only recently started to appear on the screens. Kinemacolor is a two-toned process inspired by research carried out by the great French scientists Gabriel Lippmann and Louis-Arthur Ducos du Hauron. Patented in June 1907, this new technique, designed by Smith, has perfectly reflected the variegated and contrasting colors of the English landscape. The first public demonstration took place on 26 February last at the Palace Theatre in London, followed by other showings elsewhere before it was demonstrated in the hall of Civil Engineers in Paris a month later. Kinemacolor has been an undoubted success, and it will probably not be long before this new system is shown on European screens, where it would bring more visual variation to the programs.

Emile Cohl and the arrival of the puppets

A Drama of the Puppets, the beginning of animated drawings in France.

Paris, 12 November
A Drama in Fantoche's House is the third animated film to be produced by Gaumont in the last four months, which follows hard on the heels of *Phantasmagoria* and also *Fantoche's Nightmare*. They are all the work of a single man, Emile Courtet, whose *nom de plume* is Emile Cohl. Born in Paris in January 1857, Cohl was apprenticed as a jeweler and began drawing caricatures during his military service. He went on to become a political cartoonist for numerous publications, wrote for the theater, acted, dabbled in conjuring and took up photography. He also designed some of the flip books which anticipated the arrival of animated film. The story goes that one day

Cohl stormed into the Gaumont offices to protest that the company had plagiarized one of his cartoons in a film poster. Cohl's reward was the offer of a job at Gaumont from Louis Feuillade, then the head of production at the studio. Cohl started at Gaumont as an ideas man and writer, graduating to the direction of animated films which exploit the relatively recent American invention of stop-go photography. One of Cohl's most popular creations is Fantoche, the engaging little man who makes regular appearances in his films. These animated frolics have all the freshness and innocent vigor of children's drawings, which is a most remarkable achievement for a man in his fifties.

The Pumpkin Race, which blends poetry and fantasy with realism.

The cinema is caught in the grip of respectability

The Kiss of Judas, directed by Armand Bour, with Mounet-Sully as Judas and Albert Lambert as Christ.

The men of letters turn to Daudet

Paris, 1 October

The Pathé company has put on sale *l'Arlésienne*, a picture based on Alphonse Daudet, and filmed by Albert Capellani in Arles. It is the first big production following some more, and some less, successful experiments, from the company made up of composers and men of letters. This company (SCAGL), founded on 23 June by the bankers Saul and Georges Merzbach, has the popular novelist Pierre Decourcelle and the playwright Eugène Gugenheim on staff. They took their inspiration and aims from Film d'Art, which attempts to bring plays and novels to the screen starring famous actors. Their leanings are toward populist works. The Bank of Industry and Commerce is giving financial support to the business, in which one discovers once again the hand of Charles Pathé. He is one of the principal shareholders and has assisted SCAGL by lending them his cameramen and putting at their disposal his building materials and his hiring service. He has even provided them with the blueprint for a photographic studio that the new firm will build in Vincennes. Thus Pathé has gained control over the activities of SCAGL, as he does with Film d'Art, which was rapidly obliged to give up its freedom by signing a contract with Pathé, the ogre whose appetite never seems to be satisfied.

The Comédie-Française and the Academy give backing to Film Art

Paris, 17 November

The Film d'Art company, which was founded on 14 February by businessman Paul Lafitte, the academician Henri Lavedan, the architect Jean-Camille Formigé, and actor Charles Le Bargy of the Comédie-Française, is showing its first program tonight at the Charras Hall. All the films were shot at the Film d'Art studios in Neuilly. It is expected that an elegant crowd will be present at this event, which will mean the coming together for the first time of the French elite and members of the Academie Fran-çaise with the world of the Cinematograph, that stunted offspring so criticized by high society. Film d'Art will show *Myrto's Secret*, acted by Régina Badet; *The Impression*, a mime drama with Max Dearly and Mistinguett, who dances the famous swaying waltz; and the most eagerly-awaited film, *The Assassination of the Duc de Guise*. The latter was directed by Charles Le Bargy and André Calmettes, from a scenario by Henri Lavedan, with an original music score by Camille Saint-Saëns. Charles Le Bargy, Albert Lambert, Gabrielle Robinne and Bertha Bovy perform in this film of astonishing restraint, with a skillful and tragic scenario, and polished decor. Compared with the historic scenes produced by Pathé or Gaumont, this interpretation appears to be a masterpiece. Nevertheless, there are those who are wary: the theater risks stifling the cinema, which usually tries to avoid copying its rival. But with the success of Film d'Art, the cinema has come of age.

The Assassination of the Duc de Guise dramatizes an episode of history.

Film director Albert Capellani.

Europeans await George Eastman

Paris, 10 December
Twenty representatives of the most important European film companies have arrived at the Paris offices of the Eclair company to meet George Eastman, the American inventor and businessman on a visit here. As he is the leading manufacturer of film stock, they hope that Eastman might be able to influence the Edison company in their favor. After waging a patents war for many years to protect his rights, Thomas Edison created the Film Service Association earlier this year – a cartel which brings together the leading American companies. Although Pathé was invited to join, all the other European producers were excluded. For them this has proved disastrous, since fully three-quarters of their income is generated in the United States. In response to Edison, they formed their own association in Paris on 9 March but have been far from united in their views. Some of the leading companies in France, including Gaumont, Urban and Cines, even tried to join the cartel, but found that their way was barred by Pathé, the company that continues to pull the strings in Europe.

Building of world's biggest studios

The Gaumont company, with its financial position strengthened, is now proving to be a worthy rival to Pathé.

Paris, 31 December
At Buttes-Chaumont there is a vast assemblage of offices, workshops, laboratories and also photo studios, which has now been christened the Cité Elgé, after the initials of Léon Gaumont. Since 1905, these buildings have been spread out over more than 10,000 square metres. "It's the largest studio in the world," the advertisements proclaim. Louis Feuillade is still directing productions with help from an unrivaled team: Roméo Bosetti, Etienne Arnaud, Léonce Perret and a newcomer, the designer Emile Cohl, all of whom juggle with camera technique. The basement of the glass-topped studio has been converted into artists' dressing rooms, and a second workshop has been constructed exclusively for the shooting of sound films. The warehouses for props have been enlarged and so have the workshops for the building of decor. Gaumont presides ruthlessly over his domain. The gates are closed firmly at 8 a.m. sharp each morning. Members of the staff must be punctual if they want to keep their jobs.

Edison's maneuvers cause disturbance

New York, 24 December
A serious crisis has hit the film exhibitors of New York City: pending the decision of the mayor George McClellan, as many as 500 nickelodeons may be forced to close as the result of an unprecedented citywide inspection. In an operation beginning at dawn and continuing throughout the day, a large number of inspectors were instructed to call on virtually every film hall in the city, without warning, to assess their current safety precautions. It is, of course, well-known to all that reels of film are highly inflammable, and there is always a risk of fire. Only last June, the Police Commissioner Bingham raised the possibility of revoking the nickelodeons' licenses, both for reasons of morality and public safety; fortunately for the film business, this suggestion was not taken up by the mayor. It is worth noting that the date of the current operation comes just a week

or so after the formation of the Motion Picture Patents Company, or MPPC, a kind of film industry cartel set up by the Edison Co. in league with Biograph. In addition to these two leading companies, the other members of the trust include Vitagraph, Selig, Kalem, Essanay, Lubin, George Kleine, and the two largest French companies, Pathé Frères and Méliès Star Films. Aside from these signatories, no one else is allowed either to produce or to sell a single foot of film in the U.S. without the special authorization of the trust, which also asserts the right to impose its own fees and other conditions on all film renters, exchanges and exhibitors. On top of that, the trust has also drafted an exclusive agreement with the Eastman Kodak Company for the supply of new, less inflammable film, and Edison is able to use this to control the activities of exhibitors countrywide. No wonder they are ready to rebel.

A special Marguerite

On 14 January, the clerk of the Commercial Court of the Seine registered the Gaumont emblem, a daisy with the name Gaumont through the center. Inspiration came from the first name of Léon Gaumont's mother.

1909

★ ★ ★ ★ ★ ★ ★ ★

Russia, 1 January
Cameramen from Pathé and Edison have filmed Leo Tolstoy at his home in Jasnia Polonia.

Turin, January
The Itala Film Company is producing the first films in a comic series played by André Deed, a French actor who was formerly a star with the Pathé company.

Paris, 1 February
Georges Demenÿ has delivered his version of "the origins of the cinematograph." He has put forward a defense of his own research and has sharply attacked the memory of his former master Etienne Marey.

USA, 8 February
Release of D.W. Griffith's *Edgar Allan Poe*, with Linda Arvison.

Rome, 2 March
The newly created Film d'Arte Italiano, a joint stock company, is a branch of Pathé's French firm.

Paris, 4 March
Eclair has released *les Dragonnades sous Louis XIV* (*The Dragonnade under Louis XIV*), made by Jasset.

Paris, 5 March
Representatives from 32 European production companies are meeting at Méliès' Robert Houdin Theatre. The participants, particularly the fairground showmen, were unable to agree on terms for film hire.

Paris, 11 March
Eclair has released *les Nouveaux exploits de Nick Carter* (*The Latest Exploits of Nick Carter*), in three episodes, by Victorin Jasset. The king of the detectives is played by Pierre Brussol.

Paris, 11 March
Albert Kahn, founder of Archives of the Planet, and his cameraman Alfred Dutertre are back from a film trip during which they visited many countries in the world, including China and Japan.

New York, 12 March
Cinema owner and distributor Carl Laemmle and film director William Rainous have founded a breakaway company from Vitagraph, Independent Motion Pictures (IMP). The imp has been chosen as its emblem.

Paris, 15 March
The measures taken by the International Congress of Film Producers concerning film hire have come into force. Films are to be rented out for a period of four months and then returned to the original production company for destruction.

New York, 14 April
The distributors Adam Kessel and Charles Baumann have founded the new Bison Life Films with the aim of producing Westerns.

Boston, April
Louis B. Mayer, formerly a scrap metal dealer turned cinema owner, founds The Gordon-Mayer Circuit with Nat Gordon.

Paris, 6 May
Maury, the owner of a franchise, has put the Ciné Multiphone Rousselot on the market, a type of piano used to produce sound effects for films.

Paris, 4 June
American Vitagraph is distributing *Napoleon – The Man of Destiny*, produced by James Stuart Blackton, the first American producer to move toward the "art film".

New York, 10 June
Following her debut screen in *The Violin Maker of Cremona* for D.W. Griffith, 16-year-old Mary Pickford is starring in the same director's *The Lonely Villa*. She had been a triumph on Broadway for two years, in a play by William De Mille, when Griffith took her on at the beginning of the year for a part in his new film *Her First Biscuits*.

New York, 15 June
Independent American film producers have made a secret agreement with the Eastman-Kodak company for supplies of safety film.

New York, 1 August
Edwin S. Porter has resigned his position as the head of Edison productions. He has now founded Rex Motion Pictures, in partnership with William H. Swanson.

Paris, 9 August
Gaumont has just released a tinted version of Louis Feuillade's *The Death of Mozart* and Etienne Arnaud's *Trait de bonté de Napoléon I* (*Napoleon I's Act of Goodness*).

Paris, 24 August
The Hippodrome in the place de Clichy has been turned into a skating rink by its new owners, Crawford and Wilkins Ltd of Liverpool, England. Henri Iclès, who already runs the Moulin Rouge and Luna Park, is the director.

Berlin, 4 September
The UT circuit has opened a giant cinema with seating for 1,000 in Alexanderplatz.

London, 19 September
The British weekly paper *The Kinematograph and Lantern Weekly* has launched the idea of film stories.

New York, 10 October
Pippa Passes, by the prolific director D.W. Griffith and starring Mary Pickford, is the very first film to rate a notice in the *New York Times*, thanks to its technical innovations.

St. Petersburg, 6 October
The Death of Ivan the Terrible, a film by Vassili Goncharov and produced by Pathé's Russian branch, has had a public screening.

Paris, 7 November
Emile Cohl has released his *les Lunettes féériques* (*The Magic Eyeglasses*), that was made by adapting the principle of the Chromatrope, or magic lantern, for the cinema.

Paris, 14 November
Harry Baur, a young actor from the Odéon Theatre, makes his screen debut in the new Eclair release *la Légende du bon chevalier* (*The Legend of the Good Knight*).

Paris, 19 December
Gaumont has released two films, which have been toned and tinted under the supervisorial eye of Louis Feuillade: *Noël d'artiste* (*The Artist's Christmas*), and *Noël du chiffonier* (*The Ragman's Christmas*).

New York, 23 December
After the success of his two-reel *Napoléon*, J. Stuart Blackton has released the first part of *The Life of Moses* a five-reeler (50 minutes), to be shown in five separate parts.

Vienna, 31 December
Erich Pommer has been named the general manager of Gaumont for the whole of central Europe.

Hong Kong, 31 December
The American Benjamin Polaski has founded The Asia Film Company. He is filming *The Pot's Revelations* and *To Steal a Roast Duck*.

Stockholm, 31 December
Charles Magnusson and Julius Jaenzon, directors of Svenska, have released a film by Carl Engdhal, *The People of the Värmland*.

BIRTHS

Wisconsin, 14 January
Joseph Losey

France, 3 February
André Cayatte

Paris, 10 February
Henri Alekan

Pennsylvania, 11 February
Joseph Mankiewicz

Egypt, 24 February
Riccardo Freda

Scotland, 1 March
David Niven

England, 15 May
James Mason

Austria, 17 May
Magda Schneider

Tasmania, 20 June
Errol Flynn

France, 23 June
Georges Rouquier

Milan, 5 July
Isa Miranda

Paris, 18 August
Marcel Carné

Istanbul, 7 September
Elia Kazan (Elia Kazanjoglou)

Stockholm, 13 November
Gunnar Björnstrand

New York, 9 December
Douglas Fairbanks Jr.

---

*The six films in the popular police series **Nick Carter**, made by Victorin Jasset, stars André Liabel in the title role, and Marise Dauvray. The films have made a fortune for Eclair.*

Extravagant congress of international executives

This group photograph, taken after the closing banquet, disguises the deep conflict between the various parties. In the front row, left to right: George Rogers, Charles Pathé, George Eastman, Georges Méliès and Charles Urban.

Paris, 4 February

"The Dupes' Congress" was how Georges Dureau, a journalist attached to *Ciné Journal*, described the International Congress of Film Producers, which has just finished after two days of debates. George Eastman has managed to come to France after the establishment by the Edison Trust in the U.S. of the Motion Pictures Patents Company, which has amalgamated nine new companies, including those of Pathé and Georges Méliès. In future, only the films of the MPPC can be shown in America. The founding of the company, with strong, authoritarian ambitions, has met with resistance from small and large operators within certain firms. Last October, both Nordisk in Denmark and Vitagraph, the business rival of Edison managed by Stuart Blackton, proposed the convening of a new international congress in Paris. This idea was welcomed enthusiastically because the European companies were not happy about the MPPC decisions. The stakes are high since the American market constitutes an inexhaustible outlet for all the companies. If this market is closed to certain firms, it might spell ruin for many of them. Thus, the idea of setting up a partnership of producers, a sort of rival trust, copying the American model. George Eastman has encouraged this plan, because he sees Europe as an excellent market. A skilled diplomat, he is trying to reconcile all the parties involved. His presence at the Congress was as much an event as that of Charles Pathé, the king of the cinema world. Pathé had originally cynically refused to collaborate in the Association of Filmmakers. The crisis in the industry, according to him, "will not be resolved by catastrophes and by the inevitable ruin of certain firms which are more financial than industrial." Clearly, the more bankruptcies the better! George Eastman had been persuaded to participate at the Congress. Eastman and Pathé were there together with some 200 significant, and less significant, people of European cinema: Léon Gaumont, Georges Méliès, Charles Jourjon and Marcel Vandal of Eclair, the American-born pioneer of British cinema Charles Urban, as well as the representatives of Vitagraph, Lux, Cines, Ambrosio, Hepworth, Warwick, Nordisk, Messter, the Russian company Drankoff, etc. At the start of the meeting presided over by Méliès, the creation of the International Committee of Filmmakers (CIDEF) was proposed and agreed. Therefore, a new consortium was born, bringing together 30 different firms. The main decision was that producers will rent out films only to members who have committed themselves in writing to returning their copies after four months. The fairground-stall owners are up in arms again. The Congress not only wishes to monopolize the hiring out of films, but also wants to eliminate those who arrange the hiring, the intermediaries between the producers and the stall owners. In fact, the Congress ended in great confusion. Despite the agreements signed, interests diverged totally. Even a decision on a just tariff for rentals could not be reached. Intended to avert a serious cinema crisis, the Congress resolved nothing. It set up a trust which can stifle the small operators. In reality the only winner of the day was Eastman, who now becomes the sole supplier of the Congress members.

Georges Méliès savors his day of glory

Paris, 4 February

George Méliès, president of the International Congress of Film Producers, proudly poses for a photograph. He is seated among a group of 50 well-known figures from the cinematographic world. On his right are George Eastman and Charles Pathé; on his left Léon Gaumont. Méliès the independent amidst the three giants of the industry! During the two days of the Congress, he performed his duties perfectly with good humor and his celebrated cordiality. This exceptional honor was the crowning achievement for him. Nevertheless, certain decisions taken by the Congress risked destroying Star Film, whose finances are increasingly troubled. The industrialization of cinematograph production on a vast scale could crush the modest firm in Montreuil, which functions on a small scale. Méliès is a brilliant artist but not a good businessman. Although very happy to have presided over the Congress, Georges Méliès has no doubt of the dangers that lie in store for him. For the moment, however, he can savor his glory, smiling with his friends of the day.

George Eastman is formidable as an industrialist and technician.

The independents stand up to Edison

New York, 20 March
The long-running dispute between Thomas Edison and the smaller, independent companies has suddenly taken on a new twist. Apparently, all those companies excluded from his trust, the Motion Picture Patents Company (or MPPC) have organized themselves into a powerful cartel of independents. And, in order to operate with maximum effectiveness, this new cartel has taken many precautions. The most notable is to make use of the special patents held by P.A. "Pat" Powers, which will protect them against the multiple threats made by Edison and his lawyers. By far the most important is the non-patent-infringing camera developed by Joseph Bianchi, a recording expert with the Columbia Phonograph Company. If the smaller companies continue to make use of this camera, there is no way that Edison will be able to stop them from filming. In addition to this, the French Lumière company has offered to supply the members of this "anti-trust" with a new type of less inflammable film stock as an alternative to the highly publicized new film from the Eastman Kodak Co. which has been specially reserved for the members of Edison's trust. It is highly likely that this new association will also be able to do a thriving business with all those film halls that have been excluded by Edison – an unexpected new lease on life here for the many small renters left out in the cold by the restrictive practices of the cartel.

'Pathé faits divers' marks the launching of a weekly newsreel

Barrère's view of Emile and Charles.

Paris, 31 March
Encouraged by the public's insatiable curiosity about the details of daily life in far-flung parts of the world, Pathé has launched a weekly newsreel, with exciting documentary footage provided by an army of cameramen dispatched to the four corners of the globe. From now on the company's film cameras will venture into savage and unexplored regions. Always on the lookout for the sensational, Pathé's cameramen also follow the important events of the week: disasters, murders, trials and sporting events. The newsreel, entitled *Pathé faits divers* and edited by Albert Gaveau, aims to act as an historical witness to contemporary events. *Pathé faits divers* is the first newsreel produced for general distribution. A British daily predecessor called *Day by Day* was shown only at London's Empire Theatre in Leicester Square.

One of the film news cameramen at work, sketched by a journalist.

Charles Pathé defies George Eastman

New York, 16 March
Emerging from the recent international congress held by film industry executives, Charles Pathé has decided on the course which he must follow in the future. He will challenge the virtual monopoly currently enjoyed by George Eastman and the American Eastman Kodak Company. Pathé is determined to produce his own supply of film stock to replace that of Eastman who has, up until now, provided most of the film used by European companies as well as by those in the United States. Having convinced the board mem-

bers of his company of the value of investing in this new area – the expensive stock supplied by Kodak has clearly eaten into profits – he has already purchased the small Blair factory in England for this purpose. He has also been exploring the possibility of recycling or reusing old reels of discarded film by peeling off the layer of sensitive emulsion. Although the results thus far have not been of the very best quality, Pathé is determined to pursue his new course, come what may, effectively declaring war on the monopolistic practices of Eastman.

Film Art finds itself at the center of a storm

Paris, 15 June
In spite of having produced many remarkable films, the Film d'Art company founded by Paul Lafitte has run into serious financial difficulties. Since the last annual meeting, debts of about 80,000 francs have been declared and the outlook is extremely grave. (Charles Pathé's position is not clear, and he has not yet offered to bail out the company.) Film d'Art will have produced the impressive total of 26 films by the end of this year, but Paul Lafitte has now been replaced by dramatist Paul Gavault as company head.

Wilbur Wright links flying to the cinema

Pau, 22 March

The Radios Society, founded in August 1907 by Clément Maurice and Félix Mesguich, has signed a contract with the famous aviator Wilbur Wright, whose heavier-than-air machine *Flyer* made the very first powered flight in December 1903. Last September Mesguich exclusively filmed Wright's flights from a race course near Le Mans, which created quite a sensation in France. Wright was also filmed receiving the Aviation Commission's prize for having stayed airborne for over an hour and a half. At Pau, on the little airfield at Pont-Long, Mesguich has just completed an astonishing film. After giving a demonstration flight for King Edward VII, Wright suggested that he take Mesguich aloft. The intrepid cameraman accepted the invitation and strapped the camera to one of the flying machine's wings, ensuring that the crank was within reach of his hand. Wright shouted, "Let's go!" and the motor burst into life while Mesguich hung on to his camera. The ground fell away. On the horizon the Pyrenees seemed to pitch and roll. With a thumping heart Mesguich cranked the camera. After a three-minute flight Wright gently landed and skidded to a halt. The numbed Mesguich had shot over 100 feet of film. He is the first to film from an aeroplane in flight.

The machine used by the famous American aviator to break several records.

Important film company opens in New York

New York, 14 April

Thomas Edison's formation of his film industry cartel toward the end of last year does not appear to have frightened off the independents. On the contrary, the independent sector continues to grow, its most important new addition being the New York Motion Picture Company. Founded by Adam Kessel Jr. and Charles Baumann, who had previously run the Empire Film Exchange, together with cameraman Fred Balshofer, the new company's offices are located at 426 Sixth Avenue. They have already begun shooting their first film, *Disinherited Son's Loyalty*, which is due to be released next month. Apparently, when the three men met over dinner to set up their new business, they had not yet decided on a name or trademark for their production arm. Then Kessel spotted an American buffalo on the $10 bill, and Bison Films was born. Also known as "Bison" Life Motion Pictures, the new logo fits in well with plans to include many Westerns among their future productions.

Hollywood gives a welcome to filmmaking

Open Californian spaces bathed in sunlight on the road to Hollywood.

Los Angeles, 1 November

The sleepy town surrounded by orange groves in the northern suburbs of Los Angeles seems likely to become a more lively place if an assumption can be made by the interest shown in it by filmmakers. They have already been spotted in the area, and many popular films have been shot here by crews from New York. So far the most famous is Kalem's *The Count of Monte Cristo*, adapted from Dumas' famous novel, in which director Francis Boggs cast a hypnotist found in a local fairground as the count. The film was released in New York and then around the country at the beginning of 1908 and has been such a popular and critical success that producer William Selig has decided to return to California to make more films. This will also have the happy by-product of putting a great deal of distance between Kalem and Edison, whose demands are becoming increasingly unbearable. Last May Francis Boggs and his team once again traveled to Hollywood for the filming of the new *In the Sultan's Power*. This time the leading role has been entrusted to a well-known actor, Hobart Bosworth, a Broadway star who was forced to leave the stage after temporarily losing his voice. Initially a bit reluctant to cast his lot with the cinema, Bosworth is now extremely happy with the new medium. He has reconciled himself to working conditions far removed from those he enjoyed on Broadway. Compromises include improvised sets, inexperienced leading ladies, few if any creature comforts.

Nevertheless, Selig sees a great future for filmmaking in California. Now in his forties, Selig, who likes to be called Colonel, is a veteran showman. A former magician, he toured with a successful minstrel show before moving into the fledgling movie business in 1896. Selig's base is in Chicago, but today sees the opening of a new Selig studio, and California's first, on the site of a Chinese laundry in Hollywood. Meanwhile, Colonel Selig can bask in the runaway success of his studio's recent *Hunting Big Game in Africa*, an exploitation of Theodore Roosevelt's safari. The ingenious Selig re-created the African jungle on his Chicago lot, using a mangy hired lion, some local blacks who played natives and an actor who impersonated Roosevelt.

Hobart Bosworth, former stage actor and producer, is one of the screen's new popular breed, the cowboy.

The rise and rise of Broncho Billy Anderson

A great comic talent for the French cinema

A characteristically tense moment for tough cowboy Broncho Billy Anderson.

*One of Max Linder's successes, in Louis Gasnier's **The Life of Punch**.*

Niles, 30 December

Cinema's cowboy hero G.M. Anderson is about to assume a new persona in the name of of Broncho Billy, based on the character in a Peter B. Kyne story, *Broncho Billy and the Baby*. The film will be called *Broncho Billy's Redemption*. The burly Anderson is already one of cinema's bright new stars. Born Max Aronson in Little Rock, Arkansas, in March 1882, he was briefly a traveling salesman before trying his luck as an actor in New York using the stage name Gilbert M. Anderson. While working as a male model in 1902, he was hired by the Edison studio to play the lead in a one-reeler directed by Edwin S. Porter, *The Messsenger Boy's Mistake*. A year later Anderson played several parts in Porter's trail-blazing Western, *The Great Train Robbery*. He was

originally cast as the outlaw leader but was disqualified by the fact that he could not ride. On the first day of filming he parted company with his horse – and the role of the outlaw leader! In 1907, after stints of writing, directing and acting at Vitagraph and Selig, Anderson went into partnership with George K. Spoor, the operator of a big nickelodeon chain. Together they formed the Essanay Company (after the first letters of their last names) which was originally based in Chicago. However, at this point Anderson was now more comfortable in the saddle, and he soon began filming Westerns in Colorado and comedy shorts with Ben Turpin in California. He is currently based in California, at Niles. Appropriately for a producer of Westerns, Essanay's trademark is an Indian in a war bonnet.

Broncho Billy displays the gentler side of his nature with the fair sex.

Vincennes, 31 December

Following a difficult debut, Max Linder has become one of the most flourishing stars of the French comedy school and is now one of the best known performers in Pathé's troupe. Born in 1883, Linder, who was mad about theater, left high school to study drama and was soon acting on the Bordeaux stage. He then left his native Gironde to tackle the Paris Conservatoire, where he failed three successive exams. But thanks to his friend Adrien Caillard, the young and ambitious comedian was hired by the Ambigu Theatre, under his real name of Gabriel-Maximilien Leuvielle, playing supporting parts in melodramas. The Ambigu has provided Pathé studios with a great number of its actors over the years.

Max Linder was then taken on by Ferdinand Zecca and paid 20 francs a day on his debut. It was in July, 1905 that Linder appeared for the first time in front of the cameras, in *A Schoolboy's First Day Out*, directed by Louis Gasnier. The film attracted attention, as did *The Life of Punch* two years later, yet they still failed to launch Linder. Thus he continued to work on stage for three years, using his real name in the theater and his pseudonym for the screen. Eventually, at the end of 1907, one of Pathé's comic actors, René Gréhan, decided to go over to Eclair. Max Linder replaced him and put on the costume of a dandy which Gréhan had worn. The little comedian had finally found his personal style. With his striped trousers and morning coat, his top hat, his gloves and cane, Linder appeared in

A Skater's Debut directed by Louis Gasnier. Ferdinand Zecca judged the film so mediocre that he preferred to postpone its release. However, the films that followed, directed by Gasnier and also by Georges Monca, found favor with the public at the beginning of the year. Linder played leading roles in all of them, dressed in diverse garb: an old man in *The Duel of a Shortsighted Man*, a Parisian tough in *A Cinematographic Show*, and even a young girl in *A Romantic Mademoiselle*. It was then that the actor adopted his permanent image – the elegant and worldly, idle dandy and woman chaser. *Don't Kiss Your Maid*, *The Mother-in-Law's False Teeth* and *The Barometer of Faithfulness* were great successes. Linder, small and delicate in spite of his athletic torso, has at last gained glory.

Dandy Max in search of a character.

Birth of an Industry

In 1895 the Lumière brothers held the first exhibitions of films to paying customers in the Indian Room at the Grand Café in Paris. Audiences, unprepared for the illusion of cinema, fled in panic as the screen was slowly filled by a train trundling into a station. *Arrival of the Train in the Ciotat Station* was baldly titled, but its locomotive was pulling behind it the infant film industry.

Five years later, at the Paris Exhibition of 1900, the industry was entering its adolescence. On display were color films tinted by hand; sound films in which the great actor Coquelin declaimed from *Cyrano de Bergerac*, his voice haphazardly synchronized on a cylindrical phonograph record; a screen 53-feet high and 70-feet wide on to which were projected spectacular scenes; and a Cinéorama that used 11 projectors to show a 360-degree image photographed from a balloon. The audience, who were standing on the roof of the drum which housed the projectors, must have felt as if they themselves were being transported in a giant balloon whose canopy swelled above them.

These modern marvels were harbingers of things to come: Technicolor, the talkies and wide-screen cinema. But in 1900, ambition outran technical development. The big screen came down in a storm, and the Cinéorama's 11 projectors generated so much heat that they violated fire regulations.

Until the outbreak of World War I (the Great War) in August 1914, the French led the way in film. The early 1900s saw the industrialization of filmmaking and, in 1898, George Méliès, the former magician and great pioneer, opened the first truly professional film studio at Montreuil near Paris. Here, in a large glasshouse, he created his cinema of illusion, displaying amazing special effects and trick photography in such films as *Voyage to the Moon* and *The Conquest of the Pole*. Gaumont studios in Paris arose around another great glasshouse, expanded by 1912 into a complex of offices, laboratories and factories, producing everything needed to make film. Even more lavish were the Pathé studios at Vincennes, run by Ferdinand Zecca.

Charles Pathé, a shrewd French businessman who had made his first fortune charging fairground crowds a fee to listen to early phonograph records, understood instinctively the dynamics and potential of the film business. He created a monopoly of production, distribution and exhibition at home, while simultaneously opening branches in every part of the world where films were shown. By 1908 Pathé was an international empire, distributing twice as much film in the U.S. as the entire American film industry. Pathé introduced the serial 'cliffhanger' to American audiences, combining the release of the weekly episode with syndicated publication in the local press. French performers had, in fact, an important impact on American film. The short films of the diffident and

by Thomas Talley, a former cowboy. His Electric Theater promised 'An Hour's Amusement and Genuine Fun for 10 Cents Admission.' The Electric Theater was then followed by thousands of 'nickelodeons', a term first used in 1905 which stemmed from the five-cent price of admission. The nickelodeons sprang up in small stores, ballrooms and disused halls all over America. By 1908 there were about 9,000 of them providing escapist fare for millions of working-class Americans, particularly immigrants from Southern and Central Europe whose lack of English naturally discouraged them from theatergoing.

The mushrooming of these nickelodeons revolutionized the organi-

Carl Laemmle at Universal with a group of his actors and directors.

dandified comedian Max Linder prompted American producers to tap their native music-hall and vaudeville talent and influenced the early career of Charles Chaplin.

French pre-eminence was undermined by the outbreak of the Great War. Export markets in Europe were suddenly closed, with materials and manpower diverted into the war effort. As the French retreated, the film industry in the United States, uninvolved in the bloodletting until 1917, moved in to fill the vacuum.

Until about 1900, American motion pictures were mostly straightforward records of stage acts of the day, usually screened in vaudeville theaters. In 1902 America's first true movie house was opened on South Main Street in Los Angeles

zation of the American film industry. Previously, exhibitors bought films outright from the manufacturers on the East Coast, or from local agents, at a standard price of about 10 cents a foot. Audiences, however, tired of the films long before the prints wore out. The answer was the 'film exchange', the first of which was opened in San Francisco in 1902 by Herbert and Harry Miles. The new film rental business, full of fly-by-night operators, was no place for the commercially squeamish. And it was in the typically American rough and tumble of this world that many of the industry's future moguls cut their teeth.

They were immigrants, too, most of them Jews from the ghettos of Central Europe. Above all, they

were entrepreneurs searching for ground-floor entry into a business which required little initial investment. Motion pictures presented them with a perfect opportunity.

The most durable of them all was Adolph Zukor, who died in 1976 at the ripe old age of 103. Zukor came to America from Hungary when he was 16 years old, with $40 sewn into the lining of his waistcoat. As with many Jewish immigrants, he went into the garment business, learning English while selling furs. In 1903 he went into the amusement arcade business, a diminutive man in a fur-collared coat. Later Zukor formed a partnership with another furrier, Marcus Loew, but struck out on his own as a showman and distributor in 1912. Zukor had long pondered how best to entice into the cinema the middle classes to whom he had once sold furs. The one and two-reel films churned out on breakneck shooting schedules by companies like Biograph and Vitagraph were seen as shoddy products, profitable, but fit only for the amusement of the masses. Zukor had other ideas. In 1912 he distributed the hour-long French Film d'Art production of *Queen Elizabeth*, starring Sarah Bernhardt. The film was leased on a States Rights basis, and the middle-class audiences it drew provided the clinching argument in the battle to convince the movie business that the American public would accept 'feature' films of far greater length than the standard one and two-reelers.

The Film d'Art re-creations of French classical theater were inert entertainments doomed to early extinction, but the success of *Queen Elizabeth* encouraged Zukor to form a production company to film 'Famous Players in Famous Plays'. He hired Edwin S. Porter to duplicate the Film d'Art approach by bringing Broadway stars to the screen in films such as *The Prisoner of Zenda*, starring James Hackett, and *The Count of Monte Cristo*, with James O'Neill. The resulting feature-length films were stilted and stagy, but the new audiences they attracted led to the construction of more lavishly appointed theaters to accommodate them. It was left to D.W. Griffith, enthused by spectacular Italian epics like *Quo Vadis?* (1912) and *Cabiria* (1914), to exploit fully in

The Birth of a Nation (1915), the possibilities opened up by the mass-audience appeal of the feature-length film.

In 1903 the four young Warner brothers opened a 99-seat store cinema in Newcastle, Pennsylvania. Harry Warner had been born in Poland and his brothers in a succession of American cities as the family followed their traveling-salesman father. The Warner brothers moved next into distribution and by 1912 were making their own films. Carl Laemmle was already 40 when he went into the picture business. Born into a middle-class Jewish family in Germany in 1867, he came to America when he was 17. In anticipation of a quick profit, in 1906 he opened a nickelodeon, the White Front Theater, on Chicago's West Side. Thereafter, he made up for lost time, expanding rapidly into distribution to service the Midwest chain he created. This brought him into conflict with the Motion Pictures Patent Company (popularly known as the Edison Trust), an association of the leading American production companies and the U.S. branches of the French majors. By pooling their patents claims and assigning them to Edison, and by declaring that no one was entitled to produce, distribute or exhibit films in the U.S. without their license, these companies aimed to sew up the film business and drive out the independents who challenged their monopoly.

Laemmle was one of the leaders of the crusade against the Trust. Writs flew in all directions, smear campaigns were waged and violence flared. Amid the tumult Laemmle began to produce his own pictures under the banner of the Independent Motion Picture Company of America (IMP), founded in 1909. Soon, an amalgamation with a few smaller companies meant that he was presiding over his own little film empire. In large part that empire was created by the emergence of the star system, in which Laemmle played a crucial role. In the early days of cinema the corporation lawyers and businessmen who financed the film companies aimed to produce a cheap, standardized product. Preserving the anonymity of film actors was a simple way of keeping salaries, and overheads, down. In this they were helped by the actors, many of whom regarded film work as a last resort. When the young Mary Pickford expressed

horror at working in 'the flickers', her mother reassured her that "It's only to tide us over."

This attitude changed as the public grew ever more fascinated with film. Exhibitors, and the entrepreneurs who ran the film exchanges, quickly grasped that the familiarity of popular players was an asset. In April 1909, in *The Moving Picture World*, an early trade magazine, Ben Turpin appeared under his own name in an article describing the life of a 'Moving Picture Comedian'. The corpulent comic John Bunny and the ersatz cowboy Broncho Billy Anderson starred in their own films. (Bunny was already an established stage performer, and Anderson owned his own production company). However, the most popular actress at Biograph, Florence Lawrence, was billed simply as 'The Biograph Girl'.

according to the drawing power of the box office." By 1915 Pickford was on a salary of $10,000 a week and her drawing power was the foundation of the evolving Zukor empire which, in a series of complex deals, became Paramount studios. Stars like Pickford and Chaplin became the collateral on which the film companies could borrow huge sums of money. If you could not find a star, you created one. William Fox was another German-Jewish immigrant who had made a fortune in the film exchange business, beaten off the Edison Trust, and gone into film production in 1915 as head of the Fox Film Corporation. It was Fox who transformed a dumpy stage actress named Theodosia de Coppet, born Goodman, into the screen's first 'vamp' and million-dollar star, Theda Bara.

The growth of the star system was

*Helen Holmes in **The Hazards of Helen** (1914), made for the Kalem Co.*

In 1910 Lawrence fell out with Biograph and into the welcoming arms of Laemmle's IMP. He then planted a fictitious news story that Lawrence had been killed in a streetcar accident in St. Louis. This was immediately followed by an advertisement in the trade press – headlined WE NAIL A LIE – in which the blame for the story was laid at the door of IMP's competitors. Lawrence was triumphantly produced in St. Louis to make the first personal appearance by a film star. She was mobbed by a huge crowd of fans, who tore the buttons off her coat. A star was born.

The stars rapidly moved center stage. In 1913 Adolph Zukor told Mary Pickford's mother, "if feature pictures succeed, we expect to pay

accompanied by the shift of filmmaking from the East Coast to California. Films had been made in and around Los Angeles from 1907, when the Selig company of Chicago shot *The Count of Monte Cristo* on Santa Monica Beach and in an improvised studio in the back of a Chinese laundry. The attractions for filmmakers were twofold: the pleasant climate and varied scenery, and California's considerable distance from the reach of the Edison Trust. Many films were shot in Hollywood, a sleepy suburb of Los Angeles surrounded by orange groves. In 1913 an ambitious young director arrived in Hollywood to shoot a film version of a popular Western novel, *The Squaw Man*. Named Cecil B. DeMille, he was a stage actor and

playwright who had formed a partnership with Jesse L. Lasky and Lasky's brother-in-law Samuel Goldfish (later Goldwyn). Disappointed with the locations that had been chosen out in Arizona, DeMille and his company boarded a train and rode to the end of the line, where they stumbled on to Hollywood. There, they shot *The Squaw Man*, the picture that helped to put Hollywood on the map.

In 1912 Carl Laemmle's IMP had metamorphosed into the Universal Film Manufacturing Company, later known simply as Universal. On 15 March 1915, amid a blaze of publicity, Laemmle used a golden key to open the new Universal studios built at a cost of $165,000 on the north side of the Hollywood Hills.

Hollywood was now a factory town producing dreams for sale. The money stayed on the East Coast but the films were made on the West Coast. In 1915 alone over 250 pictures, most of them two-reelers and serials, poured out of the studios at Universal City. Later this same year, after a long legal battle, the Edison Trust bit the dust. Meanwhile the power of the stars continued to grow apace. The Famous Players were now more important than the Famous Plays. Mary Pickford's status was such that she was able to force Zukor to set up a subsidiary, Artcraft, initially for her own productions, and triple the rates he charged exhibitors for her films. In 1915, alarmed by this trend, the industry's three leading independent producer-directors, Mack Sennett, Thomas Ince and D.W. Griffith, formed Triangle, which offered them the opportunity to make films free from what they saw as the tyranny of the stars.

The Triangle company proved the forerunner of United Artists, which was founded in 1919 by Mary Pickford, Douglas Fairbanks, Charlie Chaplin and D.W. Griffith, with the object of making and distributing their own films (and the quality product of others). This move reflected its founders' suspicion of the growing corporate control of the film business pioneered by Zukor. Under his aggressive leadership, Paramount became a force in the three branches of motion pictures – production, distribution and exhibition – consolidating the vertical integration of the studio system which would emerge in the 1920s.

ROBIN CROSS

1910

★ ★

London, 1 January
The Cinematograph Act of Great Britain comes into force today. Designed to protect cinemas from fire resulting from the inflammable nature of film, the Act demands the provision of a separate, fire-resistant projection box and buckets of sand in auditoriums.

Paris, 16 January
Edison has released *Faust*, adapted from Goethe, and directed by J. Searle Dawley. Copies of the 302-metre film are to be sold at 1.25 francs per metre.

Los Angeles, 20 January
D.W. Griffith has arrived in California with the Biograph troupe. He is here to complete the filming of *The Newlyweds*, a comedy he started shooting in New York.

Paris, 30 January
Gaumont have completed editing of a toned and tinted copy of *André Chénier*, "the life of a poet who died during the Revolution," made by Louis Feuillade.

Paris, 1 February
An auction sale of Pathé Frères cameras and 500 films is being held at the Hotel Drouot.

New York, 10 February
In an attempt to counter the Independents, the MPPC is trying to control regional distributors by creating its own distribution company, The General Film Company.

Paris, 12 February
Vitagraph are distributing *A Midsummer Night's Dream*, a 303-metre film adapted from the works of Shakespeare by J. Stuart Blackton.

Paris, 12 February
The firm Raleigh and Robert are distributing a new series done in six episodes, *Dr. Phantom*, directed by Victorin Jasset for Eclair.

Paris, 19 February
Louis Feuillade has undertaken a series of biblical films for Gaumont. The first of these, *Balthazar's Feast*, is now showing.

Paris, 28 February
Gaumont, like Pathé, has stopped selling films. From now on, they are only to be available for rent.

Rome, 7 March
El Cid, adapted from the play by Corneille and produced by Mario Caserini, Cines' specialist in period films, has had a public screening.

Neuilly, 27 March
Henri Pouctal is currently filming an adaptation of Goethe's *Werther*, at the Film d'Art studios. André Brulé plays the title role.

Paris, 2 April
George Eastman has put the Eclair Company in charge of his main continental warehouse. The unexposed Eastman films will be stored at the Epinay factory.

Paris, 23 April
From now on, all films supplied to France by Vitagraph will be on the new film from Eastman-Kodak that is non-inflammable.

Paris, 30 April
Eclair has created the Actors' and Writers' Association to compete with Film d'Art. It has released *Barberine,* by Emile Chautard, a former actor from the Odéon and artistic director of the Association.

New York, 16 May
Charles Pathé is making films here for the local market, under the production banner Pathé-American. The first of these, *The Girl from Montana*, starring a young blonde named Pearl White, opens today.

London, 20 May
Cameramen from Pathé, Gaumont, Eclipse, Raleigh and Robert were in the capital to film King Edward VII's funeral today.

Marienbad, 1 June
Count Alexander Kollovrath has created the Sasha-Film company, at Horni Plana, near Marienbad.

Paris, June
Franchise owners for the Enterprise Optical Company from Chicago are launching the Motiograph projector. The advertisements claim that it produces a perfectly steady picture and has 40 percent more luminosity than all other machines.

Berlin, 3 June
City cinema owners are protesting against the performance tax being considered by the mayor.

France, 18 June
The American film company Bat Films, whose emblem reflects the name, has set up business in Lyon.

Paris, 18 June
Gaumont is launching a series of art films to compete with Film d'Art. The first work is *Le Pater*, produced by Louis Feuillade.

New York, 2 July
A fire has devastated Vitagraph's studios. Numerous negatives have been destroyed.

Paris, July
The Optique Company here has launched Multicolor, a new process which adds color to films during projection.

Paris, 15 August
The 19-year-old journalist Louis Delluc is contributing articles to *Comœdia Illustré*, a glossy weekly of Parisian life, run by Maurice de Brunoff. His personal love of the theater is reflected in his articles.

Berlin, 20 August
The UT network has just opened its second cinema on the Unter den Linden, Berlin's main thoroughfare.

St. Petersburg, 21 August
Release of *The Life and Death of Pushkin* filmed by Vassili Goncharov and produced by Gaumont.

Paris, 27 August
Release of *The Samouraï's Punishment*, which presents actors from the Imperial Theatre, produced by Pathé's Japanese branch as part of the Japanese Art Film series.

Paris, 1 October
Pathé has edited a film in its "art series", *la Tragique aventure de Robert le Taciturne, duc d'Aquitaine* (*The Tragic Adventure of Robert the Taciturn, Duke of Aquitaine*), directed by Ferdinand Zecca and Henri Andréani.

Paris, 29 October
Pathé has launched a big advertising campaign for its new comic character Rigadin who is played by Charles Petit-Demange, known in the theater as Prince. The film, *Rigadin va dans le grand monde* (*Rigadin Goes into the Wide World*), directed by Georges Monca, is now available.

France, 10 November
The press has announced that Pathé's star Max Linder has undergone an emergency operation for appendicitis. The actor is reported to have said to his surgeon, "I'm not afraid... After all, I'm used to being under lights!"

Meudon, 12 November
Screening of No. 4 of Gaumont's weekly "Newsreel" series which was started last month. The sculptor August Rodin, who has just celebrated his 70th birthday and agreed to be filmed at home, is featured in the newsreel.

Paris, 26 November
Opening of the Cinérama-Théâtre at 83 avenue de la Grande-Armée, run by a pioneer of the cinema industry, Gabriel Kayser. The screening of a Gaumont newsreel was followed by Pathé's *l'Inventeur* (*The Inventor*), directed by Michel Carré.

Korea, 31 December
Opening of Seoul's first cinema.

BIRTHS

Chicago, 28 February
Vincente Minnelli

Tokyo, 23 March
Akira Kurosawa

Bordeaux, 23 June
Jean Anouilh

France, 14 July
Annabella (Suzanne Charpentier)

Tokyo, 15 July
Satsuo Yamamoto

France, 8 September
Jean-Louis Barrault

Belgium, 24 September
Jean Servais

Japan, 28 November
Kinuyo Tanaka

Italy, 11 December
Carlo Ponti

The popular 'Biograph girl' has been revealed by producer Carl Laemmle to be Florence Lawrence. She has been lured away by Laemmle to join his production company IMP.

Biblical epic shown in four parts

New York, 2 February
In recent years Vitagraph has produced a number of split-reelers with Biblical subjects, but it has taken a great commercial gamble with a new film, *The Life of Moses*. It is reported that the company has lavished $50,000 on a five-reel epic, shown in four parts, which advance publicity proclaims is a "reverent and dignified portrayal of the Wonderful Story of Moses revealed by the Greatest Triumph of Photographic and Mechanical Art ever achieved." And lovers of spectacle are promised "The Miracle of the Red Sea. A $10,000 Water Scene." To ensure the film's religious and historical accuracy, Vitagraph engaged a clerical celebrity, the Reverend Madison C. Peters, to write the script for the first reel and advise on the authenticity of the entire project. Although various clergymen have expressed their doubts about cinematic representations of Bible stories, *Moving Picture World* comments that *The Life of Moses* is "a graphic reproduction of the main events in the life of Moses, corresponding closely to the conception which has been inculcated in those who have attended church and Sunday school."

Sound scenes are making the screen sing

Paris, 5 March
"Toreador, on guard, a dark eye scrutinizes you!" At the moment, Gaumont phonoscènes are showing *Carmen*, a sound film projected by the Chronomégaphone, the apparatus on which Léon Gaumont has been working since 1902. It contains the toreador's aria that's just 83 metres long. Not only *Carmen*, but also *Faust, Mireille, la Traviata* and *The Barber of Seville* have been adapted by Gaumont. His catalogue caters to all tastes: *la Tonkinoise, la Marseillaise, O Sole Mio, The Crucifix, le Rire du nègre* and the most celebrated songs by Mayol (*Viens Poupoule*), by Dranem (*le Trou de mon quai*) and by Polin (*le Frotteur de la colonelle*). Since 1906, the volume of sound has been improved by Elgéphone on the air as well as on phonograph records by amplifying the sound using compressed air. People at the fairs are now singing: "The newest attraction – I'll take you there Bobonne – is the Chronomégaphone!"

Bizet's Carmen is the tragic heroine of this phonoscène by Alice Guy.

Plans to preserve early French films

Paris, 27 February
What has become of the thousands of films which have been made in the last 15 years? For the most part they have been mutilated, dispersed, lost and melted down. The weekly *Ciné Journal* has urgently demanded the establishment of a Cinematographothèque – a copyright registration and storage place for films just like the one for books at the National Library. "What can one say about the negligence of our contemporaries? They are not concerned that the most thrilling spectacles of their lives have disappeared without a trace." It's not a new idea. In 1898 the Pole, Boleslaw Matuszewski, requested the foundation of an "historic cinematographic library", but it failed to catch on. Manufacturers and cameramen continue to massacre their old films; the large companies are content to deposit scenarios, with only a sample of a dozen stills in the National Library. In the United States, by contrast, a storehouse for films exists in the Library of Congress where the deposited copies are printed on paper to avoid risks of fire. The paper prints also serve a legal purpose in case of counterfeit.

Frankenstein's monster comes to life

New York, 18 March
The Edison studio has produced a remarkable adaptation of Mary Shelley's macabre tale, *Frankenstein or the Modern Prometheus*. Written and directed by J. Searle Dawley, the film reinterprets rather than condenses the original, and the makers claim that they have attempted to "eliminate all the actually repulsive situations and to concentrate on the mystic and psychological problems that are to be found in this weird tale." Augustus Phillips plays Frankenstein, a young medical student whose chemical attempts to create a perfect human being produce a hideous monster, played with great relish by Charles Ogle. A veteran of the stage, Ogle has created his own makeup for the part which echoes Shelley's monstrous creation, with a ghastly chalk-white face under a wild mass of wispy hair and hands that clutch like talons. While the monster struggles with Frankenstein, he catches his reflection in a mirror and, sickened by the sight, stumbles into the night. The film reaches a terrifying climax when the monster returns to attack Frankenstein's bride-to-be, played by Mary Fuller, in her bedroom. Her agonized screams bring Frankenstein running to the rescue, only for him to find his own image in the mirror replaced by that of the horrible creature he has created. But the power of love ensures that the monster's image fades away to restore the chastened scientist to the arms of his beloved, so ending the film with an embrace. This movie is crammed with clever special effects, particularly the scene in which the half-formed monster rises from a bubbling cauldron in Frankenstein's laboratory, growing ever larger as it acquires its crude flailing arms and its ghostly face.

Actor Charles Ogle is transformed into the monster by brilliant makeup.

D.W. Griffith assured a place in the sun

Griffith, now a celebrated director.

New York, 14 April
David Wark Griffith and his famous team of actors and technicians have returned today from filming in sun-drenched California to the studios of American Mutoscope and Biograph Company in New York. During this four-month working vacation, Griffith's ensemble shot 25 films in a list of locations that gives rise to dreams: Los Angeles, Santa Monica, Pasadena, Glendale and the Sierra Madre, to name but a few. The group traveled in train coaches marked "Biograph Special", and they each had $3 a day to spend in the dining car. The original backgrounds inspired the actors who were invited on the trip. Mary Pickford and her brother Jack, Marion Leonard, Linda Arvidson (Griffith's wife), Blanche Sweet and Mack Sennett, to mention only the most

famous. It was a happy company en route and a happy company once all had settled down in Los Angeles. There they rented a studio at the corner of Grand Avenue and Washington Street, which contained two small dressing rooms for the men and similar facilities for the women across the lot. When large numbers of extras were required, they were provided with a tent for dressing. A loft nearby was rented for laboratory space. At Santa Monica and at Port Los Angeles, they made *The Unchanging Sea*, a variation on the Enoch Arden story, featuring Linda Arvidson Griffith. The penultimate film on this first Californian trip was a version of Helen Hunt Jackson's *Ramona*, in which Mary Pickford portrayed the Indian maiden. *Over Silent Paths*, about a lone miner and his daughter making the trip to California by prairie schooner, was shot in the San Fernando Valley. All the members of the company enjoyed the Californian stay and expressed their hopes that they could return. It is nearly two years since Griffith first presided over the artistic fortunes of the celebrated New York company. Biograph had fallen on hard times when Griffith joined the ranks as scenarist, but his energy and initiative gave it a new lease on life, and it earned him the chance to direct his first motion picture, *The Adventures of Dollie*. Made in 1908, it was an immediate success. Since then Griffith has directed more than 200 films, and his Californian experience seems to have motivated him even further.

An exquisite detail from *Romance of a Butterfly*, which has been made by the English pioneer of stop-motion photography, Percy Smith.

A personal vision of the French Revolution

A scene from De Morlhon's colorful film about France's ill-fated queen.

Paris, 10 June
Charles Pathé's company has been on location shooting its new film, *The Secret Adventure of Marie Antoinette*, directed by Camille de Morlhon. This comedy-drama is almost entirely colored by stencil, and represents the aristocratic De Morlhon's personal view of the French Revolution. Introduced to the cinema by Edmond Benoît-Lévy, De Morlhon has quickly carved out an important niche at Pathé under the wing of Ferdinand Zecca. He handles all the different genres with ease and brings a characteristic vigor to each new project.

A new lease of life for German production

Berlin, 1 May
The German cinema is struggling to wake from a long sleep. In recent years it has been dominated by foreign imports, mostly from America, France and Italy. Now Paul Davidson has announced the formation of the Projection Aktien Gesellschaft Union (PAGU), the aim of which is to gather together all of the small production companies which are hostile to the monopolistic ambitions of the German industrialist Von Schack. Last April Von Schack founded FIAG (Film Industrie Anonym Gesellschaft) with the aim of uniting all the German exhibitors in

a single organization. This move is likely to increase the number of foreign films flooding the German market, and Von Schack's plans have met with widespread opposition from the industry whose spokesman, Davidson, recently took over the UT circuit as well as a big cinema in Berlin's Alexanderplatz which holds 1,000 spectators. PAGU has now been given the unconditional support of the Bayerische Anilin Aktien Gesellschaft fur Anilin Fabrikation (AGFA), which is also fighting hard against American opposition in the form of the powerful Kodak company.

▷

1911

★★★★★★★★★ **1911** ★★

Chicago, 12 January
Creation of the Majestic Motion Picture Company by Harry Aitken and John Freuler.

New York, 16 January
His Trust, part one of a film by D.W. Griffith, is now screening. Part two, *His Trust Fulfilled*, should come out in three days time. Griffith wanted them shown simultaneously, but Henry Marvin, the manager of Biograph, was against the idea.

Los Angeles, 31 January
Vitagraph has opened a film studio in California.

St. Petersburg, 16 January
Alexander Khanjonkov has released *The Kreutzer Sonata*, adapted from the novella by Leo Tolstoy. Ivan Mosjoukine takes the leading role.

Istanbul, 1 February
Léon Gaumont has opened a new branch of Comptoir-Ciné-Location, a rental firm for films produced and distributed by Gaumont. He already owns branches in Paris, Brussels and Cairo.

St. Petersburg, 2 February
The Demon, an adaptation by the Italian filmmaker Giovanni Vitrotti of Lermontov's work, produced by the Gloria company, is currently screening. Filming took place in the Tiflis studios in Georgia.

Paris, 4 February
Gaumont has released Léonce Perret's *Dans la vie* (*In the Midst of Life*). The film, a "poignantly emotional story," stars Perret himself, and Yvette Andreyor.

Paris, 17 February
Léon Gaumont has once more demonstrated the Chronophone to the Photographic Society. A film was projected during the session, and Mr. d'Arsonval explained how the invention worked, while a rooster let out a loud cock-a-doodle-do through the powerful Elgéphone.

New York, 25 February
The Vitagraph company has just released *A Tale of Two Cities*, adapted from the Charles Dickens novel and produced by J. Stuart Blackton and William Humphrey. The first three-reeler made by Vitagraph, each reel will be shown separately.

Paris, 4 March
Pathé, who is the French distributor for the Russian Drankov company's documentary about Tolstoy, has just released *Anna Karenina*. The film was produced by Pathé's Russian branch and used Russian actors who worked under the direction of Maurice André Maître.

France, 11 March
The Anti-Pornography League in Lille, La Maison de la Bonne Press, and Cardinal Coullié, the archbishop of Lyon, are leading a vigorous campaign against the cinema. In Paris, the league against licentiousness has asked audiences to whistle their disapproval during immoral films and to deface posters of a questionable nature.

Paris, 16 March
Cinema Rochechouart is presently screening Guiseppe De Liguoro's adaptation of Dante's *Inferno*.

Paris, 16 March
Gaumont's new talking film, *la Vie reconstituée*, is currently showing at the Olympia.

Paris, 18 March
The Geographical Society has presented the Alfred Molteni prize to Martel, the cameraman from Lion Films, for his shots of Abyssinia.

Paris, 1 April
The Jougla Company, manufacturers of film negative, has merged with the Lumière establishment.

Paris, 7 April
Itala Films is now distributing its major production, *The Fall of Troy*, by Giovanni Pastrone.

Prague, 1 May
The producer Antonin Pech has founded the Kinofa company.

Paris, 6 May
Italian films are flooding French screens. *La Jérusalem delivrée* by Enrico Guazzoni, adapted from Le Tasse, is now screening at La Cinès.

Paris, 20 May
Pathé has released a "social drama", *les Victimes de l'alcool* (*The Victims of Alcohol*) by Ferdinand Zecca (adapted from Zola's novel *l'Assommoir*) to compete with Gaumont's "Life as it really is" series.

New York, 14 June
Enoch Arden, a two-reel film from D.W. Griffith is now screening. The Biograph company has decided to show both parts at the same session.

Paris, 17 June
Ciné-Journal has disclosed that old films are sold off to boot makers. After a treatment with celluloid they are used to glaze high quality boots.

China, 30 June
The Imperial Government here has brought in regulations concerning the cinema industry: authorization must be obtained to open a theater, men and women must be seated apart, immoral films are forbidden and the last session has to finish before midnight.

Paris, 14 July
Film d'Art has released *Camille Desmoulins*, a color-tinted film produced by Henri Pouctal.

Paris, 1 August
Gaumont has launched its 35mm, metal, X series "projection box", equipped with all the latest technology and selling for 900 francs. Pathé is selling a similar machine, the No. 4 projection box, for 876 francs.

Paris, 19 August
Gaumont has released *la Fin de Paganini* (*The End of Paganini*), the script for which was purchased by Louis Feuillade from Abel Gance.

Copenhagen, 28 August
The new Danish company Kinografen has released *De Fire Djaevle* (*The Four Devils*) by Alfred Lind and Robert Dineson, two renegades from Nordisk.

New York, 30 August
The French production company Eclair has set up its first American branch here.

Hollywood, 2 October
David Horsley, the head of a New Jersey production company, has begun building a film studio here. The Nestor will be situated at the intersection of Sunset Boulevard and Gower Street.

Rome, 27 October
Release of Luggi Maggi's *Nozze d'Oro* (*The Golden Wedding*), a gold medal winner at the World's Fair.

Paris, 10 November
First release of the 810-metre long *Notre Dame de Paris*, a SCAGL-Pathé production, an adaptation from Victor Hugo's novel by Albert Capellani, with Stacia de Napierkowska and Henry Krauss playing the main parts.

Paris, 27 December
Abel Gance has signed a contract with the Alter Ego company for the making of four films in a small studio in Neuilly.

Paris, 29 December
Pathé has released its *Little Moritz chasse les grands fauves* (*Little Moritz Hunts Big Game*), part of the "Comica" series directed by Roméo Bosetti, with the music hall actor Maurice Schwartz.

Berlin, 31 December
The production company Deutsche Bioskop has built a glass studio in Babelsberg on a block measuring 40,000 square metres.

BIRTHS

Illinois, 6 February
Ronald Reagan

Missouri, 3 March
Jean Harlow (Harlean Carpenter)

New York, 3 June
Paulette Goddard (Marion Levy)

Missouri, 16 June
Ginger Rogers
(Virginia Katherine McMath)

Paris, 13 July
Jean-Pierre Aumont

Monte Carlo, 20 July
Mireille Balin

Wisconsin, 7 August
Nicholas Ray (Raymond Kienzle)

Mexico, 12 August
Cantinflas (Mario Moreno Reyes)

Milan, 3 December
Nino Rota

Publicized under the name of its most famous character, director Gerolamo Lo Salvio's film version of Shakespeare's **The Merchant of Venice** *is a Franco-Italian co-production.*

Leading man Maurice Costello loses his head!

New York, 25 February
Vitagraph has just released *A Tale of Two Cities* in three parts. According to *The Motion Picture World*, "It seems safe to say that this production of one of the most famous stories will go down in motion picture history as one of the most notable of photoplay productions." Maurice Costello takes the role of Sydney Carton, Charles Dickens' hero who goes to the guillotine in his friend's place. "The Dimpled Darling", as the matinee-idol Costello is known, gives one of his finest performances in what must be his greatest triumph on screen. When Costello joined the Vitagraph company two years ago, part of his agreement was that he would not be required to perform the other production tasks expected of actors. "I am an actor, and I will act, but I will not build sets and paint scenery," he declared. With portrayals such that of Sydney Carton, Vitagraph has no cause for complaint. Costello's partner in the film is the "Vitagraph Girl" herself, Florence Turner, in the poignant role of Lucie Manette. They had appeared together previously in another classic, *The Merchant of Venice*, but this film is far superior.

'This is a far, far better thing I do...' Sidney Carton (Costello) on the scaffold awaiting his death by guillotine.

Winsor McCay animates his comic-strip

New York, 12 April
Since 1905 readers of the *New York Herald* have delighted in the magical world of the *Little Nemo in Slumberland* strip drawn by Winsor McCay. Now the strip has come to life in an animated film which is being shown tonight at the Colonial Theater as part of McCay's celebrated vaudeville act in which he sketches "The Seven Ages of Man." McCay has been experimenting with animation for almost as long as he has been drawing Little Nemo, the youthful Everyman who travels throughout space and time. The origins of his animated film, entitled *Little Nemo and the Princess*, lie in a wager the prolific McCay made with fellow cartoonists that he could not produce enough drawings to sustain a five-minute animated cartoon. The 4,000 hand-tinted drawings for the cartoon were made on transparent rice paper, mounted on thin cardboard and then photographed on to one reel at the Vitagraph studios in Brooklyn. The cartoon is preceded by a live action sequence, directed by James Stuart Blackton, in which McCay appears with Vitagraph's star comedian, John Bunny, in a fanciful re-creation of the famous wager in a saloon under the Brooklyn Bridge. In an equally humorous vein, it also provides a brief glimpse of the painstaking methods the cartoonist used to make the film. As a result, McCay's characters, Little Nemo, Flip, Impy and Dr. Pill, go through their paces with an almost uncanny smoothness. Little Nemo himself is formed by lines which resemble steel filings drawn on to a magnet. He sketches the Princess and presents her with a rose which grows just in time to be plucked. They are then carried off to Slumberland in a splendid dragon chariot. The film ends with another live action sequence which shows the happy McCay collecting his bet.

Allan Dwan and Co. take off with 'Flying A'

Chicago, 5 June
"Flying A" is flying high. Although the formation of this new company was first announced in *The Moving Picture World* just eight months ago, it has been quick to make its mark. Formally known as the American Film Manufacturing Company of Chicago, it has assembled a talented production team and roster of players, some of them poached from Essanay. Three different stock companies have been operating simultaneously, filming comedies, dramas and Westerns, with two one-reelers a week released under the Flying A banner since November. Most interesting of those three is the company which headed west to film, first in Tucson, Arizona and then in Southern California. Scenario writer Allan Dwan has become the director since the departure of Frank Beal, while the leading players of note are J. Warren Kerrigan and Pauline Bush. Some idea of the range of recent releases can be gleaned from the titles alone, included among which are *Rattlesnakes and Gunpowder*, *The Sheepman's Daughter* and – on a split reel with *The Elopements on Double L Ranch* – *The Sagebrush Phrenologist*.

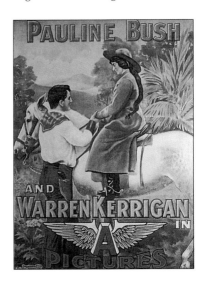

Max and Rigadin struggle for the top spot

Paris, 17 June
Max Linder's new film *Max and his Mother-in-Law* has given rise to howls of laughter. Always elegant, Max is married to a charming woman, but his enormous mother-in-law is there to ruin the honeymoon trip. She doesn't know how to skate or ski. With distaste, Max must always prop her up. Finally, Max pushes his mother-in-law down a snow-covered slope. Alas, the hardy creature survives! The film, nevertheless, ends in all-round reconciliation. Max's films have been very successful for a year, and he is now known throughout Europe. The dandy he impersonates even appeals to working-class audiences, because he doesn't hesitate to effect variations on risqué subjects.

Pathé pays him 1,000 francs per film, and directors include Linder himself, Lucien Nonguet and Armand Massart. Rigadin, another Pathé actor, has sometimes stolen Max's limelight. Already popular in the theater under the name of Prince, he also directs spicy comedies. Rigadin, like Linder, shoots 150 to 200-metre films and deals with complicated situations. In *Rigolade and his Sons*, he plays three different characters simultaneously, thanks to special effects. Linder has an undeniable superiority over rival Rigadin in being handsome, smart and pleasing to women. Rigadin is frankly ugly, but his gags have more imagination. Who will win the title of King of Laughter?

The celebrated music-hall star, Mistinguett, here plays second fiddle to Rigadin.

'New' Gaumont Palace seats 3,400 people

Paris, 30 September
Gaumont is growing increasingly more powerful. In addition to studios and laboratories, it has now moved aggressively into film exhibition. Today Léon Gaumont opens the doors of the biggest cinema in the world. The former Hippodrome, on the place Clichy, has become the Gaumont Palace. The distinguished architect Auguste Bahrmann has completely transformed the theater, which can seat up to 3,400. Films will be accompanied from behind the screen by a 30-piece orchestra and choir under the musical direction of Paul Fosse. There are two projectors, which will allow reels to be changed without any interruption to the program. Air conditioning maintains a constant temperature in the theater. The heating system, which must work overtime in such a vast space, gobbles up a daily diet of five tons of coal. During the interval the cinema's patrons can meet and eat in the Gaumont Palace's buffet, which has been placed at the center of a spacious, circular walkway. Lighting is provided by 10,000 incandescent lights and 50 arc lamps. This Saturday's program runs to over 2,000 feet of film, including tinted and sound films, the latter utilizing Gaumont's Chronophone device, newsreels and comic and dramatic scenes – in short the cream of Gaumont's output. Screened in three sessions, the Gaumont's program compares favorably with those offered by the city's other leading music halls.

Pathé releases its answer to Nick Carter

Paris, 5 August
Pathé continues to expand into new areas. It is now shooting *Nick Winter contre Nick Winter*, a comic film directed by Gerard Bourgeois and featuring Georges Winter, a leading actor from the Châtelet Theatre. The inspiration for *Nick Winter* is the *Nick Carter* series directed by Victorin Jasset for Eclair, which has been running for the last three years and stars Pierre Bressol as the debonair turn-of-the-century sleuth. The Nick Winter adventures for Pathé are comedy-thrillers with a detective background. Pathé's attempts to exploit the success of Jasset's series is a tribute to the successful formula developed by the former sculptor and stage designer who has been making films since 1905.

Georges Winter, the well-known stage actor plays Nick Winter.

The cinema causes tumult amid the orange groves

Los Angeles, 1 October

Thomas Harper Ince, one of the most enterprising and dynamic of the new breed of independent producers, has been stirring things up in California. He was initially hired by Bison Pictures (the New York Motion Picture Company) to direct Westerns at their Edenvale studios, and arrived in California just a few months ago with his actress wife Alice Kershaw. However, it was not long before Ince was making some basic changes. Dissatisfied with the simply plotted and cheaply made Westerns which are currently being turned out, he made a deal with the Miller Brothers whose 101 Ranch Wild West Show had just arrived in California for the winter. At a stroke he acquired the services of a large number of authentic cowboys and cowgirls, Indians and their squaws, trained horses, oxen and buffalo, along with wagons, stagecoaches, prairie schooners, and other invaluable accessories. He also bought almost 20,000 acres of land on which to film his Westerns so as to give them a more authentic and convincing appearance. Already, Thomas Ince's first two-reeler, entitled *War on the Plains*, has set a new standard for all Western productions of the future.

Thomas Ince has come a long way in just a few short years. An actor on the stage from an early age like his younger brother Ralph, he first became attracted to films when he realized that he would never make a real success of the theater. Having

Blanche Sweet in **The Lonedale Operator**, *the ninth film to be made by D.W. Griffith in California during January.*

played a few small movie roles around 1908-1909, Ince was signed up by Biograph in 1910 and appeared in a number of films. But he soon grew discontented with merely being an actor. With the help of his actress wife, he was hired by Carl Laemmle's IMP Co. to write and direct films featuring the company's newest star, Mary Pickford. He quickly turned out a number of one-reelers, including *Her Darkest Hour* and *In Old Madrid*, before he received his most recent (and best) offer from Bison. It is quite clear that much can still be expected of this man who has not yet reached his thirtieth birthday.

Live news footage of Scott expedition

London, 1 November

For several days cinema audiences in the British capital have been watching film reports of Captain Robert Scott's expedition to the South Pole. The screening of this fascinating documentary footage has coincided with the news that Captain Scott has set off in his assault on the South Pole from his base camp on the coast of Antarctica, where he has been wintering for several months. Now that news events are being reported with greater frequency and in greater detail, the British public has become familiar with these heroic explorers and their techniques in conquering the Pole. The film was shot between the end of May 1910 and January of this year by cameraman Herbert G. Ponting, who has been with the expedition since it set sail. He has brought the remote figure of Scott close to the public.

Florence La Badie and Lionel Barrymore in Griffith's **Fighting Blood**.

Striking out: Thomas Harper Ince.

Georges Méliès loses independence

Paris, 11 November

Georges Méliès' new film *The Hallucinations of Baron Münchhausen* is now available to customers. This 235-metre work of special effects is distributed by Charles Pathé. The greedy producer, who invested in the film which was shot at the Montreuil studio, is not really happy to be exploiting it. In truth, Pathé has risked little, because poor Méliès has given Pathé his property and his studio at Montreuil as a guarantee. If his films fail to make a profit, Pathé will be able to sell the whole lot. Alas, Pathé has reason to be cautious, because Méliès' work is no longer fashionable. Between 1896 and 1909, he directed nearly 500 films, but in 1910 his marvelous productions totally ceased. As a result, the magician has returned to his former love, the old Robert Houdin Theatre. At the beginning of the year, Méliès received a visit from Claude Grivolas, one of the various financiers backing Pathé. Grivolas has a great passion for magic and appreciates Méliès' works, so it was perhaps he who convinced Pathé to put his trust in Star Film. Méliès accepted Grivolas' offer, the latter requesting him to direct a film at Pathé's expense.

The workshop at Montreuil has now restarted its familiar activities. *The Hallucinations of Baron Münchhausen*, which began shooting in May, launches the legendary German baron into a fantastic world, by turns comic and frightening. The source of all the phantasmagoria is a large mirror. Méliès was responsible for the excellent special effects and the decor. The final result, colored by stencil, was shown to Ferdinand Zecca and Charles Pathé, but only dead silence followed the screening. Without a doubt, Zecca sees a rival in Méliès. After burying his head in his hands, Zecca eventually said that he thought the film was too short and that Méliès could improve it. Pathé kept quiet but was visibly in agreement with his artistic director. Criticized and humiliated, Méliès was furious. *The Hallucinations of Baron Münchhausen* will be hired out to theaters, but if the film fails to meet with success, it seems clear that Méliès' future as a director and proprietor will be at stake.

Feuillade gives us 'life as it really is'

Paris, 23 December

A new Gaumont film directed by the immensely prolific Louis Feuillade, *The Destiny of Mothers*, is attracting attention. It tells the story of a widow, played by Renée Carl, who initially gives up all thought of remarrying for the sake of her daughter, the beautiful Suzanne Grandais. She relents, however, and her new husband, played by the sombre René Navarre, destroys all her hopes of happiness. *The Destiny of Mothers* is the tenth film in a series which introduces cinemagoers to scenes from "Life as It Really Is". Launched in April with *The Vipers*, it is a satire against vicious gossip. Feuillade has gone on record saying that the aim of his new series is to bring to the cinema screen the kind of realism that has long been associated with literature, theater and painting. However, Feuillade's first tentative steps fall somewhat short of the work of Zola or Maupassant; the prudish Gaumont insists on maintaining a high moral tone in his films. Nevertheless, the press has af-

*Renée Carl and Suzanne Grandais, partners in **The Destiny of Mothers**.*

firmed that one of the films in the series, *The White Mouse*, is clearly leaning toward the pornographic: "One sees here two devout old girls flirting with two old paillards in a house de luxe to which morals object, but which the police tolerate."

Louis Feuillade is in his element with this series. Films Esthétiques was launched in May 1910 to compete with the quality output of both Film d'Art and SCAGL, while at the same time avoiding long and boring Biblical or historical scenes.

Newly liberated Film Art ventures into production with Réjane

Gabrielle Réjane's first film appearance, opposite Edmond Duquesne.

Paris, 10 November

The General Cinematic Agency, which distributes Film d'Art productions, has just released *Madame Sans-Gêne*, an excellent 940-metre comedy in color, directed by André Calmettes and inspired by the famous play by Victorien Sardou and Emile Moreau. The celebrated actress Gabrielle Réjane plays the title role with Edmond Duquesne as Napoleon, and Georges Dorival as Lefebvre. Since 30 December 1909, Film d'Art has been freed from Pathé's stifling surveillance. Paul Gavault succeeded Paul Lafitte, but the account books continued to look extremely unhealthy. The 1908-1909 financial trading ended in failure with a deficit of 283,000 francs. Le Bargy was also dismissed, to be replaced by André Calmettes and the former actor Henri Pouctal, who arrived at the Neuilly studios in 1910. And in spite of the release of *Madame Sans-Gêne*, the year ended badly for Film d'Art, and Paul Gavault was forced to withdraw. Charles Delac now presides over the new administrative council.

1912

★ ★

Paris, 5 January
Eclipse has released the film *Dans la solitude*, which was produced by Méliès' American Wild West Films.

Norway, 16 January
H. Nobel Roede has released a documentary, *All for Norway*. Strangely enough, despite the rich theatrical tradition in this country, fiction films are non-existent.

Paris, 19 January
Eclair has released *Au pays des ténèbres*, made by Victorin Jasset and based on Zola's novel *Germinal*.

St. Petersburg, 24 January
The producer Yakov Protazanov has filmed *Anfissa*, an adaptation of Leonid Andreyev's play.

Paris, 27 January
Gaumont has released a Western, *Cent dollars mort ou vif*, filmed in the Camargue by Jean Durand.

Budapest, 1 February
The Hunnia company has opened the first studio in Hungary.

Paris, 8 March
After the failure of *Tosca*, Sarah Bernhardt, aged 60, is making a comeback with her *la Dame aux camélias*, filmed by Henri Pouctal and Paul Capellani.

Paris, 9 March
From now on, Abel Gance is devoting himself to the cinema. He has published his first article in *Ciné-Journal* under the title "What is the cinema? A sixth art form!"

Monaco, 1 April
Maess and Richmann, cameramen from *Pathé-Journal*, have succeeded in filming a hydroplane race. They filmed aboard the flying machine of Eugene Renaux at an altitude of 50 metres.

Paris, 13 April
Eclair has released a new series *les Bandits en automobile*, inspired by the misdeeds of the "Bonnot band".

Denmark, 30 April
Nordisk's director Urban Gad has married his favorite actress, Asta Nielsen, the woman he brought from stage to screen. They are leaving for Germany to make several films for producers there.

Paris, 3 May
Bison Life is distributing a new Western from Thomas H. Ince, *The Battle of the Redskins*, a follow-up to *Indian Mother*.

Paris, 4 May
Gaumont has released a newsreel, which boasts that it tells *The Whole Story of the Tragic Capture of the Bonnot and Dubois bandits*.

Paris, 11 May
SCAGL-Pathé have released *Tragique amour de Mona Lisa*, written by Abel Gance.

Berlin, 15 May
A municipal by-law has been passed forbidding smoking in cinemas. It also forbids entry to children.

USA, 17 May
Carl Laemmle has organized the merger of several independent production companies to form the Universal Film Manufacturing Company.

Bombay, 18 May
The first Indian fiction film entitled *Pundalik*, by R.G. Torney and N.G. Chitre, is showing in the city.

Lyon, 14 June
Criminality on the screen is causing anxiety. Mayor Edouard Herriot has forbidden the screening of films depicting criminal acts.

Paris, 28 June
SCAGL-Pathé have released *les Mystères de Paris* (*The Mysteries of Paris*), by Albert Capellani, adapted from Eugène Sue.

Paris, 12 July
In competition with *Pathé-Journal*, Eclair has brought out the very first issue of its own weekly newspaper, *Eclair-Journal*.

San Francisco, 24 July
Gaston Méliès, with his wife and the team from the Gaston Méliès Manufacturing Company, are aboard the *Manuka* en route for Tahiti – part of a world film tour.

Los Angeles, 28 August
Mack Sennett and his troupe have started filming the first Keystone comedies. Some of the team, Fred Mace, Ford Sterling and Mabel Normand, left Biograph to work with Sennett.

New York, 1 September
Adolph Zukor, who presented the French film *Queen Elizabeth* with Sarah Bernhardt, has founded a new company called Famous Players.

Paris, 6 September
The music-hall stars Mistinguett and Maurice Chevalier are sharing the top billing in Pathé's film, *la Valse renversante* (*The Amazing Waltz*).

New York, 9 September
Biograph has released *An Unseen Enemy*. Directed by D.W. Griffith, it stars 16-year-old Lillian Gish and her 14-year-old sister Dorothy.

Budapest, 14 September
Release of Odon Uher's *The Sisters* (*Noverek*). It is the first full-length fiction film to be made in Hungary.

Hungary, 1 October
Sandor Korda, a young journalist, has founded a magazine here called *le Cinéma de Pest*.

Los Angeles, 1 October
Thomas H. Ince has created Kay Bee Motion Pictures with Adam Kessel and Charles Baumann.

Budapest, 14 October
The young actor Mihaly Kertesz has directed his first film, *Today and Tomorrow* (*Ma es Holnap*).

New York, 1 November
D.W. Griffith has used a panning technique to produce a panoramic effect in *The Massacre*. The film is showing here today.

Spain, 15 November
Pathé's stars Max Linder, André Deed and Stacia Napierkowska are touring the country. Max, dressed as a matador, drove the public wild at the arena in Barcelona by fighting a calf with fake horns. The memorable scene was filmed.

New York, 5 December
The New York Hat is now showing. It was made by D.W. Griffith with Mary Pickford and a relative newcomer to films, Lionel Barrymore.

London, 24 December
Despite a downturn in British production, quality films *are* being made. The latest of these is *Oliver Twist*, a film version of Dickens' novel released by Cecil Hepworth.

Paris, 27 December
The Swedish firm Svenska has released Mauritz Stiller's *The Black Masks*, starring Victor Sjöström.

New York, 31 December
Charlie Chaplin has been offered a contract by Keystone but has had to refuse owing to his stage commitments with the Fred Karno troupe.

Peking, 31 December
Benjamin Polaski has set up here a branch of the Asia Film Company.

Prague, 31 December
The architect Max Urban and his wife, the actress Anna Sedlackova, have founded the Asum company.

Warsaw, 31 December
Several actors, including Apolonia Chalupiec, have gotten together under the direction of the filmmaker Alexander Hertz to form their own production company, Sfinks.

Berlin, 31 December
Paul Davidson's production company, Projection-AG Union (Pagu), has transferred its offices to Berlin. Work has started on the Tempelhof studios.

BIRTHS

Oslo, 8 April
Sonja Henie

France, 12 April
Georges Franju

Mexico, 9 May
Pedro Armendariz

France, 4 July
Viviane Romance
(Pauline Ortmans)

England, 23 July
Michael Wilding

Pittsburgh, 23 August
Gene Kelly
(Eugene Joseph Curran Kelly)

Italy, 29 September
Michelangelo Antonioni

Having completed his ambitious new film in color, **The Conquest of the Pole**, *Georges Méliès has been forced to halt production at his Montreuil studio.*

Pornography poses a moral problem

Paris, 18 March
The Congress of the Federation of Businesses Against Pornography, presided over by Senator René Bérenger, opened its doors for two days. The cinema was one of the subjects discussed. Members of the church and the bourgeoisie complained about the popular pastime being a "stratagem used by the devil" which "competes with alcohol for the ruin of the public." Risqué films of "piquant interest" as well as comic scenes unleashed much anger. "Immodesty is spread shamelessly everywhere, religion is ridiculed in a manner that is most odious. It attacks the church's history, its sacraments and its ministers." The spicy films produced by Pathé or Mendel are nothing compared with the type of pornography which circulates undercover. On 7 March last, Valet, the head of the mobile brigade of Paris, accompanied by six inspectors, threw 25 kilometres of licentious films into the Seine. Unwarned, a policeman of the river brigade decided to bring a court action against them for "the throwing of refuse" into the Seine.

Zigomar's triumph, or the extraordinary luck of an adventurer

*Josette Andriot, Alexandre Arquillière and Camille Bardou in Victorin Jasset's **Zigomar Against Nick Carter**.*

Paris, 22 March
Who said that Zigomar was dead and buried in the ruins after the release of the first title of the series in September 1911? The next episode in the adventures of the Master of Crime, the wicked Zigomar played by Alexandre Arquillière, has just been released by the Eclair and Victorin Jasset film company. *Zigomar against Nick Carter*, with the king of detectives played by Henry Krauss, is a large cinematographic novel in four parts. The first chapter, *Zigomar Succeeds*, is being released today and is already in great demand by theater owners. Its success seems to be assured.

From Mutual to Universal, turmoil reigns in the American cinema

Los Angeles, 17 May
It appears to be the case that a total reorganization of the American film industry has been taking place during the past few months. Most important of all, the leading independents have regrouped themselves into two powerful consortia. The rivalry between them seems likely to set the pace for future developments within the industry, with Edison's monolithic trust the Motion Picture Patents Company, left behind. First of the key developments was the formation of the Mutual Film Corporation in March, headed by Harry Aitken (president) and John R. Freuler (vice president) and backed by a number of leading financiers. As an independent film exchange, it now handles pictures from a large number of companies that include Thanhouser, Reliance, American, Majestic, Great Northern, Eclair, Lux and Comet. But at this very moment, Carl Laemmle is putting the final touches to his own new and formidable company, set to rival Mutual in the independent sector. Known as the Universal Film Manufacturing Company, it will merge Laemmle's IMP with Pat Powers' Picture Plays, Bison Life and Rex, along with Nestor and Champion. The independents are obviously flourishing, and Edison's domination has been broken.

*Mary Pickford has now left the Biograph company and plans to return to the theater after completing her last film, **The New York Hat**, for D.W. Griffith.*

Abel Gance moves behind the camera

Paris, 24 May
The young actor and scenarist Abel Gance has signed a contract with the firm of Alter Ego for the shooting of four films. The latest, *The Mask of Horror*, will be screened tonight. It features the celebrated actor Edouard de Max, a friend of Gance's. Everything is strange and bold about this film. The scenario is unlike anything audiences have seen before. A mad sculptor, searching for the perfect realization of "the mask of horror," places himself in front of a mirror after smearing blood over himself with the glass of an oil lamp. He then swallows a virulent poison to observe the effects of pain. Gance, using multiple variations of color, changes the screen from blue to blood red as the terror-stricken face of the actor moves menacingly toward the spectator. An avant-garde, intense, frightening and spectacular work.

American audiences pay homage to Queen Sarah

New York, 12 July

There was a gala evening last night at the Lyceum Theater here in New York. The new organization called the Famous Players Film Company and founded last April by Daniel Frohman, Adolph Zukor and Edwin Porter, presented to a select public *Queen Elizabeth*, Sarah Bernhardt's latest film, a year after *la Dame aux camélias*. The four-reel spectacle, produced by the Franco-German firm Eclipse and directed by Louis Mercanton in London, is the longest cinematographic work presented in the United States to date. The scenario, based on a play by Emile Moreau, retraces the last moments in the life of Elizabeth, Queen of England and Ireland from 1558 to 1603. The re-creation is brilliantly done, with the tints and color evoking the tonalities of certain paintings by Rembrandt. The film has helped give artistic dignity to the cinema. An appropriate musical accompaniment, composed by Joseph Carl Breil and interpreted by the Lyceum Theater Orchestra, added solemnity to the proceedings. One can judge the French tragedienne's enormous popularity in this country from the

Bernhardt originally created her role as Queen Elizabeth I for the theater.

public's reaction. The spectators only have eyes for Sarah Bernhardt, although her partners, Lou Tellegen, Max H. Maxoudian and Marie-Louise Dorval, among others, reveal their worth. The new administrator of the Famous Players Film Company, Adolph Zukor, fought tooth and nail for the acquisition of this sensational film. He obtained, for a certain fee, the exclusive film rights for the world premiere. The work was therefore presented here for the first time before both London and Paris, where the film will not been seen until August. After lengthy negotiations, *Queen Elizabeth* received the visa of the Motion Pictures Patent Company with a license to operate. Zukor, who had wanted to do something sensational, has proven the interest of the American public in long films, provided that they are as attractive as this one. The showman has also given proof that the cinema can leave the nickelodeons behind and survive in large theaters before discerning audiences. The latter are ready to hand over more than the habitual 25 cents to see a film – something which evidently doesn't seem to spoil their pleasure.

Cinema rediscovers art of movement

Turin, 5 August

Giovanni Pastrone is not only the enlightened administrator of Itala Film as well as a talented director who has already offered us the spectacular *The Fall of Troy* – notable for its skilled handling of crowds – but he is also an unrivaled engineer. The proof is his latest invention, the Carello, which he recently patented. The Carello is a platform mounted on wheels constructed to hold the camera, permitting it to be moved around the set of a film without jolting it. Therefore, the movement of the apparatus, if manipulated by a vigilant cameraman, can give rise to stereoscopic effects of extraordinary originality. The image obtained, when projected on a screen, gains in depth and scope. Giovanni Pastrone, who has a practical mind, is to put his invention to work in his next film, provisionally entitled *The Flaming Roman*.

England's mighty Queen Elizabeth (Sarah Bernhardt) exhorts her loyal and valiant troops to courage before battle.

Magical mirth from Mack and Mabel

Hollywood, 23 September

The newly-formed Keystone Pictures Corporation has released its first two films, *Cohen Collects a Debt* and *The Water Nymph*. The driving force behind this newcomer, which will specialize in comedies, is a refugee from Biograph, Mack Sennett, born Michael Sinnott in Canada in 1880. As a youth Sennett had ambitions to be an opera singer, but his search for fame and fortune in New York brought him only modest work as a chorus boy in Broadway musicals and a performer in burlesque. But his luck changed in the summer of 1908 when he began working at the Biograph studios in Manhattan. He was soon taking lead roles in one-reelers directed by D.W. Griffith, contributing scripts and eagerly absorbing all the technical aspects of the new medium of cinema from men like cameraman Billy Bitzer. By the winter of 1910 Sennett was directing as well as acting in Biograph films.

When Sennett decided to strike out on his own this year, he had gained the experience to gather around him a stable of remarkable performers who had cut their comic teeth at Biograph: Ford Sterling, Fred Mace and, above all, the enchanting Mabel Normand, whom Sennett had directed in many films at Biograph and whose vibrant personality has already turned her into a big favorite with cinema audiences. Sennett has a particularly soft spot for Normand, whom he has described as being "as beautiful as a

spring morning." On 4 July, Independence Day, the die was cast for the troupe of comedians to gain their own independence. It was on that day that Sennett finalized his business agreement with two former bookmakers, Charles Baumann and Adam Kessel, to form the Keystone production company with a working capital of $2,500, and the Keystone cameras are set to roll in California, in the old Bison Life studio in the Edendale district of Hollywood. In the meantime, profiting from sunny weather, Sennett's team have been filming a project at Coney Island. *Cohen Collects a Debt* is set in the make-believe world of Luna Park and much use is made of its scenic railway. In a side-splitting comic chase, an unfaithful man is relentlessly pursued by a jealous woman. *The Water Nymph* has a similar premise, with Mabel Normand cast as a bathing beauty harassed by a group of old satyrs. Max Linder's influence can be detected in these early Sennett offerings, but they also have a frenzied energy that owes much to the vaudeville experience of the director and his talented troupe.

For Keystone's brilliant comic duo of Mabel Normand and Mack Sennett, any time and any place will do in which to raise a few laughs.

Famous actors for proven subjects

New York, 9 December

"Famous Actors In Famous Plays" is the new publicity slogan for the Famous Players Film Company, which is busy preparing to make *The Prisoner of Zenda*, based on the celebrated romantic novel and play by Anthony Hope. The star of the film will be the great stage actor James Hackett, who triumphed in the double role of Rudolph and the King of Ruritania at the Lyceum Theater in 1895 and then toured the United States. The director Edwin S. Porter, who has just sold his interest in the Rex Film Company, which was in dire straits, was approached to undertake this ambitious project. Porter (who will co-direct with Hugh Ford) should certainly benefit from the excellent working conditions provided by Famous Players. *The Prisoner of Zenda* will be filmed in a specially converted studio at the top of the Ninth Regiment Armory situated on 26th Street. There is sufficient space and the advantage of being able to shoot, whatever the weather, under the immense glass roof. All the details have already been planned, including the many decor changes.

The Famous Players Company, which became known to the public by releasing *Queen Elizabeth* last July, has profited from its audacity. Founded earlier this year with an initial capital of $250,000, Daniel Frohman and Adolph Zukor's company gained $80,000 in profits from being the sole distributors of the highly-successful Sarah Bernhardt film. The company benefited primarily because the promotion had been entrusted to a real businessman, Al Lichtman. All the big U.S. cities snapped up the French film, and Zukor, the first active partner, has largely regained his investment. From now on, the Famous Players Company has decided to produce its own films and to present the great actors of the American theater in the roles which have brought them glory and fame. It is an experiment modeled on Film d'Art in France. James Hackett, the first actor to be hired, seems delighted to be starring in his favorite role. Even if he fears the realism of the cinema, he is willing to dive into water if the scene requires it.

Colette Willy falls for the cinematograph

Paris, 18 October

"You would like my impressions of the cinema? They are extremely favorable. Lack of time has prevented me from making any films, but I hope that I will soon be able to rectify this." The charming young writer of these sentiments, relayed in the columns of the weekly *Cinema* magazine, is called Colette Willy. In June 1910 she divorced her husband, the writer Willy, and now lives with Henry de Jouvenel. The multitalented Colette is famous not only for her *Claudine* books but also for such works as *l'Ingenue libertine* and *la Vagabonde*. Since 25 April, she has been appearing at the Ba-Ta-Clan in *la Chatte amoureuse* (*The Amorous Cat*), a mime show devised by Roger Guttinger and directed by Georges Wague, a talented mime who has learned all the tricks of his art at the hands of Colette Willy. Wague also has his foot in the door of cinema having appeared in a number of films, notably *l'Enfant prodigue* (*The Infant Prodigy*) made for Film d'Art in 1907. Will Colette allow herself to be seduced by the siren song of cinema? She is always on the lookout for money-making propositions, and her friend and costar in *la Chatte amoureuse*, the comedienne Musidora, has already received an intriguing offer from some producers, said to be anarchists, to make a film with them next year. Will Colette decide to follow in Musidora's footsteps?

The magician from Montreuil in dire straits

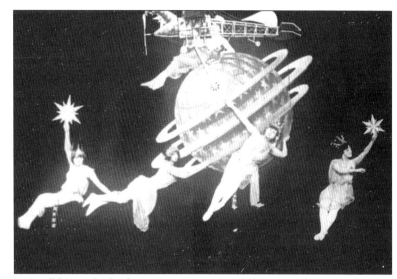

As in all his work, the fantastic is present but the magic no longer works.

Louis Feuillade has had enough of Bébé

The meeting between Bébé and Bout-de-Zan has had fatal consequences.

Paris, 12 December

A big internal struggle has blown up at Gaumont. Louis Feuillade has terminated the contract of little Anatole Clément Mary, the pint-sized star of the *Bébé* series! Feuillade loves children but his patience has reached breaking point. Anatole Clément Mary has played Bébé in 77 films, appearing in turn as an apache, a Negro, a moralist, a millionaire, an insurance agent, a socialist and a sleepwalker. But in spite of Bébé's vast popularity, he remains a mere employee of the studio. His parents have decided to take matters into their own hands, presenting Gaumont with their own assessment of Bébé's commercial value and pestering Feuillade with repeated demands for a salary increase for their son. However, Gaumont's artistic director is cunning; to speed the painless removal of Bébé's name from the Gaumont catalogue, he has acquired the services of yet another child, four-year-old René Poyen. As Bout-de-Zan (Licorice Stick) Poyen made his debut alongside Bébé in *Bébé Adopts a Little Brother* and *Bébé, Bout-de-Zan and the Thief*. The undermining of Bébé went ahead smoothly because his parents were unaware of Feuillade's scheming. Once Bout-de-Zan had proved his worth, Feuillade was free to kiss Bébé goodbye. His departure has caused Feuillade some regret as Anatole Mary possesses genuine talent. He can continue his career, nonetheless, but only under another name, as that of Bébé has been copyrighted by Gaumont. Mary now has to cede supremacy at the Gaumont studio to his four-year-old rival, for whom stardom is now beckoning.

Bout-de-Zan is a charming little scrap, swathed in clothes several sizes too big for him. With his battered top hat or enormous bowler and his gigantic dilapidated shoes, he is the incarnation of the paupers of Paris – a combination of misery, malice and mischief. Ironically it was Bébé himself who coined his name. When they met for the first time, he cried out on seeing his rival's grubby face, "Oh, how black he is, like a licorice stick!"

Montreuil, 31 December

It has been a black end to the year for Georges Méliès. The films financed by Pathé did not meet with the hoped-for success. Nevertheless, *The Conquest of the Pole*, a color film of 650 metres released on 3 May last, attempted to revive the popularity of his famous and inventive earlier films. It contains a Giant of the Snows, an immense animated figure, built of papier mâché. But this is not enough to give Méliès' reputation new life. His films cut a poor figure next to those of Jasset, Feuillade or the Americans. Méliès has also given *Cinderella* and *The Knight of the Snows* to Pathé, but both have been complete failures. Theater managers have refused to show them, and Zecca has become increasingly critical of his rival. Now Méliès is currently preparing *The Journey of the Bourrichon Family*, based on Eugène Labiche's comedy. However, he is too distracted at the moment and is leaving the direction to his assistant Manuel, who really doesn't have his boss's imagination. The result risks being disastrous. Poor Méliès's mind is elsewhere – his wife Eugénie has just died, and his brother in the U.S. is on the verge of bankruptcy.

*Méliès, as always, is both creator and actor in **The Conquest of the Pole**.*

1913

★ ★

Paris, 17 January
The Bébé-Cinema (380 seats) was opened today by M. Mary whose son Clément stars in the *Bébé* series.

Rome, 7 February
A cinema reserved for the clergy has opened at the Vatican. The Pope has forbidden Catholic priests to attend public cinemas.

France, 15 February
The Catholic paper *la Croix du Pas-de-Calais* has published an article criticizing the film *Notre Dame de Paris* and reminding readers that Hugo's book is blacklisted.

New York, 18 February
Opening of *The Prisoner of Zenda*. This film of Anthony Hope's popular novel has been made by Edwin S. Porter for Adolph Zukor's new Famous Players company.

Santa Monica, 1 March
Vitagraph has made a permanent move from New York and is setting up its studios in California.

Brussels, 4 March
Isidore Moray, the producer and cameraman who created the *Journal belge d'actualité*, filmed a house in rue de la Montagne being destroyed by a gas explosion. The film was on the screen five hours after shooting.

New York, 5 March
Thomas H. Ince has produced *The Scourge of the Desert*, directed by Reginald Barker. It is the first Western in a series with William S. Hart.

Vincennes, 17 March
Louis Lépine, the prefect of police in Paris, today visited Pathé's factories to watch the inflammability tests of celluloid-based "safety" film.

London, 31 March
At the instigation of the Minister of the Interior, the cinema profession has created the British Board of Film Censors to classify films into two classifications: U for suitable for all ages and A for adults.

London, March
Release of H.G. Ponting's second film on *Scott's Expedition to the South Pole*. The reels were found last December next to the frozen bodies of Captain Scott and his companions, nine months after their deaths.

Berlin, March
Erich Pommer, the managing director of Deutsche Eclair (Decla), a joint venture with Eclair, has bought up the majority of the capital from the mother company.

Paris, 19 April
The Minister of the Interior has forbidden the screening of all films depicting recently commited crimes or capital punishment.

Bombay, 3 May
A film inspired by the epic Mahabharata *King Harishchandra* and produced by Dhundiraj Govind Phalke is screening. It is the first full-length (four reels) Indian fiction film.

California, 1 June
D.W. Griffith has started filming his first four-reeler for Biograph, *Judith of Bethulia*. The film has a budget of $36,000, his highest to date.

Paris, 26 June
Eclair and Pathé have published their annual reports for 1912. Both companies show a healthy profit: 943,590 francs for Eclair and 7.3 million francs for Pathé.

Cologne, 1 August
Dekage (Deutsche Kinematograph Gesellschaft) which has extended its cinema circuit interests and become a production company is offering a fortune to actors to sign up. It has already won over the Dane Vigo Larsen and two promising French actresses, Suzanne Grandais and Yvette Andreyor.

Havana, 6 August
Producer Enrique Diaz Quesada has made Cuba's first feature film, *Manuel Garcia or the King of the Cuban Fields*, the story of a national hero in the war of independence.

Berlin, 22 August
Opening of Stellen Rye's film *The Student from Prague* starring Paul Wegener and adapted from Hans Heinz Ewers' book. The cameraman is Guido Seeber.

New York, 10 September
The Famous Players Film Company has released *In the Bishop's Carriage* by Edwin S. Porter and J. Searle Dawley. Mary Pickford who stars in the film was signed on by Adolph Zukor for $2,000 per week.

Rochester, 15 September
Eastman-Kodak have released the first panchromatic film, with sensitivity to the whole tonal range. But it is expensive and has several faults: it lacks stability, and processing takes longer than for orthochromatic film.

New York, 1 October
D.W. Griffith, who recently left Biograph, has signed a contract with Reliance-Majestic, a branch of the Mutual Film Corporation. He will be taking over the artistic direction and will be able to devote himself to full-length films, directing two to three projects a year.

Berlin, 3 October
The avant-garde producer and director of the Deutsches Theatre Max Reinhardt has made his first film since accepting Projeektion-AG Union's fabulous contract. The big-budget film *The Island of Happiness*, was shot in Corfu with an original film script.

Prague, 10 October
The Asum company has released Max Urban's *The Bartered Bride*, based on Smetana's opera, the first full-length Czechoslovakian film.

Stockholm, 3 November
Svenska has just released Victor Sjöström's eighth film, *Ingeborg Holm*, which stars Hilda Borgström. Sjöström's sensitivity and talent as a filmmaker are revealed against a background of social criticism.

New York, 24 November
One of America's first full-length films (2,000 metres) *Traffic in Souls*, by George Loane Tucker is a smash hit. It has been programmed in 28 cinemas in the country's main cities.

Paris, 25 November
Gaumont has released the first film in its "Vaudeville Comedies" series, *les Millions de la bonne* (*The Housemaid's Millions*), with the actresses Marguerite Lavigne and Madeleine Guitty. Louis Feuillade directed.

New York, 1 December
Gaston Méliès has returned from his extremely costly Pacific expedition ($50,000) to find his firm on the edge of bankruptcy. The documentaries filmed in Oceania have met with little success and many of the reels were destroyed by the heat.

Paris, 5 December
The Gaumont Palace cinema is currently screening Gaumont's first Chronochrome films, one of the first trichromatic processes to be developed in France.

Paris, 13 December
The Lux Company has been dissolved. Its film lab in Gentilly, which used to process 10,000 metres of film per day, is up for sale.

USA, 29 December
Release of the first episode of F.J. Grandon's *The Adventures of Kathlyn*, a 13-part serial starring Kathlyn Williams and produced by Selig.

Peking, 31 December
Asia Film Company has released the first full-length Chinese film *An Ill-Fated Couple*, a satire on arranged marriages from producers Zhang Shichuan and Zheng Zhengqiu. In the course of this last year, Asia Film was taken over from Benjamin Polaski by the Americans, Essler and Lehrman.

BIRTHS

Brooklyn, 18 January
Danny Kaye
(David Daniel Kaminsky)

Germany, 25 February
Gert Froebe

New York, 4 March
John Garfield
(Julius Garfinkel)

Bordeaux, 18 March
René Clément

London, 6 May
Stewart Granger (James Stewart)

New York, 2 November
Burt Lancaster

India, 5 November
Vivien Leigh
(Vivian Mary Hartley)

Cherbourg, 12 December
Jean Marais

The great British actor, Sir Johnston Forbes-Robertson, now gives his acclaimed Hamlet to posterity. The tale of Shakespeare's prince has been filmed by E. Hay Plumb.

'Quo Vadis?' brings ancient Rome to Broadway

New York, 21 April

An Italian film entitled *Quo Vadis?* is being shown from today to an enthusiastic public at the Astor Theater on Broadway. It runs for no less than nine reels, making it the longest film ever presented in the United States. Reflecting the importance of the event, the cost of the seats is $1 instead of the usual 25 cents. *Quo Vadis?*, the adaptation from the novel by the Polish writer Henryk Sienkiewicz, needed many months shooting and an enormous investment, estimated at around 80,000 lira, on the part of the Cines production company. The first set of scenes was recorded last July and, among the many rather unusual expenses, it was necessary to get a hold of 20 lions for the arena sequences. The New York spectators have been particularly impressed by the crowd scenes, where innumerable extras have been used. The results do justice to the director, Enrico Guazzoni, who also designed the sets and the costumes.

Lia Orlandini and Gustavo Serena in a meticulous reconstruction by Guazzoni, who holds the rights to the book.

Impressive Indian film hits the jackpot

Bombay, 5 May

The infant Indian cinema industry has produced an epic to rival those made in Hollywood. At four reels, *Raja Harishchandra*, directed by D.G. Phalke, marks the beginning of feature film production on the subcontinent. Based on a Hindu legend surrounding the trials of the righteous King Harishchandra – a story resembling that of Job in the Old Testament – the film contains many spectacular scenes, including a forest fire and the apparition of the God Siva. It is now playing at the Coronation Theatre as part of a one-and-a-half-hour variety program of dancers, jugglers and comedians.

The king (center) and his small son in Phalke's enthralling Indian film.

The Gaumont Palace and the daisy emblem have been together for two years. The building, again renovated, reopens on 5 September.

Parisians tremble before Fantômas

Paris, 9 May

The whole capital is fascinated by the new posters which have just appeared on the boulevards. They portray an elegantly-dressed Fantômas, the Master of Crime, rendered popular by the detective novels of Pierre Souvestre and Marcel Allain. All around Paris his sinister, masked face can be seen. These posters are not marked with the name of the books' publishers, Arthème Fayard, but with the Gaumont symbol. The film company acquired the rights to the successful first novel for the sum of 6,000 francs, and got Louis Feuillade to direct the adventures of this dark, mysterious character. *Fantômas*, a drama in three episodes containing over 30 scenes, was released today, and it has already captivated the public. Contained in its 1,146 metres are murders, attempted murders, robberies, blackmail and kidnappings. The three episodes are entitled *The Robbery at the Royal Palace Hotel*, *The Disappearance of Lord Beltham* and *Around the Scaffold*. The 33 chapters of the book have been condensed with great skill by Feuillade himself, though Gaumont, always the puritan, asked the director not to bring the most terrifying scenes to the screen. Despite that, Feuillade has managed to create an eerier atmosphere than that in the book. Fantômas is interpreted by the disturbing René Navarre, with his eagle's profile, who continues to baffle the poor police inspector Juve, portrayed by Bréon. Young actor Georges Melchior impersonates Jérôme Fandor,

*René Navarre in **Juve Against Fantômas**, the second instalment of the series.*

journalist and sleuth, in association with Juve, and Renée Carl is Lady Beltham. The adventures of the arch criminal and genius of disguise in a labyrinthine Paris are unforgettable. There are powerful poetic images such as the rooftop chase on the Gaumont Palace against a background of gray sky, roads with wet stones, collapsing walls and billboards behind which ruffians in black hoods are concealed. The end of the film is distressing: Juve believes he has finally arrested Fantô-

mas, but an innocent man is substituted for the real criminal and has to mount the guillotine. Juve catches sight of the unfortunate one in time, and he is saved. But the Master of Crime has escaped. The last shot shows the miserable Juve, sitting at his desk, promising to find Fantômas. Suddenly he jumps. A superimposed image of Fantômas laughing appears before him. The policeman moves toward it quickly, but the image disappears. The story continues in the next episode.

A weighty recruit for Mack Sennett

New York, 5 June

Two new Keystone comedies *Help! Help! Hydrophobia!* and *Passions He Had Three* feature bulky, baby-faced comic Roscoe "Fatty" Arbuckle, who has recently been signed to the studio by Mack Sennett. The 26-year-old Arbuckle is a vaudeville veteran who has tried just about everything possible during his show business career, from singing ballads in a nickelodeon to performing in a blackface act. But the breakthrough to the big-time has proved elusive. He made an early start in films in 1907 when he made some one and two-reelers for Selig. After another stint treading the boards, Arbuckle approached Sennett for a job at Keystone. Apparently Sennett was not overly impressed with the moon-faced comic but was nevertheless shrewd enough to spot that the public might find a fat policeman funny. So Arbuckle became a Keystone Cop at the princely sum of $3 a day. Impressed with Roscoe's performance in *The Gangsters*, directed by Henry "Pathé" Lehrman and starring Fred Mace, Sennett has moved the Fat Man up into featured roles. Fatty's contract looks likely to finally catapult him out of obscurity and into the limelight. Cinemagoers are warming to the nimble way so big a man negotiates the non-stop slapstick of Sennett's films. Arbuckle's combination of truculence and breezy good humor, which audiences find particularly appealing, marks him out as a man to watch. The Fat Man is a heavyweight addition to Sennett's stable of comedy stars, skillfully brought together on his Edendale lot.

Filming of 'The Glue' places Mistinguett in sticky situation

Albert Capellani found his inspiration here in a work by Jean Richepin.

Paris, 19 July

There has been some eventful filming in Vincennes at the SCAGL studios. Albert Capellani has adapted Jean Richepin's story *la Glu* as a vehicle for Mistinguett. The legendary music-hall star has been lured into films with a fat fee of 2,500 francs. Her money has been well earned; in one scene another actress was supposed to knock her out with a prop hammer wrapped in cotton wool. Was the blow a little too strong? Mistinguett, blood running down her face, fainted dead away in front of an astonished crew.

French film industry mourns loss of Jasset

Paris, 5 September
Victorin Jasset's final film *Protéa* has received a warm welcome from the public since it was released, but with a certain sadness. The great director of the Eclair company died prematurely last 22 June. For the film, Jasset took advantage of the tense situation in the Balkans to shoot a spy film, which has an atmosphere that comes very close to reality. The role of the spy, Protéa, is played by Josette Andriot, who must get hold of a secret treaty between Celtia and Slavonia. With the assistance of Anguille, alias Lucienne Bataille, the beautiful heroine manages to steal the document, after having been disguised as a cat burglar, as a society woman, an aide-de-camp, an ambassador of Albania, a gypsy and a wild-animal tamer. Jasset's Dr. Phantom, Zigomar and the disturbing image of Protéa in a black leotard, will be long remembered by the public.

History and romance comes Italian style

Turin, 31 October
The Italian cinema continues to grow steadily stronger and is currently profiting from the problems of the film industry in other parts of the world. Last August, Ambrosio of Turin released *The Last Days of Pompeii*, a particularly careful and impressive adaptation from the historical novel by Bulwer-Lytton, and one of many Italian motion pictures that has found inspiration in ancient Roman history. Today, it is the turn of Gloria, also situated in Turin. This company has produced a sentimental drama entitled *But My Love Does Not Die*. The star, the elegant and sophisticated diva Lydia Borelli, has succeeded to perfection in her transition from stage to screen. Unlike the historical panoramas, which were based mainly on novels, this film was derived from a boulevard stage play. Surprisingly, these two very differently conceived films were made by the same director, Mario Caserini. Celebrated for his historical pageants such as *Joan of Arc, Beatrice Cenci, Lucretia Borgia* and *The Last Days of Pompeii*, Caserini has proven himself equally at home with romantic melodrama. A former painter, Mario Caserini entered films as an actor in 1905 before turning to directing. *But My Love Does Not Die* is a good example of a film of passion, which should thrive alongside the costume epics. The mixture of genres has been a success in Italy, where Turin, not Rome, continues to be the most important film production center in Italy. It was Arturo Ambrosio who led the way when he built a glass-roofed studio there and commenced production in 1906. The biggest competitor for Ambrosio in Turin is Giovanni Pastrone's Itala-Film.

Literary classics enrich the English cinema

London, 29 October
The release this month of *Hamlet*, with Johnston Forbes-Robertson as the Prince of Denmark, is another example of the English cinema's passion for adapting literary classics. Last year we saw *Oliver Twist*, produced by Cecil Hepworth and directed by Thomas Bentley, the self-styled "great Dickens impersonator and scholar." This year the same team has repeated their success with *David Copperfield*, a film in six reels. Architectural and natural exteriors, said to be the actual places "immortalized by Dickens," were chosen for their pictorial as well as their period atmosphere. A few months ago, Mrs. Henry Wood's sentimental novel *East Lynne* was also shown to acclaim. William Barker's ambitious two-hour production has many scenes, lavish decor and sweeping photography. Now Cecil Hepworth has topped all the previous literary adaptations with his production of *Hamlet*. It cost 10,000 pounds to make and marks the final appearance of Johnston Forbes-Robertson before the great romantic actor retires at the age of 60. The film was shot mainly at Hepworth's studio at Walton-on-Thames, though considerable use was made of outdoor locations both at Hartsbourne Manor in Hertfordshire and at Lulworth

David Copperfield with Dora.

Cove in Dorset, where structures representing Elsinore Castle were built. Despite his age, Forbes-Robertson's lean face is still handsome and very expressive, and his appearance on screen will be an invaluable record of his performance in the role he first played at the Lyceum Theatre in 1897. Directed by E. Hay Plumb, it is based on Forbes-Robertson's celebrated production, now in repertory at Drury Lane. Ophelia is played by the actor's wife Gertrude Elliott, who acts her mad scene in a garden. The film was enthusiastically received and should lead to more film versions of the classics.

*A scene from Caserini's version of **The Last Days of Pompeii**.*

Hamlet berates his mother, Gertrude. A famous scene from a famous play.

Universal depicts horrors of white slave traffic

New York, 24 November
This afternoon a huge crowd laid siege to Weber's Theatre on Broadway in the frantic rush to see *Traffic in Souls*, a sensational release from the recently formed Universal Film Manufacturing Company. Ticket prices for the show have been raised to an exhorbitant 25 cents. This film's theme, the sinister menace to American womanhood from gangs of white slavers, is currently the subject of what the *New York World* has called "popular hysteria". Lurid stage plays like *The Lure* have dealt with the subject, and public debate has been further inflamed by the June publication of the long-awaited Rockefeller Report on Commercialized Prostitution in New York City. The talented director of *Traffic in Souls*, George Loane Tucker, has drawn on this report and a similar probe launched by New York district attorney Charles S. Whitman. The result is a powerful six-reel drama in which plucky Jane Gail and her policeman-fiance Matt Moore save her sister from the clutches of a white slave trader masquerading as

*Ethel Grandin (left) and Matt Moore star as victim and rescuer respectively, in **Traffic in Souls**.*

a moral reformer. Tucker's original proposal for the film, and request for a budget of $5,000, had been turned down by Universal chief Carl Laemmle. Undeterred, Tucker then raised the money from friends and was able to make *Traffic in Souls* surreptitiously, working around his regular shooting schedule. Then the director suddenly left the studio after quarreling over another matter. There was a huge battle at Universal when Laemmle discovered the existence of *Traffic in Souls*, but, nevertheless, the film is a hit.

Cecil B. DeMille and Jesse L. Lasky join the Hollywood brigade

Hollywood, 29 December
With Oscar Apfel as his co-director and Al Gandolfi behind the camera, Cecil B. DeMille has begun shooting *The Squaw Man* in a converted barn located at Selma and Vine in Hollywood, California. Dustin Farnum is the star and the film is based on the well-known play by Edwin Milton Royle. It is the tale of an Indian girl

From left: DeMille, Oscar Apfel, Dustin Farnum, Lasky, Edmund Breese.

who saves the life of a British aristocrat in the old West, and bears him a child before committing suicide. Since most of the story takes place outdoors, *The Squaw Man* was selected as being the easiest subject to film without the use of full studio facilities. In fact, the small film company was already headed for Flagstaff, Arizona, but after one look at the built-up city, they decided to get back on the train and continue on to California instead. This is the first film to be produced by the Jesse L. Lasky Feature Play Company, founded by Lasky, his brother-in-law Samuel Goldfish, Cecil B. DeMille, and Arthur Friend earlier this year. DeMille and Lasky are both new arrivals in the film industry, having previously been involved in the theater and vaudeville respectively, but they seem to know what they are doing. Since the rights to the film have already been sold to a number of regional distributors for a substantial sum, reputedly $40,000, it is likely that the newcomers will earn themselves a good profit.

Keystone seduces hesitant Chaplin

New York, 29 December
The Keystone Picture Corporation has signed a young British comedian, Charles Chaplin. About a year ago Mack Sennett and Mabel Normand were impressed with Chaplin's comic virtuosity when they saw him playing a gentlemanly drunk in *A Night in an English Music Hall*, one of the highlights of the touring Karno Company's revue showing at the American Music Hall on New York's 42nd Street. Fellow Keystone director Adam Kessel also claims to have seen the 24-year-old Chaplin and spotted his potential, and the result was an offer to join the Keystone company as a "moving picture actor" at a salary of $150 a week. The contract was signed on 25 September and Chaplin officially left the Karno troupe, with whom he has appeared for seven years, at the end of November. Early in December he arrived in Los Angeles and has been settled in to a room at the Great Northern Hotel.

1914

★ ★ ★ ★ ★ ★ ★ ★ **1914** ★

Paris, 2 January
Eclair has released the first film directed by former actor Maurice Tourneur, *le Système du Dr. Goudron et du Professeur Plume*.

California, 10 January
Filming has commenced at Venice Beach of *Kid Auto Races at Venice*. Directed by Henry Lehrman, the film is a vehicle for the British comedian Charlie Chaplin, who completed his first film *Making a Living* last week.

Paris, 17 January
Charles Pathé, who has just received the Legion of Honor, has released *Napoléon: du sacre à Sainte-Hélène*. The film, directed by the Belgian Alfred Machin, was made with the participation of the Russian and Belgian armies.

Paris, 24 January
The Italian firm Celio Films is distributing a film with music, *Histoire d'un Pierrot*, starring Francesca Bertini and from the producer Count Baldassare Negroni, who is better known for his high society films.

Berlin, 31 January
The Little Angel, produced in Germany by Urban Gad and starring his wife, Asta Nielsen, is now on view to the public.

London, 2 February
Opening of *The World, the Flesh and the Devil*, a film in Kinemacolor made by Lawrence Cowen with Frank Esmond and Rupert Harvey.

New York, 10 February
The Famous Players Film Co. has released the first of its films to be made in California, *Hearts Adrift*, directed by Edwin S. Porter and starring Mary Pickford.

Paris, 27 February
The first issue of *le Film*, by André Heuzé and Georges Quellien, is now on sale.

St. Petersburg, 5 March
Screening of *The Child from the Big City* by Evgeni Bauer, with Ivan Mosjoukine.

Copenhagen, 23 March
Benjamin Christensen has produced his first film *The Mysterious X*, with himself in the leading role.

Paris, 29 March
Sarah Bernhardt has refused a role in Abel Gance's play *la Victoire de Samothrace*. Her film *Adrienne Lecouvreur*, directed by Louis Mercanton, has just been released.

New York, 11 April
The Spoilers, a Selig production by the director Colin Campbell, was screened for the opening of the new Strand Theater here. The first purpose-built cinema for new releases, it is able to seat 2,900 people.

France, 18 April
Various cinema organizations have published pamphlets attacking the cinema tax voted in by the Chamber of Deputies on 23 March.

Paris, 24 April
Louis Aubert has released the Danish film *Opium Dreams*, by Forest Holger-Madsen.

California, 4 May
Release of Charlie Chaplin's *Caught in the Rain*. This is the first film entirely written and directed by him.

Los Angeles, 4 May
Home Sweet Home has been released by Reliance-Majestic, with the Gish sisters, Mae Marsh and Henry B. Walthall. The film was directed by D.W. Griffith in the company's Hollywood studios.

Paris, 22 May
In *le Film*, Rémy de Gourmont criticizes film versions of literature: he feels "it is a shame to see the classics reduced to trembling shadows."

Paris, 23 May
Pathé has just brought out *Maudit soit la guerre!* (*A Curse on War*). The courageous though quite brutal film, made in Belgium by Alfred Machin, has been finished since 1913; however, Pathé held back its release fearing that the underlying pacifist message might offend.

Paris, 30 May
Gaumont has released Louis Feuillade's *le Calvaire*, with Musidora, a dancer from the Folies-Bergère.

New York, May
The French director Maurice Tourneur has arrived in Fort Lee to take up his position as director of Eclair's American production.

Paris, 3 June
Raymond Poincaré unveiled a monument in memory of Etienne-Jules Marey at the Parc des Princes. According to Charles Richet, winner of the Nobel Prize in medicine, Marey invented the cinematograph.

USA, 8 June
Opening of the Ebbets Field Theater, the first drive-in cinema.

Paris, 1 July
The director André Antoine has been signed up by Pathé.

California, 4 July
After months of preparation and having raised a budget of $40,000, D.W. Griffith has started filming *The Clansman*.

Austria, 16 August
The Government is worrying about the impact of the cinema on public opinion. From now on, only patriotic films may be shown. Films from enemy countries are banned.

France, 25 August
Abel Gance, who is serving as a stretcher-bearer, is horrified by the sight of the first wounded arriving from the Front. He was exempted from active military service for health reasons.

California, 5 September
Having exceeded his budget, D.W. Griffith has temporarily stopped production on *The Clansman*.

New York, 15 September
Winsor McCay has released *Gertie the Dinosaur*. The 10-minute cartoon is made up of 10,000 drawings.

Austria-Hungary, 30 September
Rival film companies are engaged in a ruthless battle for the sale of newsfootage of the war.

St. Petersburg, 7 October
Vladimir Gardine has released *Anna Karenina*, adapted from Tolstoy.

New York, 31 October
Pathé America is now a production and distribution company under the new name Pathé Exchange. Charles Pathé, who is retaining 60 percent of the capital, was in the States last month to reorganize the branch, which had been put in financial difficulty by the Edison Trust.

Belgium, 14 November
The German director Stellan Rye, who was wounded in the fighting at Ypres, has died in a French hospital at Flanders.

Washington, 19 December
Cartoonist Earl Hurd has registered his animated cartoon technique of superimposing figures drawn on "cellulos" over a background.

New York, 20 December
Among this year's output of motion pictures was the first ever American film to be directed by a woman – Lois Weber's screen version of *The Merchant of Venice* for the Rex Co.

Berlin, 31 December
An actor from the Deutsches Theatre, Emil Jannings has made his screen debut in *In the Trenches*. He was motivated to find film work by financial need.

Paris, 31 December
Parisian cinemas have been patronized by 788,000 spectators since they reopened in November.

BIRTHS

London, 2 April
Alec Guinness

Scotland, 11 April
Norman McLaren

Marseilles, 23 April
Simone Simon

France, 31 July
Louis de Funès
(Louis de Funès de Galarza)

Italy, 14 September
Pietro Germi

Vienna, 9 November
Hedy Lamarr
(Hedwig Eva Maria Kiesler)

Turkey, 13 November
Henri Langlois

Milan, 13 November
Alberto Lattuada

The Battle of Elderbush Gulch is an ambitious film from Griffith about an Indian attack on a settlement. In the cast are Mae Marsh, Lillian Gish, Robert Harron and Henry Walthall.

England warmly embraces her native son

*Charlie's tramp emerges during filming of **Kid Auto Races at Venice**.*

London, 30 June
Charlie Chaplin's first films for Mack Sennett's Keystone company have definitely been a hit with the British public. There is no bitterness that he has yielded to the temptations of the New World. In the United States Chaplin has already become a star, although his film career is barely six months old. Within a month of his screen debut in *Making a Living*, Chaplin developed a distinctive screen character – the engaging little outcast in baggy pants, oversize shoes and battered derby hat whose jaunty cane signals his pretensions to the status of a swell. The effect is completed with a small black crepe moustache which, like his cane, seems to have a life of its own. This original little personality has already captured American hearts and looks certain to conquer Europe in turn.

Paramount intends to reach the summit

New York, 15 July
A giant new distribution company has just been born, under the name of Paramount Pictures. The brainchild of W.W. Hodgkinson, it intends to operate as a nationwide distribution network with a central office located in New York City. The venture brings together a number of well-known independents, grouped under the Paramount logo of a snow-capped mountaintop surrounded by stars. Members include Adolph Zukor's Famous Players and Lasky, also Oliver Morosco, Bosworth and Pallas. Hodgkinson arrived in New York earlier this year where, drawing on his experience in operating film exchanges in the far West, he was soon involved in negotiations which led to the formation of Paramount. Not only is this new company designed to challenge such rival distribution combines as Mutual and Universal, but also to institute a new, more efficient and profitable system of exploitation and distribution to replace the current "states rights" arrangement. This latter refers to the leasing of exclusive film rights exchanges operating in the different regions of the U.S. It is then the responsibility of each exchange to promote the film in its own area and to rent it out to individual exhibitors in order to earn a profit. However, in the case of Paramount, Hodgkinson has created a system with the member companies whereby an advance of around $30,000 would be paid for the rights to each feature film handled by the company, with the rental earnings received from exhibitors to be divided with 65 percent to the original producer and 35 percent to Paramount. If this new arrangement proves successful, it will have a major influence on all future film deals in America.

DeMille and Lasky excel with the Western

Hollywood, 10 August
With the release of the latest Lasky production *The Call of the North*, the continuing success of his company is assured. This entertaining and dramatic adventure Western stars Robert Edeson, Winifrid Kingston and Theodore Roberts and was directed by Cecil B. DeMille. As its name implies, the Jesse Lasky Feature Play Co. has made its mark by concentrating its efforts on feature-length films of real quality, especially Westerns. Set up less than one year ago, the company got off to a good start earlier this year with the highly successful Western called *The Squaw Man*, co-directed by DeMille and Oscar Apfel. Then each director was given his own project. Apfel did well with a lively comedy subject, *Brewster's Millions*, while DeMille opted to produce another Western, *The Virginian*, adapted from the well-known novel by Owen Wister and re-teaming the two lead players from *The Squaw Man*, Dustin Farnum and Winifred Kingston. Apparently, *The Virginian* has turned out so well that the company has held back its release until early next month to take advantage of its new distribution deal with Paramount, and prefers to screen first DeMille's most recently completed feature (*The Call of the North*). Although DeMille enjoys filming Westerns on location in California, as director-

*Farnum (right) in **The Squaw Man**.*

general of the Lasky company he, too, obviously wishes to avoid being typecast and consequently has already begun shooting his first comedy subject, *What's His Name?*, adapted from the novel by George Barr McCutcheon. Having previously announced a policy of completing one film per month, Lasky has already contracted to deliver double this amount for Paramount release – a tall order for a new company, but it has come such a long way in so short a time that anything seems to be possible.

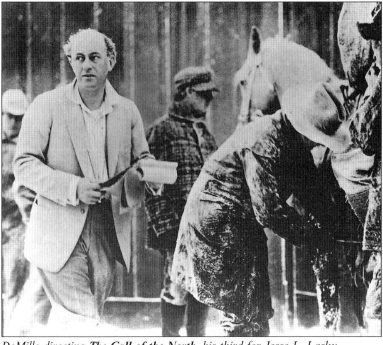

*DeMille directing **The Call of the North**, his third for Jesse L. Lasky.*

Griffith completes mammoth task of filming 'The Birth of a Nation'

Pasadena, 31 October
D. W. Griffith has now finished *The Birth of a Nation*, a film unlike any other. The scenario, based on two of Thomas Dixon's stories, *The Clansman* and *The Leopard's Spots*, concerns the history of two different families, the northern Stonemans and the southern Camerons. Griffith's intention was to recount the whole truth regarding the War of Secession in order to rehabilitate the Southerners. This was an ambitious and expensive project, financed by the Mutual Film Corporation and its head Harry E. Aitkin. The final cost was over $100,000, but the film had gone over budget, and only loans from friends permitted its completion. The shooting of the film was done mainly at the Reliance-Majestic studio in Pasadena, California and lasted nine weeks. The number of war scenes, for which Griffith needed approximately 500 extras, often take place where the actual battles occurred. Perched on a 10-metre high tower, Griffith gave out his orders like a great military strategist. When the noise of the cavalry and the booming of cannons grew louder, the instructions were totally inaudible. Extras placed at more than three kilometres from the camera were directed with the aid of

Ben Cameron (Henry Walsall) is horrified by the death of his sister (Mae Marsh).

mirrors and luminous signs. During the shooting, Griffith made constant use of Mathew Brady's Civil War photographs for historical reference. For example, the surrender of General Lee at Appomatox, the signing of the proclamation freeing the slaves, and Sherman's march to the sea have been very faithfully reconstructed from some of the negatives. He also had to recreate the interior of Ford's Theater where President Abraham Lincoln was as-

sassinated. Lincoln is played by a near-perfect double, Joseph Henabery, while Raoul Walsh with a revolver in hand, is the reincarnated personification of the murderer, John Wilkes Booth. One of the most spectacular scenes is the uprising of the riders of the Ku Klux Klan towards the climax of the film. For this sequence, Griffith had a hole dug under the place where the horses passed by, so that he could film the clamoring hoofs at ground level.

Keystone loses Chaplin to Essanay

Hollywood, 30 November
Charlie Chaplin has just signed a contract with Gilbert M. Anderson and George K. Spoor, directors of the Essanay company. The 24-year-old actor is bidding farewell to Keystone, where he enjoyed his first success in the movies. When his contract with Keystone's boss Mack Sennett came up for renewal, Chaplin demanded a raise from $175 to $1,000 a week. Sennett replied with a counteroffer of a three-year contract at $500 in the first year, rising to $1,500 in the third, but Chaplin had already decided that it was time to move on. Essanay, which up till now has thrived on a diet of Anderson's Broncho Billy Westerns, has offered him $1,250 a week plus a $10,000 bonus. In addition Anderson and Spoor have promised Chaplin complete artistic control of his films, of which he will be the star. Chaplin has truly come a long way in a year. With 35 Keystone films behind him, 23 of which he directed himself, he has already created his own comic universe. Now he will be exchanging the balmy climate of sunny California for breezy Chicago where Essanay are still making films in their original studio.

New Yorkers are delighted by McCay's 'Gertie the Dinosaur'

New York, 28 December
Winsor McCay has created a new cartoon heroine, Gertie the Dinosaur, whose adventures are the toast of the town. The inspiration sprung from an approach made to the artist by the American Historical Society to draw pictures of prehistoric animals. This is the first of McCay's animated films to have a detailed background, all of which has been created by the hand of John Fitzsimmons. Gertie makes a shy debut, peering from behind some boulders. But she soon asserts herself as she devours trees, rocks and fruit, then drinks a lake dry, tosses a mammoth over her shoulder and dances. When she is admonished for her boisterous behavior, she bursts into tears, melting the stoniest of hearts. The cartoon is accompanied by a live action sequence in which McCay and some of his cronies visit New York's Museum of Natural History and prowl

through the dinosaur exhibits. Later, resplendent in tuxedoes, they visit a restaurant where McCay bets that he can make a dinosaur movie and sets to work drawing. Gertie has

also become part of McCay's stage act. He invites Gertie to eat an apple which he holds up. She lowers her neck and swallows the fruit to the delight of the audience.

Already popular as a comic strip, Gertie comes to life on the cinema screen.

China suffers from lack of film stock

Peking, 31 December
Cinema is just one of the victims in a country that is becoming increasingly isolated internationally. Because of the war in Europe, the young republic of Sun Yat-sen has for some time experienced ever greater difficulties in obtaining the most basic materials from the West. Unused film stock has become an extremely rare commodity because of the fact that the ingredients that constitute film, and also the money needed to then manufacture it, have ceased to arrive in Peking. As a result local production, still in its infancy, has sadly diminished. Unfortunately, in this context, the pioneer Chinese works such as the films of the Spanish cameraman Antonio Ramos or of Ling Shao Po or the Li brothers might well become relegated to the secret dungeons of cinema history.

1915

★ ★

Chicago, 10 January
Charlie Chaplin's first film for Essanay titled *His New Job* is receiving a spectacular advertising campaign.

New York, 12 January
Theda Bara has made an explosive debut in *A Fool There Was*, directed by Frank Powell, an adaptation of Rudyard Kipling's *Vampire*. America's first vamp is born, helped by a publicity campaign which owes a great deal of its exoticism to the imagination of both the press and advertising agencies.

Paris, 28 January
The French branch of the German optical manufacturer Karl Zeiss has been officially impounded.

Los Angeles, 1 February
The producer, distributor and businessman William Fox has founded the new Fox Film Corporation with Winfield Sheehan.

Los Angeles, 8 February
D,W. Griffith and Harry Aitken have created the Epoch Producing Corporation on the same day as the world premiere of *The Birth of a Nation*.

Paris, 20 February
Abel Gance has accepted a proposition, by Louis Nalpas from Film d'Art, to film *Un drame au château d'Acre* in five days with a budget of 5,000 francs.

Rome, 28 February
Screening of the first film in a detective series based on the Za la Mort character, *Nellie the Gigolette*. The film is produced by Emilio Ghione and stars the diva Francesca Bertini.

Paris, 1 March
The prefect of police has banned the screening of all films depicting the scenes of desolation created by the enemy in certain regions.

Washington, 15 April
The Supreme Court has delivered a final blow to Thomas Edison by canceling all the Motion Picture Patent Corporation's patents.

Paris, 17 April
In protest against censorship, the Union of Cinematograph Directors has organized a private screening of banned films at the Palais des Fêtes.

Boston, 21 May
As a result of the campaign against *The Birth of a Nation*, the State of Massachusetts has voted in favor of creating a board of censors.

Berlin, 21 May
Ernst Lubitsch, who has already acted on stage (with Max Reinhardt) and on the screen in Carl Wilhelm's comedies for Union-Film, has gotten behind the camera to make *On the Slippery Slope*.

Paris, May
Charles Pathé has returned from a trip to the United States where he opened 22 new distribution agencies in as many states. Pathé-Exchange is now the leading firm for exporting American films to France.

Boston, 2 June
Black organizations have presented the Mayor with a petition bearing 6,000 signatures asking him to ban *The Birth of a Nation*.

California, 6 June
Harold Lloyd has completed the first film in a series of short comedies made by his friend Hal Roach. Here he portrays a character named Lonesome Luke, clearly drawing inspiration from Chaplin, and likely to displace the previous character of the Lloyd-Roach collaboration, "Willie Work".

Paris, 21 July
Abel Gance has signed up with Louis Nalpas for Film d'Art. Under the terms of his contract he has to produce nine films a year, based on senarios written by himself. Nalpas was won over by Gance's ideas and spirit in his *Un drame au château d'Acre* (*A Drama at the Château of Acre*) and *la Folie du Dr. Tube* (*The Madness of Dr. Tube*).

Paris, 30 July
Louis Feuillade has been discharged from active service due to a heart problem. He can now return to the Buttes-Chaumont studios.

Rome, 31 July
Opening of *Maciste*, directed by Vincent Denizot and Luigi Romano Borgnetto and with Bartolomeo Pagano who created the role. The film was inspired by Giovanni Pastrone's internationally acclaimed epic *Cabiria*.

Montreuil, 8 August
Gaston Méliès has turned part of his old film studio into a theater in aid of the Montreuil hospital. *The Arlesienne*, by Alphonse Daudet is playing at the moment.

France, 19 August
The Gaumont Palace in Paris and the Majestic Cinema in Lyon have reopened.

Copenhagen, 18 September
Forest Holger-Madsen's *Put Down Your Arms* is screening today in Denmark.

Paris, 1 October
French cinema production is slowly picking up after the interruption caused by the outbreak of war. As René Navarre has been called up for duty, the *Fantômas* series has been dropped. However, Louis Feuillade has started filming a new series, *les Vampires*, with Edouard Mathé, Marcel Lévesque and Jean Ayme, in the hope of forestalling the probable success in France of the highly popular *Mysteries of New York*.

Boston, 1 October
The Philarmonic Hall is screening Cecil B. DeMille's *Carmen*, with Wallace Reed and Geraldine Farrar. The prima donna, who was taken on for a fabulous sum, is making her screen debut, but... the famous voice is silent.

New York, 15 October
Release of J. Stuart Blackton's *The Battle Cry of Peace*. Financed with silent backing from the arms manufacturer Hudson Maxim, it is the first propaganda film for America's participation in the war.

New York, 31 October
Douglas Fairbanks has been signed up by D.W. Griffith. Fairbanks has just finished making *The Lamb* under Griffith's supervision at Triangle for a salary of $2,000 a week.

Paris, 12 November
Gaumont has released the first two episodes of *Vampires* from Louis Feuillade: *la Tête coupée* (*The Decapitated Head*) and *la Bague qui tue* (*The Ring that Kills*).

Paris, 25 November
First release of Giovanni Pastrone's *Cabiria* at the Vaudeville Theatre.

London, 20 December
Abel Gance is extremely impressed by D.W. Griffith's highly controversial *The Birth of a Nation*, which has not as yet been screened in France.

Paris, 23 December
The Chamber of Deputies has voted a resolution to form a committee to encourage the use of films in the education system.

Paris, 25 December
AGC is distributing Charlie Chaplin's film *Work*.

Poland, 31 December
Alexander Hertz has directed Pola Negri, formerly known as Apolonia Chalupiec, in *The Woman* and *The Little Black Book*.

Prague, 31 December
Vaclav Havel has taken over Antonin Pech's Kinofa assets and has formed the Lucerna company.

BIRTHS

Wisconsin, 6 May
Orson Welles

Rome, 15 May
Mario Monicelli

Siberia, 12 July
Yul Brynner (Julius Brynner)

Paris, 31 July
Henri Decaë

Stockholm, 15 August
Signe Hasso

Stockholm, 29 August
Ingrid Bergman

Stockholm, 10 September
Gösta Ekman

New Jersey, 12 December
Frank Sinatra

Munich, 13 December
Curt Jurgens

Paris, 19 December
Edith Piaf

Four months in the making, the first American movie epic, about the War between the States, is a testament to the ambition and genius of director D.W. Griffith.

A huge and exciting studio rises from the desert

San Fernando Valley, 21 March
Carl Laemmle, the president of Universal Manufacturing Corporation, is today a very happy man. He has just inaugurated an ensemble of prestigious studios in the San Fernando Valley in Southern California, which he has named Universal City. More precisely, these studios are situated on the 230-acre Taylor ranch across the Cahuenga Pass. Laemmle was presented with an outsize gold key by actress Laura Oakley, "chief of police" designate of the only city in the world built exclusively for the purpose of motion picture production. After announcing that there would be no long drawn-out speeches or "meaningless ceremony", Laemmle unlocked the front gates to the main entrance and pronounced the studio, and its two days' festivities, open. As he did so, the thousands of spectators marched onto the impressive new premises, gaily singing "The Star-Spangled Banner" as they went. By the afternoon the crowd had swelled to 20,000, and still they flooded in. Carl Laemmle's dream had at last become a reality. It is a tremendous triumph for this immigrant, who left Laupheim in Ger-

A flamboyant sightseeing tour of the new studio on its opening day.

Happy Mr. and Mrs. Carl Laemmle.

many 30 years ago at age 17, and who had never previously given motion pictures a thought. The large complex employs several hundred people, and the equipment, such as revolving sets, is in the forefront of modern innovation. Among other things, the truly exceptional location of this cinema city facilitates the

shooting of exteriors. This is largely thanks to the extraordinarily temperate climate which makes it "the greatest outdoor stage in the world." With the opening of Universal City, the cinema business has taken on new dimensions, though it is not clear whether Laemmle plans to expand and upgrade his productions,

too. The new studio is prepared to commence a full production schedule immediately. Some stars under contract include Pauline Bush, J. Warren Kerrigan, Francis Ford, Lon Chaney, Grace Cunard, William Clifford and Gertrude Selby. Robert Cochrane is Laemmle's vice president and Pat Powell, treasurer.

'The Lady with the Lamp' brightens up the screens of London

London, 11 March
With British soldiers fighting in the trenches in Flanders and Gallipoli, it is hard to imagine a more inspiring subject for a film than the story of Florence Nightingale, who did so much for the efficiency of military hospitals during the Crimean War. The B. and C. Company have risen to the occasion with their production *Florence Nightingale*, starring Elizabeth Risdon as the Lady with the Lamp. Starting with the earliest stories of Florence Nightingale's childhood we are even shown the infant heroine in her mother's arms in 1820 – the film documents her philanthropic and social work in England as well as her heroic efforts during the Crimean War. There are harrowing scenes of the appalling conditions she encountered in the Army's hospital at Scutari when she arrived in the Crimea, and a moving account of how she brought order out of chaos. The film ends with a

A grateful army pays homage to Florence Nightingale (Elizabeth Risdon).

scene in which the aged Florence Nightingale receives the Order of Merit from King Edward VII. This has been hailed not only as a triumph of makeup but also as testi-

mony to Risdon's sympathetic interpretation. Director Maurice Elvey's careful attention to detail and skillful handling of light and shade mark him out as one to watch.

The exotic allure of a new star

Hollywood, 12 March
With the opening of *A Fool There Was*, directed by J. Gordon Edwards for producer William Fox, the film community offers the public a new star of very unusual allure. The sultry Theda Bara, it is said, was "born in the shadow of the Sphinx" and purports to be the daughter of a desert princess and an Italian sculptor. However, those more enlightened know that Miss Bara was born Theodosia Goodman, the daughter of a Cincinnati tailor. Be that as it may, with her air of a predatory tigress and her exaggerated and exotic makeup, she has already been dubbed "The Vamp", a dangerous temptress who is bound to attract hordes of paying male customers to the theaters where her films are shown. Plans are already afoot for several more to follow her first sensational appearance.

Feelings run high over 'The Birth of a Nation'

D.W. Griffith, from now on one of the 'greats' of the world cinema.

The dramatic and exciting ride to the rescue by the Ku Klux Klan provides a suitably rousing climax to this film.

Boston, 10 April

D. W. Griffith's controversial film *The Birth of a Nation* has just been released at the Tremont Theater. Thousands of black activists opposed to the film marched on the capital, where clashes occurred because of a counter-demonstration by white supporters of the film. The police proceeded to make numerous arrests. This hullabaloo came as the result of the decision by the mayor to allow the film to be shown, whatever the cost, and despite a petition of some 6,000 signatures gathered by the Boston section of the National Association for the Advancement of Colored People (NAACP). Since 3 March, the date of the New York premiere of the film at the Liberty Theater, the dispute continues to rage on. Oswald Garrison Villard, the grandson of the famous abolitionist and New York *Post* editor, even accused the film of being "a deliberate attempt to humiliate millions of American citizens by portraying them as complete animals." In addition, the NAACP alluded to numerous scenes where white actors, blacked up, committed the worst atrocities. The leader of the protest was William Monroe Trotter, the Harvard-educated editor-publisher of a strong-minded Negro paper, *The Guardian.* Nevertheless, everything started well for this undoubtedly magnificent 180-minute work. Simultaneously with its release, *The Birth of a Nation* was shown at the White House to President Woodrow Wilson, who stated, "It is like writing history with lightning. And my only regret is that it is all so terribly true." The next day another screening was held for 300 selected guests, including the chief Supreme Court magistrate Edward D. White and Thomas Dixon, on whose work this film was based. Their reaction was particularly enthusiastic. Despite, or because of, the vocal opposition, Griffith's film today is still drawing crowds. For the first time, millions of spectators are ready to pay $2 for their cinema seat. The movie, which cost over $100,000, including shooting, advertising and distribution, should rapidly see a substantial profit.

Henry B. Walthall and Lillian Gish, two lovers separated by circumstance.

Joseph Henabery (right) as Lincoln, America's controversial president.

Charlie's partner is young typist

Los Angeles, 21 June

Charlie Chaplin's eighth film for Essanay, *Work*, has been released. Filmed at the Bradbury Mansion studio at 147 North Hill Street in San Francisco, it features Chaplin as a down-trodden decorator whose attempt to refurbish peppery Billy Armstrong's house ends in a huge explosion which buries everyone under a mountain of rubble. Co-starring once again with Charlie is an attractive 22-year-old blonde, Edna Purviance, who first joined forces with Chaplin last February in *His New Job*, appropriately the comedian's first film for Essanay. She had originally been recommended to Chaplin by one of Broncho Billy Anderson's cowboy actors, Carl Strauss, who had spotted her at a restaurant in San Francisco. She was located working as a secretary and Chaplin was instantly captivated by her and her ebullient sense of humor. At a party the night before she made her debut in front of the

With Edna Purviance in **Work**.

cameras, she bet Chaplin $10 that he could not hypnotize her. She then played along with him, pretending to fall under his hypnotic spell. There is little doubt, however, that it is Chaplin who has fallen under the spell of the petite beauty with the sensual mouth. In addition to his lovely new leading lady, Charlie is assembling a talented stock company to work with him at the Essanay studios at Niles, outside San Francisco. They include cross-eyed Ben Turpin, former Karno comic Billy Armstrong and another Englishman, Fred Goodwins, a former journalist and stage actor.

Mack Sennett's 'Bathing Beauties' revive the art of burlesque

These lovely 'Bathing Beauties', revealing themselves in swimsuits are now inseparable from the Keystone image.

Los Angeles, 31 July

Keystone's Mack Sennett has created a curious *corps de ballet*. Christened his "Bathing Beauties", they are pretty young women dressed in an increasingly extravagant range of swimsuits. Always pictured in a group, they will from now on grace Keystone comedies, popping up in the most unlikely situations something like the hilariously incompetent Keystone Cops, of whom Ford Sterling and Chester Conklin are the most famous. With the advent of the "Bathing Beauties", cinemagoers are promised a treat for the eyes. The flood of Keystone films on the market has left both audiences and the studio somewhat breathless of late. But audiences will nonetheless welcome the comic reinforcement this new group is certain to add to performances of Keystone's leading lights, Mabel Normand and Roscoe "Fatty" Arbuckle, both now established as international stars.

Ford Sterling is the police chief (left) taking the call, while Fatty Arbuckle is far right in the line of Keystone Cops ready to spring into action.

Deathblow at last for Edison's trust

New York, 15 October

The U.S. Supreme Court reached a decision today on the anti-trust case brought against the Motion Picture Patents Company has sealed the fate of Edison's trust. In fact, this decision has merely confirmed what everyone already knows, since the power of the trust has been declining for many years. The members of the trust have been unable (or unwilling) to adapt to changing conditions in the production, distribution and exhibition of films. Their business has been declining during a period when the total size of the industry has been increasing, led by such independents as Paramount, Fox and Universal. In fact, a number of its own members, such as Pathé and Kleine, have already begun to distance themselves from the trust. Both Kalem and Biograph have substantially reduced their filmmaking activities, while earlier this year Vitagraph, Lubin, Selig and Essanay joined together to form the new V-L-S-E Co. to release features made by its member companies.

Sacha Guitry films his famous compatriots

A jewel of a heroine gleams in a serial

Sacha Guitry and Sarah Bernhardt, mutual admirers and now close friends.

Mysteries of New York *adapt the exploits of Elaine to French tastes.*

Paris, 22 November
The film that the young playwright Sacha Guitry is presenting at the Varietés Theatre, stars a dazzling cast. In *Ceux de chez nous*, we see the sculptor Auguste Rodin; the composer Camille Saint-Saëns; the writers Edmond Rostand, Anatole France and Octave Mirbeau; the actors Sarah Bernhardt, Lucien Guitry (Sacha's father) and André Antoine; and the painters Claude Monet, Edgar Degas and old Auguste Renoir. Afflicted by arthritis, Renoir holds his paintbrush with the help of his son Jean, at his side.

Paris, 3 December
Cinemas in Paris are now screening the first episode of *Mysteries of New York*, an American film produced in the United States by Donald Mackenzie and Louis Gasnier for Pathé-Exchange, the U.S. subsidiary of the French Pathé company. It has been eagerly awaited, and the press has been full of stories of the American infatuation with Pearl White, the serial's heroine. For several days now the daily newspaper *le Matin* has been publishing its own serialization of the film, adapted by Pierre Decourcelle. For the French market they have compiled edited versions of three original Pearl White serials, *The Perils of Pauline*, *The Iron Claw* and *The Exploits of Elaine*, 36 episodes in all. The French version runs to 22 episodes, each of which is about 1,800-feet long. In the story, Pearl White plays Elaine Dodge, a ravishing young heiress menaced by Wu Fang, the leader of a Chinese underworld gang. However, at the moments of greatest danger she is invariably rescued by Arnold Daly and Creighton Hale. Elaine's father is played by Lionel Barrymore, a talented actor of stage and screen, already well-known for his projects with the director D.W. Griffith. In America Pearl White has become a star, and the serials have been smash-hits. Their appeal lies primarily in the vibrant personality of the young actress, for it has to be said that the version produced by Mackenzie and Gasnier shows signs of haste. Meanwhile, Elaine Dodge's millions of fans are impatiently waiting for the second episode entitled *le Sommeil sans souvenir*. Blonde and lithe, our plucky, tender-hearted heroine suffers the ordeal of clutching hands, mysterious voices, threatening rays and deadly kisses, always surviving unscathed to rejoin the fray in the next episode.

Cecil B. DeMille achieves stylistic refinement with 'The Cheat'

New York, 12 December
Two men and a woman are the lead characters in Cecil B. DeMille's new film, a refreshing change from the enormous casts and extras that today's cinema now takes for granted. The title is *The Cheat*, and it heralds the paring down of *mise-en-scène*. This story is a melodrama involving sexuality and perversion. A foolish young society woman borrows a considerable sum of money from a rich Japanese collector on the condition that she give herself to him. The promise is not kept. Furious, the man brands the young woman with a hot iron. The woman hides the exact circumstances from her husband, and he is accused of the crime. The trial which follows is going against the couple until the victim, in a display of heroism, bares her shoulder and shows the horrified jury the mark of a cheat. This Jesse L. Lasky Feature Play Company production has been a great success and has confirmed the talent of the young director Cecil B. DeMille, who shot *The Cheat* in a few weeks, at the same time as another long feature entitled *The Golden Chance*. While *The Cheat* was shot from nine to five during the day, *The Golden Chance* was filmed at night, sometimes till dawn. In such conditions, one cannot fail to be astonished by the aesthetic quality of *The Cheat* – the lighting and the framing of the images. The tragic scene of the red-hot branding iron was filmed in chiaroscuro, using close-ups and exciting editing. The young woman who attempts to deceive both men, and the lecherous Japanese villain are played respectively by the pretty Fannie Ward and the enigmatic Sessue Hayakawa. The excellence of their interpretation, especially a restrained one by the latter, should soon place them both in the firmament of stars.

The Cheat *has brought stardom to Sessue Hayakawa and Fannie Ward.*

Paris, 8 January
The Italian film version of *The Lady of the Camelias*, by Gustavo Serena and starring Francesca Bertini, is to be distributed in France.

Paris, 22 January
Jacques Feyder, a young Belgian actor, has been taken on as a director by Léon Gaumont on the recommendation of Gaston Ravel.

France, 18 February
Several business magazines have remarked on the number of foreign films invading the French market at a time when French production is suffering from a lack of work.

New York, 25 February
The first cartoon in the "Krazy Kat" series, *Krazy Kat and Ignatz Mouse Discuss the Letter G*, is being shown. It was produced by Frank Moser from an adaptation of George Herriman's comic strip.

Los Angeles, 26 February
Charlie Chaplin has signed a year's contract with the Mutual Film Corporation. He is to receive $10,000 a week plus the lump sum of $150,000 on signing.

New York, 12 March
Release of *The Habit of Happiness*, directed by Allan Dwan and starring Douglas Fairbanks, an attractive newcomer to the screen.

Chicago, 27 March
The young actress Gloria Swanson has married Wallace Beery, who is always cast in brutish roles due to his rough-hewn features.

Los Angeles, 27 March
The Lone Star studios have been equipped by Mutual to make Chaplin films.

Paris, 29 March
The committee formed to study the use of films for educational purposes has been appointed by decree.

England, 31 March
The American firm Triangle has taken control of 882 cinemas within the block booking system.

Rome, 1 April
Actress Pina Menichelli is setting the screen ablaze in Giovanni Pastrone's *Il Fuoco*.

Paris, 7 April
The French Union of Cinematographers has published its first official journal, *l'Ecran*.

Paris, 22 April
Two young girls, who are appearing in court for attempted murder, have stated that their crime was inspired by a film.

Paris, 13 May
The German-owned cinema Palais Rochechouart has now reopened its doors under the management of Alphonse Frank.

New York, 15 May
Screening of Charlie Chaplin's first film for Mutual, *The Floorwalker* with Edna Purviance and Eric Campbell.

Paris, 18 May
Gaumont has released *le Pied qui étreint* (*The Grasping Foot*). The film is a parody of *Vampires*, directed by Jacques Feyder, which starred André Roanne, Georges Biscot and Musidora.

Paris, 29 May
The National Cinema Board has met to decide on import duties for foreign films. French film producers want to be protected but need to avoid a heavy tax on the importation of unexposed film.

Paris, 16 June
Gaumont has presented *Têtes de femmes, femme de têtes* from the director Jacques Feyder. The cast includes the young Françoise Rosay, Kitty Hott and André Roanne.

New York, 16 June
The Jesse Lasky Feature Play Co. and Famous Players have merged to form the Famous Players-Lasky Corporation. Adolph Zukor takes the post of president.

Paris, 1 July
Georges-Michel Coissac has published an article in *Cine-Journal* "moralizing about the cinema and calling for the banning of vulgarity on the screen."

California, 6 August
A selected public was invited to the preview of *Intolerance* (originally entitled *The Mother and the Law*), directed by D.W. Grifffith.

Paris, 11 August
Pathé is screening the two first episodes of Louis Gasnier's new American serial, *The Exploits of Elaine*, once again starring Pearl White. A Pathé-Exchange production, it has been made as a follow-up to *Mysteries of New York*.

Stockholm, 14 August
With the release of his latest film, *Karlek och Journalistic* (*Love and Journalism*), interpreted by Jenny Tschernichin-Larsson and Richard Lund, the prolific director Mauritz Stiller has created a new genre of film: domestic comedy.

Los Angeles, 15 August
Creation of The Artcraft Pictures Corporation at Paramount. This new distribution company is to devote its main energies to distributing Mary Pickford films.

Rome, 11 September
Filippo Tommaso Marinetti has published a manifesto labeled *The Futuristic Cinema*.

Los Angeles, 14 September
Samuel Goldfish has resigned his position as administrative president of Famous Players-Lasky due to a series of disagreements with the new president Adolph Zukor.

Paris, 15 September
André Antoine is filming the street scenes for *Coupable* (*Guilty*) in the place du Tertre in an attempt "to catch life in full flight."

Prague, 20 October
Lucerna has released *A Little Heart of Gold*, produced by the playwright and actor Antonin Fencl.

Berlin, 31 October
Gustav Streseman, a deputy, has asked for a parliamentary debate on the importation of foreign films.

USA, 9 December
Charlie Chaplin has won his case to prevent publication of an unauthorized biography, *Charlie Chaplin's Own Story*. He instigated proceedings in October.

Paris, 16 December
The press has had a preview of the first episodes of Louis Feuillade's *Judex*, with Musidora, Yvette Andreyor and René Cresté.

Los Angeles, 16 December
Samuel Goldfish has formed a new production company, Goldwyn Pictures Corporation, in association with Edgar and Arch Selwyn, the Broadway producers.

Johannesburg, 31 December
Harold Shaw is making *The Voortrekkers: Winning a Continent* for African Film Productions. The film is a historical fresco recording the history of South Africa's "Afrikaaners", as the settlers of Dutch descent became known.

BIRTHS

Buenos Aires, 11 January
Bernard Blier

Japan, 4 February
Masaki Kobayashi

California, 5 April
Gregory Peck
(Eldred G. Peck)

Quebec, 1 May
Glenn Ford
(Gwyllin Samuel Newton)

Italy, 8 June
Luigi Comencini

India, 15 September
Margaret Lockwood

England, 26 September
Trevor Howard

London, 28 September
Peter Finch
(William Mitchell)

Paris, 5 November
Madeleine Robinson
(Madeleine Svoboda)

New York, 9 December
Kirk Douglas
(Issur Danielovitch Demsky)

Milan, 23 December
Dino Risi

Paris, 31 December
Suzy Delair

---

*D.W. Griffith's **Intolerance**, boasting spectacular settings and spanning four epochs, is the filmmaker's reply to those who criticized **The Birth of a Nation** as racist and bigoted.*

'Civilization': a passionate plea for peace

New York, 17 April
Thomas Ince has released his most ambitious picture to date. Produced by the Triangle Corporation and symbolically entitled *Civilization*, it draws its inspiration from *The Battle Cry of Peace*, a James Stuart Blackton film adapted from the Hudson Maxim book *Defenseless America*. The message of this ten-reel film is determinedly pacifist. A portrait of Woodrow Wilson, who has just been re-elected to the U.S. presidency on a non-interventionist ticket, makes a significant appearance at the beginning of the film. In one of the most effective scenes in *Civilization*, the commander of one of the warring powers' submarines refuses to sink a passenger ship. Clearly, this is a barely-veiled allusion to last year's torpedoing of the liner *Lusitania* in which 124 Americans died. The first half of the film is superbly controlled, depicting war sweeping over the landscape by using a succession of striking images: the silhouetted troops, ranks of charging cavalry, guns strewn over the hillside – all seem to sink through a pall of smoke as though descending into a pit of hell. At the climax of the picture, Christ returns as a submarine engineer to preach peace at the head of an army of pacifist women. Equally memorable are the less rhetorical images, such as the old woman who stares in grief as the men are taken off to war, and a shepherd boy trying to release a dove.

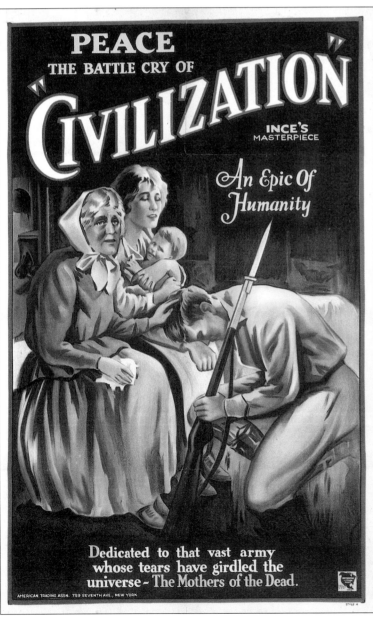

Actor William S. Hart directs 'The Aryan'

Seventeen-year-old newcomer Bessie Love co-stars with Hart in his new film.

New York, 13 April
Today sees the release of a new William S. Hart film. Entitled *The Aryan*, it has been written by the Triangle Corporation's celebrated cowboy star. Steve Denton, better known to the public as Rio Jim, is a renegade who scorns law and morality until the day when he is redeemed by the love of a young woman, in the beautiful form of Bessie Love. The "good bad man" character is a role which Hart has turned into his own. Now in his fifties, Hart's image of a Man of the West was honed by 20 years of stage experience before entering films in 1914, at which time he began working for his friend Thomas H. Ince. Hart made an immediate impression in his first season of two-reelers and has since moved on to feature-length films which he directs himself. In 1915 he followed Ince to Triangle, where his popularity now rivals that of Broncho Billy Anderson.

Censors are hot on the murderers' trail

Paris, 17 May
With the appearance of Zigomar, Fantômas and the vampires, has the cinematograph become a school for crime? Several gangsters recently caught by the police have confessed that the latest episodes of *Mysteries of New York* had influenced them in their criminal activities. Brenier, the member of parliament for Isère, climbed onto the rostrum of the Chamber and demanded that the government prohibit the screening of "cinematographic performances which, in the guise of fantastic adventures, teach the most skillful means of killing and robbing." The Minister of the Interior, Louis Malvy, agreed and is currently in charge of setting up a special commission charged with the examination and control of films. Film censorship is not a new phenomenon. For quite some time, mayors and departmental police chiefs have made the decision, independently of Paris, to ban the showing of *The Adventures of Bonnot* or *The Grasping Hand* in their districts. From now on, the officials at the Place Beauvau will be responsible for the morality in films, even to the extent of cutting them. Many have given hypocritical reasons for their decisions. It is said that the chief commissioner requested the cutting of a suicide scene, declaring, "No violent deaths must be shown while there is a war on."

Chaplin loses case over 'Carmen'

Washington, 24 June
Charles Chaplin's long legal battle against Essanay has ended in defeat. The case has gone all the way to the Supreme Court, which has ruled in Essanay's favor. The litigation was caused by a film entitled *Charlie Chaplin's Burlesque on Carmen*, a send-up of Cecil B. DeMille's *Carmen*, with Charlie capering around as "Darn Hosiery" and playing a realistic death scene with Edna Purviance before showing the audience how it was done with a prop dagger. After the comedian's departure to Mutual, Essanay decided to turn the squib into a four-reeler, inserting new scenes directed by Leo White and featuring Ben Turpin as well as salvaging material discarded by Chaplin. When the film was released in April, Chaplin immediately went to the courts to seek a remedy. In May his attorney Nathan Burkan appealed for an injunction to prevent Essanay from distributing the film, claiming that it was a fraud on the public and that Chaplin's rights as an author had been infringed. The application for an injunction was dismissed by Justice Hotchkiss of the Supreme Court of the State of New York, and Essanay launched a counter-suit against Chaplin for an estimated half-a-million dollars in lost profits on films which they claimed he still owed them. Now the Supreme Court in Washington has upheld Hotchkiss' decision, and Chaplin has emerged from the experience a sadder but wiser man. In the future the comedian's contracts will stipulate that there will be no modification or mutilation of his movies after they have been made.

*Chaplin and Edna in **Carmen**.*

The poisonous charms of Musidora

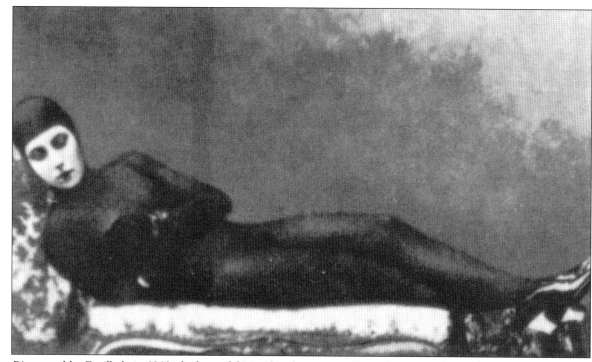
Discovered by Feuillade in 1913, the beautiful Musidora brings a totally modern sensuality to the 'Vampires' series.

Paris, 30 June
The tenth and final episode of *The Vampires*, entitled *Nights of Blood*, directed by Louis Feuillade, is now to be seen on our screens. Since the release of *The Red Code*, the third episode in the series, the whole of France has passionately followed the misdeeds of the splendid Irma Vep, a brown-eyed brunette whose name is an anagram of vampire. Musidora plays the evil-doing character, who is under the orders of the Grand Vampire, interpreted by Fernand Hermann. Dressed as a simple maid, shorthand typist or as a man, Musidora has, above all, stirred audiences in the part of the female cat burglar, because "her black tights cling to her ivory body," as the song goes. Musidora has been endowed with a provocative figure, which allows Irma Vep to glide swiftly through the shadows to steal and murder, the exact opposite of the sweet and docile Elaine Dodge. At the climax of the film, morality triumphs, because the vampire is killed by a revolver shot. Louis Feuillade has moderated the tone of the serial, primarily because the commissioner of police, Lépine, did not appreciate the failure of justice in the previous episodes. Musidora herself has been vigorously active in trying to persuade the authorities not to ban *The Vampires*. She has been successful. How can one possibly resist the charms of Irma Vep?

'Cheat' disparaged

Paris, 21 July
Critics and public alike have been knocked sideways by the latest Cecil B. DeMille film, *The Cheat*. Some have vigorously condemned the now notorious scene in which the rich and evil Japanese, played by Sessue Hayakawa, brutally bares the shoulder of a young American woman, the fragile Fannie Ward, to brand her with a red-hot iron. And one either loves or hates the director's tricks with light and shadow, enhanced in tinted copies of the film. Among *The Cheat*'s most fervent admirers is the writer Louis Delluc, who claims that the film is not only a revelation but also proof that cinema is an art form.

Jean Ayme in one of the demonic incarnations of the 'Great Vampire'.

Artistic control for Fatty Arbuckle

Atlantic City, 1 August
Roly-poly comedian Roscoe "Fatty" Arbuckle has just signed a truly unprecedented contract. Powerful producer Joseph Schenck has effectively offered Arbuckle a film company over which the comedian will maintain complete artistic control. Called The Comique Film Corporation, it will be financed and distributed by Paramount. As writer, director and star, Arbuckle will be

The chubby comedian with Phyllis Allen and Minta Durfee at Keystone.

earning $7,000 a week plus 25 percent of the profits. This deal will secure him a yearly income of over $1 million. Life is sweet for the Fat Man. After years in the wilderness he has at last been transformed into a big star.

Abel Gance to make ten new films

Paris, 5 September
Abel Gance has just completed *The Right to Life*, a psychological drama shot in nine days on a small budget for Film d'Art. Relations are tense between Abel Gance and Louis Nalpas, the head of Film d'Art, who often refers to the young director's "disordered and odd" imagination. Nevertheless, Nalpas has faith in Gance: he has just signed a year's renewable contract with him. Gance is to provide him with 10 films for which the director will be paid 1,500 francs each.

'Intolerance' is a monument to love

*Even more ambitious than the controversial **The Birth of a Nation**, Griffith's new film is a highly complex work.*

New York, 5 September
The title of D.W. Griffith's new film, *Intolerance*, resounds as a response to the polemics aroused a year and a half ago by the release of *The Birth of a Nation*. Curiously, this work mixes four historical periods: The Mother and the Law, set in the present; The Nazarene, which recounts the crucifixion of Christ; The Medieval Story, which tells of the massacre of protestants on Saint Bartholomew's Day, 1572; and The Fall of Babylon, about the betrayal of Prince Belshazzar to the Persians. Punctuating the film is the symbolic image of a woman (Lillian Gish) rocking a cradle; the intention here is to help unite the various episodes. These dissimilar events have only one point in common – love. The film cost about $400,000 to make and evolved over a period of almost two years, beginning as a short feature called *The Mother and the Law*. The gigantic decor erected for the Babylonian period required several months work from the craftsmen who built it, supervised by the brilliant production designer Walter L. Hall and his assistant Huck Wortman, while the photography was in the capable hands of Billy Bitzer, assisted by Karl Brown. In the program notes for the premiere at the Liberty Theater, Griffith explained that "the purpose of the production is to trace a universal theme through various periods of the race's (*sic*) history – ancient, sacred, medieval and modern..." At the conclusion of the screening, the audience gave this ambitious work its due when both the director and the film were heartily applauded.

Walter Hall designed the spectacular and elaborate sets for the film.

Max Linder answers the call of America

Paris, 30 September
Max Linder is leaving France and the exceptional state of affairs caused by the war. The star has just embarked on the liner *Espagne* for a long and daring crossing to the U.S. The journey is the result of his new contract which binds him for a year to Essanay, the famous Chicago film company. A few weeks ago, George K. Spoor was at Max's bedside in a Swiss military hospital. At that time Max was suffering abysmally from pneumonia, which he had contracted two years previously during the battle of the Marne. In addition, earlier in the war, Linder had been a victim of gas poisoning and suffered a serious breakdown. Spoor gave him the golden opportunity to replace Charles Chaplin who had left Essanay to go to Mutual. Once in America, the French comedian will earn $5,000 per week and should be able to direct 12 films. His health will benefit from the sea voyage, and he hopes to be able to shoot the first scenes of his new film, *Max In America*, on arrival.

'Daughter of the Gods' born from a wave

Australian swimmer Annette Kellerman's nude appearance caused a sensation.

New York, 30 October
There is a siren among the stars: Annette Kellerman, the fish-woman of *A Daughter of the Gods*, has met with unprecedented screen success. Directed by Herbert Brenon in Jamaica, the film features 10,000 extras, 2,000 horses and... 20 camels! Producer William Fox had to build a small town there to accommodate all those involved in this remarkable and daring spectacle.

An exploit in the name of an emperor

Vienna, 30 November
The pomp and circumstance surrounding the funeral of Emperor Franz Joseph, who died on 21 November in Schönbrunn Castle, has already been shown in the majority of the cinema theaters around Austria. It was Alexander Kollovrath and Sacha-Film which succeeded in filming the event. In the record time of three days, they made 255 copies, immediately distributing them all over the country. Sacha-Film was founded in 1910 by Count Alexander Kollovrath, the former parliamentarian. A big fan of cinema, Kollovrath is attached to the cinematographic archives of the War Ministry. His official duties have included facilitating the acquisition of material and film stock necessary for production. Sacha-Film is the first large production company in Austro-Hungary. There is also Lucerna, which presented *A Little Heart of Gold (Zlate Sredeck)* on the 20 October, directed by playwright Antonin Fend and played by Antoinie Nedosinska.

The more Charlie falls, the higher he rises

Hollywood, 4 December
Charlie Chaplin, happily, never fails to astonish us. His eighth film for Mutual, *The Rink*, is a madcap comedy set in a skating rink, around which Charlie glides with almost balletic ease. Embroiled in Chaplin's antics are the delightful Edna Purviance and the hulking Eric Campbell, instantly recognizable by his beetling eyebrows, bristling beard and a forbidding moustache.

*Charlie Chaplin on ice, with Edna Purviance and Mack Swain, in **The Rink**.*

Farrar, from Met stage to burning stake

Hollywood, 25 December
Geraldine Farrar has become very successful in the cinema. The ebullient opera singer is the star of a new super-production by Cecil B. DeMille, *Joan the Woman*, a sumptuous reconstruction inspired by the life of the French heroine. Last year, around the same time period, she triumphed in *Carmen*, a powerful adaptation of the Prosper Merimée novel, also directed by DeMille. At that time, her employment contract with Jesse L. Lasky created quite a brouhaha because she was paid an exhorbitant salary, had numerous material advantages and was offered a large percentage of the profits. This famous prima donna of New York's Metropolitan Opera was under contract to appear in up to three films per year, during her summer vacations. Deprived of her beautiful voice because of the limitations of the cinema, Farrar, nevertheless, has gained a huge following. Since 1 November last at the Boston Symphony Hall, where the unforgettable presentation of *Carmen* marked her screen debut, the success of the films has been boundless. At the present, Geraldine Farrar is known worldwide and her reputation as an attraction has grown almost to rival that of Sarah Bernhardt.

1917

★ ★ ★ ★ ★ ★ ★ ★ ★ ★ **1917** ★

China, 1 January
Supplies of unexposed film are once more available. The producer Zang Sichuan has founded the Huei Hsi production company.

Germany, 1 January
The Deulig (Deutsche Lichtbild Gesellschaft) production company has set itself the following goal: to act whenever possible in defense of German economy and culture throughout the world.

Paris, 5 January
A psychological drama le Droit à la vie (The Right to Life), made by Abel Gance, the director of les Gaz mortels and le Périscope, with Paul Vermoyal, Léon Mathot and Andrée Brabant, is now screening.

New York, 6 January
Joseph M. Schenck has released Panthea, with his wife Norma Talmadge playing the lead and directed by Allan Dwan.

Los Angeles, 8 January
Maurice Tourneur has directed Mary Pickford in Pride of the Clan, produced by Artcraft.

New York, 28 January
Douglas Fairbanks' last film for the Triangle Corporation The Americano, directed by John Emerson, is now showing.

Stockholm, 29 January
Director Victor Sjöström explores the hidden language of film in Terje Vigen (A Man There Was), a cinematographic adaptation of Henrik Ibsen's poem. This dramatic film captures the unleashed elements with superb lyricism.

Italy, 27 February
Gioacchino Mecheri, the director of Tiber Film and Celio Film has just bought out Itala Film. Giovanni Pastrone has decided to retire from the cinema.

India, 1 March
J.F. Maden has given a preview of the first Bengali fiction film, Satyawadi Raja Harishchandra.

California, 3 March
Release of The Tornado directed by Jack Ford, a relative newcomer to the cinema, who wrote the script and also played a role in the film.

France, 29 March
Emile Reynaud, the pioneer and inventor of cartoons, is without means and seriously ill. He has been confined to a hospice for the incurable at Ivry-sur-Seine.

St. Petersburg, 30 March
The union of patriotic filmmakers has released The Great Days of the Russian Revolution, by Vyatcheslav Viskovsky and Boutch Tovmarchersky, a film about the events leading up to the Czar's abdication. Evgeni Bauer has already released an anticzarist film, The Revolutionary.

Paris, 5 April
Creation of the French League for the Cinema, by Tristan Bernard, Edmond Benoît-Levy and Léon Gaumont. Its aims are to develop the cinema industry and to define its interests before Parliament.

Los Angeles, 14 April
Twenty-seven regional distributors, with over 2,000 cinemas under their control, have grouped together in an attempt to rival Adolph Zukor's Famous Players-Lasky and Artcraft company. They have formed a new production company: First National Exhibitor's Circuit.

New York, 23 April
The Butcher Boy is the first film Roscoe Arbuckle has made for his own Comique Film company. The film features a talented newcomer, Buster Keaton.

Los Angeles, 25 April
Samuel Goldfish, who from now on wishes to be known as Goldwyn, and his partners have created the Goldwyn Distribution Corporation.

New York, 30 April
Now that the United States has entered into the war, D.W. Griffith's film Intolerance has been withdrawn from distribution. It was already misunderstood by the public and is considered to be undesirable under the present circumstances. This move has resulted in enormous losses for the producer and distributor, Harry E. Aitken.

Los Angeles, 14 May
Cecil B. DeMille has co-written, directed and edited A Romance of the Redwoods for Artcraft, with Mary Pickford.

Paris, 15 June
The actor who created Fantômas, René Navarre, has now founded his own production company and has released The Adventures of Clémentine, a series of cartoons by Benjamin Rabier.

France, 22 June
An article has been published recently in le Cinéma criticizing the distracting background noises on sound tracks.

Indochina, 1 July
The governor-general, Albert Sarraut, has brought back numerous films from his recent visit to France, in order to show locals the "genius of the French nation."

Paris, 6 July
The first series of cartoons by Emile Cohl called les Aventures des Pieds-Nickelés has been produced by the Eclair film company.

Los Angeles, 12 July
Screening of The Little American, by Cecil B. DeMille with Mary Pickford and two newcomers, Wallace Beery and Ramon Novarro.

France, 26 July
Director Jacques Feyder has married actress Françoise Rosay.

Los Angeles, September
The Chaplin-First National contract has been made public. The total amounts to the sum of $1,075,000. Chaplin is to be paid $125,000 for each of the eight films that he is contracted to supply to the company over a period of 18 months, from January 1918.

New York, 16 October
D.W. Griffith is back from Europe with his film crew and numerous scenes for his new film Hearts of the World. The sequences were shot in England and on the French Front. The remaining scenes will be filmed in California.

Prague, 19 October
Lucarna has released les Adamites de Prague, by Antonin Fencl, with the actor Josef Vosalik.

New York, 20 October
Release of Charlie Chaplin's last film for Mutual The Adventurer, with Edna Purviance.

Shanghai, 31 October
The publishers of The Commercial Press, run by Pao Ching-chia have created a cinema section.

Paris, 14 November
Marcel L'Herbier has made his debut as a scriptwriter with a film for Eclipse, le Torrent, produced by Jean Mercanton and René Hervil.

Berlin, 16 November
Ernst Lubitsch has written and directed a comedy Wenn Vier das Selbe Machen (When Four do the Same Thing), with his faithful partner Ossi Oswalda.

Budapest, 31 December
Sandor Korda and Miklos Pasztoory have bought up the Corvin production company from Jeno Janovicz. The company is being transferred to Budapest where a studio is already under construction.

BIRTHS

Stockholm, 3 February
Arne Sucksdorff

Bordeaux, 1 May
Danielle Darrieux

Paris, 31 May
Jean Rouch

France, 27 July
Bourvil (André Raimbourg)

Connecticut, 6 August
Robert Mitchum

Prague, 11 September
Herbert Lom

Paris, 20 October
Jean-Pierre Melville (Grumbach)

Tokyo, 22 October
Joan Fontaine (Joan de Beauvoir de Havilland)

DEATHS

Paris, 20 December
Georges Demenÿ

Theda Bara is Cleopatra for William Fox. Born Theodosia Goodman in 1890 and now famous as 'The Vamp', her debut in **A Fool There Was** (1915) caused a sensation.

King of the Cowboys joins Queen of the Vamps

Company founder William Fox.

Gordon Edwards directed Theda Bara in the role of Egypt's sultry queen.

Hollywood, 17 October

The Fox Film Corporation, headed by the former penny arcade owner, exhibitor and distributor William Fox, continues to grow and prosper. Its latest feature *Cleopatra* has just opened, the newest vehicle for the studio's most famous and glamorous female star Theda Bara, following on her success in such roles as *Carmen*, *The Eternal Sappho*, *The Vixen*, and *The Tiger Woman*. The titles say it all! In addition, the company has just signed up popular Western star Tom Mix, formerly at Selig and now added to the Fox roster of stars headed by William Farnum, Valeska Suratt and George Walsh. Fox has succeeded in consistently increasing the number of his feature releases every year since he first ventured into production late in 1914. Having produced almost 40 features during his first year, Fox has continued to sign up new stars and directors. In the early days his studio was located on Staten Island before moving to New York City, and many of the scripts were written by Fox's wife. Last year alone the company released 50 features and opened a larger and newly improved Hollywood studio at the corner of Western Avenue and Sunset Boulevard. With the shift in production from the East Coast to the well-equipped West Coast facility, the company appears well on course to complete over 60 films during the current year, while the 1918 output will obviously be bolstered by a selection of Westerns starring Fox's new acquisition, Tom Mix. Fox is hardly short on directing talent either. Oscar Apfel, Frank Powell and British director Herbert Brenon have shared the directing honors during the early years with J. Gordon Edwards, who has himself handled most of the Theda Bara productions. There is also Raoul Walsh, older brother of George Walsh, whose creative output ranges from drama and social comment films to comedy and Westerns.

Very important year for Abel Gance

Gance, an established filmmaker.

*Emmy Lynn and Firmin Gémier, the principals in **Mater Dolorosa**.*

Paris, 12 October

Abel Gance's new film *la Zone de la mort* (*Death Zone*), has just been released today. This year has been decisive for the director. He met Charles Pathé in Nice on 21 January last. At a private screening, the great industrialist saw *Mater Dolorosa*, the film which Gance shot for Film d'Art. Pathé was very impressed by the direction and promised his moral and financial support. When it was released it aroused great enthusiasm. Gance and his cameraman Léonce Burel had taken an immense amount of care with the editing, lighting and interpretation, intensifying the tragedy of this social drama. Afterwards, he shot *Death Zone* and *The Tenth Symphony*, two very original works. During a second meeting on 8 July, Gance expounded his ideas to Pathé. He dreams of a film called *The Scars* and also a trilogy – a huge spectacle which would denounce the horrors of war and would be called *J'accuse*. Pathé is almost as enthusiastic as the young director and has agreed to finance the project.

Top Western star Tom Mix is a valuable acquisition for Fox.

Newly powerful Paramount has raised the stakes

Hollywood, 30 November
Whether the company is now referred to as Famous Players-Lasky or Paramount Pictures, it is clear that this large and growing film corporation is setting the pace for the rest of the movie industry. And it is the new company president, the small and quiet-spoken but shrewd Adolph Zukor, who masterminded it all. It was only 16 months ago that Zukor first arranged the key merger between his Famous Players Co. and Lasky, then organized Artcraft Pictures for the release of the prestigious Mary Pickford features, and finally succeeded in integrating the production and distribution sides of the business under the brand-new Paramount company logo. With the departure of W.W. Hodgkinson and Chairman Sam Goldwyn not long after, Zukor's consolidation of power was complete, which left Jesse Lasky in place as vice president in charge of production and Cecil B. DeMille as director-general. During the past year the company has taken advantage of the decline of a number of other studios, Triangle in particular, and has acquired several new stars to bolster its already strong lineup. Among the most notable recent arrivals are comedian Fatty Arbuckle, cowboy William S. Hart, Charles Ray and Douglas Fairbanks. In addition, Zukor has succeeded in strengthening Paramount's position even further, at the expense of other, smaller companies, through his use of the practice of block booking, i.e. forcing exhibitors to commit themselves to the whole Paramount package – in other words, requiring them to take the less desirable films in order to get the Mary Pickford or DeMille features which they want most. But perhaps most important of all is the way in which Zukor has succeeded in opening up new sources of capital. By turning to Wall Street for help in financing his plans for the studio, which include a major increase in film production, he has recently convinced his bankers and especially Otto Kahn, head of the leading New York financial firm of Kahn, Loeb and Company, that Paramount, as Zukor has reorganized it and as the spearhead of a rapidly growing industry, is an excellent financial risk. The result is a stock issue of $10 million dollars.

l to r: Lasky, Adolph Zukor, Samuel Goldwyn, DeMille and Albert Kaufman.

German cinema in the hands of the State

Berlin, 18 December
The German cinema is anticipating the end of the war. A trust has been set up to unify the different elements in an industry which is coming to a boil. It is to be called the Universum Film Aktien Gesellschaft (UFA). The new organization will regroup in the bosom of Mester and Pagu, with the support of the Deutsch Bank and powerful chemical, steel and power combines. The driving force behind this important development is General Erich Ludendorff, the German Army's Chief of Staff. Ludendorff has grasped the importance of the new medium, not only as a means of entertainment but also as a weapon of propaganda and social control. In a letter to the Minister of War, dated 4 July, Ludendorff urged that the state should move swiftly to take a controlling interest in the German film industry. "The extraordinary power of cinema", he wrote, "has been demonstrated during the war. It is now logical to centralize and control this power exercised over the masses." Several months earlier, under heavy pressure from the armed forces, the German high command had formed a picture and film bureau entitled BUFA, similar in form to the Service Cinématographique provided by the French Army. The troops at the Front will be given regular film shows. Nearly 500 cinema halls will be opened on the Western Front and about 300 on the Eastern Front. Feeding this new circuit with a diet of educational and entertainment films will present BUFA with a formidable challenge. On 29 October a top-level conference was held in Berlin between the German high command, the directors of BUFA and the Deutsch Bank. It was there that the decision was made to implement Ludendorff's recommendations without delay. State control of cinema is effectively a *fait accompli* and the German film industry a vital part of the war effort.

..The end of Rebecca's circus career.

MARY PICKFORD
IN
REBECCA OF SUNNYBROOK FARM
FROM THE PLAY BY KATE DOUGLAS WIGGIN... and CHARLOTTE THOMPSON
SCENARIO BY FRANCIS MARION... DIRECTED BY MARSHALL NEILAN
PRESENTED BY
ARTCRAFT PICTURES CORPORATION

1918

★ ★ ★ ★ ★ ★ ★ ★ ★ **1918** ★

Paris, 1 January
Gaumont's film-hire service called the Comptoir, has signed a contract with Paramount Pictures regarding exclusive rights to the American company's productions.

Paris, 4 January
The film that Albert Capellani made in the United States, *Scènes de la vie de Bohème* (*Scenes of Bohemian Life*), adapted from Murger with Paul Capellani, Alice Brady and Juliette Clarens, is now released here.

Hollywood, 21 January
Opening of the new Charles Chaplin Film Company's studios on the corner of La Brea Avenue and Sunset Boulevard.

California, 18 February
Rio Jim alias William S. Hart has cast himself in *Blue Blazes Rawden*, with Maude George and Robert McKim as his partners.

Copenhagen, 22 February
Screening of *400 Million Leagues under the Earth* by Forest Holger-Madsen, with Nicolai Neiiendam and Gunnar Tolnaes for Nordisk. However, the company is suffering financially due to competition from the rapidly expanding German film company UFA.

Paris, 3 March
Les Travailleurs de la mer (*The Sea Workers*), a Pathé-SCAGL project, adapted from Victor Hugo's work by André Antoine, with Romuald Joubé and Andrée Brabant, was screened for the Maritime League's Charity Gala at the Trocadero.

Paris, 22 March
Musidora, who stars in the film version of her great friend Colette's *The Vagabond*, also collaborated on the script and direction.

Paris, 22 March
Eclipse has released *Un roman d'amour*, by Louis Mercanton and René Hervil, with Sacha Guitry (in front of the camera), Yvonne Printemps and Fred Wright.

Los Angeles, 2 April
The king of the jungle is brought to life by Elmo Lincoln in *Tarzan of the Apes* adapted from Edgar Rice Burroughs' book, which was published in 1912.

Paris, 20 April
French producers have decided to strike from today until 23 May in protest against the difficulties they experienced with importations of unexposed reels and foreign films.

New York, 26 May
D.W. Griffith has been elected president of the Motion Picture War Service Association, which is in charge of increasing the United States' war effort by selling bonds.

Moscow, 1 June
Dziga Vertov, working under the supervision of Lev Kuleshov, is the chief editor of *Kino-Nedelia* (*Cinema Weekly*), a filmed news periodical on various aspects of Soviet life.

Berlin, 30 June
The UFA, which took over Pagu and Messter Film last year, has now taken control of the cinemas previously held by the Danish film company Nordisk.

Paris, 12 July
Clubs are Trump, one of several American films made last year by Hal Roach with Harold Lloyd is now released here by Pathé.

Moscow, 27 July
The Soviet Cinema Committee is undertaking the first state produced fiction film, *The Signal*, directed by Alexander Arkatov.

Paris, 9 August
Press magnate William Randolph Hearst's favorite, the actress and former dancer Marion Davies, has made her screen debut in *Runaway Romany*, from the director George Lederer. The film has just been released in France.

Nice, 25 August
Abel Gance, with the backing of Pathé, has started filming *J'accuse*, the first film in his trilogy about war and peace, with Romuald Joubé and Séverin-Mars. The poet Blaise Cendrars is the assistant director.

Marseilles, 31 August
The aviator Rouit has been killed during the filming of *Twenty Thousand Leagues under the Sea*, for the Jules Verne film company. He had to throw himself into a river but was caught in a whirlpool and did not reappear on the surface.

Paris, 6 September
Poor Little Rich Girl, directed in the United States by Maurice Tourneur and starring Mary Pickford, is being distributed in France.

Paris, 22 September
A gala evening has been held at the Trocadero for the opening of the Franco-American propaganda film *Lest We Forget*, directed by Léonce Perret, with Norma Talmadge.

Paris, 27 September
Charles Pathé has suggested to the Cinema Employers' Federation that a percentage of the takings replace the present film hire system. He also called for the imposition of heavy import taxes on foreign films.

Germany, 30 September
The Decla Company, which was founded by Erich Pommer with financial backing from the French company Eclair, has become 100 percent German after buying up all stock held by the mother company.

New York, 13 October
Release of *The Romance of Tarzan*, by Wilfred Lucas and starring Elmo Lincon, Cleo Madison and Enid Markey. It is a sequel to *Tarzan of the Apes*, with a prologue showing scenes from the first film.

New York, 9 November
After appearing in 34 films for Adolph Zukor, Mary Pickford has signed a contract with First National for three films to be made before 31 July 1919. She is to be paid an advance of $150,000 and then will receive $250,000 for each film. The Mary Pickford Company, which is producing the films, will select the directors and actors.

France, 11 November
According to the latest issue of *le Cinéma*, André Antoine is leaving France for Italy, where he is to film an adaptation of Henry Bernstein's play, *Israel*, for Tiber Film.

France, 30 November
The release of *The Tenth Symphony*, a new film made by Abel Gance, with Jean Toulot, Emmy Lynn and Séverin-Mars, has received a mixed reception. It has been showered with praise by some and criticized by others for its grandiloquence and visual artifices.

Paris, 30 November
The Pathé company has split into the Sound Reproduction Machine company to be run by Emile, and Pathé-Cinema Company, under the direction of his brother Charles.

Czechoslovakia, 4 December
Suzanne Marwille has made her screen debut in the film *Demon Rodu Halkenu*, produced and directed by Vaclav Binovec.

California, 15 December
Cecil B. DeMille has finished filming his latest production, a remake of his first film, *The Squaw Man*, starring Elliot Dexter and Katherine McDonald.

Berlin, 20 December
Release of Ernst Lubitsch's adaptation of Merimée's *Carmen*, with Pola Negri. This is their first film together since making *The Eyes of the Mummy*.

Hollywood, 31 December
An increasing number of talented filmmakers from France have come to the United States. Some, such as Maurice Tourneur, Emile Chautard from Film d'Art, Léonce Perret from Gaumont (who has been busy making various propaganda films) and Louis Gasnier, have already met with success here.

BIRTHS

London, 4 February
Ida Lupino

Denmark, 8 April
Gabriel Axel

France, 18 April
André Bazin

Italy, 18 May
Massimo Girotti

Sweden, 14 July
Ingmar Bergman

New York, 17 October
Rita Hayworth
(Margarita Carmen Cansino)

---

*Elmo Lincoln is the first screen Tarzan. Weighing 200 pounds, he brings Edgar Rice Burroughs' jungle hero to life in **Tarzan of the Apes** and **The Romance of Tarzan**.*

Tragedy played out in Iceland's mountains

The Outlaw and His Wife stars director Victor Sjöström and Edith Erastoff.

Stockholm, 1 January
Victor Sjöström's impressive new film, *The Outlaw and His Wife*, has just been released here. It is an adaptation from a play by the Icelandic writer Johann Sigurjonsson, and the action takes place in 19th-century Iceland. The story centers on Berg-Ejvind (Sjöström), wanted for stealing sheep to feed his starving family, and who falls in love with Halla, a rich land-owning widow (Edith Erastoff, the director's third wife). She abandons her estate and they flee to the mountains, pursued by the law. After spending an idyllic summer together, the lovers perish in a snowstorm. Most impressive are the superb landscapes, a primitive setting for this tempestuous, passionately performed melodrama. The film was shot in the mountains of Lapland, close to the Norwegian border. An expedition to the actual locale of the tale proved to be too dangerous because of the German submarines relentlessly tracking the Atlantic Ocean and the North Sea. One of the most impressive scenes in the long film has Edith Erastoff, driven back by the posse, throwing her baby from the cliff top. It is the most ambitious and impressive of the 34 films made by the 38-year-old actor-director, whose debut behind the camera was in 1912.

Feuillade renews the contract for Judex

René Cresté, who created the role of Judex, is every woman's dream.

Paris, 18 January
After the triumph of *Judex*, Gaumont and Louis Feuillade have begun their sequel to the adventures of the handsome heartthrob René Cresté, *le Mystère d'une nuit d'été* (*The Mystery of a Summer Night*). The first episode of Judex's "new mission", a romantic adventure in 12 parts, has been launched in a blaze of publicity. The screenplay is once more by Arthur Bernède and Feuillade, but, sadly, it is inferior to the original. Perhaps this is due to the absence of the captivating Musidora. The film is beautiful but lacks pace and is hampered by a combination of moralizing and melodrama. Feuillade seems to have abandoned the lyricism he gave his first serials. Yvette Andreyor is in tears from start to finish and René Cresté spends far too much time flashing his romantic profile. The only saving grace is the comic relief provided by Marcel Lévesque. The critics have not minced their words. Louis Delluc has called the production an "abomination", adding for good measure that "Judex's latest adventure perpetrates a crime greater then those regularly condemned by the council of war." Warming to his task, Delluc claims that he was taken to see the film by "some friends of mine." What friends?

Emile Reynaud dies in a hospice

Ivry-sur-Seine, 9 January
Emile Reynaud (born 1844), pioneer of animated film, has just died in a hospice on the banks of the Seine, where he had been cared for since 29 March 1917. His last years were little short of tragic, from the day in 1910 when, crushed by the Cinematograph and dejected and penniless, he threw the greater part of his irreplaceable work and unique equipment into the Seine. By then the public had deserted the showings he gave of his poetic work at the "Théâtre Optique", which had been a celebrated attraction at the Musée Grevin between 1892 and 1900.

'The Count of Monte Cristo' remains seductive and disturbing

Paris, 1 March
In Paris two spectacular productions are competing for audiences: Judex's latest adventure and a new adaptation of *The Count of Monte Cristo*, an eight-part serial produced by Louis Nalpas' Film d'Art and directed by Henri Pouctal. The seventh episode of the Judex serial, *la Main morte* (*The Dead Hand*), is released today, as is the last episode of the adventures of the Count of Monte Cristo, a role played by Léon Mathot. The public has delivered its verdict. The Count has won hands down and Gaumont is now licking its wounds. Pouctal, the artistic director at Film d'Art, has delighted the public with an ambitious and brilliantly photographed film. But it helps having Alexandre Dumas provide the scenario.

Léon Mathot is Edmond Dantes in Henri Pouctal's Monte Cristo.

D.W. Griffith plunges America into the heart of Europe's conflict

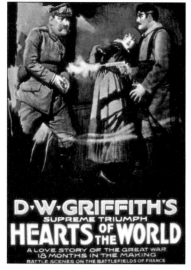

*The director of **Hearts of the World** also turns actor for the occasion.*

Los Angeles, 12 March
"Do you want to go to France?" That is the slogan of D.W. Griffith's new film *Hearts of the World*, which has just been shown at Clune's. This anti-German propaganda film, shot in England, France and California, has bowled the public over and has aroused great waves of sympathy for the Allies. The action unfolds in a small French village, before and during the war. Douglas and Marie, played respectively by Robert Harron and Lillian Gish, are separated by the war. The couple are reunited after a long period, and are saved in extremis by the intervention of the Allied troops. Griffith has had no

qualms about presenting the Germans as cynical and brutal, almost to the point of caricature. Erich von Stroheim has found a dream role as a Horrible Hun. Poor Lillian Gish has to suffer from bombardments throughout, as she tries to guide her confused grandfather to safety, and then later wanders dazed through the landscape carrying her wedding dress carefully in her arms. Her sister, Dorothy Gish, has a comic role as The Little Disturber, a street-singer, which she makes truly amusing with her elastic face and jaunty movements. Audiences have been particularly impressed by the realistic images of the Front. Certain

scenes were shot by Captain Kleinschmidt and Billy Bitzer, with the aid of the cinematographic department of the French army, near the Front, amidst the ruins and shelling. For the few months spent in France, Griffith filmed all types of arms and military equipment used in the conflict. For a director of his caliber, it was a golden opportunity to film history as it was being made. In October 1917, Griffith brought his company back to the U.S. to finish the film in California. *Hearts of the World* is Griffith's first film for Adolph Zukor's Artcraft company, but he continues to retain artistic control of his work.

Russian films boast a glorious star

Moscow, 27 April
Vera Kholodnaya, the "queen of the Soviet screen", will be starring in two films opening in Moscow next month – *Still Sadness... Still* and *The Last Tango*. She alone among Russian motion picture actresses can guarantee the success of a film. Because of her appeal, she is paid a salary of 25,000 rubles ($12,500) for each production. It was in the early spring of 1915 that Vera Kholodnaya, the wife of a poorly paid officer, applied to work at the Khanzhonkov studios as an extra. Her outstanding beauty caught the attention of director Evgeni Bauer, who gave her the leading role of Valeriya in *Song of Triumphant Love*, based on Turgenev. It was a triumphant debut, and the actress went on to make five more films under Bauer's direction, the most notable being *Children of the Age* (1915), *Beauty Should Rule The World* and *A Life for a Life* (both 1916). Because she usually plays poor girls who have managed, by good fortune, to rise up the social ladder, Kholodnaya has become an ideal for many young girls who see, in her grace, style and beauty, someone to emulate. "My eyes are my bread," she has said. As if to prove to those who believed she could not act without the direction of her mentor, Evgeni Bauer, Kholodnaya gave a moving performance last year in *Tormented Souls*, directed by Vladimir Kas'yanov. Who can forget the moment when she reads the telegram from her lover, informing her that he will not return? Kholodnaya falls helplessly onto the piano, her shoulders shaking from her wracking sobs.

The Russian cinema is flourishing amid post-revolution chaos

Moscow, 31 May
Ever since their first days in power, the Bolsheviks have been aware of the importance of cinema, mainly for propaganda purposes. Almost all the early films dealt with the recent revolutionary struggle, or with historical events seen in a revolutionary context. But the titles of some of the most recent and forthcoming films indicate a wider subject matter: *The Young Lady and the Hooligan*, *The Woman Who Invented Love*, *Maids of the Mountain*, *Jenny the Maid* and *Creation Can't Be Bought*, an adaptation of Jack London's *Martin Eden*. This month, *Father Sergius*, based on a story by Leo Tolstoy, has been released. The film's anti-clerical stance profited from the decree in January this year, which officially broke the connec-

tion between church and state. Another new film, *Still, Sadness... Still*, a spectacular drama in two parts, recounts the history of the cinema's birth. *The Last Tango* also opened

this month, a melodrama that is set in Argentina. Both the latter films are enhanced by the presence of the Soviet cinema's most popular star, Vera Kholodnaya.

*Yakov Protazanov's seven-reel **Father Sergius** is adapted from Tolstoy.*

Kholodnaya, beautiful and talented. ▷

'Hell Bent' comes heaven sent for Jack Ford and Harry Carey

*Harry Carey (center) in **Hell Bent** from the Ford partnership.*

Hollywood, 6 July

Hell Bent, the latest Western from the director-star team of Jack Ford and Harry Carey at Universal, has just opened and has already been well received. A writer in the *Motion Picture News* noted last week, "few directors put such sustained punch in their pictures as does this Mr. Ford." In fact, Jack started out in the movies acting in two-reelers directed by his older brother, Francis, in 1915 and 1916 before teaming up with Harry just over a year ago. This is their ninth feature together in which Carey plays the by now familiar role of "Cheyenne Harry", an easygoing Western character who is more of a saddle tramp than a typical movie hero. Audiences, however, don't seem to mind that at all.

Russian prodigy

Lev Kuleshov, born in 1899 has completed his first film, *The Project of Engineer Prite*.

Lenin enlists help of cinema for Revolution

Moscow, 13 August

Communism is off to war and so is the cinema. Today, Lenin is sending off the first propaganda train. Its carriages are covered with allegorical frescoes to the glory of the worker and Bolshevik soldiers. Inside, there is a conference hall, a school, a library stocked with some 7,000 books, an autonomous printworks and a cinematic installation, consisting of projector equipment, darkrooms, printing and editing rooms, as well as a significant stock of film. The experimental train is leaving for the Kazan region to capture the struggles of the civil war.

The government of the Federal Republic of Soviet Russia and its head, Vladimir Ilyich Ulyanov, known as Lenin, think that they can rally the population who have been misled by counter-revolutionary propaganda to the Bolshevik cause. During the journey, the mobile studio will produce a weekly newspaper to be run by director of photography Edouard Tissé and his young editor Denis Arkadievitch Kaufman, known as Dziga Vertov. This original undertaking reflects a growing interest in the power of the cinema. An Institute of Photography, the first in the world, is also being set up.

The Lady and The Ruffian, made by Mayakovsky and Slavinsky.

Buster Keaton to act with Fatty Arbuckle

The two skilled comedians and a lady, at work for Comique Films.

Long Beach, 15 September

Roscoe "Fatty" Arbuckle's newest film, distributed by Paramount, is entitled *The Cook*. In the swirl of slapstick around the Fat Man is a curious little newcomer to films, Buster Keaton. This latest addition to the Arbuckle stock company began performing as a toddler in his parents' vaudeville act. Billed as "The Human Mop", he spent much of the time being tossed around the stage, acquiring in the process a remarkable physical elasticity. As befits a trouper and exponent of daredevil falls, he was given the name Buster by no less a person than Harry Houdini. In March last year, the 21-year-old Keaton was introduced to Arbuckle while the latter was filming his first Comique Film comedy, the two-reeler *The Butcher Boy*. Arbuckle co-opted him on to the film and, without any rehearsal, Keaton appeared as a kind of village idiot. In one scene he demonstrated his remarkable flair for physical comedy by absorbing the shock of a flying sack of flour without even a flicker of effort. He was immediately snapped up by producer Joseph Schenck at the modest salary of $40 a week, a fraction of what he could earn on Broadway. Keaton is in love with films, and *The Cook* is his twelfth for Arbuckle.

Mauritz Stiller brings 'Thomas Graal' back to Swedish cinema

Thomas Graal's Best Film.

*Karin Molander in Stiller's 1916 hit **Love and Journalism**.*

Stockholm, 21 October
Thomas Graal's Best Film was such a great success last year that the director, Mauritz Stiller, has reassembled the same brilliant cast and production team for an equally entertaining sequel, *Thomas Graal's Best Child.* Both films revolve around the hero's various domestic difficulties. The best scene in the more recent picture has Thomas Graal (portrayed by Victor Sjöström) overdressing for his wedding, then having to undress in front of a shocked congregation in order to find the ring. Another

amusing episode takes place when he and his bride (Karin Molander) argue on the way home from the church about whether their first child should be a boy or a girl. With the two Thomas Graal films, and the sparkling comedy *Love and Journalism* that also stars vivacious Karin Molander, the 35-year-old Stiller has established himself, together with Sjöström, as the most popular director in Sweden. Of course, both men benefited greatly from the growth of a national cinema due to the dearth of foreign imports during the war.

Mauritz Stiller was born in Helsinki to Jewish Russian-Polish parents, who died when he was only four. He was trained by his adoptive parents to be a haberdasher, but entered the cinema in 1912 after fleeing to Sweden to avoid conscription in the Russian Czar's army. One of his earliest films was *Song of the Scarlet Flower*, a pastoral drama adapted from a Finnish source, and his other films were undistinguished thrillers, but it is Mauritz Stiller's comedies that have brought him fame at home and recognition abroad.

A sixteen-year-old wife for Chaplin

Hollywood, 1 November
Charlie Chaplin has returned from his honeymoon. His wife is 16-year-old Mildred Harris, who passes herself off as 18 and who Chaplin met at a party held by producer Sam Goldwyn. At the time Mildred was just another little actress on the make in Hollywood. The two were married at a simple ceremony on 23 October. Since that happy event, Mrs. Chaplin has been bombarded with offers. Louis B. Mayer came up with a contract for six films worth $50,000, something that could have only before been in the dreams of this young woman. The news of the marriage has inevitably caused a stir, not least because Charlie seems to be at the summit of his career. In June 1917 he signed a million-dollar contract with First National for eight two-reel films in 18 months. Already made are *A Dog's Life* and *Shoulder Arms*. The latter, an answer to criticism about Chaplin's lack of involvement in the war effort, took the Tramp to the Western Front, where he bombarded the enemy with grenades made from foul-smelling Limburger cheese. In between, Chaplin made a propaganda short, *The Bond*, for the Liberty Loan Committee. It has produced a flood of subscriptions, testimony to Charlie's popularity and drawing power as the greatest screen comedian of the day.

Tempestuous Pola is Ernst Lubitsch's answer to Theda Bara

*Negri, with Harry Liedtke as Don Jose in Lubitsch's version of **Carmen**.*

Berlin, 17 December
Ernst Lubitsch's new film version of *Carmen*, recently completed at the UFA studios here, has just opened to great acclaim. This is only the director's second feature-length production, after *Die Augen der Mumie Ma* (*The Eyes of the Mummy*) which was released earlier this year. Both films paired the young Polish actress Pola Negri with Harry Liedtke, who appears here in the role of Don Jose. But this is Miss Negri's picture and she makes the most of it. The stylish handling by director Lubitsch is worth noting, but it is the superb performance of Pola Negri, by turns darkly intense then passionate and lively, that excites the viewer and makes this a film to remember.

Enjoying a cruise with Mildred.

Czechoslovakia, 31 January
Gustav Machaty has directed his first short film at the age of 18. He wrote the burlesque-style scenario for *Teddy Wants to Smoke* in collaboration with Jean S. Kolar.

Paris, 26 February
The Cinema Director's Union has decided to ban the screening of all German and Austrian films for a period of 15 years.

Paris, 15 March
Marcel L'Herbier's first film for Gaumont, *Rose-France*, has been receiving severe criticism. The journal *la Cinématographie française* describes it as "feeble, limp, long-winded and maudlin."

Paris, 24 March
Release here of *The Turn in the Road*, American King Vidor's first full-length film, produced by the Brentwood Film Co. which was created for its production.

Berlin, 3 April
Halbblut (*The Half-Breed*), the first film directed by Fritz Lang is now screening. Until now, Lang has been writing film scenarios for Decla, but dissatisfied with the treatment given to his scripts he decided to turn to directing them himself.

Germany, 17 April
The engineers Hans Vogt, Joe Engl and Joseph Massolle are patenting their sound-recording system, the Tri-Ergon, which makes use of Lee de Forest's electrode tubes.

Paris, 20 April
Charlie Chaplin's *Shoulder Arms* is screening at the Gaumont-Palace and 10 other cinemas.

Paris, 15 June
Pierre Henry, a friend of Louis Delluc's, has started up a bi-monthly magazine *Ciné pour tous*.

Paris, 15 June
A cinema bank with a capital of 3 million francs has been created to rebuild the cinemas that were destroyed by the war.

France, 20 June
André Antoine is filming an adaptation of Emile Zola's novel *la Terre* (*The Earth*). He is assisted by Julien Duvivier.

France, 26 June
The mayor of Lyon, Edouard Herriot, is bringing into force the decree ordering all that all cinematographs, including fairground shows, are to use inflammable film.

Versailles, 28 June
The only cameraman allowed to enter the Gallery of Mirrors to film the signing of the peace treaty was corporal André A. Danton, the Armed Services cinematographic attaché. He placed his camera eight metres from the table and caught the historical occasion on 360 metres of film.

Los Angeles, 1 July
The 17-year-old Mary Miles Minter has signed a contract with Adolph Zukor. The head of Paramount intends to build her up as a rival to Mary Pickford.

Los Angeles, 1 July
Charlie Chaplin has started work on his first full-length film, *The Kid*, with 4-year-old Jackie Coogan.

Budapest, 1 August
With the fall of the Communes and the subsequent repression of its partisans, many actors and filmmakers are emigrating, among them Sandor Korda and Mihaly Kertesz.

Nice, 18 August
Germaine Dulac is directing Eve Francis in *la Fête espagnole* (*Spanish Holiday*). Louis Delluc wrote the scenario for this Nalpas independent production.

Moscow, 1 September
The State School of Cinematography has opened here to train film directors, actors, cameramen and lighting technicians. It is believed to be the first such institution founded anywhere.

California, 7 September
Release of *Back Stage* directed by Fatty Arbuckle and starring himself, Molly Malone and Buster Keaton.

France, 20 September
Jacques de Baroncelli is filming *The Secret of Lone Star*, with the American star Fanny Ward, Rex MacDougall and Gabriel Signoret. With this type of film, Delac and Vandal from Film d'Art are hoping to gain a bigger slice of the American cinema market.

Paris, 30 September
Bernard Grasset has edited *Cinéma et Cie*, a collection of articles by Louis Delluc from *le Film*. It is the first book of a critical nature to be published about the French cinema.

Hollywood, 30 September
Charlie Chaplin and Douglas Fairbanks, partners in the new United Artists Company, are planning a film in South America. They hope to work on location in Santiago, Chile for several months.

New York, 18 October
Marcus Loew, who has been at the head of an extensive cinema circuit since 1912, has now set up Loew's Incorporated, with a capital of $27 million. Negotiations are under way for the new outfit to take control of Metro Pictures.

Nice, 25 October
René Navarre has created a production company for "ciné-romans", popular films adapted from the serialized novels published simultaneously in all the main daily papers. The first film is already planned from a story by Gaston Leroux.

Stockholm, 8 November
Mauritz Stiller's latest comedy titled *Erotikon* is proving highly popular. The film, starring Karin Molander, draws its inspiration from a play by Hungarian writer Ferenc Herczeg.

Milan, 25 November
The beautiful Italian star, Francesca Bertini has been signed to a contract by Richard A. Rowland, a producer and the president of Metro Pictures, for a series of films to be made in Italy for the American market. If they are a success Francesca will be leaving for Hollywood.

Prague, 1 December
Sixteen-year-old Anny Ondra has made her silver screen debut in *The Woman with Small Feet*, directed by Jean S. Kolar from a scenario by Gustav Machaty.

New York, 7 December
Screening of *Blind Husbands* at the Capitol Theater. It is the first film to be written and directed by Erich von Stroheim, who also takes a leading role. Universal went against Stroheim's advice and changed the original title, *The Pinnacle*.

Hollywood, 15 December
Gloria Swanson, divorced from Wallace Beery, has married Herbert Somborn. Her last two films, made with Cecil B. DeMille, are *After the Rain, the Sunshine* and *The Admirable Crichton*.

Nice, 15 December
Having come here to make *Ecco Homo*, Abel Gance has given up the idea and is working on the scenario of *la Rose du rail*. But his companion, Ida Danis, who had a relapse of Spanish influenza, is now suffering from galloping consumption.

Stockholm, 27 December
Svenska Biografteatern has merged with Skandia. The new trust is to be known as the Svensk Filmindustri.

Seoul, 31 December
The premiere has taken place of the first film to be made in Korea. Directed by Do-San Kim, *Eurichok Koutou* is 3,280 metres in length.

USA, 31 December
The Famous Players-Lasky have released the first issue of *Paramount Magazine*, a filmed news weekly.

BIRTHS

Paris, 29 April
Gérard Oury
(Max Gérard Houry)

Rome, 15 June
Alberto Sordi

Marseilles, 19 June
Louis Jourdan
(Louis Gendre)

Italy, 14 July
Lino Ventura
(Angelo Borrini)

Paris, 10 November
François Périer (Pilu)

Italy, 19 November
Gillo Pontecorvo

Sweden, 12 December
Arne Mattson

The Viennese actor, Erich von Stroheim (left), with Sam de Grasse in **Blind Husbands**, *his impressive directorial debut, made 10 years after his arrival in America.*

The Italian cinema is in a ferment

Rome, 9 January
The Italian cinema is attempting to recover from the damage to the industry caused by the war and increased competition from the many available American films. To this end two Italian lawyers, Gioacchino Mecheri and Giuseppe Barattolo, have recently formed a new organization, the Union Cinematografica Italiana (or UCI), bringing together all the leading Italian producers. Unfortunately, the two organizers had a falling out after only a few months. Mecheri, the head of Tiber, has taken over first Celio and then Itala, while Barattolo, managing director of Caesar, has gained control of Cines, then Ambrosio and finally Film d'Arte Italiana (FAI). Each one of these rival "holding companies" has been given substantial financial backing from banks and each has big plans for the future. It will be interesting to see if they succeed in giving a much needed boost to Italian production.

With United Artists, four great reputations are put on the line

Hollywood, 17 April
A new cinematographic company has been established in the USA: The United Artists Corporation, whose management has been entrusted to Hiram Abrams, a former member of the board at Paramount. The firm originated with four of the great names of Hollywood who are active partners – Mary Pickford, Douglas Fairbanks, Charles Chaplin and D.W. Griffith. They knew it was their personalities that had made the major film companies rich. Although they had retained considerable control over their productions, they were still subject to the will of distributors, who also took a large slice of the profits. Therefore, toward the end of 1918, the four decided to found their own company. In their opinion, it was the only way to oppose the all-powerful producers, who had monopolist ambitions. At the time, there were rumors of large mergers and salary reductions. Pickford, Fairbanks, Chaplin and Griffith met at Fairbanks' home in Beverly Hills

l to r: Douglas Fairbanks, Mary Pickford, Charles Chaplin and D.W. Griffith.

in January. At their side was a particularly well-considered man, William Gibbs McAdoo, the son-in-law of President Wilson, who is former Secretary of the Treasury, and President of the Federal Railway Board. United Artists, on this occasion, could be established as a distribution company, with the five personalities owning shares. Assured of sizable financial support, the company, still in its infancy, is seeking to reorganize itself. McAdoo has given up his place to Hiram Abrams, but the three stars and D.W. Griffith remain United Artists' greatest asset.

Pacifist Abel Gance wants to see arms laid down once and for all

Paris, 31 March
The press has been enthusiastically praising Abel Gance after the showing of *J'accuse*, a tragedy of modern times in three episodes, financed by Charles Pathé and by the cinematographic department of the army. This immense work, Gance's biggest budget film to date, begun prior to the Armistice, is an anti-war indictment. A patriotic film, where the love of France is lyrically extolled, *J'accuse* is also a poignant melodrama. It begins in happiness and peace, but step by step Gance leads the audience into a bloody drama: war in all its horror. The director shows the separation of two human beings who love each other, villages in ruin, the dead, the charge of soldiers in the mud and under fire. The hero, the poet Jean Diaz played by Romuald Joubé, returns from the Front to see his dying mother. Diaz, delirious, protests, "I accuse!" Then he sees a crowd of mothers mourning and in despair. The vision is even more strongly repeated in the last part; this time Diaz the visionary, the Christ of the trenches, as Gance names him, resurrects the war dead in the film's most powerful scene. Here corpses leave their tombs and march toward the villages to find out if their deaths served a purpose. Those who benefited from the war by getting rich, flee terrified. Jean Diaz dies amidst the general madness. The sober and pacifist film has shocked chauvinists, who have accused Gance of defeatism and antimilitarism. But the critics have been unanimous in declaring *J'accuse* a masterpiece. Gance calls it "a human cry against the bellicose din of armies." One discerns the influence of the American school, notably Thomas Ince. The photography by Léonce Burel is admirable as is Gance's editing, helped by the poet Blaise Cendrars.

The director considers J'accuse to be a tragedy of modern times.

A chaste heroine for Louis Feuillade

Paris, 25 April
Louis Feuillade has recovered his inspiration and his audience with *Tih Minh*, a serial in 12 episodes which is coming to the end of its successful run today. The title role of the fragile and innocent young Annamite is played by an English actress, Mary Harald. A gang of criminals plans to kidnap her, but René Cresté intervenes...

First National revels in the possession of Pickford

*Mary Pickford (center) sparkles in First National's film version of the popular bestseller **Daddy Long Legs**.*

Hollywood, 18 May

With the opening of *Daddy Long Legs*, a delightful new feature produced by her own company, and with the creation of United Artists just a few weeks ago, it's been a good year so far for Mary Pickford. By far the most important female star in Hollywood, Miss Pickford has become increasingly involved in the production of her films. She has looked forward to gaining full independence and, late last year, accepted a lucrative new offer from First National that Zukor at Paramount was unable (or unwilling?) to match. Thus, she started off in 1919 starring in a characteristically charming, real "Little Mary" role as the orphan who finds happiness with her benefactor in *Daddy Long Legs*, from Jean Webster's novel. Marshall Neilan directed, with Charles Rosher as cameraman in this first film for the Mary Pickford Corporation. At the same time, Mary has been one of the prime movers in the formation of UA, a new style of distribution company for the independents.

'Intolerance' freed, but it's mutilated

Paris, 12 May

Intolerance, considered the major work by D. W. Griffith, has finally reached Parisian screens. The film, made in the United States nearly three years ago, was at the time banned by the French military censors. The reason given was that the representation of French history was seriously one-sided and bigoted, in particular the dramatizing of the Saint Bartholomew Day massacre. In a period of the Sacred Union, the picturalization of the murder of the Huguenots by Catholics would have opened old wounds. However, since the Armistice was signed, Griffith's greatness has become universally recognized, and the French authorities have relented. Nevertheless, many scenes have still been cut from *Intolerance*. In an article today from the journal *Paris-Midi*, the young film critic Louis Delluc rails against the arbitrary cuts, which he claims have distorted the director's work and have rendered the film more or less incomprehensible.

Lillian Gish moves America to tears with her sensitive acting

New York, 1 June

The latest Griffith film, *True Heart Susie*, is the story of a naive country girl, too shy to find herself a husband. In the starring role, Lillian Gish confirms her exceptional talent. She personifies a sort of Cinderella, wearing a shapeless long dress, an apron and a ridiculous little hat.

Rarely has there been a more convincing and simple presence. Her skillful acting makes the sentimental story genuinely moving, and the character grows in stature from a funny, happy adolescent to become a dignified woman. And, a little more than two weeks ago, Gish had an even greater triumph in *Broken*

Blossoms, another admirable melodrama directed by Griffith. In this, she played a little girl battered to death by her alcoholic father. The distinguished director seems to be the young actress' Pygmalion, and she has never left him since their joint debut with *An Unseen Enemy* in 1912 at Biograph.

*Gish with Robert Harron in **True Heart Susie** (left), and with Richard Barthelmess in **Broken Blossoms**.*

Anita Stewart, star of this film, under contract to Vitagraph since 1911.

Bout-de-Zan (1912) replaced Bébé.

1914. At the start of his career, Chaplin's face was advertised by this poster.

Made by French-Belgian Abel Gance in 1912, this film was never released.

1918. One of eight films directed by Roscoe Arbuckle that year.

Adrien Barère's poster for George Monca's 1911 film starred Chevalier.

By 1910, Nickelodeons were giving way to cinema theaters, and production companies such as this one were mushrooming across the U.S.

A French poster for a 1912 comedy made by the prolific Mack Sennett.

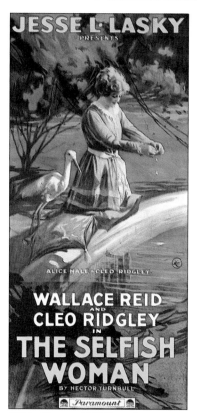

1916. Cleo wed Wallace for money.

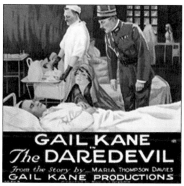

1918. Gail Kane played a French girl forced to live as a boy in the U.S.

1919. Chaplin was a hotel odd-jobs man, with Edna Purviance as his co-star.

1918. The first film from star Mabel Normand's new company.

1916. Two reformed crooks...

1914. Bobby inherited $300,000...

1919. Madge Evans as an orphan.

THE GIRL, THE COP, THE BURGLAR

1914. Wally Beery, Ruth Hennessy.

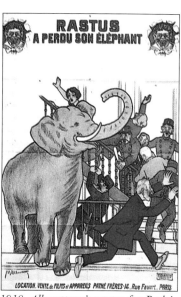

1910. Allouetteau's poster for Pathé.

The Silent Era

The American film industry grew out of the rivalry of a handful of streetwise immigrants. Like small boys squabbling in a sandpit, they staked out their territory, and in the process transformed a turn-of-the-century novelty into a multi-million-dollar business. By the early 1920s motion pictures were America's fifth-ranking industry.

For the next 25 years the movies were dominated by the studio system which had evolved during the years of the First World War. While European and, later, American troops were locked in the trench warfare of the Western Front, Adolph Zukor, Carl Laemmle and William Fox consolidated their grip on the motion picture business. When the U.S. emerged from the conflict, physically unscathed and economically buoyant, the movie moguls were able to draw on, and reflect the feeling of, a country on the move. Douglas Fairbanks' ebullient go-getters had caught the confident mood of America in the war years. Soon Clara Bow's Jazz Age flappers, Tom Mix's daredevil chases and Harold Lloyd's cliff-hanging encounters with skyscrapers would celebrate the rapidly changing social and physical landscape of America in the 1920s.

A key moment came in 1924 with the merger of Marcus Loew's Metro Picture Corporation with the Goldwyn Company and Mayer Pictures, (in both of which Loew had a controlling interest) to form Metro-Goldwyn-Mayer, or MGM as it became universally known. The head of Mayer Pictures was Louis B. Mayer, a Russian-Jewish immigrant who in 1907 had moved from scrap-dealing into motion pictures, turning base metal into gold. He made his money distributing D.W. Griffith's landmark film, *The Birth of a Nation*, on the Northeastern seaboard and then moved into production, displaying an early interest in leading actresses in romantic melodramas, handled by director John M. Stahl. Mayer was appointed as vice president and general manager of MGM. As part of a financial empire with powerful banking connections and a ready-made market in the form of Marcus Loew's extensive chain of movie theaters, MGM was well placed to challenge the

supremacy of Adolph Zukor's creation called the Paramount Pictures Corporation.

At MGM, Mayer's right-hand man and production supervisor was a 25-year-old graduate of business studies, Irving Thalberg. Six years earlier Thalberg had so impressed Carl Laemmle, head of Universal, that he had become Laemmle's private secretary. A year later he accompanied Laemmle to California and, at the age of 20, was appointed studio manager at Universal City. When Laemmle was away in New York, Thalberg was effectively in charge. The upward trajectory of Thalberg's career shows how the studios developed in the early 1920s as the expanding scope of their

Thalberg was that of the spiraling cost of the Goldwyn Company's *Ben-Hur*, which was being shot on location in Italy. Thalberg moved swiftly to replace its leading man, George Walsh, with Ramon Novarro, and director Charles Brabin with Fred Niblo. Then he brought the unit back home and filmed the chariot race sequences in California before closely supervising the editing. The strain on Thalberg's weak constitution (he had been sickly since childhood) was so great that he watched the rushes from a hospital bed. The $4 million *Ben-Hur* made no money but it attracted huge audiences, and the prestige won by its production values rubbed off on MGM and set its future tone.

Gold Diggers of Broadway (Warner Bros., 1929) directed by Roy del Ruth.

activities demanded ever-increasing supervision and control. At Universal, Thalberg locked horns with the *enfant terrible* of Hollywood, Erich von Stroheim, when the costs of *Foolish Wives* climbed over $1 million in 1920. Similarly, when costs began escalating on *Merry-Go-Round* (1923), Thalberg replaced Von Stroheim with the less interesting but more pliable Rupert Julian. Shortly afterwards Mayer poached Thalberg from Universal, reportedly after the latter declined to marry Laemmle's daughter Rosabelle. In the newly created MGM, Thalberg found himself toe-to-toe with his old sparring partner Von Stroheim, whose 42-reel epic *Greed* he ordered to be cut to a manageable length.

Another problem inherited by

Thalberg's tact and discretion, and his tidy accountant's mind, contrasted with Mayer's vulgar bluster, enhancing the status of an industry which craved respectability. It was as if Mayer and Thalberg were playing a variation on the old interrogation theme – that of the nice and the nasty policeman. Those who were appalled by Mayer's bullying and crassness were sure to be disarmed by Thalberg's apparent rapport with MGM's creative personnel. But 'The Boy Wonder', as Thalberg was nicknamed, could not singlehandedly shoulder this burden. Control was exercised by a system of producers. At MGM production values would always remain high, if slightly hollow, so that beneath the studio's gloss lay an un-

derlying blandness.

Despite his intimate involvement, Thalberg's name rarely appeared on screen. He once observed, "Credit you give yourself isn't worth having." The names that filmgoers looked for were those of the stars, of whom MGM boasted that they had 'more than there are in heaven'. In 1927 Thalberg married one of the brightest of them all, Norma Shearer, MGM's 'First Lady of the Screen'. The studios were sustained by the star system, and enormous care was taken to package and present stars as fabulous creatures who inhabited a world far removed from the daily lives of their fans. The public wanted its idols to be different, and many of them were, though image and reality were often hopelessly confused. The remarkable wedding which independent producer Sam Goldwyn arranged in 1927 for two of his stars, Vilma Banky and Rod La Roque, was stage-managed as if it were the climax of one of the romantic melodramas in which Banky shared top billing with Ronald Colman. Even the wedding cake, rivaling a small baroque church, turned out to be a papier maché prop. Indeed, when asked by a journalist what names she favored for her first child, Banky replied, apparently without irony, "I don't know, you'll have to ask Mr. Goldwyn."

The rewards for such compliance included huge and virtually untaxed salaries. Mary Pickford, of whom Adolph Zukor remarked that she had a mind like a cash register, began her movie career at Biograph in 1909 at a salary of $5. When, in 1919, she left First National to co-found United Artists, she was earning $350,000 a picture. Her negotiating skills, and those of Chaplin, not only paved the way for other high salary earners but also enabled stars to become independent producers. In 1926 Gloria Swanson turned down Paramount's offer to renew her contract at $18,000 a week and went to United Artists to produce her own films at a salary of $20,000 a week, bankrolled by her then-lover Joseph Kennedy.

Dreams of independence could also lead to disaster. Charles Ray was, in the early 1920s, the archetypal 'Country Boy' star of pictures which celebrated the rustic innocence of America. Success went to Ray's head. He formed his own company and went spectacularly bankrupt after the failure of the million-dollar epic, *The Courtship of Miles Standish*. Threatened with ruin, he threw a lavish party. When asked how he was going to pay for it, Ray replied, "Credit."

Credit was seldom extended to fallen stars, but the studios happily encouraged them to overspend. By putting themselves in debt, they effectively mortgaged any prospect of independence. In the early years of Hollywood, the movie colony lived in unpretentious hotels. Now these were forsaken for the comic opera châteaux and mock baronial mansions which their owners considered appropriate to their elevated status.

Night life arrived in Hollywood to cater to celebrities and would-be celebrities. In May 1921 the Cocoanut Grove opened at the Ambassador Hotel, decorated with palm trees left over from *The Sheik*, but scandal was bubbling away beneath the glittering surface. Anita Loos wrote of the early 1920s, "To place in the limelight a great number of people who ordinarily would be chambermaids and chauffeurs, and give them unlimited power and wealth, is bound to produce lively results." Successive scandals rocked Hollywood: the manslaughter trial of Roscoe 'Fatty' Arbuckle; the drug addiction which killed Wallace Reid; and the unsolved murder of director William Desmond Taylor, to name but three. In the wake of the Arbuckle affair, Will Hays, President Harding's Postmaster General, was appointed as a kind of moral watchdog over Hollywood, and studios introduced 'morality clauses' into their contracts. It was left to Elinor Glyn to supply a tart assessment of the underlying Hollywood dynamic. After Arbuckle's fall from grace, she was asked what would happen next. Miss Glyn replied, "Whatever makes most money."

Hollywood money enabled the major studios to raid Europe for talent, particularly Germany, where postwar angst had fueled a 'golden age' of Expressionist film whose environments of stylized sets, lighting and performances were well-suited to silent cinema. At Paramount the heavyweight German star Emil Jannings hovered over the studio like a giant Zeppelin. Other Paramount imports included the ex-

otic Pola Negri, the first big European star to be lured to California; art directors Hans Dreier and Ernst Fegte and, finally, director Ernst Lubitsch of the legendary lightness of touch, who worked at Warners but naturally gravitated to Paramount, where he found his true home. The marriage between Berlin and Hollywood reached its apogee at Fox in 1927 with *Sunrise*, directed by F.W. Murnau, adapted from a Hermann Sudermann novel by Carl Mayer, designed by Rochus Gliese, and played by a typical American cast led by Janet Gaynor. The result was a remarkable combination of American optimism and German pessimism, in which Murnau's mobile camera moved majestically through exquisitely lit sets.

Sunrise was one of the last great peaks of silent cinema. In 1926 a John Barrymore vehicle, *Don Juan*,

*Laurel (right) and Hardy in **Early to Bed** (1928), supervised by Leo McCarey.*

was the first feature film to be released with sound effects and music, but no dialogue, synchronized on disc. In October 1927 the sound barrier was finally broken by the Warner brothers and Al Jolson informing ecstatic audiences that "you ain't heard nothin' yet!" in *The Jazz Singer*. It was essentially a silent film tricked out with a few dialogue and musical sequences, but its success encouraged Warners to release their first all-talking film, *Lights of New York*. Reluctantly, the other studios followed suit, and within a matter of months silent cinema was virtually a thing of the past.

In the early days of cinema the insensitive, orthochromatic film stock, requiring strong light, had mercilessly exposed every line and

wrinkle in the faces of the middle-aged stage stars who tried their hand in the movies. The intimacy of the medium, and its punishing schedules, demanded the fresh faces, youthful energy and well-defined personalities of the young hopefuls assembled by Griffith at Biograph. The arrival of the microphone created a new friction between the stars and the technology which brought them to the screen. When Douglas Fairbanks recorded a spoken prologue for his last silent feature, *The Iron Mask* (1929), his stentorian delivery drove the microphone back 10 yards. Clara Bow's habit of restlessly dashing about the set posed acute problems for the crude new apparatus. Above all, survival or a ticket to oblivion depended on the marriage of voice and screen personality. Norma Talmadge was betrayed by her Brooklyn twang in the 18th-century setting of *Du Barry, Woman of Passion* (1930). John Gilbert's intense style – so electrifying opposite Garbo in *Flesh and the Devil* (1927) – seemed absurd when he wooed a wooden Catherine Dale Owen in his first talking feature, *His Glorious Night* (1929). His voice, light but by no means the laughable squeak of legend, was simply not the voice that Gilbert's silent fans had heard in their minds when he had melted into the arms of Garbo. His acting, choreographed to the rhythms of the universal language of silent cinema, now seemed like so much posturing.

Gilbert succumbed to the ravages of disappointment and alcohol in 1936. Fairbanks, Pickford, Bow and Swanson made a handful of talkies, but they were now too closely asso-

ciated with a cinema of the past to survive the arrival of sound. Swanson's subsequent comeback as the crazed silent movie queen Norma Desmond in *Sunset Boulevard* (1950) was ripe with irony. Nevertheless, there were far more survivors than casualties of sound. Among the stars who made the transition were John Barrymore, Laurel and Hardy, Ronald Colman, Gary Cooper, Mary Astor, William Powell, Norma Shearer, Adolphe Menjou and, after an agonizing wait, Greta Garbo. (Chaplin was by some years the last).

In the 1920s, France recovered from the ravages of World War I to foster a cinema which accommodated the extravagant technical ambitions of Abel Gance, the whimsical comedy of René Clair and the surrealist experiments of the avant-garde, the first people to recognize film as an art form – the most notable product of which was the collaboration between Spaniards Salvador Dali and Luis Buñuel on the film *Un chien andalou* (1928).

In 1920 a copy of *The Birth of a Nation* reached Moscow. Three years later Griffith was invited to take charge of film production in the Soviet Union. He declined this intriguing offer, but his work exercised a profound influence on another great director, Sergei M. Eisenstein. Like Griffith, Eisenstein was a man of the theater who turned to films in 1924, at a time when Russian cinema was at a very low ebb. However, the decision in 1925 to permit non-naturalistic and avant-garde expression in the arts in the Soviet Union paved the way for a burst of creative energy in Soviet film led by the stirring propagandist Eisenstein, the fiercely theoretical V.I. Pudovkin, the intensely lyrical Dovzhenko and the bustling Bolshevik idealist and pioneer of *cinéma vérité*, Dziga Vertov. Sadly, by 1928 the dead hand of socialist realism was starting to exert a stifling grip on Soviet cinema. The last masterpiece of the silent era was Alexander Dovzhenko's *Earth*, made in the Soviet Union in 1930. In America preparations were being made to show Eisenstein's *October*, which had already met a hostile reception from the Party hierarchy. But the talkies were now all the rage, and *October* was not screened in the U.S. until years later. A new era in cinema was about to begin.

ROBIN CROSS

1920

★ ★

France, 24 January
Jean Renoir has married Andrée Heuschling, known as Dédée. She was formerly the model for the filmmaker's famous artist-father, Auguste Renoir.

London, 25 January
Doctor Elias, who is renowned for his research in optics, has developed Colorama, a new process for the cinema using natural colors.

New York, January
Loew's Incorporated have taken over the five-year-old company, Metro Pictures. Marcus Loew is to continue as president.

Paris, 1 February
After the referendum by the daily *Comœdia* for the five best films – Cecil B. DeMille's *The Cheat* and Charlie Chaplin's *Shoulder Arms* topped the list – *Filma* magazine has given up the idea of an opinion poll for the five worst films: there are too many of them.

Washington, 5 February
The undersecretary of state for the interior, F.K. Lane, has suggested to the heads of film companies that they help their country by making anti-Bolshevik propaganda films.

Copenhagen, 9 February
Carl Dreyer has released his film *President* (*Praesidenten*), which stars Halvard Hoff and Elith Pio.

Paris, 10 February
Cinema professionals gathered at the Palais d'Orsay in order to celebrate Louis Lumière's election to the Académie des Sciences on 15 December. But Auguste Lumière declined the invitation, acknowledging his brother as the inventor of the Cinematograph.

Rome, 9 March
Giuseppe Barattolo and his UCI group have signed an agreement with German counterpart UFA with the goal of eventually controlling the European market.

Hollywood, 16 March
The release of Maurice Tourneur's screen adaptation of Robert Louis Stevenson's novel, *Treasure Island*. This has been made into a 55-minute film starring Lon Chaney, Shirley Mason and Charles Ogle.

California, 31 March
The celebrated Belgian-born writer Maurice Maeterlinck, author of *Pelléas and Mélisande*, has been invited to Hollywood under contract to producer Samuel Goldwyn.

Paris, 5 April
In his editorial in the daily *Paris-Midi*, Maurice de Waleffe is severely critical of the American invasion of French screens. He suggests these films be banned.

Brussels, 20 April
In *la Libre Belgique*, the journalist Vendabole qualifies cinema lovers as "clods" and concludes that "the cinema is harmful because it renders people mindless."

Pennsylvania, 30 April
The first trains containing cinema carriages have been put into service by the Pittsburgh Harmony Butler Rail Company.

Cairo, 7 May
The Egyptian financier Talat Harb Pacha has created the Misr Bank and has announced plans to develop the cinema industry here.

New York, 31 May
Louis B. Mayer has set up Louis B. Mayer Productions Incorporated with a capital of $5 million.

Hollywood, 15 June
Max Linder has sold his car and mortgaged various personal effects to finance his new film, *Seven Years' Bad Luck*. Filming has started at Universal City.

Shanghai, 30 June
The opera singer Mei Lanfang is playing a servant in *The Fragrance of Spring Makes it Difficult to Study*, produced by the Commercial Press company from an adaptation of the play *The Pavillion of Peonies*.

New York, 13 July
D.W. Griffith has floated 500,000 shares in the new D.W. Griffith Corporation to order to finance his new studios at Mamaroneck, near New York.

Paris, 18 July
The market porters from Les Halles have invited Mary Pickford and Douglas Fairbanks to come visit the "stomach of Paris".

London, 31 July
According to a competition planned by *The Picture Show* magazine, Mary Pickford and Douglas Fairbanks are Britain's favorite stars.

Berlin, 1 September
Ernst Lubitsch's *Sumurun*, adapted from an oriental pantomime by the producer Max Reinhardt, with Pola Negri, Jenny Hasselquist and Paul Wegener, with Lubitsch himself in the role of the little hunchback, is currently showing.

Paris, 5 September
The young American star, Olive Stone, has been found dead from bichloride poisoning in her hotel room at the Ritz. She was on vacation in Paris with her husband Jack Pickford, Mary's brother. It is still not known whether it was suicide or an accident.

London, 10 September
During his visit to London, the American producer Jesse L. Lasky signed up a number of well-known writers such as Sir James Barrie, the author of *Peter Pan*, and H.G. Wells to work with future film projects for Paramount. He is even attempting to persuade George Bernard Shaw to come into the fold.

Paris, 10 September
The philosopher Henri Bergson has been quoted in *le Cinema*: "The cinematograph interests me, as do all inventions. It is capable of suggesting new thoughts to the philosopher. It could help in the synthesis of memory or thought."

Hollywood, 25 October
Film director Rex Ingram has started shooting the super-production entitled *The Four Horsemen of the Apocalypse*, at Metro studios. His wife Alice Terry is playing the lead with Wallace Beery and a young unknown, Rudolph Valentino.

Berlin, 29 October
Paul Wegener has brought out his second adaptation of Meyrenk's novel of the fantastic, *The Golem*.

France, 30 October
Abel Gance has continued filming on *la Rose du rail* at Arcachon. The film continues to be made under a cloud – Gance's companion Ida Danis is dying.

Paris, 30 November
Fatty Arbuckle, the American comedian was given a warm welcome by his fans at Saint-Lazare station. But they decided against carrying him in triumph: he weighs 120 kg.

New York, 28 December
The cinema, one of America's leading industries, is in a crisis due to a lack of overseas markets. Production has been reduced by 50 percent, putting 5,000 people out of work.

China, 31 December
To date, China has produced 35 full-length films (33 in Shanghai and two in Hong Kong), numerous short films and documentaries.

BIRTHS

Italy, 20 January
Federico Fellini

Sweden, 28 February
Alf Kjellin

France, 29 February
Michèle Morgan (Simone Roussel)

France, 21 March
Eric Rohmer (Maurice Scherer)

China, 1 April
Toshiro Mifune

Paris, 15 May
Michel Audiard

Paris, 24 August
Jean Desailly

New York, 23 September
Mickey Rooney (Joe Yule Jr.)

Nebraska, 17 October
Montgomery Clift

New York, 20 November
Gene Tierney

Sweden, 29 December
Viveca Lindfors

DEATHS

Mario Caserini

The Cabinet of Dr. Caligari, directed by Robert Wiene, has been received with enthusiastic acclaim. Its imaginative narrative and visual effects reflect German Expressionism.

Robert Wiene reveals Germany's weird fantasies

Werner Krauss as the sinister Doctor Caligari, with Lil Dagover.

Conrad Veidt as the mad doctor's unfortunate servant, made to murder.

Berlin, 27 February
An extraordinary film, *The Cabinet of Dr. Caligari*, has opened in Germany. Following the recent successes of Ernst Lubitsch and Pola Negri and of new director Fritz Lang, it appears that the German cinema is making a remarkable and rapid postwar recovery. *Caligari*, produced by Erich Pommer, written by Hans Janowitz and Carl Mayer, and directed by Robert Wiene, is an astonishing attempt to translate the imagery of German Expressionist painting and design to the cinema screen. Most impressive of all are the stylized and painted canvas sets. Designers Herman Warm, Walter Reimann and Walter Röhrig collaborated closely on the production, in which they make remarkable use of deliberately distorted perspectives – narrow slanting streets that slice across each other at unexpected angles – that are matched by the mesmerizingly strange performances of Werner Krauss as Caligari and Conrad Veidt as the somnambulist.

The 1001 nights of Louis Nalpas

Paris, 2 January
The Sultan of Love, a tale from *A Thousand and One Nights*, directed by René Le Somptier and Charles Burguet, has been one of the great successes of French cinema since its release last December. The producer, Louis Nalpas, invested a great deal of money in this film including inviting 50 artists to stencil-color all the images to render it even more sumptuous. It will be an enormous task, which should be completed in one to two years. For the moment, *The Sultan of Love* continues to seduce the public. Nalpas has managed to compete with Hollywood.

Charlie Chaplin and Max Linder, each a student, both masters

Los Angeles, 16 February
At the airport, while they waited to catch an airplane together, Charlie Chaplin and Max Linder were interviewed by the American correspondent of the French weekly magazine *Comœdia* about the recent poll on the world's five best films. Asked about their personal favorites, the two famous comedians paid each other diplomatic homage. Chaplin opined that the five most notable films were, naturally, made by Max Linder. His traveling companion averred that, on the contrary, the best ones could only be films featuring Charles Chaplin. At the end of this whimsical exchange, Chaplin and Linder talked about the close

Their mutual professional admiration has grown into friendship.

friendship they have enjoyed since 1917, which began when the French actor-director put in a brief stint at Essanay where Charlie was at work. Linder's wartime sojourn in America came to an abrupt end in mid-1917. He had completed only three films when, sadly, he contracted double pneumonia and was forced to spend nearly a year convalescing in a sanitarium in Switzerland. His health has never fully recovered from gas poisoning sustained during war service. Now Max Linder has crossed the Atlantic again in a fresh attempt to reconquer the American market – no easy task and one in which he might benefit from Charlie Chaplin's counsel.

John Barrymore delivers an awesome incarnation of pure evil

New York, 2 April
John Barrymore, sweet prince of Broadway's leading family, has been dabbling in films since 1913 when he made his screen debut in Famous Players' *An American Citizen*. He has saved his serious energies for the stage, but now, with his twelfth film *Dr. Jekyll and Mr. Hyde*, he has come into his own. The 38-year-old Barrymore makes a handsome Dr. Jekyll, but when he downs the doctor's fatal potion he turns into a monstrous vision of pure evil before our very eyes. The chilling effect is completed with some skillful screen trickery. The sight of Jekyll's fingers dissolving into claws is followed by a close-up of Barrymore's Hyde in terrifying makeup. This Hyde is a hideous spider-like creature who scuttles on crooked legs. Soon, the transformation begins to take place unaided by the evil elixir. While Dr. Jekyll sleeps, an enormous phantom spider crawls across the floor of his bedroom, settles on top of him and melts into his body. Jekyll wakes from feverish sleep as Hyde. In a strong supporting cast, sultry Nita Naldi is outstanding as the sexual temptation placed in Jekyll's way by Brandon Hurst's cynical Sir George

Carewe. At Hyde's hands she becomes, quite literally, a shadow of her former self. *Dr. Jekyll and Mr. Hyde* will cement Barrymore's popularity with cinemagoers, although his theatrical posturing throughout the film has attracted some adverse comment. The reviewer in *Variety*

observed that, for all the makeup, Hyde "was always Jack Barrymore", adding somewhat carpingly that "in one instance of alteration of personality, the director and/or star found it necessary to change the star's clothes as well as his individuality with the aid of drugs."

Louis Wolheim (left) in the clutches of Barrymore's hideous Mr. Hyde.

America's favorite little sweetheart could be guilty of bigamy

Hollywood, 14 April
There has been another Hollywood scandal. The Attorney General of California has decided to prosecute Mary Pickford, whom he accuses of perjury and bigamy. This odd circumstance has followed the actress's recent marriage to Douglas Fairbanks on 28 March. For some years, the extramarital liaison between the two stars, both among the highest paid of the American cinema, has filled the gossip columns of newspapers. Pickord had been married to the charming actor Owen Moore, whom she met on the set at Biograph in 1913. Their divorce, announced in Minden, Nevada last March, upset the innumerable admirers of "America's Sweetheart". At the time, she declared that she did not envisage any remarriage in the immediate future. Nevertheless, less than a month later, the two co-founders of United Artists were married secretly in a small Hollywood church. Fairbanks himself had

just divorced Ann Beth Sully. To those who were astonished to see the star's recent statement contradicted, she replied, "Yes, I've changed my mind! Isn't that a woman's prerogative?" These light-hearted comments

were badly timed, as the law is taking an even greater interest in the escapades of Hollywood. Ignoring the controversy, the young couple are getting ready to pay an extended visit to Europe.

The two stars have regularized a liaison which was the talk of the town.

Harold impaired but not disabled

Hollywood, 10 July
Comedian Harold Lloyd, who suffered a serious accident one year ago, has been making a remarkable recovery, and his latest two-reeler, *High and Dizzy*, co-starring Mildred Davis and directed by Hal Roach, has just opened. While Lloyd posed for a gag photo at the Witzel studio in downtown L.A. last August, a prop bomb exploded and almost killed him. Forced to spend a long period in the hospital and convalescing thereafter, the actor has made a complete recovery but has lost the thumb and forefinger of his right hand. Since Lloyd had finished four two-reelers prior to his accident, Pathé was able to spread their release to meet the growing demand for his comedies during his absence. By last autumn Harold was already back at work at the newly constructed Roach studio in Culver City, completing *Haunted Spooks*, the comedy he was filming at the time of his accident. In fact he had only graduated to two-reelers early in 1919, the first of which, the appropriately named *Bumping into Broadway*, had a special New York opening in November. At that time Lloyd made a rare trip back East to meet Charles Pathé and to celebrate the signing of a new contract with producer Hal Roach – and beheld his name in lights for the first time on the marquees of two of the largest movie theaters, the Strand and the Rialto. He can now only move forward on the road to success.

Harold Lloyd with Bebe Daniels.

Gish sisters on both sides of the camera

Dorothy Gish remodeling her husband, James Rennie, for director Lillian.

Hollywood, 13 July
Lillian Gish, that wonderful star of so many D.W. Griffith films, has taken to directing. Although there is little evidence in *Remodeling Her Husband* that she will become a rival to her master and mentor, she has managed to demonstrate her imagination and competence. Admitted-ly, most of the laughter is provoked by the brilliant comic performance given by her sister Dorothy Gish in the main role as the vivacious heroine who, in a series of amusing episodes, teaches her smug husband (James Rennie) to appreciate her. She dominates the picture with her gift for pantomime.

Erich von Stroheim unlocks another door

Hollywood, 20 August
Stroheim has done it again! If there were ever any doubts regarding the quality of his talent as a director, they can now be set to rest. His latest film, *The Devil's Pass Key*, has just opened here to rave reviews and enthusiastic applause following the New York premiere earlier this month. According to the correspondent of *Billboard* magazine, who was present at that event, "Despite sweltering heat an SRO audience was held rapt with the enthralling interest, realism and charm so admirably pictured." Based on a story by the Baroness de Meyer entitled *Clothes and Treachery*, the new film is set in Paris immediately after the Great War and continues Stroheim's Universal studio formula of sophisticated sex, seduction and intrigue within a Continental setting. Stroheim himself does not appear as an actor in this one, however, as in *Blind Husbands*, the heroine is a dissatisfied wife (played by Una Trevelyan) who gets herself into trouble, and her well-meaning husband is played by Sam De Grasse, the husband from the previous film. Although the picture was completed and even previewed earlier this year, the Universal publicity department has been so eager to get the greatest possible mileage out of Stroheim's name that the release was delayed until now. The director has, in fact, signed a new and lucrative contract with the studio.

Fillmore, George and Busch.

Maurice Tourneur attacked by French press

*Maurice Tourneur (wearing glasses) on the set directing **Treasure Island.***

Paris, 16 July
Louis Delluc is furious. Using his *Paris-Midi* column, he has clearly lambasted those who, in their profession as journalists, have been challenging the right of the director Maurice Tourneur to return to the U.S. On 21 April, Jean-Louis Croze, in his contribution to *Comœdia*, reproached Tourneur for having spent the war years in America, and for having thus "saved his life, while so many of his compatriots lost theirs." Delluc believes that there is an arbitrary smear campaign motivated by "a treacherous chorus of bitter, sick, jealous and rancorous failures." In 1914, because he spoke English well, Maurice Tourneur (real name Maurice Thomas) was sent to the United States to direct the American productions of Eclair at its Fort Lee, New Jersey, studios. He had been an assistant director with the company since 1911. The following year, he graduated to director and quickly gained a reputation for the pictorial quality of his work. During the last six years, he has become one of Hollywood's most respected directors, ranking only behind Griffith and Thomas Ince in popularity. The films of Tourneur (formerly a book illustrator and poster designer) are remarkable for their decors and composition. This is well-suited to fantasies such as *The Wishing Ring* (1914), *Trilby* (1915) and *The Blue Bird* (1920), outstanding examples of his ability to create a fairy-tale world. His latest picture is an adaptation of Stevenson's *Treasure Island*. As a young man, Tourneur served with the French artillery in North Africa, afterwards working as an assistant at the atelier of the sculptor Rodin. Instead of criticizing Tourneur's decision to work in the United States, the French should feel proud to have a compatriot of such stature.

The tragic death of Suzanne Grandais

One of France's best-loved stars.

Paris, 1 September
The funeral of Suzanne Grandais was held this morning at the cemetery in Montmartre. A large crowd of mourners came to pay their last respects. On 28 August the popular young actress was tragically killed in a car accident while returning with director Charles Burguet from shooting her last film, *l'Essor*. She was born Suzanne Gueudret in Paris on 14 June 1893.

Great loss for Griffith as Gish goes

New York, 20 September
A few days after the release of the highly praised film, *Way Down East*, D.W. Griffith temporarily broke Lillian Gish's contract. Gish, considered to be too independent, rejoined the Frohman Amusement Company on a three-year contract. It is thought that because of Grif-

fith's financial difficulties, he can no longer afford her salary. The director's decision, whatever the reasons, could have dire results. Lillian Gish is shocked, because she has always regarded their association as sacrosanct. Together, Gish and Griffith have made dozens of successful films. The triumph of *Way Down*

East, for example, owed much to the charismatic actress, overpowering in her role as an unmarried young mother, pushed to despair. To try and fill the gap left by her absence, Griffith has now returned to Carol Dempster, whom he first directed in *The Girl Who Stayed At Home* and in two films since.

Lillian Gish and Richard Barthelmess in the poignant Way Down East.

Gabrielle Réjane is, sadly, no more

Paris, 29 October
The last film made by the great actress Gabrielle Réjane, who died on 14 June, has been released. In *Miarka, la fille à l'ours*, which is directed by Louis Mercanton, Desdemona Mazza plays Miarka, a little gypsy raised by the sorcerer Vougne who sees the future with the aid of her magic books. Réjane is Vougne and handles the part with her usual skill. Born Gabrielle Réju, she had a glittering theatrical career, covering half a century, and many compared her with Sarah Bernhardt. She was able to move easily between a comedy like *Madame Sans-Gêne* (which was also adapted for the screen) and tragedy such as *Germinie Lacerteux*. The public loved her cheeky banter, and the Parisian accent which she could drop at will. Sadly, heart trouble has meant that she has not been seen in public since 1919. In *Miarka*, which was shot in the South of France, the famous writer Jean Richepin, author of the book on which the film was based, takes on the role of the lord of the manor.

Wife trouble turns Charlie into kidnapper

Los Angeles, 19 November
Mildred Harris can draw grim satisfaction from the fact that the divorce proceedings which she opened against Charlie Chaplin last August have come to a conclusion. She has been awarded $100,000 and a share

of the community property acquired since their marriage in October 1918. The ruling is the outcome of protracted wrangling between Chaplin and his wife's lawyers. From the outset, her lawyers threatened to attach the negatives of Chaplin's latest film, *The Kid*, as part of the settlement. Chaplin made his own arrangements. At the beginning of August he left California in conditions of the greatest secrecy, taking with him over 200,000 feet of the completed film. Holed up with two assistants in a hotel in Salt Lake City, Chaplin set to work editing the film. Mildred's lawyers eventually relented, waiving all claim to *The Kid* and leaving Chaplin in sole possession of the rights to the film. *The Kid*, in which Charlie co-stars with six-year-old Jackie Coogan, has cost Chaplin $300,000 and taken 18 months to film. The emotional cost of the divorce has been as high, to which must be added a public brawl between Chaplin and producer Louis B. Mayer, who has been promoting Harris' career.

With six-year-old Jackie Coogan.

United Artists makes its mark with 'Zorro'

Los Angeles, 5 December
Crowds are already forming to see *The Mark of Zorro*, the latest film starring Douglas Fairbanks. The energetic actor has taken a risk by breaking the embargo on costume pictures. It has been a common belief in the motion picture industry that period pieces play to empty theaters. In case his new venture

failed, Fairbanks decided to make it quickly and cheaply. He need not have worried. The story tells of Don Diego Vega, an effete nobleman in 19th-century California, who disguises himself as the dashing masked Zorro, protector of the weak and innocent. Doug is at his bouncy best, and the director, Fred Niblo has kept the pace lively.

Douglas Fairbanks protects Marguerite de la Motte from Robert McKim.

1921

★ ★ ★ ★ ★ ★ ★ ★ **1921** ★

Stockholm, 1 January
Victor Sjöström has released his film version of Selma Lagerlöf's popular novel, *Körkärlen* (*The Phantom Carriage*), starring himself and Hilda Borgström.

Paris, 10 January
Daniel Bompard's film *Une brute* (*A Beast*), with André Noix, has been banned by the censors.

Paris, 9 March
A Gaumont documentary on the transformation of engines of war into tractors was shown to deputies at the Palais-Bourbon.

Paris, 26 March
The opening session (by invitation) of the Madeleine cinema took place yesterday evening. Two American films were screened: *Wolves of the Night* with William Farnum and a Mary Pickford offering, *Little Lord Fauntleroy*.

France, 25 April
To the delight of all the inhabitants of Pérouges, Henri Diamant-Berger and his film team have arrived at the town's medieval site to continue filming *The Three Musketeers*.

Montceau-les-Mines, 1 May
René Leprince seized the occasion of the local Labor Day parade to take shots for his film *l'Empereur des pauvres* (*Emperor of the Poor*).

New York, 10 May
Abel Gance has held a preview of the American version of his film *J'accuse* (*I Accuse*), for the press and cinema owners at the Ritz. The title is already well known because of the acclaim it received from critics after its London release.

Paris, 15 May
There has been an alarming drop in cinema attendance in the capital due to the current heat wave. Very few cinemas are equiped with adequate ventilation.

Pompeii, 24 May
Luitz-Morat, the French filmmaker, received special permission from the Italian Minister for Fine Arts to shoot scenes for *la Terre du diable* among the famous ruins. The stars are Gaston Modot and Yvonne Aurel, and even Vesuvius played its role by erupting.

Pyrenees, 7 June
Pearl White has been found safe. The famous American star lost her way during an excursion on horseback in the mountains. After finding a rough shelter, she slept for 16 hours before being rescued by a local shepherd.

Paris, 10 June
A memorable quote appears in the latest issue of Louis Delluc's magazine, *Cinéa*. "There is", it says, "a great actor in *l'Atlantide* made by Jacques Feyder: it is the sand."

Paris, 15 June
According to *Ciné-Journal*, the biggest cinema in the world is the 8,000-seat Capitol in New York.

Hollywood, 1 July
Douglas Fairbanks has vowed "never to put a foot in France again." The reason is that his interpretation of D'Artagnan, in the American version of *The Three Musketeers*, directed by Fred Niblo, received bad press from the French.

Berlin, 14 July
The actress Henny Porten has married Dr. Wilhelm von Kaufmann, who has finally decided to give up his medical practice to devote himself to producing his wife's films.

France, 17 July
Séverin-Mars, the well-known star of Abel Gance's *J'accuse* (*I Accuse*) and the yet to be released *la Roue* (*The Wheel*), has died unexpectedly while vacationing on the banks of the Seine. He just made his debut as a filmmaker with *le Cœur magnifique* (*The Magnificent Heart*).

Paris, 22 July
The French public may never see the boxing match between Frenchman Georges Carpentier and the American Jack Dempsey which finished in the latter's favor. French distributors are refusing to pay Fox, who hold the rights to the match, the asking price of 700,000 francs.

New York, 31 August
D.W. Griffith has spent $150,000 building a replica of an 18th-century French village at the Mamaroneck studios for his film *Orphans of the Storm*, based on a popular French melodrama. The set is to be burned as soon as filming is over.

Paris, 5 September
Aimé Simon-Girard, D'Artagnan in Henri Diamant-Berger's film *The Three Musketeers*, has bought the horse he rode in the film. They can be seen together in the Bois.

Moscow, 15 September
S.M. Eisenstein has been admitted to the GVIRM (State Filmmakers Institute of Higher Education), headed by V.E. Meyerhold.

Nice, 19 September
The prefect of the Alpes-Maritimes, Armand Bernard, has decided to ban all films with scenes of crime, theft or murder from his region.

Paris, 20 September
Louis Delluc's criticisms and notes on Chaplin's work have been published under the title *Charlot*.

Paris, 15 October
Sirène have published *Bonjour Cinéma*, the first book by Jean Epstein. Epstein has also just made his debut in films as director Louis Delluc's assistant director on *le Tonnerre*.

Moscow, 18 November
Lenin has published his *Thesis on Propaganda and Production*: the cinema must be used in the service of ideological development.

Paris, 2 December
Abel Gance is still editing *la Roue* (*The Wheel*). Shooting finished last year, but cutting is a long process. The filmmaker is said to have exposed 277,863 metres of negative.

New York, 6 December
Release of *Be My Wife*, produced and directed by Max Linder, who also stars alongside Alta Allen and Caroline Rankin.

Paris, 16 December
The film *Pour Don Carlos* (*For Don Carlos*), co-directed by Musidora and Jacques Lasseyne, is still not having much success with the public, despite having been cut by a fifth of its original length.

Berlin, 22 December
Hintertreppe (*Backstairs*), an allegorical and Expressionist work that is directed by Leopold Jessner and Paul Leni and stars Henny Porten, Wilhelm Dieterle and Fritz Kortner, opens today.

Paris, 27 December
A gala evening to help War Widows and Orphans was held at the Opéra de Paris with a screening of *l'Agonie des aigles* (*The Agony of Eagles*), from director Dominique Bernard-Deschamps. The date was carefully chosen by the organizers to coincide with the centenary of Napoleon I's death.

Berlin, 31 December
The number of films made by German production companies during the year was 600.

Hollywood, 31 December
Paramount Pictures has announced that it made a total of 101 feature-length films during the year. This is the highest output to date achieved by a single studio.

BIRTHS

London, 1 March
Dirk Bogarde

London, 4 March
Joan Greenwood

Germany, 25 March
Simone Signoret
(Simone Kaminker)

France, 25 April
Jean Carmet

Calcutta, 2 May
Satyajit Ray

France, 19 May
Daniel Gélin

Italy, 31 May
Alida Valli
(Alida Maria Altenburger)

Minnesota, 21 June
Jane Russell

Italy, 13 October
Yves Montand
(Ivo Livi)

Scotland, 20 October
Deborah Kerr
(Deborah Kerr-Trimmer)

Henri Diamant-Berger has met the high hopes of his producers, Pathé Consortium, with the success of **The Three Musketeers** *in a year when it has been filmed by the Americans.*

Ecstatic reception for little Jackie Coogan

Since its New York opening, **The Kid** *has proved to be a major success.*

New York, 6 January

Charlie Chaplin's first feature film, *The Kid*, has opened in New York to instant and resounding success. For once Chaplin has found a foil worthy of his mettle, the bewitching little Jackie Coogan, whom he had spotted parodying his father's tap-dance routine at an Annette Kellerman revue. After meeting Jackie two days later, Chaplin declared, "This is the most amazing person I ever met in my life." As Chaplin watched the child, the idea for the six-reel film sprung into his mind. After testing the little boy in a two-

reeler called *A Day's Pleasure*, he cast Coogan as the bright-eyed ragamuffin in battered cap and oversized trousers who is reared, lost and then finally regained by the Tramp. Coogan provides a miniature version of the Tramp's pathos and artfulness and at times it seems as if the "Little Fellow", as Chaplin calls the Tramp, is walking hand-in-hand with his infant self. For his own part, Chaplin has suggested that the orphaned Coogan represents all those children orphaned by the Great War. While watching the film, it is hard not to be struck by the remarkable rapport between Chaplin and his small co-star. Jackie Coogan Sr. has also played his part in the production, appearing in several roles including a bum who picks the Tramp's pocket and the Devil in a dream sequence.

The Kid has placed Chaplin in a very strong financial position. Already confident that he had a winner on his hands after giving the film a trial showing in Salt Lake City, he asked First National for an advance of $1.5 million plus 50 percent of the net after the company had recovered the advance. First National stalled, and displayed a studied lack of enthusiasm even after seeing the film. But Chaplin stuck to his guns, and the stubborn executives were forced to acknowledge that *The Kid* had given him an unbeatable hand. *The Kid* is also certain to make a worldwide star of Jackie Coogan, and Chaplin has stated that though they will not work together again, he will not hold Coogan back.

Jackie Coogan, a real heartbreaker.

Filmmakers proclaim the 'seventh art'

Paris, 27 May

The cinema has given rise to unprecedented debates on aesthetics, and the writings of the Italian poet Riccioto Canudo have only added fuel to the discussions. However, since 6 May, a new weekly magazine, *Cinéa*, has entered the fray. Louis Delluc, the editor, is a theoretician of the Impressionist school and an opponent of Canudo's somewhat woolly writing. Canudo has coined the word "screenist" to describe film directors. Delluc prefers the better-sounding "cinéaste", and expresses the hope that "the seventh art" (Canudo's expression) will be capable of giving an "accurate impression of truth and a study of mankind." The more abstract and lyrical Canudo speaks about the "rhythm of light" that the camera must provide. The Italian poet has brought a worldly air to the discussions, and has attracted an elegant and refined following to Poccardi's restaurant as well as to his residence at 12 rue du Quatre-Septembre. Last March, Canudo founded *Le Casa*, a club for the friends of "the seventh art". At the club, one can encounter

Riccioto Canudo, sketched after the war by his friend Pablo Picasso.

the intellectual set: Léon Moussinac, Jean Cocteau, Blaise Cendrars, Fernand Léger, Robert Mallet-Stevens, Jean Epstein, Abel Gance, Marcel L'Herbier, Germaine Dulac and even "screenists", that is, commercial filmmakers, such as René Pouctal and Léonce Perret, among the social elite.

Darkness shrouds Pathé Consortium studio

At Vincennes, artificial light is systematically and effectively used in filming.

Vincennes, 14 June

Pathé Consortium, the production company spawned by the break-up of the Pathé empire, is opening a new film studio on the rue du Cinématographe. One of the most arresting features of the studio is the artificial light provided by banks of extremely powerful lamps. To mark the opening, several scenes from

The Three Musketeers were filmed in front of an audience of notables and members of the press. The versatile producer-director of this expensive 12-part serial is Henri Diamant-Berger. The new company has yet to establish itself, and its management allege that the rival Pathé-Cinéma has done all in its power to undermine its launch.

Fairbanks plays the leading Musketeer

'Musketeer' Doug has found his new role made to measure.

Hollywood, 28 August
America's idol, Douglas Fairbanks, was born to play D'Artagnan, "the best swordsman in France", and does so in Fred Niblo's new film *The Three Musketeers* which is based on Alexandre Dumas' novel. This second historical legend, following *The Mark of Zorro*, is confirmation of the recent change that has come over the energetic actor. Turning his back on contemporary comedies, Fairbanks has decided to project his American dynamism into distant times and places. As a triumphant and optimistic D'Artagnan – in his plumed headgear, long curly wig and moustache – Fairbanks has given an American flavor to Richelieu's France. And as proof of how popular the actor has become in the U.S., a mountain peak in Yosemite National Park in the Sierra Nevada has been named after him. Now that's certainly what's known as reaching the heights!

Lovely Musidora is not just a pretty face!

Paris, 8 July
Thanks to *Judex* and Louis Feuillade, Musidora is now a big star. But she is not just another run-of-the-mill actress. She has the talent to both amuse and shock, as is demonstrated by this photograph that appeared in *Cinéma* magazine. She supplied a caption which is worthy of a long article: "It is vital to be photogenic from head to foot. After that you are allowed to display some measure of talent." Musidora has plenty of both qualities.

Musidora, the complete artist, believes in intelligence as well as beauty.

England welcomes back its prodigal son

An enthusiastic welcome for his first visit to the land of his birth since 1912.

London, 15 September
Charles Chaplin's visit to Britain has proved an even bigger event than the Armistice! He decided to go on a sudden impulse several weeks before the American release of *The Idle Class*. The return to his native land of this "prodigal son" has generated a huge wave of enthusiasm. From the moment of his arrival at Waterloo Station on 10 September, the King of Comedy was engulfed by wildly excited crowds surging through the police cordons which vainly tried to hold them back. It was little short of a miracle that no one was trampled in the ensuing crush. Accompanied by actor Donald Crisp, Chaplin made a sentimental pilgrimage to the scenes of his deprived childhood. He was followed everywhere, at a respectful distance, by curious crowds. Installed in the agreeable surroundings of the elegant Ritz Hotel, he has held court to a never-ending stream of journalists and personalities come to pay homage. The great and the good have extended their hospitality. At the invitation of E.V. Lucas, he dined at the Garrick Club where he sat next to Sir James Barrie, who told Chaplin that he would like him to play Peter Pan. His encounter with the writer H.G. Wells has also been widely reported. The two men watched a new film of Wells' novel *Kipps* and dined afterwards with Rebecca West. Chaplin is now an immortal among immortals.

Fatty indicted on culpable homicide charge

San Francisco, 10 September
Grave charges have been leveled against comedian Roscoe "Fatty" Arbuckle after the death under suspicious circumstances of a young actress, Virginia Rappe. She died yesterday in the hospital where she was admitted after becoming ill at a wild 48-hour party thrown by Arbuckle in three adjoining suites at the Saint Francis Hotel. The party was held to celebrate Arbuckle's three-million-dollar move to Paramount to make full-length features. Now the deal, and Fatty's future, are imperiled by Rappe's death. The doctors diagnosed acute peritonitis caused by a ruptured bladder, but one of Virginia's friends, Maude Delmont, who was also at the party, has told police that Arbuckle raped Miss Rappe, or at least attempted to do so. On the basis of these serious allegations, Arbuckle was arrested on a homicide charge. Throughout his interrogation by the police, the comedian has vigorously protested his innocence, but a large black cloud threatens the career of the film industry's favorite Fat Man. The press has not been supportive. A Hearst newspaper has already written that Rappe, once voted the Best-Dressed Girl in the Movies, "today wears the oldest garment in the world. It is a shroud."

Reid and Swanson shock with Schnitzler

New York, 18 September
The Austrian playwright Arthur Schnitzler's first play *Anatol*, performed in 1890, was pretty shocking at the time. This was not only because of its risqué subject matter – the amorous adventures of a young Viennese man-about-town – but also because of its impressionistic technique and psychological insights. Now Cecil B. DeMille has brought it to the screen under the title *The Affairs of Anatol*, with Wallace Reid as the irresponsible gallant. Though

still able to send shock waves out to audiences, the director has tried to play down the risqué elements by giving the story a moral lift. DeMille has achieved this by devoting a great deal of the footage to Anatol's wife, played by Gloria Swanson, to whom the philanderer keeps returning. Who could complain! Gorgeously dressed, Miss Swanson is once again more sinned against than sinning. Particularly pleasing are the lavish sets that create the ambiance for the teasing boudoir tale to be told.

*Wallace Reid and Gloria Swanson in DeMille's **The Affairs of Anatol**.*

Feyder's risk with 'Atlantide' pays off

Jean Angelo, Stacia Napierkowska, and Manuel Orazi's striking decor.

Paris, 30 September
At the moment, *l'Atlantide*, directed by Jacques Feyder and based on Pierre Benoit's novel, is showing here in the large auditorium of the Gaumont Palace. "A Man Who Dared..." is how the advertisers are characterizing Feyder, who did not hesitate to shoot the film in the middle of the Sahara, against the advice of all and sundry, and under extremely difficult conditions. It was worth it, because the magnificently photographed Hoggar desert is the

real star of the film, more so than the mysterious Antinéa, played by Stacia Napierkowska. Screen actors Jean Angelo and Georges Melchior, in the roles of Captain Morhange and Lieutenant Saint-Avit, have been swift to capture female hearts. Jacques Feyder and Louis Aubert, who financed the picture on a budget of 2 million francs – making it the most expensive French film to date – have carried it off. The exotic *l'Atlantide* has already become a great popular success.

Richard Barthelmess and Henry King find inspiration in the hills

Los Angeles, 21 September
Richard Barthelmess has formed his own film production company, Inspiration Pictures, in partnership with the director Henry King. D.W. Griffith had acquired the rights of Joseph Hergesheimer's novel of small-town life, *Tol'able David*, for Barthelmess but, on the advice of Lillian Gish, he abandoned it to make *Orphans of the Storm* instead. Because there was no role in the latter suitable for him, Barthelmess bought the rights from Griffith for $7,500 and produced it himself. With Henry King directing his first important film, from a scenario by Edmund Goulding, *Tol'able David* is extremely successful. Richard Barthelmess is perfectly cast in the title role of a plucky and good-natured mountain boy, suspected of cowardice, who triumphs over three bullying brothers, saves the U.S. mail and

becomes a man of character and strength. The film delivers a splendid evocation of rural America, with a nostalgic love of the landscape. Before the premiere this week, this

star of many Griffith films showed it to his former mentor. Griffith embraced and kissed Barthelmess at the end, such was his unbegrudging admiration for the film.

Barthelmess, already a star, formed Inspiration Pictures to make this film.

Critical triumph for Fritz Lang

Berlin, 7 October
After the success of *The Spiders* last year, the 30-year-old Viennese film director Fritz Lang has triumphed once again with a dark and mystical three-episode allegory entitled *Destiny (Der Müde Tod)*. The story, co-written with Thea von Harbou, tells of a honeymoon destroyed when the husband disappears with a sinister stranger who turns out to be Death. (The German title literally means The Tired Death.) The wife pleads with Death for her husband's life, and he strikes a series of bargains with her, until love finally wins out. The film is even more impressive for its mastery of visual composition than some of the director's previous work, and confirms Lang as one of the most exciting directors working in Germany today.

America's fair sex seduced by Italy's Latin lover

Los Angeles, 30 October
Almost the entire female population of America has fallen in love with Rudolph Valentino, the dashingly romantic star of Metro's *The Four Horsemen of the Apocalypse*. In Rex Ingram's adaptation of the novel by Blasco Ibañez, Valentino plays a wastrel who becomes a war hero. When he swoops across the screen in a sensual tango, women in the audience are seen to faint dead away in the aisles.

The object of all this adulation was born Rodolfo Guglielmi in Italy in May 1895, the son of a veterinary surgeon. He arrrived in America, traveling steerage, in 1913. After a spell as a gardener in New York's Central Park, he became a nightclub dancer, briefly replacing Clifton Webb as the partner of exhibition dancer Bonnie Glass. At this time Valentino was moving in fast company, and New York became a little too hot for him when he found himself involved in a scandalous society divorce. He made his way west to San Francisco with a touring theatrical company and then finally on to Los Angeles and the world of the movies. Mae Murray, an old friend,

Valentino: a classic pose.

found Valentino work in *Alimony* (1918), and he soon carved a niche for himself playing oily heavies. In *Eyes of Youth*, he was cast as a professional co-respondent hired to romance Clara Kimball Young. Then shortly afterwards, his marriage to actress Jean Acker collapsed on their wedding night. Valentino's big

The dangerously mesmeric gaze of Rudolph Valentino's seductive sheik.

break came earlier this year when June Mathis, chief of Metro's script department and a powerful figure at the studio, suggested him for the second lead in Rex Ingram's *The Four Horsemen of the Apocalypse*. By the end of shooting, Valentino's part had been built up into the starring role. Success, however, has only

soured relations between Metro and their new star. While playing Armand opposite Nazimova in the film *Camille* he was refused a salary increase from $350 to $450 a week. The studio's stinginess could cost it dear, as both Valentino and the valued June Mathis are now contemplating a move.

Four Horsemen still galloping at box office

New York, 21 November
Box-office tills are still ringing for Metro's *The Four Horsemen of the Apocalypse* months after its sensational premiere in New York. Originally Rudolph Valentino had only featured billing, but all prints were

recalled after the hoopla that surrounding its opening, and the credits altered to make him the star. There is general agreement in the movie world that the huge audience the film has reached will help to make picture-going respectable.

*Sensationally dancing the tango with Alice Terry in **Four Horsemen**.*

Rudy takes talent to Paramount

Hollywood, 27 November
The love affair between Rudolph Valentino and Metro has ended. Disenchanted with the studio's reluctance to reward his huge drawing power at the box office with a commensurate salary, the biggest new star in Hollywood took himself to Paramount, who secured his services at the bargain price of $500 a week. They already had the perfect property for him, *The Sheik*, adapted from the lurid bestseller by E.M. Hull. Valentino plays the prince of the desert, Ahmed Ben Hassan, and Agnes Ayres is the object of his erotic emoting. The Latin's flashing eyes and magnificently flared nostrils are sending shock waves of "Sheik mania" racing across America. Paramount has rewarded him by more than doubling his salary to $1,250 a week. His next project is *Moran of the Lady Letty*, co-starring Dorothy Dalton.

Director Lubitsch crosses the Atlantic

New York, 24 December
Ernst Lubitsch, the brilliant German director of *Carmen*, *Madame Dubarry*, *Anna Boleyn* (known here as *Deception*) and many other notable films, has arrived on his first visit to the U.S. He has just completed his latest screen epic, *The Loves of Pharaoh*, and he hopes to be around long enough to help promote it. During the course of his visit, Lubitsch also plans to make important contacts within the film industry and to familiarize himself with the latest American production techniques. It appears that he has already received offers from a number of Hollywood producers, including Mary Pickford, but he has not yet committed himself. Clearly, this young man, who has not yet reached his thirtieth birthday, has a bright future ahead, while it is likely that his favorite star, Pola Negri, will also soon be lured here.

Paris, 1 January
Henri Diamant-Berger's *The Three Musketeers* has proved to be a boon for the Pathé Cinéma Consortium, despite its enormous budget. A few weeks ago, the company showed its appreciation by throwing a banquet to celebrate reaching the grand total of 1,000 copies rented to exhibitors.

Paris, 10 January
Louis Delluc has written his final critique for *Paris-Midi*. He is going to devote himself to *Cinéa* and the filming of *la Femme de nulle part* (*The Woman From Nowhere*) in the Gaumont studios at la Villette.

Paris, 13 January
First release of *la Vie et l'œuvre de Molière* for the 300th anniversary of Molière's birth. The production was made by Jacques de Féraudy on the orders of the Minister for Public Education.

Los Angeles, 2 February
Inauguration of a new series of cartoons, "Laugh-O-Grams" by Walt Disney, with *Four Musicians of Bremen*, a parody of the fable.

Copenhagen, 7 February
World premier of *Die Gezeichneten* (*Love One Another*), filmed in Germany by Carl Theodor Dreyer and starring Polina Piekovska and Vladimir Gadjarov.

Paris, 28 February
The court case of André Legrand versus Marcel L'Herbier has drawn to a close in favor of L'Herbier. The jury decided that his film *Villa Destin* was not based on Oscar Wilde's work *The Crime Of Lord Arthur Saville*, to which Legrand has the exclusive rights.

Marseilles, 31 March
The Cabinet of Dr. Caligari, the Expressionist film directed by Robert Wiene which was banned by the prefecture only three days after its release due to complaints from ex hibitors, can once more be shown provided that certain scenes are cut.

Shanghai, 31 March
The filmmaker Zhang Shichuan has recently created the Mingxing Company. Production has already started on three comic films, two of them inspired by Charlie Chaplin and Harold Lloyd.

Hollywood, 1 April
Douglas Fairbanks has started work on *Robin Hood* under the direction of Allan Dwan.

Prague, 7 April
Release of Karl Anton's first film *Cikani* (*The Bohemians*), inspired by the romantic poet Karel H. Macha.

Paris, 4 May
The Cocorico Cinéma has opened in the Bellville district. The artistic director is actor René Cresté, who is best known for his roles in films by Léonce Perret and as Louis Feuillade's *Judex*.

Paris, 16 May
The news that Berthe Dagmar was seriously wounded by a panther during filming of *Marie chez les fauves*, was only made public today, when the director Jean Durand presented the film to the public.

Paris, 17 May
Baron Gabet, who chaired Pathé Cinéma's annual board meeting, has announced that the profits for the year 1921–1922 amounted to a net profit of 16,153,203 francs.

Moscow, 21 May
Kino-Pravda, still edited by Dziga Vertov has replaced *Kino-Nedelia*.

Marseilles, 31 May
Inhabitants watched in astonishment as a naval battle between 18th-century ships took place just off the coast. It had been organized by Louis Feuillade for a scene in *Fils de flibustier* (*The Buccaneer's Son*).

Paris, 6 June
It was decided at the French Entertainment Industry's annual meeting that all cinemas in France will shut on 15 February 1923 if nothing is done to reduce the crippling charges imposed on the profession.

Rome, 1 September
Release of *A noi* (*Ours*), a fascist propaganda film from the director Umberto Paradisi.

Paris, 5 September
Presentation of *l'Ouragan sur la montagne* (*Storm on the Mountain*), by Julien Duvivier, with Gaston Jacquet and Lotte Loring. This film marks the first Franco-German co-production since the Great War.

Berlin, 7 September
Marlene Dietrich is playing the lead in the revival of the play *Pandora's Box*, by Franz Wedekind, a major exponent of expressionism.

Stockholm, 18 September
Häxan (*Witchcraft Through the Ages*), directed by Benjamin Christensen with himself and Elisabeth Christensen, is now screening in the Swedish capital.

Germany, 22 September
The government is suffering a loss of 2 million marks a day because of the cinema industry's general strike against taxes.

Hollywood, 5 November
The Headless Horseman, by Edward Venturini, is the first film in the U.S. that has been shot entirely on panchromatic film.

Paris, 15 November
At the annual Cinema Festival that is organized by the Cinema Lovers' Club, Léon Moussinac gave a warmly applauded speech followed by excerpts from the most outstanding films of the year.

Paris, 2 December
In an editorial entitled "Theatre and Truth" for *Ciné-Journal*, written following the immense success of the film *Nanook of the North*, Georges Dureau remarked on "the over-all weakness of theatrical style films, and the obvious need felt by the public to see real life on the screen."

Paris, 11 December
The Chamber of Deputies is the scene of heated debates after the decision made by the president of the Censorship Board to ban Ernst Lubitsch's *Madame Dubarry*.

New York, 22 December
According to the editorial in today's *New York Times*, "Arbuckle has become a symbol of the vices indulged in by the world of cinema."

Sofia, 22 December
The first full-length Bulgarian film *Pod staroto nebe*, by Nikolai Larine, was shown at the Theatre Moderne.

Paris, 27 December
Jean Epstein's film *Pasteur*, was shown at the Sorbonne to commemorate the scientist's 100th birthday.

Germany, 31 December
Sixty-four percent of films shown during the past year were home-grown productions.

Germany, 31 December
The number of production companies has now reached the 300 mark.

Paris, 31 December
There are now 207 cinemas in the French capital and 2,959 in the entire country, including Morocco and Algeria.

BIRTHS

England, 21 January
Paul Scofield

Italy, 22 February
Giulietta Masina

Italy, 5 March
Pier Paolo Pasolini

Italy, 5 March
Serge Reggiani

Italy, 22 March
Ugo Tognazzi

France, 16 May
Martine Carol
(Maryse Mourer)

France, 3 June
Alain Resnais

Minnesota, 10 June
Judy Garland
(Frances Gumm)

Paris, 22 August
Micheline Presle
(Micheline Chassagne)

Italy, 1 September
Vittorio Gassman

Italy, 15 November
Francesco Rosi

Cannes, 4 December
Gérard Philipe

North Carolina, 24 December
Ava Gardner

---

*Valentino went largely unnoticed in several films before reaching stardom. This year sees him in four films, of which **Blood and Sand** is the most successful.*

Stroheim's new film disturbs and seduces

*Patsy Hannen is the actress co-starred with Stroheim in **Foolish Wives**.*

New York, 11 January
The latest film written and directed by Erich von Stroheim, who also plays the lead, is *Foolish Wives*. It has just opened here at the Central Theater and is his most ambitious production by far. The film looks great with its convincing re-creation of the Monte Carlo setting and use of atmospheric photography, while the plot represents a natural culmination of the theme of the naive American wife deceived by an unscrupulous adventurer, as explored in Stroheim's previous film projects. Here, he gives his most sustained performance as the leading character, a bogus count, a seducer and a swindler, who is aided in his nefarious schemes by two cynical young ladies who pose as his cousins. Unfortunately, the film was beset by problems from the beginning and went far over budget. Worst of all, Stroheim's completed version, running 18 reels or more, was considered too long and was severely cut by the studio to its present length of 14 reels. Nonetheless, Universal's publicists have been working overtime, erecting giant billboards in New York with such advertising slogans as "He's going to make you *hate him* even if it takes a *million dollars* of our money to do it!" Undoubtedly, this is by far the most expensive film that Laemmle's Universal studio has yet made.

America gets first look at Lubitsch's Egypt

New York, 22 February
Americans have been fortunate to see the German film *The Loves of Pharaoh*, by the director Ernst Lubitsch, before it has been released in Germany. It is true, however, that the film was partly financed by an American company, the Famous Players-Lasky Corporation and that Lubitsch's previous films have all been great successes in the U.S. A grandiose epic, with vast decors and impressive crowd scenes – it used 126,000 extras and took 10 months to shoot – *The Loves of Pharaoh* is also a personal work of immense charm and sensitivity. Actor Emil Jannings, the larger-than-life Titan of the German cinema, has created a tyrannical yet pathetic Pharaoh Amenes, unhappy in love. By not neglecting any detail of the luxury and debauchery of the period, Lubitsch has succeeded in reaching the apotheosis of the historical film. In refining his style, the director of *Anna Boleyn* and *Madame Dubarry* has managed to circumvent, in a virtuoso manner, the traps inherent in this type of production. Here, he has confirmed his reputation for being able to bring a human dimension into a historical tale, sustaining the atmosphere throughout. And to lighten a rather somber story, Lubitsch has treated certain scenes as comedy, a genre in which he is a master. Participating in the achievement of the film were the cameramen, Theodor Sparkuhl and Alfred Hansen, and the decorators, Ernst Stern and Kurt Richter. Apart from Jannings, there are also good performances by Dagny Servaes (who replaced Pola Negri) as a slave with whom the Pharaoh falls in love, and Harry Liedtke as the young man whom the slave prefers.

The Loves of Pharaoh, a German film made in the grand American style.

Art the most important weapon for Lenin

Moscow, 1 February
In order to emerge from the chaos of a Russia hungry and in ruins, newspapers and novels are seeking to mobilize the population, but the vast country is 80 percent illiterate. How then can one explain, convince and educate them? How does one forge men and women anew, to create a new society? Thankfully, the cinema is accessible to all. Lenin told Lunatcharski, the people's commissar of education, an intellectual and highly-considered screen writer, "Of all the arts, the cinema is for us the most important." Indeed, he can and must relay the propaganda as widely as possible. Now that the creators of bourgeois melodramas and their clientele have left for Europe, the cinema has ceased to be a way of passing the time, and has become more a tool of social and moral progress – an art to be put to use for the benefit of the masses. The dilapidated state of the studios is an obstacle, but this ambitious task will be tackled.

Hollywood is embroiled in another scandal

Hollywood, 2 February
With the last rites being read over Fatty Arbuckle's career, another scandal has erupted at the accident-prone Paramount studio. This time it looks like murder. The victim is top Paramount director William Desmond Taylor, whose lifeless body police have discovered at his luxurious Westlake bungalow. They arrived to find the place a hive of activity. Two Paramount executives were burning papers in the fireplace while the instantly recognizable figure of lovely comedienne Mabel Normand, a close friend of Taylor, was feverishly ransacking the dead man's bureau for compromising documents. The circumstances of Taylor's life and death are bizarre. Taylor had claimed to be an English gentleman, but he was in fact of Irish descent, born William Deane-Tanner in 1877, who abandoned his family in New York in 1908 and resurfaced in Hollywood. The police have found his closets crammed with pornographic material and also lingerie that bears the monogram "M.M.M.", the initials of actress Mary Miles Minter. There are more questions than answers to the affair.

Vampire Dracula reinvented as Nosferatu

*Max Schreck (left) and Max Nemetz in Murnau's **Nosferatu, the Vampire**.*

Berlin, 5 March
Having left his sinister castle in the Carpathian mountains, in a coffin filled with earth, the vampire Nosferatu is now throwing his menacing shadow across the cinema screens of the world, and frightening audiences. Freely adapted from Bram Stoker's 1897 novel *Dracula*, the film entitled *Nosferatu, the Vampire*, was made by the great German director, Friedrich Wilhelm Murnau. Although it was shot for the most part in actual locations instead of in the usual stylized studio sets, and has used realistic interiors, the film is marked by the influence of German Expressionism. This is notable in the choice of the strange camera angles and eerie images in the photography of Fritz Arno Wagner and Gunther Krampf, as well as in the expressive decor of Albin Grau. All this makes *Nosferatu*, a "strange symphony of terror", which is the German subtitle of the work. It also uses the special effects of negative film and speeded-up motion to suggest a ghostly ride. The disturbing and fascinating vampire is brilliantly interpreted by Max Schreck. His spectral gaunt figure – shaven head, pointed ears sticking out, cavernous eyes and sharply-pointed finger nails – is unforgettable. Besides its capacity to shock, the supernatural tale is a work of poetry and immense plastic beauty.

American film industry under surveillance

Hollywood, 10 March
For some time, various voices raised against the film industry have called for some form of film censorship and industry regulation. This has escalated since the recent scandals concerning comedian Fatty Arbuckle and director William Desmond Taylor. In order to forestall such pressures, the leading studios have decided to institute a system of self-regulation, to be administered by a new organization, the Motion Picture Producers and Distributors of America (MPPDA), which will also serve as a liaison between the industry and the public. Will H. Hays, the former postmaster general, will head the organization, and has stated its aims as follows: "To foster the common interest of those engaged in the industry by establishing and maintaining the highest possible moral and artistic standards in motion picture production, by developing the education as well as the entertainment value and general usefulness of the motion picture... and by reforming abuses relative to the industry..." It seems that from now on, the industry's morals will be under close scrutiny.

Dwan and Doug dazzle in Sherwood Forest

Hollywood, 1 April
Douglas Fairbanks' new film, *Robin Hood*, has turned out to be as exciting as United Artists promised it would be... and more. The movie bowls one over with its sheer exuberance and technical wizardry. Almost entirely financed by Fairbanks himself, it cost over $1.5 million to make. Inside a new studio located on Santa Monica Boulevard, art director William Buckland built the biggest sets ever conceived for a motion picture, including a gigantic castle with 90-foot-high walls, which needed 500 workmen to construct. It seems even more immense on the screen because the top of the castle was painted onto glass before being photographed by Art Edison. Many of the action scenes surpass any Fairbanks has done before, with hidden trampolines being used to give more lift to his leaps, particularly one across a 15-foot moat. There is plenty of bounce in Alan Dwan's direction as well. Dwan agreed to work for 5 percent of the profits, which was a shrewd move when one considers the public acclaim the film has already received. Ironically, Fairbanks first refused to play the hero of Sherwood Forest, who robs the rich to give to the poor. "I don't want to play a flat-footed Englishman," he said when the project was first brought to him. Fortunately, his entourage were not afraid to argue, and they pointed out the romantic ingredients: the Merrie Men, the wicked sheriff, the evil prince and, of course, Maid Marian (Enid Bennett). Doug, at 39, seems stronger and more agile than ever, his heels hardly ever touching the ground. Fairbanks couldn't be flat-footed if he tried. *Robin Hood* is the best Fairbanks picture yet, and one wonders what further heights he will be able to scale.

Fairbanks, the perfect folk-hero.

Fatty is cleared but remains blacklisted

Hollywood, 18 April
It has taken three trials, stretching over four months, to clear Roscoe Arbuckle of the charges brought against him after the death of Virginia Rappe last September. At the first trial in December, the judge reduced the main charge to that of involuntary homicide, but the jury was unable to reach a unanimous decision. A new jury remained hung at the retrial in February. Third time around, on 12 April, it took the jury only five minutes to clear the Fat Man of all blame. They put it on record that, "We feel that a great injustice has been done to him... Roscoe Arbuckle is entirely innocent..." However, Arbuckle's acquittal has not rescued his career. He has sold his house and cars to pay his lawyers' fees. Paramount has withdrawn his movies from circulation and consigned two others

Fatty Arbuckle, now disgraced.

recently completed to the vaults. It has reportedly cost them $1 million. Reviled by both press and public, Fatty can no longer find work in the world where he briefly reigned as one of the Kings of Comedy.

▷

1923

★ ★

Paris, 3 January
The chemist Berthon has demonstrated a new color film process. The negative is covered with thousands of microscopic flecks and is made sensitive by panchromatization: a screening process which filters the three primary colors.

Paris, 20 January
The Chamber of Deputies has voted to adopt an amendment, reducing taxes on those cinemas which devote at least 25 percent (in footage) of their total program to French films.

Paris, 26 January
Max Linder is presenting the first release of his latest American-made film at the cinema named after him. The film is titled *The Three Must-Get-Theres* and is a parody of *The Three Musketeers*.

Brussels, 31 January
Belgian authorities have banned Jacques Feyder's latest screen project *Crainquebille*, on the grounds that it demonstrates a lack of respect for the country's laws.

New York, 3 February
The production of *Salome* with Alla Nazimova has just been released. The costumes by Natasha Rambova were inspired by the drawings of English artist, Aubrey Beardsley.

Paris, 14 February
The Railway Union has demanded that certain scenes be cut from Abel Gance's *la Roue* (*The Wheel*) as they paint an unfavorable picture of railway workers. However, Gance has vigorously refused to comply.

Tokyo, 20 February
Kenji Mizoguchi's directorial debut *Furutaso* (*Homeland*) is now showing. The film deals with the differences between rural and urban life.

Paris, 20 February
Paramount President Adolph Zukor has told the press that his company will no longer be making films with Fatty Arbuckle.

Paris, 27 February
The committee against the danger of venereal disease has released a film *Syphilis, A Social Disease: How To Make It Disappear*, made by Gaumont, Pathé-Consortium and Dr. Comandon.

San Francisco, 13 March
Erich von Stroheim has started filming *Greed* on location.

Paris, 26 March
The great actress Sarah Bernhardt has died. She made a total of eight films including *The Clairvoyant*, which remains unfinished.

Switzerland, 30 March
Premiere of *The Call of the Mountain*, directed by the pioneer Arthur Porchet and starring Emile Crettex and Ernette Tamm.

Moscow, 25 April
In the middle of his adaptation of Ostrovsky's play *The Wise Man*, Eisenstein has inserted a film sequence of the *Journal du Gloumov*, a parody of detective films.

Nice, 30 April
Max Linder lost control of his car at high speed on a bend of the promenade des Anglais and overturned. He was thrown clear of the vehicle and only suffered minor bruising.

Paris, 30 April
Robert Florey's book *Filmland* has now been published in France.

Paris, 1 June
The young writer Louis Aragon has written in the magazine *Théâtre et Comœdia illustré* that he would like to see the creation of "real films without hypocrisy. The perfecting of techniques are of no interest to me." The ironic reply from filmmakers: "Let's get together to offer the youngster a magic lantern."

Berlin, 12 June
The actress Marlene Dietrich has made her screen debut in *Der Mensche am Wege* (*A Man on the Path*), written and directed by Wilhelm Dieterle, who also acts in it.

Paris, 30 June
The Committee for the Protection of Entertainment is worried about the growing success of a new device, the wireless telegraph. The question they are asking their members to consider is this: does the arrival of radiotelephony pose a threat to the entertainment industry?

Cairo, 12 June
Authorities have promulgated the first law on film censorship.

Paris, 1 August
In the latest issue of *Crapouillot*, M. Lebedinsky has let his irritation show. Here he writes that "there are moments when one wishes one were deaf, so as to avoid hearing the orchestra relentlessly playing *Do You Know the Country Where Orange Trees Blossom?* while the dogs in *Nanook* are freezing to death in a snow storm!"

Paris, 2 August
Forty-year old Max Linder has wed for the first time. His young bride, the 20-year-old Hélène Peters, has known Linder since her childhood.

France, 11 August
Gaumont has obtained the exclusive rights for the distribution of Buster Keaton's film projects throughout the French Territories.

Japan, 1 September
All film studios, including that of Shochiku, have been destroyed in the earthquake which has ravaged the Tokyo and Yokohama regions. Film companies have grouped together to make use of Nikkatsu's old studios in Kyoto.

Berlin, 11 September
The last film Ernst Lubitsch directed in Germany called *Die Flamme* (*The Flame*) with Pola Negri, has been released here. Lubitsch is at present pursuing his career in Hollywood.

Paris, 20 October
The Birth of a Nation, which has been showing at the Marivaux since 17 August, has been banned by the prefect of police due to its racist scenes. Police fear they might result in disturbances of the peace.

Rome, 24 October
A new statutory order increases the Fascist Government's powers of censorship. From now on they have the right to intervene both before filming and once the film is finished.

Soviet Union, 25 October
The cinema section of the Georgian Education Board screened a film by Ivan Perestiani, *Citeli Esmakudeni* (*The Little Red Devils*).

New York, 21 December
The grand opening of Cecil B. DeMille's epic spectacular, *The Ten Commandments*.

Paris, 27 December
Alexandre Volkoff has released his latest film, *Kean, désordre et génie* (*Kean, Dissoluteness and Genius*), an adaptation of Alexander Dumas's book produced by the company Albatross Films, which stars Ivan Mosjoukine, Nathalie Lissenko and Nicolas Koline.

Paris, 28 December
Release of *Légende de sœur Béatrix* (*The Legend of Sister Beatrix*), with Sandra Milowanoff and Suzanne Bianchetti, directed by Jacques de Baroncelli with the assistance of René Clair, who joined him after giving up his project for *Geneviève de Brabant*.

La Paz, 31 December
The first Bolivian fiction film to be made here was banned by the censors the day after its release due to the scandal caused by the plot. The scenario, which centers on a love affair between an important landowner and an Indian servant, was based on real events.

BIRTHS

Senegal, 1 January
Ousmane Sembene

Italy, 23 February
Franco Zeffirelli

Texas, 8 March
Cyd Charisse
(Tula Ellice Finklea)

India, 4 May
Mrinal Sen

England, 29 August
Richard Attenborough

Italy, 29 September
Marcello Mastroianni

New York, 1 October
Walter Matthau
(Matuschanskavasky)

Illinois, 4 October
Charlton Heston
(Charles Carter)

The Ten Commandments, a monumental achievement, confirms that Cecil B. DeMille is a master of spectacle, inspired variously by religion, history and legend.

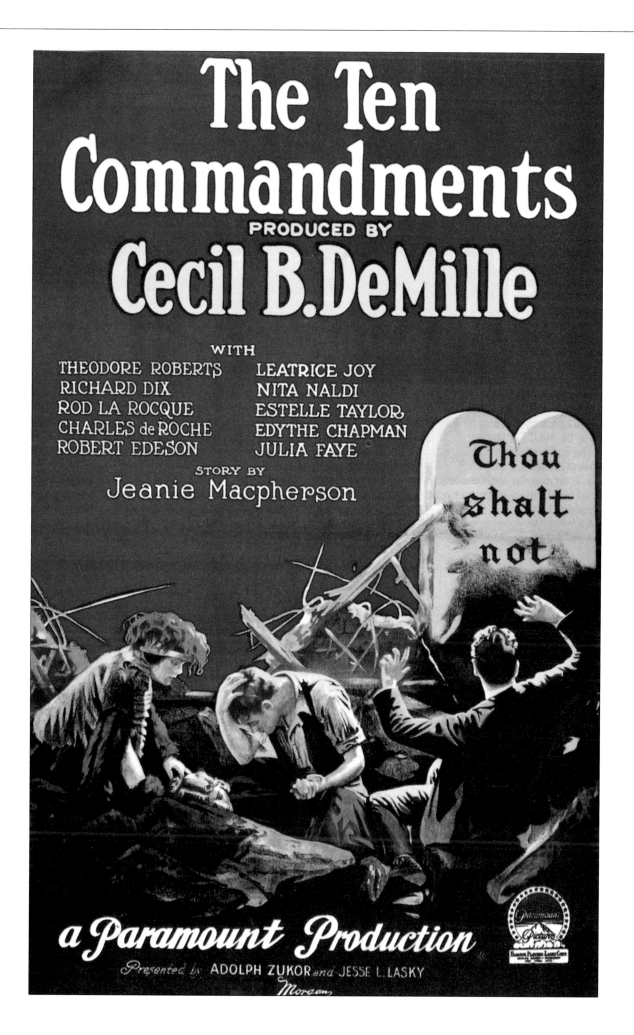

1924

★ ★ ★ ★ ★ ★ ★ ★ **1924** ★

Los Angeles, 10 January
The producer Harry Cohn and his brother Jack, in association with Joe Brandt, have founded Columbia Pictures. The studios are situated at 6070 Sunset Boulevard, Hollywood.

Paris, 15 January
Release of a short puppet film *la Petite chanteuse des rues*, directed by Ladislas Starewitch, with his daughter Nina.

Paris, 25 January
For Pierre Gilles of the *Matin*, "the cinema is an industrial commodity that the silent partner can manipulate with impunity." But the Film Authors' Society has replied that "the artistic qualities of a film remain the property of the director."

Rome, 30 January
Due to the crisis in the Italian film industry, the producer Giuseppe Barattolo has withdrawn his financial participation in Abel Gance's *Napoleon*. If Gance wants to continue with the project he will have to find a new backer.

Canton, 1 February
Lin Minwei, who specializes in political documentaries, has finished filming Sun Yat-sen's first Kuomintang congress.

Hollywood, 3 February
The eminent Swedish director, Victor Sjöström, signed to a contract by the Goldwyn Co., has completed his first American film. *Name The Man* stars Mae Busch and Conrad Nagel, and its director is now to be known here as Victor Seastrom.

Hollywood, 4 February
The comic actor Harry Langdon has made his film debut in a Mack Sennett film, *Picking Peaches*. He intends to make 10 more films in the coming year.

Paris, 8 February
Louis Delluc, who has been ill since filming *l'Inondation* (*The Flood*), has submitted his latest article to the daily *Bonsoir*.

Hollywood, 1 March
Walt Disney has released *Alice's Day At The Sea*, the first in the series called "Alice in Cartoonland". The films are a mixture of cartoons and live action scenes.

Moscow, 1 April
Sergei Eisenstein and Pletniev have convinced the Prolekult to tackle the cinema with a cycle of films under the title of *Towards Dictatorship*. Eisenstein will be directing the first episode called *Strike*.

Paris, 15 April
The actor Camille Bardou has left for Marseilles to make *le Lion des Mogols* (*The Lion of the Mogols*). Jean Epstein is directing for Albatros, with Ivan Mosjoukine and Nathalie Lissenko.

Paris, April
Under the terms of their five-year agreement, Gaumont have formed a partnership with the American film company Loew's-Metro and will distribute their works in France. The new entity will, among other things, be taking charge of the Gaumont cinema circuit.

New York, 10 May
Reports show there are now 578 cinemas in the city with seating for 428,926 people.

Los Angeles, 28 May
Louis B. Mayer has offered Erich von Stroheim a bonus of $10,000 if he completes shooting of *The Merry Widow* in less than six weeks. Shooting has not started as yet.

Paris, 5 June
The Cinema Club has organized a special showing, at the Colisée, of an unreleased film made by André Antoine in 1920. The film, *l'Hirondelle et la mésange* (*The Sparrow and the Tit*), is based on a scenario by Gustave Gillet and was filmed entirely in the open air.

Los Angeles, 10 June
Worried by the length of time the filming of *Ben-Hur* is taking in Italy and by the mediocrity of the scenes that are already done, the directors of Metro-Goldwyn-Mayer have decided to employ radical means: the dismissal of the entire film crew.

Versailles, 7 July
Police interrupted the shooting of an Austrian-directed production in the park. Artists from the Paris Casino were being filmed in the nude in orgiastic scenes of the most liberal kind. The film's directors have been imprisoned.

Paris, 19 August
Charles Desvaux of the town council has asked the prefect to ban the Danish film *Hamlet* by Sven Gade, with Asta Nielsen. According to him it is "a vulgar melodrama with a pathetic scenario." Apparently the director made the mistake of imagining a feminine Hamlet.

New York, 9 September
Release of *The Iron Horse*, a historical fresco by John Ford with George O'Brien and Madge Bellamy.

Moscow, 25 October
The extravagant sets designed for Yakov Protazanov's *Aelita*, based on Tolstoy, have caused a sensation.

Berlin, 26 October
The Danish filmmaker Carl Dreyer has unveiled his latest film, *Michael*. It was filmed in Germany with Benjamin Christensen, Nora Gregor and Walter Slezak in the cast.

Paris, 31 October
Screening of Léon Abrams' film *la Voyante* (*The Clairvoyant*), starring Sarah Bernhardt, Harry Baur, Mary Marquet and Georges Melchior – the last one made by the great star.

Paris, 12 November
Max Linder is taking a stand against the invasion of American films in France. His attitude is exacerbated by United Artist's opposition to the American release of his last film, *Au Secours* directed by Abel Gance.

Berlin, 13 November
Release of *Das Wachsfigurenkabinett* (*Waxworks*) by Paul Leni, with Werner Krauss, Emil Jannings, Conrad Veidt and Lupu Pick.

Paris, 15 November
American actress Gloria Swanson has arrived in France to star in *Madame Sans-Gêne*, for director Léonce Perret.

Paris, 28 November
Preview of Raymond Bernard's historical fresco *The Miracle of the Wolves*, featuring 20 savage wolves.

New York, 4 December
Louis B. Mayer and Irving Thalberg have refused to release the initial 20-reel version of *Greed*. Instead, a 10-reel version disowned by Erich von Stroheim was shown at the preview.

Moscow, 10 December
The centralization of the Soviet film industry has finally been achieved with the creation of Sovkino. The move is planned to give new impetus to flagging film production by attracting increased financial backing from the government.

Hollywood, 13 December
The young actor Clark Gable has gotten married to his drama teacher Josephine Dillon. She is 14 years his senior.

Berlin, 23 December
Release of *Der Letzte Mann* (*The Last Laugh*), directed by F.W. Murnau and starring Emil Jannings as the proud doorman.

New York, 31 December
The most successful films of the year are: *The Sea Hawk*, *Secrets*, *The Thief of Bagdad* and *Girl Shy*.

Italy, 31 December
This entire year's output of film production does not exceed 20 titles (as compared to 921 films in 1912 and 220 in 1920): the Italian cinema is dying.

Zurich, December
A production company, Praesens Film, has been set up by Lazare Wechsler, an engineer and aviation pioneer of Polish origin.

BIRTHS

Nebraska, 3 April
Marlon Brando

Paris, 22 May
Charles Aznavour
(Shanoun Aznavourian)

New York, 16 September
Lauren Bacall
(Betty Joan Perske)

Illinois, 17 November
Rock Hudson
(Roy Fitzgerald)

Morocco, 27 November
Michel Galabru

---

*Mae Murray, 'The Girl with the Beestung Lips', is one of the screen's most popular glamour figures. The year sees her in **Mademoiselle Midnight** and **Circe the Enchantress**.*

1925

★ ★

Los Angles, 9 January
After having a serious difference of opinion, Paramount chief Adolph Zukor has terminated the producer-director Cecil B. DeMille's contract.

Hollywood, 10 January
A compromise has been reached between D.W. Griffith and United Artists: in exchange for his freedom, the director is to provide the company with a final film, and the shares he owns in the company are to be placed in a fiduciary deposit.

Berlin, 31 January
Release of *Orlacs Hände* (*The Hands of Orlac*) by Robert Wiene, adapted from Maurice Renard, with Fritz Kortner and Conrad Veidt.

Hollywood, 31 January
A struggle between Erich von Stroheim and actress Mae Murray, has caused problems on the set of *The Merry Widow*. Louis B. Mayer fired and then re-hired the director.

New York, 7 February
Release of *The Salvation Hunters*, directed by Josef von Sternberg.

Rome, 16 March
Gabriellino d'Annunzio and Georg Jacoby's remake of *Quo Vadis?* has been badly received here. Despite the presence of Emil Jannings as Nero and financial backing from UFA, who co-produced the film, it is a pale copy of the 1913 version.

Paris, 31 March
Launching of the book *Two Years in the Studios of America*, written by Robert Florey, French director and Hollywood correspondent for the weekly *Cine-Magazine*.

Paris, 15 May
Judgment was passed today on the director and actresses arrested during an orgy at Versailles on 7 July 1924. The Austrian impresario was condemned to a month's imprisonment and was also fined 22 francs. The actresses Lucienne Schwartz, Yvonne Savaille and Lucienne Legrand received suspended sentences and were fined 16 francs each.

Berlin, 22 May
Fritz Lang has commenced filming *Metropolis* in the UFA studios. The scenario was written by the director and his wife Thea von Harbou.

Paris, 15 July
L'Histoire du cinématographe (*The History of the Cinematograph*), written by Georges-Michel Coissac, is the first historical study to be made on the origins of the cinema.

Paris, 22 July
Max Linder has been elected president of the Filmwriters Society in the place of Michel Carré who has resigned. It seems Linder's position in defense of the cinema industry in France last November explains this unexpected election.

Paris, 29 July
Release of *Feu Mathias Pascal*, a film version of the work by Pirandello, directed by Marcel L'Herbier, and starring Ivan Mosjoukine. The latter, who is under contract to Ciné-France Film, is at the moment on location in Lettonia with Victor Tourjansky for *Michael Strogoff*.

Los Angeles, 2 August
Adolph Zukor has given the go-ahead to United Artists to distribute the film directed and produced by D.W. Griffith for Paramount, *Sally of the Sawdust*, starring the popular comic actor W.C. Fields and Carol Dempster.

New York, 16 August
MGM has released *The Unholy Three*, an unusual thriller with some amazing scenes of the fantastic, directed by Tod Browning with Lon Chaney and Mae Busch.

New York, 29 August
Samuel Goldwyn has signed a contract with United Artists: he is to supply from two to four films a year and in return will receive 75 percent of the gross takings.

Paris, 22 September
The release of *The Phantom of the Opera*, directed by Rupert Julian, adapted from the novel by Gaston Leroux and starring Lon Chaney. For this lavishly produced historical drama, a replica of the entire Paris Opera was constructed at Universal Studios near Hollywood.

Copenhagen, 5 October
Carl Dreyer has made *Master of the House*, with Johannes Mayer and Astrid Holm. This film, made in Dreyer's native Denmark, is in the German *Kammerspiel* tradition.

Geneva, 9 October
Michel Simon, a photographer and actor with the Pitoeff troupe, is causing a sensation with his performance in *The Vocation of André Carrel*. From director Jean Choux, and with Blanche Montel and Camille Bert, it is Simon's first screen role.

Paris, 30 October
Max Linder, who was obsessed by death, first killed his wife Hélène and then committed suicide today.

New York, 1 November
As of today, Warner Bros. owns Vitagraph, the company created in 1896 by J. Stuart Blackton and Albert E. Smith. Under the agreement that was signed in February, Warners inherits all research undertaken by Vitagraph in the field of sound.

Paris, 3 November
Max Linder's will was read today in the Seine Civil Court. The star has bequeathed all the films produced by him to the president of the Cinema Press Association, J.L. Croze.

Paris, 4 November
Backing for Abel Gance's project *Napoleon* has been taken up by the General Film company, which was set up for this purpose. Filming was interrupted on 21 June after the main backers, the German group Stinnes, were declared bankrupt.

Rome, 5 November
Luce Institute (Educational Cinematographic Union) has been nationalized by the Facist government.

Hollywood, 7 November
The independent producer B.P. Schulberg has joined Paramount. He brings with him Clara Bow, John Gilbert and the director William Wellman.

Moscow, 21 November
Release of *Chess Fever*, the first film directed by Vsevolod Pudovkin, an actor who has previously assisted in the making of several films.

New York, 29 November
The young actress Louise Brooks has spoken to the *Daily Mail* about a series of nude photos taken of her two years ago. She wants to prevent their publication. She also alluded to her relationship with Charlie Chaplin whom she met last summer.

Paris, 25 December
Release of Henri Fescourt's version of *les Misérables*, filmed in four episodes with Gabriel Gabrio and Sandra Milowanoff.

Berlin, 31 December
UFA has signed a reciprocal agreement with Paramount and MGM for the importation of films between the two countries. A 'progressive' company has been created to distribute Soviet documentaries.

BIRTHS

Ohio, 26 January
Paul Newman

France, 12 March
Georges Delerue

Sweden, 24 May
Mai Zetterling

New York, 3 June
Tony Curtis
(Bernard Schwartz)

France, 31 August
Maurice Pialat

England, 8 September
Peter Sellers
(Richard Henry Sellers)

France, 23 September
Jean-Charles Tacchella

Athens, 18 October
Melina Mercouri

Algiers, 20 October
Roger Hanin (R. Lévy)

Paris, 6 November
Michel Bouquet

Wales, 10 November
Richard Burton
(R. Jenkins)

Paris, 27 December
Michel Piccoli

Germany, 28 December
Hildegard Knef
(aka Hildegarde Neff)

---

*The highly popular Richard Dix plays the lead in **The Vanishing American**. This Western epic, from Zane Grey's novel on a theme of racial injustice, was directed by George B. Seitz.*

'The Jazz Singer' heralds end of silent cinema

The rabbi's son a hit in blackface

New York, 6 October
Wild excitement has greeted the premiere of Warner Brothers' *The Jazz Singer*, the first motion picture in which spoken dialogue is heard. The studio had been in serious financial difficulties for some time. But, emboldened by the success of their John Barrymore vehicle, *Don Juan*, released last summer and the first feature film to use Warners' Vitaphone sound-on-disc system for sound effects and synchronized score, they staked everything on *The Jazz Singer*. The story of a cantor's son torn between the synagogue and show business, *The Jazz Singer* was originally a stage hit for George Jessel, who had already appeared for the studio in a 1926 silent picture entitled *Izzy Murphy*. Jessel wanted too much money to move into the uncharted territory of the "talkers", and comedian Eddie Cantor proved to be equally unwilling. Consequently, Warners turned to the greatest entertainer in the world, Al Jolson, who agreed to play the role of Jakie Rabinowitz for a fee of $75,000. It

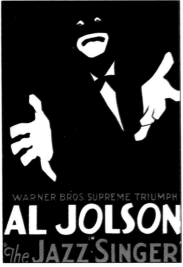

Al Jolson and May McAvoy star in a film that marks a successful first attempt at sound for the Warner brothers.

was inspired casting because Jolson brings all of his legendary attack to a piece of undiluted *schmaltz*, which remains a silent film on to which certain songs and snatches of dialogue, most of the latter improvised, have been none too subtly grafted. However, the moment that Jolson launched himself into "Toot, Toot, Tootsie Goodbye" and the show-stopping blackface "Mammy" routine, the audience went wild. And when he told them, "You ain't heard nothin' yet!" pandemonium broke out in the theater. It's unfortunate that none of the four Warner brothers was able to attend this successful premiere. Tragically, Sam Warner, the driving force behind the Vitaphone experiment, died of a sinus infection just 24 hours earlier. Harry, Albert and Jack Warner traveled immediately by train to Los Angeles for the funeral, missing a historic, and clearly defining, moment in a new era of cinema.

Bittersweet night for the Warners

New York, 6 October
The death of Sam Warner from a sinus infection resulting from an old broken nose injury has deprived the Warner brothers of their moment of triumph with *The Jazz Singer*. The sons of Polish immigrant parents, the Warner brothers took their first steps in the movie business in 1903 when their father acquired a nickelodeon in Newcastle, Pennsylvania. Eleven-year-old Jack, the youngest of 12 children, sang to the audience during intermissions. Two years later, he joined his brothers Harry, Albert and Sam in a film distribution venture which was soon forced to sell out to the Patents Company. They returned to exhibition and also moved into production, but with little success until 1918, when they released their first feature film, *My Four Years in Germany*. In 1919 they established Warner Brothers West Coast Studio in Burbank, California. By the spring of 1923, the studio was fully incorporated as Warner Brothers and big enough for the simultaneous shooting of six films. In 1925 they absorbed Vitagraph with its New York studio, and then in 1926 formed a subsidiary, called Vitaphone, in association with Western Electric, to develop a sound-on-disc system for motion pictures. This gamble has produced *The Jazz Singer*.

New Yorkers throng ten-deep to purchase tickets outside the most famous marquee in American cinema history.

A new stage for Murnau in the glowing splendor of his 'Sunrise'

Murnau, wearing a white cap, filming a scene for his first American movie.

New York, 29 November
With the quality of films such as *Nosferatu* and *The Last Laugh*, F.W. Murnau established himself as one of the great German directors. Now he is being placed on an equal footing with the most talented of his American colleagues. Seduced by *The Last Laugh*, William Fox did not wait long to invite the brilliant young cinéaste to come and work for his company. The "German Genius" arrived here together with two of his habitual collaborators, scenarist Carl Mayer and set designer and costumer Rochus Gliese. Side by side, the trio worked on their first American film, *Sunrise*, which the Carthay Circle Theater is showing at a gala premiere. Despite the fact that Fox imposed certain scenes and a happy ending against the director's will, as well as cutting the film by 20 minutes, it remains a splendid work. *Sunrise* is a poetic melodrama, adapted from the German writer Hermann Sudermann, about a farmer's wife (Janet Gaynor) whose husband, played by actor George O'Brien, is urged to drown her by a city woman. But the husband thinks better of it, and the couple go on a second honeymoon to the metropolis. The most impressive sequence is the trip to the big city by trolley car, where she sits transfixed while the scenery whizzes by.

A rich crop from USSR this year

Moscow, 13 December
The vitality of the Soviet cinema has been very much in evidence this year with the release of a number of excellent films: some experimental, some naturalistic, some more traditional, and some all three. One of the first of the films commissioned to celebrate the tenth anniversary of the Revolution is Pudovkin's *The End of St. Petersburg*, which includes spectacular scenes showing the storming of the Winter Palace. Another truly splendid film that pays homage to Russian revolutionary history is Yacov Protazanov's *The Forty First*, about a woman serving in the Red army who takes prisoner a soldier of the retreating White army. In contrast, films such as Abram Room's *Bed and Sofa* and Boris Barnet's *Girl with the Hatbox* concentrate on the housing shortage in Moscow and the devastating effect it has on relationships.

Janet Gaynor and George O'Brien, the sad and tender married couple.

Wonderful 'Wings' flies higher and higher

Los Angeles, 23 December
Since its premiere in August, *Wings*, with its spectacular and unfaked aerial sequences, has had a rapturous reception whenever it is shown, and is now set for a nationwide general release early next month. Paramount executives, who took a $2 million chance on young director and ace flying man William Wellman, are rubbing their hands in glee at the box-office lines. The cast, too, have reason to be delighted. Small-part player Gary Cooper, following his success in *The Winning of Barbara Worth*, excels in his one scene and has been signed to a contract, while Charles 'Buddy' Rogers and Richard Arlen are no longer up-and-coming but have arrived.

Jack London's novel, filmed in 1923 for Hal Roach, with Jack Mulhall.

*A French art deco poster, 1928, for G.W. Pabst's **Pandora's Box**.*

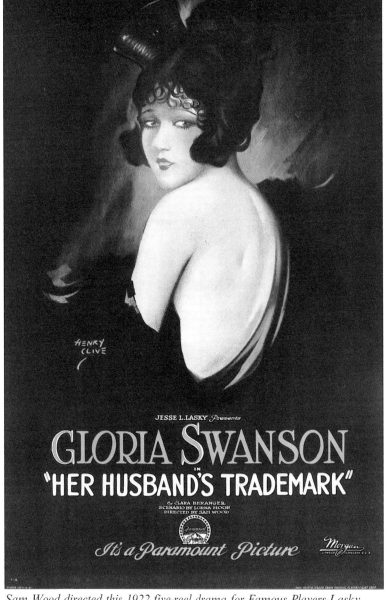

Sam Wood directed this 1922 five-reel drama for Famous Players-Lasky.

1924. Comedy-drama about a small-town boy in Hollywood.

1926. Actor Gary Cooper impressed.

1922. Melodrama of self-sacrifice.

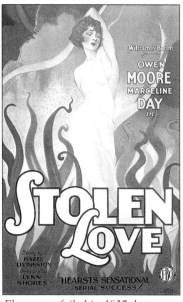

Elopement failed in 1927 drama.

1928. Garbo's top billing over Gilbert.

Universal's 1921 crime melodrama.

1929. John Barrymore's first talkie.

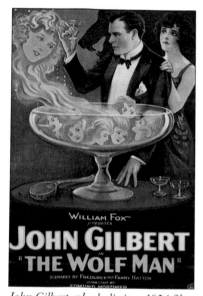

John Gilbert, alcoholic in a 1924 film.

In this 1929 third film version, Ruth Chatterton played the tragic heroine.

Colleen Moore is social climber Mary Brown in this First National comedy.

1926 Warner-Lubitsch moneymaker.

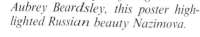

1923. In the style of English artist Aubrey Beardsley, this poster highlighted Russian beauty Nazimova.

In 1927 Georges Scott composed a fresco illustrating Abel Gance's **Napoleon**.

The 1925 sequel to **The Rag Man**.

Handsome, athletic Tom Tyler began his career in 1924, first as a stunt man.

Documentary about the Ubangi tribe.

Raoul Walsh directed this musical comedy-drama for William Fox.

Universal's biggest and most serious film to date, and a landmark war movie.

Villains, chases and a prison escape enlivened this popular action serial from director Richard Thorpe.

The Metropolitan Opera soprano and Broadway star Grace Moore makes her silver screen debut.

Top left: Richard Arlen rescued Nancy Carroll from villains in a South Seas island hotel in this blood-and-thunder movie, whose plot was suggested by Joseph Conrad's novel **Victory**.

Above: Spectacular aerial sequences and the presence of 19-year-old Jean Harlow were among the major attractions of this $3 million movie.

Far left: This barbed romantic comedy, based on a stage hit, had a young lawyer switching his affections to his fiancee's more sympathetic sister.

The tempestuous Lupe Velez, known as the 'Mexican Spitfire' (and who was educated in a convent), starred in her seventh feature film.

Moscow, 5 January
Director Vsevolod Pudovkin has disconcerted audiences with his first sound film *la Vie est belle* (*Life is Beautiful*), due to his exaggerated use of slow motion and an overly extravagant scenario.

Los Angeles, 30 January
Charlie Chaplin's latest film *City Lights*, with himself, Virginia Cherrill and Harry Myers, has been given a triumphant reception. The sound track was added after shooting was completed on the film with an over $1.5 million budget.

Paris, 25 February
The newly fitted out Pagoda cinema has opened in the Chinese Pavilion, rue de Babylone. A Spanish film, *The Price of a Kiss*, was scheduled for the opening.

Hollywood, 5 March
Carl Laemmle, founder and president of Universal has just celebrated his 25th anniversary in the movie business. He opened his first nickelodeon 25 years ago in 1906.

Marseilles, 10 March
A group of cinemagoers is offering to teach audiences how to whistle down bad films. The initiative is worrying local advertising agencies.

Toyko, 25 March
The Nippon Gekkyo, with its three screens, immense organs and 4,000 seats, is advertised as being more modern than the Gaumont Palace.

Algiers, 20 April
Charlie Chaplin has arrived from Nice to join his older brother Sydney. This is his first visit to North Africa and he intends among other things to visit the Casbah.

London, 30 April
French director René Clair is fast becoming one of Britain's favorite filmmakers. His film *le Million* is a triumphant success.

Paris, 30 April
The press has echoed rumors about the international crisis in the cinema industry. The problem seems to be an apparent lack of availablity of new releases in proportion to the cinema network's needs, exacerbated by the increase in costs incurred by the use of sound equipment.

Hollywood, 20 May
Mary Pickford has bought up all her silent films. She feels that the recent technical advances in the cinema industry has made actors in old films look ridiculous.

New York, 22 May
Premiere of *The Smiling Lieutenant*, directed by Ernst Lubitsch and starring Maurice Chevalier.

Berlin, 30 June
All Quiet on the Western Front has finally been passed by the censors here, despite violent protests from Hitlerian youth groups and the disapproval of the Reichstag. Special precautions have been taken in the cinema where it is being screened to avoid incidents.

New York, 21 August
Release of *Pardon Us*, the first short feature starring the comic actors Laurel and Hardy. It was directed by James Parrott and photographed by George Stevens.

Stockholm, 14 September
Release of *En Natt* (*One Night*), by Gustav Molander, with Uno Henning and Bjorn Berglund. The quality of the soundtrack is proof that Molander has made the transition to talking films without a hitch.

France, 15 September
Film director G.W. Pabst is deep in the coalmines in the Pas-de-Calais region where he is completing the last shots for *Kameradschaft* with the participation of local miners. The film is based on the 1906 mining catastrophe in Courrières.

Hollywood, 19 September
Release of the Marx Brothers' *Monkey Business*, by Norman McLeod.

USA, 20 September
At a recent congress, cinema managers united against the abundance of gangster films, which according to them, irritate the public. They also stated that the exhorbitant salaries paid to film stars are to blame for the high cost of film hire.

France, 30 September
The wet summer has been catastrophic for film production. Several films being shot on location had to be postponed or canceled.

New York, 8 October
Mrs. Josef von Sternberg has initiated proceedings against the actress Marlene Dietrich, wife of Rudolph Sieber, for the "alienation of her husband's affection."

Paris, 17 October
Release of Alexander Korda's film *Marius*, adapted from Marcel Pagnol's play. The Paramount-Pagnol production stars Pierre Fresnay, Raimu and Orane Demazis.

New Jersey, 18 October
Death of the inventor and cinema pioneer Thomas Alva Edison, at the age of 84.

Hollywood, 20 October
Douglas Fairbanks is putting the finishing touches on the film he made during a recent voyage. It is to be released under the title *Around The World in 80 Minutes*.

Lisbon, 20 October
The 23-year-old filmmaker Manuel de Oliveira has released his first film *Duoro, Faina Fluvial*. This project is a cut above the run-of-the-mill and mediocre documentaries which have proliferated since a new law in their favor was passed.

New York, 10 December
The Struggle, directed by D.W. Griffith, has been a serious failure both financially and in the eyes of the critics.

Berlin, 31 December
This year, UFA has experimented with a new color process for a film called *The Many-Colored World of Animals*.

*The tough, dramatic William Wellman movie, **The Public Enemy**, is another success for Warners' 'criminalversus-society' subjects. It has created a major new star in James Cagney.*

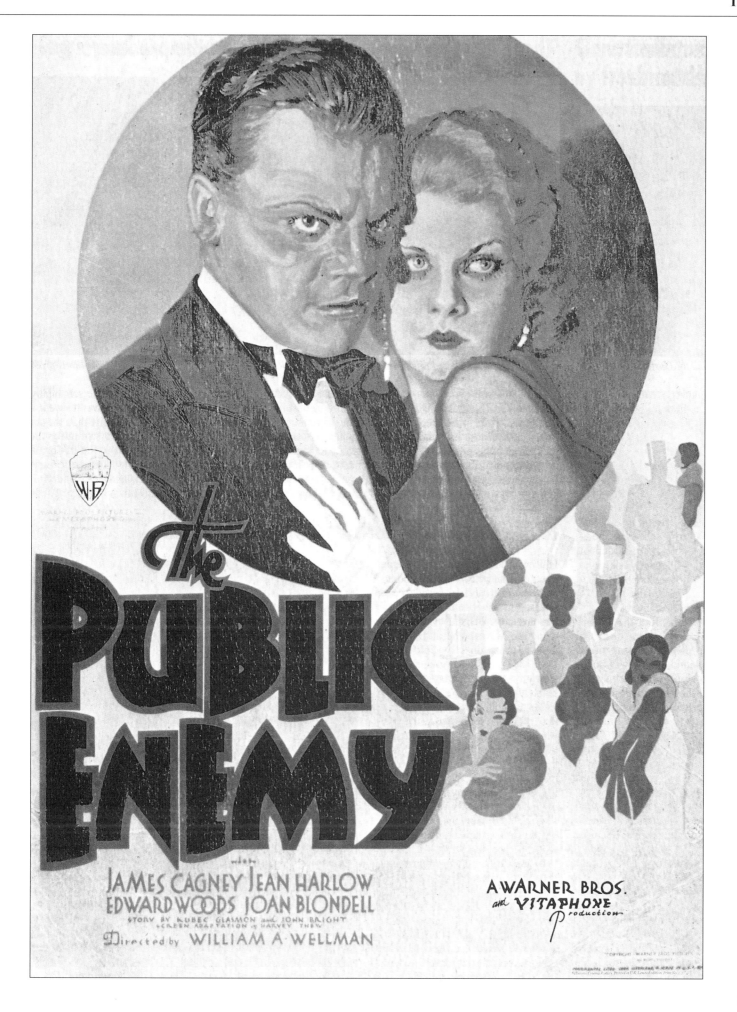

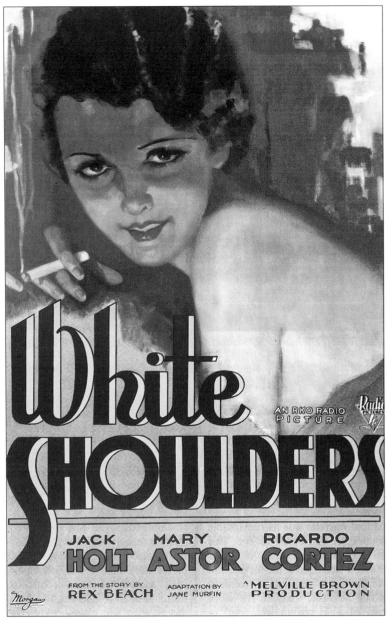

Based on a Rex Beach novel, this was a remake of the 1924 film **Recoil**.

Gable and Garbo in **Susan Lennox**.

Jean Harlow in **The Iron Man**.

This was an insipid poor gal-rich guy romance with a great Gershwin score.

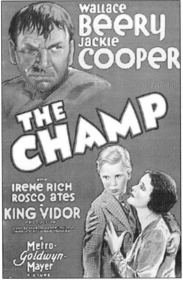

This was MGM's biggest box-office success in 1931.

Brown as botanist in campus capers.

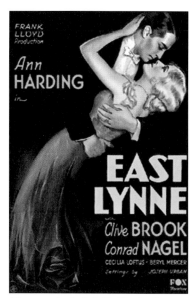

The cast included Cecilia Loftus, an actress considered 'one of the greatest mimics the stage has ever known'.

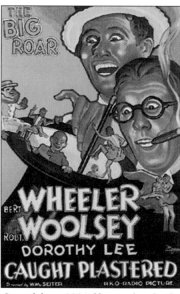

One of three 1931 films with Wheeler & Woolsey, a successful partnership since **Rio Rita** (1929).

Spanning 1889 to 1929, this sweeping Western cost RKO over $1.4 million.

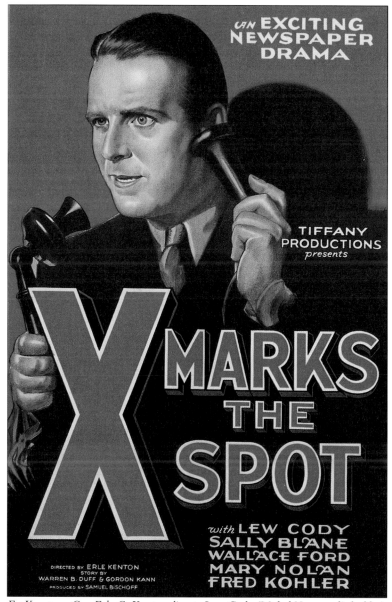

Ex-Keystone Cop Erle C. Kenton directs Lew Cody (Mabel Normand's hubby).

Gibson is a popular B-Western cowboy, fondly known as 'The Hooter'.

French René Clair's charming operetta was influencing screen musicals.

1931/2 Academy Awards, Ambassador Hotel, 18 Nov.

Best Film: *Grand Hotel* (dir: Edmund Goulding)
Best Director: Frank Borzage *(Bad Girl)*
Best Actor: Wallace Beery *(The Champ)*
Fredric March *(Dr. Jekyll and Mr. Hyde)*
Best Actress: Helen Hayes *(The Sin of Madelon Claudet)*

New York, 20 January
Hiram S. Brown has resigned as president of RKO. He will be replaced by the president of the NBC radio network, Merlin Aylesworth.

Hollywood, 2 February
Joe Brandt, Columbia's president, has sold his interest in the company to Jack Cohn and his brother Harry Cohn, who is now both head of the studio and the company president.

Los Angeles, 17 February
Release of *Shanghai Express*, directed by Josef von Sternberg, with Marlene Dietrich and Clive Brook.

Berlin, 24 February
Premiere of *Das Blaue Licht* (*The Blue Light*), made by and starring Leni Riefenstahl.

Hollywood, 28 February
Cecil B. DeMille has left MGM to return to Paramount, the company he helped found. Paramount will be financing and distributing all of his future screen projects.

London, February
The film director of Hungarian origin, Alexander Korda, has been made Paramount's representative in Great Britain and has created a production firm, London Films.

Shanghai, 3 March
Japanese bombs have destroyed numerous cinemas and studios. Thirty companies have ceased production.

Paris, 10 March
Abel Gance in association with André Debrie, the inventor of the Parvo movie camera, has lodged a new application to the patent office for his Perspective Sound process.

Rochester, 14 March
Death of the industrialist George Eastman, founder and president of Eastman Kodak as well as the inventor of flexible film with celluloid-reinforced perforations.

Paris, 17 March
The president of the republic Paul Doumer attended the premiere of Raymond Bernard's film *les Croix de bois* (*The Wooden Crosses*), based on the novel by Roland Dorgelès about the Great War.

Germany, 21 April
In response to public protest, authorities have lifted the ban on Slatan Dudow's film *Kuhle Wampe*, based on a scenario by Bertolt Brecht.

New York, 19 May
Release of Howard Hawks' *Scarface*, with Paul Muni. Hawks played a role and produced the film.

Tokyo, 27 May
Because of the success of *Mushibameru Haru* (*Lost Springtime*), Mikio Naruse can be considered one of the most talented Japanese directors.

Hamburg, 1 June
The negatives of Eisenstein's *Que Viva Mexico!*, which were on the way from America to Moscow, have been intercepted in transit on novelist Upton Sinclair's orders and sent back to Hollywood.

Hollywood, 28 June
The Movietone City studios, built by Fox on West Pico Boulevard, have been inaugurated. They consist of 10 huge movie sets and numerous large outbuildings.

Munich, 18 August
Premiere of *Die Verkaufte Braut* (*The Bartered Bride*), adapted from Smetana's comic opera by Max Ophuls, with Jarmila Novotna and Karl Valentin.

Berlin, 14 September
Release of *Der Träumende Mund* (*Melo*) by Paul Czinner, based on French author Henry Bernstein's play, with Elisabeth Bergner and Rudolph Forster. In the French version the roles are played by Gaby Morlay and Pierre Blanchar.

Berlin, 15 September
Fritz Lang has started filming *The Testament of Dr. Mabuse* in UFA's studios in Neubabelsberg.

Hollywood, 2 November
The stage actress Katharine Hepburn is making her screen debut in George Cukor's *A Bill of Divorcement*, alongside John Barrymore and Billie Burke.

Los Angeles, 8 November
Release of Lubitsch's *Trouble In Paradise*, starring Miriam Hopkins, Kay Francis and Herbert Marshall.

New York, 10 November
Mervyn LeRoy's film, *I Am a Fugitive From a Chain Gang*, with Paul Muni and Glenda Farrell has received enthusiastic press. The plot is about the inhuman treatment of a condemned but innocent man.

Paris, 11 November
Release of *Boudu sauvé des eaux* (*Boudu Saved from Drowning*) by Jean Renoir, produced and interpreted by Michel Simon, adapted from the play by René Fauchois.

Moscow, 3 December
Vsevolod Pudovkin's latest film, *A Simple Case*, is a disappointment. The script by Alexander Rjechevski is lyrical but lacks structure.

Budapest, 3 December
Release of the Franco-Hungarian co-production, *Tavaski Zapor* (*Spring Shower*), starring Annabella, in the absence of its director Paul Fejos, who has had to leave the country for political reasons.

Paris, 7 December
The release of *Poil-de-carotte* (*Redhead*), a film by Julien Duvivier, based on the book by Jules Renard, with Harry Baur and 11-year-old Robert Lynen.

Paris, 8 December
A new cinema, the Rex, has opened on the boulevard Poissonnière. Its tasteful decor and luxurious fittings make it an essential port of call for all cinema lovers.

London 20 December
The young actress Vivian Mary Hartley, who is only 19, and the lawyer Herbert Leigh Holman were married in Saint James church.

Berlin, 31 December
Under Alfred Hugenberg's management, the UFA trust has recovered from its financial crisis and is now employing 5,000 people.

BIRTHS

Philadelphia, 19 January
Richard Lester

Detroit, 22 January
Piper Laurie (Rosetta Jacobs)

France, 6 February
François Truffaut

London, 27 February
Elizabeth Taylor

Japan, 31 March
Nagisa Oshima

Texas, 1 April
Debbie Reynolds
(Mary Francis Reynolds)

Spain, 4 April
Carlos Saura

New York, 4 April
Anthony Perkins

Beirut, 10 April
Delphine Seyrig

Egypt, 10 April
Omar Sharif (Michel Shahoub)

Philadelphia, 21 April
Elaine May

Paris, 27 April
Anouk Aimée
(Françoise Dreyfus)

Algeria, 10 May
Françoise Fabian (Michèle Cortes de Leone y Fabianera)

Ireland, 2 August
Peter O'Toole

France, 10 October
Louis Malle

Detroit, 7 December
Ellen Burstyn (Edna Rae Gillooly)

*At the Academy Awards, Walt Disney was crowned king of animated film for his achievements in creating Mickey Mouse and his wonderful 'silly symphony', **Flowers and Trees**.*

The life of a poet according to Cocteau

Paris, 20 January

The debut film by the poet and novelist Jean Cocteau was shown to the public for the first time at a gala evening held at Vieux-Colombier. Originally titled *The Life of a Poet*, this medium-length movie is now called *The Blood of the Poet*. It was financed by the Viscount Charles de Noailles, Cocteau's friend, and was shot between April and September 1930. It is a poetic reverie in four episodes, in which a young poet passes through a mirror into another world where he finds his muse. Enrique Rivero plays the poet with Lee Miller as his muse. It is already referred to as "salon surrealism".

The Blood of the Poet: Lee Miller.

Eisenstein's Mexican adventure turns into a nasty nightmare

Mexico, 16 March

Finally, after a month of waiting at the Mexican border, exit visas have been issued to Sergei Eisenstein and his two comrades, photographer Edouard Tissé and assistant Grigori Alexandrov. Thus an unhappy escapade has come to an end. After the 1930 rupture with Paramount, Eisenstein joyfully accepted the offer of the left-wing novelist Upton Sinclair to finance a documentary to be shot in Mexico called *Que Viva Mexico!*, destined to tell the thousand-year history of the country divided into four thematically related episodes: The Aztec and Maya Empire, the Spanish Conquest, Colonialization and Revolution. Eisenstein had long wanted to make a film in Mexico, and so approached the novelist on the advice of Charles Chaplin. In fact, it was Sinclair's wife who backed the project, appointing her brother Hunter Kimbrough as producer. But things began badly when, upon their arrival on 8 December 1930, the trio was imprisoned for one day. Eventually, the film got under way, but as time passed they got bogged down, and Sinclair had to put pressure on them to finish. Eisenstein's project was far more grandiose than the Sinclairs had envisaged, and he greatly exceeded his schedule and modest budget. In November 1931, the novelist even received a telegram from Stalin saying that Eisenstein "is considered as a deserter, who has broken with his fatherland." Unfortunately, Sinclair was forced to withdraw his finances at the beginning of this year, owing to lack of resources. Therefore, after two and a half years absence, Eisenstein is returning to Moscow. His situation looks black after having failed to make any films in Hollywood and leaving the Mexican film unfinished.

It took a year's work and 35,000 metres of negative to make this film.

'Mountain-movie' actress turns to directing

Berlin, 24 March

Leni Riefenstahl, the leading actress in four of Arnold Fanck's *mountain* films, has turned to directing. Her first venture, *The Blue Light*, is of a similar romantic vein, shot on location and emphasizing a Germanic mystical union with nature. Riefenstahl herself plays a young woman who is thought to be a witch because she alone in the Dolomite village can reach the top of a dangerous peak. A painter falls in love with her, but when he discovers her secret route to the summit, she jumps to her death. The film's strongest point is the magnificent alpine photography by Hans Schneeberger.

*Riefenstahl, also the star of **The Blue Light**, her first film as director.*

Johnny Weissmuller is the new jungle king

New York, 25 March

Cinema's sixth and latest Tarzan is former Olympic swimming champion Johnny Weissmuller, the man who scooped a total of five gold medals at the 1924 and 1928 games. In 1929, undefeated and acknowledged as the world's finest swimmer, Johnny turned professional, appearing in a series of aquatic extravaganzas and a number of short swimming films. MGM sat up and took notice then quickly moved in to screen-test the brawnily handsome Olympian when the actor they had signed for a new Tarzan adventure fell ill. Everything went swimmingly, and Metro signed Weissmuller at $250 a week to star as Edgar Rice Burroughs' jungle hero in *Tarzan the Ape Man*. Co-starring as Jane is the sparky Maureen O'Sullivan, and the directing is capably handled by W.S. "Woody" Van Dyke, known throughout the film world as "One-Shot Woody". Weissmuller's back-projected exploits in the studio jungle play fast and loose with Edgar Rice Burroughs' original creation, whose novels portrayed the ape man as the cultivated Lord Greystoke. In contrast, Weissmuller's dialogue is confined to grunts and monosyllables. But Johnny's blithe ability to let his athletic torso do the talking has made the film a hit. MGM has signed him for seven more films.

Maureen O'Sullivan, Weissmuller.

'Grand Hotel' hosts an assembly of stars

Director Edmund Goulding, his cast and the crew during the filming.

New York, 12 April
MGM's *Grand Hotel*, directed by Edmund Goulding, is premiered today at the Astor Theater. Adapted from Vicki Baum's novel of a luxurious Berlin hotel, where "nothing ever happens", the film and its unprecedented roster of stars set out to prove precisely the opposite as the characters tangle with each other. Greta Garbo is a lonely ballerina; John Barrymore is her jewel-thief lover; Lionel Barrymore a harassed little pen pusher; Joan Crawford a brassily ambitious stenographer; Wallace Beery a ruthless businessman; and, observing all the comings and goings, Lewis Stone. This galaxy of stars gave the studio some ticklish problems. By all accounts Joan Crawford declined to be a team player, delaying filming by playing records of Dietrich (suppos-

edly Garbo's great rival). Billing also required some extremely careful handling. Garbo's contract stipulates that she alone has top billing in her films. As a means of honoring this clause while at the same time not upsetting her co-stars, MGM suggested that "Garbo" should appear alone at the top of the bill and be followed by the full names of the others. Few can remember a film so eagerly anticipated as *Grand Hotel*. It seems to have won an instant place in film history. The *New York Times* has called it the most important film since the arrival of talking pictures," and a *Morning Post* headline claims that the film is "Screen Art at its Highest". Some are less impressed. Sydney Carroll thinks the film "only worth seeing as a drum-beating exhibition of stars... each and all of them miscast".

Wallace Beery and Joan Crawford, two of **Grand Hotel**'s distinguished stars.

Carl Dreyer's vampire is given a voice

A compelling image from Carl Dreyer's atmospheric treatment of a vampire.

Copenhagen, 6 May
Denmark's Carl Dreyer has ventured into sound cinema. A perfectionist who is well-known for falling out with his backers, he has endured idleness through lack of funds since his brilliant *The Passion of Joan of Arc* was released four years ago. Now comes *Vampyr*, a horror film whose atmospheric treatment of the

supernatural, aided by magnificent photography and spare but effective dialogue, surpasses most of its predecessors. Financed by Nicolas De Gunzberg, a Dutch baron and amateur actor who insisted on playing the leading role under the pseudonym Julian West, *Vampyr* was made entirely on location near Paris in French, German and English.

Ozu elevates domestic drama with his skill

Tokyo, 3 June
The 29-year-old Japanese film director Yasujiro Ozu, has produced his finest movie to date. *I Was Born, But...*, is a fine example of *shomin-geki*, or lower-middle-class domestic drama. The story tells of two boys, ages 10 and eight, who watch their beloved father kowtowing to his boss and playing the fool in order to ingratiate himself. Disgusted, the boys go on hunger strike until things become clearer to them. Although *I Was Born, But...* reflects the melancholy theme of tainted innocence, it is also wonderfuly humorous, and the children (Hideo Sugahara and Tokkankozo) are a delight. Ozu has been directing for five years, and this is the third of his films with a similar qualified title, following *I Graduated, But...*, and *I Flunked, But...*, all of which center on the concerns of young students. Ozu's many films about college life might be accounted for by the fact that he himself never had one. However, his interest in the Japanese family de-

rives from his own experience of a close-knit domestic unit. Not very strong on plot, Ozu prefers to focus on a narrow area, using a simple but affecting style.

Mitsuko Yoshikawa, Tokkankozo in Ozu's **I Was Born, But ...**

With his horse Silver, Buck joined an outlaw gang to bring them to justice.

This risqué comedy was a hit for producer-director Ernst Lubitsch.

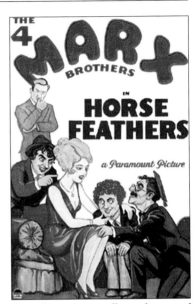

Groucho was a college dean and Zeppo his son in this crazy outing.

In this drama, March's drinking and womanizing drove Sydney to despair.

Inventor Joe hoped to make a fortune with a 'non-sinkable' swimsuit fabric.

Friendly rivalry in backstage yarn about two ex-Ziegfeld girls.

Two members of the all-star cast in MGM's **Grand Hotel**, Greta Garbo and John Barrymore played an unhappy ballerina and her lover.

Joel McCrea (left), here with Leslie Banks in **The Most Dangerous Game**.

Robert Z. Leonard directed Norma Shearer and Clark Gable in **Strange Interlude**, a 110-minute film version of Eugene O'Neill's five-hour play.

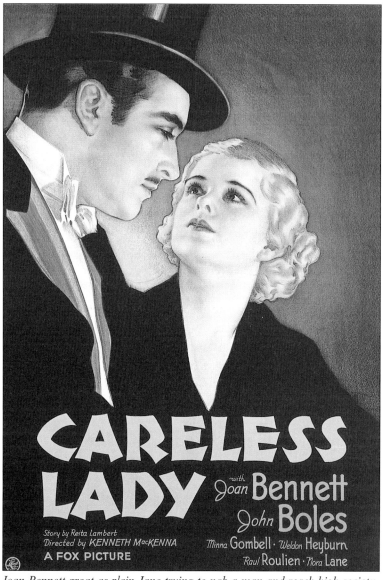

Joan Bennett great as plain Jane trying to nab a man and reach high society.

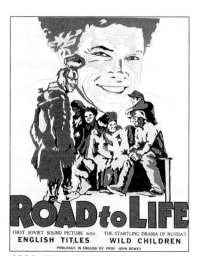

1931. First Russian film that was specially created for sound.
Right: George Arliss was a concert pianist deafened by anarchist's bomb.

Charles Laughton, Claudette Colbert, Fredric March in **The Sign of the Cross**.

1933

★ ★ ★ ★ ★ ★ ★ ★ **1933** ★

Paris, 14 January
Release of René Clair's latest film *Quatorze Juillet* (*July 14th*), which stars Annabella, Georges Rigaud, Pola Illery, Paul Olivier and Raymond Cordy.

France, 22 January
Jean Vigo has finished the location shots for *Zéro de conduite* (*Zero for Conduct*). Filming was started in the studios on 24 December but was interrupted by bad weather and the director's poor health.

Los Angeles, 23 January
RKO has declared itself bankrupt and has been placed under judicial supervision, resulting in drastic cutbacks in spending and the dismissal of a large number of employees.

Hollywood, 2 February
Louis B. Mayer, the president of MGM, has canceled actor Buster Keaton's contract for "a valid and sufficient reason." Keaton has just completed the filming of *What! No Beer?* for the studios.

Los Angeles, 1 March
The release of *Thunder Over Mexico*, presented as being Russian director Eisenstein's "American" film, has caused a violent international campaign to be waged against Upton Sinclair. The novelist, who initially backed the director's ill-fated undertaking, *Que Viva Mexico!*, is being accused of improperly using the negatives he recovered from that unfinished film.

Berlin, 3 March
Release of Max Ophuls' latest production for UFA *Liebelei*. Magda Schneider's wonderful performance and Ophuls' subtle direction transcend the plot in this film version of Arthur Schnitzler's play.

Shanghai, 5 March
There have been stormy reactions to the release of Cheng Bugao's *Wild Torrent*. It is the first Chinese revolutionary film with the peasants as the central point of interest.

California, 6 March
Under the increasing pressure of public opinion, the heads of all the major studios have undertaken to ensure that the clauses set down in the 1930 Production Code will be adhered to in the future.

USA, 9 March
Release of Lloyd Bacon's musical, *42nd Street*, with Warner Baxter, Dick Powell and Ginger Rogers.

Berlin, 23 March
The premiere of Fritz Lang's film *Das Testament des Dr. Mabuse* (*The Testament of Dr. Mabuse*) has been canceled on the orders of the government's censors.

Berlin, 29 March
After the hasty departure of Fritz Lang from Germany, Goebbels' spokesman has explained that the director's *Dr. Mabuse* was banned because of its subversive nature, which is likely to "incite people to anti-social behavior and terrorism against the State."

Paris, 4 May
Release of MGM's *Red Dust*, directed by Victor Fleming, and starring Jean Harlow and Clark Gable.

Rio de Janeiro, 23 May
Humberto Mauro, who has been making films since 1925, is presenting *Ganga Bruta*, his latest work filmed in the Cinedia studios.

Washington, 1 June
According to statistics published by the Ministry of Commerce, American cinema attendance has dropped by 56 percent since 1928.

Los Angeles, 31 July
In accordance with the directives of the National Recovery Act, the MPPDA has instituted the 40-hour week for cinema employees, a measure designed to create more jobs.

Los Angeles, 8 August
Professionals in the cinema industry have launched a series of debates and consultations to decide on the enforcement of the Motion Picture Code, in accordance with the provisions of NRA.

New York, 9 September
Release of Frank Capra's *Lady for a Day*, with Warren William and May Robson.

Sofia, 2 October
The Modern Theatre is screening the first Bulgarian sound film, *The Slaves' Revolt*, by Vassili Guendov. The film evokes the struggle for national freedom in the 19th century.

Hollywood, 4 October
20th Century, the new company owned by Darryl F. Zanuck and Joseph Schenck has released its first film *The Bowery*, directed by Raoul Walsh, with Wallace Beery and George Raft.

Prague, 13 October
Actor and director Josef Rovensky has released his second film, *Rekka*, a story of adolescent love.

Hollywood, 31 October
On signing his contract with MGM, Joseph Yule Jr. has become Mickey Rooney.

Paris, 8 November
Release of Louis Jouvet's new film *Dr. Knock*, a screen version of Jules Romain's satirical play, with Jouvet himself as Dr. Knock.

New York, 11 November
Release of *Little Women*, the film version of Louisa May Alcott's popular novel about the March family. George Cukor directed with the role of Jo played by Katharine Hepburn.

Shanghai, 12 November
As if the Japanese bombings and political disorder were not enough, a commando from the blue shirts, a fascist group, has sacked the Yi-Hua studios, which were founded by the film director Tian-Han.

Paris, 15 November
Jean Vigo has filmed the first scenes for *l'Atalante*, with Dita Parlo, Jean Dasté and Michel Simon, at Conflans-Sainte-Honorine for producers Nounez-Gaumont.

Moscow, 17 November
Release of *Velikii uteshitel* (*The Great Consoler*), by Lev Kuleshov, adapted from the novel by O'Henry.

Paris, 23 November
Jean Gabin has married Jeanne Mauchain, a dancer at the Paris Casino and the Apollo under the name Doriane.

Hollywood, 30 November
Charlie Chaplin has started work on the scenario for *Modern Times*. While on board the yacht belonging to the president of 20th Century, Joseph Schenck, he met the actress Paulette Goddard and decided to sign her up for the film.

New York, November
A committee of archbishops, presided over by the papal legate Amleto Cicognani, has founded the National Legion of Decency, with the aim of stopping all forms of "incitement to moral depravity."

Paris, 15 December
Director Fritz Lang is now shooting *Liliom* for Fox-Europa, a company run by the former production chief for UFA, Erich Pommer, who has also left Germany.

Hollywood, 22 December
Dancers Fred Astaire and Ginger Rogers are partners in *Flying Down to Rio*, directed by Thornton Freeland for RKO.

Palestine, 31 December
British censors have banned the first full-length Yiddish sound film called *Sabra*, made in Palestine by young Polish director Aleksander Ford. They consider it a "left-wing and anti-Arab" work of propaganda.

BIRTHS

England, 18 January
John Boorman

Chicago, 13 February
Kim Novak
(Marilyn Pauline Novak)

London, 14 March
Michael Caine
(Maurice Micklewhite)

Algeria, 30 March
Jean-Claude Brialy

Paris, 9 April
Jean-Paul Belmondo

Pennsylvania, 19 April
Jayne Mansfield
(Vera Jayne Palmer)

Paris, 18 July
Jean Yanne
(Jean Gouyé)

Paris, 18 August
Roman Polanski

King Kong, made by Merian C. Cooper and Ernest B. Schoedsack, has revealed to a fascinated public the scope of creative and technical achievements possible in the cinema.

240

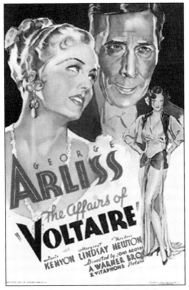

Another biopic triumph for Arliss.

New York in the gay 90s, a big hit.

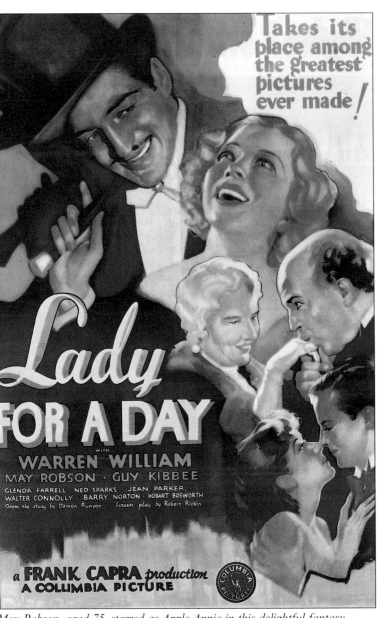

May Robson, aged 75, starred as Apple Annie in this delightful fantasy.

*Nils Asther and Barbara Stanwyck in **The Bitter Tea of General Yen**.*

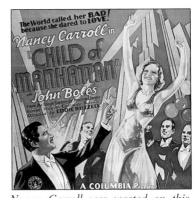

Nancy Carroll was wasted on this nonsense about a dance-hall girl in love with a millionaire (John Boles).

This Capra film opened at the new Radio City Music Hall in New York.

Watered-down version of a ménage à trois play was still thought shocking.

Chatterton as daughter of a Barbary Coast saloon keeper in tearful melo.

A joyous day at the fair for a farming family in a delightful movie.

A striking star performance from Katharine Hepburn as a lady flyer.

This 12-part Mascot serial starred the original Rinty's replacement.

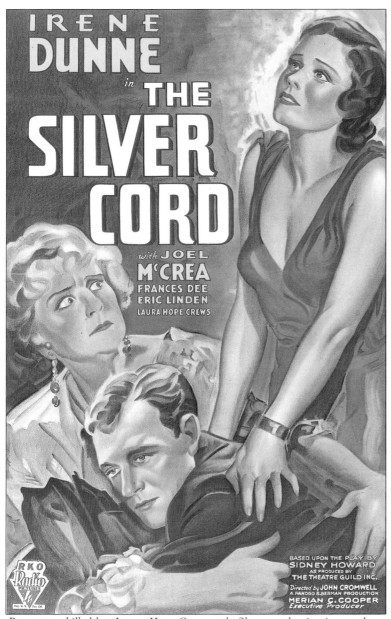

A brittle and sarcastic film from Somerset Maugham's tale of social pretension.

Dunne star-billed but Laura Hope Crews stole film as a dominating mother.

Gary Cooper and Joan Crawford in **Today We Live**, a film with a wartime love triangle that wasted an all-star cast on a poor script.

Dancing Lady is chiefly memorable for introducing dancer Fred Astaire (above, with star Joan Crawford) to the silver screen.

★★★★★★★★ 1934 ★★★★★★★★★★★★★★★★★★★★★★★★★★★★★★★★★★★★★

1932/3 Academy Awards, Ambassador Hotel, 16 Mar.

Best Film: *Cavalcade* (dir: Frank Lloyd)
Best Director: Frank Lloyd
Best Actor: Charles Laughton
(The Private Life of Henry VIII)
Best Actress: Katharine Hepburn *(Morning Glory)*

Prague, 1 January
Gustav Machaty, who has decided to leave the country, has held a preview of his film *Nocturne*. Shooting was done in Austria with photography by Jan Stallich.

Paris, 4 January
Premiere of Jean Renoir's new film *Madame Bovary* at the Ciné-Opéra. The film stars Valentine Tessier and the director's brother Pierre Renoir.

Berlin, 16 January
Minister Josef Goebbels has instituted an official prize, the Film Of The Nation, for works of merit, with propaganda as the obvious theme. He quoted the film *The Battleship Potemkin* as an example.

London, 10 February
Cary Grant has married the actress Virginia Cherrill at Caxton Hall.

Berlin, 16 February
Promulgation of the cinema law prepared by Goebbels' staff. The law gives the government the power to intervene in all phases of film production and absolute control over the choice of subject matter, authors and directors.

Paris, 26 February
The French version of *Liebelei*, made by Max Ophuls with Magda Schneider, has been released here under the title *Une histoire d'amour (A Love Story)*.

London, 30 April
Robert Flaherty was invited to make *The Man of Aran* by John Grierson, the leader of the English documentary school. The film was released a couple of weeks ago and is proving very successful.

Los Angeles, 3 May
Release of *Twentieth Century*, based on the play by Ben Hecht and Charles MacArthur, and directed by Howard Hawks. John Barrymore and Carole Lombard are the stars.

Paris, 15 May
The first film directed by Fritz Lang since he left Germany, has been released today. *Liliom* was adapted from the play by Hungarian writer Ferenc Molnar and stars Madeleine Ozeray and Charles Boyer.

Switzerland, 29 May
Filming has started in St. Moritz on *The Man Who Knew Too Much*, the English director Alfred Hitchcock's latest film, which stars Peter Lorre, Leslie Banks and Edna Best.

New York, 9 June
Release of W.S. Van Dyke's new film *The Thin Man*, based on the novel by Dashiell Hammett, starring William Powell and Myrna Loy as the amateur detectives Nick and Nora Charles.

Los Angeles, 13 June
A new code has been introduced to set down production guidelines in regards to censorship and morality. Cinema owners are authorized to refuse all films produced prior to the code which they consider to be in contravention of it.

Los Angeles, 12 July
The president of the MPPDA, William H. Hays, has announced that a fine of $25,000 will be the penalty for any changes made to screenplays once they have been passed by the Commission.

Berlin, 22 July
The censors have banned *Nana*, filmed by the French director Jean Renoir from the novel by Zola. The film stars Catherine Hessling in the title role, with the Germans Werner Krauss and Valeska Gert also cast. Jewish actress Gert had to emigrate to America last year.

Hollywood, 24 July
Release of Cecil B. DeMille's work *Cleopatra*, with Claudette Colbert as the legendary beauty, Warren William and Henry Wilcoxon.

Shanghai, 31 July
The film now showing at the Jingcheng cinema, *Yu Guang Qu (The Song of the Fisherman)*, written and directed by Caï Chusheng, has been an instant success. The exquisitely beautiful song of the title is on its way to becoming one of the most popular melodies in China.

Cairo, 15 September
The cinematographic branch of the Misr Bank, which at the moment is already involved in film production, is now building new studios.

Moscow, 15 September
The Moskino-Kombinat studio has released Mikhaïl Romm's first feature, *Pyshka*, a silent film based on Maupassant's *Boule-de-suif*.

Los Angeles, 2 October
Release of *Our Daily Bread*, by King Vidor, tells of the vicissitudes of an agricultural cooperative during the Great Depression.

Moscow, 5 October
German thespian Erwin Piscator has made his first film *The Revolt of the Fishermen*, in the Soviet Union.

Hollywood, 13 October
Ernst Lubitsch has released his screen adaptation of the famous operetta *The Merry Widow*, by Franz Lehar, with Maurice Chevalier and Jeanette MacDonald.

Prague, 26 October
Release of *Hej Rup!*, a satirical film by Martin Fric, which takes a long and bitter look at the problems caused by unemployment.

Moscow, 7 November
Lenfilm has released *Chapayev*, by Sergei and Georgi Vasiliev, a patriotic epic set during the civil war.

Tokyo, 23 November
Premiere of Yasujiro Ozu's *Ukigusa Monogatari (A Story of Floating Weeds)*. The film deals with the difficult relationship between a father and son in a traveling troupe.

Los Angeles, 28 November
Members of the board of directors for Paramount-Publix (undergoing bankruptcy) have resigned, and a new Board has been elected. The Company has submitted its recovery plan to the courts.

Paris, 19 December
Julien Duvivier's *Maria Chapdelaine*, with Jean Gabin and Madelaine Renaud, has been awarded the major French film prize.

Hollywood, 28 December
Charlie Chaplin has shot several scenes with dialogue between himself and Paulette Goddard for *Modern Times*, a film he has been working on since 1933. However, none of these sequences have been retained.

BIRTHS

New York, 13 February
George Segal

England, 17 February
Alan Bates

Algeria, 26 February
Mohamed Lakhdar Hamina

New York, 26 March
Alan Arkin

Virginia, 24 April
Shirley MacLaine
(Shirley MacLean Beaty)

Italy, 1 May
Laura Betti

Wisconsin, 19 June
Gena Rowlands

Paris, 1 July
Claude Berri (Claude Langman)

Canada, 17 July
Donald Sutherland

Ohio, 16 September
George Chakiris

Rome, 20 September
Sophia Loren
(Sofia Scicolone)

Paris, 28 September
Brigitte Bardot

DEATHS

California, 28 July
Marie Dressler

---

*The runaway success of **It Happened One Night** has proved the jewel in the crown of the director Frank Capra's career as the creator of a truly unique brand of American comedy.*

Another airing for the Queen of the Nile, with a top-notch cast and Cecil B. DeMille's customary panache.

Françoise Rosay, the wife of director Jacques Feyder, in **le Grand jeu**.

Raft and Lombard's dance, plus Ravel's music, was a sizzler for Paramount.

This well-meant social drama was a box-office failure.

A memorable musical with Fred, Ginger and a Cole Porter score.

A slice of small-town Americana.

Theatrical hit came to the screen.

Moody mix of jealousy and murder.

Miraculous Powell-Loy chemistry.

*Peter Lorre (left), Leslie Banks in Hitchcock's **The Man Who Knew Too Much**.*

*l to r: J.M. Kerrigan, Victor McLaglen and Reginald Denny in **The Lost Patrol**.*

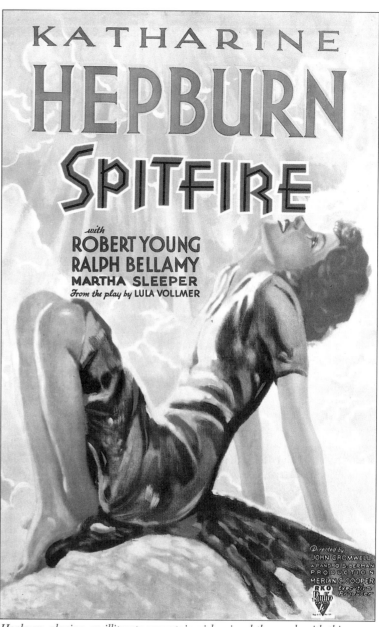

Hepburn, playing an illiterate mountain girl, missed the mark with this one.

Top British director Victor Saville had a great cast for this WWI drama.

Sam Goldwyn's new Russian-born star failed to make an impression.

Catherine the Great: the luxurious sixth collaboration.

Audiences wept buckets over this tale of mother love and racism.

1935

★ ★

1934 Academy Awards, Biltmore Hotel, 27 Feb.

Best Film: *It Happened One Night* (dir: Frank Capra)
Best Director: Frank Capra
Best Actor: Clark Gable *(It Happened One Night)*
Best Actress: Claudette Colbert *(It Happened One Night)*

Washington, 12 January
RKO, Warner Bros. and Paramount have been summoned to appear before a grand jury on charges of monopolistic practices.

Hollywood, 28 February
Douglas Fairbanks and Mary Pickford's divorce is now final.

Moscow, 28 February
The Chinese film, *The Song of the Fisherman*, by Caï Chusheng has taken the prize of honor at the Moscow Festival.

Hollywood, 2 March
Friz Freleng has directed *I Haven't Got a Hat*, a short cartoon for Leon Schlesinger's "Merrie Melodies", featuring a wonderful new character called Porky Pig.

USA, 24 April
Release of Richard Boleslawski's *les Misérables*, with Fredric March, Charles Laughton, Florence Eldridge and Rochelle Hudson. This film is the third American adaptation of Victor Hugo's novel.

New York, 3 May
Release of *The Devil is a Woman*, Josef von Sternberg's adaptation of the novel by Pierre Louys, with Marlene Dietrich, Lionel Atwill and Cesar Romero.

Hollywood, 10 May
Who is Frankenstein's promised one? Those who are interested can find out in James Whale's *The Bride of Frankenstein*, which is being released today. Boris Karloff again stars as the poor creature, with Colin Clive and Elsa Lanchester.

Paris, 11 May
Abel Gance has released a sound version, with a few extra scenes, of his 1927 silent film *Napoleon*. Paramount helped bring out this new version using the Perspective sound process for the first time. The result is sensational.

Hollywood, 27 May
Joseph M. Schenck and Darryl F. Zanuck have bought a controlling interest in the Fox Film Corporation which has merged with their own company; this new company has been named 20th Century-Fox.

Hollywood, 17 June
Paramount-Publix has finished its financial reorganization. Having been bought up by its own circuit's Cinema Union, it emerges under the name of Paramount Pictures Inc.

Berlin, 2 July
A ministerial order decrees that all silent or sound films made before 30 January 1933 must once more be submitted to the censorship Commission before 31 December 1935.

London, 14 August
The actress Vivien Leigh has signed a contract with Alexander Korda, the most influential producer in Great Britain. He has granted her the privilege of being able to act on the stage for six months each year.

Tokyo, 15 August
Release of a sentimental comedy, directed by Mikio Naruse *Tsuma Yo Bara No Yo Ni* (*Wife, Be Like a Rose*), starring Sachiko Chiba, the director's companion.

New York, 13 September
Mark Sandrich's musical comedy *Top Hat*, starring Fred Astaire and Ginger Rogers, has beaten box-office records for Radio City Music Hall. Takings reached $245,000 in the first two weeks.

Paris, 20 September
Release of Julien Duvivier's *La Bandera*, which stars Jean Gabin, Annabella and Robert Le Vigan.

Copenhagen, 28 September
Paul Fejos describes the torments of an admired actress' conscience in *Det Gyldne Smil* (*The Golden Smile*), which is being released today.

Tokyo, 30 September
Nikkatsu, the oldest of the major Japanese production firms, has fallen victim to a stock-market crash. Henceforth, the firm is giving up the production side of its business to concentrate on distribution.

Cairo, 10 October
All the most important people in Cairo attended the inauguration of the final stage of Misr's studios in Giza. Egyptian cinema has now become a full-fledged industry.

New Jersey, 11 October
Joan Crawford has married the actor Franchot Tone at Englewood. The star was previously married to Douglas Fairbanks Jr.

Moscow, 6 November
The production companies Ukrainfilm and Mosfilm have released Alexander Dovzhenko's latest film, *Aerograd*.

Hollywood, 7 November
Paramount has released *Peter Ibbetson*, inspired by the novel by George Du Maurier, with Gary Cooper, Ann Harding and Ida Lupino. The film is Henry Hathaway's second for 1935, the first being *The Lives of a Bengal Lancer*.

Hollywood, 8 November
Release of *Mutiny on the Bounty*, directed by Frank Lloyd, with Clark Gable as the bare-chested Fletcher Christian and Charles Laughton as the unyielding Captain Bligh.

Rome, 9 November
The Italian authorities have drawn up the constitution for the ENIC (National Board for the Cinema Industry). This new organization is in charge of film production, distribution and cinema management.

Hollywood, 15 November
The Marx Brothers have starred in their first film for MGM, *A Night at the Opera* directed by Sam Wood. Their films were previously produced by Paramount.

London, 17 December
René Clair's first English film, *The Ghost Goes West*, with Robert Donat and Jean Parker, was screened during a gala evening attended by Queen Mary. The guests were completely won over by the film.

Los Angeles, 26 December
Release of *Captain Blood* with Errol Flynn in his first starring role and Olivia De Havilland. Michael Curtiz directed.

Berlin, 31 December
Average production costs in Germany have doubled since 1933. This is mainly due to the inflated salaries paid to actors and directors.

BIRTHS

Hollywood, 5 March
Dean Stockwell

Los Angeles, 31 March
Richard Chamberlain

London, 19 April
Dudley Moore

Pennsylvania, 21 April
Charles Grodin

Athens, 27 April
Theo Angelopoulos

Wisconsin, 11 June
Gene Wilder
(Jerry Silberman)

Paris, 25 June
Laurent Terzieff

England, 1 October
Julie Andrews
(Julie Elizabeth Wells)

France, 8 November
Alain Delon

Stockholm, 11 November
Bibi Andersson
(Brigitta Andersson)

New York, 1 December
Woody Allen
(Allen Stewart Koenigsberg)

Massachusetts, 14 December
Lee Remick

DEATHS

Alaska, 15 August
Will Rogers

The Devil is a Woman marks another exotic and successful collaboration between Josef von Sternberg and Marlene Dietrich. It is a romantic tale of love, jealousy and betrayal.

Clark Gable, Rosalind Russell, C. Aubrey Smith and Jean Harlow: *China Seas*.

This chorus-girl story mirrored its star Harlow's own unhappy off-screen life.

Groucho, Chico, Allan Jones, Harpo in Marx brothers' *A Night at the Opera*.

*Victor McLaglen appeared in John Ford's powerful **The Informer**.*
*R: Peter Lorre in sinister **The Hands of Orlac** about a dead concert pianist.*

Flynn, and a great Korngold score.

A superb, big box-office melodrama.

Cagney on the right side of the law.

Charlie Ruggles, Charles Laughton in **Ruggles of Red Gap**.

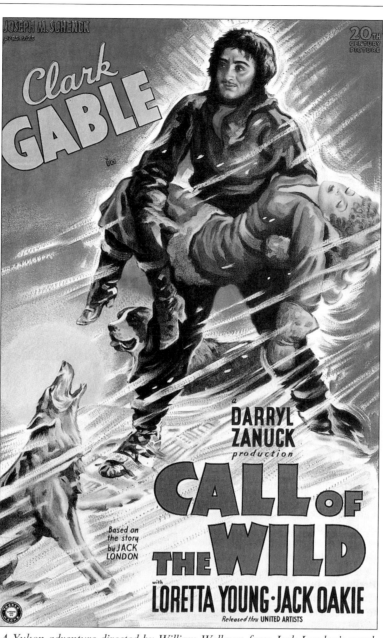

A Yukon adventure directed by William Wellman from Jack London's novel.

A smoldering love triangle in Mexico.

The Kordas went to Africa for this.

A smash-hit action adventure, both humorous and exciting, set in India.

The first, warmly applauded pairing of songbirds MacDonald and Eddy.

This account of the famous Empire-builder was more fiction than fact!

Coalminer Muni battled for better conditions in this controversial film.

265

Fritz Lang, Germany's great filmmaker, joins Hollywood's ranks

*In **Fury**, Spencer Tracy portrays the innocent man, unjustly hunted down by a crazed mob in search of vengeance.*

New York, 5 June
The first American film by the great German director Fritz Lang, *Fury*, has been successfully released. It stars Spencer Tracy and Sylvia Sidney in a somber tale of a lynching. In 1933, following the banning of *The Testament of Dr. Mabuse* in Germany and Goebbels' suggestion that he become head of the new Nazi cinema, Lang fled to Paris. After a brief sojourn in France, where he shot *Liliom* with Charles Boyer, the director accepted David O. Selznick's invitation to come to the U.S. Under contract to MGM, the mon-

ocle-wearing Lang familiarized himself with the local mores, learned English by talking to cab drivers, waitresses and gas station attendants, and lived for almost eight weeks with the Navajos. Many of his script suggestions were turned down until his adaptation of a four-page synopsis by Norman Krasna called *Mob Rule* was finally given the go-ahead by the studio. The shooting of *Fury* took place under some difficulties. Lang had to adapt to American methods of filming that were so different from German practices. Used to absolute control at the UFA stu-

dios, he had no idea that union rules demanded that food and rest breaks were called for in his unrelenting schedule. Even Tracy sided with the hordes of extras who felt they were being exploited. Producer Joseph L. Mankiewicz rewrote some of the dialogue, and MGM, imposing a happy ending on the film, prevented Lang from editing it. (Scenes showing blacks victimized by a gang of whites were cut.) Nevertheless, *Fury* is a powerful statement about an innocent man arrested as a suspected kidnaper, who escapes lynching, but returns to prove his innocence.

W.C. Fields is Eustace McGona-gle, carnival man extraordinaire again! Fields first played the role on stage in *Poppy*, then again in a silent movie version, *Sally of the Sawdust*, in 1925. This time is indisputably the funniest.

San Francisco collapses in smoking ruins for our entertainment

Hollywood, 26 June
MGM has a habit of hitting the screen with spectacular entertainment, and there's spectacle aplenty in the second half of the studio's *San Francisco*, which features the earthquake that devastated the city in 1906. The first half is some fluff about nightclub czar Clark Gable, one of his "chantoosies" Jeanette MacDonald and his boyhood chum, a priest played by Spencer Tracy. For the climactic quake in the second half, MGM special effects men Arnold Gillespie and James Basevi constructed full-size buildings on top of hydraulically operated rocker platforms. During filming the set shook and disintegrated, panicking the extras when the first tremors hit, but injuring no one as walls collapsed and bricks rained down.

Pius XI calls for moral standards

Rome, 15 July
The church is worried about the bad moral influence which the cinema can have on a worldwide scale. The Pontifical Encyclical *Vigilanti Cura*, sent to American bishops, recommended the boycotting of indecent films and congratulated the Legion of Decency on their activities. Pope Pius XI is particularly concerned about the influences on youth, and has expressed his desire for a rigorous classification system. The demands of the Pope coincide with those of the Fascist censors, who are leaning toward a more edifying cinema. Above all else, the portrayal of women must be circumscribed. A heroine in a melodrama has to be a virgin, or faithful wife and mother.

Leni Riefenstahl and the Berlin Olympics

The official chronicler of the Games.

Berlin, 17 August
Berlin's Olympic Games have finished. It was an occasion for Germany to show the world the power of Hitler's regime. Leni Riefenstahl was commissioned by the Fuhrer to film the Games "as a song of praise to the ideals of National Socialism." To capture the great event, she had over 30 cameramen, as well as many planes and airships at her disposal. It will be edited into two parts – the Festival of Nations and the Festival of Beauty – and will be, in the director's words, "a hymn to the power and beauty of Man."

Langlois creates the Cinémathèque

Paris, 2 September
Frenchman Henri Langlois is fighting to prevent the destruction of silent films, along with ensuring the existence of future safeguards of this country's rich cinematographic heritage. Thus he has just registered the constitution of a non-profit French Cinémathèque whose headquarters are located at the premises of Paul-Auguste Harlé's *La Cinématographique Française*. More than a year has passed since Harlé backed young Langlois' efforts. Now the Cinémathèque has become a vital link with the Cinema Circle film club founded by Langlois and Georges Franju last year. Harlé has been appointed president and Langlois and Franju are joint secretary generals.

Jean Renoir abandons country pleasures for the slums of the city

France, 20 August
What should have been a sunny rural idyll for Jean Renoir and his cast and team of friends, filming *A Day in the Country* beside the river Loing in the Ile de France, was dampened by the one of the wettest summers for years. As a result, this screen adaptation of a Guy de Maupassant short story had to be abandoned, with only two sequences left to be shot. The director had been happy to make a film in the sort of location dear to the Impressionists, and to compose images worthy of his father's paintings. Reluctantly, Renoir has had to desert the countryside to take up work on *The Lower Depths*, for which he has been contracted. A story of urban squalor, it is based on the play by Maxim Gorky.

*Jane Marken is charmed by Jacques Brunius in Renoir's **A Day in the Country**.*

Astaire and Rogers fly on wings of dance for the sixth time

Hollywood, 27 August
Fred Astaire and Ginger Rogers have attained the summit of their terpsichorean talents in *Swing Time*, which marks their sixth pairing since *Flying Down to Rio* three years ago. More than ever have the dancing duo of RKO musicals demonstrated their virtuosity. The number "Never Gonna Dance" has Fred trying to win Ginger over in dance. They hold each other closely, but she achingly spins away from him and the dance ends in separation. Their numbers are not merely the gems that stud rather simple stories, but, far more than dialogue, also trace the emotional development of the two characters and even advance the plot. For example, in order to get to meet dancing teacher Ginger, Fred pretends he can't dance a step. Blaming her for her pupil's two left feet, her boss fires her. Fred gets her job back by demonstrating the skills she has taught him in one lesson. The music is by Jerome Kern, a favorite composer of the two stars who have both danced, separately, in Kern shows on Broadway.

*The twinkle-toed partners in **Swing Time**, directed by George Stevens.*

'Boy Wonder' of MGM dies at thirty-seven

Irving Thalberg: taste and brilliance.

Los Angeles, 15 September
"The Boy Wonder" of Hollywood, Irving Thalberg, has died of pneumonia. The son of German-Jewish immigrants, he suffered ill-health from childhood and had a severe heart attack toward the end of 1932, which forced him to take off several months from MGM where he was production chief. Thalberg began his career as a humble secretary at Universal, but his exceptional qualities of judgment and organization led to a meteoric rise which prompted Carl Laemmle to appoint him to head of production before he was much past age 20. At Universal, the toughness beneath his frail exterior was evidenced in his stormy confrontations with Von Stroheim over *Foolish Wives* and *Merry-Go-Round*, a situation which later repeated itself at MGM over the editing of *Greed*. Thalberg and Laemmle fell out early in 1923 when the former refused to marry the latter's daughter. The young tyro joined Louis B. Mayer and, with the formation of MGM in 1924, he became the new studio's production chief, marrying actress Norma Shearer in 1927. He wielded immense power as a brilliant hands-on producer and his loss will be keenly felt. He leaves behind a fortune estimated in millions.

Chilling view of future from Korda's stable

London, 14 September
The celebrated writer H.G. Wells has adapted his novel, *The Shape of Things to Come*, for the screen. The result is a visually superb science fiction film, *Things to Come*, directed by William Cameron Menzies, which takes a sobering look at the future and climaxes with humanity venturing into space.

Françoise Rosay helps Carné to success

*Vanel, Barrault, Préjean and Toutain with Françoise Rosay in Carné's **Jenny**.*

Paris, 16 September
The first full-length film by Marcel Carné, *Jenny*, has been released. During the shooting of *Carnival in Flanders* last year, Carné was merely an assistant to Jacques Feyder. The film's star, Feyder's wife Françoise Rosay, offered the young man her services free of charge for his first film, an agreement that was decisive in helping him realize the project. *Jenny* has had a rather cool reception, some judging it as no more than a conventional melodrama, but thanks to the superior dialogue by Jacques Prévert, and an excellent use of locations, the film is an auspicious debut for Carné.

Sacha Guitry and the morality of a cheat

Actor-director Sacha Guitry, here in his role as the cheat, his fourth film.

Paris, 19 September
For having stolen a few francs, a young lad is deprived of mushrooms for dinner, and thus escapes from the poisoning which destroys his whole family: so begins *le Roman d'un tricheur (The Story of a Cheat)*, Sacha Guitry's new film, which can be seen at the Marignon. Adapted by the director himself from his own novel published in 1934, the film is a stylish and witty comedy about the art of cheating, which nevertheless ends on a moral note. The story is narrated in the first person by Guitry himself, who portrays the character of a repentant conman in his own inimitable way.

The Prix Louis Delluc gives its first nod to 'The Lower Depths'

*Jean Gabin, Louis Jouvet and Vladimir Sokoloff in **The Lower Depths**.*

Paris, 22 December
The first ever winner of the Prix Louis Delluc, created on the initiative of the group of Young Independent Critics in homage to the critic and director who died recently, is Jean Renoir's *The Lower Depths*. The film won by three votes over Marcel Carné's *Jenny*. Among the panel of judges present were Marcel Achard, Maurice Bessy, Claude Aveline, Pierre Bost, Henri Jeanson and Georges Altman. In one sense, the prize is meant to counterbalance the academicism of the Grand Prix du

Cinéma Français. The Prix Louis Delluc will try to reflect the tastes of the man who first coined the word "cinéaste" (meaning filmmaker), and one of the first critics to consider film as an art form and work out a theory. Delluc would certainly have approved of *The Lower Depths* with its flowing camerawork, superb

sets and locations, and splendid performances, particularly those from Louis Jouvet and Jean Gabin. Although ostensibly situated in Moscow, the movie is very French in flavor. According to Renoir, "I was not trying to make a Russian film. I wanted to make a human drama based on Gorky's play."

A few surprises in new popularity poll

London, 31 December
The year ends with some revealing polls as to who are the most popular stars. And from the studios' point of view, of course, this means WHO equals Big Bucks at the Box Office! Especially interesting is the fact that America's favorites are not necessarily tops with the rest of the world. The major Quigley poll, whose results were published in *Variety* last week, list the U.S. Top Ten, starting from No. 1 as follows: juvenile curly-top Shirley Temple, dashing he-man Clark Gable, dancing duo Fred As-

*French-born Claudette Colbert, the effervescent star of **It Happened One Night**, in at No. 9.*

No Roach, but a double dose of comedy from Laurel and Hardy

New York, 10 November
Unhappy with *The Bohemian Girl*, their last film made for Hal Roach, Stan Laurel and Oliver Hardy decided to break out on their own. It was Stan who wanted more control

over their pictures, and set up Stan Laurel Productions. The first one released under this banner, *Our Relations*, is also one of their best. In it, Stan and Olly play themselves and their twin brothers, Alfie Laurel and

Bert Hardy, causing double trouble when they turn up at different times at Denkers' Beer Garden. It is impossible to describe the twists and turns of this comedy of errors, but, needless to say, it is hilarious.

taire and Ginger Rogers, handsome Robert Taylor, jug-faced comedian Joe E. Brown, somber Dick Powell, glamorous Joan Crawford, sparkling Claudette Colbert, songbird Jeanette MacDonald and perennial favorite Gary Cooper. Precocious moppet Temple supersedes glamour and sex appeal outside the U.S. as well, but gorgeous Gary Cooper moves in to No. 2 elsewhere while Robert Taylor drops down to 10, with Charlie Chaplin, Garbo, Dietrich, diva Grace Moore and the Fat man and the Thin man – Laurel and Hardy – joining the world popularity list from No. 5 to No. 9. The top international box-office film for the year was Chaplin's *Modern Times*, MGM's W.S. Van Dyke is the director who brought in the most dollars for his combined output (which included both *San Francisco* and *Rose-Marie*), and finally the New York Film Critics voted *Frank Capra's Mr. Deeds Goes to Town* as the year's best film.

*The comic duo in **Our Relations**.*

*The fat man and the thin, spying on Mae Busch in **The Bohemian Girl**.*

Gorgeous Carole Lombard in one of her three sparkling 'society' roles this year.

Jean Gabin, Louis Jouvet and Vladimir Sokoloff in Renoir's **The Lower Depths**.

Director Saville and star Matthews teamed again for British musical charmer.

Olivia De Havilland and Errol Flynn in **The Charge of the Light Brigade**.

Charles Laughton was Rembrandt.

Marlene Dietrich and Basil Rathbone in **The Garden of Allah**.

An instant winner: MGM spared no expense to make this dazzling, lavish biopic of the Broadway impresario.

Technicolor was the real star of this largely disappointing costume musical.

The aggressive pioneer John Wayne opened up the frontier in one of seven films he made this year.

An imaginary romance between Wild Bill Hickok and Calamity Jane.

'Dr.' Jean Hersholt delivered quins!

Ouida's tale filmed for the third time.

Detective Chan, based on real-life sleuth Chang Apada, in one of four filmed outings this year.

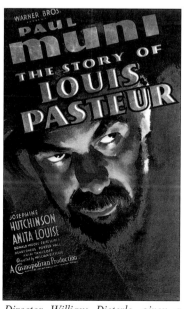

Director William Dieterle, given a scant budget, created a prestigious biopic of the famous scientist.

Founding of the great insurance co.

1937

★ ★

1936 Academy Awards, Biltmore Hotel, 4 Mar.

Best Film:	*The Great Ziegfeld*
	(dir: Robert Z. Leonard)
Best Director:	Frank Capra *(Mr. Deeds Goes to Town)*
Best Actor:	Paul Muni *(The Story of Louis Pasteur)*
Best Actress:	Luise Rainer *(The Great Ziegfeld)*
Best Supp. Actor:	Walter Brennan *(Come and Get It)*
Best Supp. Actress:	Gale Sondergaard *(Anthony Adverse)*

Paris, 15 January
Abel Gance has been forced to accept the release of an entirely altered version of his film *The Life and Loves of Beethoven*. Despite the court decision allowing cuts to 55 sequences, the film has been given a highly favorable reception. Harry Baur is memorable as Beethoven.

France, 31 January
Jean Renoir has begun filming *The Grand Illusion*, in the town of Colmar's barracks, Pierre Fresnay has accepted to play the role of Captain de Boëldieu.

Moscow, 2 February
The Mosfilm production company held a preview of *The Last Night*, by the filmmaker Yuli Raizman.

Paris, 8 February
The CGT has announced that Jean Renoir is to make a new film about the French Revolution. The project, already supported by the Union, *Ciné-Liberté* magazine and the Popular Front government, will be financed by a national subscription.

Hollywood, 9 March
Captain Dreyfus' son, Pierre Dreyfus, has approved the script inspired by the Dreyfus case that Warner Bros. want to produce under the title *The Life of Emile Zola*. Paul Muni will play Zola, and William Dieterle will direct.

London, 21 March
Alexander Korda has abandoned *I, Claudius* with only 20 minutes of expensive filming completed. Adapted from Robert Graves' bestseller, this major production, directed by Josef von Sternberg with Charles Laughton in the title role and Merle Oberon playing Messalina, has been dogged by both dispute and disaster. Sternberg's obsessive perfection upset Laughton, and his disregard for the budget alarmed Korda. To top it all, Miss Oberon has received serious injuries in a car crash.

Hollywood, 17 April
Release of *Porky's Duck Hunt*, a Tex Avery cartoon for Warner Bros.' "Looney Tunes", introducing the character of Daffy Duck.

Paris, 8 June
Premiere of Marc Allégret's *Gribouille*, with Michèle Morgan, Jean Worms, Raimu and Julien Carette.

Hollywood, 30 June
Rita Cansino, who married the millionaire Edward Judson just three months ago, has adopted the screen name Rita Hayworth during the shooting of her 13th film *Criminals of the Air*.

Hollywood, 30 June
Actor Ronald Reagan has signed a seven-year contract with Warner Bros. for $200 per week.

Shanghai, 10 July
For the first time, scriptwriter Tian Han's name has appeared officially in the credit titles. The film, *The Youth March*, was directed by Shi Dongshan. Until now Tian Han has been under suspicion due to his left-wing sympathies and has been forced to work under a pseudonym.

Prague, 30 July
Release of *Svet patri nam*, by Martin Fric. The film appeals for a mobilization against Nazism.

New York, 22 August
Alfred Hitchcock has arrived on board the *Queen Mary*. According to news reports he is on holiday in the United States.

Munich, 1 September
Jacques Feyder is undertaking the filming of *les Gens du voyage* (*Wanderers*) for Tobis, with Françoise Rosay and André Brulé.

London, 10 September
René Clair is filming *Break the News* at Pinewood studios, with Jack Buchanan and Maurice Chevalier.

France, 25 September
Popular French actress Danielle Darrieux has embarked for Hollywood to make a film for Universal, while director Julien Duvivier has been taken on by MGM for a trial period of six months.

New York, 30 September
Hedy Kiesler, who fled to America to escape the Nazi regime and her husband – the arms manufacturer Friedrich Mandl – has decided to take Hedy Lamarr as her new stage name, in memory of Barbara La Marr, the star of silent films.

Paris, 22 October
Release of Max Ophuls' film *Yoshiwara*, with Pierre Richard-Willm and Sessue Hayakawa.

Paris, 25 October
Censorship has been tightened up. From now on, visas from the censorship commission will be refused to all films which make the army look ridiculous or could upset the national feelings of foreigners. The latest changes are directly aimed at war and spy films.

Washington, 11 November
President Roosevelt has enjoyed a private view of *The Grand Illusion*, screened at the White House, and has declared that in his opinion "every democratic person in the world should see this film".

California, 30 November
The French film *Club de femmes* (*Women's Club*), by Jacques Deval, has been accused of immorality by the American censors who have demanded several cuts. The film has already been banned by the censors in Great Britain. Other films under attack are: *Faisons un rêve* (*Let's Dream a Dream*), by Sacha Guitry and *Lucretia Borgia*, a historical drama by Abel Gance.

Los Angeles, 24 December
After seeing the new Swedish film *Intermezzo*, from director Gustav Molander, David O. Selznick is reported to be very taken with the young actress Ingrid Bergman.

Los Angeles, 24 December
Premiere of Walt Disney's wonderful cartoon *Snow White*. The film is the first full-length cartoon in the history of the cinema.

Mexico, 31 December
Among the 38 films produced in Mexico during the year, 20 were based on the "rancheros", a mixture of folklore and country life. The success of these films in all Latin American countries puts the Mexican cinema on the top rung of the Spanish-speaking cinema industry.

BIRTHS

London, 30 January
Vanessa Redgrave

England, 25 February
Tom Courtenay

Virginia, 30 March
Warren Beatty (Henry W. Beaty)

New Jersey, 22 April
Jack Nicholson

Nebraska, 27 April
Sandy Dennis

France, 28 July
Francis Veber

Los Angeles, 8 August
Dustin Hoffman

California, 18 August
Robert Redford

Moscow, 20 August
Andrei Mikhalkov-Konchalovsky

Paris, 13 October
Sami Frey (Samuel Frei)

Paris, 30 October
Claude Lelouch

New York, 21 December
Jane Fonda

Wales, 31 December
Anthony Hopkins

DEATHS

Hollywood, 7 June
Jean Harlow

Hollywood, 11 July
George Gershwin

---

*Walt Disney's **Snow White and the Seven Dwarfs**, made at vast expense over a three-year period, is the first full-length animated feature. It has received a rapturous welcome.*

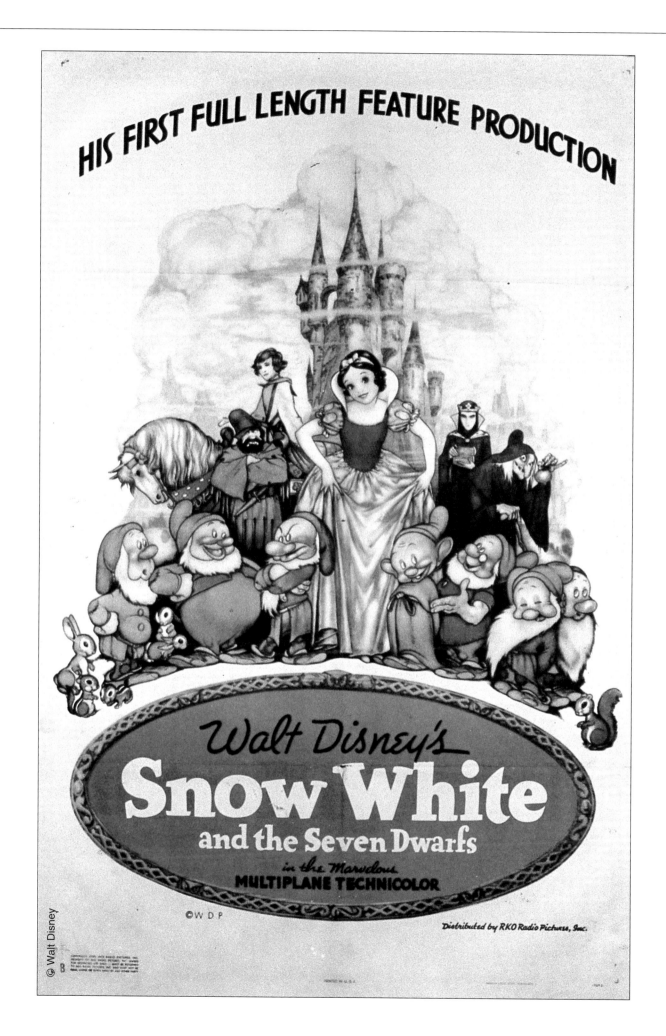

Garbo a luminous Lady of the Camelias

Greta Garbo and Robert Taylor are Marguerite Gauthier and Armand Duval.

New York, 22 January
Greta Garbo has given her most intensely moving performance as Dumas' consumptive courtesan in the movie *Camille*, which co-stars Robert Taylor, who made his first big impression in 1935 with *Magnificent Obsession*. In his piece in the *New York Herald Tribune*, writer Howard Barnes says, "With her fine intelligence and unerring instinct, she has made her characterization completely credible, while giving it an added poignancy that, to me, is utterly irresistible." Seeing Camille's death scene, it is hard to imagine the difficulty skilled director George Cukor had in shooting it. His leading lady required several takes, as she repeatedly burst into uncontrollable fits of nervous laughter the moment the cameras began to roll.

Inventive gags for seedy stationmaster

London, 3 January
Gainsborough Pictures bring the music-hall magic of comedian Will Hay to the screen in the comedy film *Oh, Mr. Porter!* Directed by Marcel Varnel, Hay plays a bungling station master sent to remote Northern Ireland, where gun-running with the Free State is rife. Sterling support comes from crazed Moore Marriot and, joining Hay for the first time, cheeky fat boy Graham Moffatt.

César joins Marius and Fanny in trilogy

A card game worthy of record played by friendly but argumentative companions. L to r: Raimu, Charpin, Paul Dullac and Robert Vattier (back view).

Nice, 23 January
The Escuriel and the Rialto, who have been simultaneously showing Marcel Pagnol's *César*, the last part of his Marseilles trilogy, have netted their largest box-office takings since *Ben-Hur* – a total of 315,000 francs. All of the 58 copies that Pagnol made of the film in his Marseilles laboratories are circulating throughout Provence, gaining huge success everywhere. The Trilogy, begun six years ago with *Marius*, was an adaptation of Pagnol's play, with no real thought to any sequel. But the popularity of the film, directed by Alexander Korda, encouraged the author to do a follow-up by transposing *Fanny* to the screen, directed by Marc Allégret. Pagnol decided to direct *César* himself, which is the only one of the three to have been written directly for the cinema. This transformation of a single work into a diptych and then a triptych has been justified because Pagnol's characters are so alive, and the actors who embody them so brilliant, that the public demanded more of them. Who could forget Raimu as César, the crabby but lovable proprietor of the Marine Bar, whose son Marius (Pierre Fresnay) runs away to sea, leaving a pregnant Fanny (Orane Demazis). Poor Fanny then marries Panisse (Charpin), a kindly widower who then dies, leaving the way for reconciliation all around. The three films are fictionalized portraits of Marseilles life described by a wonderful storyteller who creates pathos without sentimentality.

Will Hay observes Moore Marriott's efforts to milk a cow in **Oh! Mr. Porter**.

l to r: Charpin, Alida Rouffe, Orane Demazis and Raimu in **Fanny**.

André Fouché with Raimu in **César**, *which completes the trilogy.*

Gabin in the skin of 'Pépé-le-Moko'

Paris, 29 January

Jean Gabin and Mireille Balin have been brought together again in *Pépé-le-Moko*, Julien Duvivier's new film. Gabin, who was seen recently in Jean Renoir's *The Lower Depths* and in Duvivier's *la Belle équipe*, is appearing in his twenty-fifth film in less than five years. He is now the highest paid actor in France, getting fees of 100,000 francs per film. With dialogue by Henri Jeanson, adapted from the novel by Roger D'Ashelbé, *Pépé-le-Moko* is an exotic tale set in Algiers. Gabin plays Pépé, a high-powered jewel thief and bank robber forced to flee from his beloved Paris and live in the Algerian Casbah as his only means of avoiding arrest. When he falls in love with a beautiful visiting Parisienne (Balin), he leaves the Casbah to seek her and is caught. Gabin, at his most attractively roguish, brilliantly portrays the quintessential loner in a film that teems with life, romance, suspense

Jean Gabin with Mireille Balin and Lucas Gridoux, two faces of treason.

and humor. The studio-constructed Casbah, under Duvivier's expert direction, is beautifully lit and photographed (by Jules Kruger), with songs sung by Fréhel, who herself plays an old singer in the film. *Pépé-le-Moko* is the fourth motion picture on which Gabin and Duvivier have worked, and they obviously make a perfect team.

Sergei Eisenstein admits his 'errors'

Moscow, 25 April

No one will ever see Sergei Eisenstein's first sound feature, *Bezhin Meadow*. Inspired by a Turgenev tale, it tells of the youthful organizer of a village Young Pioneer group who is killed by his own *kulak* father while guarding the collective harvest against sabotage. The film's troubled production began in the spring of 1935 but has been constantly interrupted by Eisenstein's ill health and orchestrated political interference. And drastic revisions in the screenplay to conform to the Soviet doctrine of Socialist Realism have proved unavailing. All work on the film was stopped in March, followed by a vicious attack on Eisenstein in *Pravda*. The director has now been forced to make a public admission of his "errors" and to disown his film. The state-sponsored campaign to humiliate Eisenstein has reached new and shameful heights.

Docu-drama makes star of young Indian

London, 9 April

An intriguing collaboration between Zoltan Korda and celebrated documentary filmmaker Robert Flaherty has thrown up a new star, Sabu, an enchanting 13-year-old Indian boy. Flaherty discovered Sabu, a former stable boy at the court of an Indian maharajah, and immediately cast him in the title role of *Elephant Boy* to play the native lad who claims he knows the location of a mythical

elephant herd. The movie is loosely based on a Kipling story. Flaherty filmed the exterior scenes on location in India, and the interiors were shot by Zoltan Korda. Flaherty has given the film the required authenticity, the Kordas have provided the polish and Sabu has supplied bags of unforced charm. Director Zoltan Korda, younger brother of Alexander Korda and also a product of the vanished Austro-Hungarian empire, has played an enthusiastic part in the celebration of the slowly vanishing British empire. His *Sanders of the River*, adapted from an Edgar Wallace story, cast Paul Robeson as an African chief, but was fashioned into a hymn for British imperialism which so upset the black American star that he walked out of the London premiere when asked to make a speech. One suspects, however, that Korda is more interested in picturesque adventure than the politics of empire. But the more pliable Sabu proves the perfect centerpiece for *Elephant Boy*'s romantic view of India. He was paid a living wage during filming, and was grateful for it, but fame and fortune beckon, and it seems unlikely that he will return to the maharajah's stable.

Young Sabu scrubs his elephant.

On 4 March *The Great Ziegfeld*, directed by Robert Z. Leonard, was awarded the Best Film Oscar and its female star, Luise Rainer, the Best Actress award. Frank Capra won the Best Director Oscar for *Mr. Deeds Goes to Town*, and Paul Muni was named Best Actor for *The Story of Louis Pasteur*.

Jean Renoir and the illusion of peace

Cinecittà biggest studio in Europe

Commanding officer Von Stroheim.

Gabin, Fresnay and Dalio represent differing classes united in War.

Paris, 8 June

Jean Renoir's latest film, *la Grande illusion*, has just opened to a warm reception from the public and critics alike. After his *The Lower Depths*, Renoir has returned to a more personal subject and created an antiwar masterpiece in the process. The story was inspired by the adventures of General Pinsard, whom Renoir met in 1916 when they served in the same squadron. The director also added many of his own memories of the war. For him, "the Frenchmen in the film are good Frenchmen, and the Germans are good Germans. It is not possible for me to take the side of any of my characters." A wonderful cast has been assembled to play these characters: Jean Gabin, Marcel Dalio and Pierre Fresnay are three French prisoners of war, and Erich von Stroheim is the sympathetic German Commandant.

Rome, 28 April

Italy has just opened its own "dream factory" called Cinecittà. It has been set up in the Roman countryside, 10 kilometres from the via Tuscolana, and covers 60 hectares filled with workshops, auditoria, laboratories, nine sound stages, and villas to accomodate the casts, crews and directors. Just like Hollywood, Cinecittà enjoys a mild climate and an exceptional quality of light. All of it took over a year to construct, making it the largest cinematographic complex in Europe. Mussolini laid the first stone at 9 a.m. on the morning of 29 January 1936. The studio has been created with the intention of breathing new life into Italian film production, because the cinema has recently been recognized as an important means of propaganda. A prestigious workplace was needed to entice the filmmakers, and Il Duce hopes it will become an international attraction, an ambitious Fascist Hollywood. Above the gates of the studio, an aggressive motto has been inscribed: "The Cinematograph is the Strongest Weapon."

Sacha Guitry finds riches in stolen jewels

Paris, 11 May

Sacha Guitry's new film, *The Pearls of the Crown*, is a trilingual story – French, English and Italian – about seven pearls given to a range of famous personages over the ages, and a number of contemporary people of different nationalities who search for them. As usual, Guitry has provided a film of style and wit, with most of the pearls in the dialogue, rather than in the plot.

Jean Harlow cut off in the prime of life

Los Angeles, 7 June

Jean Harlow has died in the hospital of a cerebral edema. She became seriously ill during the filming of *Saratoga* and had been treated for uremic poisoning. Some blame her mother, a Christian Scientist, for preventing Harlow from receiving the treatment that might have saved her. Anita Loos claims that Harlow was severely depressed by the end of her affair with William Powell.

*Filming of **The Pearls of the Crown**, with Arletty as the Queen of Ethiopia.*

*Harlow with Clark Gable in **Saratoga**, her last film made just before she died.*

Chinese cinema is inspired by Hollywood

*With **Malu Tianshi**, Yuan Muzhi has made a recognizable Chinese classic.*

Peking, 24 July
A new Chinese film, *Malu Tianshi* (*Street Angel*), is a highly original work, even if it's been influenced by Frank Borzage's 1928 Hollywood drama of the same title. Its 28-year-old director, Yuan Muzhi, had a distinguished career on stage before entering films as an actor and writer. The movie captures the atmosphere of one of Shanghai's poorest areas, where a young man is in a chaste affair with a woman pressed into prostitution. The tragi-comic film is firmly rooted in reality, and explicit in its criticism of Chinese society.

Jean Gabin proves capable of vulnerability

Paris, 29 September
In his latest film, *Gueule d'amour*, Jean Gabin assumes his habitual role of pessimistic anti-hero, playing an army officer who is betrayed by the woman he loves. But this time he allows himself to suggest vulnerability in his screen persona which has previously been concealed from cinema audiences. Nevertheless, he remains cinema's quintessential loner, doomed in life and love.

Gabin's seducer who becomes a melancholy victim is a departure for the actor.

Search for memories in 'Un carnet de bal'

Marie Bell finds Louis Jouvet during her search for her lost dance partners.

Paris, 7 September
The scenario of Julien Duvivier's new film, *Un carnet de bal* (*Dance Card*), focuses on a rather original idea. A wealthy, middle-aged widow (Marie Bell) finds an old dance card dating back to her sixteenth year, and decides to find out what has happened to the men whose names are on it. She discovers an epileptic doctor (Pierre Blanchar), a monk (Harry Baur), a hairdresser (Fernandel), a crooked nightclub owner (Louis Jouvet), a skiing instructor (Pierre Richard-Willm) and a small-town mayor (Raimu). Her quest reveals the indifference and pettiness of the world, and she finds her existence meaningless. However, when she adopts an orphan boy, her life takes on new meaning. The optimistic ending does not efface the pessimism that precedes it. This elegant film allows a galaxy of French stars to do short turns, doubtless contributing to its great success.

On 3 September, Italy's *Scipione the African*, directed by Carmine Gallone, was voted best film at Venice. Duvivier's *Dance Card* (*Un carnet de bal*) was best foreign film and, despite protests from the Italian government, Renoir's *The Grand Illusion* was chosen as best film for overall artistic quality.

Françoise Rosay and Marie Bell.

Carné and Prévert, victims of the 'bizarre'

*Jouvet and Michel Simon in **Drôle de drame**, aptly known as **Bizarre, Bizarre**.*

Paris, 20 October
The new film from Marcel Carné, *Bizarre, Bizarre (Drôle de drame)*, was greeted with whistles and boos when it opened at the Colisée. The public failed to appreciate the craziness of the humor which recalls *It's in the Bag (l'Affaire est dans le sac)* by the Prévert brothers. This connection is not accidental because *Bizarre, Bizarre* is Jacques Prévert's second collaboration with Carné.

The film, set in Edwardian London, tells what happens when a mystery writer (Michel Simon) has to pretend to a visiting Bishop (Louis Jouvet) that his wife (Françoise Rosay) has been called away. The failure of this witty and anarchic farce is even more bitter for Carné because it was shot in an unpleasant atmosphere. Jouvet and Simon didn't think much of it, and spent their time making nasty comments on the set.

Ruined village gets a face-lift from Pagnol

*Fernandel and Orane Demazis in **Regain**, from the novel by Jean Giono.*

Paris, 28 October
Audiences who go to see Marcel Pagnol's *Harvest (Regain)* will be astonished to learn that the ruined village, in which the action of the film unfolds, was built entirely from scratch in Provence by Marius Broquier, the art director. Drawn from a novel by Jean Giono, the film tells the story of a poacher (Gabriel Gabrio), longing for fatherhood, who coaxes an itinerant girl (Orane Demazis) away from her simple knife-grinder companion (Fernandel). He sets up house with her in a deserted village, which they bring back to life. The film contains superb pantheistic images, and atmospheric music by Arthur Honegger. *Harvest* will be given a gala showing tonight at the Marignan cinema, for the benefit of the country's war orphans, and will be attended by the President of the Republic, Albert Lebrun.

First award given of new acting prize

Paris, 31 October
The first winner of the new Suzanne Bianchetti Prize is a young actress from Marseilles, Junie Astor. She has won the award for her performances in Raymond Bernard's film *Coupable*, Jean Renoir's *The Lower Depths*, and Jean de Limur's work *la Garçonne*. Junie made her screen debut three years ago, sparring with Noël Noël's gloriously befuddled soldier in *Ademai aviateur*. This prize has been set up by the critic René Jeanne as a memorial to his wife, Suzanne Bianchetti, who tragically disappeared without trace in November 1936 at age 47. A star of the silent screen she appeared in many films, including Jacques de Baroncelli's *le Père Goriot* in 1921, Léonce Perret's *Madame Sans-Gêne* in 1925 and finally in Abel Gance's *Napoleon* in 1927.

A sweet, light soufflé of American comedy from Leo McCarey

Hollywood, 4 November
Director Leo McCarey has scored a tremendous success with an hilarious Columbia comedy, *The Awful Truth*, which stars Cary Grant and Irene Dunne. They play a married couple whose decision to divorce leads to innumerable romantic complications. A graduate of the Hal Roach studio and the man responsible for pairing Stan Laurel with Oliver Hardy, McCarey has found in Grant and Dunne the perfect combination of warmth and comedy technique. If proof is required that, for the moment at least, Columbia need not rely solely on Frank Capra, then McCarey has demonstrated it.

*Sophisticated banter between Cary Grant and Irene Dunne in **The Awful Truth**.*

Selznick goes from strength to strength

Selznick: a force to reckon with.

A Star is Born: March and Gaynor.

Hollywood, 26 September
This has been a good year for producer David O. Selznick. Two years after leaving MGM to form his own independent production company, Selznick International Pictures, he has begun to fulfill his promise. Two outstanding new films have already opened, *A Star is Born* with Janet Gaynor and Fredric March, and *The Prisoner of Zenda*, based on the novel by Anthony Hope and with an all-star cast headed by Ronald Colman, Douglas Fairbanks Jr., Raymond Massey, Madeleine Carroll and Mary Astor. In addition, a third project, *Nothing Sacred*, has been finished for a November premiere. This last is from the same team as *A Star is Born*: director William Well-

man, art director Lyle Wheeler, actor Fredric March starring (with Carole Lombard), and color specialist W. Howard Greene behind the camera. Both pictures were filmed in Technicolor and demonstrate that it can enhance the look of a modern drama or comedy, and need not be restricted to costume pictures, musicals or exotic subjects. Most of all, these films reflect Selznick's commitment to top quality stories and scripts – not only published works such as *Zenda* or *The Adventures of Tom Sawyer* (currently filming), but to film originals like *Nothing Sacred* from Ben Hecht, and *A Star is Born* from Wellman and Robert Carson, and scripted by Dorothy Parker and Alan Campbell.

*Carole Lombard, Walter Connolly and Fredric March in **Nothing Sacred**.*

Disney's Snow White even silences Grumpy

Hollywood, 21 December
Judy Garland, Marlene Dietrich and Charles Laughton are among the stars attending the premiere, at the Cathay Circle Theater, of Walt Disney's *Snow White and the Seven Dwarfs*, the first feature-length animated film in three-strip Technicolor. Disney, who hit the road to fame and fortune in 1928 when he created Mickey Mouse, has taken an enormous artistic and financial risk in

the creation of *Snow White*, which has been four years in the making at a cost of $1.5 million. In addition to the pioneering animation techniques employed by the Disney studio, under the supervision of David Hand, music plays an important part in the production, and tunes like "Whistle While You Work" and "Some Day My Prince Will Come" look like they will become immediate big hits with the public.

Walt Disney has published a comic book of his 1928 creation, Mickey Mouse.

Flora Robson was Elizabeth I, but Laurence Olivier and Vivien Leigh got raves.

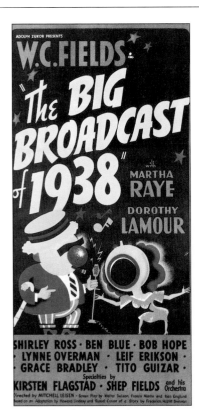

Empty-headed excuse for star turns.

Vehicle for a much-loved British star.

Exciting, emotional whaling yarn.

Paramount's amusing and zippy musical had Ida Lupino pretending to be a socialite, and then soliciting Jack Benny's assistance to become Queen of the Ball. Raoul Walsh directed.

Wells Fargo was a fictionalized account of the famous coach company of the same name. Joel McCrea was a Unionist, married to a Confederate. She was played by his real-life wife Frances Dee.

The inimitable Peter Lorre played a spy, out to secure secret documents in this successful thriller.

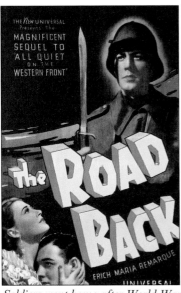

Soldiers went home after World War I to problems and disillusion. This time they were German.

Katharine Hepburn, Franchot Tone in **Quality Street** from J.M. Barrie's play.

Dietrich, Herbert Marshall in **Angel**.

Fred, no Ginger, but Gershwin score.

Great special effects created meteorological mayhem and drew big audiences.

The Marx brothers scored another comedy success in **A Day at the Races**.

Taut adaptation of Emlyn Williams' play about a psychopath.

Utopia in magnificent deco sets.

Méliès and Cohl: two magicians gone

Paris, 25 January

Among the mourners who accompanied Georges Méliès to his final resting place at Père Lachaise cemetery, were the two young founders of the French Cinémathèque, Georges Franju and Henri Langlois. There were also many other admirers of Méliès, most of whom have only recently rediscovered this pioneer of cinematographic art. This fervent group had paid homage to the modest and forgotten magician in his old age after he had been found in a little toy shop at the Gare Montparnasse. Méliès died at the age of 78 on 21 January. Ironically, the day before, Emile Cohl died tragically at an old people's home at Villejuif, a candle having set his beard on fire. Thus, by an astonishing accident, he was reunited in death, after an interval of a only few hours, with another early enchanter of the cinema, two sprites with white goatee-beards and sparkling eyes.

Delluc prize goes to 'The Puritan'

Paris, 16 February

After having impressed the public and critics on its release last December, *The Puritan*, Jeff Musso's first film, has become the second recipient of the Prix Louis Delluc. Adapted from a story by the Irish writer Liam O'Flaherty, it tells of Francis Ferriter, a journalist who belongs to a secret society dedicated to cleansing the country of moral impurities. When a fellow member refuses to denounce his own son's affair with Molly, a woman of easy virtue, Ferriter murders her, only realizing much later that he was motivated by his own sexual desire. There is a superb performance by Jean-Louis Barrault in the title role, leading a fine cast that includes Viviane Romance as Molly and Pierre Fresnay as the probing and perceptive police chief. The re-creation of the atmosphere of Dublin also, quite obviously, influenced the panel of judges in their choice.

'Marseillaise': a modern-day revolution

A film born of a trade union initiative and partly financed by public money.

Paris, 9 February

The Parisian public are at last able to enjoy *la Marseillaise*, the great film about the French Revolution that Jean Renoir has promised for a year. The originality of the screenplay lies in the events of 10 August 1792, and not those of 1789. There must have been a tremendous temptation to deal with the leading figures of the epoch. Instead, Renoir has preferred to cast his eye over the ordinary people who made up the Marseilles Batallion, the group of volunteers who marched to Paris. Pierre Renoir plays Louis XVI and Lise Delamare is Marie-Antoinette, but the real heroes of the popular fresco are a peasant, a customs official, a mason and a house painter.

The collective production, financed by the French trade unions is "the film of the union of the French nation against a minority of exploiters, the film of the rights of man and of the citizen." In commemorating the 150th anniversary of the Revolution, Renoir is celebrating, at the same time, the Popular Front. One should ask, however, if this idea has arrived too late, as the enthusiasm for the Popular Front is not what it was in 1936. Originally, the idea was to finance the film by issuing public subscriptions at two francs apiece; however, it fell short of the total required. In addition, financial support was lost when Léon Blum's government fell last year. Nevertheless, Renoir's film is a triumph.

Mark Twain's Tom Sawyer is back again

Hollywood, 11 February

The producer David O. Selznick has brought Tom Sawyer back to the silver screen in *The Adventures of Tom Sawyer*, starring Tommy Kelly in the title role. There is, perhaps, a little more slapstick in this handsome production than Mark Twain would have liked, but the cave sequence with evil-eyed Victor Jory as Injun Joe captures the chilling mood of the original. Photographed in Technicolor by James Wong Howe and designed by Lyle Wheeler and William Cameron Menzies, the film presents a highly romanticized view of life in the American South from the producer who is about to embark on his production of *Gone With the Wind*. Norman Taurog directed.

Tommy Kelly, here with May Robson, is Twain's irrepressible Tom Sawyer.

Louis XVI (Pierre Renoir, center) with the Royal family in the Tuileries.

Bette Davis sizzles as rebellious 'Jezebel'

Luise Rainer pulls off an Oscar double

Henry Fonda (right) is an appropriately distinguished co-star for Bette Davis.

*Tracy and Bartholomew in **Captains Courageous**; Rainer in **The Good Earth**.*

Hollywwod, 10 March

Her bitter contractual battles with Warner Brothers behind her, Bette Davis has hit her stride with *Jezebel*, directed by William Wyler. She delivers a magnetic performance as tempestuous Southern belle Julie Marston, "half-angel, half-siren, all woman!" as the posters shriek, who goes a tad too far in attempting to arouse fiance Henry Fonda's jealousy. Davis' extraordinary conviction ensures that the red dress she wears to scandalize New Orleans society loses none of its impact in a black-and-white picture.

Hollywood, 10 March

Luise Rainer was content to stay at home on the evening of the tenth annual Academy Awards ceremony held at the Biltmore in front of over 1,000 guests. After all, although she had been nominated for her role in *The Good Earth*, she had already won the Best Actress Oscar last year for *The Great Ziegfeld*. And on top of that, her rivals this time around were Greta Garbo (*Camille*), Barbara Stanwyck (*Stella Dallas*), Janet Gaynor (*A Star is Born*) and Irene Dunne (*The Awful Truth*). However, at 8:35 p.m., the names of the winners were given to the press, and Rainer was telephoned at home and told she had won. Quickly changing into an evening dress, she dashed downtown to receive her second statuette. She therefore becomes the first star to win two Oscars in succession. The evening's other big winners were Spencer Tracy (*Captains Courageous*), director Leo McCarey (*The Awful Truth*) and *The Life of Emile Zola*, voted the Best Picture.

Leonid Moguy has warm regard for his 'Prisoners without Bars'

Paris, 16 February

The former news cameraman and Russian emigré, Leonide Moguy, is extremely content with the enthusiasm which has greeted his second feature, and second French film, *Prison Without Bars*, at the Max Linder cinema. This social drama takes place in a woman's prison, and relies heavily on its brilliant female cast. It includes Annie Ducaux of the Comédie Française; rising star Ginette Leclerc, who portrays a depraved prisoner, and also Corinne Luchaire, a young 17-year-old actress with a strange beauty who is the daughter of the journalist Jean Luchaire. Among this group of talented women, the male lead, Roger Duchesne, has some difficulty getting himself noticed. *Prison Without Bars* should enable the director, who came to France in 1929, to continue to make a successful career here.

*Corinne Luchaire (left) and Ginette Leclerc (center) play the two principal roles in Moguy's **Prison Without Bars**.*

*Best Film: Henry O'Neill (right), Paul Muni in **The Life of Emile Zola**.*

World of cinema demonstrated by Pagnol

Fernandel and Orane Demazis in **The Schpountz**, *from an original screenplay.*

Paris, 15 April
The curious title of Marcel Pagnol's new film playing at the Olympia, *The Schpountz*, was borrowed from Slavonic slang that means a simple or screwy person, and was originally suggested by Pagnol's photographer Willy Faktorovitch. In this case it refers to Fernandel as a cinema-mad grocer, who becomes the victim of a practical joke played on him by a cynical film crew touring his district of Provence. He arrives at the studio in Paris on their false promises, but reveals himself as a successful comedian. Apparently, this ironic, very amusing, self-mocking and acerbic satire was based on a true story. Fernandel in the title role is wonderfully "schpountzy" and is encircled by a rich gathering of characters, among them the Pagnol favorites Charpin and Orane Demazis, the Panisse and Fanny of his trilogy.

'Olympia' celebrates German athleticism

Goebbels (left) and Leni Riefenstahl at a press reception for the Olympics.

Berlin, 20 April
For those who could not attend the Berlin Olympics, the event has been stunningly captured on film by Leni Riefenstahl, chronicler of the Nazi rallies at Nuremberg in *Triumph of the Will*. Her *Olympia*, backed by all the resources of the State, is a virtually delirious celebration of the postures of German physical vitality, divided into two parts: the Fest de Völker is an evocation of Ancient Greece utilizing a combination of "strength through joy" and Isadora Duncan; the Fest der Schönheit celebrates the games itself, emphasizing athletic shape rather than the details of competition. However, this hymn to glistening muscle has been marred by the demand of Nazi ideology that the minimum of attention be paid to the highlight of the Olympics, the triumphs of the black American sprinter Jesse Owens.

Abel Gance looks to Latin America

Paris, 6 May
Abel Gance, director of *Napoleon*, has never concealed his preference for screenplays of vast historic frescoes. Unfortunately for him, there are not many producers capable of financing his unbounded ambitions. However, it seems as though this state of affairs may be on the verge of change. Following an announcement in the press today, Gance is preparing to make three large films for the Sud company. The trio will highlight three significant historical figures: Christopher Columbus, the Genoese who discovered America; Ignatius Loyola, the Spanish theologian who founded the Jesuit order, and finally the Cid Campeador, the eleventh-century Castilian knight, already the hero of a great many literary works, of which Corneille's play is the most famous. According to the director, the films will be a huge "Latin Gesture".

A dashing, daring Errol Flynn follows in Fairbanks' footsteps

Hollywood, 12 May
Already this looks like Errol Flynn's year. Warner Brothers' swashbuckling star has stepped into the shoes of Douglas Fairbanks in *The Adventures of Robin Hood*, a high, wide and handsome story of Sherwood Forest shot in glorious three-strip Technicolor and directed with immense panache by Michael Curtiz,

Errol Flynn as the legendary Robin Hood in a film of superb color quality.

who took over the director's chair from William Keighley after filming began. The legendary medieval outlaw was originally supposed to be played by James Cagney, but the project was shelved after one of the feisty star's disputes with the studio. However, after Flynn's triumph in the 1935 *Captain Blood*, it was only a matter of time before Jack Warner dusted off the property for his athletic new star. Flynn is backed by a superb supporting cast, including Olivia De Havilland as a meltingly lovely Maid Marian, Alan Hale as a rumbustious Little John, and aquiline Basil Rathbone as the silkily villainous Sir Guy of Gisbourne, perishing at the sharp end of Flynn's sword after an epic battle to the death. Erich Wolfgang Korngold's stirring score spurs the action along, and Carl Jules Weyl's magnificent sets provide the perfect backdrop to a $2 million extravaganza which can boast of sufficient stunts for at least six adventure yarns.

Jean Gabin on the 'Quai des brumes'

The 'Rage of Paris' is rage of Hollywood

Jean Gabin and Michèle Morgan are threatened with destruction by the violent jealousy of Michel Simon-Zabel.

Paris, 1 July
The young French film star Danielle Darrieux, known in France simply as "D.D.", has recently returned from Hollywood, which she set out to conquer last autumn. Accompanied by her husband, director Henri Decoin, she intends to resume her career in Europe. Her return coincides with the French release of her first American film, *The Rage of Paris*, a fast-moving comedy that co-stars Douglas Fairbanks Jr. and has been smoothly tailored by Universal to introduce the charming star to the American public. Director Henry Koster heads the same team who shot Deanna Durbin to stardom.

The great filmmaking team surrounds the stars, left to right, Alexander Trauner, Jacques Prévert, Carné, Eugen Schüfftan and Simon Schiffrin.

Paris, 18 May
Marcel Carné's third feature, *Quai des brumes*, is now showing at the Marivaux. This story, adapted by Jacques Prévert from the novel by Pierre Mac Orlan, tells of an army deserter (Jean Gabin), who is driven to murder by evil forces and flees to Le Havre. It is there that he meets and falls in love with Nelly (Michèle Morgan), but their plan to escape together is foiled by her guardian (Michel Simon). In the end, he is shot and killed by a gangster (Pierre Brasseur) whom he had humiliated. When Gabin tells the 18-year-old Morgan, in trench coat and beret, that she has beautiful eyes, nobody in the audience could disagree. The doomed and poetic atmosphere of the film is created by muted lighting and the somber, fog-bound sets designed by Alexander Trauner. All the characters give the impression of living in suspense, in a world where corruption has triumphed. Perhaps it is this quality which has annoyed some of the critics. Both those on the left and right have reproached *Quai des brumes* for being totally pessimistic. In his column in the Communist newspaper *l'Humanité*, Georges Sadoul referred to "the politics of deadly nightshade running downstream". Jean Renoir felt antipathy toward the film, seeing it as "Fascist propaganda", and believing that the immoral characters were "fascist at heart", who would happily shake the hand of a dictator. Prévert, who considers himself violently anti-fascist, was incensed by his friend's remarks.

*With Douglas Fairbanks in **The Rage of Paris**, directed by Henry Koster.*

Film archives united

Paris, 15 July
This month sees the establishment of the Fédération internationale des archives du film (FIAF). The driving force behind this new organization has been Henri Langlois, a film archivist who founded the Cinémathèque Française along with George Franju in 1936. Langlois believes most passionately that the true key to safeguarding the heritage of the world cinema lies in establishing close links between national film libraries. Outside France there are film archives in Britain, the United States and Germany. FIAF's headquarters will be in Paris, but its first congress will be held in New York. ▷

Famous set designer Lazare Meerson dies

London, 30 June
The celebrated art director Lazare Meerson has died at the age of 38. Born in a part of Poland long dominated by Russia, he left Eastern Europe after the Bolshevik revolution, spending several years in Germany before settling in France in 1924. From working for directors such as Jacques Feyder amd Marcel l'Herbier, Meerson revolutionized the look of French films, moving away from the pervasive expressionism to achieve a "poetic realism" which has dominated the French cinema in recent years. The huge studio-built cityscapes Meerson created for such movies as René Clair's *Sous les toits de Paris* have influenced art directors in Europe and Hollywood. His career ended on a high note, working for Alexander Korda on *The Citadel* in England.

*Meerson (right) photographed with Georges Auric (left) and René Clair during the filming of **le Million**.*

Raimu makes a colorful and moving baker

![With Ginette Leclerc in The Baker's Wife based on a story by Jean Giono.](placeholder)

*With Ginette Leclerc in **The Baker's Wife** based on a story by Jean Giono.*

Paris, 8 September
Filmgoers have been flocking to see Marcel Pagnol's new film, *la Femme du boulanger* (*The Baker's Wife*). Inspired by an episode in the Jean Giono novel *Jean le Bleu*, the film received its first public showings in Marseilles, in a theater rented by Pagnol and renamed Le César for the occasion. Thanks mainly to its star, Raimu, this acutely observed drama dealing with infidelity has been an instant popular and critical success. Having played the irascible César in Pagnol's Marseilles trilogy, Raimu is cast as a baker bewitched, bothered and bewildered when his young wife (Ginette Leclerc) leaves him for the handsome shepherd Charles Moulin.

'Alexander Nevsky' is an epic film-opera

Moscow, 1 December
After years of failure and fruitless projects, Sergei Eisenstein has finally succeeded in creating his first sound film. The action of *Alexander Nevsky* takes place in 1242, when Holy Russia was invaded by the armies of Teutonic knights. Prince Alexander Nevsky (Nikolai Cherkassov) forms a people's army to drive the brutal invaders from their land. Eisenstein, combining aesthetic demands with a popular theme, has placed his ideas about musical counterpoint and sound at the service of a patriotic epic. The result offers stirring images and a "symphonic structure" (with the dramatic music of Prokofiev), particularly during the Battle of the Ice.

Rumors of film festival in Cannes

Paris, 19 September
It was while on the train headed to Venice, where they would attend the Mostra film festival, that Emile Vuillermoz and René Jean, two journalists, had the idea for an international film festival to be held in France. When put to Jean Zay, the Minister of Education and Arts, he was very interested. And in fact, the transformation of the Mostra of Venice into a highly politicized event has necessitated the creation of another film festival. That is why the Americans and the British have let it be known that they would encourage the setting up of an international festival in France. Already, many towns have put forward their candidature, notably Vichy, Biarritz and Algiers. Nevertheless, it looks as if the town of Cannes has won this race. Its sunny Mediterranean climate and its refined atmosphere would be an excellent shop-window for France and her cinema.

Classic Shaw play looks to be a 'bloody likely' hit in the USA

New York, 2 December
Audiences at Radio City Music Hall give thumbs up to Leslie Howard's production of the Bernard Shaw play *Pygmalion*. Howard is perfectly cast as the unworldly philologist, Professor Higgins with the delightful Wendy Hiller co-starring as the Cockney flower girl he turns into a lady. Bernard Shaw's original screenplay was adapted by Ian Dalrymple, Cecil Lewis and W.P. Lipscomb. Three men have had a hand in the direction of *Pygmalion*, Howard, Anthony Asquith and the volatile central European, Gabriel Pascal, whom Shaw has entrusted with the filming of his plays. Shaw had previously rejected various Hollywood suitors, including Sam Goldwyn, to whom he personally delivered the tart observation,"The trouble, Mr. Goldwyn, is that you are only interested in art, and I am only interested in money." Little love was lost between Howard and Pascal during filming, but none of this can be discerned in the final product. Indeed, after completing the film, Howard and Pascal announced their plan for Howard to play two real-life British heroes, Nelson and also Lawrence of Arabia. Howard's co-star Wendy Hiller has been on stage since the age of 18, and in 1935 scored a personal triumph in London and New York in the Depression drama titled *Love on the Dole*.

Professor Higgins (Leslie Howard) picks up Eliza Doolittle (Wendy Hiller).

MacDonald and Eddy romance in triple color

Hollywood, 26 December
MGM has chosen *Sweethearts* for its first three-tone Technicolor picture. Starring Nelson Eddy and Jeanette MacDonald, the film is based on Victor Herbert's 1913 operetta and not only introduces the singing lovebirds in color, but also places them into a contemporary setting for the first time. MacDonald has bright red hair and green eyes, and is dressed throughout by Adrian in pale pink shades. In the title number, the fair-haired Eddy wears a bright uniform, and she is in a gold sequined gown. Of course, the stars' voices make the film as much of a joy to the ears as to the eyes.

Carné's brilliant cast shines in poetic drama

Louis Jouvet and Arletty in the striking 'atmosphere' scene in **Hotel du Nord**.

Paris, 16 December
"Atmosphere, atmosphere... I've had a gutsful of atmosphere!" so says Arletty in Marcel Carné's "atmospheric" new film *Hôtel du Nord*. Although this time Carné has used a screenplay penned by Henri Jeanson and Jean Aurenche instead of Jacques Prévert, the dialogue is as eloquent and incisive as in *Quai des brumes*. The writers have given the director ample opportunity to create a poetic bittersweet drama, and the splendid cast the chance to shine. Adapted from the populist novel by Eugène Dabit, the film focuses on the residents of a rundown hotel on the Canal Saint-Martin in Paris. They include a young couple (Jean-Pierre Aumont and Annabella) who make a suicide pact, and a cynical murderer on the run (Louis Jouvet) with his lively mistress (Arletty). In order to create the atmosphere required, Carné got his art director Alexander Trauner to construct the hotel and the Quai in the studio. The subtly-lit and perfectly designed sets are well photographed by Armand Thirard, except when a bus, passing a scaled-down hotel facade, reaches up to the first-floor windows.

Jean Renoir returns to Emile Zola twelve years on from 'Nana'

Paris, 21 December
Jean Renoir's new project entitled *The Human Beast* (*la Bête humaine*) came about because Jean Gabin wanted to work with Renoir again, and because of the star's love of locomotives. Like *Nana*, which Renoir directed for his wife Catherine Hessling 12 years ago, *The Human Beast* originates from Emile Zola's Rougon-Macquart series of novels, though the style of the film is vastly different. While *Nana* was close to German Expressionism, the recent film is full of the fatalistic mood of French realism. Renoir's beautifully crafted screenplay that has been updated to contemporary France, does remain faithful to the 1890 novel and provides opportunities for the powerful, brooding presence of Gabin and the enchanting Simone Simon, and allows Gabin to actually drive a train from Paris to Le Havre.

Jean Gabin with his iron friend.

Prix Louis Delluc

Paris, 23 December
A bit in advance of the customary award date, the jury for the Prix Louis Delluc, currently in its third year, has named Marcel Carné's *Quai des brumes* as the winner of its award. Carné's film was chosen from a prestigious selection of pictures that include: *les Disparus de Saint-Agil*, *l'Etrange Monsieur Victor*, *Entrée des artistes*, *Hôtel du Nord* and *la Bête humaine*. Meanwhile, *Alerte en Mediterranée* from director Leo Joannon has won the Grand French prize.

Margaret Lockwood, Paul Lukas, Philip Leaver, Michael Redgrave and Mary Clare in Hitchcock's splendid **The Lady Vanishes**.

Charles Boyer and Hedy Lamarr in **Algiers**, *based on the classic* **Pépé-le-Moko**.

This wonderfully well-acted screwball comedy was actually an affectionate satire on Hollywood.

Colman's French poet Villon pitted his wits against, and was outacted by, Rathbone's King Louis XI.

This popular period melodrama was a $2 million **San Francisco** *lookalike.*

Alexander Nevsky, *directed by Eisenstein, used music instead of natural sound.*

Despite critical indifference, strong public enthusiasm greeted this swash-buckling movie.

*Tyrone Power, with Norma Shearer as **Marie Antoinette**, in the lavish film of that name.*

Aerobatics and romance made this one of the year's top ten moneymakers.

Mae doubled as both a blonde and a brunette, and wore seventeen gowns!

*David Niven, Claudette Colbert, Tommy Ricketts in **Bluebeard's Eighth Wife**.*

Morris, a real-life Olympic medalist.

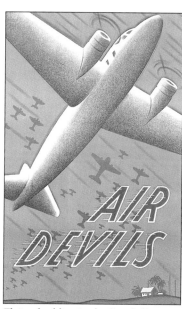

Flying buddies in the South Seas.

1938 Academy Awards, Biltmore Hotel, 23 Feb.

Best Film:	*You Can't Take It With You* (dir: Frank Capra)
Best Director:	Frank Capra
Best Actor:	Spencer Tracy *(Boys Town)*
Best Actress:	Bette Davis *(Jezebel)*
Best Supp. Actor:	Walter Brennan *(Kentucky)*
Best Supp. Actress:	Fay Bainter *(Jezebel)*

Paris, 25 January
First screening of *Trois de Saint-Cyr*, directed by Jean-Paul Paulin. Love becomes inextricably tangled up with heroism in Paulin's version of the archetypal colonial-cum-military adventure so greatly appreciated by the French public.

Moscow, 2 February
Release of *The Vyborg Side*, by Grigori Kozintsev and Leonid Trauberg, the last part of the trilogy which started in 1935 with *The Youth of Maxim*.

Billancourt, 6 February
Marcel Carné has started shooting the studio footage for *le Jour se lève* (*Daybreak*). Carné is back working in collaboration with Jacques Prévert on this film.

Madrid, 15 February
The producer G. Renault-Decker has obtained permission from Franco's government to film *Christopher Columbus* in Granada. Abel Gance will be directing the film in several languages.

Villars-de-Lans, 27 February
Jacques Feyder is on location in the Vercors for the film *la Loi du nord*. The action is actually supposed to take place in the far North of Canada in the world of the trappers.

Moscow, 7 March
Release of the second part of *Peter the Great*, by Vladimir Petrov, and with Nikolas Simonov and Nikolai Cherkassov.

Warsaw, 8 March
Opening of *Trois valses* at the Napoléon, a cinema reserved exclusively for French productions. The film was made by the German Ludwig Berger now working in Paris.

Los Angeles, 17 March
Release of *Love Affair*, by Leo McCarey, starring Charles Boyer, Irene Dunne and Maria Ouspenskaya.

Epinay, 22 March
Claude Autant-Lara and Maurice Lehmann have started shooting *Fric-frac* in the Eclair studios. Arletty and Michel Simon are once again playing the roles that made them famous in the theater.

Paris, 21 April
Premiere of Marcel L'Herbier's *Entente cordiale* at the Marivaux. The film is based on André Maurois' book *Edward VII and His Time*. Gaby Morlay interprets the role of Queen Victoria.

New York, 11 May
Release of *Only Angels Have Wings*, directed by Howard Hawks, with Jean Arthur, Cary Grant, Richard Barthelmess and Rita Hayworth heading the cast.

Hollywood, 19 May
The cameras had scarcely started turning for *Ninotchka*, when Greta Garbo, who usually has a very good relationship with the director Ernst Lubitsch, suddenly decided she was speaking too loudly. She snapped at him, in German, "Could you be so kind as to speak more softly when you address me." Lubitsch was apparently quite taken aback.

Soviet Union, 1 June
Sergei Eisenstein and his cameraman Edouard Tissé have just started shooting the short documentary *The Grand Canal of Fergana*.

Washington, 9 June
German actress, Marlene Dietrich, who came to work for Paramount in 1930, has now officially become an American citizen.

Paris, 20 June
A special evening was held at the university in honor of Charlie Chaplin on his 50th birthday. It was organized by Laure Albin-Guillot from the National Cinema Archives and Henri Langlois from the French Cinematèque.

Brussels, 31 July
The History of the Cinematic Art, written by Carl Vincent, has been published by Trident. The book is one of the first attempts at a general history of the cinema.

Cannes, 1 August
Preparations for the International Film Festival are actively underway. The supplementary funding has been voted by the municipal council to finish equipping the casino. The opening is planned for 1 September.

Los Angeles, 14 August
Janet Gaynor, who was the winner of the first-ever Academy Award for Best Actress in 1929, today married top designer Adrian.

Paris, 24 August
The Paramount cinema has released *Louise*, by Abel Gance, based on the opera by Charpentier, with the American soprano Grace Moore, tenor Georges Thill, André Pernet and Robert Le Vigan in the cast.

Paris, 28 August
With the threat of war approaching, a censorship law has been passed to control all printed matter, written work, radio transmissions and film projections. This law is aimed at titles such as *le Déserteur*.

New York, 1 September
Release of *The Women*, by George Cukor. This adaptation of Claire Booth Luce's hit play stars Norma Shearer, Joan Crawford, Rosalind Russell, Joan Fontaine and Paulette Goddard plus a host of other actresses from the MGM stable.

Washington, 20 October
Frank Capra's newly released political satire, starring James Stewart, *Mr. Smith Goes to Washington* has been given a hostile reception by certain politicians.

New York, 21 December
The film critic for the *Daily Worker* has been dismissed because editors thought he wasn't harsh enough in his review of *Gone With the Wind*. The paper considers the film to be an apology for slavery.

Paris, 29 December
The Cinematographic Service for the army is to hold recreational film sessions for soldiers on campaign.

Hollywood, 31 December
At year's end, the top three box-office grossers in America are *Babes in Arms*, Ford's *Drums Along the Mohawk* and *Goodbye, Mr. Chips*.

England, 31 December
This year's production is down to 40 films compared to 228 in 1937.

BIRTHS

Brazil, 14 February
Glauber Rocha

New York, 23 February
Peter Fonda

Oklahoma, 10 March
Chuck Norris

New York, 26 March
James Caan

Germany, 31 March
Volker Schlöndorff

Detroit, 7 April
Francis Ford Coppola

Tunis, 15 April
Claudia Cardinale

London, 19 May
James Fox

London, 23 July
Terence Stamp

New York, 30 July
Peter Bogdanovich

France, 9 August
Bulle Ogier

Detroit, 1 September
Lily Tomlin

Boston, 28 October
Jane Alexander

Tokyo, 16 December
Liv Ullman

DEATHS

New York, 28 October
Alice Brady

After many problems, including 'the search for Scarlett', and a change of director (Victor Fleming replaced George Cukor), **Gone With the Wind** *is a monumental success.*

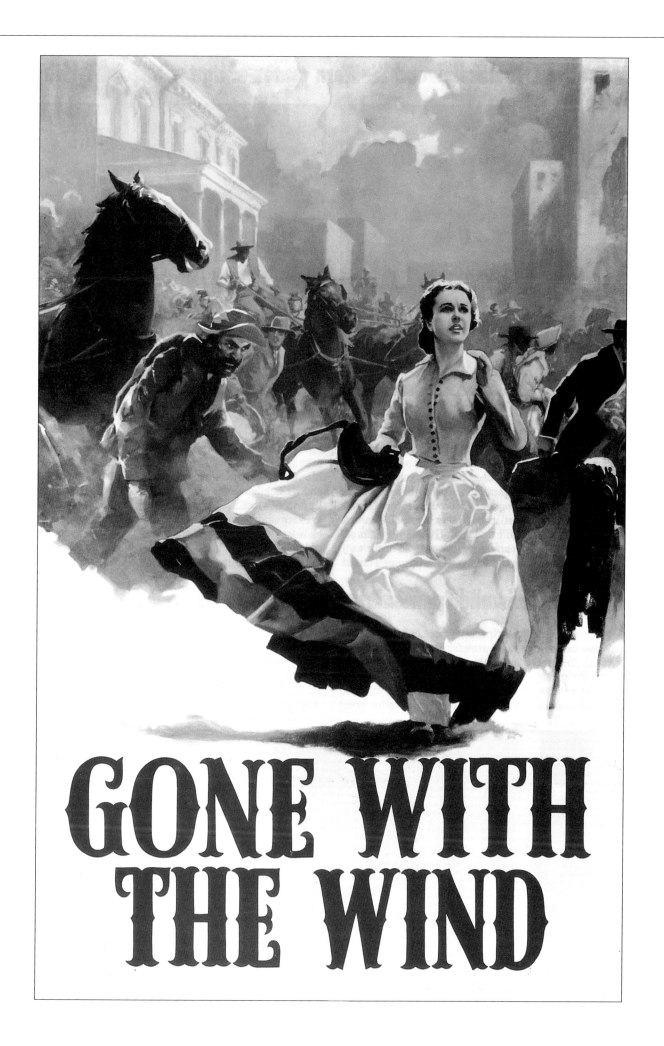

Marcel Carné fashions an intriguing drama from a workaday idea

*Gabin and Arletty in **le Jour se lève (Daybreak)**, a tragedy played out in everyday surroundings designed by Trauner.*

Paris, 9 June
Marcel Carné's new film, *Daybreak* (*le Jour se lève*), is a rather commonplace story of tragic love, but its treatment has drawn a lot of attention. The scenario came about after Carné received a visit from his neighbor Jacques Viot. Viot suggested the plot and wrote the synopsis, which

Jacques Prévert then adapted for the screen. It tells of a worker (Jean Gabin) who gets involved with the mistress (Arletty) of a shady showman (Jules Berry), and kills him in a jealous confrontation over an innocent flower seller (Jacqueline Laurent). He then barricades himself in his small room during the night as

the police and crowds wait below. Most of the film is told by flashing back and forth between the past and the present. Memorable atmospheric use is made of the dark tenement set designed by Alexander Trauner, and Gabin's tragic stature is almost matched by the hypnotically suave villainy of Berry.

A new film from René Clair

Paris, 17 July
René Clair's first French film since *le Dernier milliardaire* in 1934 is the new *Air pur*. The director came back to France last November and admitted that he was rather disappointed by his experience in England, where he made *Break the News* starring Maurice Chevalier and Jack Buchanan. Clair worked hard over the winter creating the scenario of *Air pur*, searching for new inspiration and a new style. This film centers around a young welfare officer who has dedicated his life to sending children of the poor people of Paris to the countryside in order to improve their health. It is a departure for the director of *Sous les toits de Paris* in that most of the film takes place in natural surroundings in the Massif Central, the mountainous region in central France. Also, the fact that the performers in the film are relatively unknown, or are playing themselves, including 15 children, and that he uses a hand-held camera for the first time, points to Clair's new interest in realism.

Cool reception for 'The Rules of the Game'

Paris, 22 July
After Jean Renoir's new film, *The Rules of the Game*, was loudly booed at its gala showing at the Colisée two weeks ago, it has been withdrawn. With a budget of 2.5 million francs, much of it from the director's own pocket, the film was eagerly awaited. Even if the critics were not unanimous, the public seems to be totally against it, despite Renoir having reduced the film by a sizable 23 minutes. Because of the poor reception of this bitter social satire, Renoir has even thought about quitting the cinema. In the meantime, however, he has departed for Italy, where he is to make *La Tosca*.

Director Jean Renoir appears in his new film. Here, with Nora Grégor.

'Beau Geste' looks set for socko box-office

Hollywood, 24 July
One of Paramount Pictures' greatest box-office successes in the silent era was *Beau Geste*, filmed in 1926 and starring Ronald Colman in the title role. Now the same studio looks as though it will even surpass that hit of yesteryear with its spectacular remake of the P.C. Wren colonial adventure story, directed by William Wellman. It closely follows the earlier picture's flashback format, with its memorable opening scene of a desert fort manned by corpses. The three well-born English Geste brothers, who join the Foreign Legion to escape disgrace, are played by Gary Cooper, Ray Milland and Robert Preston. Although they seem unlikely siblings, and even more unlikely Englishmen, these three stars have made the trio of heroes believable and spirited. Brian Donlevy makes a splendidly sadistic sergeant. Only one of the brothers (Cooper) survives the sergeant, an abortive mutiny and an attack by Arab tribesmen. After again demonstrating his comic talents in his last two films, Ernst

Lubitsch's *Bluebeard's Eighth Wife* and H.C. Potter's *The Cowboy and the Lady*, it is good to finally see Gary Cooper back in a full-blooded adventure yarn again. *Beau geste* was filmed on location in Buttercup Valley, west of Yuma in Arizona, a landscape that stands in perfectly for the Arabian desert.

Gary Cooper and Ray Milland.

Magic trip with Judy down the yellow brick road

Hollywood, 17 August

The gala premiere of *The Wizard of Oz* will take place tonight at Grauman's Chinese Theater. MGM has created a magical Technicolor musical fantasy, based on the famous children's story by L. Frank Baum. It is also a wonderful vehicle for a bright new star, Judy Garland. But this most expensive production in the studio's history was not made without many difficulties. Producer Mervyn LeRoy started with Richard Thorpe directing, but he stopped shooting after a few weeks, scrapping all the footage. It restarted under George Cukor, who stayed three days. Victor Fleming then took over with a new script. King Vidor completed the project, when Fleming moved on to direct *Gone With the Wind*. In addition, there were several problems before the right cast was chosen. MGM initially tried to get Shirley Temple to play Dorothy, but 20th Century-Fox would not loan her out. Then Universal refused to part with Deanna Durbin for one picture. Hence Judy Garland, who began her work in a fancy blonde

Scarecrow (Ray Bolger), Tin Man (Jack Haley) and Dorothy (Judy Garland).

wig, wearing heavy cherubic make-up. It was Cukor, during his brief stint on the picture, who insisted Judy look like a real Kansas farm girl. Buddy Ebsen was originally cast as the Tin Woodman, but the aluminium dust he was covered in coated his lungs, and he had to be hospitalized. His replacement, Jack Haley, had to wear a painful costume, and was in agony throughout. Then, too, the crowd of Munchkins, played by midgets and Lilliputians, were up to all sorts of tricks, drinking and gambling on the set.

The story follows the dream adventures of Dorothy who, after being knocked unconscious during a tornado, makes her way, with her dog Toto and some bizarre companions she meets on the Yellow Brick Road, to the Emerald City to find the Wizard of Oz. The song, *Over the Rainbow*, that Judy sings at the beginning, was supposed to be cut, but producer Arthur Freed argued vehemently for it to remain. We should be grateful, because it is a charming melody, touchingly delivered. A treat for all ages.

RKO studios engage an 'Infant Prodigy'

Hollywood, 21 August

At the conclusion of a long and detailed series of negotiations, George Schaefer, the president of RKO, has announced that he has now signed Orson Welles to a film contract. This talented young man, who has very little prior film experience, has been offered the most remarkable terms to work for RKO as a producer, director, actor and scriptwriter on film projects of his own choosing. Although this may appear quite exceptional, Welles has already, in fact, proved the range of his abilities through his previous work in the theater and on the radio. He has, for example, shown an impressive grasp of the relatively new medium of radio, and an ability to use sound and dialogue creatively as demonstrated – perhaps all too well – in his famous broadcast version of H.G. Wells' *War of the Worlds* which turned this Welles into a celebrity overnight, vastly increased his radio audience and has led to his RKO contract.

Formidable lineup of MGM's distaff side

New York, 1 September

MGM have assembled an all-star female cast for *The Women*, directed by George Cukor. In this adaptation of Clare Boothe's successful stage celebration of bitchery, Joan Crawford, as hairdresser Crystal, leaves rivals Norma Shearer (the tear-stained socialite) and Rosalind Russell out in the cold.

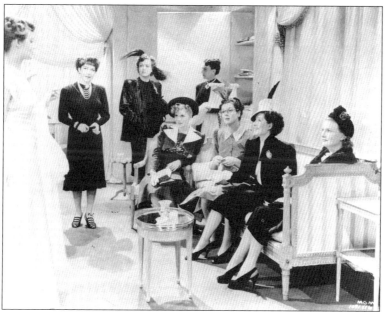

*Norma Shearer (second right) heads the lineup of MGM ladies in **The Women**.*

The war puts an end to illusions

Paris, 3 September

The currently general mobilization of all troops and reserves, and the sudden declaration of war by the French government, has taken by surprise many of France's leading producers and directors. About 20 feature films are currently in mid-production and will be adversely affected. Director Max Ophuls, for example, was just in the process of shooting the exteriors for his newest film, *From Mayerling to Sarajevo*, when he lost the actor, Gilbert Gil, who was cast to play the assassin, Prinzip. In the meanwhile, the director himself has been called up to rejoin his army unit. Others affected include Jean Grémillon, currently filming *Remorques*, Marcel Pagnol, who is in the midst of *la Fille du puisatier*, Marc Allégret with his *le Corsaire* and Christian-Jaque with *Tourelle 3*. Even the celebrated René Clair, back filming in France for the first time in five years, has not been spared these circumstances.

▷

Rathbone brings Sherlock Holmes to life

Basil Rathbone, the perfect Holmes.

London, 11 September
Sir Arthur Conan Doyle's great creation, Sherlock Holmes, has a cinema history stretching back to 1903. Now Holmes returns to the screen in 20th Century-Fox's handsome new version of *The Hound of the Baskervilles*. Basil Rathbone, whose gimlet profile usually dispenses deadly villainy in Warner Brothers' costumers, is cast as the master detective and Nigel Bruce plays the bluff Dr. Watson, courageous to a fault but usually about three steps behind the fast-moving plot. Two more Britons head the cast list: handsome Richard Greene plays Sir Henry Baskerville, heir to a dangerous inheritance; and Lionel Atwill, heavily bearded and bespectacled in a sinister red herring role. The film is briskly paced by director Sidney Lanfield, a specialist in comedies rather than period thrillers, and the fog machine works overtime to disguise the fact that much of the outdoor action takes place on a single master set. When the production was announced, fans were alarmed by Lanfield's stated aim to "pep up the story" and make Holmes more "up to date". In fact, *The Hound of the Baskervilles* is a respectful version of the original. And, in Rathbone, Fox has discovered such an incisive Holmes that a sequel is inevitable.

Selznick unveils his new Swedish find

*With Leslie Howard in the remake of her Swedish success, **Intermezzo**.*

Hollywood, 5 October
After protracted negotiations with David O. Selznick, the Swedish actress Ingrid Bergman left her doctor husband and baby daughter at home in Stockholm, and arrived in New York aboard the *Queen Mary* on 6 May. At Selznick's behest, little fanfare attended her coming, but her first American film opens today. Entitled *Intermezzo: A Love Story*, co-starring Leslie Howard and directed by Gregory Ratoff, it is the emotional tale of a concert violinist who falls in love with a young piano teacher and runs away with her – a remake of the film that made Miss Bergman a star in her native land.

'Comrade' Garbo laughs for Lubitsch

Hollywood, 3 November
The posters for MGM's *Ninotchka* bear the slogan "Garbo Laughs!" Seeking to restore Garbo's sagging popularity, the studio has cast her in a romantic comedy which guys her solemn image. The ploy has worked.

Garbo plays a high-minded Soviet official charmingly won over to Western ways by debonair Melvyn Douglas. It's by no means the first time that Garbo has laughed on screen, but MGM's accountants are laughing all the way to the bank.

Any moment now, Melvyn Douglas will have Garbo laughing at his silly jokes!

Deanna Durbin has grown up at last...

Hollywood, 10 November
Universal's lovely, youthful singing star and most bankable asset, Deanna Durbin, has slowly but surely blossomed into young womanhood in *First Love*, in which she receives her first screen kiss. The lucky man is Robert Stack, making his screen debut, and that kiss has created headlines throughout the country. The major box-office star is coming up to her eighteenth birthday, and Universal Pictures decided that Deanna should be allowed to grow up. *First Love* is a Cinderella story in which she plays an orphan adopted by a rich, uncaring family. Snubbed by relatives, and prevented from going to the gala ball, she gets to meet her Prince Charming, with the help of servants. It is now three years since Durbin started on her career in *Three Smart Girls*. She has continued to wow audiences with her bell-like voice and Pollyanna personality. Whether their loyalty will follow her into adulthood remains to be seen.

Deanna Durbin and Robert Stack.

Lavish treatment given to 'Gone With the Wind'

Scarlett O'Hara (Vivien Leigh) in the gardens of her beloved mansion, Tara.

The spectacular burning of Atlanta was the first scene of the film to be shot.

With Rhett Butler (Clark Gable).

Swashbuckler Doug lays down his sword

Atlanta, 14 December
The most eagerly-awaited film of the year, *Gone With the Wind* has just been given its world premiere in the city where a great deal of the story unfolds. This was the culmination of the most intensely publicized production ever. It was introduced by the producer David O. Selznick, in the presence of the principal cast members and the author Margaret Mitchell who wrote the bestseller from which this super-production was adapted. The credited director, Victor Fleming, who considered himself neglected, was absent. It is true that Selznick appears to be the film's real creator. Since June 1936,

when he bought the rights to the novel for $50,000, about 15 screenwriters and four directors have been employed on it at various times. The original scenario, written by Sidney Howard who, sadly, died last June, was reworked by Ben Hecht and Scott Fitzgerald, among others, each of them working on a different colored script.

Production began in January and ended on 1 July. The first director, George Cukor, was fired scarcely two weeks into shooting after several disagreements with Clark Gable, the male lead. Fleming worked on the film until May when he left ill and exhausted, handing on the baton to Sam Wood who completed it. As for the stars, the choice of Gable as Rhett Butler was automatic, due to a poll held among the public. Casting Scarlett O'Hara proved far more problematic. Some of the biggest female stars who wanted the role had screen tests: Bette Davis, Katharine Hepburn, Paulette Goddard, Susan Hayward and Loretta Young, among dozens of others, as well as 1,400 unknowns. Selznick was still undecided until his brother Myron introduced him to Vivien Leigh, an English actress who had had a brilliant stage career prior to appearing in a number of British films before the war. Selznick immediately fell under her charm, and courageously decided to cast her in the much sought-after role. For the sequence depicting the burning of Atlanta, Selznick ordered more than

30 acres of the old Pathé backlot of tinderbox sets to be put to the torch. Every Technicolor camera in Hollywood, all seven of them, were used to record the conflagration from different angles. All in all, *Gone With the Wind*, which runs three hours and 42 minutes plus an intermission, and cost over $4 million, is a magnificent achievement. What lifts the film into the highest category is not only its spectacular depiction of the American Civil War, but also its range of strongly drawn characters, seen especially in the central relationship between Rhett and Scarlett – a monument to devouring passion.

Santa Monica, 13 December
The legendary screen star Douglas Fairbanks died yesterday at his California home at the age of 56. After making his last film, the 1934 *The Private Life of Don Juan*, Fairbanks distanced himself from the movies. His burial was an intimate ceremony attended by members of the family and a few faithful friends. Among them were Charles Chaplin, who closed his studio to attend, Doug's wife and son, Douglas Fairbanks Jr., born in 1909 during Fairbanks' marriage to Ann Beth Sully. Fairbanks was born Douglas Ullman in Denver, Colorado on 23 May 1883. When he was signed by the Triangle Corporation in 1915 he was already

a successful juvenile lead on Broadway. Fairbanks quickly established himself in a series of fast-paced satirical comedies, artfully scripted by Anita Loos, which crystallized the impulses and daydreams of American moviegoers. By 1917 he had his own production company, and two years later joined Chaplin, Griffith and Mary Pickford to form United Artists. His marriage to Pickford followed, along with a string of classic roles, all of them infused with Doug's athletic grace and abundant good humor: Zorro, Robin Hood, the Black Pirate and the Thief of Bagdad. No one exemplified better than Doug the maxim that motion pictures are all about movement.

Leslie Howard, Olivia De Havilland.

Vengeful killer, gripping suspense.

MGM's much-loved gang in another mischievous caper.

Dave and Max Fleischer created their first full-length challenge to Disney.

l to r: Michel Simon, Arletty and Fernandel in Autant-Lara's **Fric-Frac**.

Fred Astaire (2nd left), Ginger Rogers in **The Story of Vernon and Irene Castle**.

MGM's British unit scored with this poignant film adaptation of James Hilton's bestseller.

A fourth, and less successful, outing for the charming and gentlemanly English society thief.

Sympathetic outlaw wows audiences.

McCrea built first transcontinental track in DeMille's tribute to rail pioneers.

Tarzan: O'Sullivan and Weissmuller.

Mireille Balin and Sessue Hayakawa in **Macao, l'enfer du jeu**.

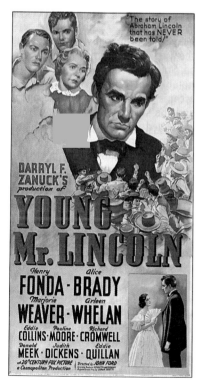

Inspiring view of a historical giant.

Rich depiction of settler life in upstate New York proved to be one of the year's biggest successes.

Billy Wilder scripted this deliciously witty film about a penniless American girl in Paris.

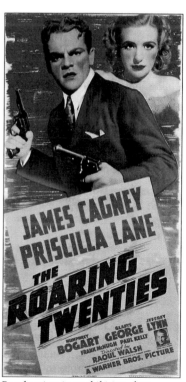

Bootlegging in prohibition days.

Controversial exposé offended the French, who delayed its release for a year.

Lubitsch charmer reunited the stars.

By Hungarian director John H. Auer.

*Outrageous pairing: W.C. Fields and Mae West in **My Little Chickadee**.*

Keye Luke replaced Boris Karloff in this sixth film of the 'Wong' series.

Popular, costly adventure lost money.

Tyrone Power in **The Mark of Zorro**.

Lavish showcase for Alice Faye.

Leigh in tear-jerking wartime melodrama of superb quality, set in London.

Henry Daniell and Errol Flynn dueled in Michael Curtiz's **The Sea Hawk**.

Rogers a hit in straight dramatic role.

Charles Halton in **Dr. Cyclops**.

Island tale blew up box-office storm.

Livingston mounts again as Western hero Stoney Brooke in popular series.

Sanders' stylish copy of his 'Saint' persona landed RKO with a lawsuit.

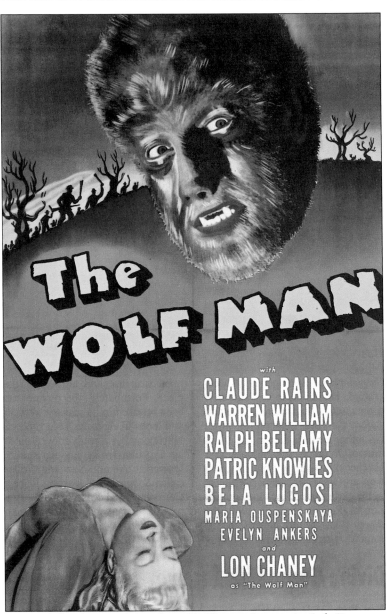

Lupine chiller showcased the talent of brilliant makeup artist Jack Pierce.

l to r: Jean-Louis Barrault, Edith Piaf, Roger Duchesne: **Montmartre-sur-Seine**.

A delightful 1910 Sunday afternoon spent with a perfect cast, sharply photographed by James Wong Howe.

Despite the casting, and a plot from James Hilton's novel, this was a stilted and disappointing melodrama.

Judy Garland and Mickey Rooney were effervescent in **Babes on Broadway**.

*Charles Boyer and Olivia De Havilland in **Hold Back the Dawn**, an affecting romance directed by Mitchell Leisen.*

*Rita Hayworth and Tyrone Power in Mamoulian's drama **Blood and Sand**.*

Breezy musical was one of three 1941 films with soldiers' sweetheart Grable.

Umpteenth version of this well-loved Victorian farce gloriously showcased lace-clad Jack Benny.

The svelte Gene Tierney found herself miscast as the most notorious female outlaw.

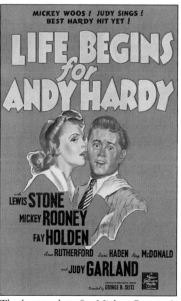

The best to date for Mickey Rooney's small-town wisecracker.

Bogart as the sympathetic fugitive in a high-class gangster drama.

No real heroes in solemn, impressive, unromantic reinterpretation of the West.

Overheated World War II action picture of Marines fighting for Pacific base was blatant propaganda.

This was a departure for George Sherman, a prolific director known for low-budget Republic Westerns.

The musical **Cabin in the Sky** was Vincente Minnelli's film directing debut.

One of the year's musical highs with gorgeous George and Ira Gershwin score.

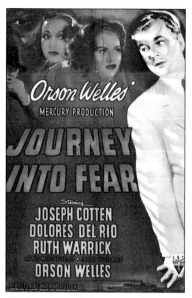

Welles scripted this enjoyable melo, and co-directed with Norman Foster.

Two fairground showmen vied for singer's affections in big hit.

Paramount paid $150,000 for the rights to Ernest Hemingway's famous novel.

The 'Lubitsch Touch' was much in evidence in this charming period fantasy.

Nazi-resistance tale set in Norway.

Big talent overcame a weak storyline in this all-black revue.

1944

★ ★

1943 Academy Awards, Grauman's Chinese Theater, 2 Mar.

Best Film:	*Casablanca* (dir: Michael Curtiz)
Best Director:	Michael Curtiz
Best Actor:	Paul Lukas *(Watch on the Rhine)*
Best Actress:	Jennifer Jones *(The Song of Bernadette)*
Best Supp. Actor:	Charles Coburn *(The More the Merrier)*

Poland, 1 January
Filmmaker Aleksander Ford is shooting *Majdanek,* a documentary on the Nazi extermination camp, which has just been liberated by the Soviet army.

New York, 12 January
Release of Alfred Hitchcock's film *Lifeboat*, with William Bendix, Tallulah Bankhead, John Hodiak and Walter Slezak in the cast.

Paris, 15 January
After the release of Pierre Billon's *Vautrin* (*Vautrin the Thief*), with Michel Simon, a newspaper published the following: "The cinema has condemned us to seeing the base, disgusting, revolting face that Michel Simon gives to Vautrin." Denounced by *le Pilori* as a Jew, his photo is on view at the anti-Semite exhibition at the Berlitz Palace.

Rome, 17 January
With the liberation of the capital, Roberto Rossellini has started filming *Roma Città Aperta* (Rome, Open City), starring Anna Magnani and Aldo Fabrizi.

Moscow, 24 January
Release of director Mark Donskoi's *Radouga*, which portrays life in a Ukrainian village subjected to atrocities by the German troops during the Occupation.

Paris, 31 January
Death of Jean Giraudoux – author, playwright, scriptwriter and the former Commissioner of Information.

Los Angeles, 4 February
Little 11-year-old Elizabeth Taylor is making *National Velvet* for MGM's Clarence Brown.

Los Angeles, 6 February
Jean Renoir has married Dido Freire. One of the witnesses was Charles Laughton, who stars in Renoir's latest film about the French Resistance, *This Land is Mine*.

California, 14 April
Marlene Dietrich has undertaken a tour of the American bases in Italy and North Africa.

Los Angeles, 2 May
Release of *Going My Way*, a musical comedy about the conflict between a priest (Barry Fitzgerald) and his young replacement (Bing Crosby). Leo McCarey directs.

New York, 4 May
Premiere at the Capitol Theater of George Cukor's *Gaslight*, starring Charles Boyer and Ingrid Bergman.

Italy, 3 June
Partisans have managed to free director Luchino Visconti from the prison in San Gregorio where he had been transferred for acts of resistance. His political connections have made him a popular target for the fascist regime.

Hollywood, 29 June
Otto Preminger has finished filming *Laura* with Gene Tierney in the title role and Dana Andrews. Laura's portrait in the film is in fact a photograph done over with oil paint.

Hollywood, 1 July
Leon Schlesinger, the producer of "Merry Melodies" and "Looney Tunes", has decided to retire. He has sold his studio to Warner Bros.

Paris, 22 August
Henri Langlois, under the aegis of the French Cinémathèque, has just screened Victor Fleming's *Gone With the Wind* before the cinemas have even had time to reopen. It is the first American film to be shown in Paris since the Liberation.

Paris, 25 August
The actor Charles Dauphin, a colonel with the Leclerc division, took part in the liberation of Paris. Having served in London and in the U.S., he arrived in France with the Allied forces on 14 July.

New York, 1 September
Warner Bros. have finally released *Arsenic and Old Lace*, directed by Frank Capra before he offered his services to the U.S. Government to supervise the production of a series of propaganda films to explain the America's war commitment.

Paris, 24 September
Fred Astaire is giving a show for the allied forces at the Olympia Theatre. It is the first time the famous dancer and actor has appeared on stage in France, but unfortunately, the show is not open to the public.

Paris, 27 September
The actor Roger Duchesne has been arrested in the 18th arrondissement, where he has been in hiding since the Liberation. He is accused of having worked for the Gestapo.

Stockholm, 2 October
Release of *Hets* (*Torment*), by Alf Sjöberg, who is considered to be Sweden's leading filmmaker, with Stig Jarrel, Alf Kjellin and Mai Zetterling. Ingmar Bergman wrote the impressive screenplay.

Paris, 4 October
Marlene Dietrich has arrived in the capital to take part in a show at the Olympia for the allied forces.

Paris, 13 October
Actress Odette Joyeux, who was arrested at home yesterday following a denunciation, has been released. The charges proved groundless.

New York, 16 October
Release of *Spies on the Thames* (aka *Ministry of Fear*), by Fritz Lang, adapted from a Graham Greene novel. The film stars Ray Milland, Marjorie Reynolds and Dan Duryea.

Paris, 24 October
Charles Vanel's appearance in Paris has put an end to the rumors about his disappearance.

Paris, 6 December
After a long four-year break, the activities of the Cercle du Cinéma, organized by Henri Langlois, have started up again. A screening will take place at 8:15 p.m. in the Studio de l'Etoile, with a program of films by Méliès, Emile Cohl, René Clair, Luis Buñuel and Jean Vigo.

Madrid, 20 December
Due to financial problems encountered by the producers, Abel Gance has had to stop work on the film he started two weeks ago, starring the famous matador Manolete.

Germany, 31 December
In a country ruined by the war, producers, nevertheless, managed to turn out 75 full-length films during the past year.

BIRTHS

California, 1 January
George Lucas
(George Walton Lucas Jr.)

Netherlands, 23 January
Rutger Hauer

New York, 13 February
Stockard Channing
(Susan Stockard)

England, 14 February
Alan Parker

Paris, 5 May
Jean-Pierre Léaud

Indochina, 10 May
Marie-France Pisier

California, 31 July
Geraldine Chaplin

Australia, 21 August
Peter Weir

England, 13 September
Jacqueline Bisset

New York, 25 September
Michael Douglas

New York, 8 October
Chevy Chase
(Cornelius Crane Chase)

New Jersey, 17 November
Danny DeVito

DEATHS

Los Angeles, 22 December
Harry Langdon

Laurence Olivier as Shakespeare's Henry V in the stirring and visually magnificent film version of the play, with which this compelling actor has also made his directing debut.

*Eric Portman in **A Canterbury Tale**.*

Lush, funny psychoanalytic musical.

*Spencer Tracy and Signe Hasso in **The Seventh Cross**.*

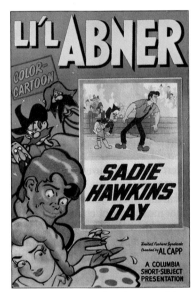

In first film, Bogart and Bacall were an explosive combo on-screen and off.

Li'l Abner frolicked with Daisy Mae.

*Mary Anderson and William Bendix, all at sea in Hitchcock's unusual **Lifeboat**.*

*Ingrid Bergman and Charles Boyer in George Cukor's remake of **Gaslight**.*

Nazi officer's career in flashback.

Fritz Lang tried out Graham Greene.

Judy Garland and Lucille Bremer in **Meet Me in St. Louis.**

Pleasant backstage musical purporting to be biopic of vaudevillian Nora Bayes.

Jane Frazee did many B-musicals.

Captive Wild Woman's *weak sequel.*

Robert Young (left) in Jules Dassin's **The Canterville Ghost.**

Critical raves greeted Alexander Knox's portrayal of U.S. President **Wilson.**

This film from Raymond Chandler's **Farewell, My Lovely**, with Powell as Philip Marlowe was an RKO success.

Meredith was real-life correspondent Ernie Pyle, in one of the best war films.

FBI foiled Nazi spies in New York.

Bernard Lancy's original poster for Bresson's symbolic melodrama.

Karloff and Lugosi in classic thriller about grave-robbers.

Frank Morgan with Fred Astaire in MGM's **Yolanda and the Thief**.

Another from King of the Cowboys.

Vaudevillians June Haver (left) and Betty Grable shone in **The Dolly Sisters**.

John Wayne, Donna Reed and Robert Montgomery in **They Were Expendable**.

Ingrid Bergman and Gregory Peck in Hitchcock's psychodrama **Spellbound**.

James Dunn and Peggy Ann Garner in Elia Kazan's **A Tree Grows in Brooklyn**.

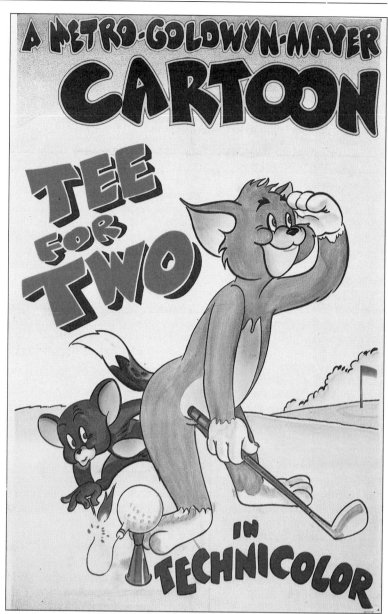

Hilarity and hi-jinx on the golf course with MGM's much-loved cat and mouse.

Ann Todd and James Mason: concert pianist and guardian in **The Seventh Veil**.

1945 Academy Awards, Grauman's Chinese Theater, 7 Mar.

Best Film: *The Lost Weekend* (dir: Billy Wilder)
Best Director: Billy Wilder
Best Actor: Ray Milland *(The Lost Weekend)*
Best Actress: Joan Crawford *(Mildred Pierce)*
Best Supp. Actor: James Dunn
                 (A Tree Grows in Brooklyn)
Best Supp. Actress: Anne Revere *(National Velvet)*

Switzerland, 15 January
Jean Delannoy has started filming *The Pastoral Symphony*, based on André Gide's novel, with Michèle Morgan and Pierre Blanchar.

Paris, 15 February
Jean Vigo's *Zéro de conduite* has finally been passed by the film control commission. The work was banned on its release in 1933.

London, 23 February
Jean Delannoy's *l'Eternel retour* (*Love Eternal*) has had a negative reception from British film critics. They find the blond hero, played by Jean Marais, "too Aryan".

Paris, 27 February
The first full-length film by director René Clément *la Bataille du rail*, has been greeted with enthusiasm. The project, which was originally begun as a clandestine documentary of work being carried out by the Resistance, gradually developed into a full-scale film accurately dramatizing wartime events.

New York, 15 March
Release of the film *Ziegfeld Follies*. This musical extravaganza, directed by Vincente Minnelli, has William Powell as impresario Florenz Ziegfeld, with guest appearances from a huge all-star cast that includes Fred Astaire, Esther Williams, Lucille Bremer, Lena Horne, Judy Garland and Gene Kelly.

Hollywood, 23 April
Shirley Temple, who won an Academy Award when she was only six, has given a party for her 18th birthday. As a symbolic gesture to the passing of her famous childhood, she burned a red school tunic in front of the 100 guests.

Marseilles, 1 May
The Capitole cinema has reopened its doors to the public. It had been requisitioned, first by the Germans and then by the Americans.

Shanghai, 23 May
Audiences at *One Night's Kiss* will see the first screen kiss in the history of Chinese cinema. But, out of respect for the public's sense of propriety, the couple in Yasuki Chiba's film do so behind an open parasol.

Paris, 23 May
The actors Daniel Gélin and Danièle Delorme have married. They met while attending René Simon's acting classes.

Atlantic City, 3 July
Jerry Lewis, who is doing a music hall number at Club 500, has come across a new singer with talent in Dean Martin.

France, 8 July
Servicemen on leave are no longer entitled to free cinema tickets.

Paris, 13 July
The professional weekly *la Cinématographie française* has devoted an article to the French cinema's rising stars: Simone Signoret, Gérard Philipe, Martine Carol, Yves Montand and Daniel Gélin.

Hollywood, 16 July
Fox has signed up the 20-year-old photographic model Norma Jean Baker at a salary of $75 a week. She will now be known professionally as Marilyn Monroe.

Rome, 9 August
Premiere of *Desiderio*, co-directed by Roberto Rossellini and Marcello Pagliero, starring Elli Parvo and Massimo Girotti and filmed before the making of *Roma Città Aperta* (*Rome, Open City*). The shooting, which started in Rome in 1943, was interrupted by the fall of Mussolini, then restarted at the end of 1945.

France, 10 August
The producer and distributor Léon Gaumont, a major pioneer of the cinema industry, has died at his property in the Var.

New York, 22 August
Alfred Hitchcock's *Notorious* is being advertised as the film with the "longest screen kiss in the history of the cinema." Two-and-a-half minutes of passion between Cary Grant and Ingrid Bergman, broken here and there by the words necessary to satisfy the 30-second contact limit imposed by the censors.

Paris, 20 September
The French film world is in mourning for Raimu, the wonderful character actor of the Pagnol trilogy.

Hollywood, 30 September
In the opinion of the vice president of the American Federation of Labor, Matthew Woll, Hollywood is the "third largest Communist center in the United States." He has also warned studios that the unions will not countenance actors and scriptwriters "guilty of treason."

New York, 24 October
Ava Gardner has been granted a divorce from the musician Artie Shaw on grounds of mental cruelty.

Paris, 6 November
The release of Walt Disney's new cartoon *Fantasia* has given rise here, just as in the U.S., to a debate on the cinematographic interpretation of musical works.

Paris, 16 November
Actor Robert Vigan has received a 10 year sentence with hard labor for open collaboration with the enemy and their program of anti-Semitic propaganda on Radio Paris. All the actor's belongings have also been confiscated.

Hollywood, 3 December
Release of John Ford's *My Darling Clementine*, starring Henry Fonda, Linda Darnell, Victor Mature and Walter Brennan.

Tokyo, 17 December
Kenji Mizoguchi's *Five Women Around Utamaro*, that is currently screening, is a stylized portrayal of the legendary 18th-century artist Edo.

Paris, 22 December
French gala premiere at the Palais de Chaillot of Vittorio De Sica's *Sciuscia* (*Shoeshine*), with Rinaldo Smordoni and Franco Interlengi as the two enterprising shoeshine boys.

Los Angeles, 31 December
At a staggering $120 million, the combined profits of the eight biggest studios have almost doubled in comparison with the already record figures for 1945.

BIRTHS

Los Angeles, 5 January
Diane Keaton (Diane Hall)

Missouri, 20 January
David Lynch

London, 5 February
Charlotte Rampling

France, 17 February
André Dussollier

Los Angeles, 12 March
Liza Minnelli

Algiers, 22 April
Nicole Garcia

Los Angeles, 9 May
Candice Bergen

California, 20 May
Cher (Cherilyn Sarkisian)

New York, 6 July
Sylvester Stallone

New York, 15 September
Oliver Stone

New York, 4 October
Susan Sarandon (Susan Tomaling)

California, 6 November
Sally Field

DEATHS

London, 5 February
George Arliss

California, 19 April
Mae Busch

Los Angeles, 23 June
William S. Hart

Los Angeles, 25 December
W.C. Fields

*Columbia has a hit with **Gilda**, due in no small measure to Rita Hayworth in the title role as a nightclub owner's wife and her tangled relationship with his manager (Glenn Ford).*

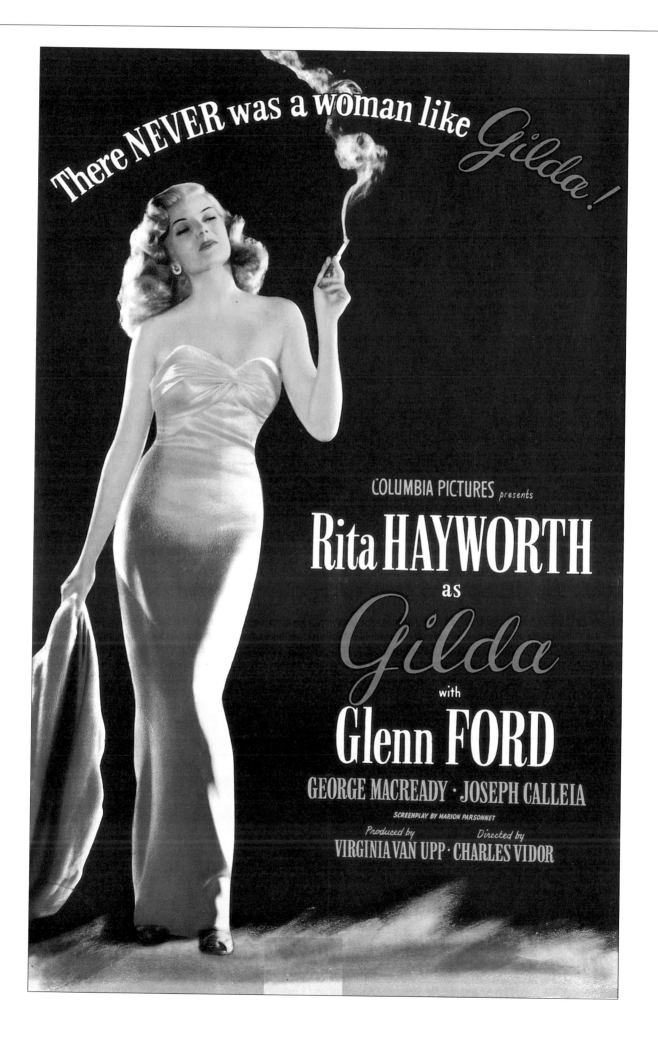

Howard Duff (left) and Burt Lancaster starred in Jules Dassin's **Brute Force**.

Great film noir about a detective tangling with a homicidal woman.

Grable fought for women's rights, with her famous legs covered!

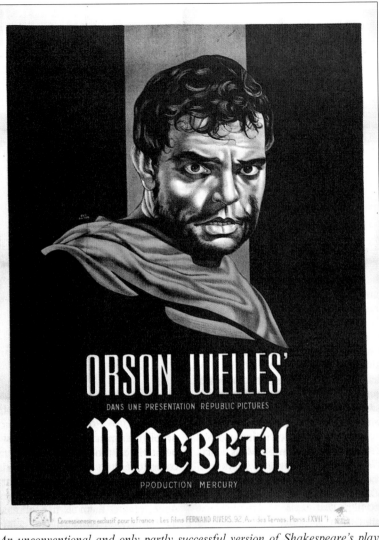

An unconventional and only partly successful version of Shakespeare's play, made in 21 days by cinema's **enfant terrible**.

l to r: Brian Donlevy, Richard Widmark and Victor Mature in **Kiss of Death**.

Rex Harrison was the sea captain who haunted Gene Tierney in the unusual **The Ghost and Mrs. Muir**, directed by Joseph L. Mankiewicz.

*French poster for **Forever Amber**.*

*Clair's **Silence is Golden**: a delight.*

*Joan Crawford in **Daisy Kenyon**.*

Another great Dickens adaptation.

*Jiri Trnka's **The Czech Year**.*

A woman destroyed by alcoholism.

Enchanting story about Santa Claus.

Garfield played a boxer in this uncompromising drama about the fight game.

***Five Women Around Utamaro**.*

***Unconquered**: Cooper and Karloff.*

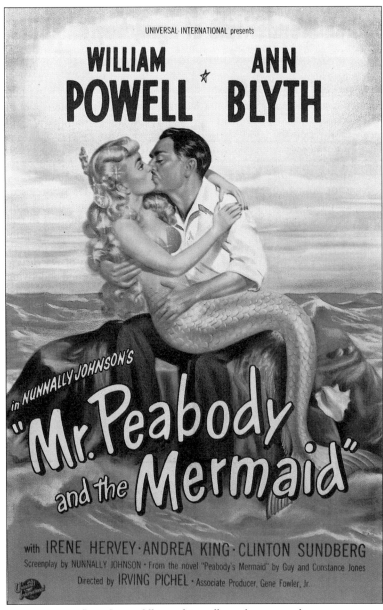

An amusing trifle with a middle-aged Powell caught in an underwater romance.

Geoffrey Keene, Jack Hawkins, Bobby Henrey, Bernard Lee: **The Fallen Idol**.

Jean-Louis Barrault in Christian-Jaque's **D'homme à hommes (Man to Men)**.

Max Ophuls at his stylish best.

Olivier, Jean Simmons in **Hamlet**.

Luchino Visconti's **La Terra Trema**.

Bogart, Bacall in the Florida Keys.

Rossellini's **Germany, Year Zero**.

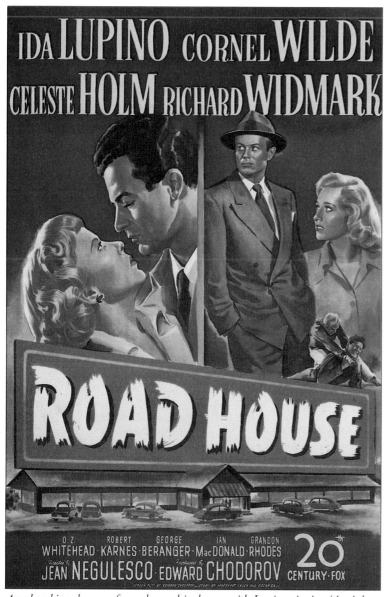

Johnny Belinda: Jane Wyman's back at Warners in a brilliant performance as a deaf mute, called the 'dummy'.

Ingrid Bergman and Charles Boyer in Milestone's **Arch of Triumph** about an unhappy love affair in Paris.

An absorbing drama of murder and jealousy, with Lupino singing 'Again'.

*Gene Tierney and Dana Andrews in Preminger's **Where the Sidewalk Ends.***

Famous for Scarlett O'Hara, Vivien Leigh played Tolstoy's Anna Karenina.

Old-timer yearned for vaudeville.

Stars in top form in comedy Western.

1949

★ ★

1948 Academy Awards, Academy Awards Theater, 24 Mar.

Best Film:	*Hamlet* (dir: Laurence Olivier)
Best Director:	John Huston
	(The Treasure of the Sierra Madre)
Best Actor:	Laurence Olivier *(Hamlet)*
Best Actress:	Jane Wyman *(Johnny Belinda)*
Best Supp. Actor:	Walter Huston
	(The Treasure of the Sierra Madre)
Best Supp. Actress:	Claire Trevor *(Key Largo)*

Hollywood, 3 January
Alfred Hitchcock has just signed a contract with Warner Bros., in which he agrees to make four films in the next six years.

Los Angeles, 6 January
Humphrey Bogart is a father. Wife Lauren Bacall has just given birth to their first child, Stephen.

Paris, 10 January
Yves Allégret has started shooting *Manèges* (*Wanton*), starring Simone Signoret and Bernard Blier.

Los Angeles, 20 January
Release of *A Letter to Three Wives*, by Joseph L. Mankiewicz, starring Jeanne Crain, Linda Darnell, Kirk Douglas and Ann Sothern.

Paris, 20 January
Premiere of *Une si jolie petite plage* (*Riptide*), by Yves Allégret, with Gérard Philipe and Madeleine Robinson. Hunted by the police for the murder of a dancer, a man returns to the scene of his childhood.

England, 26 January
Release of *The Passionate Friends*, directed by David Lean, with Ann Todd and Claude Rains.

Washington, 25 February
Paramount has signed the anti-trust agreement, aimed at separating production and distribution, whereby it will hand over its cinema network interests. The 1,450-strong cinema circuit is to be be taken over by a new company and reduced by one third to 600 cinemas by 1952.

Paris, 25 February
The Eclair company has launched the portable Camiflex 300, using André Coutant's patents.

Paris, 9 March
Release of Henri-Georges Clouzot's *Manon*, a transposition of Prévost's chivalric novel *Manon Lescaut* to the postwar years.

Paris, 28 March
Jean Gabin has married Christiane Fournier, known as Dominique. It is the great French star's third marriage, his former wives were Gaby Basset and Doriane. His new wife, one of the top models for Lanvin, was introduced to Jean at a dinner party. According to the happy couple, the meeting was a case of love at first sight. She has been seen every night, since 9 February, at the Ambassadeurs Theatre where Jean is currently playing in *la Soif*.

Peking, 31 March
A Cinema Board has been set up by the People's Liberation Army, which has been in control of the capital since January. Yuan Muzhi, the head of the army's cinematographic section since 1938, has been chosen to run the Board.

Sicily, 4 April
Roberto Rossellini is shooting on location on the volcanic island of Stromboli, just off the straits of Messina, for *Stromboli, terra di Dio*, to star Ingrid Bergman and non-actor Mario Vitale, a fisherman.

Paris, 21 April
Jean-Pierre Melville's first feature film *le Silence de la mer*, succeeds in transposing Vercor's practically unfilmable parable of the Resistance to the screen. The film is virtually a monologue by the German officer, but a great deal of what is going on beneath the surface is suggested by look and gesture. The actors, most particularly the Swiss Howard Vernon, are all excellent.

New York, 12 May
The press have attended a preview of Mark Robson's latest effort *Home of the Brave*. It is the first film to deal with the problem of racial hatred in the army.

Vallauris, 27 May
Rita Hayworth has married Prince Aly Khan.

Rome, 18 June
Abel Gance and producer Georges de la Grandière have been given a private audience by Pope Pius XII at the Vatican, where they discussed their project on the life of Christ, *The Divine Tragedy*.

Berlin, 15 July
The direct control of German film production exercised by the Allies has been replaced by a production code based on the American one.

Paris, 3 September
After a widely talked about affair, Micheline Presle has finally married the American director Bill Marshall, formerly married to another French actress, Michèle Morgan.

Hollywood, 29 September
Singer Dean Martin and comedian Jerry Lewis have made a film together, *My Friend Irma*, directed by George Marshall.

Stockholm, 17 October
In the newly released *Torst* (*Thirst*), Ingmar Bergman invites audiences to follow the tortured journey taken by a couple who are torn apart by their inability to communicate.

Padua, 26 October
Pier Paolo Pasolini has been expelled from the Italian Communist Party in disgrace for "morally and politically unacceptable behavior" after members received a police report on his homosexuality.

Los Angeles, 4 November
Director Nicholas Ray's first film *They Live by Night*, with Cathy O'Donnell and Farley Granger in the leading roles, has been released today in the U.S. Unusually, it had already been released in Europe.

Los Angeles, 8 November
Premiere of *All the King's Men*, directed by Robert Rossen, with Broderick Crawford, Joanne Dru and John Ireland. The film is based on the hard-hitting novel about corruption by Robert Penn Warren.

Washington, 9 December
Congressman J. Parnell Thomas, former chairman of the HUAC and leader in the fight against Communist influence and lax morals, has been sentenced to 10 months imprisonment for embezzlement.

Mexico, 20 December
Congress has answered the demands of professionals by voting in a law to protect the cinema industry from the importation of films. This measure is aimed especially at American productions.

New York, 25 December
Release of George Cukor's *Adam's Rib*, starring Katharine Hepburn, Spencer Tracy and Judy Holliday.

Rome, 29 December
A new law designed to promote the cinema industry has been passed on the initiative of Giulio Andreotti. The law will increase subsidies but also strengthens government control over film censorship.

BIRTHS

Chicago, 24 January
John Belushi

France, 22 March
Fanny Ardant

Minnesota, 20 April
Jessica Lange

New Jersey, 22 June
Meryl Streep (Mary Louise Streep)

California, 8 August
Keith Carradine

Philadelphia, 29 August
Richard Gere

New York, 8 October
Sigourney Weaver (Susan Weaver)

Los Angeles, 4 December
Jeff Bridges

Texas, 25 December
Sissy Spacek
(Mary Elizabeth Spacek)

DEATHS

Hollywood, 6 January
Victor Fleming

Hollywood, 15 April
Wallace Beery

---

*Carol Reed's **The Third Man** not only splendidly pairs Joseph Cotten with Orson Welles, at the peak of his acting talent, but raises the British cinema to a high level of achievement.*

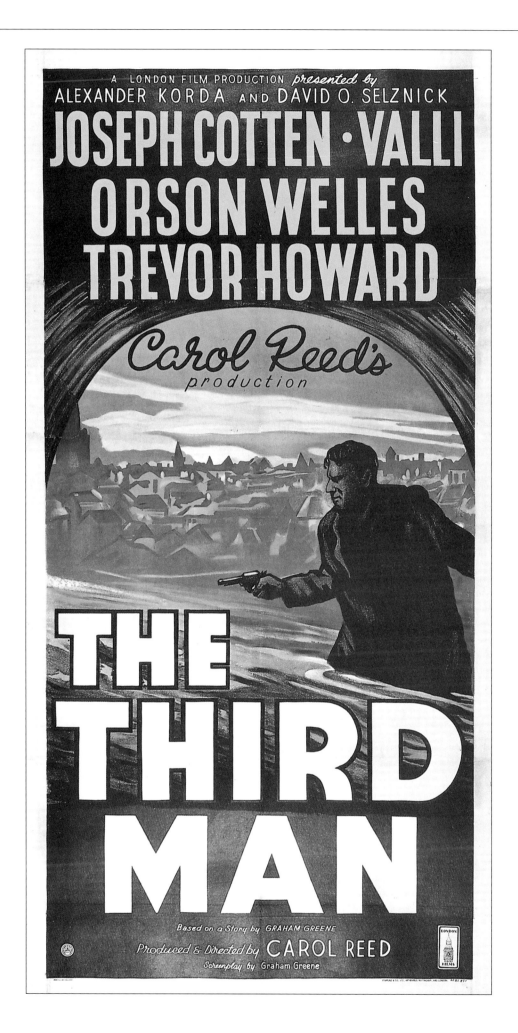

Scott adventure chills and moves

London, 7 March
In January 1945, as the war drew to a close, Michael Balcon, the head of Ealing studios, outlined a bold program for postwar British cinema: "British films must present to the world a picture of Britain as a leader in social reform, in the defeat of social injustices and a champion of civil liberties... Britain as a questing explorer, adventurer and trader... " Part of this pledge has been fulfilled in Ealing's *Scott of the Antarctic*, directed by Charles Frend. The British are curiously attached to heroic failures, and in this sad canon there are few more notable than that of Captain Robert Falcon Scott's doomed attempt to race the Norwegian explorer Amundsen to the South Pole. Scott and his party perished on the return journey, just short of a supply dump which might have saved them. The film, heavily based on Scott's diaries and shot in Technicolor on location in Switzerland and Norway, is a measured, slightly stilted account of the expedition, in which the stiff upper-lip reaction to disaster dominates, and the mood is one of wry understatement. John Mills portrays Scott, an English amateur bested by the professional Norwegians, with solid support coming from Harold Warrender, Reginald Beckwith, Derek Bond and James Robertson Justice as his doomed companions. The unrelenting drama of Scott's terrible journey across the icy wastes is underpinned by Ralph Vaughan Williams' evocative score.

Star-crossed love elevates young Anouk

Anouk Aimée and Serge Reggiani are the 'Romeo and Juliet' of Cayatte's film.

Paris, 7 March
During the shooting of a film version of Shakespeare's *Romeo and Juliet*, the two understudies of the leads fall in love. This is the basis for the scenario of André Cayatte's new film, *The Lovers of Verona*. Written by Jacques Prévert, it brings a fresh quality to the updating of the classic story. It was Prévert who had the idea of writing the part of the modern-day Juliet for 16-year-old Anouk Aimée. Her glowing beauty, the intensity of Serge Reggiani as her Romeo, the brilliant acting of Pierre Brasseur and Martine Carol, and the stunning location photography of Venice, should assure the film a wide success.

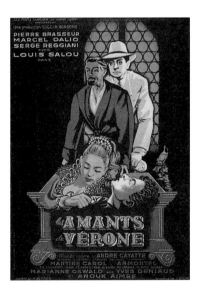

First time for Oscars at Academy Theater

Hollywood, 24 March
This year's Academy Award presentation ceremony turned out to be a chaotically cramped affair. The decision to relocate the show from larger venues to the 950-seat Academy Theater was admirably motivated – the major Hollywood studios, sensitive to charges of having previously brought their influence to bear on the voters, had withdrawn all direct financial support of the event. But it resulted in an undignified scramble for places and the resignation of Academy President Jean Hersholt. Nevertheless, during the evening, presented by Robert Montgomery and Ava Gardner, there were lively musical interludes from Doris Day, Gordon Macrae and Jane Russell, and most of the awards were well deserved. Laurence Olivier's *Hamlet* was not only the first British, but also the first non-American, film to win the Best Picture prize. Though Olivier lost out to John Huston as Best Director for *The Treasure of the Sierra Madre* (in which the director's father, Walter Huston, won Best Supporting Actor), the great Shakespearean walked away with the Best Actor award for his performance in the title role of his film. Jane Wyman, who used to play pert chorines, obtained the Best Actress Oscar for her heartbreaking portrayal of a deaf-mute farm girl in *Johnny Belinda*.

Zany satire on British eccentricity is good-humored entertainment

London, 1 April
After four years of postwar austerity there is an atmosphere of mild anarchy in the air, perfectly caught by Ealing's *Passport to Pimlico*, directed by Henry Cornelius. In this pointed social satire, a small district in London wakes up to discover that it is part of the ancient dukedom of Burgundy. "Blimey, I'm a foreigner," gulps the local copper. So the inhabitants immediately establish their new kingdom as an independent, ration-free state, with hilarious results. This warm-hearted celebration of an embattled but united community, a metaphor for Ealing itself, keeps the spirit of the studio's wartime films burning in a Britain that's edging from austerity into affluence.

*Margaret Rutherford, Stanley Holloway, Philip Dupuis in **Passport to Pimlico**.*

John Mills as the heroic explorer.

Hard-hitting exposé of the fight racket

![Arthur Kennedy and Kirk Douglas in Champion, a Stanley Kramer production.](arthur-kennedy-kirk-douglas)

*Arthur Kennedy and Kirk Douglas in **Champion**, a Stanley Kramer production.*

New York, 10 April

Kirk Douglas takes the title role in United Artists' *Champion*, an adaptation of Ring Lardner's story of the rise and fall of a cocksure boxer whose savage fight scenes belie its soft center. Douglas, reveling in his role as a heel, double-crosses his manager Paul Stewart, two-times his wife Ruth Roman for blonde floozie Marilyn Maxwell and then dumps her for Lola Albright. However, he does send money to his Mom and helps his crippled brother Arthur Kennedy. But this fails to save him from a KO come-uppance in the final reel, swiftly followed by madness and death.

Tati offers the French cinema a real feast

*Guy Decomble, Jacques Tati (on cycle) and Paul Frankeur in **Jour de fête**.*

Paris, 4 May

Made in 1947, Jacques Tati's first feature film, *Jour de fête*, has only now been released. Tati has already appeared as an actor in Claude Autant-Lara's *Sylvia and the Phantom*, and is the director/performer of several short films, one of which, *School for Postmen*, was a rough sketch for *Jour de fête*. As the postman in a French village who decides to emulate the high-speed delivery of mail in the U.S., Tati proves himself to be the true descendant of the silent movie comedians, relying as he does on sight gags. Shot with modest means, the film is packed with comic invention.

Hollywood blacklist grows ever longer

Washington, 8 June

In a cartoon published in the British newspaper *Reynolds News*, David Langdon shows Hollywood Boulevard packed with Stalin lookalikes. If the FBI is to be believed, this satirical vision is likely to come true. In the middle of a spy trial, the Bureau has released a confidential document which accuses a number of stars of being Communist sympathizers. Among those named are John Garfield, Paul Muni, Edward G. Robinson and Sylvia Sidney. In addition, a Senate committee that is investigating anti-American activities has published an astonishing list of several hundred people alleged to have "followed the Communist Party line." Some of the biggest names in Hollywood crop up on this list: Charles Chaplin, Gregory Peck, Katharine Hepburn, Gene Kelly, Danny Kaye, Fredric March, Frank Sinatra and Orson Welles. Most of them are well known for their liberal and progressive views, but the notion that the rich pastures of Beverly Hills have been colonized by hardline Bolsheviks is absurd.

Crime as practised by Dennis Price is most definitely a fine art!

Alec Guinness in six of his eight roles as members of the D'Ascoyne family.

Price: in search of wealth and title.

Guinness as Admiral D'Ascoyne.

London, 16 June

Certainly influenced by Chaplin's *Monsieur Verdoux*, Ealing director Robert Hamer has produced a brilliantly barbed comedy of murder, *Kind Hearts and Coronets*. Adapted from Roy Horniman's Wildean novel of decadence, *Israel Rank*, the film stars suave Dennis Price as a social outcast who murders his way to a dukedom through an entire family of unspeakable relatives. All eight D'Ascoynes are portrayed by Alec Guinness in a series of neatly observed cameos, from ferocious suffragette Aunt Edith, whose ballooning activities are brought to an abrupt end by a well-placed arrow, to blustering General D'Ascoyne who meets his end while digging into a booby-trapped pot of caviar. The film's feline script, by John Dighton, Hamer's elegant interplay between word and image, and the smooth visual surface provided by cameraman Douglas Slocombe, have created a masterpiece of black comedy. Above all, Dennis Price's coolly considered performance as the calculating and self-possessed murderer Louis Mazzini marks him out as an actor to watch.

'The Fountainhead' diluted but still daring

Architect Roark (Cooper), Dominique (Neal) and the New York skyline.

New York, 8 July
Ayn Rand's best-selling 1943 novel, *The Fountainhead*, has been brought to the screen by King Vidor, with a script by Rand herself. Although the film version has diluted some of the book's more extreme views, it has, nevertheless, retained much of its powerful symbolism – the phallic buildings and tools employed, the hero's climactic ascent by construction elevator to the top of the cloud-surrounded tower. The normally taciturn Gary Cooper is somewhat miscast as Howard Roark, the uncompromising architect based on Frank Lloyd Wright. Yet, Patricia Neal as the architecture critic who is sexually drawn to him, and Raymond Massey as her unscrupulous publisher, deliver the verbose dialogue with gusto. The musical score by Max Steiner perfectly underlines the drama, and Edward Carrere has provided brilliant sets and designs. Vidor wanted Lloyd Wright himself to design the film, but studio head Jack Warner vetoed the idea.

Ingrid sends shock waves through USA

Los Angeles, 6 August
Reports from the Italian newspaper, *Corriere della Sera*, confirming the details of Ingrid Bergman's liaison with Roberto Rossellini are causing a scandal in the film community and is a shock to the American people, who took the Swedish star to their hearts after the release of *Intermezzo* 10 years ago. Miss Bergman arrived in Rome on 20 March this year, prior to filming *Stromboli* for the Italian director. Their collaboration began when the actress wrote to Rossellini expressing her admiration for his film, *Rome, Open City*, and making clear her desire to work with him. They met in Paris last summer, and in January this year Rossellini came to Los Angeles for further discussions, staying with Ingrid and her husband, Dr. Peter Lindstrom. Close observers noted the growing bond between the actress and her guest, and Lindstrom was not happy about his wife's visit to Rome. Now, having completed location filming on the island of Stromboli (after which the film is named), Bergman is back in Rome. Throughout the arduous shoot, financed by Howard Hughes, rumors ran wild about the

*In Hitchcock's **Under Capricorn**.*

adulterous nature of the relationship between Bergman and Rossellini. The rumors are now confirmed: the couple are living together as man and wife and, worse still, the star, who already has a small daughter by her husband, is pregnant. The situation is now a "cause célèbre" here, with Americans unwilling to forgive a once much-loved star whose reputation has been built on an image of moral purity and family values.

Stalingrad tribute lasts nearly four hours

*Vladimir Petrov's **The Battle of Stalingrad**, 3 hours and 40 minutes of history.*

Moscow, 7 August
The war has been over for four years, but the USSR has not forgotten the high price it paid for victory. The first part of Vladimir Petrov's immensely long *The Battle of Stalingrad*, released in Moscow last May, has just won the Grand Prix at the Karlovy-Vary Festival in Czechoslovakia. Here, Petrov, a specialist in historical frescoes, has impressively re-created the heroic struggle.

James Cagney red-hot in 'White Heat'

Virginia Mayo, with gangster James Cagney in typically violent mood.

Los Angeles, 2 September
"Top of the world, Ma!" shrieks psychopathic mobster James Cagney as he goes up in flames at the end of Raoul Walsh's pulsating *White Heat*. As the mother-fixated Cody Jarrett, Cagney delivers an electric performance as a helpless, manic outlaw running wildly out of control. Cornered by the cops, he goes out with a bang as he turns a petrol tank into a colossal fireball.

New headquarters for the Cannes Festival on the famous Croisette

Only a few weeks ago, the Festival Palace was still a huge building site.

The Third Man, *voted best film, boasts brilliant atmospheric photography.*

Luis Buñuel is now making films in Mexico

Luis Buñuel's second Mexican film.

Cannes, 17 September

Since the creation of the Cannes Festival, the mayor of the city and the organizers of the festival have wanted to open the Festival Palace on the Croisette, which they had claimed to be "worthy of good taste and French art." It was with pride then that they were finally able to inaugurate the building in the presence of celebrities from around the world. But the edifice, started hastily in 1947, still resembles a building site, as it continues to be patched up. Meanwhile, sightseers could catch a glimpse of Martine Carol, Orson Welles, Joseph Cotten, Alida Valli and many other international stars, entering the unfinished Palace. This year's festival saw 80 countries participating, some with a single short film, and others such as France, the U.S., England and Italy with full-length features. It was, therefore, expected that those four countries mentioned should have shared the bulk of the awards. English director Carol Reed's *The Third Man* walked off with the Grand Prix, while the Frenchman René Clément took the best director prize for *The Walls of Malapaga*, co-produced by Italy. Isa Miranda was presented with the best actress award for her role as the lonely waitress in the latter film. America's consolation came in the form of Edward G. Robinson's best actor performance in Joseph Mankiewicz's *House of Strangers*, and also Virginia Shaler's award for her best screenplay, *Lost Boundaries*, directed by Alfred Werker, which deals with racism.

Mexico, 25 November

After dropping out of sight since his departure from the United States, Luis Buñuel has been discovered living in Mexico where two films he made here have just been released. They are a musical, *Gran Casino*, and a melodrama called *El Gran Calavera*. It has been 15 years since Luis Buñuel last directed a film. Between 1944 and 1946, the Spanish emigré had worked at Warner Bros. dubbing and supervising foreign versions of Hollywood films. He had been under consideration for the assignment of director of *The Beast With Five Fingers*, but the job went to Robert Florey. After another abortive project, Buñuel was welcomed by Mexico.

A natural beauty in the rice fields

*Mangano in **Bitter Rice**, a new star.*

Rome, 1 November

New director Giuseppe De Santis, a friend of Luchino Visconti and the screenwriter on Visconti's *Ossessione*, has retained the passion he had when he was a critic for the magazine *Cinema*. His first film, *Tragic Hunt* (*Caccia Tragica*) in 1947, placed him among the leading Italian neo-realists, the movement which he had helped formulate as a critic. In *Bitter Rice* (*Riso Amaro*), De Santis has returned to the countryside of his youth in the Po Valley. The slightly melodramatic storyline deals with one of the many urban women who come each year to work in the rice fields, wading up to their waists in the water. The girl falls for a petty thief (Vittorio Gassman) who hopes to steal the rice crop. There is no doubt that *Bitter Rice* will make the 19-year-old Silvana Mangano, Miss Rome of 1946, into a star. The voluptuous Mangano in thigh-revealing shorts and torn nylons, her ample breasts thrust forward, her seductive head held high, standing in a rice paddy, is the film's most memorable image and the one that audiences will take with them. Ostensibly a neo-realist exposé of the exploitation of women workers, the steamy film in reality exposes more of Mangano than its subject. ▷

Superb evocation of greed and corruption

Broderick Crawford (center), a superb performance in Robert Rossen's film.

New York, 8 November
Since returning from war service, burly Broderick Crawford, the son of thespians Lester Crawford and Helen Broderick, has been mostly confined to parts in cheap Westerns. Now Robert Rossen has cast him as the demagogic Southern politician Willie Stark in *All the King's Men*, adapted from the Pulitzer Prize-winning novel by Robert Penn War-ren. Stark is closely modeled on the Louisiana "Kingfisher" Huey Long. It's a part perfectly tailored to fit Crawford's belligerent and bullying style, and provides an example of actor and character becoming completely one. There is strong support from Mercedes McCambridge, and from John Ireland as the cynical journalist who narrates this cautionary political tale.

Becker explores Saint-Germain-des-Prés

Paris, 6 December
Jacques Becker's new film, *Rendez-vous de juillet*, tells the story of a group of young people planning to make an anthropological documentary in Africa, and who attempt to find maturity and happiness through love, theater and jazz. The film presents a vivid picture of French youth marked by the war, and evokes the Saint-Germain-des-Prés jazz clubs, which they frequent. Since getting a cool reception at the Cannes Film Festival, Becker has re-edited and reduced its length. This more concise and lucid version has been sufficiently appreciated to win this year's Prix Louis Delluc.

The Lorientais jazz cellar, a perfect milieu for Jacques Becker's Parisian film.

Kelly and Sinatra, sailors on the loose

*Frank Sinatra, Gene Kelly and Jules Munshin about to go **On the Town**.*

Hollywood, 8 December
The dancer Gene Kelly, who made *The Pirate* last year under Vincente Minnelli, has now become a director himself. Conceived balletically and co-directed by Kelly's colleague and friend, the choreographer Stanley Donen, *On the Town* is a joyous and innovative musical which follows three sailors (Kelly, Frank Sinatra and Jules Munshin) on a 24-hour leave in New York. The opening number "New York, New York" was actually filmed on location in that "wonderful town". After the trio has paired off with three girls (Vera-Ellen, Betty Garrett and Ann Miller), the six go visit the Empire State building, this time a Hollywood set, more exciting and colorful than the real thing. Full of dynamic dance numbers and produced for MGM by Arthur Freed, the film was freely adapted by Betty Comden and Adolph Green from the Leonard Bernstein Broadway hit.

Clark Gable remarries after seven years

Santa Barbara, 21 December
Clark Gable has never been the same man since the tragic death of Carole Lombard in 1942. Now it seems that he has rediscovered a measure of happiness with Sylvia Hawkes, former wife of Lord Ashley, Douglas Fairbanks Sr. and Baron Stanley of Alderly. Clark and Sylvia have known each other for only a few weeks. Their whirlwind romance became a marriage when Gable, fortified by a bottle of champagne, whisked Hawkes off to a quiet wedding by the sea. The witnesses were Gable's secretary Jean Garceau and MGM publicity man Howard Strickling. Gable's sudden decision to tie the knot has caused alarm among his family and friends.

The Studio System

Among the most famous company names in the history of the cinema are Warner Bros., MGM, Paramount, United Artists (or UA), Fox (20th Century-Fox), Universal, Columbia and Disney. Indeed, the history of the cinema in the United States can be understood through observing the ups and downs of these giant Hollywood studios. But their beginnings were very different from their present corporate stature.

As with other countries, the American cinema started out as a diverse collection of small, competing companies. In 1908 a number of industry leaders, including Biograph and Vitagraph, joined together under Edison to set up a restrictive Trust to control the production, distribution and exhibition of films. These companies, however, had become set in their ways, often opposed to making longer films at a time when the film market was growing and becoming increasingly competitive. This opened the way for a few enterprising independents to risk the production of feature-length pictures. Thus, several famous movie moguls first made their mark at this time, notably Carl Laemmle, Adolph Zukor, William Fox, Jesse Lasky and Cecil B. DeMille. A key event was the merger of Zukor's Famous Players with Lasky and the Paramount Distribution Co. in 1916. Other companies such as First National (1917)

Photographed in the 1930s, the 20th Century-Fox studio complex.

and United Artists were formed to meet the threat of Paramount. However, the real challenge didn't come until 1924 with the formation of Loew's Metro-Goldwyn-Mayer, headed by Marcus Loew and Louis B. Mayer. By the end of the 20s the classic Hollywood lineup had taken shape. The costly changeover to sound had caused a shakeout among the smaller companies and led to a further consolidation of power by the large studios. Filmmaking was now concentrated more than ever within the studio walls, with stars, directors and other personnel bound by long-term contracts. The five largest companies were Paramount, MGM, Fox, Warner Bros. (who had just taken over First National)

and the new RKO Radio – followed by the three mini-majors – Universal, United Artists and Columbia.

Despite the problems caused by the Depression, the studio and star system flourished in Hollywood throughout the 1930s, with MGM the clear industry leader. But the outbreak of war in 1939 marked the beginning of the end. Studios cut back on production and made changes in the restrictive contract system. During the postwar era many leading stars and directors decided to go independent, films were increasingly made on location, and the government's 1948 Consent Decree forced the majors to sell off their movie theaters and give up other monopolistic practices. RKO,

headed by the eccentric Howard Hughes, was the only studio to fold, however, and in the 1950s, the three mini-majors, along with Disney, began challenging the top group for the first time. UA in particular was revitalized by a new management team. Production continued to decline, but studios diversified into other areas such as TV and music, a process continued in the 1960s when there were a number of takeovers and mergers. Studios suffered in the late 1960s with audiences at a record low, but soon recovered with the aid of a new generation of successful directors (Francis Ford Coppola, George Lucas, Steven Spielberg, etc.). The main casualties in the 1980s were MGM and United Artists who had merged, then collapsed after a number of complicated deals. But Disney, with a big boost from its Touchstone subsidiary, had the most remarkable success in the 1980s. The list of majors still includes some of those very familiar names which go back 70 years or more: Columbia (paired with Tristar and owned by Sony), 20th Century-Fox (now owned by Rupert Murdoch), Warner Bros. (joined up with Time Magazine in Time-Warner), Universal/MCA (now owned by Matsushita) and Paramount Pictures (taken over by Viacom in 1994). Owners may change and managements reshuffle, but these Hollywood giants appear to be indestructible.

The producing team of Richard Zanuck and David Brown in 1973.

l to r: Harry Warner, Joan Crawford, Jack Warner and Michael Curtiz.

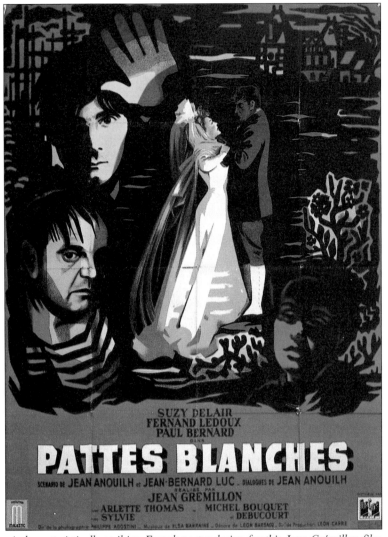

*Cathy O'Donnell and Farley Granger in Nicholas Ray's **They Live By Night**.*

A characteristically striking French poster design for this Jean Grémillon film.

Capturing the spirit of Tati's film.

*The French poster for **Bitter Rice**.*

*Jean Gabin and Isa Miranda in René Clément's **The Walls of Malapaga**.*

*Fred Astaire danced 'Shoes with Wings On' from **The Barkleys of Broadway**.*

Olivia De Havilland and Montgomery Clift co-starred in the film **The Heiress**.

The poignant story of a girl who fell hopelessly in love!

Racial problems exposed as a Southern black girl passes for white.

Odd follow-up from **King Kong** team.

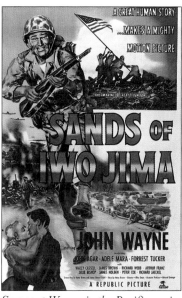

Sergeant Wayne in the Pacific again.

Kind Hearts and Coronets: Alec Guinness got ill to the delight of Dennis Price.

Great photography by Winton Hoch.

An immensely successful war drama with Peck losing his nerve.

1950

★ ★

1949 Academy Awards, RKO Pantages Theater, 23 Mar.

Best Film:	*All the King's Men* (dir: Robert Rossen)
Best Director:	Joseph L. Mankiewicz *(A Letter to Three Wives)*
Best Actor:	Broderick Crawford *(All the King's Men)*
Best Actress:	Olivia De Havilland *(The Heiress)*
Best Supp. Actor:	Dean Jagger *(Twelve O'Clock High)*
Best Supp. Actress:	Mercedes McCambridge *(All the King's Men)*

London, 1 January
Release of Basil Dearden's *The Blue Lamp*, starring Dirk Bogarde and Jack Warner.

Moscow, 21 January
Mosfilm studios present Mikhail Chiaureli's two-part super production *Padeniye Berlina* (*Berlin Falls*).

Stockholm, 20 February
Premiere of Ingmar Bergman s *Till Gladje* (*To Joy*) with Maj-Britt Nilsson, Stig Olin, Victor Sjöström and, in a minor role, Erland Josephson.

Cannes, 25 February
A decision reached at the Film Producer's Conference will change the Cannes Film Festival to take place in the spring from now on, rather than in September; consequently, there will be no festival this year.

Madrid, 8 March
Franco's government has announced the creation of the National Office of Entertainment Classification to give a morality rating (on a scale of one to six) to all films.

Washington, 10 April
The Supreme Court is refusing to comment on the condemnation of screenwriters Dalton Trumbo and John Lawson for their contempt of Congress. This effectively upholds the condemnation. It also affects the eight other hostile witnesses.

Los Angeles, 12 April
After making its reputation in Cannes, the British director Carol Reed's *The Third Man* is now seeing release in the U.S. Here, too, Anton Karas' haunting zither music will no doubt captivate the public.

Buenos Aires, 13 April
The powerful influence of certain European films and a strong literary sensibility are discernible in Leopoldo Torre Nilsson's first feature film, *El Crimen de Oribe* (*Oribe's Crime*), which starts screening today.

Hollywood, 20 April
Alfred Hitchcock has bought the rights to Patricia Highsmith's first novel *Strangers on a Train*.

Peking, 30 April
Effective immediately, the Central Office of Cinematographic Control is now attached to the Ministry of Culture. Mao Tse-Tung's wife Jian Quing, who was herself an actress in prewar Shanghai, is a member of a committee set up to advise and control the film industry.

Los Angeles, 20 June
Singer Judy Garland, who has been suffering from deep depression, has attempted suicide by cutting her throat with a piece of glass. Her family raced to her aid, and she is reported to be out of danger.

Hollywood, 30 July
Mary Pickford and Charlie Chaplin have decided to sell 3,600 of their 4,000 shares in United Artists.

Prague, 4 August
Director Jiri Weiss has released his new film *Posledni vystrel* (*The Last Shot*), filmed with a cast of non-professional actors.

Tokyo, 25 August
Release of Akira Kurosawa's film *Rashomon*. An intriguing work with forceful performances from Toshiro Mifune and Takashi Shimura.

Paris, 26 August
With producer Georges Grandière failing to honor his commitments, and the backing for the film not yet assured, Abel Gance has canceled his contract for *The Divine Tragedy*. The film will not be made.

Tokyo, 1 September
American occupational authorities have instituted a purge among the Japanese cinema circles where numerous key figures were, and are still, very involved with militarist and ultra-nationalist movements.

Venice, 10 September
This year's awards have been given to films addressing social problems. Best Italian film goes to Leonide Moguy's work *Domani è troppo tardi* (*Tomorrow is Too Late*), and André Cayatte's handling of a euthanasia case in *Justice est faite* takes off with the Golden Lion award. Eleanor Parker receives the best actress nod for her role as the moving victim in John Cromwell's pessimistic film *Caged* and Sam Jaffe is named best actor for *The Asphalt Jungle*.

New York, 14 September
During a reception in his honor, Joseph L. Mankiewicz violently denounced the current blacklisting as well as Cecil B. DeMille's demand that members of the Screen Directors' Guild swear an oath of loyalty.

Paris, 29 September
Jean Cocteau has made a screen version of his play *Orphée*. Jean Marais and Marie Déa portray Orpheus and Eurydice. It is the second film in Cocteau's Orphic trilogy, the first being *The Blood of the Poet*.

Monaco, 31 October
Accused of "libidinous relations" with a 17-year-old girl, actor Errol Flynn has just been acquitted by the Monaco court.

Rio de Janeiro, 1 November
The Vera Cruz company, created and run by director Alberto Cavalcanti, who has recently returned from Europe, has released its first film, Adolfo Celi's *Caiçara*.

Hollywood, 21 November
RKO has yielded to injunctions from the Ministry of Justice regarding the integration of its activities. The organization will split into two distinct companies: RKO Pictures Corporation, which takes over film production, and RKO Theaters Corporation to manage the cinemas.

Mexico, 23 November
Luis Buñuel's *The Young and the Damned* has to close after only four days. It has been widely attacked and has failed to attract the public.

Milan, 15 December
Roberto Rossellini's newest work *Flowers of St. Francis*, played by Aldo Fabrizi, is an honest portrayal of the saint's spiritual quest.

Washington, 31 December
According to the latest census there are approximately 71,500 cinemas in the world, a figure which includes America's 11,300 cinemas and its 4,700 drive-ins.

BIRTHS

Algiers, 24 January
Daniel Auteuil

Tennessee, 18 February
Cybill Shepherd

Paris, 22 February
Miou-Miou (Sylvette Hery)

England, 22 February
Julie Walters

Ireland, 25 February
Neil Jordan

West Virginia, 18 March
Brad Dourif

Washington D.C., 20 March
William Hurt

Chicago, 31 May
Tom Berenger

Germany, 2 August
Mathieu Carrière

Paris, 9 August
Anémone (Anne Bourguignon)

Toronto, 31 October
John Candy

Missouri, 15 December
Don Johnson

DEATHS

California, 7 April
Walter Huston

Hollywood, 22 July
Rex Ingram

San Francisco, 23 October
Al Jolson

Hollywood, 28 October
Maurice Costello

Swanson makes an amazing comeback to the screen, virtually playing herself and doing it brilliantly, in Billy Wilder's scathing view of early Hollywood titled **Sunset Boulevard***.*

SUNSET
BOULEVARD
A
HOLLYWOOD
STORY
starring
WILLIAM HOLDEN · GLORIA SWANSON · ERICH von STROHEIM
with NANCY OLSON · FRED CLARK · LLOYD GOUGH · JACK WEBB
and CECIL B. DeMILLE · HEDDA HOPPER · BUSTER KEATON · ANNA Q. NILSSON · H. B. WARNER · FRANKLYN FARNUM
Produced by CHARLES BRACKETT · Directed by BILLY WILDER

Faithful screen version of hit comedy play with Stewart as Elwood P. Dowd.

Alfonso Mejia (l) and Roberto Cobo in Buñuel's **The Young and the Damned**.

Raf Vallone (left), the lead in Pietro Germi's **The Path of Hope** (Italy).

Toshiro Mifune and Machiko Kyo in Akira Kurosawa's **Rashomon**.

James Stewart (center), Jay C. Flippen (rt) in Anthony Mann's **Winchester 73**.

Dad Tracy, daughter Taylor... bliss!

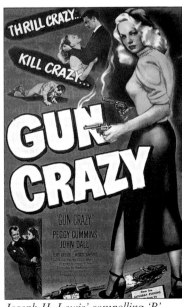

Joseph H. Lewis' compelling 'B'.

MGM boss Mayer hated this one.

Mitchum finds himself in trouble.

Webb brilliant as Frank Gilbreth, father of 12 children based on a true story.

Anne Baxter, Bette Davis, Marilyn Monroe, George Sanders: *All About Eve.*

Princess of Death (Maria Casarès), Orpheus (Jean Marais): Cocteau's *Orphée.*

Outlaw Gregory Peck seeks reconciliation with his wife and son.

A man arrives at a police station to report his own murder...

Superb treatment by Powell and Pressburger of Offenbach's fantastical opera.

*Daniel Gélin, Anne Vernon in Becker's wicked satire, **Edward and Caroline**.*

*Anna Magnani and Tina Apicella in Luchino Visconti's **Bellissima**.*

*French poster for Alfred Hitchcock's **Strangers on a Train**.*

*Evelyn Keyes and Van Heflin in Joseph Losey's taut thriller, **The Prowler**.*

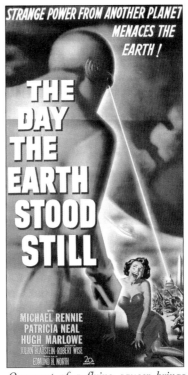

Occupant of a flying saucer brings a dire warning to Washington D.C.

*Alec Guinness (l), Stanley Holloway in **The Lavender Hill Mob**.*

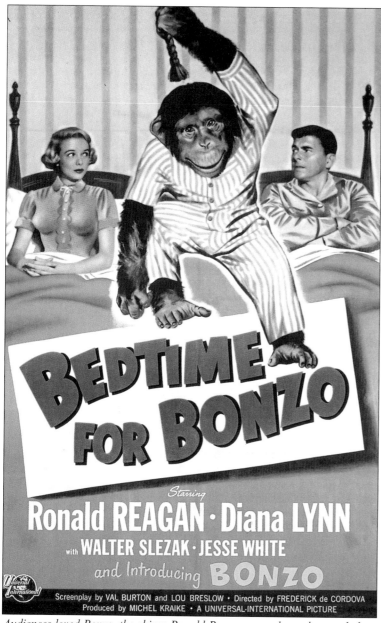

*Kirk Douglas plays the newsman in Billy Wilder's **Ace in the Hole** aka **The Big Carnival**.*

*The French poster for **A Streetcar Named Desire**.*

Audiences loved Bonzo, the chimp Ronald Reagan reared as a human baby.

*Fredric March triumphed as tragic Willie Loman in **Death of a Salesman**.*

*Marilyn Monroe, Albert Dekker in the affable comedy **As Young as You Feel**.*

Another frothy, forgettable but fun outing featuring Marilyn Monroe.

*Peter Ustinov as the mad Nero and Patricia Laffan in **Quo Vadis?***

1952

★ ★

1951 Academy Awards, RKO Pantages Theater, 20 Mar.

Best Film:	*An American in Paris* (dir: Vincente Minnelli)
Best Director:	George Stevens *(A Place in the Sun)*
Best Actor:	Humphrey Bogart *(The African Queen)*
Best Actress:	Vivien Leigh *(A Streetcar Named Desire)*
Best Supp. Actor:	Karl Malden *(A Streetcar Named Desire)*
Best Supp. Actress:	Kim Hunter *(A Streetcar Named Desire)*

Bombay, 24 January
The opening of the Indian International Film Festival marks the first festival of cinema in Asia. Forty feature-length films from 21 countries will be screened.

Paris, 13 February
Jean Gabin and Danielle Darrieux share the top billing in *la Vérité sur Bébé Donge (The Truth About Baby Donge)*. Darrieux is directed once again by her ex-husband, Henri Decoin, with whom she has made six films in the past.

Hollywood, 5 April
Howard Hughes has announced the temporary closure of RKO Studios to facilitate the dismissal of close to 100 employees suspected of having Communist sympathies.

Washington D.C., 10 April
Today Elia Kazan denounced 15 of his former colleagues to the HUAC. Earlier this year, Kazan had admitted membership of the Communist Party from 1934 to 1936, but had refused to name any of his friends. He claims that his change of heart is due to a new appreciation of the dangers inherent in the Communist doctrine. His recent picture *Viva Zapata!*, with Marlon Brando, is openly anti-Communist.

Tokyo, 24 April
Completed in August 1945, Akira Kurosawa's film, *The Men Who Tread on the Tiger's Tail*, is only now released in Japan, as the American Army censors had prohibited it because of its feudal ideology.

Washington D.C., 25 May
The Supreme Court has delivered a unanimous verdict in favor of the distributor of Rossellini's film *The Miracle*. The Court ruled that the cinema has the right to constitutional guarantees protecting freedom of expression. Until now, the law has regarded the cinema as "a purely commercial venture".

New York, 1 July
The new projection system known as Cinerama was put on display for the first time last night before an invited audience at the Broadway Theater. Thrills and scenic wonders combine to impressive effect on this sweeping wide-angle (146 degree) screen which is also higher than ordinary screens, and added impact is provided by "stereophonic" sound. The tri-panel panoramic picture is thrown from three projectors but looks like a single picture.

Mexico, 14 July
Luis Buñuel has begun shooting *Robinson Crusoe*, from the novel by Daniel Defoe, with Dan O'Herlihy. Produced by Oscar Dancigers, it is Buñuel's first feature film in color.

Quebec, 21 August
Alfred Hitchcock begins shooting for *I Confess*, starring Montgomery Clift in the role of a priest.

Venice, 1 September
At this year's festival here, the Golden Lion has been won by René Clément for *Jeux interdits (Forbidden Games)*, while Fredric March won the Volpi award for best actor for *Death of a Salesman*. The jury's special prize went to a French cartoon by Paul Grimault, *la Bergère et le ramoneur*, from a script by Jacques Prévert. No prize was given to an actress this year.

London, 4 September
Opening of *Operation Burma*. The controversial film was accused of being a travesty of the Burma campaign by the British. It was taken off a week after its opening in 1945.

Washington D.C., 19 September
James McGranery, U.S. Attorney General, has announced that he has ordered the immigration services to refuse Charles Chaplin entry to America until the conclusions of the inquiry into his political activities are known.

London, 23 September
Charlie Chaplin has been warmly welcomed by his countrymen on his return to England with his wife and family after a 21-year absence.

London, 9 October
Gala premiere at the Empire Theatre in Leicester Square of David Lean's semi-documentary British film, *The Sound Barrier*.

Paris, 15 October
The 87-year-old actress formerly known as Jehanne d'Alcy and now Madame Charlotte Méliès, widow of Georges Méliès, appears in some scenes in Georges Franju's documentary film *le Grand Méliès (The Great Méliès)*.

Germany, 1 November
Charlie Chaplin has refused to allow *Limelight* to be distributed here unless German audiences are first able to see *The Great Dictator*.

London, 23 November
French actress Edwige Feuillère has been elected "Star of Stars" by *The Sunday Graphic*.

Hollywood, 28 November
The Hollywood premiere of Arch Oboler's much advertised 3-D film *Bwana Devil*, which co-stars Robert Stack and Barbara Britton, brought screams from the audience as a lion appeared to leap from the screen. The audience wore polaroid glasses to obtain the full 3-D effect.

London, 1 December
Serge Reggiani, Claude Dauphin and Simone Signoret are in the British capital to dub Jacques Becker's film *Golden Marie (Casque d'or)* themselves.

Hollywood, 20 December
Opening of Harry Horner's anti-Communist, science fiction film called *Red Planet Mars*, in which two scientists, an American and a German, captured by the Soviets, must persuade the Martians to incite revolution in the United States.

Paris, 21 December
Eighteen-year-old actress Brigitte Bardot married director Roger Vadim in a civil ceremony yesterday. The couple will celebrate a religious ceremony in the parish church in Passy today.

BIRTHS

Paris, 27 March
Maria Schneider

Paris, 15 April
Josiane Balasko

Ireland, 7 June
Liam Neeson

France, 16 June
Michel Blanc

Rome, 18 June
Isabella Rossellini

Rome, 18 June
Ingrid Rossellini

Missouri, 20 June
John Goodman

Canada, 1 July
Dan Aykroyd

Chicago, 21 July
Robin Williams

Texas, 18 August
Patrick Swayze

New York, 27 August
Pee Wee Herman
(Paul Rubens)

New Jersey, 22 September
Paul Le Mat

New York, 25 September
Christopher Reeve

Holland, 28 September
Sylvia Kristel

Pittsburgh, 22 October
Jeff Goldblum

DEATHS

New York, 8 May
William Fox

New York, 21 May
John Garfield

Hollywood, 27 October
Hattie McDaniel

Twelve years on, the Tom and Jerry cartoons continue to delight. This year's **Smitten Kitten** *uses a series of flashbacks to amorous adventures enjoyed by Tom.*

1954

★ ★ ★ ★ ★ ★ ★ ★ ★ **1954** ★

1953 Academy Awards, RKO Pantages Theater, 25 Mar.

Best Film:	From Here to Eternity (dir: Fred Zinnemann)
Best Director:	Fred Zinnemann
Best Actor:	William Holden (Stalag 17)
Best Actress:	Audrey Hepburn (Roman Holiday)
Best Supp. Actor:	Frank Sinatra (From Here to Eternity)
Best Supp. Actress:	Donna Reed (From Here to Eternity)

Paris, 1 January
Cahiers du Cinéma has published an outspoken attack on "certain trends in French films" written by André Bazin's young protégé François Truffaut, in which Truffaut compares the rejected scenario of Pierre Bost and Jean Aurenche's *Diary of a Country Priest*, adapted from Georges Bernanos' work, with the film made by Robert Bresson. And he concludes with: "Of what value is an anti-bourgeois film made by a bourgeois for the bourgeoisie?"

Paris, 8 January
American screen comedian and filmmaker Buster Keaton, taken on by the Medrano Circus, makes his debut with the company tonight, when he will perform a sketch.

New York, 8 January
The New York critics have voted André Cayatte's French film, *Justice is done* (*Justice est faite*) as the best foreign film shown in the United States during 1953. Cayatte and Charles Spaak co-wrote the script for this ironic examination of the French legal system. Both of them are former lawyers.

New York, 26 January
The film rights to Charles A. Lindbergh's autobiography *The Spirit of St. Louis* have been acquired by director Billy Wilder and Broadway producer Leland Hayward for what is reported to be the highest price paid by Hollywood for a literary work – an estimated $1 million.

Korea, 1 February
Marilyn Monroe is on a tour of the battle front, boosting morale by entertaining the troops.

Hollywood, 16 February
David O. Selznick voiced his anger over use of a *Gone With the Wind* clip in a birthday salute to MGM on the Ed Sullivan Show. Selznick feels it is misrepresentation as the film was not an MGM production.

Hollywood, 2 March
Clark Gable has announced that he is leaving MGM after 23 years there under contract. His annual salary was $500,000. It is not yet known whether other studios have made an approach to the star.

Los Angeles, 19 March
Responding to rumors predicting an imminent breakup, Dean Martin and Jerry Lewis state: "We do indeed intend to dissolve our team... on 25 July 1996, for the 50th anniversary of our partnership."

Los Angeles, 25 March
At this year's Oscar ceremony, the Academy honored the Bausch and Lomb Optical Company with a special award for their contributions to the advancement of the motion picture industry. On the artistic side, Greta Garbo, who never won the Oscar despite her legendary success, was finally honored with a statuette for "her unforgettable screen performances", as was Danny Kaye "for his unique talents, his service to the Academy, the motion picture industry and the American people".

New York, 2 May
The *New York Times* today has published a letter from Robert Bresson protesting against the cuts made by the American distributor of his film *Diary of a Country Priest*, which, in his view, render the film incomprehensible. According to the paper the slow pace of certain foreign films is alien to American taste.

Hollywood, 28 May
Dial M for Murder, Alfred Hitchcock's last film for Warner Bros. is released today in a "flat" version although it was filmed in 3-D. Is the vogue for stereoscopic films over?

Hollywood, 20 September
Walt Disney has terminated his distribution agreement with RKO. All his films will in future be distributed by his own subsidiary, Buena Vista.

Stockholm, 4 October
Premiere of Ingmar Bergman's film *Lesson in Love*, which co-stars Eva Dahlbeck and Gunnar Björnstrand. The work is one of Bergman's rare excursions into comedy.

Los Angeles, 5 October
Opening of Otto Preminger's film *Carmen Jones*, inspired by Bizet's opera and retaining its score with a new libretto. The press revealed that the composer's heirs refuse to allow the film to be shown in France.

Paris, 18 November
Two French stars, Stéphane Audran and Jean-Louis Trintignant, were married today.

Tokyo, 23 November
Opening of Kenji Mizoguchi's film *Chikamatsu Monogatari* (*The Crucified Lovers*). Set in 17th-century Japan, the word is that it is one of the great director's best films.

Hollywood, 30 November
The Screen Actors Guild has sent a letter to the Immigration Bureau urging a "stricter application", by the United States Immigration and Naturalization Service, of regulations governing "alien actors coming into this country to take supporting or even minor roles in movies being made here." The letter stressed that the protest was aimed at "non-resident aliens" who are employed for lower salaries than American actors and not at "stars of distinguished merit and ability".

Hollywood, 1 December
Yesterday, Darryl Zanuck, the production chief at 20th Century-Fox, declared that the attitude of foreign exhibitors and producers to his company's wide-screen process was one of "eagerness and enthusiasm". To substantiate his claim he cited increases in receipts of over 50 percent in all British theaters showing CinemaScope films with similar figures from France. So far orders for CinemaScope photographic lenses have come from West Germany, Italy, England and France.

New York, 26 December
Release of *Vera Cruz*, directed by Robert Aldrich and the first film made in Superscope, a process akin to CinemaScope. Burt Lancaster and Gary Cooper head the cast.

New York, 28 December
The New York Critics have voted Marlon Brando best actor for Elia Kazan's *On the Waterfront*, and Grace Kelly best actress for George Seaton's *The Country Girl*.

BIRTHS

Ohio, 22 January
Jim Jarmusch

New Jersey, 18 February
John Travolta

Oklahoma, 1 March
Ron Howard

Houston, 9 April
Dennis Quaid

New York, 16 April
Ellen Barkin

Toronto, 18 April
Rick Moranis

Chicago, 15 May
James Belushi

Missouri, 19 June
Kathleen Turner

Canada, 16 August
James Cameron

Minnesota, 29 November
Joel Coen

England, 15 December
Alex Cox

New York, 28 December
Denzel Washington

DEATHS

Hollywood, 19 January
Sydney Greenstreet

Vienna, 4 June
Charles Vidor

Hollywood, 3 September
Eugene Pallette

California, 15 November
Lionel Barrymore

Alfred Hitchcock's **Rear Window** *is a highly ingenious thriller with a house-bound James Stewart relying on the gorgeous Grace Kelly for help with his amateur sleuthing efforts.*

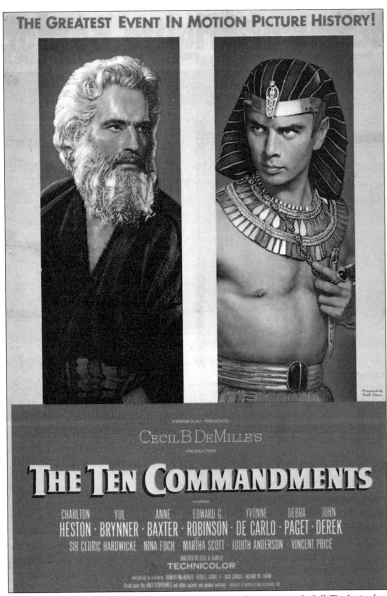

Cecil B. DeMille remade his 1923 biblical epic, this time with full Technicolor.

Marlon Brando goes Japanese.

Britain's blonde and busty bombshell.

Brigitte Bardot and Jean-Louis Trintignant: **And God Created Woman**.

George Stevens' **Giant**: James Dean.

Dana Andrews and Joan Fontaine starred in the ingenious Fritz Lang thriller, **Beyond a Reasonable Doubt**.

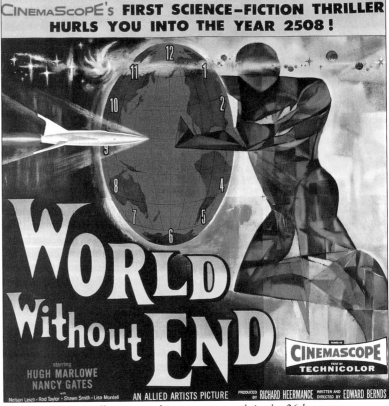

Shades of H.G. Wells as spaceship comes to earth in the 26th century.

First-class effort in a sci-fi year.

George Cukor directed in Pakistan.

Sci-fi suspense and rollicking humor, inspired by Shakespeare's **The Tempest**.

Deborah Kerr and John Kerr (no relation) starred in **Tea and Sympathy**.

Robert Hirsch, Gina Lollobrigida and Jean Danet in Frenchman Jean Delannoy's **Notre-Dame de Paris**, adapted from Victor Hugo.

Hitchcock remade his own 1934 film.

Japan's answer to current sci-fi craze.

★ ★

1956 Academy Awards, RKO Pantages Theater, 27 Mar.

Best Film:	*Around the World in 80 Days* (dir: Michael Anderson)
Best Director:	George Stevens *(Giant)*
Best Actor:	Yul Brynner *(The King and I)*
Best Actress:	Ingrid Bergman *(Anastasia)*
Best Supp. Actor:	Anthony Quinn *(Lust for Life)*
Best Supp. Actress:	Dorothy Malone *(Written on the Wind)*

New York, 2 January
The women's fashion press has just elected the best dressed women of the year. Among them are Princess Grace of Monaco, Audrey Hepburn and Marlene Dietrich.

Tokyo, 15 January
Opening of Akira Kurosawa's film *Kumonosu-Jo* (*Throne of Blood* aka *Castle of the Spider's Web*), a new version of Shakespeare's *Macbeth* set in medieval Japan, with Toshiro Mifune and Takashi Shimura.

Paris, 18 January
Actress Maria Schell has signed a contract to play the leading role in Alexandre Astruc's latest film *Une vie*, adapted from the novel by Guy de Maupassant.

Hollywood, 18 February
Orson Welles has begun filming *Touch of Evil* for Universal Studios. The cast is headed by Charlton Heston, Janet Leigh, Marlene Dietrich and the director himself. It is his first U.S. film since *Macbeth* in 1948.

Paris, 19 February
The Lutetia production company has threatened Brigitte Bardot with a lawsuit if she continues to fail to turn up on the set of *la Chatte* (*The Cat*), based on Colette's novel. The film's producers are prepared to sue her for the sum of $50 million in damages – the star's casual attitude could cost her dearly.

London, 22 February
During the shooting of Otto Preminger's *Saint Joan*, the actress Jean Seberg narrowly escaped being burnt alive while shooting the sequence where she is tied to the stake for just such a fate in the film.

Washington D.C., 26 February
James Stewart has been promoted to the rank of Brigadier General in the United States Armed Forces. President Eisenhower himself conferred this honor on the actor.

Rome, 21 March
John Huston, who had just begun filming *A Farewell to Arms* from the novel by Ernest Hemingway, has been sacked by producer David O. Selznick; the director Charles Vidor is to replace him.

Cannes, 22 April
The People's Republic of China has withdrawn from the Festival competition on learning that Taiwan is also taking part.

Paris, 18 May
At the Maison des Lettres, Claude Lelouch, a young director, is presenting *Vers une nouvelle technique* (*Towards a New Technique*), three short 16mm experimental films.

Washington D.C., 1 June
The playwright Arthur Miller has been found guilty of contempt of Congress for refusing to reveal to the HUAC the names of members of a literary circle suspected of Communist affiliations.

Paris, 7 June
At the Rex, the first escalators to be installed in a cinema were set in motion by Gary Cooper and Mylene Demongeot.

New York, 9 June
There are currently 6,000 drive-in theaters in America and operators predict this number should rise to 10,000 in two years. Many of today's drive-ins have fully-equipped children's playgrounds, supermarket-sized cafeterias and an "all weather" theater for those who prefer to sit indoors in bad weather.

New Orleans, 18 July
Robert Rossen's new film, *Island in the Sun*, opened today in spite of objections from a citizen's council chapter and an American Legion committee over the film's content – a romance between a colored man (Harry Belafonte) and a beautiful white woman (Joan Fontaine).

Rome, 7 September
After seven years of marriage, actress Ingrid Bergman and director Roberto Rossellini have decided to separate. Rossellini, who is reportedly in love with a young Indian woman, has given Ingrid custody of their three children, Roberto, Ingrid and Isabella, on the condition she stays in Europe until they are of age. The actress is leaving for Paris tomorrow to continue rehearsals for Robert Anderson's play *Tea and Sympathy* at the Théâtre de Paris.

Hollywood, 22 September
Actress Kim Novak has gone on strike. She considers her popularity to be worth more than her current salary of $1,250 per week.

Hollywood, 20 September
Lauren Bacall has formally denied rumors of a forthcoming marriage to Frank Sinatra.

Paris, 3 October
Jayne Mansfield, who is here for the opening of her film *Will Success Spoil Rock Hunter?*, directed by Frank Tashlin, happened to meet Greta Garbo at Maxims and was quick to ask for an autograph.

Hollywood, 10 October
RKO studios have been sold to Desilu, the television production company founded by Lucille Ball and Desi Arnaz, stars of the famous *I Love Lucy* series.

London, 13 October
A newspaper has disclosed that the Indian actress Anna Kashfi, whom Marlon Brando has just discreetly married, is in fact the daughter of a Welsh laborer and is named Joan O'Callaghan.

Hollywood, 29 November
Composer Erich Wolfgang Korngold, aged 60, has died. The former child prodigy from Czechoslovakia won two Oscars for film musical scores. He first came to Hollywood in 1934 to arrange the music for *A Midsummer Night's Dream*.

Paris, 4 December
Claude Chabrol, a film critic for *Cahiers du Cinéma*, has commenced shooting his first feature-length film, *Bitter Reunion* (*le Beau Serge*), starring Gérard Blain, Jean-Claude Brialy and Bernadette Lafont.

BIRTHS

Massachusetts, 21 January
Geena Davis

New York, 28 February
John Turturro

California, 20 March
Theresa Russell
(Theresa Paup)

New York, 29 March
Christopher Lambert

Swaziland, 5 May
Richard E. Grant

New York, 9 August
Melanie Griffith

Paris, 18 August
Carole Bouquet

Minnesota, 21 September
Ethan Coen

Paris, 24 November
Thierry Lhermitte

DEATHS

Hollywood, 14 January
Humphrey Bogart

California, 31 March
Gene Lockhart

Paris, 12 May
Erich von Stroheim

Hollywood, 29 July
James Whale

California, 7 August
Oliver Hardy

London, 20 October
Jack Buchanan

Los Angeles, 29 October
Louis B. Mayer

Las Vegas, 24 December
Norma Talmadge

Monte Carlo, 25 December
Charles Pathé

*Directed by Jack Arnold for Universal, **The Incredible Shrinking Man** is impressive sci-fi in which Grant Williams shrinks to micro-size after being caught in a radioactive mist.*

Humphrey Bogart succumbs to cancer

With his wife, actress Lauren Bacall, and their two children in happy times.

Los Angeles, 17 January
Three days ago Humphrey Bogart lost a long battle against throat cancer. The slide began after an operation in March last year, but Bogey, unwilling to change the habits of a lifetime, continued to smoke and drink whisky. At the end he was so weak and emaciated that a service elevator was converted to bring the wheelchair-bound star downstairs to meet friends. Today, after a short funeral service, Bogart was cremated at Forest Lawn. Beside him was a whistle as a reminder of *To Have and Have Not*.

America forgives Ingrid Bergman her sins

New York, 20 January
Ingrid Bergman has at last returned to New York and the arms of the American people. The reconciliation has been effected by the success of *Anastasia*, directed by Anatole Litvak, in which she plays an amnesiac refugee selected by Yul Brynner to impersonate the surviving daughter of Czar Nicholas II. Meanwhile, her marriage to Roberto Rossellini has hit the rocks. Bergman has been nominated for an Oscar for *Anastasia*, and has already received the New York Critics' award for her performance.

At Idlewild, the star is surrounded by eager press photographers en route to a welcome from fans who have remained loyal through the years of exile.

A new busty blonde explodes on the screen

New York, 8 February
The American male's obsession with big breasts has found its perfect incarnation in the sumptuous 40-19-36 statistics of Jayne Mansfield, who shot to stardom last year in Frank Tashlin's rock 'n' roll comedy *The Girl Can't Help It*, memorably clutching two milk bottles to her ample bosom. Today sees the release of another Tashlin picture titled *Will Success Spoil Rock Hunter?*, in which Tony Randall plays an ad-man trying to persuade movie star Jayne to endorse Stay-Put lipstick. Whether the 24-year-old former beauty queen will stay put on the movie scene remains to be seen.

Jayne Mansfield in Will Success Spoil Rock Hunter? *A parody of Marilyn.*

Entrepreneur Mike Todd marries Liz Taylor

Mexico, 2 February
Although she has not officially divorced Michael Wilding, Elizabeth Taylor has pressed ahead with her marriage to Mike Todd, tying the knot in the small Mexican village of Puerto Marquez, far away from the complications of the American legal system. It is the third time around for both Liz and Mike, who was previously married to Joan Blondell. Producer and originator of the Todd-AO wide-screen process, Todd met Taylor during the filming of *Around the World in 80 Days*. He swept Liz off her feet, presenting her with a $30,000 ring, which she has pointedly worn on her left ring-finger in the presence of the hapless Wilding. Taylor's attachment to the bauble became so great that she even tried surreptitiously to wear it during the shooting of *Raintree County*. Todd, who is 25 years Taylor's senior, laid on a characteristically opulent ceremony: over 15,000 flowers, dozens of cases of champagne and a small mountain of caviar, although there were few people present at the reception. Those guests who were there included Eddie Fisher, Debbie Reynolds and Cantinflas, who had the role of Passepartout in *Around the World in 80 Days*. The happy couple will shortly sail for Europe, where they are planning to interrupt their honeymoon to drop in on the Cannes Film Festival.

Ingmar Bergman and the question of death

Max Von Sydow (left) and Bengt Ekerot play a deadly game of chess.

Stockholm, 16 February

Ingmar Bergman's 17th film, *The Seventh Seal*, has definitely set him firmly in the pantheon of directors. After his bubbling comedy of manners, *Smiles of a Summer's Night*, which received worldwide acclaim two years ago, Bergman has now returned to explore the darker side of life. *The Seventh Seal*, shot in only 35 days, is a medieval morality tale which powerfully depicts the cruelties of the time such as witch burning and flagellation, as well as the joys and aspirations of ordinary people. This movie follows, in luminous images derived from early church paintings, the journeys of a knight (Max Von Sydow) returning from the Crusades through a Sweden ravaged by plague. In his search for God, he meets a group of strolling players, suffering peasants, and Death (Bengt Ekerot) himself, with whom the knight plays a deadly game of chess.

A trip around the world worth five Oscars

Hollywood, 27 March

The fact that flamboyant showman-producer Michael Todd, whose film *Around the World in 80 Days* carried off five Oscars, had never worked in the cinema before, was only one of the oddities at this year's Academy Award ceremony. The Best Actor Oscar was awarded to the virtually unknown, bald Yul Brynner, who claims to be a gypsy born in Outer Mongolia, for his performance as the despotic King of Siam in *The King and I*; the Best Actress went to Ingrid Bergman for the title role in *Anastasia*, after she had been ostracized by Hollywood for many years; and James Dean, for the second year running, was a posthumous nominee for Best Actor in *Giant*. Although *Around the World in 80 Days* may be the most star-studded movie of all time, it failed to gain any acting honors, its Oscars being awarded for Best Picture, Best Cinematography, Best Adapted Screenplay, Best Film Editing and Best Musical Score. Much of the film was shot around the world in 70mm Todd-AO and Eastman Color, as Inspector Fix (Robert Newton) follows Phileas Fogg (David Niven) and Passepartout (Cantinflas).

Ingrid Bergman and Helen Hayes.

Audrey's 'Funny Face' delights Fred Astaire

New York, 28 March

Audrey Hepburn has made her first screen musical, co-starring with the doyen of dance, 57-year-old Fred Astaire, who is still spry, graceful and charming. Directed by Stanley Donen, the "Cinderella" story tells of a Greenwich Village bluestocking (Hepburn), transformed into a top model by a fashion photographer (Astaire), in the face of opposition from his *Vogue*-type editor (Kay Thompson). Around this – and a subplot that takes a side-swipe at phony intellectuals – a spell is woven of song, dance, Paris locations and a spectacular Givenchy wardrobe for Hepburn, under the supervisory visual eye of photographer Richard Avedon, on whom Astaire's character is said to be based. From the first Paris number, "Bonjour Paree", where Astaire, Thompson and Hepburn run into each other atop the Eiffel Tower in triple split-screen, through the outdoor photo sessions, to the romantic finale ("S'Wonderful") in a churchyard, the film lovingly captures Paris – and the magic essence of Audrey. And it does so in a swirl of energy and high spirits, wonderfully orchestrated by Donen, a former dancer, choreographer and an integral member of MGM's famous Freed unit.

In a left-bank club in Paris.

Depressing party makes impressive movie

New York, 9 April

The team of producer Harold Hecht, director Delbert Mann and writer Paddy Chayefsky, have followed up their success with *Marty* (1955) with *The Bachelor Party*. Set in a cheerless New York at night, the film traces the attempts of five office workers to enjoy the final moments of bachelorhood of one of their number. But instead of having a good time, their emotional problems come to the surface. Each of the relatively unknown actors gives an excellent, realistic performance in a downbeat but impressive movie.

l to r: Jack Warden, Don Murray and Carolyn Jones in Delbert Mann's film.

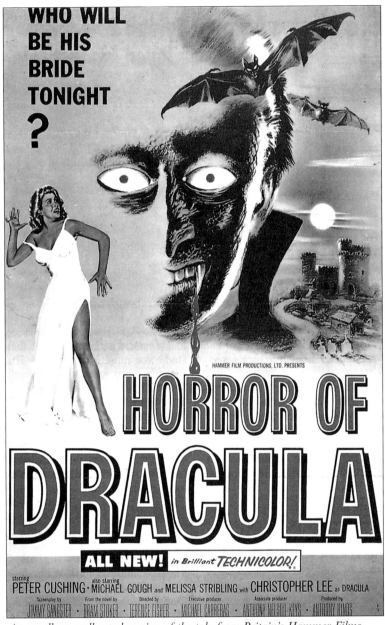

*Max Von Sydow and Ingrid Thulin in **The Magician**, Ingmar Bergman's examination of the duality of the artist, one of his favorite themes.*

An excellent, well-acted version of the tale from Britain's Hammer Films.

Another excursion into horror has a scientist turning into a monster fly.

*Kerwin Mathews and Kathryn Grant in Nathan Juran's **The Seventh Voyage of Sinbad**. This film showcased terrific special effects.*

Characteristic Saul Bass design for 1958's Hitchcock offering.

*John Gavin in **A Time to Love and a Time to Die**, made by Douglas Sirk.*

*Chabi Biswas (left) and Padma Devi in Indian director Satyajit Ray's **The Music Room**, an exquisite study of a declining aristocrat.*

Welles returns to Hollywood after long absence with atmospheric melodrama.

An all-black remake of a 1949 melo, originally a popular stage play.

Barbara Graham's true, tragic story.

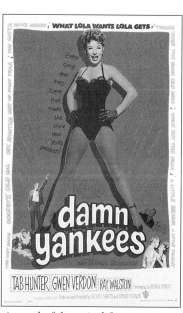

A wonderful musical fantasy.

Robot with a dead man's brain.

*Kurosawa's **The Hidden Fortress**.*

1959

★ ★

1958 Academy Awards, RKO Pantages Theater, 6 April

Best Film:	*Gigi* (dir: Vincente Minnelli)
Best Director:	Vincente Minnelli
Best Actor:	David Niven *(Separate Tables)*
Best Actress:	Susan Hayward *(I Want to Live!)*
Best Supp. Actor:	Burl Ives *(The Big Country)*
Best Supp. Actress:	Wendy Hiller *(Separate Tables)*

London, 1 January
The distinguished actor, Alec Guinness, a star of both stage and screen, has been honored with a knighthood in the Queen's New Year's List.

New York, 1 January
The MPAA has repealed a 1957 ruling that forbids persons sympathetic to communism, or those who refused to give evidence to the HUAC, from being nominated for an Academy Award.

Los Angeles, 16 January
In a television interview, the formerly blacklisted screenwriter Dalton Trumbo has revealed that he is the author, under the pseudonym of Robert Rich, of the screenplay for *The Brave One*, which won the 1956 Oscar for Best Screenplay. Nobody at the time came forward to receive the trophy.

Spain, 25 January
The filming of *Solomon and Sheba* is dogged with disaster and tragedy. Following Tyrone Power's death from a heart attack during filming, Spanish actor Luis Santana accidentally set himself on fire today by dropping an oil lamp on his clothes.

Los Angeles, 20 February
Singer Eddie Fisher has filed for divorce from his wife, actress Debbie Reynolds. Fisher and Elizabeth Taylor have apparently been inseparable since the star went to watch Eddie, the best friend of her late husband Mike Todd, perform at the Tropicana in Las Vegas.

Rome, 16 March
The Swedish actress Anita Ekberg has arrived at Cinecittà to film *La Dolce Vita* under the direction of Federico Fellini.

Cairo, 18 March
Egyptian censors have decided to ban all of Elizabeth Taylor's films as a retaliatory measure against the actress' financial support for Israel.

Hollywood, 29 March
Elizabeth Taylor, originally Protestant, has been officially converted to Judaism. The ceremony took place at a Hollywood synagogue.

France, 18 June
Brigitte Bardot and actor Jacques Charrier have disclosed that they were married in secret on 5 June. The couple, who have been hounded by journalists since making *Babette Goes to War*, left St. Tropez yesterday, hidden in two cars. The press was invited to the official ceremony at Brigitte's parents' home today.

Rome, 30 July
Fire broke out today at Cinecittà destroying the sets used for director Carmine Gallone's film *Carthage in Flames*, and injuring 20 people.

London, 5 August
Cary Grant's former chauffeur has failed in a suicide attempt. He is implicated in the divorce of the actor and his wife Betsy Drake. Grant has accused his employee of having an affair with his wife.

Moscow, 6 August
Soviet censors have banned director Christian-Jaque's *Babette s'en va en guerre (Babette Goes to War)*, even though he is a member of the jury for the Moscow Film Festival.

New York, 6 August
The French film, *Love is My Profession*, directed by Claude Autant-Lara, is to be shown here without any cuts. The American censor has passed all Brigitte Bardot's nude scenes intact.

Rome, 8 August
Sophia Loren has just returned here with her husband Carlo Ponti, who could find himself charged with bigamy. Their marriage, which took place on 17 September 1957, is not considered valid in Italy because divorce is not recognized here. Under Italian law Ponti is still married.

Paris, 9 August
It has been reported that the French actress Jeanne Moreau intends to leave the cinema and devote herself to the stage.

Brazil, 22 August
Following Italy's lead, Brazilian authorities have banned Louis Malle's *les Amants (The Lovers)*.

London, 6 September
Actress Kay Kendall has died of leukemia. Her dearest wish, "to marry Rex Harrison", was realized in 1957 as soon as he was separated from his previous wife, Lilli Palmer.

Paris, 9 September
The premiere of Roger Vadim's *les Liaisons dangereuses 1960* was canceled at the last moment. The 800 guests, among them Audrey Hepburn and her husband Mel Ferrer, left without having seen the film.

Hollywood, 19 September
The Soviet leader, Nikita Kruschev, seemed to appreciate the charms of capitalism on his visit to Los Angeles. Despite his recent criticism of American politics, he appeared relaxed and smiling at a dinner in his honor in Hollywood during which several stars, including Marilyn Monroe, Frank Sinatra and Gary Cooper, were presented to him.

Zagreb, 12 October
Abel Gance is making *Austerlitz*, a joint Italo-Franco-Yugoslav production. The project has a provisional budget of 48 million francs and prestigious international distribution deals are already in place.

New York, 22 October
Errol Flynn has bequeathed the major part of his immense fortune ($50 million) to his estranged third wife Patrice Wymore.

Tokyo, 3 November
Premiere of Kon Ichikawa's *Fires on the Plain*, a violent description of the wanderings of Japanese soldiers trapped in the jungle who end up eating their dead comrades.

Hollywood, 25 November
Eleanor Powell and Glenn Ford, who married in 1943, have divorced. One of Hollywood's greatest screen dancers, Miss Powell gave up her career for her marriage.

BIRTHS

St. Louis, 22 January
Linda Blair

Washington, 22 February
Kyle MacLachlan

Chicago, 8 March
Aidan Quinn

Paris, 18 March
Luc Besson

California, 22 March
Matthew Modine

London, 15 April
Emma Thompson

California, 29 April
Michelle Pfeiffer

Madrid, 4 July
Victoria Abril

New York, 10 August
Rosanna Arquette

Stockholm, 3 November
Dolph Lundgren
(Hans Lundgren)

DEATHS

Hollywood, 21 January
Cecil B. DeMille

Hollywood, 4 March
Lou Costello

Beverly Hills, 18 June
Ethel Barrymore

New York, 6 August
Preston Sturges

Rome, 7 October
Mario Lanza

Vancouver, 14 October
Errol Flynn

California, 7 November
Victor McLaglen

Paris, 25 November
Gérard Philipe

---

*Billy Wilder's **Some Like It Hot** starring Monroe with Jack Lemmon and Tony Curtis, turned out to be the year's most clever, original, hilarious, and even poignant, comedy.*

Brigitte follows in Marlene's foosteps

*Bardot in **la Femme et le pantin**, the third film version of Pierre Louys' novel.*

Paris, 13 February
Concha Perez, the beautiful, seductive heroine of Pierre Louys' novel *la Femme et le pantin* (*The Woman and the Puppet*) has previously been portrayed on the screen by Conchita Montenegro in 1929, in a film directed by Jacques de Baroncelli, and unforgettably by Marlene Dietrich in Josef von Sternberg's *The Devil is a Woman* in 1935. Now it's the turn of Brigitte Bardot, today's sex goddess, to play this mythical and mysterious *femme fatale* in *la Femme et le pantin*. While retaining the Spanish location – the hot atmosphere of the Seville festival – director Julien Duvivier has now updated the story, and has transformed the film's heroine into a French girl who is raised in Spain. Bardot remains a provocative creature who drives men mad.

Tense and tragic story of Anne Frank opens

Living in hiding: Joseph Schildkraut, with Millie Perkins as Anne Frank.

New York, 18 March
The director George Stevens has brought all of his meticulous preparation and shooting method to bear on *The Diary of Anne Frank*. The result is a three-hour portrait of a Jewish family's survival in an Amsterdam attic during the wartime occupation by the Germans. It has been adapted from the Broadway production which drew heavily on the real diary kept by Anne Frank, a teenager whose family underwent the ordeal depicted in the film. It ended with their discovery in 1944, following which they were sent to the death camps. Stevens' solemnity smothers Anne's remarkable gaiety and love of life, and his choice of the inexperienced former cover girl Millie Perkins to play Anne was a gamble which has not paid off.

Kirk Douglas lets Anthony Mann go

Hollywood, 13 February
Less than two weeks after shooting began on *Spartacus* in Death Valley, California, Kirk Douglas, executive producer and principal actor of the film, has fired Anthony Mann as director. The star has decided to replace him with the 30-year-old Stanley Kubrick, who had directed Douglas in the brilliant anti-war movie *Paths of Glory* a couple of years ago. At the news of Anthony Mann's sacking, many in the motion picture profession have expressed their misgivings. Mann is one of the most respected of American directors, known principally for his Westerns with James Stewart. Others have expressed their doubts as to whether Kubrick, who up until now has only made films on a limited budget, will be able to handle a $12 million project like *Spartacus*, a huge star-studded epic set during the Roman Empire.

Howard Hawks has a new angle on the Old West in 'Rio Bravo'

Angie Dickinson and John Wayne: a flirtatious moment from Hawks' Western.

New York, 18 May
In *Rio Bravo*, Howard Hawks has abandoned the sweeping exteriors of the traditional Western for the claustrophobic interiors of a frontier town's bars, hotel and jail. John Wayne plays cantankerous, loner lawman John T. Chance who reluctantly gathers a "family" around him – old-timer Walter Brennan, drunken deputy Dean Martin, professional gambler Angie Dickinson and beardless youth Ricky Nelson – in order to bring murderer Claude Akins to trial. Hawks claims that *Rio Bravo* is his response to *High Noon*. "Gary Cooper ran around trying to get help and no one would give him any. And that's a rather silly thing for a man to do. So I said, we'll just do the opposite." And the result is a laconic "indoor" Western in which Angie Dickinson is outstanding as Feathers, a warm and sexy woman moving easily in a man's world without ruffling any of its conventions.

The heat's on Tony, Jack and Marilyn

Hollywood, 29 March

Billy Wilder's new film, *Some Like It Hot*, is a high-water mark in screen comedy. Wilder and his usual screenwriter I.A.L. Diamond have created an amalgam of parody, slapstick, romance and farce – modern in its sexual approach, nostalgic in its tribute to screwball comedies and old gangster movies. The clever plot begins in the Chicago of the 1920s, where Joe (Tony Curtis) and Jerry (Jack Lemmon), two jazz musicians who are on the run from gangsters, disguise themselves as "Josephine" and "Daphne" in order to join an all-girl band on its way to Florida. They become friends with Sugar Kane, the band's singer, with whom Joe falls in love. Wilder's speedy comic style gets equal performances from the three stars and a supporting cast that includes Joe. E. Brown, George Raft and Pat O'Brien. Curtis and Lemmon give unparalleled drag portrayals: Tony in a dark wig, high-pitched voice and alluring made-up eyes, Jack in high-heeled shoes, a flapper's frock and a blonde wig. Marilyn, the genuine female article, brings sensitivity to her role, and sings two zippy numbers.

Just girls together! 'Daphne' (Jack Lemmon) and Sugar Kane (Monroe).

'Gigi' breaks record but Leslie loses

Hollywood, 7 April

The record of Oscars won by a single film, held by *Gone With the Wind* and only twice matched, has finally been beaten. By the end of the evening at the RKO Pantages Theater, *Gigi* had scored a grand total of nine Oscars: Best Picture, Director (Vincente Minnelli), Screenplay (Alan Jay Lerner), Cinematography (Joseph Ruttenberg), Art Direction (William A. Horning, Henry Grace, Preston Ames, Keogh Gleason), Film Editing (Adrienne Fazan), Song (Gigi), Musical Score (André Previn) and Costume Design (Cecil Beaton). Unusually, not one of the film's cast was honored in any category; its star, Leslie Caron, lost to Susan Hayward for her all-stops-out performance as Barbara Graham, the petty criminal executed for murder in the harrowing *I Want to Live*. The Best Actor prize went to David Niven's subtle playing as a bogus major arrested for molesting women in the cinema in *Separate Tables*. Wendy Hiller gained a Best Supporting Actress Oscar for her landlady in the same movie. The burly Burl Ives was delighted to be given the Best Supporting Actor award for his role as the obstinate patriarch in *The Big Country*.

The Jean Vigo jury honors Claude Chabrol

Paris, 11 March

Just as Claude Chabrol's second feature, *The Cousins* has been released, the Jean Vigo prize jury has chosen to honor his first film, *Bitter Reunion* (*le Beau Serge*). But that choice created certain rumblings from those in the profession who object to the young director's rapid rise. Chabrol's two films, the first set in the country, and the second in Paris, have the same excellent young actors in the leads, Gérard Blain and Jean-Claude Brialy.

Alain Delon and Romy Schneider

Switzerland, 22 March

Alain Delon and Romy Schneider got to know each other in Vienna last summer during the making of *Christine*, which was directed by Pierre Gaspard-Huit. If Delon had first described Schneider as a "little white goose", he soon fell under her spell, and enjoyed the many retakes of their screen kisses. By the time filming was completed, the couple had fallen deeply in love with each other. Romy decided not to return to Cologne but to rejoin Alain in Paris, where they are now living together in his apartment on the quai Malaquai. Magda Schneider, Romy's actress mother, expressed her disapproval of her daughter's actions, but to no avail. Romy broke all contact with her family to prove her determination and Magda has finally given in. Alain and Romy have announced their engagement, putting the affair on a legal basis.

Claude Chabrol (3rd left) making his first film le Beau Serge (Bitter Reunion).

*Susan Hayward in **I Want to Live**.*

The New Wave breaks on the shore of Cannes

Cannes, 16 May

Accompanied by their "mentor" Jean Cocteau, the hot-heads of the New Wave arrived in force for this year's Cannes Film Festival. In addition to Jean-Luc Godard, Claude Chabrol and François Truffaut, one also noticed the presence of Roger Vadim, Alain Resnais, and Marcel Camus, who could certainly be considered part of the New Wave. If Truffaut, Resnais and Camus came to speak up for their own films, others arrived to support them. It was François Truffaut, the former harsh critic for *Cahiers du Cinéma*, who carried off the Best Director prize for his first feature, *The Four Hundred Blows*. Truffaut derived the

*As the 12-year-old Antoine Doinel in **The Four Hundred Blows**, Jean-Pierre Léaud carries Truffaut's message.*

*Marpessa Dawn in **Black Orpheus**, Golden Palm winner for Marcel Camus.*

screenplay from his own deprived childhood, and follows the adventures of a 12-year-old Parisian boy, neglected by both his mother and stepfather, who plays truant and takes to petty crime. He is placed in a reform school, but escapes to the coast. The film ends with a freeze of the child's face as he runs to the sea and, perhaps, liberty. The film's freewheeling quality is refreshing, but it is the natural performance of the young Jean-Pierre Léaud that makes it outstanding. Unfortunately, Resnais' *Hiroshima mon amour*, original in concept and subject, was shown outside of competition. The Golden Palm was given to *Black Orpheus*, Marcel Camus' musical transposition of the Greek myth to the carnival in Rio.

Where will it go?

It is far too early to speculate about the arrival of the New Wave, which has been hailed by the press, radio and television in Cannes. However, one can always question the nature of this so-called "movement". Launched last year by Françoise Giroud in an article in *l'Express*, the label New Wave now embraces directors that are very different from one another, even though some of them belong to the *Cahiers du Cinéma* group. Twenty of these young directors are taking part in a symposium at La Napoule, organized by the Cannes Film Festival. This idea had originated from the communiqué they recently published which outlined the areas of "total agreement" and those of "total disagreement concerning details." It remains to be seen whether these undoubtedly talented young people will contribute something genuinely new to the art of cinema. Some commentators have recollected that, in terms of innovation, the directors of the so-called New Wave are indebted to predecessors such as Roger Leenhardt, Jean-Pierre Melville, Alexandre Astruc and Agnès Varda, who always worked alone, and never considered themselves part of a movement. The New Wave directors have team spirit. That is what gives them their strength.

*Eiji Okada and Emanuelle Riva in Alain Resnais' **Hiroshima mon amour**. Although presented out of competition the film won the Critics Prize.*

*Simone Signoret, voted best actress for the British **Room at the Top**.*

Fellini parades the sour side of the sweet life with Marcello

Marcello Mastroianni, Fellini's doom-laden hero, with sensual Anita Ekberg.

New York, 19 April

Having caused scandal and division among critics, audiences and churchmen in its native Italy as well as in Catholic Europe, Federico Fellini's *La Dolce Vita* (*The Sweet Life*) has arrived in the U.S. This study of crippling boredom, leading to artistic paralysis and loose sexual morals, played out against the decadence of postwar Roman cafe society is an undoubted cinematic masterpiece. Fellini's imagination has run riot with a series of striking, brilliantly photographed images as his central character (Marcello Mastroianni), a journalist, lives out 24 hours in search of a story. Memorable scenes include a huge statue of Christ flown over Rome, Anita Ekberg drenched in the Trevi Fountain with a kitten on her head and Nadia Gray hosting an orgy at which she performs a striptease. Here is a contrived world of shoddy pleasures in a film that amazes and enthrals.

Pity and pain from Luis Buñuel

Mexico City, 4 June

Luis Buñuel's latest film, *Nazarin*, tells of how a humble and unworldly priest attempts to live by the precepts of Christianity, but is despised for his pains, finding compassion only with a prostitute. Told in the manner of a Christian parable, the film is touching, as well as being an ironic and forceful criticism of formal religion.

Francisco Rabal and Marga Lopez.

Royal premiere for 'angry young man'

London, 29 May

Tonight sees the gala premiere of the film version of John Osborne's landmark play *Look Back in Anger*. It stars Richard Burton as "Angry Young Man" Jimmy Porter, the brooding misogynist trapped in a dreary Midlands town and raging against the fossilized state of British society. Mary Ure plays his put-upon wife Allison and Claire Bloom gives an icy edge to her friend Helena, the "unmarried Mother Superior" who temporarily takes over from Allison at the ironing board and in Jimmy's bed. Director Tony Richardson has opened up the play for the screen, and softened some of Jimmy's impotent rage, but the picture still packs a punch.

Fred Zinnemann's act of faith pays off

New York, 18 June

With the opening of *The Nun's Story*, director Fred Zinnemann's faith has borne fruit. His persistence and the securing of Audrey Hepburn for the role of Sister Luke convinced Jack Warner to make the film, based on the true story of former nun Marie-Louise Habets. Made in Rome, Belgium and the Congo jungle, the film, from its early sequences in the convent, through harrowing scenes in a madhouse, to the key Congo episodes rich in a sense of missionary selflessness, is majestic and moving. Its excellence is matched in every department, notably by Hepburn as the nun whose sense of individual self brings her into agonizing conflict with her vocation.

Jimmy Porter (Burton) with wife (Mary Ure, left) and mistress (Claire Bloom).

Sister Luke (Audrey Hepburn) in the Congo with missionary Niall MacGinnis.

Gripping courtroom drama from Preminger

*James Stewart and Lee Remick star in Preminger's **Anatomy of a Murder**.*

New York, 6 July
Otto Preminger is code-breaking again in *Anatomy of a Murder*, a courtroom drama adapted from retired judge Robert Traver's novel and filmed in Traver's hometown in Michigan. James Stewart plays the easygoing country lawyer defending Ben Gazzara, accused of shooting the man who tried to rape his wife Lee Remick, and words such as "panties" and "contraception" are daringly bandied about. Presiding over the court is real-life Boston lawyer Joseph Welch, the man who helped expose Senator McCarthy.

'Apu' concludes Ray's humanist triptych

Paris, 14 September
Satyajit Ray's "Apu Trilogy", begun in the great Indian director's mind almost 10 years ago, has reached its climax with the release of *The World of Apu*. Taken at a less leisurely pace and more conventionally structured than either *Pather Panchali* or *The Unvanquished*, it is, nevertheless, imbued with the same keen observation, beautiful performances and memorable scenes, such as Apu (Soumitra Chatterjee) scattering the pages of his novel over a mountain at dawn. Although Apu is inconsolable when he loses his wife in childbirth, this humanist triptych ends on a note of hope.

*The man Apu: Soumitra Chatterjee, Sharmila Tagore in **The World of Apu**.*

A cocktail of suspense, sex and humor

*A case of mistaken identity lands Cary Grant in danger **North by Northwest**.*

Hollywood, 6 August
Alfred Hitchcock's latest effort is a blithely implausible chase thriller in which glibly feckless ad-man Cary Grant becomes the object of a cross-country spy hunt. It's packed with artful set pieces characteristic of Hitchcock, which include Grant being pursued across the prairie by a crop-duster and a climax on Mount Rushmore, which prompted Hitch to suggest the film be called "The Man Who Sneezed in Lincoln's Nose". Eva Marie Saint smolders sexily and there's a masterclass in silky villainy from James Mason.

Frank and frothy comedy for Doris and Rock

Los Angeles, 14 October
Rock Hudson reveals a deft talent for comedy in *Pillow Talk*, in which he plays a philandering songwriter whose shared party phone line with career girl Doris Day leads to romantic complications. Directed by Michael Gordon, produced by Ross Hunter, and sleek as a brand-new Cadillac in Eastmancolor and CinemaScope, *Pillow Talk* features a superb supporting cast that includes Tony Randall as one of Day's disappointed suitors and Thelma Ritter as a tipsy maid. It's a departure for Day, too. As interior designer Jan Morrow, she swaps the suburban housewife look for *haute couture*.

Doris Day and Rock Hudson, the couple who fall in love on a party phone line.

He-man Errol Flynn dies aged 50

Vancouver, 14 October

Errol Flynn has died of a heart attack at the age of 50. A life devoted to dissipation has finally caught up with him. According to Jack Warner, the star had long been one of the living dead, ravaged by drink and drugs, bottle-nosed, bleary-eyed and wasted. Flynn's recent films have cast him as a drunk: a wastrel expatriate in *The Sun Also Rises*; with tragic irony as his old drinking partner John Barrymore in *Too Much Too Soon*; and then rambling woozily among African elephants in *The Roots of Heaven*. There were still flickers of the old charm but the lights were about to go out. Flynn's final film was a semi-documentary, *Cuban Rebel Girls*, featuring his last lover, the 16-year-old Beverly Aadland. The coroner who examined Flynn's body said that the most dashing and athletic of all screen Robin Hoods had the body of an old, sick and tired man.

Ben-Hur: even bigger, but is it better?

Ben-Hur (Charlton Heston) taken as a galley slave, the condition that inspires his fight for freedom and justice.

Affecting tale of wartime life in Russia

Moscow, 18 December

After the worldwide success of *The Cranes Are Flying* two years ago, the Soviet cinema is offering audiences another film that promises to be equally welcome abroad. Entitled *Ballad of a Soldier* and directed by Grigori Chukrai, it tells of a young soldier, on four days leave from the Front during World War II, travelling by train, truck and on foot to see his mother. En route, he meets a variety of people affected in different ways by the war, and a girl with whom he falls in love. This simple, touching and unrhetorical view of everyday life in wartime Russia, is directed with superb technical skill.

Hollywood, 18 November

Just as it was in 1925, the future of MGM is riding on a big-budget production of *Ben-Hur*. Director William Wyler, who also acted as producer after the death of Sam Zimbalist, worked as an assistant director on the chariot race in the original. This time around he has handed over the shooting of this thunderous sequence to Andrew Marton and ace stuntman Yakima Canutt. Charlton Heston's Judah Ben-Hur and Stephen Boyd's Messala battle it out to the death in the Circus Maximus, re-created at the Cinecittà studios in Rome and the largest outdoor set ever built. Everything's big about this production, and with a budget of $14.5 million it's the most expensive movie ever made. It's also a supreme test of the stamina of Charlton Heston. Will its quality justify the cost?

*Vladimir Ivashev, star of **Ballad of a Soldier**, with Antonina Maximova.*

l to r: Heston, Sam Jaffe, Martha Scott, Haya Harareet, Cathy O'Donnell.

Color and Widescreen

*Impressive example of early color in French film, **Cyrano de Bergerac** (1923).*

*Michael Curtiz made **Robin Hood** for Warners (1938) in striking Technicolor.*

Today we take color pretty much for granted in the cinema and are occasionally pleasantly (or unpleasantly) surprised by a film made in black and white. Yet color took a long time to establish itself. The first big breakthrough came in the late 30s – after the introduction of the newly developed three-strip Technicolor process – with the success of Walt Disney's first feature-length cartoon, *Snow White and the Seven Dwarfs* (1937), Warner Bros.' lively and entertaining version of *The Ad-* ventures of Robin Hood* (1938) and David O. Selznick's *Gone With the Wind* (1939). But color filming did not entirely replace black and white until the late 60s.

Color was, in fact, first introduced at the very beginning of the cinema. As early as 1894, the Edison company began adding color by hand to such films as *Annabella's Dance*, which ran for only a few seconds and were viewed in the company's Kinetoscope machines. Ten years later, in France, Georges Méliès was adding imaginative hand-tinted color, thus providing an additional, delightfully picturesque quality to the fairy-tale fantasy and special effects (transformations, explosions, etc.) found in his short films. Also in France, around 1908, the Pathé company had initiated the first ever production and distribution of color prints on a large scale, making use of assembly-line methods of stencil tinting at its Vincennes factory where over 100 young women were employed as colorists. In England the Kinemacolor company first introduced its two-color 'additive' system which involved filming through a red-orange and blue-green filter, then projecting the completed movie through matching filters.

Many filmmakers experimented with color processes throughout the silent era, but such names as Polychromide, Prizma and Chronochrome merely merit a footnote in cinema history. The most familiar form of color from 1915 to 1926 was the overall tinting or toning

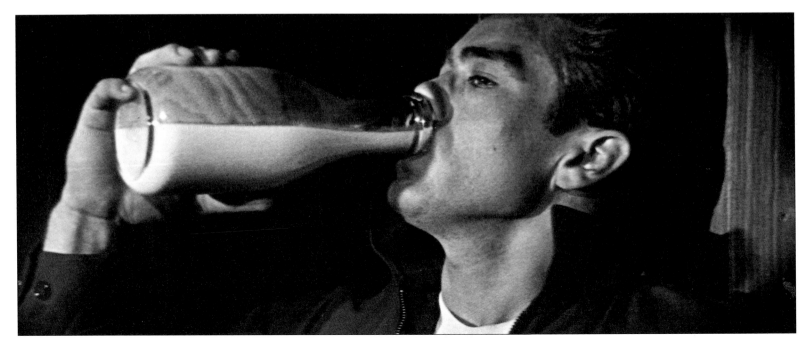

of feature films, with sepia or pink for day scenes, blue for night, and so on. The first widely adopted system of two-color subtractive photography was developed by Herbert Kalmus of the Technicolor Co. in the early 20s. This made use of a beam-splitting device behind the camera lens so that red and green exposures could be made simultaneously. It was first used for shooting special sequences in a number of major Hollywood costume movies such as *The Ten Commandments* (1923) and *Ben-Hur* (1925), and for entire features, such as *The Black Pirate* (1926), starring Douglas Fairbanks, and *The Viking* (1929), as well as for many of the spectacular early sound musicals including *Melody of Broadway* and *Show of Shows* in 1929, *Sally, Whoopie!* and *The Vagabond King* in 1930.

By 1934 a new Technicolor which recorded the entire color spectrum became available, but required filming with special three-strip cameras. Processing took place at Technicolor's labs where the three separate negatives were used to make matrix relief films in what was known as imbibition printing, and these were combined to make the final release print. The first three-strip feature, *Becky Sharp* in 1935, was followed by numerous other features in the U.S., and in England where Technicolor set up a lab. But the numbers grew only slowly since color filming was expensive, the special cameras required were large and awkward to handle and most of the leading directors and (non-musical) stars pre-

*Joan Crawford in Nicholas Ray's **Johnny Guitar**, shot in Trucolor for Republic.*

ferred black and white In the words of Bette Davies, "They gave the color to the terrible scripts as an added inducement to get the public in. My pictures brought the public in without the added expense." In the U.S. an imaginative use of color was seen mainly in the musicals where MGM was the leader, beginning with *The Wizard of Oz* (1939) and, especially, *Meet Me in St. Louis* (1944) directed by Vincente Minnelli. However, the leading creative filmmaker working in color during these years was an Englishman: Michael Powell's remarkable films, in both ideas and visual quality, included an original treatment of war themes in *The Life and Death of Colonel Blimp* (1943), *A Matter of Life and Death* (aka *Stairway to Heaven*), *Black Narcissus* (1947) and, most successful of all,

The Red Shoes (1948). Finally, in the early and mid-50s the long overdue increase in color filming took place in the U.S. and abroad, coinciding with, and stimulated by, various new technical innovations. The Technicolor monopoly was seriously challenged for the first time by a less expensive, single-strip Eastmancolor which could be used in a standard 35mm camera, while the introduction of various new widescreen and large format processes also put the emphasis firmly on color. The decade was characterized by great technical diversity, black and white existing side by side with color, 35mm with 70mm. However, there was a basic change in the screen format or height to width ratio, which has been maintained up to the present day. The old 1:33 of 'Academy' was re-

placed by 1:75, 1:85 or occasionally 1:65, with the new CinemaScope and 70mm providing a 'letterbox' shape of 2 or 2½ to 1. During these years many leading directors made features in color for the first time, among them Anthony Mann, George Stevens and William Wyler in the U.S., John Huston, Carol Reed and Alexander Mackendrick in England, Jean Renoir in France, Luchino Visconti in Italy, and, in Japan, two creative giants, Ozu and Mizoguchi. For some, their first in color was also in CinemaScope (Cukor, Kazan, Ophuls). By the mid-60s the 35mm Panavision (anamorphic) lenses had replaced those of CinemaScope, black and white was on the way out, and the last films were being shot in 70mm, for it was now cheaper and easier to film with the new improved 35mm equipment and fine-grain Eastman negative, then print up to 70mm. Thus, the main choice for filmmakers today is between a standard wide screen or anamorphic (letterbox) shape, with black and white rarely an option. A leading director such as Robert Altman likes the freedom which the extremely wide shape (and looser framing of shots) allows, while Martin Scorsese, Francis Ford Coppola and Woody Allen generally prefer the standard wide screen. And the choices made by Steven Spielberg are especially interesting: normal wide screen for the intimate *E.T.*, the wider Panavision for *Jaws*, *Close Encounters* and the *Indiana Jones* movies, and black and white for *Schindler's List*.

François Truffaut's **The Four Hundred Blows** was much praised everywhere.

Eiji Okada and Emmanuelle Riva in Alain Resnais' **Hiroshima, mon amour**.

Eiji Funakoshi (c), Mantaro Ushio in **Fires on the Plain** from Kon Ichikawa.

From Italy, **Big Deal on Madonna Street**, an impeccable social comedy that spoofs **Rififi**, directed by Mario Monicelli. Here, Renato Salvatore (left), Toto.

The most famous of gang bosses brought realistically to life.

A successful movie from the British bestseller by John Braine.

Charlton Heston got the title role sought after by Rock Hudson and Brando.

Sugar Kane (Marilyn Monroe), Josephine (Tony Curtis): **Some Like It Hot**.

Richard Widmark (l), Henry Fonda (r) in Edward Dmytryk's **Warlock**.

Günther Hoffman in Bernhard Wicki's powerful anti-war film from Germany titled **The Bridge (Die Brücke)**.

An explosive, doom-laden trip into Tennessee Williams territory.

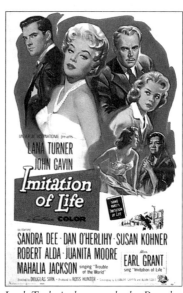

Lush Technicolor remake by Douglas Sirk of the 1934 hit.

491

One of Huston's least successful films cast Audrey Hepburn as an Indian girl. She lost her own baby in a fall from a horse during shooting.

Blue-collar hero Albert Finney in *Saturday Night and Sunday Morning*.

Laurence Olivier and Shirley Anne Field in *The Entertainer*.

The variously gifted Cocteau's own poster design for his film.

Doris Day and Rex Harrison in the thriller *Midnight Lace*.

Dina Merrill, Tony Curtis, Cary Grant: Blake Edwards' *Operation Petticoat*.

A great variation on *Dracula*, with a disciple of the Count on the rampage.

HERE COME "THE SUNDOWNERS"! They're real people, fun people, fervent people. They have a tremendous urge to keep breathing. Their rousing story comes roaring across six thousand miles of excitement...

DEBORAH KERR ROBERT MITCHUM PETER USTINOV

FRED ZINNEMANN'S PRODUCTION OF **The SUNDOWNERS**

Co Starring GLYNIS JOHNS · DINA MERRILL · Screenplay by ISOBEL LENNART · MUSIC COMPOSED AND CONDUCTED BY DIMITRI TIOMKIN
Directed by FRED ZINNEMANN · TECHNICOLOR® · PRESENTED BY WARNER BROS

An Anglo-American cast, headed by Robert Mitchum and Deborah Kerr, in a lovingly filmed saga of a pioneering family in the Australian bush.

*Judy Holliday (left) and Dean Martin (second left) in Minnelli's film of the Broadway musical **Bells Are Ringing**.*

*Singer Charles Aznavour stars in Truffaut's **Shoot the Pianist**.*

*Annie Girardot, a tragic figure in Visconti's **Rocco and His Brothers**.*

***Psycho**: Motel owner Norman Bates (Anthony Perkins) and guest Janet Leigh.*

Aristocrats of the acting profession illumine this epic of Ancient Rome.

The Italian poster for Italy's **La Notte (The Night)**, Michelangelo Antonioni's bleak and brilliant follow-up to **L'Avventura**.

Saul Bass, unmistakably, designed the witty poster for Wilder's film.

The Hustler: 'Fast' Eddy Felson (Paul Newman) shoots; George C. Scott (l).

Federico Fellini's **La Dolce Vita** (aka **The Sweet Life**) caused outrage in Italy and a sensation in the rest of the world.

Corinne Marchand as Cléo in director Agnes Varda's **Cléo From 5 to 7**.

Lucyna Winnicka, Mieczyslaw Voit: **The Devil and the Nun** (Poland).

Jerry Lewis in **The Errand Boy**; he wrote, produced and directed it.

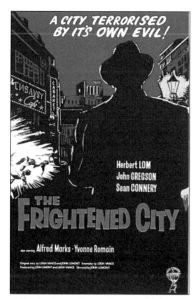

Criminal racketeering British-style was a successful formula.

The American critics gave a seal of approval to last year's British hit.

Lightweight but cheery British comedy about young marrieds and maids.

Downbeat but first-class British movie, **A Taste of Honey**, with Murray Melvin and Rita Tushingham, again directed by Tony Richardson.

Left to right: David Niven, Gregory Peck and Anthony Quinn in **The Guns of Navarone**, directed by J. Lee Thompson from Alistair Maclean's novel.

From Italy this year came Pietro Germi's delightful satire, **Divorce, Italian Style**, with Marcello Mastroianni and Daniela Rocca.

1962

★ ★

Prague, 12 May
Director Jiri Trňka has started filming *Kybernetika Babicka (Cybernetic Grandma)*, a puppet film which deals with the problems associated with man's reaction to advances in technology.

Tokyo, 2 January
Release of Akira Kurosawa's film, *Tsubaki Sanjuro (Sanjuro)*, which stars Toshiro Mifune. Eight young warriors and a wandering samurai take on a corrupt lord in this satirical historical "Eastern-Western".

Rome, 6 January
Renato Salvatori and Annie Girardot were married today. The two actors first met while filming *Rocco and his Brothers*.

Rome, 15 January
The producer Dino De Laurentiis has laid the foundation stone for the Dinocittà studio.

Los Angeles, 20 January
To allay rumors about a return to 20th Century-Fox, Darryl Zanuck has left the following memo: "I am not bitter, but I have reached the age... where I cannot spend my days with people I would not like to have dinner with..."

Paris, 27 January
In *le Monde*, François Truffaut is quoted as saying:"The thing which gives me the courage to keep going is that in the cinema industry one does not feel isolated. Solitude is one of the greatest problems facing other artists such as abstract painters and musicians."

Paris, 31 January
Opening of Louis Malle's latest film, *Vie privée (A Very Private Life)* co-starring Marcello Mastroianni and Brigitte Bardot. Critics have not failed to notice the similarity between Louis Malle's tragic heroine and the tribulations suffered in real life by Miss Bardot.

Paris, 5 February
The Empire cinema has reopened under the name Empire-Abel Gance, with a Cinerama film *la Grande rencontre*. Special homage was paid to Abel Gance's inventive genius during the opening speech.

Paris, 5 February
Roger Vadim is shooting the first scenes for his new film *le Repos du guerrier* in the Billancourt studios. It is his fourth film with his ex-wife, Brigitte Bardot, who is partnered by Robert Hossein, and likely to be his last as Bardot has said she intends to retire from the screen.

Milan, 22 February
Première of *Boccaccio '70*, a film of short vignettes, directed by Federico Fellini, Vittorio De Sica, Luchino Visconti and Mario Monicelli. The cast is headed by Romy Schneider, Sophia Loren, and Anita Ekberg.

Tunis, 2 March
The Tunisian Federation of ciné-clubs, which was created in 1950, has at last received official recognition. It now has the enviable status of a National Cultural Society.

Paris, 7 March
Release of *Cartouche*, directed by Philippe de Broca, with Jean-Paul Belmondo and Claudia Cardinale.

Sicily, 14 March
Burt Lancaster has hurt his leg and is unable to dance with Claudia Cardinale for the ball scene in *The Leopard (Il Gattopardo)*. The scene, which called for 250 extras, as well as 120 wardrobe masters, makeup artists and hairdressers, has had to be postponed. Director Luchino Visconti is apparently furious.

New York, 20 March
The *New York Times* has announced that Grace Kelly, now Princess Grace of Monaco and retired from the screen, will return to star in Alfred Hitchcock's next film, *Marnie*.

Rome, 1 April
On location here for *Cleopatra*, stars Richard Burton and Elizabeth Taylor have been seen together frequently. Despite repeated denials from their agents, their liaison is now public knowledge. The press appears to be on the side of Sybil Burton and Taylor's husband, Eddie Fisher, the wronged parties.

Prague, 12 May
Federico Fellini has started filming his latest film *8½ (Otto e mezzo)* in Cinecittà studios, with Marcello Mastroianni, Claudia Cardinale and Sandra Milo.

Paris, 25 May
The press has been showing a great deal of interest in the Tahitian liaison between Martine Carol and a young soldier named Jean-Marie Dallet, who is said to be one of Georges Pompidou's nephews.

Paris, 10 June
A quote from film critic Robert Benayoun in the magazine *Positif* – "Have you been abroad lately? There are two things other countries envy us for: De Gaulle and the *Nouvelle Vague (New Wave)*."

Paris, 13 August
Philippe Noiret has married Monique Chaumette. Both of them had worked at the National Theatre.

Los Angeles, 18 September
The Music Corporation of America (MCA) has taken over the Decca record company, the major shareholder in Universal.

Rome, 22 September
At the premiere of *Mama Roma*, in the Quattro Fontane Cinema, the film's director, Pier Paolo Pasolini, was attacked by members of fascist groups who had turned up to protest against the film.

Paris, 20 November
After three years of married life, Brigitte Bardot is divorcing Jacques Charrier. The couple's problems have been exacerbated by Brigitte's infatuation with Sammy Frey, her co-star in Henri-Georges Clouzot's *la Verité*. Charrier has been given the custody of their two-year-old son Nicholas, as Brigitte, who recently attempted suicide, feels incapable of taking on the responsibility.

Tokyo, 20 November
Yasujiro Ozu's latest film *Samma no Aji (An Autumn Afternoon)* has opened in the capital.

Paris, 10 December
Issue no. 130 of *Cahiers du Cinéma* is a special number devoted to the *Nouvelle Vague*, and includes a long interview with Jean-Luc Godard. According to the filmmaker: "The sincerity of the *Nouvelle Vague* is essentially that it deals intelligently with things it knows about, rather than speaking badly of things it knows nothing about."

California, 20 December
A real-estate firm has bought the Hal Roach studios in Culver City. The studios were built in 1920 and innumerable short comic films, including all Laurel and Hardy's early work, were made there.

BIRTHS

Los Angeles, 5 February
Jennifer Jason Leigh

New York, 21 March
Matthew Broderick

New York, 12 May
Emilio Estevez

New York, 3 July
Tom Cruise

New Mexico, 11 November
Demi Moore (Demi Guynes)

Los Angeles, 19 November
Jodie Foster

DEATHS

Hollywood, 10 April
Michael Curtiz

Hollywood, 19 June
Frank Borzage

Hollywood, 6 October
Tod Browning

California, 17 December
Thomas Mitchell

English director David Lean's desert epic on the life of T.E. Lawrence has revealed an unusual and charismatic new star in Peter O'Toole. The film's other star is undoubtedly the Sahara.

Jules, Jim and Catherine are bathed in a tender glow by Truffaut

Truffaut with Jeanne Moreau.

Paris, 24 January

A *ménage à trois* is the subject of François Truffaut's new film, *Jules and Jim*, a story that might have been sordid in anyone else's hands. It tells of how close friends, the German Jules (Oskar Werner) and the Frenchman Jim (Henri Serre), both fall in love with Catherine (Jeanne Moreau). However, Jules marries her and takes her back to Germany. World War I separates the two friends even further, and when they meet again after hostilities, Catherine decides to change

Catherine (Moreau) with Frenchman Jim (Henri Serre) in a somber moment.

partners. Although Truffaut's invigorating tale of friendship and love is full of cinematic allusions, (one to Chaplin's *The Kid*), and is a homage to Jean Renoir, it is a unique piece of filmmaking. The director, while he remains true to Henri-Pierre Roché's first novel, employs a wide range of cinematic devices to ex-

press the shifting moods of the characters and plot, including both stills and newsreels. The three leads are delightful, and Jeanne Moreau's charming singing of "le Tourbillon" is a memorable moment. Truffaut came across the novel as long ago as 1953, and determined then to film it one day. It is a dream come true.

Germany's answer to the 'New Wave'

Oberhausen, 28 February

The annual festival of short films at Oberhausen is always an exceptional event in the cinematographic calendar. This year a manifesto was presented, signed by 26 young German filmmakers. They are concerned about the evolution of their cinema and condemn its stultifying conformity, typified by the *Sissi* series and *Heimatfilme* (rural films). Like the "angry young generation" of the British Free Cinema, and those of the French New Wave, Herbert Vesely, Alexander Kluge and others are trying to make themselves heard. Their ambition is to create a new German cinema of full-length films as interesting as the shorts shown here. This generation of directors has already presented many of its short films to acclaim at other international festivals. They now wish to bring this "new cinematographic language" into features and are willing to take economic risks. Herbert Vesely's *Das Brot der Fruhen Jahre* (*Bread of Youth*) is representative of this New German Cinema.

'West Side Story' dances off with ten Oscars

Hollywood, 9 April

The Academy Awards ceremony this year, once again presented by Bob Hope with the assistance of Ann-Margret, saw the triumph of *West Side Story*, directed by Robert Wise and Jerome Robbins. This film scooped ten Oscars, including Best Picture, Best Director and both Best

Supporting Actor and Actress, the last two awards being handed, respectively, to George Chakiris and Rita Moreno. The Best Actor award went to Maximilian Schell for his strong performance as the defense attorney in *Judgment at Nuremberg*. Sophia Loren was voted Best Actress for *Two Women*.

*Spencer Tracy and Marlene Dietrich in Kramer's **Judgment at Nuremberg**.*

Cléo sees her life flash past in two hours

*Corinne Marchand and Jose Luis de Villalonga in Varda's **Cléo From 5 to 7**.*

Paris, 11 April

Two hours in the life of a superstitious young nightclub singer (played by the beautiful ex-model Corinne Marchand) as she waits for the medical verdict on whether she will live or die, is the subject of the new film

from Agnes Varda, *Cléo From 5 to 7*. The director has managed to capture Paris as seen through the eyes of the heroine, where every trivial incident takes on new significance. Part of the film's originality is that the story unfolds in real time.

Wayne and Stewart, old comrades-in-arms

James Stewart (center) and John Wayne, two old-timers reunited in the West.

San Francisco, 11 April
John Ford's newest Western, *The Man Who Shot Liberty Valance*, explores the transformation of the frontier from wilderness to garden and the myths on which the process of civilization depend. James Stewart is Ransom Stoddart, the bookish Eastern lawyer who becomes a hero, and a senator, when he confronts and kills the brutal gunslinger of the title, played by Lee Marvin. But his belated confession that Valance was shot by John Wayne's Tom Doniphon, symbol of the Old West, is dismissed by a newspaper editor who comments, "when the legend becomes fact, print the legend."

Peck and Mitchum: a fight to the death

Robert Mitchum, Gregory Peck struggle for survival in a terrifying sequence.

Florida, 12 April
Robert Mitchum is at his most powerfully malevolent as Max Cady, the vengeful, cigar-chomping ex-con stalking upright Florida attorney Gregory Peck and his family in *Cape Fear*, directed by Britain's J. Lee Thompson. Mitchum's attentions soon move from poisoning the family dog to sexually asssaulting Peck's teenage daughter Lori Martin. Finally the desperate Peck uses Martin and wife Polly Bergen as bait in a trap he sets for Mitchum in the steamy mangrove swamps of the Everglades. Not since *The Night of the Hunter* has Mitchum reveled in such rich villainy.

British realism colors 'A Kind of Loving'

London, 21 May
In *A Kind of Loving*, director John Schlesinger focuses on the kind of smoky, northern industrial environment which is rapidly becoming a cliché of British cinema. The film stars Alan Bates and June Ritchie as a young couple forced to marry when Ritchie becomes pregnant. Schlesinger explores the landscape of their lives, both interior and exterior, with some sensitivity, but the feeling remains that they are representatives of a particular kind of social thinking rather than living, breathing people.

Chinese women of war win coveted prize

Peking, 22 May
The magazine *Popular Cinema* has just created the One Hundred Flower prize, chosen by a poll of its readers. The first winner is *Detachment of Women*, directed by Xie Jin last year. Born in 1923, the director is already well-known, with *Basketball Player No. 5* being among his successes. His latest film takes place on the island of Hainan in 1930, where the Communist guerillas consist solely of women. The stirring story along with the engaging presence of the young Zhu Xijuan, has enchanted the public.

June Ritchie and Alan Bates, a bleak union in John Schlesinger's film.

*Zhu Xijuan in Xie Jin's award-winning Chinese film **Detachment of Women**.*

Antonioni and Bresson share in triumph

*Alain Delon, Monica Vitti in Special Jury prizewinner **The Eclipse**.*

Cannes, 25 May
Without taking into consideration the negative reactions of the public to both Robert Bresson's *The Trial of Joan of Arc* and Michelangelo Antonioni's *The Eclipse*, the films shared the Special Jury Prize. Neither could be called crowd pleasers. Bresson's austere work was drawn from the actual transcripts of the trial of Joan, played by Florence Carrez, a non-professional actress. *The Eclipse* completes Antonioni's trilogy of alienation, and dwells on the emptiness of modern life. To everybody's surprise, the Golden Palm went to *The Given Word*, a Brazilian film by Anselmo Duarte.

Political potboiler casts pall on U.S. Senate

New York, 6 June
The wheelers and dealers of Washington come under the skeptical scrutiny of Otto Preminger in his new film, *Advise and Consent*, adapted from a novel by Allen Drury. For the task he has drawn together a superb cast: Franchot Tone as the dying president; Lew Ayres as the disarmingly youthful vice president who succeeds him; Henry Fonda as a presidential candidate; and Don Murray and Charles Laughton as senators – the former tortured by his homosexuality and the latter in flamboyant form as a wily Southern fixer. Sadly it was Laughton's last performance. He died of cancer in a Hollywood hospital on 15 December last year, at the age of 63.

*Charles Laughton (left) and Walter Pidgeon appear in **Advise and Consent**.*

Teenage temptress Lolita arrives on screen

*James Mason and Sue Lyon in Kubrick's **Lolita** from the novel by Nabokov.*

New York, 13 June
"How Could They Make a Movie of *Lolita*?" the ads for Stanley Kubrick's latest film demand. Well, the answer must be, they have – up to a point. A significant difference between Vladimir Nabokov's screenplay and his bestselling novel is that the age of the nymphet in the book has been raised into the teens to make it more acceptable to movie audiences, thereby changing Humbert Humbert's "perverse passion" into something less shocking. This alteration, and the reduction of the American landscape's importance in the novel (the picture was shot in England) still does not diminish the impact of this acerbic tragi-comedy. Apart from the obvious differences between the novel and the film, the story is basically the same. Humbert Humbert (James Mason), a middle-aged professor of French literature in New Hampshire, rents a room for the summer in the house of Charlotte Haze (Shelley Winters), a snobbish widow whose 14-year-old daughter Lolita (Sue Lyon) he finds irresistibly attractive. He marries the mother to be closer to the daughter, and Charlotte dies in a freak accident shortly after learning the truth. Humbert takes the girl on a long car trip, but is dogged all the way by mysterious writer Clare Quilty (Peter Sellers). Both Mason and Sellers play their off-beat roles to perfection, and Shelley Winters touchingly and humorously suggests emotional starvation and middlebrow pretentions. Sixteen-year-old Sue Lyon, in her first film, wonderfully catches Lolita's blend of gum-chewing vulgarity and quivering animal tenderness and sensuality.

Jean Gabin meets his alter ego

Paris, 11 May
Two great French actors, each from a different generation, have come face to face in Henri Verneuil's film *A Monkey in Winter* (*Un singe en hiver*): Jean Gabin from the Golden Age of prewar French cinema and Jean-Paul Belmondo, the darling of the New Wave. In the course of making the film, set in Normandy in 1944, the two stars struck up a friendship. At one stage, Gabin told Belmondo, "Kid, you're me at 20."

Sue Lyon: a junior femme fatale.

The final crack-up in Marilyn Monroe's life

Los Angeles, 6 August
Marilyn Monroe has been found dead in her bed this morning in her Brentwood house on the west side of Los Angeles. The autopsy revealed that she had succumbed to a massive dose of sleeping pills. If it was a case of suicide, then numerous reasons could be given for it: a loveless and profoundly unhappy childhood; a mentally unstable mother and an unknown father; three failed marriages; two miscarriages; a number of unfulfilled romances; constant pressure from the press; and professional difficulties due to a loss of confidence in herself... In fact, very little had gone well for her since February 1961, after her divorce from Arthur Miller. It was then that

Marilyn entered a psychiatric clinic, fearful that she might suffer insanity as her mother before her.

Marilyn returned to work last April to begin shooting on her 29th movie, *Something's Got to Give*, directed by George Cukor, and with Dean Martin and Cyd Charisse as co-stars. One of her last public appearances was at Madison Square Garden in New York on 21 May. Dressed in a clinging, flesh-colored, sequined dress, she sang "Happy Birthday" to President Kennedy. Production on the film was interrupted soon after. Marilyn, who was said to be ill, seldom turned up on the set, forcing the director to shoot as much as he could around her. The studio (20th Century-Fox) began to look for a replacement, but Dean Martin, a friend of hers, threatened to quit the film if Marilyn went. She came back for a day's shooting at his instigation, but then disappeared again. This time Fox started proceedings against the star, reclaiming $750,000 from her for breach of contract. Marilyn sent a letter to the film team which read, "Please believe me, I did not do it without good cause. I would have loved to have worked with you." Just three months later, she was dead, leaving no message that would explain her final gesture. "Marilyn was the most frightened little girl," Joseph L. Mankiewicz had once commented. "And yet scared as she was, she had this strange effect when she was photographed... In fact, the camera loved her."

Marilyn's bedroom, the scene of her tragic, premature and mysterious end.

In How to Marry a Millionaire.

Crowds gathered for the star's funeral held at Westwood Memorial Park.

Darryl F. Zanuck takes the reins at Fox

Hollywood, 29 August
Darryl F. Zanuck has just been appointed as the new president of 20th Century-Fox. This comes six years after he relinquished his post as that studio's vice president in charge of production in favor of a new career as an independent in Europe, producing films such as *The Sun Also Rises* (1957), *The Roots of Heaven* (1958) and completed this year, *The Longest Day*. Unfortunately, Fox performed badly under departing president Spyros P. Skouras, and has recorded huge losses during the past three years, only managing to survive by selling off 260 acres of its

back lot. The situation has become increasingly desperate during the past year, with the costs of *Cleopatra* climbing over $30 million to make it by far the most expensive movie ever made; while the Marilyn Monroe film, *Something's Got to Give*, abandoned midway through production, involved around $2 million in cost write-offs. On his taking over, Zanuck immediately shut down the studio and dismissed most employees in order to cut costs and gain some breathing space before the release of both *The Longest Day* and *Cleopatra*, films which should replenish the company offers.

Honors for Italy and the USSR at Venice

Venice, 8 September
At this year's Mostra the jury found it impossible to decide which of two films merited the Golden Lion. They resolved this problem by giving it both to Andrei Tarkovsky's *Ivan's Childhood* and to Valerio Zurlini's *Family Diary* (*Cronaca Familiare*). The choice shows that they went for emotion rather than pyrotechnics. The Soviet film tells of the adventures of 12-year-old Ivan, whose family is wiped out by the Nazis. Hell-bent on revenge, he joins a detachment of Partisans who are able to use his size and agility for intelligence purposes. It concludes that

"childhood is made to love, and not for combat." The 30-year-old Tarkovsky's feature debut shows a rich pictorial sense, especially in the lyrical black-and-white landscapes. Also beautiful to look at is *Family Diary*, with Zurlini using color to evoke the Impressionists. It is a melancholy tale of two brothers, newspaperman Enrico (Marcello Mastroianni) and Lorenzo (Jacques Perrin), separated in childhood, but later brought together in a close and loving relationship. The film takes the form of flashback reminiscences of Enrico following the death of the younger Lorenzo from an incurable disease. ▷

Zanuck's all-star cast disembarks for longest day

Paris, 10 October
Producer Darryl F. Zanuck, who for several years has been operating as an independent based in France, has become a five-star general for *The Longest Day*, fighting the Normandy invasion all over again with a budget of $10 million, 50 international stars, 10,000 extras, 48 technical advisors and dozens of locations. No black-and-white movie has ever cost as much. Three directors were assigned to the picture – Ken Annakin, Andrew Marton and Bernhard Wicki – but there was never any doubt about who was in charge. Darting from location to location in a helicopter, the cigar-chewing Zanuck declared, "This is my picture. When one wants to take the credit for something one must also take the responsibility. I don't mind the hard work. There is plenty of compensation in the pride one can feel when it's all over." These are the words of a producer who had not had too much success lately as an independent. Carried along with

The Longest Day happened on 6 June 1944. Robert Mitchum leads his men.

Curt Jurgens (left), the German side.

Zanuck in this great executive assault on the events of 6 June 1944 are John Wayne, Rod Steiger, Robert Ryan, Henry Fonda, Richard Burton, Eddie Albert, Curt Jurgens, Peter Lawford, Gert Frobe, Robert Wagner, Sal Mineo, Richard Beymer, Richard Todd and a host of

others. It must all seem very familiar to Todd who, as a paratrooper, actually took part in Overlord. The film has been adapted by Cornelius Ryan from his best-selling book, and looks at the titanic events of D-Day from nearly every viewpoint, including that of the Germans. And a

healthy measure of authenticity has been achieved by the decision to allow the characters to speak in their own languages, with subtitles. The result receives its world premiere today. Zanuck has succeeded in his own longest day, a triumph of cinematic logistics.

Anna Karina is Jean-Luc Godard's muse

Paris, 22 September
After winning the Special Jury Prize at the recent Venice Film Festival, Jean-Luc Godard's fourth feature, *My Life to Live* (*Vivre sa vie*), has

just opened in Paris. It is the story (told in 12 chapters) of Nana S., a girl from the provinces, who gets a badly-paid job in a record shop in Paris. Then when she finds herself unable to pay the rent, she is gradually initiated into prostitution, finally becoming experienced. Using interview techniques, direct sound, long takes, texts, quotations and statistics, Godard has given this probing and dazzling examination of prostitution a documentary tone. Godard's screenplay was inspired by a survey carried out by Marcel Sacotte on the current state of prostitution in France, extracts of which are read out by Saddy Rebot, who plays a pimp. The philosopher Brice Parain also makes an appearance in which he reflects on the heroine's actions. Above all, however, the film is a passionate cinematic love letter to his wife Anna Karina, who plays Nana. Close-ups of her remind one of Louise Brooks and Lillian Gish as well as Falconetti, the latter tearfully watched by Karina in Carl Dreyer's *The Passion of Joan of Arc*. The star has become, more than ever, Godard's muse.

*Anna Karina in **My Life to Live**.*

Sean Connery a very special agent 007

London, 1 October
The current Cuban missile crisis has provided a real-life backdrop to the screen debut of Ian Fleming's secret agent James Bond in *Dr. No*, produced by Harry Saltzman and Cubby Broccoli. Sean Connery takes the part of agent 007, licensed to kill.

His combination of physical grace, classless Scots burr and hint of sadism fleshes out the perfect fantasy spy, thwarting the eponymous villain's dreams of world domination and wryly watching Ursula Andress' Honey Rider rise glistening from the sea.

*Switzerland's Ursula Andress and Scotland's Sean Connery star in **Dr. No**.*

'The Manchurian Candidate' is, simply, brilliant

New York, 23 October

"More and more I think our society is being manipulated and controlled." These words come from director John Frankenheimer whose latest screen effort, *The Manchurian Candidate*, plunges into the world of brainwashing, political extremism and the murky machinations of the

Brainwashed: Laurence Harvey.

Cold War. Adapted by George Axelrod from Richard Condon's best-selling novel, this movie stars Laurence Harvey as a returning Korean War hero who is not all he seems. "Why do you always have to look as if your head were about to come to a point?" asks his mother Angela Lansbury. But his zombie-like behavior is understandable. Harvey was brainwashed while a prisoner of the Communists in North Korea. Now Lansbury and her husband, a rabidly McCarthyite senator, are using their son to carry out a series of assassinations in America for their own nefarious purposes. Total disaster is averted by wartime buddy Frank Sinatra in a stunning set piece staged at a convention in Madison Square Garden. Unfazed by Frankenheimer's feverish direction, Angela Lansbury delivers a superb performance as the most monstrous of mothers. In reality she is only three years older than her screen son, but she looks more interested in life than the pointy-headed Harvey.

*The terrorizer terrorized: Angela Lansbury in **The Manchurian Candidate**.*

See 'Gypsy' and have 'a real good time'

New York, 1 November

The long-running Broadway hit musical *Gypsy* comes to the screen with its virtues intact, despite losing the unique Ethel Merman in favor of Rosalind Russell. The memorable score by Jule Styne, with lyrics to match from Stephen Sondheim and a great libretto, lights up this enthralling real-life tale that charts the childhood, adolescence and subsequent career of stripper Gypsy Rose Lee. Natalie Wood excels in the role, as does Russell playing Rose, Gypsy's brash, domineering showbiz mom at the center of things.

Three directors win the West in Cinerama

London, 1 November

The dramatic possibilities of Cinerama are showcased in *How the West Was Won*, an episodic history of the opening up of the American frontier directed by Henry Hathaway, John Ford and George Marshall. This film opens with the exploits of mountain man James Stewart and closes with a train robbery. Along the way the three-camera system, projected on to a huge screen, provides some breathtakingly spectacular action that includes a buffalo stampede, shooting the rapids and an Indian attack on a wagon train.

*Rose's turn: Rosalind Russell (left), and Natalie Wood in the title role in **Gypsy**.*

James Stewart and the spectacular landscape in one of Hathaway's sequences. ▷

Bette and Joan in Gothic horror melo

New York, 6 November
Director Robert Aldrich has given Bette Davis and Joan Crawford a bizarre new lease on life in *What Ever Happened to Baby Jane?*, an extraordinary extension of the sado-masochistic elements that have been running through their film careers, in which they play two elderly sisters trapped in the past. Davis was the child star of the title until Crawford became a leading lady and elbowed her out of the spotlight. Now the studio lights have been switched off for both of them, and they occupy a shuttered mansion, Crawford in a wheelchair, drink-sodden Davis gleefully serving her rats for dinner. There's heavyweight support from 300-pound newcomer Victor Buono and Aldrich works all the organ stops on this bit of sub-Gothic horror. It's ironic that rivals Crawford and Davis should join forces at War-ners, scene of their 1940s triumphs.

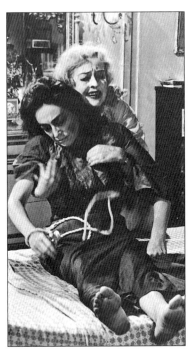

Joan Crawford and Bette Davis.

Marlon Brando plays Fletcher Christian

New York, 9 November
Marlon Brando has made a spirited but wayward attempt to reinvent an English version of Clark Gable in *Mutiny on the Bounty*. In the 1935 film, Gable and Charles Laughton were the mutinous Fletcher Christian and the martinet Captain Bligh; now Brando co-stars with Trevor Howard and a replica of the original *Bounty* which gobbled up a sizeable chunk of the $19.5 million budget.

Huston, Freud and the country of the mind

Hollywood, 13 December
Among the many biopics that have come out of Hollywood over the years, the latest one, John Huston's *Freud*, is one of the most successful. Originally, the director had asked Jean-Paul Sartre to write the screenplay, but the French philosopher and writer delivered a script that would have entailed a film of 16 hours running time. Though Huston found it unusable, he went to work on it with screenwriter Charles Kaufman and producer Wolfgang Reinhardt, picking out some of Sartre's better ideas. The end result is a fascinating portrait of the father of psychoanalysis, seen from inside the profession, mixing real biographical elements with fictional ones. The picture begins with the 30-year-old Freud taking a leave of absence from his work in the General Hospital in Vienna to delve deeper into the causes of hysteria. His work with several patients, especially a woman with a father fixation, prompts him to begin writing his theories, which are derided by his peers. Montgomery Clift, though miscast in the title role, is able to suggest a world of meaning in his soulful eyes as he stumbles to formulate the Oedipus complex. Curiously enough, during the shooting, he had an operation

Montgomery Clift plays Freud.

to remove cataracts from both his eyes. He was also suffering from a thyroid problem, and had difficulty remembering his lines. Much of *Freud* was filmed in England, and Huston, with photographer Douglas Slocombe, has evoked the texture of some of the famous paintings of the period.

*Marlon Brando (left) as Fletcher Christian and Trevor Howard as Captain Bligh in Lewis Milestone's remake of **Mutiny on the Bounty**.*

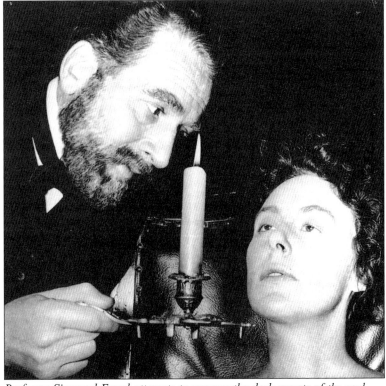

Professor Sigmund Freud attempts to uncover the dark secrets of the soul.

Peter O'Toole and the Sahara compete for beauty

Peter O'Toole and Omar Sharif.

New York, 16 December
Director David Lean has exchanged the steamy jungles of Ceylon, in which he filmed his *The Bridge on the River Kwai*, for the shimmering empty spaces of the Jordanian desert, where the subject of his latest picture fought a legendary guerrilla campaign in the First World War. In *Lawrence of Arabia*, Lean and producer Sam Spiegel have mounted an epic examination of the ambiguous war hero and writer T.E.

Lawrence which is bound to spark off a controversy. In the title role Lean has cast a relatively unknown actor, 30-year-old Irish-born Peter O'Toole, whose blond hair and staring pale blue eyes give his interpretation of the compromised hero an unnerving intensity. Here, Lean orchestrates the expansive action in leisurely style, and makes a nod in the direction of the Lawrence enigma, hinting at the repressed homosexual and sado-masochistic tendencies which lay under the surface of the warrior-scholar. The $15 million picture, which has been three years in the making, also boasts a strong supporting cast that includes Alec Guinness as Prince Feisal and Jack Hawkins as General Allenby. And, riding out of the pulsing desert haze aboard a camel, is Egyptian star Omar Sharif as Lawrence's friend Sherif Ali.

O'Toole as Lawrence, a romantic figure, leads the Arabs into battle.

Peck marvelous in 'To Kill a Mockingbird'

Los Angeles, 25 December
Critics have long contrasted Gregory Peck's exceptional good looks with his unexceptional acting talent. Now he has silenced them with his persuasive performance as the liberal Southern lawyer in Robert Mulligan's *To Kill a Mockingbird*, adapted from the novel by Harper Lee. His low-key personality is ideally suited to the part of the soft-

spoken Alabama attorney who has to defend black man Brock Peters on a rape charge, while bringing up two children on his own and patiently trying to give them an insight into the proceedings. It's a performance of quiet conviction and inner strength, well balanced by Peters' measured dignity, which culminates in a long and superbly handled series of courtroom scenes.

Destruction of 'Days of Wine and Roses'

Los Angeles, 26 December
Hot on the heels of Christmas cheer comes a harrowing reminder of the destruction that can be caused by alcohol and mutual dependency. The ironically titled *Days of Wine and Roses* follows a PR man whose drinking gets out of control. By way of being supportive, his wife joins him in his binges but, sadly, while he rehabilitates himself, she becomes

a hopeless alcoholic. This thought-provoking movie, directed by Blake Edwards, is a little uneasy in tone, veering between slick comedy, sentimentality and impending doom, but it grips the attention throughout. Above all, it confirms Jack Lemmon as one of the most impressively versatile and convincing of America's actors, and Lee Remick as an attractive and gifted co-star.

Gregory Peck, the quietly heroic lawyer, with his daughter (Mary Badham).

Lee Remick and Jack Lemmon, the unhappy couple doomed by alcoholism.

Like the poster says, 42 stars re-enacted D-Day landings for Darryl Zanuck.

Jean-Pierre Cassel (left), Claude Brasseur in Renoir's **The Vanishing Corporal**.

Luis Buñuel's surreal **The Exterminating Angel** with (left to right) Jacqueline Andere, Silvia Pinal and Enrique Garcia Alvarez.

The Loneliness of the Long Distance Runner: another from Tony Richardson and the British school of realism, with Tom Courtenay, left, and James Fox.

Thriller with two heavyweight stars.

Irene Papas in the role of **Electra**, here with Yannis Fertis.

Tom Tryon had his best part to date in Otto Preminger's **The Cardinal**.

Sam Fuller's bloody Burma war pic.

With Scotsman Sean Connery playing Ian Fleming's James Bond, Agent 007, **Dr. No** was one of the year's blockbusters.

Edward Dmytryk directed this movie set in a New Orleans brothel but, despite Stanwyck's presence, the best bit was the Saul Bass title sequence.

Elsa Martinelli and Michèle Girardon in **Hatari!**, directed by Howard Hawks.

Leon Niemczyk (left) and Zygmunt Malanowicz in Polish director Roman Polanski's gripping drama, **Knife in the Water**.

1963

★ ★

1962 Academy Awards, Santa Monica Civic Auditor., 8 Apr.

Best Film:	*Lawrence of Arabia* (dir: David Lean)
Best Director:	David Lean
Best Actor:	Gregory Peck *(To Kill a Mockingbird)*
Best Actress:	Anne Bancroft *(The Miracle Worker)*
Best Supp. Actor:	Ed Begley *(Sweet Bird of Youth)*
Best Supp. Actress:	Patty Duke *(The Miracle Worker)*

Algiers, 9 January
Authorities have decided to create an office for Algerian News under the control of director Mohamed Lakhdar Hamina.

New York, 6 February
According to *Variety* magazine, Fox has received advances of $8.35 million from exhibitors for *Cleopatra*.

Paris, 1 March
Release of Jacques Demy's *la Baie des anges* (*Bay of Angels*), starring Jeanne Moreau and Claude Mann.

New York, 26 March
20th Century-Fox shares are now at $29 compared to $15 in June 1962 before Darryl Zanuck took over.

San Francisco, 4 April
The director Jean Renoir has been made Doctor *honoris causa* of the University of Southern California.

Los Angeles, 13 April
Two new categories have been created by the Academy Award Board of Governors to replace the Special Effects Award: Special Visual Effects and Sound Effects. Emil Kosa Jr. won the visual award for *Cleopatra*, while the award for sound went to Walter G. Elliott for *It's a Mad, Mad, Mad, Mad World*.

Madrid, 8 May
New censorship norms are to be introduced. To a certain extent, they will ease the restrictions which have been in force since the civil war.

Paris, 5 June
Opening of the Cinematheque's new cinema at the Palais de Chaillot. An homage to Charlie Chaplin was followed by a retrospective on the American and Japanese cinema.

Brazil, 18 June
The filmmaker Glauber Rocha has started shooting his film, *Deus e o diabo na terra do sol* (*Black God White Devil*).

Los Angeles, 25 June
The Black civil rights organization, the NAACP, has accused film studios of racial discrimination. As an example, there is not a single black actor in the film *The Longest Day*, although 1,700 black soldiers took part in the Normandy landings.

Paris, 26 June
First day of shooting for *The Black Tulip* (*la Tulipe noire*). Christian-Jaque directs, Alain Delon stars.

New York, 8 August
Release of *The Great Escape*, a World War II film directed by John Sturges and starring Steve McQueen, James Garner, Richard Attenborough and Charles Bronson.

Hollywood, 14 August
Dramatist and screen writer Clifford Odets has died.

Hollywood, 20 August
A meeting between the representatives of the NAACP and producers, about the of employment of black actors in the cinema industry, has resulted in a quota agreement.

Rio de Janeiro, 24 August
Nelson Pereira dos Santos has held a preview of *Vidas Secas* (*Barren Lives*), adapted from the novel by Graciliano Ramos. The film evokes the plight of the poor farmers from the Northeast with a documentary style realism, and is already being hailed by the critics as the symbol of the Cinema Novo in Brazil.

New York, 10 September
For the first New York Film Festival, 31 films are being screened at the Lincoln Center and the Museum of Modern Art.

New York, 11 September
New York's first film festival opened last night at the Lincoln Center for the Performing Arts, with a screening of Luis Buñuel's *The Exterminating Angel*.

New York, 12 September
Samuel Fuller today held a preview of his film *Shock Corridor*, starring Peter Breck, Constance Towers and Gene Evans, about a journalist investigating a murder in an asylum.

Hollywood, 17 October
Under the terms of a new agreement, Frank Sinatra now owns one third of the Warner Bros. Record Company. Sinatra has announced his intention to devote himself entirely to artistic activities and to give up his questionable interests in the gambling industry.

Hollywood, 20 October
The Screen Actors Guild and other unions are accusing producers of trying to obstruct a Congressional inquiry into the recently growing trend of making films overseas.

Hollywood, 4 November
For the launching of *It's a Mad, Mad, Mad, Mad World*, producer-director Stanley Kramer and United Artists, his distributor, are organizing the most expensive press reception in the history of the cinema. Two hundred and fifty reporters from 26 countries have been invited for four days of festivities at a cost of $250,000.

Hollywood, 25 November
All film studios closed today as a mark of respect to the late President, John F. Kennedy, assassinated three days ago.

New York, 1 December
In reply to the accusations made by the unions, Eric Johnston, the president of the MPAA, has declared that the cinema industry would be unable to survive without making a percentage of its films overseas, where costs are considerably lower.

New York, 4 December
MGM has announced that its films will no longer be released under the exclusive rights system but under the Showcase system recently launched by Fox and United Artists: the film is shown simultaneously at 20 or so cinemas in each major city.

Los Angeles, 11 December
Frank Sinatra's son Frank Sinatra Jr., who was kidnapped on 9 December, has been released after the payment of a $240,000 ransom.

Prague, 20 December
Press preview of Vera Chytilova's first full-length film *O Necem Jinem* (*Something Else*). The film's loose framework and spontaneous style are reminiscent of the *cinéma-vérité*.

Italy, 31 December
Over the last year, 32 magazine covers were devoted to Claudia Cardinale, 30 to Sophia Loren and 11 to Gina Lollobrigida.

BIRTHS

Kentucky, 9 June
Johnny Depp

London, 11 May
Natasha Richardson

Florida, 30 July
Wesley Snipes

Los Angeles, 5 November
Tatum O'Neal

Oklahoma, 18 December
Brad Pitt

DEATHS

California, 2 January
Jack Carson

Hollywood, 3 January
Dick Powell

New York, 6 May
Monty Woolley

Hollywood, 7 June
ZaSu Pitts

Los Angeles, 18 June
Pedro Armendariz

New York, 17 August
Richard Barthelmess

France, 11 October
Jean Cocteau

Beverly Hills, 29 October
Adolphe Menjou

Hollywood, 2 December
Sabu

Cleopatra reached the screen this year. Dogged by delays, illness, scandal, changes of director and escalating expense, it was finally brought home by Joseph L. Mankiewicz.

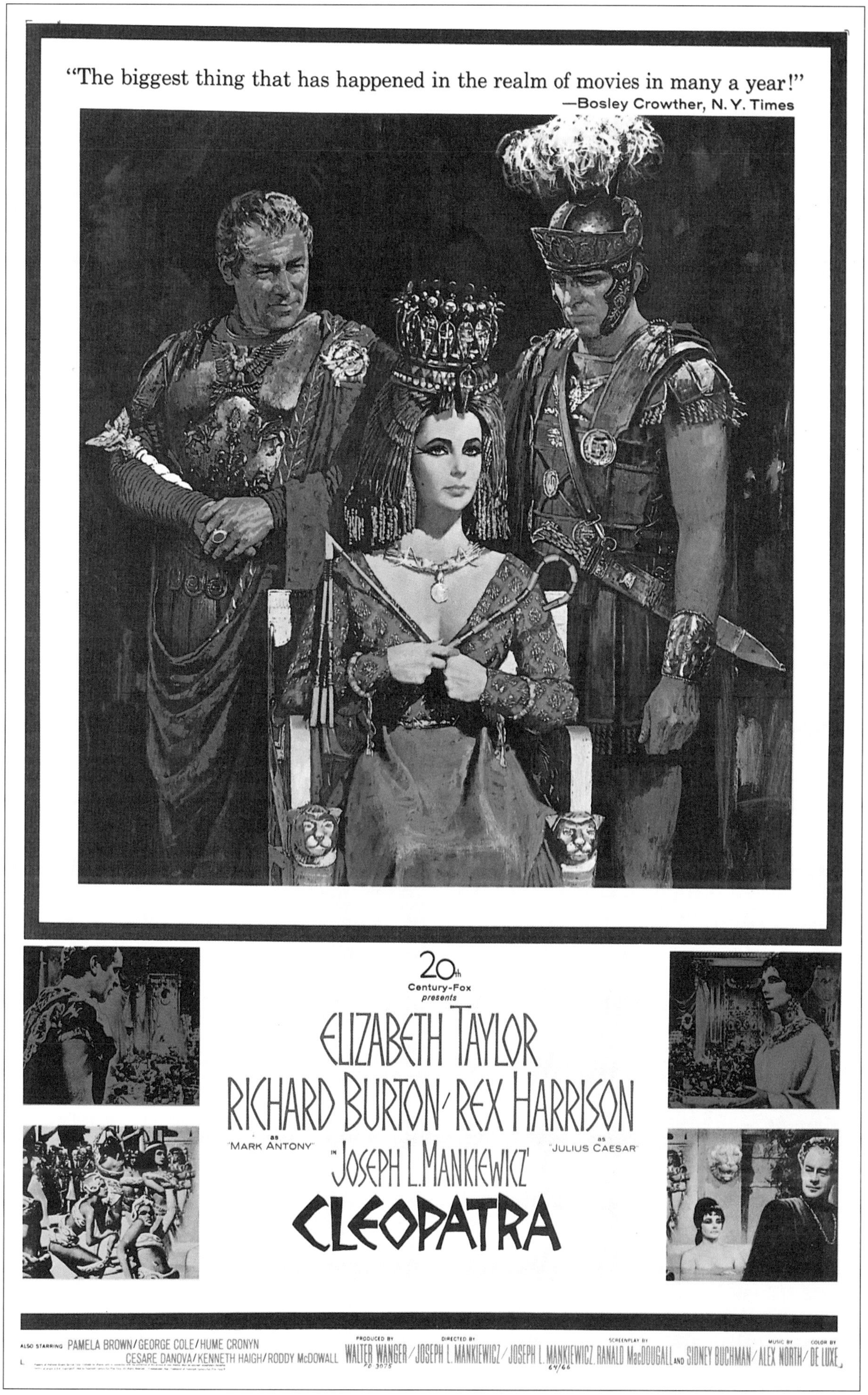
"The biggest thing that has happened in the realm of movies in many a year!"
—Bosley Crowther, N.Y. Times
20th Century-Fox presents
ELIZABETH TAYLOR
RICHARD BURTON · REX HARRISON
as "MARK ANTONY"
as "JULIUS CAESAR"
in JOSEPH L. MANKIEWICZ'
CLEOPATRA
ALSO STARRING PAMELA BROWN/GEORGE COLE/HUME CRONYN
CESARE DANOVA/KENNETH HAIGH/RODDY McDOWALL
PRODUCED BY WALTER WANGER/DIRECTED BY JOSEPH L. MANKIEWICZ/SCREENPLAY BY JOSEPH L. MANKIEWICZ, RANALD MacDOUGALL AND SIDNEY BUCHMAN/MUSIC BY ALEX NORTH/COLOR BY DE LUXE

Magic of Kabuki in 'An Actor's Revenge'

*Kazuo Hasegawa as the actor and Ganjiro Nakamura in **An Actor's Revenge**.*

Tokyo, 13 January
Kon Ichikawa, who began his career in cartoon and puppet films, uses some of these skills to conjure up the world of the Kabuki theater in his latest film, *An Actor's Revenge*. It tells of how an *onnagata* (female impersonator), during the early 19th century, takes revenge on the three men who caused the death of his parents. The veteran actor Kazuo Hasegawa not only gives an extraordinary performance as the hero-heroine, but also portrays a daring bandit in the complex subplot. The Daieiscope screen is brilliantly used in this fascinating and ambiguous study of opposites.

This Landru ignites spark of black humor

Paris, 25 January
Following the example of Charles Chaplin's work *Monsieur Verdoux*, Claude Chabrol has tackled a similar tale of a multiple murderer with cynicism and black humor. Entitled *Landru*, it recounts the true story of the notorious Henri Désiré Landru, who charmed a number of unsuspecting women, and then killed them. Charles Denner, with bald dome, bushy eyebrows and black beard, gives a strong performance in the title role, supported by a starry female cast, including Michèle Morgan, Danielle Darrieux, Hildegard Knef and Stéphane Audran. Yet critics have expressed disapproval, particularly of Françoise Sagan's awkward dialogue.

*Charles Denner in the title role, with Catherine Rouvel in Chabrol's **Landru**.*

Fellini revealed in circus of life and art

Rome, 25 February
People have been puzzled by the title of Federico Fellini's new film, *8½ (Otto e Mezzo)*, until it was explained by the director. As the picture is semi-autobiographical, Fellini has added up his seven solo features plus three collaborations, counting a half each, to get the title. The film attempts as few others have done to enter the mind of an artist (in this case a movie director) and explain the creative process. Marcello Mastroianni, in a thinly-veiled portrait of Fellini, is unable to find the inspiration for his next film. Having been immensely successful with his last picture, he is harried by his producer (Guido Alberti), his

'Film director' Mastroianni.

In this film, Federico Fellini retreats into his own fantasies and recollections.

wife (Anouk Aimée) and his mistress (Sandra Milo) to get started on a new one. Needing rest, he goes off to a spa, where he retreats into personal recollections, dreams and fantasies. He remembers his dead mother and father, an obese hooker on a beach, his Catholic school, and has an erotic wishful fantasy that involves his controlling a horde of beautiful women with a whip. In reality, he is forced to examine his relationship with the women in his life, including an actress (Claudia Cardinale), whom he believes personifies every woman he has ever dreamed of. The finale has everyone in his life, living and dead, joining hands in a circus parade. In *8½* Fellini has not only produced a cogent statement about the nature of inspiration and creativity, but has also made a sharp comment on a selfish and superficial society. In addition, it is visually stunning, exhilarating and constantly surprising, underlined by the evocative qualities of the Nino Rota score.

Pier Paolo Pasolini is taken to court

Rome, 1 March
Pier Paolo Pasolini is not only the *bête noir* of the neo-fascists, but also of the Church. *La Ricotta*, the sketch he directed for the film *RoGoPaG*, (the title made up from the names of the four directors involved: **Ros**sellini, **Go**dard, **Pa**solini and **G**reg-oretti), has got him into trouble for undermining the state religion. Pasolini's film is a vigorous satire on the contrast between the Christian message and those that propagate it. Laura Betti portrays the Virgin Mary, with Orson Welles as a director making a religious epic, during which a simple man dies on the cross. His death is due to overeating at a feast which includes ricotta, the white cheese that gives the story its title. Pasolini's only crime seems to be that he has denounced those who vulgarize religion.

Orson Welles in **RoGoPaG**.

Pasolini sentenced to four months

Rome, 11 May
The affair of *La Ricotta*, the satiric sketch in *RoGoPaG* that has been deemed blasphemous, has turned bitter for Pier Paolo Pasolini, who directed and wrote it. He lost the court case last month, about 12 days after the release of the collective film. The controversial director was found guilty of "public defamation" and has received a four months suspended prison sentence.

Visconti's sad reflections on the death of the Sicilian aristocracy

The Prince of Salina (Lancaster).

Alain Delon and Claudia Cardinale attend a ball as the old order collapses.

Rome, 27 March
Only Luchino Visconti's ninth film in almost 20 years, *The Leopard* seems destined to become his biggest success. Previously, each of his pictures divided opinion sharply. Some criticized the "father of neo-realism" for making a period piece such as *Senso*, but when Visconti returned to his own epoch with the realistic *Rocco and His Brothers*, he unleashed a scandal. The premiere of *The Leopard* resembled a reconciliatory high mass. This gorgeous evocation of the era of the *Risorgimento*, which was faithfully adapted from Giuseppe De Lampedusa's 1958 novel, is full of set pieces, particularly the final ball which takes up to 40 minutes of screen time. In order to get 20th Century-Fox to release the film internationally, Visconti had to agree to cast Burt Lancaster in the role of the Prince of Salina, the dying 19th-century Sicilian aristocrat. Lancaster delivers a rich performance while Alain Delon and Claudia Cardinale make an attractive young couple. "We are the leopards, after us the jackals will come," comments the Prince sadly, a phrase that might express the aristocratic director's feelings.

Murderous birds share star billing with Hitchcock's latest blonde

New York, 29 March
The stuffed birds which loom over Anthony Perkins in *Psycho* have proved strangely prophetic. In Alfred Hitchcock's latest, *The Birds*, they have come alive with a vengeance, swarming in their tens of thousands to terrorize the inhabitants of a small community north of San Francisco. Says Hitch, "They are the victims of Judgment Day. I felt that after *Psycho* people would expect something to top it." Rod Taylor and Tippi Hedren are the stars battling the winged terror, which presented Hitchcock's special effects team with an enormous technical challenge. They tackled it with a combination of back projection, animation and lifelike mechanical birds. However, for the scene in which Hedren is trapped in a room by a swarm of feathered enemies, real birds were attached to her body. Hitchcock, who notoriously likes to put his "ice maiden" leading ladies through several kinds of hell, was reportedly extremely pleased with the results in this scene. Hedren was less enthusiastic about the ordeal. *The Birds* reunites Hitchcock with Daphne du Maurier 23 years after *Rebecca*: Evan Hunter's spare script has been loosely adapted from one of her stories. It daringly uses the device of a science fiction apocalypse to underline the intriguing sexual and emotional insecurity radiated by the cool leading lady.

Tippi Hedren is the central victim of Alfred Hitchcock's terrifying birds.

Hepburn and Harrison charm in 'My Fair Lady'

Flower girl Eliza Doolittle sings up a storm in Covent Garden market.

'I could have danced all night...'

New York, 21 October
Alan Jay Lerner and Frederick Loewe's long-running stage musical, *My Fair Lady*, finally reaches the screen, with Rex Harrison repeating his London and Broadway performance as Shaw's Professor Higgins, who, for a bet, turns a guttersnipe into a "lady". However, English rose Julie Andrews, a fine soprano but unknown to movie audiences, is replaced by one of the world's most loved film stars, Audrey Hepburn who, her tremulous and appealing delivery of "Moon River" in *Breakfast at Tiffany's* notwithstanding, can barely sing a note.

Jack Warner, last of the old-style moguls, has staked much on this lavish production. Determined to acquire the rights after seeing the Broadway show at its 1956 opening, it took him several years to clinch a deal which cost a massive $5.5 million for the rights alone. Preparation was dogged with problems. Warner wanted Peter O'Toole and, when that idea foundered, Cary Grant – who, wisely, said that Harrison was the only possible choice. Then Alan Jay Lerner, unable to persuade Warner to cast Andrews, was left angry and disappointed at the choice of Hepburn, who Warner regarded as the surefire security for his investment. For her part, Hepburn was reportedly thrilled to get the role (and a $1 million paycheck) and, was confident that she could learn to sing it. She set about voice lessons with dedication, only to be told, after months of hard work and her songs already recorded, that musical director André Previn had decided to hire Marni Nixon to dub the famous numbers, thus inflicting a bitter blow to Audrey's professional pride. Warner personally took on the producer role, and chose veteran George Cukor to direct. The darling of screen actresses, Cukor's experience of the musical form has previously been limited to the essentially dramatic remake of *A Star is Born* with Judy Garland. However, the film has retained not only Harrison, but Stanley Holloway as Doolittle ("Get Me to the Church on Time" is a high point) and Cecil Beaton as designer, with the result that the clothes are stunning, particularly in the famous Ascot scene.

The result of this troubled history is a film which, thanks to its indestructible story, score and lyrics, cannot help but beguile. Harrison is impeccable, as is Wilfrid Hyde White as Pickering, with Jeremy Brett well-cast as luckless Freddy-Eynsford Hill. But the enterprise is marred by some obviously artificial "staginess" and an occasional disjunction between the admirable Miss Nixon's voice and Hepburn's personality. And what of Audrey Hepburn? Even the most ardent of her many fans would have to concede that as a Cockney flowerseller her efforts at authenticity simply fail to convince. However, from the moment of her transformation into a lady, all the Hepburn magic is intact: grace, dignity, charm, and vulnerability. Her appearance at the top of the stair in the white Beaton ballgown must surely become one of the iconic images of female beauty in the modern cinema, and is one that, ultimately, sends audiences home happy.

The 'lady' arrives at the ball.

A posed publicity shot in her Ascot outfit designed by Cecil Beaton.

Death of brilliant young Indian film director

*A new frontier in Indian cinema: Guru Dutt in his film **Paper Flowers**.*

Bombay, 10 October
Sensitive and tormented, resembling many of the characters he played in his own films and in those directed by others, the Indian director and actor Guru Dutt has committed suicide at the age of 39. Born in Bangalore, Dutt studied at Uday Shankar's academy of art, before entering the cinema in 1951, the year he shot his first film, *Game*. He made seven other pictures, of which two are considered to be masterpieces, *The Thirsty* (1957) and *Paper Flowers* (1959). Dutt reconciled the traditions of popular Indian cinema with more demanding fare, thus paving the way for younger directors.

Clint Eastwood in an unusual Western

Rome, 10 November
After small parts in 10 movies and seven years acting in TV's *Rawhide* series, 34-year-old Clint Eastwood is now starring in an Italian-German co-production called *A Fistful of Dollars*, which happens to be a Western. The producers had originally wanted Henry Fonda in the lead, but they couldn't afford him. The director is a certain Bob Robertson, the American-sounding pseudonym of Sergio Leone, who made such epics as *The Last Days of Pompeii* and *The Colossus of Rhodes*. Here he has taken on a genre hitherto exclusively American, and scored a success. Other Italians involved in the picture disguised themselves behind names such as Dan Savio (the composer Ennio Morricone), Jack Dalmas (the cinematographer Massimo Dallamano) and John Welles (co-star Gian Maria Volonte). Clint Eastwood had no need to change his name, although he plays the mysterious Man With No Name. The plot, taken from Akira Kurosawa's *Yo-*

*TV cowboy Clint Eastwood in Sergio Leone's **A Fistful of Dollars**.*

jimbo (1961), tells of how Eastwood, as a quick-on-the-trigger mercenary, plays off two rival gangs against each other, and then faces five gunmen alone in the final protracted shootout. With a small budget of $100,000, Leone shot the exteriors in Spain, while the interiors were filmed at Cinecittà in Rome.

Cary Grant marooned with a brood of kids

New York, 10 December
Paired with Audrey Hepburn last year in *Charade*, Cary Grant is now co-starring with Hollywood's other European gamine, the delightfully French Leslie Caron, in *Father Goose*. But the formula is not nearly as successful, thanks to a second-rate screenplay. Grant, with the aid of a beard and a sailor's cap, plays a beachcombing type forced to man a small island during World War II. Events saddle him with Caron, a schoolteacher, and half-a-dozen refugee schoolchildren. Competently directed by Ralph Nelson, the film might appeal as undemanding family viewing over the festive season.

*Cary Grant and Leslie Caron, the stars of Ralph Nelson's **Father Goose**.*

U.S. studios looking financially healthier

Hollywood, 31 December
After experiencing problems during the early 1960s, the past year has marked a recovery in the fortunes of most of the leading Hollywood film companies. Their profits have been on the rise, especially at Disney, boosted by the spectacular success of *Mary Poppins*, by far the biggest hit of the year and the most popular "live action" feature in the company's history. The movie stars Julie Andrews, who was snubbed by Warner Bros. for the role of Eliza Doolittle, and, ironically, it appears that Warners' lavish production of *My Fair Lady* has flopped at the box office, with Warners as the one top studio that has failed to share in the general recovery. Most impressive of all has been the performance of United Artists with two big James Bond hits, *From Russia With Love* and *Goldfinger*, along with Blake Edwards' *The Pink Panther* starring Peter Sellers, *A Hard Day's Night* with the Beatles, and Stanley Kramer's *It's A Mad, Mad, Mad, Mad World*, released late last year. MGM has climbed back into the black after a disastrous 1963 with the help of a couple of successful musicals, *Viva Las Vegas* and *The Unsinkable Molly Brown*, while 20th Century-Fox appears to be making a comeback under Darryl Zanuck and his son Richard. Embassy and Paramount had a big hit with Joseph E. Levine's *The Carpetbaggers*, and Columbia did well with *The Cardinal* and *Dr. Strangelove*. It looks as though the long postwar fall in audiences may at last be bottoming out. Certainly, the improvement in movie company results would indicate this.

*The success of the third James Bond film, **Goldfinger**, made a major contribution to United Artists' revenue.*

Stanley Kubrick's film used black comedy to transmit a frightening message.

Kyoto Koshoda in Teshigahara's erotic, bizarre **Woman of the Dunes**.

Jean-Paul Belmondo in **That Man From Rio**, a spoof thriller.

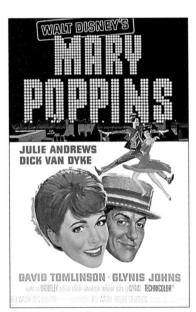

A supercalifragilistic hit!

Andréa Parisy and French heart-throb Jean-Paul Belmondo: **Greed in the Sun**.

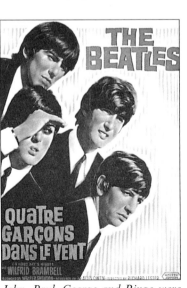

John, Paul, George and Ringo were loved everywhere. (French poster).

Jeanne Moreau in **The Diary of a Chambermaid** for Luis Buñuel.

*Left to right: Olivia De Havilland, Bette Davis, Agnes Moorehead: grotesquerie in **Hush, Hush, Sweet Charlotte**, from director Robert Aldrich.*

Sci-fi from MGM's British arm.

Black God, White Devil *comes from Brazil's Glauber Rocha.*

This wistful romance deals with a therapist/patient love affair in an asylum.

*Xie Fang and Cao Yindi were **Two Stage Sisters**, a wonderful picture from China's Xie Jin, made just before the Cultural Revolution.*

*Kobayashi's **Kwaidan**: five years to prepare, one to shoot and a huge budget.*

1965

★ ★ ★ ★ ★ ★ ★ ★ ★ **1965** ★

Copenhagen, 1 January
Release of Carl Theodor Dreyer's new film, *Gertrud*, with Nina Pens Rode and Bendt Rothe.

Madrid, 4 January
The British director David Lean has just begun filming *Doctor Zhivago*, based on Boris Pasternak's Nobel Prize-winning novel.

Hong Kong, 18 January
Philippe de Broca is on location for his new film *les Tribulations d'un Chinois en Chine*, starring Jean-Paul Belmondo, Ursula Andress and Jean Rochefort.

Genoa, 27 January
During the congress on "The Third World and the World Community", Brazilian director Glauber Rocha presented his manifesto titled *The Aesthetics of Hunger*.

Paris, 2 February
The *Bulletin d'information du CNC*, has published an alarming report on cinema attendance: 273 million spectators in 1964 as compared to 423 million in 1957.

London, 15 February
Royal Command Performance of *Lord Jim* at the Odeon cinema in Leicester Square, in the presence of Queen Elizabeth, the Queen Mother and HRH the Princess Margaret. Peter O'Toole plays the title role in writer-director Richard Brooks' adaptation of the Joseph Conrad novel, a mammoth production, wonderfully photographed by Freddie Young. Proceeds from the evening will go to the Cinema and Television Benevolent Fund.

Cairo, 3 March
Henry Barakat, one of Egypt's most prolific filmmakers, has moved off the beaten track of musical comedy and melodrama with his latest film *The Sin* (*Al Haram*). Starring Faten Hamama, it is a cruel naturalist drama on the realities of rural life.

Lisbon, 15 March
Release of *The Enchanted Isles* (*As Ilhas Encantados*), by Carlos Vilardebo, with Amalia Rodrigues and Pierre Clementi.

France, 30 March
In protest against duties and taxes, exhibitors have organized a country-wide "Free entry" operation to draw the public's attention to the problems faced by the industry.

Los Angeles, 22 June
Producer David O. Selznick has died of a heart attack (his fifth) at the age of 63. His widow is actress Jennifer Jones.

Hollywood, 13 July
Columbia has announced that Jerry Lewis is to shoot *Three on a Couch*, his first film for the studio after completing 33 films for Paramount.

London, 18 August
Catherine Deneuve and the English photographer David Bailey were married today. Despite being the mother of Roger Vadim's son Christian, it is Miss Deneuve's first marriage. Vadim has recently married actress Jane Fonda.

Los Angeles, 26 October
George Stevens has started proceedings against Paramount and the NBC television network to prevent the mutilation of his film *A Place in the Sun*, which the network is scheduled to screen on 12 March 1966. He is demanding $1 million in damages if cuts are made to the film.

Rome, 30 October
Federico Fellini has just completed *Giulietta degli Spiriti* (*Juliet of the Spirits*), starring Giulietta Masina.

London, 31 October
Charlie Chaplin called a press conference to announce his plans to make a new film, *A Countess From Hong Kong*. Marlon Brando and Sophia Loren will co-star.

Paris, 1 November
The editorial staff of *Cahiers du Cinéma* has come up with some new policy decisions: firstly to distance itself from writers' political views, secondly to refuse to systematically promote American films. The film critics' new methods are to be based on structuralism and linguistics.

Paris, 10 November
Brigitte Bardot has claimed a symbolic one-franc payment of costs and damages from several publications which published photos, taken with a telescopic lens, of La Madrague, her property near St. Tropez, and its occupants.

Prague, 12 November
Release of *Lasky Jedne Plavovlasky* (*Loves of a Blonde*), director Milos Forman's second film.

Los Angeles, 15 November
Walt Disney and his brother Roy have announced their plans for a second Disneyland in Florida. Walt Disney World, which is planned to open in October 1971, will cover an area twice the size of Manhattan. The land alone cost $5 million.

Paris, 17 November
On leaving a club in rue Princesse, the actor Peter O'Toole hit the Comte Philippe de La Fayette over the head. The latter has decided to lodge a complaint.

Paris, 22 November
Roger Vadim has started shooting *la Curée*, based on the novel by Emile Zola. The film will star American actress Jane Fonda (daughter of Henry), who has agreed to appear nude on the screen for the first time. She happens to be the director's wife.

New York, 30 November
Otto Preminger is appearing in the State Supreme Court where he has brought charges against Columbia's television subsidiary, Screen Gems, for having granted transmission rights for his highly acclaimed film, *Anatomy of a Murder*, to a Chicago station which is planning 36 commercial breaks during screening.

New York, 30 November
The Legion of Decency has been re-christened the National Catholic Office of Motion Pictures.

New York, 13 December
Brigitte Bardot's arrival at Kennedy airport today caused great excitement and jostling among the crowd assembled to greet her.

Hollywood, 22 December
The Screen Writers Guild signed a new retrospective agreement today with Universal Pictures for films made during the period 1948-1960. From now on, script writers are to receive 1.5 percent of the studio's revenue from television screening rights for their credited films.

BIRTHS

New York, 4 April
Robert Downey Jr.

New York, 31 May
Brooke Shields

Paris, 14 August
Emmanuelle Béart

Illinois, 24 August
Marlee Matlin

New York, 3 September
Charlie Sheen (Carlos Estevez)

DEATHS

Texas, 14 January
Jeanette MacDonald

California, 23 February
Stan Laurel

Hollywood, 23 March
Margaret Dumont

Hollywood, 23 March
Mae Murray

Chicago, 10 April
Linda Darnell

New York, 7 June
Judy Holliday

Hollywood, 8 September
Dorothy Dandridge

Los Angeles, 27 September
Clara Bow

Englishman Michael Caine, who combines an earnest, bemused air with cool nonchalance and a core of steel, is the perfect screen incarnation of Len Deighton's Harry Palmer.

Over two hours of knockabout comedy, set in 1910, with a huge star cast.

Charlton Heston in **Major Dundee**.

Julie Andrews: **The Sound of Music**.

France's much-loved comic, Bourvil, in Gérard Oury's **le Corniaud**.

Larisa Kadochnilova and Ivan Nikolaychuk in Sergo Paradjanov's **Shadows of Our Forgotten Ancestors** *(USSR).*

Jane Birkin and Ray Brooks star in the prize-winning British export, **The Knack... and How to Get It**.

Fists in the Pocket: Lou Castel.

Julie Christie and Omar Sharif in **Dr. Zhivago** *from Pasternak's novel.*

Content poor, visuals superb.

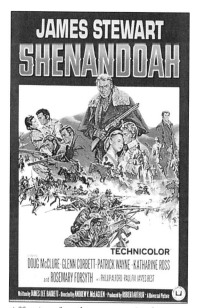

Affecting family saga in Civil War.

Lavish but tedious version of Conrad's novel which even O'Toole couldn't save.

Hungarian Gabor Argady (left), Tibor Molnar (center) and Andras Kozak (right) in Miklos Jancso's hypnotic **The Round-Up**.

Sailen Mukherjee (left) and Soumitra Chatterjee in Indian director Satyajit Ray's poignant **Charulata** *(aka* **The Lonely Wife**).

1966

★ ★

1965 Academy Awards, Santa Monica Civic Auditor., 18 Apr.

Best Film:	*The Sound of Music* (dir: Robert Wise)
Best Director:	Robert Wise
Best Actor:	Lee Marvin (*Cat Ballou*)
Best Actress:	Julie Christie (*Darling*)
Best Supp. Actor:	Martin Balsam (*A Thousand Clowns*)
Best Supp. Actress:	Shelley Winters (*A Patch of Blue*)

London, 12 January
François Truffaut has started shooting his first film in English titled *Fahrenheit 451*, which stars Julie Christie and Oskar Werner.

New York, 20 January
Otto Preminger, the director and producer, lost his case yesterday to prevent any cuts or excessive commercial interruptions during the televised showing of his film *Anatomy of a Murder*. Justice Arthur Klein rejected Mr. Preminger's suit, which had been closely watched by the television industry.

Los Angeles, 31 January
Barbara Rooney, actor Mickey Rooney's wife, and her lover Milos Milocevic were found dead at her home. Police believe that Milocevic killed Barbara in a fit of jealousy, before taking his own life.

Hollywood, 25 March
Seymour Poe, Fox's executive vice president reported yesterday that up to 16 March, *Cleopatra*, which was considered to be the disaster of the decade, had earned $38,042,000 as the distributor's share of world box-office receipts. The film, which cost $31,115,000 to produce and a fortune in lawsuits, needs to bring in $41,358,000 for Fox to break even. Mr. Poe feels confident that the film will bring in $47 million over the next five years.

Paris, 5 April
The Film Authors Federation, the French Film Critics Association and the Writers Union for Truth are all vigorously protesting about the banning of Jacques Rivette's controversial new film, *la Religieuse* (*The Nun*).

Paris, 22 April
Release of Jean-Luc Godard's film *Masculin-féminin*, a sociological view of today's youth, with Jean-Pierre Léaud, Chantal Goya, and making her debut, Marlène Jobert.

Lausanne, 18 May
Greek actress Melina Mercouri has married director Jules Dassin.

Paris, 20 May
Release of the German film *Young Torless*, starring Mathieu Carrière. Volker Schlöndorff directed, and also adapted the screenplay from the work by Robert Musil.

New York, 24 May
MGM have announced that all their surviving silents are to be transferred on to non-inflammable film.

Rochefort-sur-Mer, 31 May
Jacques Demy has started shooting *les Demoiselles de Rochefort*, a musical comedy starring Françoise Dorléac and Catherine Deneuve.

Nashville, 18 July
Police have seized *Who's Afraid of Virginia Woolf?* and arrested the manager of a local cinema for contravening a municipal order that bans all entertainment of an obscene nature.

Los Angeles, 27 July
Release of Hitchcock's new film *Torn Curtain*, with Julie Andrews and Paul Newman.

New York, 12 August
Variety has published an article stating that 62 of the 136 American films underway this year are being made overseas. Among the biggest budget films are *2001: A Space Odyssey*, filmed in Great Britain, as is *The Dirty Dozen*, while *The Sand Pebbles* is being made in Taiwan.

New York, 16 August
Jack Valenti, the recently elected president of the MPAA, has sent a confidential memo to the heads of all studios recommending that "The classification of films by the government should be avoided at all costs." He feels the film industry should have its own classification system to avoid all external censorship.

Copenhagen, 19 August
Henning Carlsen has announced the release of his adaptation of Knut Hamsen's masterpiece titled *Sult* (*Hunger*), starring Per Oscarsson and Gunnel Lindblom.

Paris, 8 October
Channel One has screened ORTF's production *la Prise du pouvoir par Louis XIV* (*The Rise of Louis XIV*), directed by Roberto Rossellini from a script by Philippe Erlanger. Cinema distribution is also planned.

San Francisco, 12 October
Shirley Temple has resigned from the Festival selection board in protest against the planned screening of the Swedish film by Mai Zetterling, *Nattlek* (*Night Games*). The film deals with the question of incest.

Paris, 18 October
Director Jean-Luc Godard has stated: "Until I am paid on a par with Clouzot, Fellini and Clément, I cannot consider myself to be a success."

Stockholm, 18 October
Opening of Ingmar Bergman's film *Persona*, with his favorite actresses, Liv Ullmann and Bibi Andersson.

London, 26 October
Elizabeth Taylor and Richard Burton have founded their own production company, *Taybur*.

Washington D.C., 2 November
The Justice Department has decided that the massive acquisition of Columbia shares by the Banque de Paris et des Pays Bas to be illegal. American law forbids the ownership of television stations by foreign companies, and Columbia owns Screen Gems, a television distribution company.

Paris, 5 November
François Truffaut's much awaited biography of Alfred Hitchcock, *Le Cinéma Selon Hitchcock*, is at last available. The biography, which is based on a series of interviews between the two men last year, traces Hitchcock's life and career from his childhood up to his 50th film, *Torn Curtain*. Apart from Hitchcock's obvious sincerity, the book's greatest quality is the importance that Truffaut gives to the filmmaker's methods rather than to an analysis of the meaning of his films.

New York City, 1 December
Andy Warhol's *The Chelsea Girls* has made history as the first ever "underground" film to play in a mainstream movie theater. Having mesmerized audiences since September at the 41st Street Basement Cinémathèque, the non-synchronized two-screen marathon movie today transfers to the Cinema Rendezvous for a limited run only. A special holiday release of *The Sound of Music* starts on 21 December.

Paris, 2 December
Release of Roman Polanski's *Cul-de-sac*, The director's second British film after *Repulsion*.

Hollywood, 7 December
Vincente Minnelli is leaving MGM after 22 years. All his films, which have ranged across a broad spectrum, were made at this studio.

BIRTHS

Los Angeles, 10 February
Laura Dern

Paris, 17 November
Sophie Marceau (Sophie Maupuis)

London, 21 December
Kiefer Sutherland

DEATHS

Hollywood, 21 January
Herbert Marshall

Hollywood, 1 February
Hedda Hopper

Hollywood, 1 February
Buster Keaton

New York, 18 February
Robert Rossen

New York, 23 July
Montgomery Clift

Hollywood, 23 August
Francis X. Bushman

Beverly Hills, 13 October
Clifton Webb

Roger Corman produced and directed this unusual film which looks at California life: motorcycle gangs, Mexicans, orgies, rape, death, etc. Peter Fonda is the wildest angel.

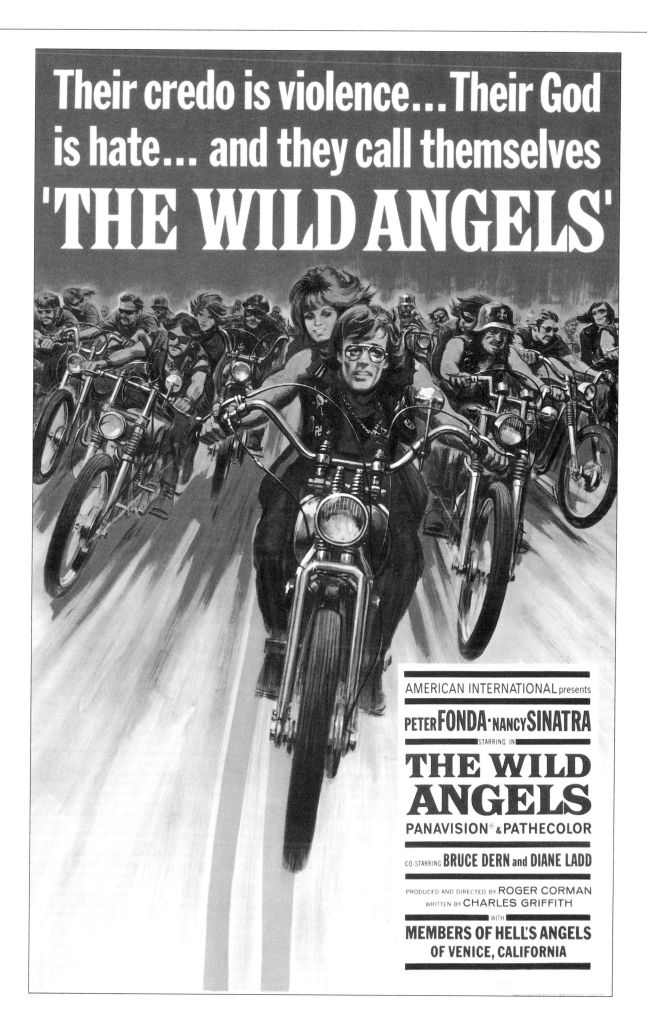

Hedy Lamarr lives out a nightmare

New York, 30 January
Fallen star Hedy Lamarr has been imprisoned for shoplifting. It's not the first time she has courted scandal. Born Hedwig Kiesler in Vienna on 9 November 1913, she was discovered by Max Reinhardt and in 1932 gained international notoriety by appearing fleetingly naked in a Czech film, *Ecstasy*. Her reputation went before her to London, from where she pursued a reluctant Louis B. Mayer to America on board the *Normandie*. Before the liner docked in New York, she had a seven-year contract and a new name. In the early Forties, Hedy was a byword for Hollywood glamour; however, although frequently cast as a woman of mystery or a *femme fatale*, she

*With Mature in **Samson and Delilah**.*

lacked the vital spark of personality. By 1949 she was virtually a back number when Cecil B. DeMille cast her to play Victor Mature's devious mate in *Samson and Delilah*, about which Groucho Marx observed that he never went to see movies where the hero's breasts were bigger than the leading lady's! By 1957, she was virtually playing herself as an aging movie star in *The Female Animal*. The much-married Lamarr has had four husbands: screenwriter Gene Markey, actor John Loder, a Texan millionaire and her own divorce lawyer. But now that she has fallen on hard times, Lamarr's private life is getting more column inches than her films.

Michael Caine scores a huge success as Cockney Casanova 'Alfie'

London, 24 March
Michael Caine is the chirpy Cockney philanderer in *Alfie* directed by Lewis Gilbert and adapted from Bill Naughton's play. He plays merry hell with the women in his life, mournful Vivien Merchant, buxom Shelley Winters and waif-like Jane Asher, but he's beginning to find the competition catching up with him. Alfie's snappy flannels and bogus regimental blazer mark him out as an old-fashioned sexual predator, but losing ground to the dandified young bucks who prowl "Swinging London". His humiliation comes at the hands of Winters, whom he finds cavorting in bed with a young musician whose guitar, like a phallic symbol, is propped up by the door. There's something of Alfie in the bespectacled Caine's background. He was born Maurice Micklewhite in London in 1933, worked as a porter in Smithfield meat market and drifted into films after stage and television work. A long string of bits and walk-ons followed before he made his mark in *Zulu*, struggling with his vowels as an aristocratic officer. He then proved that girls do

The reprobate Alfie (Michael Caine) with one of his 'harem' (Jane Asher).

make passes at men wearing glasses, playing Len Deighton's hangdog hero Harry Palmer in *The Ipcress File*. Caine's Cockney accent and good-humored bewilderment at his success are perfectly attuned to the new "classless" world promoted by Britain's media. He seems like a handsome version of the guy who pulls you a pint in the pub or sells you a pound of oranges off the barrow in a street market. And his myopia makes him the first star since Harold Lloyd to wear glasses.

The shadows of forgotten ancestors live on in new Soviet film

Moscow, 25 March
One of the most unusual and impressive Soviet films for a long time has just opened in Moscow. *Shadows of Our Forgotten Ancestors* is a variation on the Romeo and Juliet story set in the Carpathian mountains at the turn of the century. A young peasant falls in love with the daughter of the man responsible for the death of his father, but marries a woman who indulges in sorcery. The director, Sergo Paradjanov, reveals a remarkable talent for lyrical extravagance, placing him in the grand tradition of Alexander Dovzhenko. Using radiant Sovcolor, he brings a swirling, kaleidoscopic camera style to this rural folk tale. But who is Paradjanov? He was born Sarkis Paradjanian in Tbilisi in Georgia of Armenian parents in 1924. He was brought up in luxury, though the family went through hard times during the Stalin years. He studied music at the conservatoire at Tbilisi, before enrolling in the state film school in Moscow at the age of 22. After he graduated, he worked in

Kiev, where he co-directed his first feature work, *Andriesh*, in 1955, noteworthy for its use of surrealistic elements. This was followed by several undistinguished comedies and melodramas in the socialist-realist style. *Shadows of Our Forgotten Ancestors* is a striking departure from his previous work as well as from much of postwar Soviet cinema. The intense Ukrainian nationalism of the film has granted Paradjanov the patronage of Pyotr Shelest, the Ukrainian communist party boss.

*Ivan Nikolaychuk in Paradjanov's **Shadows of Our Forgotten Ancestors**.*

A second wedding for Sophia Loren

Sèvres, 9 April
Between the shooting of two films, Sophia Loren has once again married Carlo Ponti, with whom she has been together since 17 September 1957, after a marriage in Mexico. In order not to be prosecuted for bigamy in Italy, where the producer is still considered married to his first wife because divorce does not exist there, Sophia has taken French nationality. This second marriage, held at the town hall at Sèvres, has given the marriage a legal basis. After the ceremony, the couple were invited to dine at the Coq-Hardi restaurant at Bougival. The Italian star has just completed *A Countess From Hong Kong*, opposite Marlon Brando, under the direction of Charles Chaplin. She leaves in a few days for the south of Italy, where she will co-star with Omar Sharif in *More Than a Miracle* (*C'era una Volta*), directed by Francesco Rosi, and produced by Carlo Ponti. She has decided that afterwards she will put her career on hold for a while, because, at 34 years old, she is expecting her first child.

David Lean and 'Doctor Zhivago' lose out to 'The Sound of Music'

Best Supporting Actress Shelley Winters, Sidney Poitier, Elizabeth Hartman.

Hollywood, 18 April
At this year's Oscar ceremony, televised in color for the first time, the Best Picture award was one of the most closely contested ever. *The Sound of Music* and *Doctor Zhivago* entered the competition neck and neck with 10 nominations apiece, and it was to remain a tie at the end. Five Oscars went to David Lean's Russian epic (Best Screenplay, Cinematography, Art Direction, Original Musical Score and Costume Design) but the top prizes eluded it.

The Rodgers and Hammerstein musical was considered Best Picture, and Robert Wise gained the edge on David Lean for Best Director. *The Sound of Music* also won Best Musical Score, Editing and Sound. When it came to the Best Actress award, two Julies were in the running: Andrews for *The Sound of Music* and Christie for *Darling* and *Doctor Zhivago*. In the event it was Julie Christie who triumphed for her portrayal of an ambitious young model in the cynical and modish milieu created by John Schlesinger for *Darling*. Had her rival won, she would have been the first to match a record established by Luise Rainer for two Best Actress Oscars in succession. As it was, Julie Andrews accepted defeat gracefully, hugging her tearfully overjoyed fellow Brit. Best Supporting performers were the veteran trouper Martin Balsam for *A Thousand Clowns*, and second-time winner Shelley Winters as the blowzy, overbearing mother of a blind girl in *A Patch of Blue*. Lee Marvin carried off the Best Actor statuette for his hilarious, drunken, has-been gunfighter in *Cat Ballou*.

Rivette's controversial film is banned despite initial approval

Paris, 15 April
Fifteen days after the banning of Jacques Rivette's *la Religieuse* (*The Nun*), André Malraux, the Minister of Culture, has announced that he would not oppose the showing of the film at the Cannes Festival next month. He has therefore implicitly repudiated Yvon Bourges, the Secretary of State for Information. The matter has already been long drawn out. It was in 1962 that Rivette first conceived this faithful film adaptation of Diderot's novel of 1760. But for three years the project came up against official opposition. Last September, after numerous changes were made in the screenplay, Rivette and his producer, Georges de Beauregard, began shooting, with the title role going to Anna Karina. The plot concerns Suzanne Simonin, who is forced, through lack of a dowry, to enter a convent where she undergoes a great deal of suffering, including semi-starvation, beatings, lesbian attentions from the Mother Superior, and attempted rape by a priest. Even before the film was completed, and without having seen any of the rushes, the association of former nuns, and the parents of students in "free" schools demanded a banning order. At the receiving end was Yvon Bourges, who went against the Censorship Commission which had authorized the film. The banning has now set public opinion alight, and an air of scandal surrounds the film. Finally, the sole beneficiary has been Diderot. For some days copies of his novel have been selling like hot cakes.

*Anna Karina and Liselotte Pulver in Jacques Rivette's **la Religieuse**.*

Top box-office for happy film

New York, 18 April
Not only has Fox's *The Sound of Music* carried off the Oscar, but, with rentals topping the $70 million mark for North America alone, it has easily surpassed the recent box-office records set by MGM's *Ben-Hur* to become the biggest hit since *Gone With the Wind*. Mainly filmed on location in Austria in the 70mm Todd-AO process, with a budget of $8 million, the picture has played a major role in re-establishing Fox as one of the most active Hollywood studios – this only four years after it faced bankruptcy due to a series of flops and the escalating costs of *Cleopatra*. Not surprisingly, the studio intends to make more musicals, and is already planning a follow-up picture for star and director of *The Sound of Music*, Julie Andrews and Robert Wise, while *Dr. Dolittle*, starring Rex Harrison, starts filming shortly.

Lelouch's prize-winning romance opens in Paris

*Racing driver Jean-Louis Trintignant in Lelouch's **A Man and a Woman**.*

Anouk Aimée and Souad Amidou.

Paris, 27 May

Claude Lelouch's film *A Man and a Woman*, the Jury Prize winner at the Cannes Film Festival, has opened in Paris. It's a color supplement romance, starring Anouk Aimée and Jean-Louis Trintignant as a widow and widower who fall in love to the catchy strains of Francis Lai's maddeningly memorable theme song. Lelouch himself was a photographer for glossy magazines, and *A Man and a Woman*'s sleek surface is more of a trick of the ad-man's lens than an examination of the thorny reality of loss that invades the lives of real people. The pain of the principals is smoothed over by the prettiness of Lelouch's camerawork and the luxury of their lives. The film is sure to be a huge hit.

The Burtons dispense on-screen vitriol

Los Angeles, 22 June

Booze and self-disgust flow in torrents in the screen version of Edward Albee's play *Who's Afraid of Virginia Woolf?* Here, Warners have cast the world's most famous married couple, Elizabeth Taylor and Richard Burton, as one of the unhappiest ever to have tied the knot. The love-hate relationship between college history professor George and his blowzy wife Martha, daughter of the college president, has been festering for years before it explodes like a boil in the faces of the young campus couple – George Segal and Sandy Dennis – whom they invite home. As the martinis mingle with mutual loathing, both couples find themselves staring into the abyss. Choreographing this lacerating encounter, and also making his screen debut, is Broadway director Mike Nichols, who found the film a tough assignment: "There was a very unpleasant aspect for all of us. We had to keep coming back to the same damn room, over and over, every day. And the poor Burtons had to spit at each other and hit each other for days." How different from the stars' own decorous home lives.

An even-handed account of recent history

Venice, 10 September

For the Golden Lion this year, the jury of the Mostra has chosen a disturbing film which has attempted to seek out the truth of an event in recent history. Gillo Pontecorvo's *The Battle of Algiers* deals with the guerrilla war for Algerian independence from the French in 1957, as seen through the eyes of the participants. Shot in the actual locations, mixing actors with those who fought in the battle, and without recourse to any newsreel footage, the film probably comes closer to the truth and the complexities of the situation than many documentaries have. Its main strength lies in its scrupulous attention to the views and problems of both sides. The film, subsidized by the Algerian government, exploits the possibilities of the Casbah's back streets, contrasted with the smart avenues of the French quarters. The winner of the Special Jury Prize was Alexander Kluge's *Yesterday Girl* (*Abschied von Gestern*), a debut feature from Germany. This tale of a completely amoral and rebellious East German girl comes as a breath of fresh air from the moribund German film industry.

George and Martha (Burton and Taylor), a pair of experts in bitter invective.

*Jean Martin in Gillo Pontecorvo's **The Battle of Algiers**, the best film.*

Truffaut's journey to Britain with Bradbury

Paris, 16 September
Director François Truffaut has ventured into color for the first time with *Fahrenheit 451*. Adapted from a Ray Bradbury novel, it's a science fiction parable set in a future dystopia where all books are banned. Squads of firemen incinerate those that survive (the title refers to the temperature at which they ignite). Oskar Werner is the fireman who begins to have doubts about his job, seeks solace in a secret hoard of literature and finally joins the "book people", a community of fugitives who commit classics to memory. Each one is a living book. Cameraman Nicolas Roeg's photography, particularly the close-ups of blazing books, is superb.

François Truffaut during the filming.

The fire brigade as conceived in the world of Ray Bradbury and Truffaut.

The Production Code is thirty-six years old

New York, 20 September
Recognizing that many changes in mores and social standards have taken place during the 36 years since the Production Code was first established, the MPAA (The Motion Picture Association of America), headed by Jack Valenti, has announced the formulation of a new and more flexible 'code of self-regulation' to replace the more strictly enforced rules and regulations of the Hays Code. In fact, the thinking behind this new approach was suggested by a draft code published last year and follows on the controversy caused by two recent films, *The Pawnbroker* (1965) and *Who's Afraid of Virginia Woolf?* It read, in part, "Brutality, illicit sex, indecent exposure, vulgar or profane words and gestures, and offensive treatment of religions and racial or national groups, are noted as subjects for restraint, but interpretation in all cases... including nudity, is left to the discretion of the administrators." However, unlike the old Code, the wording of the new one has been left deliberately vague. In addition, it does not stress the moral obligations of filmmakers, nor does it insist on certain specific standards of moral conduct. It looks likely, therefore, that a new system of classification will be set up, designating films as "suitable for children" or "for adults only", similar to the one that is already operating in Great Britain. The code will thus meet the requirements of today's world, without the necessity for government regulation.

Ursula and the tribulations of Belmondo

*Jean-Paul Belmondo and Ursula Andress met while making **Tribulations d'un Chinois en Chine (Up to His Ears)** for director Philippe de Broca.*

Paris, 29 September
Jean-Paul Belmondo met sultry star Ursula Andress for the first time when they began filming *Tribulations d'un Chinois en Chine*, directed by Philippe de Broca. The co-stars rapidly became inseparable. Now Belmondo's wife, Elodie Constante, the mother of their three children, has filed for divorce, citing her husband's "intimate relations with a well-known actress." It would seem that Belmondo has tribulations of his own.

Flames quenched by a shower of stars

Paris, 13 October
The cast of René Clément's *Is Paris Burning?* reads like a Who's Who of international stars, among them Leslie Caron, Orson Welles, Gert Froebe, Alain Delon, Kirk Douglas, Glenn Ford, Anthony Perkins, Jean-Paul Belmondo and Simone Signoret. And that would appear to be the problem. The distinguished director's account of the historic liberation of Paris in 1944 is a tedious and disappointing muddle. Adapted by Americans Francis Ford Coppola and Gore Vidal from a French book, and backed by a stirring Maurice Jarre score, the film seems more concerned with parading its dozens of cameo performances than in delivering a coherent story.

*Orson Welles (left) and Gert Froebe in René Clément's **Is Paris Burning?***

Paramount bought by Gulf & Western

New York, 19 October
At the company's recent annual meeting, the stockholders of Paramount Pictures agreed to accept an offer of $83 per share (almost $10 over the market price) from Charles Bluhdorn's Gulf & Western Industries. This essentially means that the deal will now go ahead as expected. Paramount thus becomes the first major Hollywood film company to be owned by a corporate conglomerate. (General Tire and Rubber Company's purchase of RKO in 1955 hardly qualifies, since the studio was already in its death throes at the time.) Founded by Bluhdorn in 1957, the rapidly expanding Gulf & Western encompasses a variety of financial and manufacturing interests – not to be confused with Gulf Oil, an entirely different company. This new development represents a culmination of a battle for control of Paramount which has been waging over the past year. Under attack were the policies of executive vice president George Weltner, who had been running the company ever since longtime president Barney Balaban became chairman of the board. Weltner was challenged by a dissident group headed by Broadway producers Feuer and Martin and the chemicals mogul Herbert Siegel. While this group was making plans for a proxy overthrow of the management, Bluhdorn successfully stepped in.

Ronald Reagan is elected as governor

California, 9 November
Former movie actor Ronald Reagan, best known for *King's Row* and *Bedtime for Bonzo*, has been elected Republican governor of California, with 58 percent of the vote. Previously a Democrat, he was active in SAG (Screen Actors Guild) in the 1940s, becoming a board member and gaining his first experience of elective office as SAG president for six years. In the 1950s he worked most frequently on TV, hosting the *General Electric Theater*. Reagan first registered as a Republican in 1962, supporting Goldwater in 1964 before deciding to run for governor.

Czechoslovakia's young filmmakers brave forbidden ground

Prague, 18 November
The just-released *Closely Watched Trains* has already aroused much enthusiasm from both critics and the public. In his first feature film, 28-year-old Jiri Menzel brilliantly balances the themes of war and sexuality in a story set during the German occupation of Czechoslovakia. Menzel's screenplay focuses on the life of a young trainee railway guard at a remote country station, desperately trying to lose his virginity. He finally achieves his goal with a Partisan girl, who calls herself Victoria Freie (the underground password), before he is killed because of clumsiness and excess zeal. The director wanted a happy ending, but his co-writer Bohumil Hrabal, on whose novel this film was based, persuaded him to retain the tragic conclusion. But this closely-observed, satiric, touching and humorous film is an excellent example of the Czech New Wave.

For about three years now, the Czech cinema has continued to astonish with its freshness. There are now more than 20 directors in the country, mostly graduates from FAMU, the Prague film school founded in 1946. They have reacted against the ponderous and conformist films made during the Stalin era, drawing on everyday life for their inspiration in a realistic manner. Their humor sometimes verges on the burlesque, but it allows them to

Jiri Menzel's *Closely Watched Trains*. The films, too, are under scrutiny.

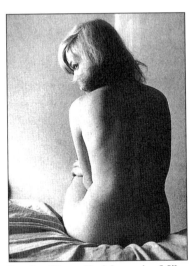

Lovely Hana Brejchova in Milos Forman's *Loves of a Blonde*.

tell the truth beneath a jokey surface. Milos Forman's *Peter and Pavla* and *Loves of a Blonde* places the characters in various hilarious situations, a pretext to show how ill at ease the younger generation feels under a repressive regime. In Vera Chytilova's *Daisies*, two bored adolescent girls destroy material goods and play some outrageous pranks on those who belong to the consumer-oriented society. And an existential anguish pervades Jaromil Jires' *The Cry* and Ivan Passer's *Intimate Lighting*. These recent films are planting the seeds of the new Czechoslovakian society, one which addresses the aspirations of the young.

Forman's first feature, *Peter and Pavla* (aka *Black Peter*), a key film.

The Cry directed by Jaromil Jires.

The Disney kingdom loses its ruler

California, 15 December
Walt Disney, one of the greatest figures of the entertainment world, has died aged 65. He suffered an acute circulatory collapse following surgery for the removal of a lung tumor. "Pleasing the public is one of the most difficult tasks, because we don't really know ourselves what we really like and what we want," he declared in 1938. He certainly knew how to please the public better than most. Born in Chicago in 1901, Walt Disney began work in a commercial art studio in Kansas City, where he met Ub Iwerks, another promising young artist. In 1923, he, Iwerks, and Walt's older brother Roy set up their own company to produce the cartoon series, *Oswald the Rabbit*. In 1928, the character that placed Disney on the road to fame and fortune, Mickey Mouse, was born. The Disney studio then grew and grew, its "stars" like Donald Duck and Goofy, becoming international favorites. In 1934, Disney had the novel idea of making an animated feature. *Snow White and the Seven Dwarfs* proved an enormous success, and it was followed by prewar classics such as *Fantasia*, *Pinocchio*, *Dumbo* and *Bambi*. Later on, the studio branched out into live-action features, such as *Treasure Island*. Even though these never quite captured the perfection of the earlier films, Walt Disney productions continued to make a vast amount of money at the box office. Not content with films and television programs, Disney fulfilled his dream in 1955 when he opened Disneyland, one of the most popular tourist attractions in the world.

Walt Disney, an original genius.

Antonioni's English film exposes the dangerous power of images

London, 18 December
The mystique of the fashion photographer in "Swinging London" has become so great that Italian director Michelangelo Antonioni has made *Blow Up*, a film about one. Former child actor David Hemmings plays the trendy, cherub-faced snapper whose photograph snatched of a couple in a park may, or may not, provide proof of a murder. His desultory sleuthing is constantly disrupted as he wanders through London's "magic village", inhabited by the beautiful people. Eventually the real and imaginary become inseparable. The body Hemmings has discovered disappears and his evidence is destroyed, with the exception of the largest "blow-up", which has become too abstract to reveal its secret. Antonioni's artful meditation on the manipulation of images has caught the mood of the moment.

*Hemmings the photographer and Redgrave the model in Antonioni's **Blow Up**.*

The director during the filming.

Tunisia holds its first film festival

Tunis, 11 December
The holding of the first Cinematographic Days at Carthage, is an important event for Arab and African cinema, which until now has been singularly lacking in international festivals. This festival, which was founded by Tahan Cheriaa, head of the cinema section of the Ministry of Culture and Information, is an ambitious project; it is hoping to become the principal meeting place for directors from Africa and Asia. Among the many films shown as part of the competition, the winner of the Grand Prix was a Senagalese film called *Black Girl*, directed by Ousmane Sembene. It tells the tragic story of a young Senegalese woman working as a maid for an affluent French family on the Riviera, concentrating on her isolation and her growing despair. Shot in a quasi-documentary style, influenced by the French New Wave, it is a remarkable first feature by Sembene, who is also a novelist of stature. Second prize went to the Kuwaiti film, *The Falcon*, by Khaled Siddiq.

Egyptian film falls foul of Nasser regime

Cairo, 30 December
Although the Egyptian film director Tewfik Saleh is the most cultivated of his generation, he has encountered nothing but hostility and incomprehension. After the commercial failure of his first two films, *Madmen's Alley* and *The Struggle of Heroes*, his third, *The Rebels*, has been censored. About a rebellion in a sanitarium, it is an allegory directed at the present Egyptian regime, and a thinly-veiled criticism of Nasserism. The Ministry of National Culture here imposes strict censorship on ideas it finds unpalatable.

*Tewfik Saleh's **les Révoltés**, the director's third attempt at gaining recognition.*

The adventure, the ecstasy, the supreme suspense of a woman wronged beyond words, almost beyond revenge...

PARAMOUNT PICTURES AND KURT UNGER PRESENT

SOPHIA LOREN

in

"JUDITH"

CO-STARRING

PETER FINCH · JACK HAWKINS

WITH HANS VERNER · TERENCE ALEXANDER · FRANK WOLFF · ARNALDO FOA · ANDRE MORELL · PRODUCED BY KURT UNGER

DIRECTED BY DANIEL MANN · SCREENPLAY BY JOHN MICHAEL HAYES · FROM A STORY BY LAWRENCE DURRELL · MUSIC SCORED BY SOL KAPLAN · TECHNICOLOR PANAVISION

Sophia suffered in glorious makeup as the avenging wife of a Nazi. Dismal.

Millionaire and mistress a topic for farce, from a Broadway hit.

*Mike Hynson and Robert August in Bruce Brown's **The Endless Summer**.*

*Jeanne Moreau in **Mademoiselle**, directed by Tony Richardson.*

A caper movie that bombed.

*Andras Balint (left) and Klari Tolnay in Istvan Szabo's **Father** (Hungary).*

*Monica Vitti and Terence Stamp in **Modesty Blaise**, directed by Joseph Losey.*

Five-star visuals and acting but dull account of General Gordon.

Kenneth Anger's underground film: *Inauguration of the Pleasure Dome*.

International Velvet stars in Andy Warhol's *The Chelsea Girls*.

Screen version of play with Paul Scofield as Sir Thomas More.

Burt Lancaster (left), Claudia Cardinale and Lee Marvin in Richard Brooks' *The Professionals*, a strong, suspenseful Western.

l to r: Candice Bergen, Elizabeth Hartman, Kathleen Widdoes, Mary Robin Redd, Jessica Walter (on the couch): *The Group*, directed by Sidney Lumet.

1967

★ ★

1966 Academy Awards, Santa Monica Civic Auditor., 10 Apr.

Best Film:	*A Man for All Seasons* (dir: Fred Zinnemann)
Best Director:	Fred Zinnemann
Best Actor:	Paul Scofield (*A Man for All Seasons*)
Best Actress:	Elizabeth Taylor (*Who's Afraid of Virginia Woolf?*)
Best Supp. Actor:	Walter Matthau (*The Fortune Cookie*)
Best Supp. Actress:	Sandy Dennis (*Who's Afraid of Virginia Woolf?*)

London, 2 January
Opening at the Carlton Theatre of Charlie Chaplin's *A Countess From Hong Kong* starring Marlon Brando and Sophia Loren. It is the second of Chaplin's films to star actors other than himself (the other was *Public Opinion*), and also the second to be made by Chaplin in Britain since his arrival from the U.S.

Paris, 20 January
The Studio des Ursulines cinema in the Latin quarter has re-opened after undergoing renovations.

New York, 20 January
MGM has published a full page announcement in several papers, pointing out that the company's shares have risen by 150 percent since Robert O'Brien took over as president in January 1963.

Hollywood, 20 February
Yakima Canutt has been awarded an honorary Oscar for his work as a stuntman and for developing safety devices to protect all stuntmen.

Paris, 22 February
Release of *le Voleur* (*The Thief of Paris*), directed by Louis Malle, with Jean-Paul Belmondo, Geneviève Bujold, Françoise Fabian, Marie Dubois and Charles Denner.

New York, 2 March
Judy Garland has announced her return to the screen in a film version of Jacqueline Susann's bestseller *The Valley of the Dolls*, which is to be filmed by Mark Robson for Fox. She made her last film in 1962.

Los Angeles, 8 March
Shirley MacLaine has won the suit she brought against 20th Century-Fox in 1966. The studio has been ordered to pay her $800,000, the total of her contract for the unmade film, *Bloomer Girl*. The star's contract stated that she was to be paid her salary whether or not the film was made.

Wilmington, 15 March
Philip Levin has begun new proceedings against MGM in the Federal court in Delaware, accusing Robert O'Brien's group of buying the votes of several shareholders in order to make sure that those supporting Levin would be in the minority at the general meeting.

San Francisco, 15 March
The Transamerica Company, an insurance and financial services giant, has made a public offer for United Artists. The company's board of directors is encouraging shareholders to accept this "friendly" offer.

Los Angeles, 10 April
At this year's Academy Awards Ceremony, both the Irving G. Thalberg Memorial Award and the Jean Hersholt Humanitarian Award, which are not always given, found worthy recipients. The Thalberg award went to Alfred Hitchcock, while actor Gregory Peck's many contributions to the film acting profession were recognized with the Hersholt award.

Lisbon, 20 April
Release of *Mudar de Vida* (*A New Life*), directed by Paulo Rocha with Isabel Ruth and Geraldo del Rei. Rocha was Jean Renoir's assistant on *The Vanishing Corporal*.

New York, 6 May
Gloria Swanson attended the first American screening of the restored version of *Queen Kelly*, directed by Erich von Stroheim, of which she was the producer and star. The uncompleted film had never been distributed in the U.S., but a short version of the film had been shown in Europe.

Los Angeles, 8 May
Robin Moore, the author of *The Green Berets*, which John Wayne intends to turn into a film, said in a radio interview that the Pentagon had done all in its power to prevent production of the film.

New York, 24 May
Release of *Cool Hand Luke*, directed by Stuart Rosenberg, starring Paul Newman.

Los Angeles, 28 May
Dyan Cannon has been granted a divorce from Cary Grant on the grounds of "brutal and inhuman treatment." Miss Cannon asserted that Grant used to lock her up and beat her, and on two occasions forced her to take LSD. The couple married in 1965.

Washington, 5 June
An official announcement has confirmed the creation of the American Film Institute. The Institute aims to train young filmmakers, to stock and conserve America's film heritage and to publish a catalogue listing all American-produced films. The $5 million annual budget will be funded jointly by the Federal Government, the MPAA, the Ford Foundation and a number of other private organizations. Headed by George Stevens Jr. the Institute has numerous filmmakers, actors and producers on its board of directors.

London, 10 June
The Queen attended the premiere of the fifth James Bond film *You Only Live Twice,* directed by Lewis Gilbert. Sean Connery stars once again as Agent 007, and the film introduces lovely newcomer Mie Hama.

England, 28 August
Britain's most prolific film director Maurice Elvey has died. During his long directorial career, which started in 1913, Elvey made over 300 feature films, including a handful in the U.S., and numerous shorts.

Paris, 13 October
Film critic and historian Georges Sadoul has died after a long illness.

London, 8 November
Roman Polanski's third English film, *The Fearless Vampire Killers*, with Sharon Tate is showing in London for the first time today.

Los Angeles, 8 December
Mike Nichols has presented his latest film, *The Graduate*, to the press. It stars Dustin Hoffman in his first major role – a role that was originally offered to Robert Redford who turned it down.

Paris, 19 September
A group of extremist right-wing youths vandalized the Kinopanorama Cinema, in the avenue de La-Motte-Piquet, which was screening *Far From Vietnam*. The manager was hurt in the attack.

Rome, 27 December
Actor Marcello Mastroianni has been honored with the Italian Republic's Order of Merit.

BIRTHS

France, 31 May
Sandrine Bonnaire

Georgia, 28 October
Julia Roberts

DEATHS

California, 21 January
Ann Sheridan

France, 6 February
Martine Carol

Berlin, 29 April
Anthony Mann

New Hampshire, 30 May
Claude Rains

Hollywood, 10 June
Spencer Tracy

New Orleans, 29 June
Jayne Mansfield

London, 8 July
Vivien Leigh

New York, 21 July
Basil Rathbone

Germany, 9 August
Anton Walbrook

Hollywood, 13 August
Jane Darwell

California, 25 August
Paul Muni

Los Angeles, 9 November
Charles Bickford

---

*Lerner and Loewe's record-breaking stage musical, **Camelot**, comes to the screen. Directed by Joshua Logan with its glorious score intact, it cost the studio a fortune to make.*

Demoiselles Deneuve and Dorléac dance for Demy

Real-life sisters Catherine Deneuve (left) and Françoise Dorléac in **les Demoiselles de Rochefort**, *a multi-colored universe.*

Paris, 8 March

The two sisters, Françoise Dorléac and Catherine Deneuve, are cast as the twins Solange and Delphine in Jacques Demy's newest film, *The Young Girls of Rochefort*. Following *Lola*, which was situated in Nantes, and *The Umbrellas of Cherbourg*, Demy has continued his exploration of the towns of the west coast of France, the area where he was born. The film was actually shot in Rochefort-sur-Mer, mainly in the Place Colbert, in the center of this charming town. Last year, Demy visited many towns along the coast looking for a square which could accommodate the vigorous choreography and sweeping camera movements, and his choice finally fell on Rochefort. Teams of painters, under the direction of the designer Bernard Evein, were assigned to redecorate the square, painting the facades of the houses in white, blue and pink. On 27 May last, Demy was ready to shoot this colorful CinemaScope picture, a direct homage to the great days of the MGM musical, which Gene Kelly's presence in the cast underlines. The plot tells of two girls who run a ballet school and who pine to meet their ideal man. Kelly, a concert pianist, and Jacques Perrin, a sailor on leave, are also looking for their ideal woman. Michel Legrand composed the melodious songs which Dorléac and Deneuve put over with enthusiasm, while the dancing, choreographed by Irishman Norman Maen, has been given a dynamic boost by Broadway hoofers George Chakiris and Grover Dale. As for Gene Kelly, at 55 nobody expected the kind of energetic dancing that informed *On the Town*, to which this film pays tribute. But he lends the film an authentic image of the Hollywood musical.

Martine Carol's sad passing

Monte Carlo, 6 February

Martine Carol has died of a heart attack, probably brought on by a mixture of alcohol and tranquilizers. Born Maryse Mourer in Biarritz on 16 May 1922, Carol made her big screen debut in 1943 in *la Ferme aux loups*. During the early 1950s she was the unchallenged sex symbol and box-office queen of French cinema before being finally overtaken by Brigitte Bardot. A voluptuous blonde whose ripe sensuality outweighed her modest acting talent, she was memorable in Richard Pottier's *Caroline chérie*, René Clair's *les Belles de nuit* and Max Ophuls' *Lola Montès*. She also appeared in a number of costume spectaculars directed by her husband Christian-Jaque. However, recent attempts to revive her flagging career met with little success.

Eric Rohmer's first feature-length 'moral tale' is set in St. Tropez

Paris, 2 March

A new art cinema on the Left Bank, the Studio Gît-le-Coeur, has been inaugurated with the first showing of Eric Rohmer's second full-length feature, *la Collectionneuse*. It is the third of the director's Six Moral Tales, the first two being *The Baker of Monceau* and *Suzanne's Career*, both short films made some four years ago. *La Collectionneuse* concerns an artist (Patrick Bachau) and an antiques dealer (Daniel Pommereulle) sharing a friend's villa in St. Tropez with a bikini-clad nymphet (Haydée Politoff), who sleeps with a different boy every night. The two older men try to resist being added to her collection. "Less concerned with what people do than what is going on in their minds while they are doing it," in the words of the director, the film is witty, intellectual and analytical, as well as erotic. Rohmer establishes the theme of resistance to sexual temptation using the hedonistic, sun-soaked and undoubtedly alluring setting of St. Tropez to underline the dangers. Eric Rohmer is now hoping to complete the series with *The Girl on the Bicycle*, *Claire's Knee* and *Love in the Afternoon*, titles which give some idea that the director will be continuing to explore the same territory.

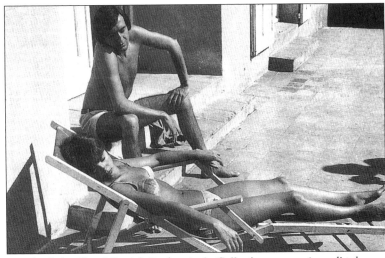

Haydée Politoff and Patrick Bachau in **la Collectionneuse**, *a 'moral' tale.*

Young boy shakes old man's prejudices

*Michel Simon and Alain Cohen in Claude Berri's touching film **The Two of Us**.*

Paris, 11 March
The Two of Us (*le Vieil homme et l'enfant*), Claude Berri's first feature, is a semi-autobiographical tale very close to the director's heart. This work is a reconstruction of Berri's own childhood experience, which he describes as "a love affair between a Jew and an anti-Semite." Set during the Nazi occupation of Paris, it tells the story of Claude (Alain Cohen), an eight-year-old Jewish boy, who is sent to stay with an elderly couple in the country. Since Pépé (Michel Simon), the old man, is a rabid anti-Semite, the boy is instructed to conceal his origins. Once there, Claude and Pépé forge a close relationship. The complex situation is handled with sensitivity and humor, seen mainly through the amused and bemused child's eyes.

Oscar ceremony almost ruined by TV strike

Los Angeles, 10 April
Only hours before the Academy Awards ceremony it was unclear whether the proceedings would be televised. The ABC network was threatened with strikes which would black out the prize-giving and leave the Academy with a financial loss of nearly a million dollars. In the end everything went ahead as planned, with Bob Hope once again acting as master of ceremonies. The most successful film was Mike Nichols' *Who's Afraid of Virginia Woolf?*, which won five Oscars, including a second Best Actress award for Elizabeth Taylor and Best Supporting Actress for Sandy Dennis, who made her screen debut six years ago in *Splendor in the Grass* but is better known as a Tony Award-winning Broadway star. Also taking home statuettes for their work on that picture were Haskell Wexler (cinematography), Richard Sylbert (art direction) and Irene Sharaff (costume). The vote for Best Picture went to *A Man for All Seasons*, directed by Fred Zinnemann, who also won the Best Director prize. His star in the picture, Paul Scofield, won the Best Actor award for his

*Robert Shaw: **A Man for All Seasons**.*

portrayal of the prickly, principled martyr Sir Thomas More. Walter Matthau, master technician of mordant comedy, was given the Best Supporting Actor Oscar for his performance as the ambulance-chasing lawyer in Billy Wilder's biting satire, *The Fortune Cookie*. And the Best Foreign Film award went to Claude Lelouch's huge international hit, *A Man and a Woman*.

Welles plays merry havoc with Falstaff

New York, 19 March
Orson Welles' third assault on Shakespeare is *Chimes at Midnight*, based on his own stage adaptation of the Falstaff scenes in *Henry IV, Parts One and Two* and filmed in Spain. His own interpretation of the role of the rascally Sir John Falstaff, hobbling on a gnarled walking stick, conjures poignant images of the tragic trajectory of Welles' own career. A bravura battle scene, filmed on a shoestring in a Madrid park, and the firelight dancing on the faces of Falstaff and Shallow remind us of the waste of this great talent.

Tragic love story lyrically filmed in Sweden

Stockholm, 24 April
The director Bo Widerberg has addressed himself to a true-life tragedy for the subject of *Elvira Madigan*. It tells of a tightrope artist (Pia Degermark) and a married army officer (Thommy Berggren) who fall in love, run away together and enjoy an idyllic time in the countryside, before the outrage of 19th-century society destroys them. This affecting film is exquisitely shot with a lyrical camera and well-acted (to the strains of Mozart's Piano Concerto No. 21). One can anticipate an overseas audience for this.

*Actor-director Orson Welles, a larger-than-life Falstaff in **Chimes at Midnight**.*

*Pia Degermark and Thommy Berggren in Bo Widerberg's **Elvira Madigan**.*

French film hits American jackpot

New York, 2 May
The winner of two Oscars at last month's Academy Awards ceremony – Best Foreign Language Film and Best Original Screenplay – Claude Lelouch's *A Man and a Woman* is one of the rare French pictures to make a hit in the United States. It opened modestly at a small art house in Manhattan last summer, immediately after its success at Cannes. The film did so well at the box office that it opened in other cities around the country. *Variety* has now devoted an entire article to the phenomenon: "According to Allied Artists, it is the most profitable film in their history, considering that it was made for a mere $100,000." *A Man and a Woman* has already made $2 million, a sum which could treble by the end of its showing. Its attraction seems to be its ultra-chic setting (Deauville), its attractive stars (Jean-Louis Trintignant and Anouk Aimée) and Francis Lai's catchy musical theme.

Cinema Novo director Rocha shocks Brazil with 'Land in Anguish'

Glauce Rocha is the bereaved mistress in **Terra em Transe (Land in Anguish)**.

Black God White Devil: *his first film.*

Brazil, 2 May
Glauber Rocha is undeniably the leader of *Cinema Novo*, the radical movement of Brazilian directors. Rocha, who created a sensation three years ago with *Black God White Devil*, has now returned to similar territory with the equally lyrical *Land in Anguish* (*Terra em Transe*). The hero of the film is a journalist and poet severely beaten up by the police. On his death bed, he recalls his past and his struggle against the destructive agents of multinational companies and the Church. Rocha has here launched a vigorous attack on the "permanent state of madness" that his country seems to be living in since the military coup d'etat in 1964. In his denunciation, he has called upon every cinematic weapon at his disposal – shock montage, jump cuts and the film-within-a-film technique.

Veteran star Spencer Tracy is laid to rest after a lengthy illness

Hollywood, 11 June
Spencer Tracy has died at his Hollywood home shortly after completing work on his last film, *Guess Who's Coming to Dinner*. Born in Milwaukee, Wisconsin, on 5 April 1900, he made his stage debut in 1922 as a robot in Karel Capek's *R.U.R.* He entered films in 1930, making two shorts for Vitaphone before John Ford cast him in *Up the River* and Fox gave him a contract. After four frustrating years at Fox, in which he gained a reputation for irascibility and heavy drinking, Tracy moved to MGM, where he established himself as a front-rank star in Fritz Lang's *Fury*. In 1942 he was teamed for the first time with Katharine Hepburn in *Woman of the Year*. Their remarkable partnership in nine subsequent films was matched by a lifelong romance, although Tracy never divorced his wife Louise Treadwell, whom he had married in 1923. Tracy was ill and exhausted throughout his final film, but, as Humphrey Bogart has said, "Spence was a natural, as if he didn't know a camera was there, or as if there had *always* been a camera there."

With Katharine Hepburn in George Cukor's **Adam's Rib**, *a huge hit in 1949.*

Tragedy strikes two stars in two days

New Orleans, 29 June
Within the space of two days, the film world has lost two of its stars in tragic accidents: the French actress Françoise Dorléac and the American sex goddess Jayne Mansfield. Dorléac had been on vacation with her sister Catherine Deneuve and brother-in-law David Bailey near St. Tropez. She left two days ago to drive to Nice in order to catch a plane. But while traveling on the slippery road leading to the airport, she lost control of the car and was killed instantly. Dorléac was only 25 but had already made 15 films, working with directors René Clair, Roman Polanski, François Truffaut, Ken Russell and Jacques Demy. Today, Jayne Mansfield, her lawyer and chauffeur died in a car accident. They were on the way to New Orleans, when they ran into the back of a truck which had stopped suddenly. The star was found decapitated. Mansfield, aged 34, had made her reputation as a busty blonde in a number of comedies such as *The Girl Can't Help It*.

The lovely Vivien Leigh dies of tuberculosis

Black and white on same side of the law

*Vivien Leigh in **The Roman Spring of Mrs. Stone** (1961) with Warren Beatty.*

*Sidney Poitier and Rod Steiger in Norman Jewison's **In the Heat of the Night**.*

London, 8 July
Actress Vivien Leigh, forever Scarlett O'Hara in *Gone With the Wind*, has died of tuberculosis. Born Vivian Mary Hartley in Darjeeling on 5 November 1913, she made her screen debut in 1934. In 1939 David O. Selznick chose her for *Gone With the Wind*, which brought fame and an Oscar. Marriage to Laurence Olivier followed in 1940 and lasted till 1960. She won a second Oscar in 1952 for her Blanche Dubois in *A Streetcar Named Desire*, but latterly her career had been dogged by depressive illness.

New York, 2 August
The theme of racial bigotry in a small, sweltering Mississippi town is wrapped around a murder hunt in Norman Jewison's *In the Heat of the Night*. Sophisticated Philadelphia homicide expert Sidney Poitier reluctantly joins forces with the swagbellied, manically gum-chewing redneck local police chief Rod Steiger to solve the killing of "the most important white man in the town." In the process they strike up an uneasy but affecting relationship. The stirring theme song is delivered with feeling by Ray Charles.

'La Religieuse' finally unbanned

Paris, 26 July
It was necessary for a change in the government, along with the replacement of Yvon Bourges by George Gorse as the Minister of State for Information, for the long ban on Jacques Rivette's *la Religieuse* to be lifted. Nevertheless, Rivette has had to make one slight compromise: the film will now be shown under the title of *Suzanne Simonin, la religieuse de Diderot*. The controversial work, completed in 1965, was originally banned from general release, but André Malraux permitted it to be shown at last year's Cannes Film Festival. Initially, it was a case of government officials giving in to certain religious and moral pressure groups, who had objected, without having seen the film, to its subject matter. Rivette's 140-minute color adaptation from Diderot's 18th-century novel of the travails of a young woman who is forced to enter a convent, is far from prurient. In fact, it is directed with an austere detachment and an authentic sense of claustrophobia and pain.

'Bonnie and Clyde' is a defiant challenge to the social system

New York, 14 August
Warren Beatty has turned producer with *Bonnie and Clyde*, which stars Faye Dunaway and himself in the title roles. They're Bonnie Parker and Clyde Barrow, the publicity-hungry bank robbers whose gang blazed its way across the Midwest during the Depression years. Beatty canvassed François Truffaut and Jean-Luc Godard before securing the services of Arthur Penn as director. Penn has given his bandits a heroic quality: Dunaway's Bonnie is a touching blend of sensuality and innocence, while Beatty's impotent and shyly limping Clyde Barrow suggests a link between sexual satisfaction and outlawry. Their death, a slow-motion ballet of blood and bullets, has caused a sensation. With strong support from gang members Gene Hackman, Estelle Parsons and Michael J. Pollard, *Bonnie and Clyde* switches back and forth exhilaratingly between comedy, melodrama and barbed social comment.

Left: Clyde Barrow and Bonnie Parker in the climactic shoot-out that ends their lives. Right: How it all began...

Dark secrets of 'Belle de jour' win the prize

*Catherine Deneuve in Luis Buñuel's **Belle de jour**, winner of the Golden Lion.*

Venice, 10 September
Luis Buñuel continues to astonish. His latest film, *Belle de jour*, shot in France, is a witty and erotic exploration into the secrets of femininity. It tells of a respectable doctor's wife, who spends her afternoons working in a high-class brothel with kinky clients. Catherine Deneuve, as the part-time *bourgeois* whore, grows more beautiful with each perversion, imagined or otherwise. The film merited the Golden Lion. Coincidentally sharing the Special Jury Prize were two films reflecting the current Western interest in Maoism: Jean-Luc Godard's *la Chinoise* and Marco Bellocchio's *China is Near*.

Newman's lonely hero tough and touching

Luke (Paul Newman) about to swallow fifty hard-boiled eggs in one session.

New York, 1 November
"What we've got here is a failure to communicate," says Strother Martin's prison boss to Paul Newman's uncooperative inmate in *Cool Hand Luke*, directed by Stuart Rosenberg. Newman takes the title role of the loner, imprisoned for decapitating parking meters, who becomes the camp hero after defeating hulking George Kennedy in a hardboiled egg-eating contest guaranteed to leave cinemagoers queasily eyeing their popcorn. A descendant of such 1930s melodramas as *I Was a Fugitive From a Chain Gang*, *Cool Hand Luke* hands Newman one of his most powerful roles to date.

Charming swan song for Tracy and Hepburn

New York, 11 December
Stanley Kramer's *Guess Who's Coming to Dinner* at first appears to be a daring approach to romantic comedy, being about a love affair that crosses the color bar. It is, in fact, devoid of real problems, as a group of very attractive protagonists easily sort out the temporary discomfort caused by the intended engagement of an eligible middle-class black man (Sidney Poitier) to an eligible middle-class white girl (Katharine Houghton, Katharine Hepburn's real-life niece). But despite its soft center, this is a heartwarming and entertaining movie, likely to be a huge hit because it marks the final collaboration of a legendary team, Spencer Tracy and Katharine Hepburn. As the bewildered parents of the girl, both are superb. That Tracy died soon after filming was completed brings an extra lump to the throat.

Left to right: Sidney Poitier, Katharine Houghton and Katharine Hepburn.

Carryings-on at King Arthur's court

Warners have lavished no less than $15 million on *Camelot*, the screen version of Lerner and Loewe's Broadway show, which was itself adapted from the Arthurian novel by T.H. White, *The Once and Future King*. However, it's hard to see exactly where the money has gone, as the sets and costumes look decidedly tacky, and they are not enhanced by director Joshua Logan's vulgar use of color filters. It also remains to be seen whether the starry cast, none of whom can exactly be described as a scintillating singer, will ensure its success at the box office. Richard Harris, Vanessa Redgrave and Franco Nero form the Round Table ménage à trois as King Arthur, Guinevere and Lancelot, and they are supported by David Hemmings as Mordred, Lawrence Naismith as Merlin and Lionel Jeffries as King Pellinore. It will require something of Merlin's wizardry for the studio to recoup its investment. There's also some very sloppy continuity work. Lionel Jeffries' King Pellinore meets King Arthur for the first time about an hour into the picture, yet about 20 minutes earlier he can be clearly spotted at Arthur's wedding.

Harris, Redgrave and Nero.

Unlikely candidate graduates to stardom

'Weekend' opening closes Godard's year

*Godard during the filming of **Weekend**, his devastating attack on our society and the horrors of the motor car, which stars Mireille Darc and Jean Yanne.*

New York, 21 December
In the midst of a cold New York winter, there are long lines of young people outside movie theaters, full of expectation at seeing a movie that addresses them and their problems. The film is Mike Nichols' *The Graduate*, and it features an unlikely new young star called Dustin Hoff-

man. He portrays 21-year-old Ben Braddock, who feels alienated from the shallow values of his wealthy parents and friends, and is lured into a relationship with a much older woman (Anne Bancroft). Hoffman is short and a bit of a *nebbish*. But it's the loser image that will make him a winner with the young.

Paris, 29 December
With the release of *Weekend*, Jean-Luc Godard has ended a particularly prolific year, during which five of his films were shown to the public. *Made in USA* and *Two or Three Things I Know About Her* were released in January and March respectively. Godard had shot both films simultaneously during the previous summer. With these pictures, the director's style has become more elliptical, and his attitudes more militant. *Made in USA* takes place in 1969, in an Americanized Paris, where Anna Karina is searching for a man involved in the assassination of the Algerian leader Ben Barka. This is Godard continually redefining cinematic images in a sponta-

neous, topical, pop art manner. *Two or Three Things I Know About Her* is about a housewife (Marina Vlady) who prostitutes herself one day a week to obtain the household luxuries she wants. The film, the title of which refers to Paris, is another advance towards Godard's desire to find an equivalent to "bourgeois cinema". With *la Chinoise*, Godard seems to have moved towards a Maoist political commitment. It concerns five young people who set up a Maoist cell to try to put their theories into revolutionary practice. (Red is the appropriately dominant color.) And a disenchantment with French society is even stronger in *Weekend*, a devastating attack on modern life and the motor car.

Sci-fi and soft porn from Roger Vadim

Paris, 25 December
Jane Fonda has been directed for the third time by her husband Roger Vadim in *Barbarella*, based on a science fiction comic book. The film has created a storm, because Miss Fonda does a striptease during the

opening credits. Although her nudity is partially hidden, this did not stop the censors from cutting some of it before releasing the film with a certificate restricted to audiences over 18. Thus critics have unfairly accused Vadim of "anti-eroticism."

*Jane Fonda in **Barbarella**, a film version of Jean-Claude Forest's comic strip.*

*Juliet Berto in **la Chinoise** which won the Special Jury Prize at Venice.*

Catherine Deneuve is the part-time prostitute in **Belle de jour**, directed by Luis Buñuel, here with one of her customers (Iska Khan).

Peter Sellers in **Casino Royale**, a misguided James Bond spoof with star cast.

THEY
MAKE
SOMETHING
WONDERFUL OUT OF
BEING
ALIVE!

20th Century-Fox presents (STAR OF "TOM JONES")

AUDREY ALBERT
HEPBURN FINNEY

in STANLEY DONEN'S

"TWO FOR THE ROAD"

Suggested For Mature Audiences

with ELEANOR BRON · WILLIAM DANIELS · CLAUDE DAUPHIN · NADIA GRAY
produced and STANLEY DONEN written by FREDERIC RAPHAEL music HENRY MANCINI
directed by
Panavision° Color by DeLuxe ORIGINAL SOUNDTRACK ALBUM AVAILABLE ON RCA VICTOR RECORDS

Chic, witty and wistful tale of marriage directed by Stanley Donen.

Mireille Darc and Jean Yanne in the nightmare of Godard's **Weekend**.

Elizabeth Taylor stars in **Reflections in a Golden Eye**.

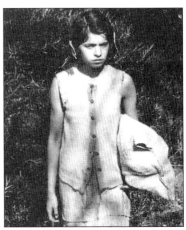

Nadine Nortier is tragic teenager **Mouchette** for Robert Bresson.

Lee Marvin, Angie Dickinson in John Boorman's rough, tough Point Blank.

Sophia Loren and Marlon Brando in Chaplin's A Countess From Hong Kong.

Schoolteacher Sidney Poitier (right) with Judy Geeson: To Sir With Love.

Peter Cook and Dudley Moore of Beyond the Fringe stage fame, are reunited on the big screen in Stanley Donen's Bedazzled.

A daring, atmospheric version of D.H. Lawrence's novel on a lesbian theme.

1968

★ ★

1967 Academy Awards, Santa Monica Civic Auditor., 10 Apr.

Best Film:	*In the Heat of the Night* (dir: Norman Jewison)
Best Director:	Mike Nichols (*The Graduate*)
Best Actor:	Rod Steiger (*In the Heat of the Night*)
Best Actress:	Katharine Hepburn (*Guess Who's Coming to Dinner*)
Best Supp. Actor:	George Kennedy (*Cool Hand Luke*)
Best Supp. Actress:	Estelle Parsons (*Bonnie and Clyde*)

New Delhi, 5 January
Louis Malle has arrived in India, where he plans to make a film.

New York, 15 January
Customs have seized a copy of Jack Smith's avant-garde film *Flaming Creatures*. The picture has been declared obscene and the Justice Department is starting proceedings against its distributor.

New York, 19 January
A Swedish film directed by Vilgot Sjoman, *I am Curious - Yellow*, has been seized by the United States Customs Service here. Arthur Olick an assistant United States attorney said yesterday that the film was seized because "...it leaves nothing to the imagination, including the act of fornication."

London, 15 February
Laslo Benedek's *The Wild One*, has at last been released here. It has been banned by the British censors for 14 years due to the activities of a group of bikers in the film which were judged likely to incite violence among the youth.

New York, 21 February
Variety has reported that the 1967 release of *Gone With the Wind* earned $7.5 million in film rentals for MGM.

New York, 25 February
MGM has launched its publicity campaign for Stanley Kubrick's new film *2001: A Space Odyssey*, with a four page advertisement in the *New York Times*, the *Los Angeles Times* and the *Washington Star*.

Paris, 8 April
George Gorse, the Minister for Information, has authorized the release of Romain Gary's *les Oiseaux vont mourir au Pérou* (*The Birds Come to Die in Peru*), starring Jean Seberg and Maurice Ronet. The Cinema Control Commission had asked for a ban on the film.

New York, 17 April
Variety has announced that Frank Sinatra and Elizabeth Taylor are to co-star in *The Only Game in Town*. Filming is scheduled to start in early September.

New York, 18 April
The popularity of film studies courses has soared in the last year. There are now 60,000 graduate and undergraduate students enrolled in 1,500 film courses at 120 colleges throughout the United States.

New York, 28 April
The American premiere of the Russian-made *War and Peace* will be held tonight at the DeMille Theater, Seventh Avenue and 47th Street. According to the Russians the seven-hour film is the most expensive ever produced. Screenings will be in two parts: alternate matinees and evenings. Admission prices are a record $7.50 for the best seats.

New York, 3 May
Producer Joseph E. Levine has sold his company Embassy Films to the Avco conglomerate for $40 million. Embassy first made a name for itself in the early 60s distributing foreign films, but soon moved into production. Its greatest success to date has been *The Graduate*.

Paris, 6 May
In an announcement made to the daily, *Combat*, Robert Favre Le Bret, the general organizer of the Cannes Festival, said: "This year's Festival will have sportsmen, musicians, festivities of all kinds and a truly exceptional selection of films."

Los Angeles, 1 June
Director Jacques Demy is making *The Model Shop*.

New York, 3 June
Andy Warhol was hit by several bullets fired by one of his entourage, Valerie Solanis. He is in a hospital, reported to be in a critical state.

Washington D.C., 16 July
The American Film Institute has embarked on an ambitious new publishing project to compile a complete catalogue of all films produced in the U.S. since the beginning of the cinema.

Hollywood, 5 August
Italian director Michelangelo Antonioni has started shooting his first American film, *Zabriskie Point*, with Mark Frechette and Daria Halprin.

USA, 31 August
Robert Redford has opened an ecological ski resort, Sundance, created and named by him.

Rome, 13 September
Director Pier Paolo Pasolini's film, *Theorem*, has been seized by order of the courts.

Stockholm, 29 September
Release of *Skammen* (*Shame*), by Ingmar Bergman, with Liv Ullmann and Max Von Sydow.

New York, 9 October
For the first time in the history of American motion pictures, the film industry has, of its own volition, opted to use a classification system. MPAA head Jack Valenti stated that the system will come into effect on 1 November. Classifications are as follows: G – general exhibition; M – mature audiences; R – under 17s only admitted accompanied by an adult; X – adults only (over 18). However, States may raise the ages of the last two ratings to comply with their own laws.

Paris, 30 October
Release of *la Chamade* (*Heartbeat*), directed by Alain Cavalier, with a screenplay based on the novel by Françoise Sagan. Michel Piccoli and Catherine Deneuve head the cast.

Paris, 11 November
The French director of Polish origin Walerian Borowczyk has won the art film prize for *Goto, l'Ile d'amour* (*Goto, the Island of Love*), with Pierre Brasseur, Ligia Branice, Ginette Leclerc and René Dary.

Paris, 12 November
From today the Institute of Advanced Cinema Studies (IDHEC), will hold its classes in the Raleigh Cinema building in rue des Vignes.

San Francisco, 21 November
Jane Fonda has taken up the cause of the American Indians who have settled on Alcatraz Island.

Italy, 29 November
Romain Gary's French film, *The Birds Come to Die in Peru*, has been banned throughout the country.

London, 30 November
Premiere of Jean-Luc Godard's film *One Plus One*, with the rock group the Rolling Stones.

Paris, 22 December
Three Parisian cinemas specializing in sex films, the Strasbourg, Rex and Bosphore have been closed by the police until mid-February.

Italy, 31 December
The total number of productions (including co-productions) for this year is 254 films, compared to 182 in 1965. About 40 films belong to the erotic comedy genre.

BIRTHS

California, 14 February
Molly Ringwald

DEATHS

California, 13 February
Mae Marsh

Hollywood, 16 April
Fay Bainter

Italy, 4 June
Dorothy Gish

Los Angeles, 7 June
Dan Duryea

New York, 26 August
Kay Francis

New York, 18 September
Franchot Tone

Hollywood, 30 October
Ramon Novarro

New York, 12 December
Tallulah Bankhead

---

*Peter O'Toole and Katharine Hepburn in **The Lion in Winter**. Hepburn won her third Best Actress Oscar, unprecedented in being a shared award with Barbra Streisand.*

The Most Significant Reserved Seat Attraction Of The Year!

JOSEPH E. LEVINE presents
AN AVCO EMBASSY FILM

Starring

PETER O'TOOLE
as Henry II, King of England

KATHARINE HEPBURN
as Eleanor of Aquitaine, His Wife

A **MARTIN POLL** Production

THE LION IN WINTER

with
JANE MERROW as Princess Alais   JOHN CASTLE as Prince Geoffrey   TIM DALTON as King Philip of France
ANTHONY HOPKINS as Prince Richard the Lionhearted   NIGEL STOCK as William Marshall   NIGEL TERRY as Prince John

Based upon the play by   Executive Producer   Screenplay by
JAMES GOLDMAN   JOSEPH E. LEVINE   JAMES GOLDMAN

Produced by   Directed by   Music composed and
MARTIN POLL   ANTHONY HARVEY   conducted by JOHN BARRY

An AVCO EMBASSY PICTURES Release   PANAVISION®   In COLOR

Roman Polanski has married Sharon Tate

London, 20 January
Last year, the Polish-born director Roman Polanski made *The Fearless Vampire Killers, or Pardon Me But Your Teeth Are in My Neck*, in London, with a young, unknown American actress, Sharon Tate. Today, aged 33, Roman married Sharon. Polanski began his career in Poland, but has since made films abroad, one in Holland (an episode of *The Beautiful Swindlers*) and three in England, the first two being *Repulsion* and *Cul-de-Sac*. He now hopes to settle in the United States with his wife. Polanski has just signed a contract to direct his first Hollywood film, *Rosemary's Baby*, a horror story set in Manhattan.

Carl Dreyer's lasting legacy

Bendt Rothe and Nina Pens Rode.

Copenhagen, 20 March
The death of Danish director Carl Dreyer, aged 79, has caused sadness and anger among his admirers, due to the negative response to his last film, *Gertrud*, released in 1965. The film, which deals with the growing awareness of a young woman (Nina Pens Rode) betrayed in love (by Bendt Rothe), has remained both unappreciated and misunderstood. Subsequent to its failure, the great director had difficulty in getting his projects realized. He never got the chance to make *Jesus Christ Jew*, which had haunted him since 1949. To quote *Gertrud*, his life was "a long, endless pursuit of dreams, one superimposed upon the other."

Charlton Heston finds himself in a strange world ruled by apes

*Charlton Heston in **Planet of the Apes**, directed by Franklin J. Schaffner.*

New York, 9 February
Franklin J. Schaffner's *Planet of the Apes* looks like it may change the course and momentum of science fiction cinema, which has been in the doldrums for most of the decade, in large part reduced to the role of a supermarket supplying decorative elements to spice up other genres. Adapted by the prolific Rod Serling and the former blacklist victim Michael Wilson from the satirical novel by Pierre Boulle titled *Monkey Planet*, *Planet of the Apes* has reworked the time travel theme, putting astronaut Charlton Heston through a timeslip and on to a post-holocaust Earth in which intelligent apes have become the defenders of "humanity". Firmly controlled by Schaffner, an old-fashioned craftsman, and strikingly photographed in the national parks of Utah and Arizona by Leon Shamroy, *Planet of the Apes* moves at a measured pace towards a memorable climax in which Heston finds the ruined, half-buried remains of the Statue of Liberty and comes to the bitter realization that he is on Earth after all. The remarkably flexible ape make-up, which has enabled the actors playing the apes to create believable characters rather than stereotypes, was created by John Chambers. Roddy McDowall and Kim Hunter are outstanding as the sympathetic ape scientists who examine Heston to discover whether he might be the "missing link" in simian development, a delightful conceit which neatly underlines the notion of rational ape confronting irrational man.

Zeffirelli's pair of star-crossed lovers are properly youthful

London, 4 March
At the ages of 17 and 15 respectively, Leonard Whiting and Olivia Hussey are as close to the ages of Romeo and Juliet as William Shakespeare intended. And, indeed, they make a very pretty couple of star-crossed lovers in Franco Zeffirelli's exuberant screen version of *Romeo and Juliet*. Alas, neither of them has a shred of acting ability, so that Shakespeare's verse is hopelessly garbled whenever they appear. Poetry takes second place to pictorial extravagance, with the rich Technicolor photography of Pasqualino de Santis and handsome costumes designed by Danilo Donati a treat for the eye. Some acting ballast is provided by Laurence Olivier's prologue, Michael York's athletic Tybalt and John McEnery's whimsical Mercutio. The Italian Zeffirelli began his career as an actor and later became Luchino Visconti's assistant on films like *La Terra Trema* and *Senso*. He has also enjoyed a successful career as an international opera designer and director in London, New York and Milan, with a reputation for opulent spectacle.

Olivia Hussey and Leonard Whiting as Romeo and Juliet in Zeffirelli's film.

Stanley Kubrick ventures into space and the future

New York, 4 April

Stanley Kubrick's *2001: A Space Odyssey*, loosely adapted from his own story *The Sentinel* by Arthur C. Clarke, explores at greater length the question taken up in *Planet of the Apes* regarding the forces which control man's evolution. *2001*, shot in England at a cost of $10.5 million, aims to restore speculative thought to science fiction film, along with a primitive sense of wonder which harks back to the early days of cinema. The result is a technical tour de force in which images of vast, complex spacecraft float infinitely slowly through deep space to the strains of Strauss' "Blue Danube Waltz". At its heart the film contains one of the most stunning jump cuts in film – the moment when an animal bone hurled into the air by a prehistoric man is transformed into a slowly turning spaceship. We follow space-age man Keir Dullea in a search for a Higher Power behind a mysterious monolith discovered on the moon. He outwits the homicidal mission computer HAL before taking a hallucinogenic ride through a star gate to reemerge as a "transcended man". Kubrick has a clinical vision of the future in which mankind is just a cipher controlled by the force embodied in the monolith. But the reclusive filmmaker remains coy about the message, claiming, "The feel of the experience is the important thing, not the ability to verbalize or analyze it. Those who won't believe their eyes won't be able to appreciate this film."

*Stanley Kubrick's **2001: A Space Odyssey** searches for the origins of man across millions of years and through space.*

Dressed for the space adventure.

Oscars promote racial tolerance in wake of King assassination

Los Angeles, 10 April

This year the Academy Award ceremony was held under unusually somber circumstances. The assassination of Reverend Martin Luther King caused the event to be postponed for 48 hours. And for the same reason, the annual post-Oscar ball was canceled altogether. It was significant, therefore, that most of the major awards went to two films that deal with racial prejudice. The Best Picture winner, Norman Jewison's *In the Heat of the Night*, takes place in a small, steamy Mississippi town where Philadelphia's number one detective Virgil Tibbs reluctantly arrives to help the redneck police chief solve a murder. The fact that the senior visitor is black – Sidney Poitier at his most dignified and passionate – and that the local cop is a white bigot, makes for an entertaining game of dominance, with a social message. Rod Steiger, behind yellow sunglasses and incessantly chewing gum, won the Best Actor prize for managing to find nuances in his role as Poitier's adversary. Katharine Hepburn was presented with her second Best Actress Oscar for Stanley Kramer's comedy of racial coexistence, *Guess Who's Coming to Dinner*. She gave a warm and touching portrayal of an understanding woman whose daughter wishes to marry a black man (Sidney Poitier again), partnered for the last time by Spencer Tracy. Both movies won screenplay Oscars. The Best Director award went to Mike Nichols for only his second film, *The Graduate*, a movie that touched a chord among the nation's youth.

Guess Who's Coming to Dinner: Hepburn and Tracy (his last film).

Jeanne Moreau a vengeful black widow

*Charles Denner and the image of Jeanne Moreau in **The Bride Wore Black**.*

Paris, 17 April
François Truffaut has paid his most direct homage to his idol Alfred Hitchcock in his new film, *The Bride Wore Black*. Based, like *Rear Window*, on a novel by William Irish (Cornell Woolrich) and with a score by Bernard Herrmann, Hitch's fre-quent composer, it relates how the widow of a man shot dead on his wedding day, tracks down the group of men responsible, and eliminates them one by one. Jeanne Moreau is superb as the seductive avenging angel, and there are splendid cam-eos from the victims.

Matthau and Lemmon, hilariously odd

New York, 2 May
Jack Lemmon and Walter Matthau are paired again in the screen ver-sion of Neil Simon's Broadway smash *The Odd Couple*, in which two divorced men share an apartment. Matthau is reprising the role he played in the original, that of sloppy Oscar, while Lemmon is cast as fus-sy Felix. With a face which resem-bles a cross between a bloodhound and Yogi Bear, Matthau spent much of the early part of his screen career playing heavies. In a memorable screen debut in 1955 he took a bull-whip to Burt Lancaster in *The Ken-tuckian*. Now, at the age of 48, he's hit the big time.

Felix Unger (Jack Lemmon, left) and Oscar Madison (Walter Matthau).

Worldwide support pours in for Langlois

Simone Signoret and Michel Piccoli join the throngs supporting Langlois.

Paris, 30 April
The affair of the Cinémathèque has been brought to an end with the re-instatement of Henri Langlois as its head. The crisis erupted last Feb-ruary, but the attempt of the state to control the Cinémathèque dates back further. When André Malraux became Minister of Culture in 1959, the government demanded represen-tatives on the administrative coun-cil. They removed control over the funds from Langlois, and appointed a deputy financial manager. Rapid-ly, the Treasury started quibbling, and the number of civil servants on the administrative council was in-creased until they had gained an absolute majority. During a meeting of the council on 9 February, Pierre Moinot was elected to the presiden-cy of the Cinémathèque, replacing the film director Marc Allégret. Moinot demanded Langlois' sus-pension and named Pierre Barbin in his place. *Le Monde* published a protest signed by 40 directors on 10 February, which mobilized the en-tire profession. French as well as foreign filmmakers (including Jean Renoir, François Truffaut, Jean-Luc Godard, Roberto Rossellini, Federi-co Fellini and Ingmar Bergman) announced they would not permit the new administration to screen their films. Four days later, there were demonstrations outside the Cinémathèque. Given the passions aroused, the state had no choice but to withdraw its control, but also its subsidies. The Cinémathèque will now be free, but poor.

Henri Langlois, the guiding light of the Cinémathèque, back in his rightful place in the rue de Courcelles, holds the keys to the future.

Cannes Festival is caught in the eye of the storm

Urged on by the recent events in Paris, young filmmakers take over the Palais.

*José Lopez Vasquez, Geraldine Chaplin in Carlos Saura's **Peppermint Frappé**.*

Cannes, 18 May
Robert Favre le Bret, president of the Cannes Film Festival, had every reason to be happy. The 1968 vintage augured well and many prestigious guests were present at the gala opening, during which *Gone With the Wind* was shown in 70mm and stereophonic sound. Meanwhile, in Paris the students were confronting police across the barricades erected in the Latin Quarter. For some days, the festival-goers seemed unconcerned with the reverberations emanating from the capital. Yet today, just before the showing of the Spanish film, Carlos Saura's *Peppermint Frappé*, an angry group of people climbed onto the stage and grabbed the curtain. "In no way are we going to allow the Festival to continue while students are endangering their lives on the barricades in Paris," they shouted. Among this group were two of the young lions of the New Wave, Jean-Luc Godard and François Truffaut, as well as Claude Lelouch, Claude Berri, the critic Jean-Louis Bory and the actor Jean-Pierre Léaud. In addition to their desire to demonstrate their solidarity with the students, the rebellion was provoked by Culture Minister André Malraux's decision to sack Henri Langlois from his post as head of the Cinémathèque. And in Cannes, as in Paris, events were moving fast. A press conference was held regarding the "Cinémathèque affair", and there were meetings in the auditorium of the Palais. Then came the news of the resignation of four members of the jury, including

Louis Malle and Roman Polanski, followed by the decision of Alain Resnais, Milos Forman and Carlos Saura to withdraw their films from the Festival.

Because of the disruptions to the Festival, many of the interesting works were not shown. The films selected bore witness to the new movements and tendencies in world cinema, particularly the emergence of a whole new generation of young directors who promise to be tomorrow's masters of the art. Among them are representatives of the young Czechoslovakian cinema. Jan

Nemec's bold Kafkaesque film, *A Report on the Party and the Guests*, was made two years ago, but was denounced by the National Assembly in Prague, and has only now been released. Milos Forman, who had astonished us with *Loves of a Blonde*, was to have screened *The Firemen's Ball*, a virulent satire on Czech society. Another example of the regeneration of the film industry in Eastern Europe is the Hungarian Miklos Jancso, whose originality is well demonstrated in *The Red and the White*. He uses the possibilities of the large screen, orchestrating

a large-scale drama of domination and submission, with the minimum of dialogue. The Spanish director Carlos Saura would have been one of the top contenders for a prize with his *Peppermint Frappé*, had the showing of his film not been interrupted. The director has dedicated his film to Luis Buñuel, whose influence is evident in his treatment of the dreams and memories of his hero, focusing on his repressive religious upbringing. However, the demonstrations heralded the death warrant of this year's potentially rich Cannes Film Festival.

Mia Farrow mesmerized by witchcraft in the heart of Manhattan

New York, 12 June
Waif-like beauty Mia Farrow gives monstrous birth to a child of the Devil in *Rosemary's Baby*, Roman Polanski's brilliant shocker adapted

from a novel by Ira Levin. When she and her husband John Cassavetes move into a Gothic apartment block in Manhattan, they are adopted by their elderly neighbors Ruth Gor-

don and Sidney Blackmer. But their kindly attentions mask a sinister purpose, for they are Satanists, and Farrow has been chosen to carry the Devil's baby. Making his Hollywood debut, Polish writer-director Polanski tells the story from Farrow's point of view, so that the audience shares the growing realization on her part that there is something horribly wrong with her pregnancy, and that the twittering, vulgar Gordon and the courtly Blackmer are not all that they seem. Even Cassavetes turns out to be party to the plot as her grisly confinement draws near. Shot on location in the creepy Dakota apartment building in New York City, *Rosemary's Baby* cleverly mingles the mundane and the macabre to suspend our disbelief in witchcraft and give the film's coven a terrible plausibility.

*Mia Farrow in Polanski's **Rosemary's Baby** from the novel by Ira Levin.*

▷

Steve and Faye play sexiest chess game!

Boston, 19 June

There's never been an insurance investigator like Faye Dunaway in *The Thomas Crown Affair*. With a wardrobe full of Paris fashions, some of them rather startling, she has been unleashed on Steve McQueen's Tommy Crown, a laid-back Boston playboy who has a nice line in bank heists. Now he's planning another one, with the full knowledge that he is being stalked by the sophisticated Dunaway, whose investigative methods are as unconventional as her clothes. When they lock horns over a game of chess in Crown's pad, the way they handle the pieces gives a new meaning to the notion of foreplay. Jewison's use of split-screen heightens the tension in a movie as sleek and self-satisfied as its protagonists.

Steve McQueen, Faye Dunaway a magnetic duo in **The Thomas Crown Affair***.*

A funny girl with a truly sensational voice

New York, 19 September

Fanny Brice, born to a Jewish New York family, grew up with one burning ambition: to succeed in the theater. That Fanny was ugly, skinny and flat-chested, and yet overcame these disabilities to reach stardom, was testament to her determination. The story of Brice was told in the hit Broadway musical, *Funny Girl*, which made a star of a Jewish girl from New York, determined to succeed – Barbra Streisand. Now *Funny Girl*, directed by William Wyler, with choreography by Herb Ross, and its terrific Jule Styne-Bob Merrill score, has been filmed, bringing 151 minutes of Streisand. She has presence, humor, acting talent and, above all, a rich and powerful voice that belts its way through the songs with considerable artistry. And co-starring as Brice's no-good husband, Nicky Arnstein, is Dr. Zhivago himself, Omar Sharif, whose collaboration has, reportedly, incurred the disfavor of Egypt's government.

Streisand: a new phenomenon.

Pasolini's 'Theorem' angers all factions

Venice, 18 September

The Festival has ended today in confusion. The Grand Prix of the International Catholic Office of Cinema has been awarded to Pier Paolo Pasolini's *Theorem*, although it was seized six days ago by the public prosecutor in Rome for obscenity. The film has thus divided believers as much as the general public and critics. It has also displeased some Marxists, who see it as an implicit attack on their ideology, and has disturbed puritans with its attitude to sexual taboos. This fable of the middle-classes tells how a handsome young man (Terence Stamp) ingratiates himself into the home of a wealthy industrialist and sleeps with every member of the family – the father, the mother, the daughter, the son, and even the maid. (The latter is played by Laura Betti, who took the best actress prize.) The QED of Pasolini's theorem might be puzzling, but there is a certain mathematical beauty in his efforts to reach it.

Terence Stamp takes his turn with wife and mother Silvana Mangano.

Warhol and Morrissey focus on 'Flesh'

New York, 26 September

Flesh is the last film to come from Andy Warhol's Factory, which has closed after the attempt on Warhol's life in June of this year. It is Paul Morrissey's first full-length feature, and has all the hallmarks of the Factory, being peopled by junkies, hookers and drag queens. However, *Flesh* is narratively more ordered than Warhol's own experimental movies, and subsequently is being given a commercial showing. It is an amusing camp exercise in the best of bad taste. The plot, such as it is, concerns a male hustler (beefy Joe Dallessandro), who sells his body to earn enough money to pay for his wife's girlfriend's abortion. Other members of Warhol's band, such as Geri Miller and Candy Darling, make striking appearances. These characters are treated sympathetically and directly, and Morrissey films them in a simple, unfussy, *cinéma vérité* manner. Morrissey joined Warhol in 1963 as production assistant and cameraman.

Joe Dallessandro, the Warhol factory's icon of easy sex, in Morrissey's **Flesh***.*

A daredevil chase through the tortuous streets of San Francisco

*Steve McQueen and new British star Jacqueline Bisset in Peter Yates' **Bullitt**.*

New York, 17 October
Impressed by Britisher Peter Yates' staging of a car chase through London in *Robbery* (1967), Steve McQueen was responsible for getting Yates to direct *Bullitt*. The hero of this thriller, a police lieutenant, spends a great deal of time speeding after villains through the undulating streets of San Francisco. McQueen is not only bucked by an ambitious politician (Robert Vaughn) but by the Mafia as well, as he picks his way through the knotted threads of a murder involving a grand jury witness. The memorable chase occurs about midway through the film, a chase with a difference, and probably the most thrilling ever committed to film, during most of which McQueen insisted on doing his own stunts. Jacqueline Bisset plays McQueen's attractive girlfriend. This thriller is put together with pace and style by Peter Yates, directing his first American film, and making stunning use of the locations.

Novarro murdered in his home

Hollywood, 31 October
The blood-spattered corpse of 69-year-old silent star Ramon Novarro has been found sprawled in the bedroom of his Hollywood home. It seems that he choked to death on a lead Art Deco dildo – a present from Rudolph Valentino – which had been rammed down his throat by his assailants, two young hustler brothers from Chicago, Paul and Tom Ferguson.

Novarro in 1930, a typical image.

'Coogan's Bluff' shows Clint ain't kidding

New York, 2 October
Director Don Siegel and Clint Eastwood form an explosive partnership in *Coogan's Bluff*, a pacy police drama which dispatches laconic Arizona lawman Eastwood to New York to extradite homicidal hippie Don Stroud. When Stroud goes on the lam, Eastwood tracks him down by using methods more appropriate to the West than the Big Apple. Lee J. Cobb plays the bemused city cop trying to keep him under control, Stroud is splendidly malevolent as Eastwood's quarry, and Tisha Sterling catches the eye as his strung-out girlfriend. Director Siegel is a durable Hollywood veteran, a montage specialist at Warners in the mid-Forties, whose features career began with *The Verdict* in 1946. Many of his films have focused on outsiders balefully at odds with society, and Clint Eastwood is the latest addition to Siegel's gallery of tough loners. The two men seem made for each other, and *Coogan's Bluff* promises an interesting partnership.

*Clint Eastwood is the toughest cop on the job in Siegel's **Coogan's Bluff**.*

Horror and beauty of 'The Living Dead'

New York, 4 December
George Romero's debut film is a Z-budget shocker, *Night of the Living Dead*, shot over several weekends in Pennsylvania. It chronicles the desperate efforts of a bunch of Middle Americans, trapped in a remote farmhouse, to beat off the attacks of an army of walking dead – zombies who have inexplicably risen from the grave or broken out of the morgue. With a skill worthy of Hitchcock, Romero undercuts the traditions of the horror movie: the apparent heroine lapses into a state of permanent catatonia early in the film; a young couple, society's hope for the future, are burned to a crisp and return as zombies; and the black hero gets all his companions killed before being mistaken for a zombie and shot by a redneck rescue party. Film freak Romero worked as a grip on *North by Northwest* when he was at college. Now his own Pittsburgh-based Latent Image Company has graduated from commercials to a drive-in smash.

'Truth rises from the grave'! A highly original film from George A. Romero.

It's flashy, trendy and well-acted but still not as good as the poster!

Ava Gardner, Omar Sharif in a tedious remake of tragic romance **Mayerling**.

The famous comic strip comes to life.

This has the best car chase yet.

Three of the four Monkees, from left to right, Mickey Dolenz, Peter Tork and Michael Nesmith in Bob Rafelson's **Head**.

**Charlie Bubbles**: Liza Minnelli made her screen debut with Albert Finney.

An epic drama of adventure and exploration

Man's colony on the Moon...a whole new generation has been born and is living here...a quarter-million miles from Earth.

2001: a space odyssey

MGM PRESENTS A STANLEY KUBRICK PRODUCTION

CINERAMA Super Panavision® and Metrocolor

Stanley Kubrick ventured into space, 'tripping' on technology and symbolism.

*Max Von Sydow and Liv Ullmann in Ingmar Bergman's parable, **The Shame**.*

*John Lennon: **The Yellow Submarine**.*

*Peter Sellers stars in Blake Edwards' comedy of disaster, **The Party**.*

*Edward G. Robinson and Vittorio De Sica: **The Biggest Bundle of Them All**.*

*David Hemmings in Tony Richardson's **The Charge of the Light Brigade**.*

1969

★ ★

1968 Academy Awards, Dorothy Chandler Pavilion, 14 Apr.	
Best Film:	Oliver! (dir: Carol Reed)
Best Director:	Carol Reed
Best Actor:	Cliff Robertson (Charly)
Best Actress:	Katharine Hepburn (The Lion in Winter)
	Barbra Streisand (Funny Girl)
Best Supp. Actor:	Jack Albertson
	(The Subject Was Roses)
Best Supp. Actress:	Ruth Gordon (Rosemary's Baby)

Prague, 1 January
Anxiety is growing among filmmakers here. The period of comparative freedom of expression, enjoyed during the "liberal spring", appears to be drawing to a close. Relations between the film industry and the state have become increasingly strained since troops entered the city. Milos Forman and Jiri Menzel have been warned about giving an unfavorable impression of the conditions of the working class and Forman, who is in Paris, has decided not to return to Czechoslovakia. His last film to be made there was *The Firemen's Ball* in 1967.

Hollywood, 12 January
Judy Garland, who divorced Mark Herron in 1967, has married again. Her husband is a young hairdresser named Mickey Deans.

New York, 15 January
Darryl F. Zanuck, the head of Fox, has refused to distribute Edouard Luntz's *le Grabuge,* from a scenario by Jean Duvignaud, which was produced by the American company. He is shocked by the anti-bourgeois violence in the film.

New York, 17 February
Hedy Lamarr, the star of Gustav Machaty's 1933 production *Ecstasy*, has instigated proceedings against the editor of her biography *Ecstasy and Me, My Life as a Woman*, and against all those who took part in the writing and publishing of the book, which the actress describes as being obscene and shocking. Miss Lamarr is demanding $21 million as compensation for the damage done to both her reputation and career.

Boston, 11 March
An exhibitor has been condemned to six months imprisonment and fined $1,000 for screening Robert Aldrich's film *The Killing of Sister George*. The film had been banned by the local censor due to its controversial lesbian love scenes.

Boston, 30 March
The Killing of Sister George continues to be shown after the court ruled against the seizure of the film. Judith Crist, one of the country's most respected film critics, stated during the trial that not only is the film not in the least pornographic but, in her view, it is among the 10 best films of the year.

Las Vegas, 8 May
Lana Turner has married the magician and hypnotist Michael Dante.

Hollywood, 26 May
Edgar Bronfman replaces Robert O'Brien as president and chief executive officer at MGM.

Washington D.C., 8 June
The State Department has just announced that Stanley Kubrick's film *2001: A Space Odyssey*, is the USA's official entry for the Moscow Film Festival in July. Selection was made by three representatives of the film industry: director-producer Frank Capra, producer Walter Mirisch and scriptwriter Michael Straight.

New York, 10 June
David Picker, aged 33, has been elected president of United Artists. He replaces Arthur Krim who has moved on to the board of directors with Robert Benjamin.

New York, 10 June
Warner Bros.-Seven Arts' shareholders have approved a merger with Kinney National Services. The cost is estimated at $11.5 million.

California, 10 June
Franklin J. Schaffner has finished filming *Patton* at the military base in Pendleton. Shooting started in Spain in February.

New York, 18 June
A great deal of controversy has arisen over the extreme violence of Sam Peckinpah's latest Western, *The Wild Bunch*, now on release.

Boston, 24 June
The Supreme Court has upheld the ban on Frederick Wiseman's feature-length documentary *Titicut Follies*, which was shot in the Bridgewater State hospital for mentally disturbed criminals in 1967. Permission has, however, been granted for the film to be shown non-commercially for groups of professionals.

Algiers, 1 July
The Algerian government has announced the nationalization of all film companies. The move is aimed at forcing big foreign companies with branches in Algeria, such as Paramount, MGM and Fox, to give up their interests in the country.

New York, 28 July
MGM has taken Kirk Kerkorian to court. The latter wants to buy $35 million worth of MGM shares. However, since finance for the purchase comes mainly from Transamerica, which already owns United Artists, this is regarded as unacceptable.

New York, 10 August
Despite the court descision, Kirk Kerkorian has acquired 24 percent of MGM by turning to alternative sources of finance.

Woodstock, 15 August
A vast outdoor rock music festival opened here today. Documentary filmmaker Michael Wadleigh has been chosen to film the concerts for Warner Bros., who have acquired the film rights.

Paris, 28 August
Release of Robert Bresson's new film *Une femme douce* (*A Gentle Creature*), based on the short story by Dostoevsky. The film reveals the talent of Dominique Sanda.

Paris, 5 September
Release of Jean-Pierre Melville's *l'Armée des ombres* (*The Army in the Shadows*), drama of the Resistance, adapted from Joseph Kessel's novel and starring Lino Ventura, Simone Signoret and Paul Meurisse.

New York, 29 September
Jerry Lewis held a press conference to announce the creation of his new cinema chain in association with Network Cinema Corp. He hopes to open 750 cinemas by 1974. The first is already under construction.

San Francisco, 14 November
Francis Ford Coppola and George Lucas have founded American Zoetrope. The main aim of the company is "to work with the most talented youngsters in all aspects of the cinema, using the latest in technology."

New York, 18 November
Director Elia Kazan's latest work, *The Arrangement*, with Kirk Douglas, Deborah Kerr and Faye Dunaway, has received scathing reviews from the critics. The screenplay was based on Kazan's own novel.

Paris, 31 December
Industry professionals are worried by the number of cinema closures. They blame the increasing popularity of TV (there are now 9,378,032 sets licensed in France) and also the programming by ORTF of 327 feature films during 1969.

BIRTHS

New York, 18 August
Christian Slater

DEATHS

England, 2 February
Boris Karloff

New York, 5 February
Thelma Ritter

England, 7 February
Eric Portman

Texas, 27 February
John Boles

Hollywood, 8 June
Robert Taylor

London, 22 June
Judy Garland

California, 5 July
Leo McCarey

Norway, 13 October
Sonja Henie

Hollywood, 22 December
Josef von Sternberg

Italian filmmaker Sergio Leone made an international star of Clint Eastwood. He now makes his first American epic, the impressive **Once Upon a Time in the West**.

The 'Lovely War' that both horrifies and amuses

A monument to senseless carnage.

London, 10 April

In his first project as a director, Richard Attenborough has restaged the First World War on Brighton pier. *Oh! What a Lovely War* is an ambitious attempt to translate to the screen Joan Littlewood's history of the 1914-18 conflict. Her Stratford East stage hit combined music-hall songs, diaries and contemporary commentary in a withering attack on the folly of war and the fatuity of the ruling class. Attenborough has retained the basic structure, anchored in a seaside pierrot show, and opened it out to take in the Victorian splendor of Brighton pier along with the rolling hills of Sussex Downs, which stand in for the Western Front. The film is full of small miracles of production design: John Mills' Field Marshal Haig directs the Battle of the Somme from the top of a helter-skelter while the mounting losses are posted on a cricket scoreboard; a member of the representative Smith family, Maurice Roeves, gets on the pier's miniature railway and leaves for the Front; at the end of the film the last surviving Smith boy follows a red tape from the trenches to a room where the Armistice is being signed.

'I'll make a man of every one of you': Maggie Smith entices boys to the call-up.

Some of the searing quality of the original has been smothered by the scale of the production and the roster of stars in cameo roles, among them Ralph Richardson, Laurence Olivier, Dirk Bogarde, Michael and Vanessa Redgrave and, memorably, Maggie Smith as the raddled old soubrette who lures young men on to the music-hall stage and straight into the welcoming arms of the recruiting sergeant.

Maurice Pialat wins the Jean Vigo prize

Paris, 20 March

The Jean Vigo prize has been awarded to the first feature by the documentary director Maurice Pialat for *l'Enfance nue*, made two years ago, and not yet released. Pialat exhibits a superb control of his subject, an examination of childhood, which is never allowed to become sentimental. Played by non-professionals, the film tells the touching story of a 10-year-old boy, abandoned by his mother, and sent to a working-class foster family where his behavior is disturbed. He is then moved to a second family, which proves more successful, though the boy's tendency to lose control of his emotions leads to a crisis. As a distant cousin to *The Four Hundred Blows* and *The Two of Us*, it is therefore not surprising to find that François Truffaut and Claude Berri are two of the film's executive producers.

Katharine Hepburn wins her third Oscar

Los Angeles, 14 April

When Ingrid Bergman unsealed the envelope containing the name of the Best Actress winner at this year's Oscar ceremonies, she exclaimed, "It's a tie!" Barbra Streisand (for her impersonation of the vaudeville queen Fanny Brice in *Funny Girl*), and Katharine Hepburn (for her portrayal of Eleanor of Aquitaine in *The Lion in Winter*) had each obtained exactly the same number of votes. Hepburn thus becomes the first performer ever to win a trio of major Oscars, and her tally of 11 nominations is the highest ever recorded in the Academy's history. The Best Actor award went to Cliff Robertson for his extraordinary performance as the mentally retarded *Charly*. The jolly Dickens musical adaptation, *Oliver!* received both the Best Picture and Best Director (Carol Reed) statuettes.

Michel Tarrizon is the adopted child at the center of Pialat's truthful film.

Mark Lester as Oliver Twist in Best Director Carol Reed's Dickens musical.

The Soviets and the British feature at Cannes

*Malcolm McDowell (center) in Lindsay Anderson's **If**, the major prizewinner.*

*Tarkovsky's **Andrei Rublev** previously banned by the Soviet authorities.*

Cannes, 23 May

Although the prizes at this year's Cannes Film Festival were spread among the British, French, Brazilian, Swedish and American entries, it was a Soviet film that created most interest. Completed in 1966, *Andrei Rublev* has been kept on the shelf by the government of the USSR, who found various pretexts to ban it, one of them being that they felt it was too "dark" for the 50th anniversary of the October Revolution. The film, directed by Andrei Tarkovsky, consists of eight imaginary episodes in the life of Rublev, the 15th-century icon painter, as he journeys through feudal Russia. Faced with the cruelty and horror of what he sees, he abandons speech and his art, until a simple act renews his faith in mankind. This slow, powerful and impressive epic, in black-and-white and CinemaScope, ends with a color sequence which does justice to the paintings.

As for those who took the prizes, the Grand Prix was awarded to Lindsay Anderson's *If*, a vitriolic attack on the British class system which owes much to Jean Vigo's *Zero for Conduct*. Karel Reisz, Anderson's colleague from the days of the Free Cinema movement in the 1950s, was represented by *Isadora*, for which Vanessa Redgrave won the prize for best actress for her role as the celebrated American dancer Isadora Duncan. Jean-Louis Trintignant was chosen as best actor for his portrayal of the honest judge in Costa-Gavras' effective political thriller, *Z*. The *Cinema Novo* from Brazil was acknowledged by the jury, headed by Luchino Visconti, with the best director award given to Glauber Rocha for his baroque *Antonio das Mortes*. The Special Jury Prize went to another film with a political theme, *Adalen 31*. Directed by Bo Widerberg, it concerns a lengthy strike at a paper mill in a small town in the north of Sweden in 1931, which ended with five workers being killed by soldiers. The actor Dennis Hopper gained the prize for a best first feature, *Easy Rider*.

Vanessa Redgrave and Karel Reisz.

Dustin Hoffman's Ratso Rizzo in 'Midnight Cowboy' is a triumph

New York, 25 May

For his role as the unattractive bum Ratso Rizzo in *Midnight Cowboy*, Dustin Hoffman was paid 10 times more than he received for his part in *The Graduate* a couple of years ago. With greasy hair, pallid complexion, bad teeth and gammy leg, he brilliantly represents a man who merges easily into the seedy and sordid atmosphere of New York as conjured up by British director John Schlesinger, making his first American movie. Opposite Hoffman is Jon Voight as a would-be stud. It is the relationship between this big, blond, likable dimwit and the small down-and-outer that is the impressive centerpiece of this comedy-drama.

*Ratso Rizzo (Hoffman) and Joe Buck (Jon Voight, right) in **Midnight Cowboy**.*

Michèle is favorite

Because of her series of *Angélique* films, Michèle Mercier has become one of France's most popular stars. To satisfy her admiring public, she can now be seen in yet another story of Angélique, *The Indomitable Angélique*. It all began in 1964 with *Angélique*, the first of the films based on the books by Serge and Anne Golon, recounting the adventures of a *Forever Amber*-like heroine in the France of Louis XIV. Then *Marvelous Angélique*, *Angélique and the King* and *Angélique and the Sultan* followed. Settings and costumes are colorful and Mlle Mercier pouts prettily throughout.

Sergio Leone takes on America's Old West

Charles Bronson in Sergio Leone's **Once Upon a Time in the West***.*

New York, 28 May
Henry Fonda makes a rare excursion into double-dyed villainy in Sergio Leone's *Once Upon a Time in the West*. The man who became a Western film icon as Marshal Wyatt Earp in John Ford's masterpiece *My Darling Clementine*, has been cast as a cold-eyed killer targeting Claudia Cardinale, a widow locked in battle with the railroad over water rights. Leone's follow-up to his "Dollars" trilogy, co-scripted with Dario Argento and Bernardo Bertolucci, is built around a complex series of references to classic Westerns – *High Noon*, *Shane* and *The Searchers* in the first 15 minutes alone – all of which are couched in Leone's bravura, operatic style. Leone calls this collision of Western stereotypes with the onward march of frontier history a "ballet of the dead." The Monument Valley locations also mark Leone's departure from the Cinecittà origins of his "spaghetti" Westerns. Reportedly, the set for "Flagstone" cost more than the entire budget of *A Fistful of Dollars*. *Once Upon a Time in the West* also boasts the longest credits sequence in the history of the Western. Originally, Leone wanted to say goodbye to his earlier triumphs by killing off Clint Eastwood, Eli Wallach and Lee Van Cleef, the stars of *The Good, the Bad and the Ugly*, at the beginning of the picture, but Eastwood wouldn't play ball.

Liberated woman and shameless Don Juan

Françoise Fabian and Jean-Louis Trintignant in **My Night With Maud***.*

Paris, 7 June
Just opened here is Eric Rohmer's *My Night at Maud's*, the fourth of his Six Moral Tales, and probably his best film to date. This witty, erotic and profound film proves that long intellectual discussions can be as cinematic as more obviously visual material. Set in snowy Clermont-Ferrand, it tells of an engineer and devout Catholic (Jean-Louis Trintignant) who spends a chaste night with the dark, seductive and free-thinking Maud (Françoise Fabian), even though they are mutually attracted. She calls him "a shameless Christian pretending to be a shameless Don Juan."

A dose of decadence from 'The Damned'

New York, 28 May
In his latest film, Luchino Visconti has set out to examine the ideological link between the Nazis and the capitalist bourgeoisie. Entitled *The Damned* (*Gotterdämmerung*), this German-Italian co-production has a fine international cast that includes Ingrid Thulin (Swedish), Dirk Bogarde and Charlotte Rampling (British), Renaud Verley (French), Umberto Orsini (Italian) and Helmut Berger (German). It deals with the conflicts within a powerful family of munitions manufacturers operating in Germany during the rise of Nazism. The film is directed in a flamboyant style, typified by a scene where Berger performs in Dietrich-style drag.

Symphonic violence in 'The Wild Bunch'

Los Angeles, 18 June
Sam Peckinpah's directing career has been in the doldrums since 1965 when he fell out with the producer of *Major Dundee*. Now he has re-established himself with *The Wild Bunch* in which William Holden stars as the aging leader of a band of outlaws driven into Mexico after an unsuccessful bank raid. They are men out of their time. Involvement in the civil war raging between the Mexican army and guerrilla forces leads to a climactic battle against impossible odds in which the gang is wiped out in a burst of sensually filmed and edited violence. It's a brutal but humane film, which confronts head-on the violence which lies at the heart of the Western.

Ingrid Thulin and Dirk Bogarde.

Helmut Berger in decadent drag.

Ernest Borgnine in Sam Peckinpah's unusually violent **The Wild Bunch***.*

Garland's star is tragically extinguished

*In **Babes on Broadway** (1941).*

Judgment at Nuremberg (1961).

London, 27 June
Judy Garland, who died of a drug overdose in London six days ago, was buried today. Her passing at the age of 47 marks the end of a difficult life which encompassed worldwide fame and adulation but was punctuated by nervous breakdowns, suicide attempts, studio suspensions, lawsuits, and five husbands (including Vincente Minnelli). Her fifth, Mickey Deans, was present at the funeral with her daughter, Liza Minnelli. From *The Wizard of Oz* (1939) onwards, she remained uniquely gifted, never more so than in *A Star is Born* (1954), in which she made a comeback after a long rough patch.

Hippie America howls across the screen

Peter Fonda (left) and Dennis Hopper, a defiant generation ill-at-ease.

New York, 14 July
Trailing clouds of glory from the Cannes Festival, where it won the directing prize for Dennis Hopper and Peter Fonda, is *Easy Rider*. Hopper co-stars with producer Fonda as two hippie bikers searching for the "real America" to the strains of a pounding rock soundtrack. Jack Nicholson, a graduate of Roger Corman's Z-budget movie academy, plays the boozy lawyer who comes along for the ride. Hopper's reputation for difficult behavior has, until recently, barred him from most of the studios. Now the majors are scrambling to emulate the sensational success of *Easy Rider*.

Assured debut from Swiss Alain Tanner

*François Simon in **Charles Dead or Alive**, a quality debut from Alain Tanner.*

Switzerland, 1 August
The award of the Grand Prix of the Locarno Film Festival to *Charles Dead or Alive*, the debut feature by the Swiss director Alain Tanner, is a rather late recognition of the emergence of the young Swiss cinema, and promises to wake the national industry out of its lethargy. Tanner, a former TV and documentary director, has been the moving spirit of the movement. *Charles Dead or Alive*, a cruel fable that questions the complacent values of Swiss society, deals with a middle-aged watchmaker (François Simon, Michel Simon's son), who abandons the rat race for a new life.

Sharon Tate killed in horrifying bloodbath

*Tate and Polanski in **The Fearless Vampire Killers** made two years ago.*

Hollywood, 9 August
With Roman Polanski in England preparing a film, his pregnant wife Sharon Tate was killed last night in a particularly shocking manner. She was in her villa in the Hollywood Hills entertaining three guests: the producer Voyteck Freykowsky, his girlfriend Abigail Folger and Jay Sebring, the hair stylist. Nobody knows exactly what happened next. When police arrived this morning they found four mutilated bodies, one of them Sharon Tate, who had been stabbed 15 times and whose breasts had been severed. On the front door, the word "Pigs" had been scrawled in blood.

▷

Newman, Redford: effervescent outlaws

Redford (left) and Newman, two outlaws exhausted from a hard day's work!

Connecticut, 23 September
George Roy Hill's *Butch Cassidy and the Sundance Kid* is not the first screen portrayal of two of the West's legendary outlaws, leaders of the "Hole in the Wall" gang, but it looks like it is the most profitable. Paul Newman and Robert Redford make an attractive Butch and Sundance (whose real name was Harry Longbaugh), laid-back outlaws for whom the West is a playground rather than the killing ground por-trayed by Sam Peckinpah. The film is full of the currently fashionable nostalgia for the passing of the West – "the horse is dead," announces a bicycle salesman – and the use Hill makes of sepia-tinted photographs glows warmly with the light of other days. At the center of the film is the relationship between Newman and Redford, frozen forever in the last frame as they break cover to die at the hands of a small army of Bo-livian soldiers.

Ken Russell unveils 'Women in Love'

Oliver Reed and Glenda Jackson are Lawrence's Gerald and Gudrun.

London, 13 November
Flamboyant director Ken Russell has fashioned a sexually frank and passionate version of D.H. Law-rence's *Women in Love*. This is fa-miliar territory for Russell, who cut his teeth making arts documentaries for British television, and he is well-served by his principal players: Glenda Jackson as the strongwilled Gudrun Brangwen; Alan Bates as the D.H. Lawrence figure Rupert Birkin; and Oliver Reed, radiating bull-like potency as the mine-owner Gerald Crich. His firelit nude wrest-ling match with Bates is one of the highlights of the film.

'Bob and Carol and Ted and Alice'... !

New York, 8 October
Paul Mazursky has made his direct-ing debut with *Bob & Carol & Ted & Alice*, a film which capitalizes on the new wave of permissiveness and the fashionable encounter group philosophy it has spawned. It's at such a group that sophisticated sub-urban swingers Robert Culp and Natalie Wood discover a philosophy of sexual freedom which they then try to sell to their uptight friends Elliott Gould and Dyan Cannon. Mazursky's sharp comedy of man-ners draws excellent performances from the principals, particularly the 30-year-old Gould, who began his career in the chorus line of the stage version of *Irma la Douce*. Broadway stardom arrived when he co-starred with Barbra Streisand in *I Can Get It for You Wholesale*, and he got Streisand wholesale when he mar-ried her in 1963. They divorced last year as her career took off while his seemed stalled. Now movie star-dom beckons for the agreeably self-deprecating actor.

Left to right: Elliott Gould, Natalie Wood, Robert Culp and Dyan Cannon.

Costa-Gavras takes a swipe at the colonels

New York, 8 December
The military regime of the Greek colonels is the target of a new poli-tical thriller, *Z*, shot in Algeria by the Greek-born director Constantin Costa-Gavras who is now a French citizen. Yves Montand, the leader of a pacifist opposition party in an unidentified Mediterranean country (which is clearly Greece), is knocked down by a van and dies after under-going brain surgery. Investigating magistrate Jean-Louis Trintignant treats the case as a murder when he uncovers a government-support-ed conspiracy to assassinate "Z". Based on a novel by Vassili Vassi-likos, *Z* is a virtuoso indictment of the junta now ruling Greece and of the methods applied by totalitarian regimes throughout the world. The son of a Greek bureaucrat, Costa-Gavras left Greece at the age of 18 to pursue a degree in literature at the Sorbonne. After attending the Institut des Hautes Etudes Cinéma-tographiques (IDHEC), he became assistant director to Yves Allégret and René Clément before making his directing debut with *The Sleep-ing Car Murders*, a taut suspenser starring Yves Montand. His second film was *Shock Troops*, a harrowing tale about the French Resistance.

Yves Montand is 'Z' and Irene Papas his wife in Costa-Gavras' film.

'Satyricon' a procession of wild orgies

Josef von Sternberg dies at age 75

Rome, 1 December
Federico Fellini has defined his new work, *Fellini Satyricon*, based on Petronius' ancient Roman fragment and other fables, as more science fictional than historical. "Decadent Rome is as far from me as the

For his **Satyricon**, *Fellini's fertile imagination has turned for inspiration to a decadent period in Rome's past culture.*

Hollywood, 22 December
Josef von Sternberg, one of the great pictorial stylists of the Golden Age of Hollywood, has died in a Hollywood hospital at the age of 75. He was born plain Josef Sternberg in Vienna in 1894 – the "von" was acquired later in Hollywood – and arrived in America with his parents at the age of seven. As a silent film director at Paramount, he quickly created his own artificial world of light and shade filled with strong men and mysterious women. He launched Marlene Dietrich in 1930 in *The Blue Angel*, and in six subsequent films she became the enigmatic centerpiece of Sternberg's obsession with light and composition. Known as a notoriously difficult man to work with, Sternberg once said, "The only way to succeed is to make people hate you. That way they remember you."

moon," the director explained. The picture tells of two students in Rome *circa* A.D. 500, who go their different ways after fighting over a pretty boy. Their separate adventures include drunken orgies, imprisonment on a galley ship and a duel fought with the Minotaur, before they meet up again. The film is really *La Dolce Vita* in Ancient Rome, with Fellini looking with disapproval at the immoral goings-on in a pre-Christian

society, and by implication today's. He emphasizes this connection by casting two unmistakably modern young men in the leading roles: Englishman Martin Potter and American Hiram Keller as Encolpius and Ascyltus, whose sole aim is the pursuit of pleasure. Fellini employed more than 250 character actors and extras and had 90 sets built, making *Satyricon* the most expensive movie made at Cinecittà since *Ben-Hur*.

Dolly years too young but full of bounce

New York, 16 December
Fox have reportedly spent $24 million on filming the smash-hit stage musical, *Hello, Dolly!* They have staked the money on hot star Barbra Streisand, who delivers the goods with exuberance, vivacity, a great line in rapid-fire patter and, of course, that voice. However, it must

be said that as Dolly Levi, matchmaker and self-appointed fixer, in search of a rich husband (Walter Matthau), she is at least 20 years too young for the role, which may disturb some. Terrific entertainment, though, with Gene Kelly directing a first-rate cast and handing the choreography over to Michael Kidd.

The great Italian director at work on what is a visually extraordinary film.

The title number: Dolly Levi is welcomed back at the Harmonia Gardens.

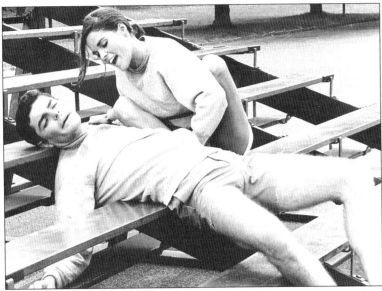

Richard Benjamin and Ali MacGraw in Larry Peerce's **Goodbye, Columbus**.

Mimsy Farmer and Klaus Grumberg in Barbet Schroeder's **More** *(France).*

Hoffman and Voight: memorable.

A small-scale, big impact movie: Dennis Hopper (r) directed **Easy Rider**; *Peter Fonda (l), Jack Nicholson (c) co-starred.*

Belmondo, mail-order bride Deneuve in Truffaut's **The Mississippi Mermaid**.

Peter Schildt in Bo Widerberg's **Adalen 31**, *a strike tragedy from Sweden.*

You never met a pair like Butch and The Kid

They're Taking Trains...
They're Taking Banks
And They're Taking
One Piece Of Baggage!

20th Century-Fox presents

PAUL NEWMAN
ROBERT REDFORD
KATHARINE ROSS

BUTCH CASSIDY AND THE SUNDANCE KID (A)

A George Roy Hill–Paul Monash Production Co-Starring STROTHER MARTIN, JEFF COREY, HENRY JONES.
Executive Producer PAUL MONASH Produced by JOHN FOREMAN Directed by GEORGE ROY HILL Written by WILLIAM GOLDMAN
Music Composed and Conducted by BURT BACHARACH A NEWMAN-FOREMAN Presentation PANAVISION® COLOUR BY DE LUXE

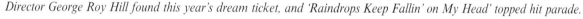
Director George Roy Hill found this year's dream ticket, and 'Raindrops Keep Fallin' on My Head' topped hit parade.

Brigitte Bardot and Xavier Gélin in **The Bear and the Doll** *(France).*

Susannah York in Sydney Pollack's **They Shoot Horses, Don't They?**

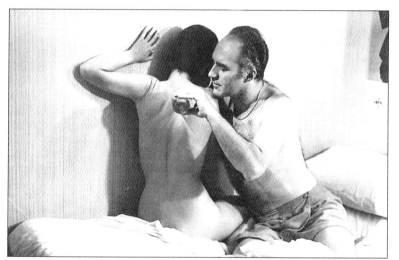
Anita Pallenberg, Michel Piccoli: **Dillinger is Dead** *from Italy's Marco Ferreri.*

Verna Bloom in Haskell Wexler's comment on 60s America, **Medium Cool**.

Michele Lee and Buddy Hackett in (and with!) **The Love Bug**, *from Disney.*

Strange Bedfellows

Though fewer Americans went to the cinema each week in the 1970s than they had done in the three preceding decades, when a movie was released that they really wanted to see, they turned out in greater numbers than ever before. Indeed, the 70s may have produced fewer feature films than at any time in Hollywood's history, but the handful of major hits, such as William Friedkin's *The Exorcist* (1973), George Roy Hill's *The Sting* (1973), Steven Spielberg's *Jaws* (1975) and George Lucas' *Star Wars* (1977) became blockbusters.

The latter grossed more than $164 million in only two years in the U.S. It also began movie merchandizing of spin-off gadgets in earnest, with sales of *Star Wars*-related goods eventually reaching around $1.5 billion per year worldwide. Hits such as the above were able to carry a dozen or so box-office flops. The decline in worldwide audiences leveled out in the decade and, with the sharp increase in ticket prices, total dollar earnings generally kept pace with the costs of production.

As the 70s began, nervous producers, unable to predict what punters would be looking for, set out to replicate some of the trends that had been initiated in the previous decade. For example, after the extraordinary success of Dennis Hopper's seminal road movie *Easy Rider*, and Arthur Penn's Arlo Guthrie-inspired *Alice's Restaurant* (both 1969), a spate of anti-heroic, predominantly youth-oriented films bombarded the market place.

George Lucas' 'coming of age mosaic', *American Graffiti* (1973), which was set in a small town in 1962, made a star of Richard Dreyfuss, and was the best of an impact-making bunch that also included Bob Rafelson's *Five Easy Pieces* (1970), Stuart Hagman's *The Strawberry Statement* (1970), Terrence Malick's *Badlands* (1973), Michael Wadleigh's rock music documentary *Woodstock* (1970) and David and Albert Maysles and Charlotte Zwerin's *Gimme Shelter* (1970), a chilling account of the Altamont Freeway concert by the Rolling Stones that ended in murder.

The cinema's new permissiveness was also luring audiences away from the tamer, more strictly censored fare offered at home on television. Hard-hitting cop movies such as Don Siegel's *Dirty Harry* (1971), Robert Aldrich's *Hustle* (1975) and *The Choirboys* (1977), Roman Polanski's remarkable *noir*-like *Chinatown* (1974), and Friedkin's *The French Connection* (1971) were tough, efficient and uncompromising entertainments that brought out the macho best in actors like Clint Eastwood, Jack Nicholson, Gene Hackman and Burt Reynolds, building up their star status.

Violence also featured prominently (and quite startlingly) in Stanley Kubrick's frightening adaptation of Anthony Burgess' novel *A Clockwork Orange* (1971), Michael Ritchie's *Prime Cut* (1972),

Robert De Niro (l), Harvey Keitel in Martin Scorsese's **Mean Streets** *(1973).*

John Boorman's *Deliverance* (1972), Tobe Hooper's influential *The Texas Chainsaw Massacre* (1974), John Schlesinger's *Marathon Man* (1976) and Alan Parker's disturbing *Midnight Express* (1978).

For the first time in Hollywood's checkered history there was also an outspoken approach to sex, demonstrated in Mike Nichols' *Carnal Knowledge* (1971), Hal Ashby's *Shampoo* (1975) and Louis Malle's first American movie, *Pretty Baby* (1978). From Europe and elsewhere came Just Jaeckin's *Emmanuelle* (1975), Bernardo Bertolucci's *Last Tango in Paris* (1972), Pasolini's *The Decameron* (1971) and *Salo* (1975), Nicholas Roeg's *Don't Look Now* (1973) and Oshima's explicit *In the Realm of the Senses* (1976).

With the Warren Report on the assassination of President Kennedy and the murk that was Watergate, the eternal verities so deeply embodied in the American way of life came into question. If the elected representatives of the country's welfare could no longer be trusted, who could? With no satisfactory answers forthcoming, Americans during the 70s were nervous and insecure about the state of the nation, and saw their fears made manifest in a series of 'conspiracy' movies. These pitted individual integrity and vulnerability against corporate might and political corruption.

Among the best movies which reflected this near-paranoia were Sidney Lumet's *The Anderson Tapes* (1972), Francis Ford Coppola's *The Conversation* (1973), Sydney Pollack's *Three Days of the Condor* (1975), Alan J. Pakula's *The Parallax View* (1974) and *All The President's Men* (1976, directly about Watergate) and James Bridges' *The China Syndrome* (1979), which articulated the unease about the dangers of nuclear power. From Europe came Elio Petri's *Investigation of a Citizen Above Suspicion* (1970), Costa-Gavras' *State of Siege* (1973) and Francesco Rosi's *The Mattei Affair* and *Illustrious Corpses* (1975), proving that corruption was not an exclusively American preserve.

The other major event addressed by American cinema was the Vietnam War – a subject that would prove increasingly fertile and dis-

turbing in the 1980s. The first crop dealt either with the war itself – as in Ted Post's underrated *Go Tell the Spartans* (1978), Sidney J. Furie's *The Boys in Company C* (1978) and Coppola's remarkable *Apocalypse Now* (1979) – or, as in Martin Scorsese's controversial *Taxi Driver* (1976), with the traumatic after-effects on individual soldiers.

Other movies that dealt with the domestic problems of the physically and mentally war-scarred included Jeremy Paul Kagan's *Heroes* (1977), Hal Ashby's *Coming Home* (1978) and Michael Cimino's *The Deer Hunter* (1978). Set before, during and after the war, and, arguably, the finest of the Vietnam movies of the period, this last film drew attention to Meryl Streep, and confirmed Robert De Niro's status as one of the screen's finest actors.

The majority of those people who went to the cinema with any regularity in the 70s were in their teens and early twenties, and, in order to cater to their tastes, the studios turned to a quartet of talented young film-school graduates who would not only dominate the cinema of the decade but that of the 1980s and 90s, and whose films would be among the biggest grossers in the history of motion pictures.

The oldest was Francis Ford Coppola (born 1939), who, in 1969, founded his own (ultimately ill-fated) production company, Zoetrope, and whose two most notable movies in the 70s were *The Godfather* (1972) and *Apocalypse Now*.

George Lucas (born 1944) came to prominence with the influential (and profitable) *American Graffiti*, though its financial returns were as nothing compared with the millions earned by *Star Wars*, the most financially successful movie of the decade, which brought Harrison Ford to prominence, and spawned two equally successful sequels.

The third of the 'movie brats', as they came to be known, was Martin Scorsese (born 1942). After making a handful of independent features, this NYU graduate made his breakthrough with *Mean Streets* (1973), a critically acclaimed drama about young men in Manhattan's Little Italy, which turned De Niro into a star and elevated Harvey Keitel. Scorsese reinforced his reputation as one of the boldest, most exciting young directors of his generation with his 1976 New York-based *Taxi Driver* with De Niro and featuring an adolescent Jodie Foster.

But the most successful of these *wunderkinder* was Steven Spielberg (b. 1947) whose surreal, low-budget, made-for-TV horror picture *Duel* (1971) – in which a businessman on the freeway is terrorized by a behemoth with an invisible driver – led the production company, Universal, to offer him his feature debut in 1974 with the road movie *The Sugarland Express*. He followed this with the phenomenally successful *Jaws* (1975) and, even more of a contrast, *Close Encounters of the Third Kind* (1977), arguably the most intelligent sci-fi film ever.

The radical change that characterized the movies of the 70s was also reflected in the Hollywood musical. Though a large part of the decade saw several Broadway hits – *Fiddler on the Roof* (1971), *Man of La Mancha* (1972), *1776* (1972), *Jesus Christ Superstar (1973), Mame (1974), The Wiz (1979)* – receiving the big screen treatment, director-choreographer Bob Fosse redefined this hitherto escapist genre. He, and screenwriter Jay Presson Allen, did this with a radical adaptation of the long-running Broadway success *Cabaret* (1972), which made a superstar of Liza Minnelli, gave birth to the "adult" musical, and was rewarded with several Oscars.

Fosse explored his own life in *All That Jazz* (1979), the first musical to deal with the subject of death; while Mark Rydell's *The Rose*, in which Bette Midler made an astonishing screen debut, also eschewed escapism for gritty realism in a story loosely based on the life of doomed singer Janis Joplin.

The most commercially successful musicals of the decade, though, were *Saturday Night Fever* (1977) and *Grease* (1978), both starring a newcomer called John Travolta and trend-settingly placing the accent squarely on youth. Another discernible trend in the 70s was the big-budget "disaster" movie such as *Airport* (1970), *The Poseidon Adventure* (1972), *The Towering Inferno* (1974), *Earthquake* (1974), *The Hindenburg* (1975) and *The Swarm* (1978). Martial arts movies also abounded, their chief exponent being Bruce Lee in such actioners as *Fists of Fury* (1972) and *Enter the Dragon* (1973).

In complete contrast were actor-director Woody Allen's sophisticated and hilariously angst-ridden New York movies. The cycle took off with *Annie Hall* in 1977, introducing the most persuasive (and pervasive) strand of Jewish neurosis yet into screen comedy.

This was the decade in which it became clear that producers believed the maxim, if at first you succeed, try, try again. Hence the rash of sequels to hits, among them *The Godfather*, *Airport*, *Star Wars*, *The Exorcist* and *Rocky* (1976).

The European cinema was well represented throughout the 70s, especially by France, some of whose most notable achievements included Eric Rohmer's *Claire's Knee* (1970) and François Truffaut's *Day for Night* (1973). Also from France came Jacques Tati's inventive *Traffic* (1970), Louis Malle's *Lacombe*

*Donald Sutherland, a brutal fascist in Bertolucci's epic **1900** (Italy, 1976).*

Lucien, Claude Chabrol's *Violette* (1977) and Bertrand Blier's *Get Out Your Handkerchiefs* (1977).

Luis Buñuel continued to contribute significantly to world cinema with *The Discreet Charm of the Bourgeoisie* (1972) and *That Obscure Object of Desire* (1977), while the decade saw in the New German Cinema. Its main exponent, Rainer Werner Fassbinder, directed such highly individual films as *The Bitter Tears of Petra von Kant* (1972), *Fear Eats the Soul* (1974), *Effie Briest* (1974) and *The Marriage of Eva Braun* (1978), which made a star of Hanna Schygulla. Also from Germany came Werner Herzog's *Aguirre, The Wrath of God* (1973), *The Enigma of Kaspar Hauser* (1974) and a striking new version

of *Nosferatu* (1979); and Wim Wenders' *Kings of the Road* (1976) and *The American Friend* (1977).

Italy relied largely on its veterans to keep its seriously depressed industry from drowning in mediocrity. The most notable films of the decade were Vittorio·De Sica's *The Garden of the Finzi-Continis* (1971), Fellini's *Roma* (1972), *Amarcord* (1974) and *Casanova* (1976), and Bertolucci's *The Conformist* (1970) and *1900* (1976).

Nor was this a particularly fruitful decade for British cinema which, after the boom period of the 'Swinging Sixties', found itself fighting for its life. The best of British – many of which were produced or directed by Americans – included Schlesinger's *Sunday Bloody Sunday* (1971), Kubrick's *A Clockwork Orange* and *Barry Lyndon* (1975), Melvin Frank's *A Touch of Class* (1973),

Lindsay Anderson's *O Lucky Man!* (1973), Nicolas Roeg's *Don't Look Now* and *The Man Who Fell to Earth* (1976) and Richard Lester's *Robin and Marian* (1976), which brought Audrey Hepburn back to the screen after a nine-year absence.

Like Britain, the Swedish film industry found itself beset with problems (mainly financial). With the exception of Jan Troell's *The Emigrants* (1971) and *The New Land* (1973), it was Ingmar Bergman who, as always, dominated the scene with such complex dramas as *Cries and Whispers* (1972), *Scenes From a Marriage* (1974), his enchanting vision of Mozart's *The Magic Flute* (1975) and *Autumn Sonata* (1978). This last one brought him together, on the only occasion in both their

careers, with his countrywoman and namesake Ingrid Bergman.

The two principal filmmaking countries of Eastern Europe, Poland and Czechoslovakia, were still suffering from the effects of 1968's tumultuous events – the student demonstrations in Poland and the Russian invasion of Czechoslovakia – and the political purges that followed in their wake, and produced little of cinematic value in the 70s.

For signs of renewed hope in the art of cinema, one had to look further afield, mainly to the former French colonies of Africa. Because of increased investment in the film industry, pictures from Senegal, Mali and Mauritania began to appear with success at festivals, and gradually gained an admiring international audience. Directors leading the way were the Senegalese Ousmane Sembene with *Xala* (1974) and *Ceddo* (1976), comedy-dramas that dug deeply into African society, and the Mauritanian Med Hondo, who turned a savage eye on the French colonial past beginning with *Soleil Ô* (1970). There was also a breakthrough for Algerian cinema when director Mohammed Lakhdar-Hamina's 175-minute epic *Chronicle of the Burning Years*, one of the most expensive productions ever to come from the Third World, won the Golden Palm at Cannes in 1975.

Meanwhile, back in Hollywood, Columbia, suffering the worst losses in its history, gave up its long-established Gower Street studio and, as Columbia Pictures Industries Inc., moved to Burbank where it shared facilities with Warner Bros., which had become Warner Communications Inc. Around the same time, MGM sold two of its largest back lots totaling 100 acres and, in October 1973, it ceased to exist as an individual maker and distributor of feature films.

The terminal decline of the studio system and huge diminution of output was symbolized by an event which took place in May 1970. A fabulous auction of thousands of movie props and costumes was held at MGM Studios, the once-proud giant and industry leader. It was reminiscent of the opening scene of *Citizen Kane*, when all the multi-millionaire's goods are put under a hammer. Hollywood, like Xanadu, was being sold off, but it still retained a certain grandeur and its power lingered on.

CLIVE HIRSCHHORN

595

1970

★ ★

1969 Academy Awards, Dorothy Chandler Pavilion, 7 Apr.

Best Film:	*Midnight Cowboy* (dir: John Schlesinger)
Best Director:	John Schlesinger
Best Actor:	John Wayne *(True Grit)*
Best Actress:	Maggie Smith *(The Prime of Miss Jean Brodie)*
Best Supp. Actor:	Gig Young *(They Shoot Horses, Don't They)*
Best Supp. Actress:	Goldie Hawn *(Cactus Flower)*

New York, 11 February
The trade journal *Variety* has revealed that Walt Disney's *Song of the South* (1946) was withdrawn from circulation in 1958 due to the racist attitudes reflected in the roles played by Negroes.

New Jersey, 17 February
Frank Sinatra has been forced to give evidence at a hearing of the State of New Jersey's Commission of Inquiry into Organized Crime. Sinatra, who was questioned about his association with certain well-known members of the Mafia, has denied any contact with the organization. He insists that a misunderstanding arose due to shares he once held in a Las Vegas casino. The actor has been exonerated.

France, 1 March
Jacques Demy has started shooting *Peau-d'ane* (*Donkey Skin* aka *The Magic Donkey*), based on the tale by Charles Perrault, on location at the Château de Chambord. Shooting of this fairytale is next scheduled to move to the castles of Plessis-Bourré and Gambais.

Paris, 9 March
The Armand Tallier prize for the best film book has been won by the Swiss film critic and historian, Freddy Buache for his work *The Italian Cinema from Antonioni to Rosi*, published by The Age of Man.

New York, 23 March
CBS held a demonstration of a color video recording and announced that the first commercial distribution of videotapes would begin next fall. Darryl Zanuck has declared that 20th Century-Fox intends to sell films on videotape five years after their release in cinemas.

New Jersey, 25 March
The first Jerry Lewis cinema opened in Wayne. Lewis, who now plans only 355 cinemas instead of 750, is seeking investors.

Paris, 27 March
An article representing the views of the French "workers party", which appeared in the professional weekly *le Film français*, attacked the "unhealthy nature" of today's French films: "A small group of neurotic intellectuals and film merchants show no hesitation in corrupting our nation and, in particular, our young people."

Denver, 16 April
Jane Fonda slept outdoors and fasted for 36 hours in protest against the war in Vietnam and against John Wayne's film, *The Green Berets*, to the displeasure of her father, Henry Fonda.

Los Angeles, 26 April
The celebrated stripper and burlesque queen of the 30s, Gypsy Rose Lee (Rose Louise Hovick), has died.

Lyon, 23 May
A group of 40 conservationists from the International Federation of Film Archives (FIAF) are working on the problems related to film preservation. High on the agenda is the necessity of raising the awareness of authorities and the public to the importance of restoring and protecting art treasures hidden away in film libraries.

Los Angeles, 15 June
The trial of Charles Manson and five members of his sect opened today. They stand accused of the murder of actress Sharon Tate and four other people on 9 August in Hollywood. They confessed to the "ritual killings" when first arrested last November.

Paris, 20 June
Although François Truffaut denies being a "revolutionary", he has been selling *la Cause du peuple* (*The People's Cause*) on the streets, in the company of Jean-Paul Sartre and Simone de Beauvoir, to uphold the cause of freedom of expression.

Los Angeles, 24 June
Dennis Hopper has started proceedings against Peter Fonda and his Pandro Company. Hopper is asking for 3 percent of the profits of *Easy Rider* as payment for his contribution to the screenplay.

Pakistan, 10 July
Jean-Luc Godard's *Alphaville* has been banned in all cinemas throughout the country.

Paris, 5 August
The first drive-in cinema in the Paris region has opened in Rungis.

London, 7 August
Actor Albert Finney has married French star Anouk Aimée.

Paris, 14 August
Abel Gance has signed a contract with Claude Lelouch for a new release of his reconstructed silent film *Napoleon*, following an unsuccessful attempt in 1968.

New York, 29 August
Paramount's Vice President Stanley Jaffe has been named president, making him, at age 30, the youngest man to hold such a position in the cinema industry.

Los Angeles, 27 August
The Screen Actors Guild has promised to help Chicanos improve their image. Following a meeting between Charlton Heston, Guild president, and representatives from a group called Justice for Chicanos, the Guild resolved to review and demonstrate against films judged demeaning to Mexican-Americans, such as *Butch Cassidy and the Sundance Kid* and *El Condor*, which depict a handful of whites gunning down entire armies of Latin Americans.

Paris, 29 August
Release of *Candy*, a film directed by the actor Christian Marquand from Terry Southern's best-selling novel, with Richard Burton, Marlon Brando, Ringo Starr, Charles Aznavour and John Huston.

Hollywood, 8 September
All the major studios except Fox have started proceedings against ABC and CBS. The television stations have started making their own films, and it is alleged that this is a contravention of the anti-trust law.

Culver City, 5 October
MGM has started selling off its back lot by auction. The third lot of 34 hectares sold for $7.25 million.

Tokyo, 31 October
Release of *Dodes' kaden*, director Akira Kurosawa's first film since 1965, with Yoshitaka Zushi and Junzaburo Ban. The film runs for four hours and is Kurosawa's first to be made in color.

Cleveland, 9 November
Jane Fonda has appeared in court for possession of narcotics. She was arrested on her return from Canada on 3 November. Some see this as another anti-government ploy by the star who has been protesting against racial prejudice in the U.S., the war in Vietnam and the invasion of Cambodia by U.S. troops.

Paris, 12 November
All cinemas are closed today as a sign of respect to General de Gaulle who died on 9 November.

Paris, 7 December
Henri Duchemin, an employee at the Simca factory, has demanded the seizure of Claude Lelouch's film *le Voyou* because one of the characters has the same name as he.

Los Angeles, 31 December
The 10 hits of the year, including *Airport*, *M*A*S*H*, *Patton*, and *Bob & Carol & Ted & Alice*, account for 40 percent of the distributors' total takings for 1970.

BIRTHS

Boston, 29 April
Uma Thurman

DEATHS

Los Angeles, 14 May
Billie Burke

Indiana, 1 August
Frances Farmer

California, 29 September
Edward Everett Horton

Set in Ireland against a background of magnificent seascapes, David Lean brought his characteristic epic sweep to what was essentially a love story during the Irish Rising.

Two heart-throbs join forces in 'Borsalino'

A return to 1930s Marseilles. Alain Delon (left) and Jean-Paul Belmondo.

Paris, 20 March
A recent popularity poll in France placed Alain Delon and Jean-Paul Belmondo in equal first place. Now, for the first time, they are appearing together in the same film, *Borsalino*. The two stars play a couple of petty crooks, who join up and rise in the underworld of 1930s Marseilles until they control all meat supplies.

Delon and Belmondo got on well while making this jaunty, tongue-in-cheek gangster movie. However, their relationship has subsequently deteriorated. As Delon was also the producer of *Borsalino*, his name appears twice on the billboards, much to the chagrin of Belmondo, who intends to sue. It is doubtful we will see them on screen together again.

Theaters rock to the sounds of 'Woodstock'

New York, 26 March
For three days in August 1969, a 600-acre farm in upstate New York was invaded by half a million people who flocked to the Woodstock Festival, a feast of rock music presented on an unprecedented scale. If you didn't make it to Max Yasgur's farm, you can now get something of the flavor of this remarkable event in Michael Wadleigh's documentary account of the great gathering of the tribes of youth culture. With a team of 12 cameramen using 16mm film, Wadleigh shot some 120 hours of film which has been edited down to 184 minutes. There's arresting footage of the festival's once-in-a-lifetime lineup, which included Jimi Hendrix, Joe Cocker, Joan Baez, The Who, Crosby, Stills and Nash, Arlo Guthrie, Santana, Country Joe and the Fish, and Sly and the Family Stone. But Wadleigh also turns the camera's eye on the raggle-taggle army encamped in the mud who came to watch, dance and dream the festival away amid the Purple Haze conjured up by the Jimi Hendrix Experience.

The flower children at Woodstock.

Joe Cocker: one of the top acts.

Unconventional characters win Oscar votes

Los Angeles, 7 April
This year no fewer than 17 stars hosted the Oscars ceremony. In an evening full of surprises, none of the favorites won an award. The Best Picture Oscar went to *Midnight Cowboy*, which also won the Best Director award for John Schlesinger. Maggie Smith was voted Best Actress for her superb performance as the mesmerizing schoolmarm in *The Prime of Miss Jean Brodie*. Thirty years after he played the Ringo Kid in *Stagecoach*, John Wayne received his first Academy Award, that of Best Actor for his warm performance as the boozy lawman Rooster Cogburn in *True Grit*. Costa-Gavras' *Z* was voted the Best Foreign Film.

Costa-Gavras attacks the Czech Stalinists

Paris, 29 April
Because he had closed his eyes to certain crimes committed by communist regimes at the time he was a member of the French Communist Party, Yves Montand has long wanted to atone for his past errors. This explains the conviction with which he threw himself into Costa-Gavras' *The Confession*. After attacking the far Right with enormous success in *Z*, the director has now turned his attention to the Czech Stalinists. Montand plays Artur London, who was arrested, imprisoned and tortured during a political purge in 1951. The true story packs a punch, especially during the interrogation scenes which lead to the false confession of the title.

Maggie Smith as Jean Brodie with a group of her admiring students.

*Yves Montand in the trial scene from **The Confession**, a Stalinist critique.*

Public and critics at Cannes greet Uncle Sam's medics with delight

Mae goes west with Welch in 'Myra'

l to r: Elliott Gould, Robert Duvall and Donald Sutherland in M*A*S*H.

*Florinda Bolkan in Elio Petri's **Investigation of a Citizen Above Suspicion**.*

Cannes, 16 May

Can one make a comedy today out of a situation as tragic as war? The American director Robert Altman has shown it can be done with *M*A*S*H*, a hilarious, iconoclastic, anti-war satire, which has won the Grand Prix at this year's Festival. After he'd directed four forgettable movies, the 45-year-old Altman was then offered *M*A*S*H* because "14 more acceptable directors turned it down." The film has struck a responsive chord with audiences, who see the film's Korean War setting as a reference to Vietnam. It deals with two surgeons (Donald Sutherland, Elliott Gould) at a mobile hospital at the Front, who spend their time chasing women and bucking authority in order to keep themselves sane. The other Festival winners were all Italian: Elio Petri's *Investigation of a Citizen Above Suspicion* (Special Jury Prize); Marcello Mastroianni in *Drama of Jealousy*, and Ottavia Piccolo in *Metello*.

New York, 23 June

Mae West has not made a movie since 1943, although she has not wanted for offers – she was the first on Billy Wilder's list for *Sunset Boulevard*, but was reported to be "insulted" by the notion that she might play mad old movie star Norma Desmond. After all, Miss West was very much alive and kicking. To prove it she has made her long-delayed comeback, at the age of 78, in Fox's version of Gore Vidal's sex-change fantasy, *Myra Breckinridge*, directed by former English pop singer Mike Sarne. Raquel Welch stars as Myra, who was Myron and looked like Rex Reed in a former

Mae, with Raquel Welch (Myra).

20th Century-Fox plunges to all-time low with Russ Meyer feature

Los Angeles, 17 June

In spite of its title, Fox's *Beyond the Valley of the Dolls* has nothing to do with the novel by Jacqueline Susann. It's a sexploitation movie directed by "skin flick" king Russ Meyer, a World War II combat cameraman and former *Playboy* photographer who has made millions out of drive-in fodder like *Faster, Pussycat! Kill! Kill!* featuring lots of sex and violence dealt out by Amazonian women with huge breasts. For years the cheerfully vulgar Meyer has been ridiculed by the Hollywood establishment as a peddler of schlock, but the huge success of his 1968 *Vixen*, which took $5 million in rentals on an investment of $75,000, excited the interest of profit-hungry Fox who let him loose as producer-director on *Beyond the Valley of the Dolls*, which he has co-scripted with film critic Roger Ebert. The result – decidedly less raunchy than Meyer's usual offerings – follows the bizarre adventures of a three-girl rock group called the Carrie Nations as they go in search of fame and fortune in the cynical, scheming and, it would seem, largely bisexual music world of Los Angeles. However, Meyer's particular brand of playful perversity and sense of the surreal (absolutely anything can happen in a Meyer movie and usually does) have been smothered by the size of the budget. Low-rent genius flourishes best when operating on a shoestring.

life, but is now a woman who looks like Marlene Dietrich in *Seven Sinners*. West is a Hollywood agent, surrounded by studs and resembling a faintly blurred version of her old self, although her legendary drawl has survived the passing of the years. Mae's fee of $335,000 for 10 days' work (in addition to writing her own dialogue) was almost certainly worth every penny in publicity to Fox, but the film has emerged as a frightful farrago, stitched together with clips from old Fox movies and torpedoed by Sarne's inexperience. Inevitably, perhaps, a feud developed between its two stars. Raquel Welch was reported to be enraged by West's top billing. But West has had the last laugh. At the New York premiere she was mobbed while the fans ignored Welch.

l to r: Marcia McBroom, Dolly Read and Cynthia Myers in Russ Meyer's movie.

Mixed reception for film of 'Catch 22'

Jack Nicholson drifting in search of himself

Left to right: Austin Pendleton, Orson Welles, Martin Balsam, Buck Henry, Bob Newhart, Norman Fell and Alan Arkin in Mike Nichols' film.

*Middle-class intellectual turned truck driver: Nicholson in **Five Easy Pieces**.*

New York, 24 June
Eighteen years after it was published, Joseph Heller's *Catch-22*, a black comedy set in wartime Italy, has hit the screen. At one point it looked as if it would be filmed by Stanley Kubrick, but the man at the helm of this $10 million Paramount production is Mike Nichols. Alan Arkin heads a starry cast as Yossar-ian, the pacifist American bomber pilot trapped in the coils of military double-think contained in the title and personified by Orson Welles' monstrous General Dreedle. The picture represents a considerable technical triumph for Nichols, but he is only intermittently successful in transferring Heller's bleakly sur-real vision to the screen.

New York, 12 September
Bob Rafelson's *Five Easy Pieces* is a road movie built around the evasive charm of Jack Nicholson. Screen-writer Adrien Joyce has partly fash-ioned the character around the ac-tor's own personality. He is Bobby Dupea, a middle-class drifter who briefly abandons oil-rigging and a sluttish girlfriend (Karen Black) to return to his middle-class, musical family – the title refers to five pieces by Chopin. In the end he forsakes his family, the pregnant Black, and the chance of happiness with Susan Anspach, for the road to Alaska. It's a poignant tale of wasted intelli-gence and American restlessness, and one of the few Hollywood films to explore the theme of class.

James Earl Jones explodes onto the screen

Festival opens with Chahine's new film

New York, 11 October
Howard Sackler's Broadway suc-cess, *The Great White Hope*, comes to the screen directed by Martin Ritt and stars the original leads, James Earl Jones and Jane Alexander. The film is a thinly disguised biopic of the great black boxer Jack Johnson, here called Jefferson. He becomes a sporting hero when, in 1910, he wins the world heavyweight champi-onship. But fame, riches and sport-ing honor are insufficient to keep racism at bay, and he is cruelly hounded for his relationship with his white girlfriend. James Earl Jones' towering central performance is matched by that of striking new-comer Jane Alexander. Their trag-edy is a plea for racial tolerance.

Tunis, 18 October
Most of the African and Arab film-makers and critics gathered at the third "Days at Carthage" Festival, consider Egyptian director Youssef Chahine to be a master. So it was no surprise when loud applause greeted the announcement that the Grand Prix was to be awarded to him for the ensemble of his work. His new film, *The Choice*, which opened the Festival, is a denunciation of the failure of the intellectual elite to take on their social responsibilities. Constructed like a hall of mirrors, which reflects the hero's split per-sonality, it is as far from commercial Egyptian cinema as one can get. Second prize was given to the Syrian film, *Men of the Sun*.

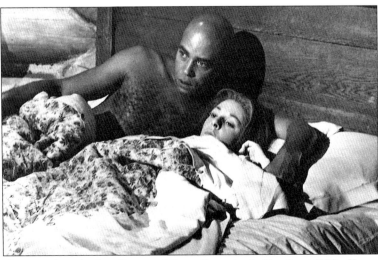

*Crossing the color bar: Jones and Jane Alexander in **The Great White Hope**.*

*Soâd Hussny, Isat El Alâli in **The Choice**, Chahine's impressive new film.*

Sherlock Holmes given new life by Wilder

Robert Stephens as Sherlock Holmes.

New York, 29 October
The Private Life of Sherlock Holmes is an amusing attempt by Billy Wilder, along with his co-writer I.A.L. Diamond, to debunk the legend of Sir Arthur Conan Doyle's famous sleuth. Holmes (played sardonically by Robert Stephens) complains that he only wears the deerstalker and cape and smokes a pipe because the public has come to expect it of him. Happier taking cocaine and playing his violin than solving mysteries, he finds that almost every one of his conclusions are inaccurate. In two unrelated plots, he and Dr. Watson (Colin Blakely) get mixed up with the Russian Ballet and a beautiful German spy (Genevieve Page).

'Love Story' guarantees public a good cry

New York, 16 December
"The death of a beautiful woman is always a poetic subject." So says Paramount executive Robert Evans, who encouraged writer Erich Segal to write the best-selling novel *Love Story* and has now brought it to the screen. It's just an old-fashioned three-handkerchief weepie, with a dash of *Romeo and Juliet*, in which banker's son Ryan O'Neal woos and wins Italian immigrants' daughter Ali MacGraw in the face of parental opposition, only to lose her to a tastefully fatal illness. Everyone's repeating the picture's catchphrase, "Love means never having to say you're sorry."

Ali MacGraw and Ryan O'Neal as Jenny and Oliver in the hit tearjerker.

Rural romance and rebellion from Lean

*Trevor Howard, Sarah Miles and John Mills in Lean's **Ryan's Daughter**.*

London, 9 December
MGM has recently been racked by crisis brought on by the abandonment of Fred Zinnemann's latest project, *Man's Fate*, and the spectacular box-office failure of Antonioni's *Zabriskie Point*. Now the studio is pinning its hopes on David Lean's film, *Ryan's Daughter* – 10 months in the writing and nearly a year in the filming on location on Ireland's Dingle peninsula. Set in 1916, in the time of The Rising, it stars Sarah Miles as the village schoolmistress married to dull Robert Mitchum and falling for British officer Christopher Jones. The film is just as plodding as the Mitchum character. A simple love story has been swollen by Lean's cinematic elephantiasis and cannot be rescued by Freddie Young's superb photography or a wordless performance by John Mills as the village idiot.

Dustin remembers 121 years on earth

New York, 14 December
If one were going to cast anyone in the title role of a movie called *Little Big Man*, there would not be many actors in Hollywood besides Dustin Hoffman who come to mind. It was also inevitable that the actor who seems to epitomize the New Hollywood should work with Arthur Penn, one of the directors most attuned to young audiences. *Little Big Man* continues Penn's preoccupation with the outsider by seeing the Cheyennes as "ethnic" hippies who contrast favorably with white civilization. Hoffman plays Jack Crabb, a 121-year-old survivor of Custer's Last Stand, who reminisces over his long and eventful life. In order to play the old man, Hoffman had to suffer under a 14-piece latex mask, which took five hours a day to apply under the hot makeup lamps. He is brilliantly convincing as the centenarian, as well as managing to look and behave like a very young man when the movie goes into flashback. The plot follows Crabb from the time when, as a 10-year-old white orphan, he is found and adopted by the Cheyenne, and is later made a brave. Penn's film has been seen as an obvious analogy between the treatment of the Indians and the Vietnam War.

Hoffman, a stunning performance.

*Delphine Seyrig, Catherine Deneuve: **Donkey Skin**, Jacques Demy's fairy tale.*

*Pole Jerzy Skolimowski's English film **Deep End** stars Jane Asher.*

*A sad boy and his pet bird: David Bradley in **Kes** (Great Britain).*

*Barbra Streisand is the wacky hooker in **The Owl and the Pussycat**.*

*Fabrice Lucchini with Béatrice Romand (Claire's sister) in **Claire's Knee**.*

*Edy Williams, David Gurian in Russ Meyer's **Beyond the Valley of the Dolls**.*

*Cliff Gorman and his poodle attract glances in **The Boys in the Band**.*

Hilarious army antics, smash-hit.

An amiable, all-black caper.

Expensive, faithful but boring account of Pearl Harbor, seen from both sides.

James Earl Jones is the beleagured champ in **The Great White Hope**.

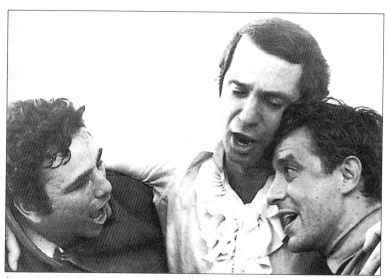

l to r: Peter Falk, Ben Gazzara and John Cassavetes in the latter's **Husbands**.

Hackman makes an unpleasant connection

Gene Hackman has caused a stir as tough cop Popeye Doyle in Friedkin's film.

New York, 8 October
After having dealt with drug traffic in the United States, the American cinema has now turned its attention to the supply route from Europe in *The French Connection*. This tough crime movie, realistically directed by William Friedkin, is based on a true case, and contains an incredibly exciting train chase through New York. As "Popeye" Doyle, the cop who passionately hates all drug pushers, Gene Hackman creates a thoroughly convincing portrait of a crude and violent man, rare in its total lack of concession to audience sympathy. Roy Scheider is perfect as his sidekick.

Subtle treatment of inflammatory subject

*Benoît Ferreux and Lea Massari in **Murmur of the Heart**: forbidden love.*

New York, 17 October
French director Louis Malle's film *Murmur of the Heart* is a triumph of delicacy in dealing with the uncomfortable subject of incest. In truth, the film is about the pains of adolescence as experienced by 15-year-old Laurent (Benoît Ferreux). After an illness leaves him with a heart murmur, his mother (Lea Massari) takes him to a spa. There, each meets with sexual rejection, and their mutual sympathy and love culminates in bed. Set in the context of 1950s middle-class family life, this is a truthful, funny and affectionate work, in which Massari handles her task with exquisite finesse.

'Fiddler' introduces a new star from Israel

New York, 3 November
"If I Were a Rich Man" laments Tevye the Jewish milkman in the best-loved song from *Fiddler on the Roof*, the long-running stage hit about the trials and tribulations of a family who survive the pogroms of pre-revolutionary Russia. Topol, the Israeli actor who created the role in London, will not have to share Tevye's longings. In the film version, just opened here, he is a powerhouse of attractive charm, humor, vitality and passion. In short, a star. Norman Jewison's lumbering film cannot destroy the Jewish jokes, poignant story and appealing music of the original, nor dampen Topol.

Israeli star Topol as Tevye the milkman, dreams of being a rich man.

Clint Eastwood makes his directing debut

New York, 3 November
Clint Eastwood's fruitful collaboration with Don Siegel has produced *Play Misty for Me*, Eastwood's directing debut, in which Siegel plays a small role as a laconic barman. He is a confidant of Clint's laid-back Monterey-based late-night disc jockey who gets more than he bargained for when he has a casual fling with psychotic admirer Jessica Walter. Walter, a highly regarded Broadway actress who makes occasional forays into films, gives a riveting performance as a woman who just won't take no for answer, sliding from edgy infatuation into homicidal hysteria as she stalks her increasingly twitchy prey. Eastwood's portrayal of the beleaguered hero chimes with his recent performance in Siegel's *The Beguiled* in which Geraldine Page amputated one of his legs. In *Play Misty for Me*, Walter threatens to dismember him with a meat cleaver before a well-aimed sock to the jaw sends her floating face-down out to sea to the strains of Errol Garner's title song. Since coming together in *Coogan's Bluff*, Siegel and Eastwood have enjoyed a particularly productive partnership, but it now looks as if the latter's strong, commercial personality will overwhelm his mentor. Eastwood looks as comfortable behind the camera as he does in front of it.

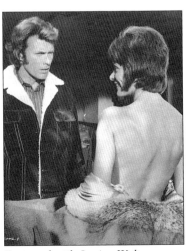

Eastwood with Jessica Walter.

The poison spreads in an Italian garden

Dominique Sanda comforts grandmother Inna Alexeiff before being led away.

Tel Aviv, 2 December
Italian director Vittorio De Sica emerged from a period in the creative wilderness with *The Garden of the Finzi-Continis*, a haunting and tragic testament to Italy's involvement in the Holocaust. Brilliantly cast (Dominique Sanda, Lino Capolicchio, Helmut Berger) and photographed, the film won the Foreign Film Oscar and was voted best at Berlin, before its acclaim in U.S. and European cinemas. However, its opening here has particular emotional resonances for an audience all too familiar with the fate of Jews under Fascism, whose wealth and position offered no protection.

Harold and Maude: a very bizarre affair

New York, 20 December
Safely settled ideas of taste have been disturbed by Hal Ashby's new film *Harold and Maude*, an oddball love affair between death-obsessed 20-year-old Bud Cort and speed-obsessed 80-year-old Ruth Gordon. She lives in a disused railroad car, he stages an hilarious succession of suicide attempts to ruffle the placid feathers of his unflappable mother, Vivian Pickles. Harold and Maude meet at a funeral – they both like attending the last rites of total strangers – and they get married on Ruth's 80th birthday. The screenplay is by Colin Higgins and the score is from rock troubador Cat Stevens. Thirty-five-year-old Ashby hitchhiked to California in his teens and worked his way through the movie business to be an assistant director on several William Wyler and George Stevens pictures. He won an editing Oscar for his work on Norman Jewison's *In the Heat of the Night*, then acted as associate producer on the same director's *The Thomas Crown Affair*, and it was Jewison who gave him his chance to direct. *The Landlord*, made in 1970, was a quirky comedy-drama starring

Bud Cort and Ruth Gordon.

Beau Bridges as the rich kid who buys a Brooklyn tenement intending to turn it into his own home and then, touched by the plight of his tenants, changes his mind.

Stanley Kubrick discomforts with a devastating look at the future

London, 20 December
Stanley Kubrick's latest project, *A Clockwork Orange*, will no doubt shock those who believe in the reassuring prospect of social progress.

Malcolm McDowell in Kubrick's adaptation of the Anthony Burgess novel.

Adapted from the novel by Anthony Burgess, it's a frightening, prophetic vision of a Britain of the future in which roaming gangs of young men have adopted violence as their only way of life. In one sequence, Alex (Malcolm McDowell), a brutal teenage hood, the head of the band of Droods, beats a woman to death with a giant phallic sculpture. Sent to prison for murder, Alex becomes a guinea pig in a rehabilitation program based on aversion therapy, and emerges having lost his soul. The film's controversial message seems to be that free will and individuality must be preserved at any cost. The violence, though explicitly shown, is given a stylized unreality, mainly through the use of music, such as the voice of Gene Kelly crooning "Singin' in the Rain" while the gang beat up an old tramp, or the choral movement from Beethoven's Ninth which becomes Alex's stimulation to sadistic pleasures. Kubrick also makes stunning use of color – harsh and glossy for the first part of the film, muted and more naturalistic after Alex has been brainwashed. Malcolm McDowell is remarkable as an inverted Candide, seemingly irredeemably amoral.

Clint Eastwood is *Dirty Harry*, a tough San Francisco cop as brutal as the psycho criminals he nails – except that he's on the right side of the law. Don Siegel's film is stylish, ambiguous and violent; Eastwood is compelling.

Left to right: John Cleese, Eric Idle and Graham Chapman in **...And Now for Something Completely Different** (Monty Python).

Gian Maria Volonte in Francesco Rosi's **The Mattei Affair** (Italy).

Jon Voight and Ned Beatty in John Boorman's **Deliverance**.

Paul Winfield, Kevin Hooks and the title hound **Sounder**.

Pier Paolo Pasolini in his film of **The Canterbury Tales**.

A suitably stark and somber ad.

Malcolm Tierney, Sandy Ratcliffe in **Family Life**: attacking British psychiatry.

Paul Morrissey's **Heat** for Andy Warhol: Sylvia Miles and Joe Dallesandro.

Michael Caine and Laurence Olivier in Joseph Mankiewicz's cunning **Sleuth**.

Animator Ralph Bakshi wrote and made his first feature, **Fritz the Cat**.

Scatman Crothers (left) and Jack Nicholson in **The King of Marvin Gardens**.

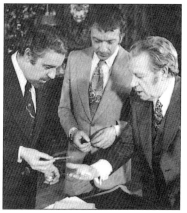

Fernando Rey (left) in **The Discreet Charm of the Bourgeoisie**.

Diana Ross is singer Billie Holliday in **Lady Sings the Blues**.

Barry Foster is the psychopath in Hitchcock's British film **Frenzy**.

Gian Maria Volonte (l), Jean-Louis Trintignant in Boisset's **l'Attentat (Plot)**.

1973

★ ★

1972 Academy Awards, Dorothy Chandler Pavilion, 27 Mar.

Best Film:	*The Godfather* (dir: Francis Ford Coppola)
Best Director:	Bob Fosse *(Cabaret)*
Best Actor:	Marlon Brando *(The Godfather)*
Best Actress:	Liza Minnelli *(Cabaret)*
Best Supp. Actor:	Joel Grey *(Cabaret)*
Best Supp. Actress:	Eileen Heckart *(Butterflies Are Free)*

Hollywood, 7 January
Paramount is celebrating its founder Adolph Zukor's 100th birthday. Over a thousand people have been invited to a party in his honor. The estimated cost of the reception is $100,000.

Paris, 14 January
The 30th Louis Delluc Prize has been awarded to Costa-Gavras for *State of Siege*, with Yves Montand, a political film dealing with CIA involvement in Latin America.

Malibu, 19 January
Jane Fonda has married political activist Tom Hayden.

Rome, 2 February
A Bologna criminal court today lifted a ban on *Last Tango in Paris*, and acquitted the director of the film, Bernardo Bertolucci, its stars Marlon Brando and Maria Schneider and two others of obscenity charges. The trial started on 15 December, and on 21 December the movie was seized throughout Italy on orders from a deputy prosecutor in Rome. Bertolucci welcomed the news not just for the film but "for the freedom of expression in Italy."

Los Angeles, 31 March
The American Film Institute has honored John Ford with its Lifetime Achievement Award. President Nixon attended the ceremony and personally handed the Liberty medal, the country's highest civil award, to the film director.

Washington D.C., 6 April
The American Institute's inaugural film festival was marred by confusion and charges of censorship. Only hours before the opening a New York distributor announced that a third of the films scheduled were to be withheld as a protest against the withdrawal of Constantin Costa-Gavras' picture *State of Siege*. New York film critics have harshly criticized the affair.

San Diego, 21 April
Pioneer Merian C. Cooper, who, with Ernest B. Schoedsack, directed exotic adventure films including the memorable *King Kong*, has died.

New York, 24 April
Jerry Lewis has removed his backing from the Network Cinema group (about 200 cinemas) due to its serious financial difficulties. He blames the failure on a lack of suitable films for general viewing.

Stockholm, 25 April
Ingmar Bergman's *Cries and Whispers* (*Viskningar och Rop*), released here last month, is set to be picked up for international release.

New York, 10 May
Abel Green, the chief editor of the weekly show-biz bible *Variety*, has died at the age of 72.

Rhode Island, 6 June
Jack Clayton has started filming *The Great Gatsby*, based on the novel by F. Scott Fitzgerald and starring Robert Redford and Mia Farrow.

New York, 12 June
Marlon Brando let fly with his fists in anger at a photographer who was annoying him, and broke his jaw. Brando himself had to be hospitalized with a swollen hand.

Washington D.C., 21 June
The Supreme Court has voted in a decision (six to three) which drastically modifies its previous attitude toward pornography. Henceforth, it will be left to the state governments to decide what constitutes obscenity and whether a film should be protected by the First Amendment of the Constitution.

Hollywood, 24 June
Seventy percent of Screen Writers Guild members have voted to end the strike which started on 7 March, bringing to an end the longest strike in the history of Hollywood.

New York, 3 July
A spokesman for Richard Burton and Elizabeth Taylor has announced that the couple have decided to separate, despite numerous attempts at a reconciliation.

Cairo, 4 July
The opening of Salah Abou Seif's film *The Baths of Malatili* (*Hammam el Malatili*), has caused a sensation because of its author's daring exploration of all forms of sexuality.

New Jersey, 4 July
Georgina Spelvin, star of the erotic film *The Devil in Miss Jones*, has been arrested. She was making a promotional visit to a cinema showing her film.

New York, 25 July
Alan Hirschfield, one of Herbert Allen's protégés, has replaced Leo Jaffe as president of Columbia Pictures Industries. Jaffe has become chairman of the company's board of directors.

Hollywood, 28 September
Metro-Goldwyn-Mayer's lion is not roaring as loudly under James T. Aubrey Jr.'s new streamlined regime as it did in the old Louis B. Mayer days. But Leo still intends to be heard from for the next 10 years under a new distribution deal with United Artists. The deal includes distribution to movie theaters and TV syndication. Distribution fees are confidential, but UA have also agreed to purchase MGM's Robbins, Feist and Miller music publishing company and its half interest in Quality Records of Canada for about $15 million.

New York, 31 October
Release of the American Film Theater's first production, *The Iceman Cometh*, a film version of Eugene O'Neill's play directed by John Frankenheimer, with Lee Marvin, Robert Ryan and Fredric March. Ely Landau founded the AFT with the idea of producing film adaptations of American theater classics.

Paris, 30 November
A tax inspector, Edouard Dega, has been accused of laxity in dealing with certain taxpayers, including the film directors Bernard Borderie and Alain Cavalier, who have been under investigation.

Las Vegas, 5 December
Inauguration of the MGM-financed MGM Grand, the biggest hotel and casino complex in the U.S.

London, 7 December
Technicolor is reported to have sold a film processing lab to Communist China for around $7 million.

New York, 19 December
American premiere of Charlie Chaplin's *A King in New York*. Chaplin had always refused to release the film in the U.S. (it came out in Europe in 1957) until last year's reconciliation.

DEATHS

Hollywood, 26 February
Edward G. Robinson

Switzerland, 10 March
Robert Siodmak

Jamaica, 26 March
Noel Coward

California, 2 July
Betty Grable

Vermont, 7 July
Veronica Lake

New York, 11 July
Robert Ryan

London, 18 July
Jack Hawkins

Hong Kong, 20 July
Bruce Lee

California, 31 August
John Ford

Rome, 26 September
Anna Magnani

Tokyo, 23 November
Sessue Hayakawa

London, 25 November
Laurence Harvey

Los Angeles, 20 December
Bobby Darin

Director George Roy Hill re-teamed the smash-hit duo of Newman and Redford in **The Sting**. *This engaging tale of two 30s con-men ended up walking away with seven Oscars.*

PAUL NEWMAN · ROBERT REDFORD
ROBERT SHAW

IN A BILL/PHILLIPS PRODUCTION OF
A GEORGE ROY HILL FILM

THE STING

A RICHARD D. ZANUCK/DAVID BROWN PRESENTATION

...all it takes is a little Confidence.

Written by	Directed by		Produced by
DAVID S. WARD ·	GEORGE ROY HILL ·	TONY BILL, MICHAEL	and JULIA PHILLIPS

Music Adapted by MARVIN HAMLISCH · A UNIVERSAL PICTURE · TECHNICOLOR®   ORIGINAL SOUNDTRACK AVAILABLE EXCLUSIVELY ON MCA RECORDS AND TAPES   PG PARENTAL GUIDANCE SUGGESTED

74 / 8

Werner Herzog in the heart of Eldorado

Klaus Kinski in Aguirre, the Wrath of God, Herzog's mythic adventure.

Paris, 5 January

With *Aguirre, Wrath of God*, the German director Werner Herzog has offered us a spectacle far from his earlier experimental films. Inspired by the insane exploits of 16th-century conquistador Don Lope de Aguirre, who led a hazardous expedition through the wilds of Peru in search of El Dorado, the film does not attempt a mere historical reconstruction. Herzog, through the delirium of his hero, wishes to reveal, not the story of conquest, but the fevered fascination of the lure of gold and of power. The final shot, an aerial view of a lone survivor on a raft, is masterly. Like his protagonist, Herzog had to overcome extremely difficult conditions during the shoot in the Peruvian Andes. He made the film in six weeks at extraordinary risk to the lives of his cast and crew. The director also had problems dealing with Klaus Kinski, whose intense performance in the title role is one of the great strengths of the film. Kinski, a temperamental man, often threatened to abandon the whole project.

The fantastic found in the snow of Avoriaz

Avoriaz, 11 February

The ski resort of Avoriaz in the French Alps has been invaded by a very different type of tourist from the usual. For the last 12 days, fans have been gathering for the first International Festival of Horror and Fantasy Films, initiated by journalist and publicist Lionel Chouchan. The jury, headed by director René Clément, has given the first prize to an American film, *Duel*, made for television by a talented young director named Steven Spielberg. Written by Richard Matheson, adapting his own novel, it is an immensely effective man vs. machine thriller about a salesman driving along a highway who gradually realizes he is being chased across the country by a huge and menacing truck, the driver of which is never seen. The Special Jury Prize went to *Themroc*, an extremely strange French film directed by Claude Faraldo, in which the characters communicate only in a series of formless noises. It tells of a factory worker, living in a squalid apartment, who suddenly rebels, causing anarchy.

Dennis Weaver in Duel, a terrifying allegory made for TV by Steven Spielberg.

Luchino Visconti completes his trilogy of 'German decadence'

Rome, 18 January

As a Marxist, Luchino Visconti should, in principle, be dedicated to the destruction of the class and culture he represents, and yet it is bourgeois European art that attracts him most – Mahler, Bruckner, Lampedusa, Thomas Mann, Wagner... He is both repelled by and drawn to the decaying society that he depicts in such impressively loving detail. Visconti's latest film, *Ludwig*, which completes his trilogy of "German decadence", following *The Damned* and *Death in Venice*, is no exception. This long (186 minutes) and unhurried look at the life and premature death of Ludwig II of Bavaria, revels in the Bavarian locations and castles, and the costumes and manners of the mid to late 19th century. Helmut Berger, who has gained the nickname Ham Berger, is excellent in the title role, and looks uncannily like the tortured king. He ages convincingly from the young Ludwig who ascends the throne to the 41-year-old madman who drowns himself. Naturally, much of the film is taken up with Ludwig's patronage of Richard Wagner (Trevor Howard), and his platonic relationship with his beautiful cousin, Elizabeth of Austria (Romy Schneider).

Romy Schneider, with Helmut Berger as King Ludwig, in Visconti's film.

Sissi exorcised

Italy, 18 January

While still in her teens, during the mid-1950s, Romy Schneider became the most popular young star of the German-speaking world as "Sissi", the future Empress Elizabeth, in three romantic and sentimental films about the Austro-Hungarian royal family. Usually shown cut together in the U.S. as one movie under the title *Forever My Love*, they are part-operetta, part-Hollywood style biopic. The role of "Sissi" has haunted Romy ever since, and is one which she has always mocked. Therefore, it took some convincing on Luchino Visconti's part to persuade the lovely star to reprise the role in *Ludwig*, this time as a more mature and cynical Empress, cousin to the King of Bavaria, in a very different kind of film.

'Deep Throat' has to swallow a heavy fine

New York, 1 March
As expected, a New York court has judged the sexploitation movie *Deep Throat* to be obscene. A stiff fine has been imposed – twice the picture's box-office receipts. This judgment follows action taken against *Deep Throat* in a number of cities, notably in Miami and Toledo, Ohio, where it was seized by police on the day it was released. Directed by Gérard Damanio, *Deep Throat* follows the erotic adventures of a young woman, Linda Lovelace, who discovers that one of her most important erogenous zones, her clitoris no less, is located in her throat. This unique medical condition leads to a feast of fellatio. Released in New York last June in a Times Square theater that specializes in such fare, *Deep Throat* enjoyed such a phenomenal success that, like *The Devil and Miss Jones*, it transferred to an East Side art

Linda Lovelace, the protagonist.

house. It is, indeed, rarely that a film of a pornographic nature manages to escape from the low-rent ghettos to which such movies are normally confined.

'Godfather' Marlon's message to Indians

Los Angeles, 27 March
Francis Ford Coppola's *The Godfather* has been voted Best Picture at this year's Oscar ceremony at Los Angeles Music Center. Marlon Brando won the Best Actor award for his performance in the same movie. This was no surprise, but his reaction certainly was. The star did not attend the ceremony. In his place he sent an Indian girl called Sasheen Littlefeather (in reality an actress named Maria Cruz). Littlefeather read out a statement from Brando accusing the motion picture industry of "degrading the Indian and making a mockery of his character." It seems you can't even give Oscars away these days. This year's Best Actress was Liza Minnelli for her performance in *Cabaret*, which won seven other Oscars, including Best Supporting Actor (Joel Grey), Director (Bob Fosse) and Cine-

Fernando Rey in Buñuel's **The Discreet Charm of the Bourgeoisie**.

matography (Geoffrey Unsworth). Best Supporting Actress was Eileen Heckart for *Butterflies Are Free* and Best Foreign Film was *The Discreet Charm of the Bourgeoisie*.

Marriage put under Bergman's microscope

Liv Ullmann and Erland Josephson are the couple in **Scenes From a Marriage**.

Stockholm, 11 April
Ingmar Bergman began working for television around the mid-1960s, a medium which he found stimulated his imagination. His latest TV production is a series consisting of six 50-minute episodes, collectively titled *Scenes From a Marriage*. It analyses the traumatic breakup of the 10-year marriage between Marianne (Liv Ullmann) and her husband Johan (Erland Josephson), who is seriously involved with a younger woman (Bibi Andersson).

The rupture is painful for both, and each of them deals with it in a different way. The years pass, but they seem closer than ever since the divorce. Played largely in close-up, it creates a claustrophobic, hermetically-sealed atmosphere, while the terse exchanges and bitter silences convey a sense of bleak aridity in the beleaguered marriage. Though depressing, it is undeniably absorbing, with the director's style everywhere evident, especially in the sensitive handling of his accomplished cast.

This Ryan's daughter steals the show

New York, 16 May
Cheerfully ignoring the old theatrical warning to avoid acting with dogs or children, Ryan O'Neal has embarked on a movie which co-stars his *own* daughter Tatum. In *Paper Moon*, directed by Peter Bogdanovich, he plays a Bible-selling con man in Depression-era Kansas who falls in with a sassy, cigarette-smoking little girl who proves to be as sharp, if not sharper, than he is.

It's a variation on the relationship between Charlie Chaplin and Jackie Coogan in *The Kid*, and while not quite in that class, *Paper Moon* nevertheless threatens to be a runaway hit. Inevitably, Tatum O'Neal steals the show as the self-possessed nine-year-old who succumbs to childish jealousy when grown-up girl Madeline Kahn (superb) comes along for the ride. She's already being tipped for an Oscar nomination.

Little Tatum O'Neal practically eclipses her daddy, Ryan, in **Paper Moon**.

The Cannes Festival is rocked by controversy

*Jean-Pierre Léaud, Françoise Lebrun and Bernadette Lafont in **The Mother and the Whore**. Jean Eustache's film won the Special Jury Prize.*

*Andrea Ferreol and Michel Piccoli in Marco Ferreri's **la Grande bouffe**.*

Cannes, 25 May

When they chose Jean Eustache's film *The Mother and the Whore* and Marco Ferreri's work *Blow-Out* (*la Grande bouffe*) to represent France at this year's Cannes Festival, the selection committee could not have foreseen the furor that would ensue. Eustache's work provoked loud protests during and after the screening, primarily because of its crude dialogue. The director was almost physically assaulted when he exited the auditorium with Jeanne Moreau, who had taken his arm in friendship. The 215-minute film of a *ménage à trois* is witty, verbose and erotic, and consists mainly of monologues, conversations and confessions. The showing of *Blow-Out* was the last straw. This story of four middle-

*Gene Hackman and Al Pacino in Jerry Schatzberg's **Scarecrow**.*

aged men literally eating themselves to death, seems to have offended the defenders of good taste, morality and national pride, and there were cries of "Nauseating! Disgusting!" during the film.

As if all this were not enough, Robert Bresson was furious that his picture, *Lancelot of the Lake*, was not selected in competition. He declared: "The Cannes Festival has sunk deep into mediocrity and error." After Bresson's film received almost as noisy a reception as those of Eustache and Ferreri, Michel Piccoli, one of the stars of *Blow-Out*, acted as spokesman for the director. "Monsieur Robert Bresson, in accord with his producers and the Society of French Directors, has decided not to show *Lancelot of the*

Lake this evening. Out of respect for the jury and the public, he would like to reverse his decision, but he wishes to express his indignation at the conditions under which the Festival is taking place. The spirit that reigns over the selection and the organization of the Festival seems to him to be contrary to the best ideals of cinema." The selectors explained that they wanted to make the Festival an "event", and chose French films which are "daring and original". This has gone beyond their wildest dreams, because the French entries have eclipsed all others, even the two films that shared the Grand Prix – Jerry Schatzberg's *Scarecrow* and Alan Bridges' *The Hireling*, American and British productions respectively.

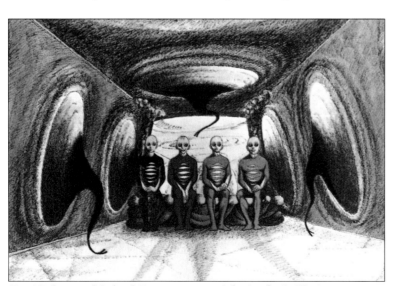

*René Laloux and Roland Topor won a special prize for **la Planète sauvage**.*

The jury on the terrace of the Palais surround their president, Ingrid Bergman.

Anglo-American relations a real romp

George Segal tries to teach Glenda Jackson baseball in London's Hyde Park.

London, 24 May
George Segal and Glenda Jackson strike sparks in *A Touch of Class*. He's the married executive who whisks prim Jackson off to Spain for a bit of sun and sex but finds her more than a mite quarrelsome. *A Touch of Class* harks back to many

an older, and better, movie in which a meeting cute is followed by a long battle before the final clinch and fade-out. Segal dispenses lots of shaggy charm as the besotted businessman, dislocating his back in bed, but Jackson, essaying her first film comedy, is far too shrill.

Sixties America revisited by George Lucas

Los Angeles, 5 August
The second feature from 29-year-old George Lucas, *American Graffiti*, is a dreamy vision of adolescent life in a small Californian town in 1962, before Vietnam and the drug scene; a time of comparative innocence. Using the rock 'n' roll hits of the period on the soundtrack and with

brilliant hyper-realist photography, the movie creates a finger-lickin' golden past. It also draws on memories of teen-pix of the 1950s, on which the director grew up. The refreshing little-known cast includes Richard Dreyfuss, Ronny Howard, Paul Le Mat, Cindy Williams, Candy Clark and Harrison Ford.

*Paul Le Mat (left), Cindy Williams and Ronny Howard in **American Graffiti**.*

François Truffaut's tribute to filmmaking

Paris, 24 May
It was while cutting *Two English Girls* (aka *Anne and Muriel*) at the Victorine Studios in Nice, that François Truffaut got the idea for his new film, *Day for Night*. The sight of the decor for *The Mad Woman of Chaillot*, Bryan Forbes' British film, awoke his desire to make a film about making a film. The screenplay revolves around the shooting of a melodrama called "Meet Pamela", during which the juvenile lead (Jean-Pierre Léaud) falls hopelessly in love with the married international star (Jacqueline Bisset); an Italian actress (Valentina Cortese) keeps forgetting her lines; the male lead (Jean-Pierre Aumont) is killed in an automobile crash; time and money begin to run out; and someone has a baby.

*Dani and Jean-Pierre Léaud in **Day for Night**. Truth or fiction?*

"Are films more important than life?" Léaud asks at one stage. Truffaut, himself playing the director called Ferrand, answers in the affirmative. Despite all the difficulties it reveals, *Day for Night* is an exuberant celebration of filmmaking. Never before have the atmosphere and techniques of filming been so lovingly and vividly presented. The title itself is a term for simulating night by the use of filters in daylight. We see how crowd scenes are organized, how crane and tracking shots are set up, dialogue agreed, actors and actresses encouraged and placated, props gathered and stunt work carried out. In one sequence, derived from his own *la Peau douce* (*The Soft Skin*), Truffaut shows the

problems of introducing animals into a film, by using a stubborn kitten. *Day for Night* also wittily explores the relationship between the audience and the film-within-a-film. Georges Delerue's cod baroque music adds vitality to the already springy editing. The movie abounds with references to other films, directors and books (the novelist Graham Greene appears in an uncredited bit part as a money man), and special tribute is paid to Hollywood – the film is dedicated to the Gish sisters, and Truffaut-Ferrand dreams of stealing stills of *Citizen Kane* from outside a movie theater. Truffaut is at the center, soothing everyone from the stars to the continuity girl, and communicating his enthusiasm.

Director Truffaut (right) with Jean-Pierre Aumont and Jacqueline Bisset.

Bob and Barbra act out thirty years of nostalgia

New York, 17 October
Barbra Streisand and Robert Redford are an unlikely pairing in Sydney Pollack's *The Way We Were*, a romantic drama set against three decades of American political history. She's a left-wing activist and he's a Waspish literary type who meet, marry and divorce as the Second World War gives way to the Cold War and the menace of McCarthyism. The screenplay is by Arthur Laurents, who lived through the days of fear and betrayal in Hollywood in the early 50s. However, director Pollack has been quick to reassure moviegoers that the film is a romance rather than a political tract, adding, "but I hope that audiences also ponder some of the movie's serious undertones." Redford gracefully plays second fiddle to Streisand, who apparently insisted on some of his scenes being cut. The film features a strong and haunting title song, belted out by Streisand.

Barbra Streisand as the young, left-wing idealist in the early sequences.

Robert Redford as the screenwriter with Barbra Streisand as the girl he marries.

Eight-year-old Ana Torrent as the lonely little girl in Victor Erice's impressive debut film, *The Spirit of the Beehive*. Her wide brown eyes reflect the world of her imagination, in which most of the film's events take place, especially centered on her obsession with Boris Karloff's good-bad monster in the film of *Frankenstein*.

Film colony loses major figures

California, 31 August
It has been a black summer for the film world with the announcements of the deaths of Betty Grable, Veronica Lake, Robert Ryan and Bruce Lee. Martial arts star Lee died on 15 July, aged only 33. Three weeks ago, French director Jean-Pierre Melville died in his mid-50s. Born Jean-Pierre Grumbach, he changed his name because of his fondness for the great American writer Herman Melville. But it was the American gangster novel and *film noir* that were the main influences on his films. Now today, John Ford has died of cancer at Palm Desert, his Californian ranch. Arguably the greatest American-born Hollywood director, Ford was known principally for raising the Western to artistic status, starting with *Stagecoach* (1939). But it was for non-Westerns that he won his four directing Oscars: *The Informer*, *The Grapes of Wrath*, *How Green Was My Valley* and *The Quiet Man*.

The brilliant French filmmaker, Jean-Pierre Melville: a loss.

Bardot says her farewells to the screen

L'Histoire très bonne et très joyeuse de Colinot Trousse-chemise.

Paris, 25 October
On the release of her latest film, *l'Histoire très bonne et très joyeuse de Colinot Trousse-chemise*, Brigitte Bardot has announced her retirement from the screen, soon after having celebrated her 39th birthday. She reached the decision because of the recent failure of *Don Juan 73 or If Don Juan Were a Woman*, directed by her ex-husband Roger Vadim.

She told a magazine: "I've made 48 films of which only five were good. The rest are not worth anything. I will not make another, and I will never visit a plastic surgeon." One of the great beauties of the cinema, she has refused to allow herself to be seen aging on screen. In fact, Bardot never really enjoyed acting, and will now be able to devote her time to the cause of animal welfare.

Pacino superb in police corruption drama

*Sidney Lumet's **Serpico** stars Al Pacino, here in uniform and undercover.*

New York, 5 December
Al Pacino, recently seen to such good effect in *The Godfather*, which gained him an Oscar nomination for Best Supporting Actor, takes the title role in *Serpico*. It's based on the true story of a brave New York cop whose revelations in 1970 of institutionalized corruption rocked the police establishment to the core. In his role as the whistle-blowing cop, Pacino deftly subverts the tepid realism of director Sidney Lumet with an idiosyncratic portrait of a loner, isolated from his comrades by his incorruptibility and turning into a maddeningly modish hippie with beard, bobble hat and Old English sheepdog in tow. Man and dog survive the film, which was pacily scripted by Norman Wexler and Waldo Salt from Peter Maas' biography.

Brutality of prison life on Devil's Island

New York, 17 December
The semi-autobiographical bestseller by Frenchman Henri Charrière, *Papillon*, has been made into a $13 million Hollywood movie directed by Franklin J. Schaffner. This paean of praise to survival stars Steve McQueen as the convict determined to escape from Devil's Island where he has been sentenced to life imprisonment, and Dustin Hoffman as his feeble, thickly bespectacled friend. The suffering of the prisoners is particularly well depicted.

*Steve McQueen and Dustin Hoffman in Franklin J. Schaffner's **Papillon**.*

Ludicrous horror pic pulls out all the stops

Los Angeles, 26 December
Twelve-year old Linda Blair is the child of every parent's nightmare in *The Exorcist*, vomiting jets of green bile over a priest and masturbating with a crucifix. William Friedkin's messy parable of demonic possession is packed with startling effects, not least the chilling moment when, almost subliminally, one realizes that Blair's head has turned around way beyond human limits. The demon's mocking voice was provided by Mercedes McCambridge.

Max Von Sydow, the exorcist of the title, with distraught mother Ellen Burstyn.

*Tom Laughlin as half-breed **Billy Jack**. Huge at the box office.*

*Edward Fox (left) and Cyril Cusack: **The Day of the Jackal**.*

*Joe Don Baker (right) in **Walking Tall**, the true story of a vigilante.*

*From France, Roland Topor and René Laloux's animated **la Planète sauvage**.*

***Enter the Dragon**: a new kind of actioner based on Kung Fu, with Bruce Lee.*

*Eustache's **The Mother and the Whore**: Jean-Pierre Léaud, Bernadette Lafont.*

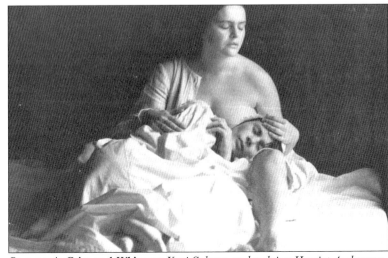

*Bergman's **Cries and Whispers**: Kari Sylwan and a dying Harriet Andersson.*

l to r: Randy Quaid, Otis Young, Jack Nicholson in Ashby's **The Last Detail**.

Jane Fonda as Nora in Joseph Losey's version of Ibsen's **A Doll's House**.

Max Von Sydow (left) and Jason Miller in William Friedkin's **The Exorcist**.

Andréa Ferreol, Marcello Mastroianni: **la Grande bouffe (Blow Out)**.

Marcello Mastroianni with Sophia Loren in **The Priest's Wife**.

Helmut Berger as the mad Bavarian king, with Romy Schneider in **Ludwig**.

Robert Shaw, Robert Redford, Paul Newman in George Roy Hill's **The Sting**.

★ ★ ★ ★ ★ ★ ★ ★ 1974 ★

1973 Academy Awards, Dorothy Chandler Pavilion, 2 Apr.

Best Film:	*The Sting* (dir: George Roy Hill)
Best Director:	George Roy Hill
Best Actor:	Jack Lemmon *(Save the Tiger)*
Best Actress:	Glenda Jackson *(A Touch of Class)*
Best Supp. Actor:	John Houseman *(The Paper Chase)*
Best Supp. Actress:	Tatum O'Neal *(Paper Moon)*

Paris, 10 January
The Communist Deputy Jack Ralite protested in the National Assembly about the meager share of the state budget (0.049 percent) allocated to the French film industry.

Mexico, 17 January
The Mexican Cinémathèque, which has been organized on the French Cinémathèque model, opened today with great ceremony.

Avoriaz, 28 January
The main prize at the second International Festival of Fantasy Films was awarded to Richard Fleischer's *Soylent Green*.

France, 20 February
Funds of 3.6 million francs have been allocated to the Film Archives Service to build three new special storage vaults to take 55,000 reels of highly inflammable nitrate film.

Hollywood, 7 March
Wildwood Productions, Robert Redford's company, has acquired the rights to the Carl Bernstein and Bob Woodward book, *All the President's Men*, for $450,000. About the events in the Watergate scandal, it was published in February.

Los Angeles, 13 March
The American Film Institute has honored James Cagney with its Lifetime Achievement Award. This is the second year this award has been given to reward and acknowledge exceptional careers in film.

Paris, 18 April
Marcel Pagnol has died at his home in Paris. The 69-year-old writer and filmmaker leaves us with the image of a man deeply attached to his native Provence, which he depicted with honesty and warmth in films such as *la Femme du boulanger*, *Manon des Sources* and the early classic *Topaze*. Pagnol was also the first film director to become a member of the Académie Française.

Massachusetts, 2 May
Steven Spielberg has started filming *Jaws* on location at Martha's Vineyard. The movie, based on a book by Peter Benchley, is the first independent production from Richard Zanuck and David Brown.

Hollywood, 6 May
A fire has destroyed part of the Samuel Goldwyn studios, causing $3 million worth of damage.

Cambridge, 10 May
The satirical magazine *The Harvard Lampoon* has awarded the prize for the worst actor of 1973 to Barbra Streisand for her performance in *The Way We Were*.

Washington D.C., 23 June
The Supreme Court ruled against a city ordinance as "unconstitutional interference" today. The ordinance made drive-in theaters criminally liable for showing films with nude scenes if they are visible outside the theater grounds. Justices ruled that while such films may be offensive to some, they could easily be avoided, and were no more likely to stop the traffic than scenes of violence.

Washington D.C., 24 June
The Supreme Court has ruled that the film *Carnal Knowledge* is not obscene. This ruling quashes a previous decision handed down by a court in Georgia.

Chicago, 13 July
Chicago's best-known cinema, the Biograph, has gone out quietly almost 40 years to the day after the violent death of its most famous patron John Dillinger. The flamboyant Dillinger, known as "Public Enemy No. 1" died in a gunfight with Federal agents outside the movie theater where he had been watching Clark Gable in *Manhattan Melody*. Trivia fans will remember that he sat in the middle of the 12th row handy to the exit. Sadly, the Biograph was no longer economically viable.

Paris, 27 August
The President of France, Valéry Giscard d'Estaing, said during an interview on television that film censorship would be abolished in the near future.

Paris, 2 October
A special soiree in honor of Woody Allen was held at the Chaillot Cinémathèque. The film chosen for the evening, *Sleeper*, was selected by Allen himself: "Perhaps my least successful film with the French public but the one I like the best."

London, 30 October
Charles Chaplin has compiled a companion volume to *My Autobiography* (1964). The new book, *My Life in Pictures*, comes out today.

Los Angeles, 1 November
Release of *Earthquake*, directed by Mark Robson, with Charlton Heston, Ava Gardner and Geneviève Bujold. The film is the first to be made in "Sensurround". This process works by emitting such deep sound that it is almost inaudible but at extremely powerful levels so that the vibrations are felt by the body.

New York, 8 November
Frank Yablans has surprised the film world by resigning from his position as president of Paramount Pictures. Barry Diller, who became chairman last October, now finds himself in charge of the studio.

Chile, 29 November
Actress Carmen Bueno and leading cameraman Jorge Muller have been arrested in Santiago by the DINA, Pinochet's political police.

London, 6 December
World premiere of Guy Hamilton's latest James Bond, *The Man With the Golden Gun*, with Roger Moore once again playing agent 007.

Hollywood, 11 December
MGM's profits for the year 1973-74 have risen by 190 percent compared to the previous year. This result is in large part due to its hotel-casino, the MGM Grand in Las Vegas.

Rome, 20 December
Release of Luchino Visconti's latest film, *Conversation Piece* (*Gruppo di Famiglia in un Interno*), with Burt Lancaster and Silvana Mangano.

New York, 25 December
An editorial criticizing *The Godfather I* and *II* has appeared in the *New York Times*. The films are described as "breaking the record for pornography and violence." The article is concerned with the television screening of the first *Godfather* and its effect on young viewers.

New Delhi, 30 December
Opening of the fifth Indian Film Festival, presided over by Satyajit Ray. From now on the festival is to be held annually. The Indian film *Siddhartha*, is causing controversy due to a semi-nude scene.

Paris, 31 December
Four American films – *The Hustler*, *The Exorcist*, *Robin Hood* and *Papillon* – appear in the list of France's Top Ten box-office hits for the year.

New York, 31 December
Cinema receipts, unadjusted for inflation, appear to be the highest on record, while distribution receipts are up 25 percent from last year.

DEATHS

Palm Springs, 1 January
Edward Sutherland

Los Angeles, 31 January
Samuel Goldwyn

California, 24 April
Bud Abbott

Minnesota, 30 April
Agnes Moorehead

California, 21 September
Walter Brennan

Paris, 13 November
Vittorio De Sica

London, 17 November
Clive Brook

Paris, 15 December
Anatole Litvak

Beverly Hills, 26 December
Jack Benny

The Godfather Part II enjoyed the distinction of repeating the huge success of the original. Al Pacino memorably and brilliantly stepped into Brando's shoes as the new Don.

French screens are assailed by pornography

Paris, 28 August

The announcement yesterday by President Valéry Giscard d'Estaing of the lifting of most film censorship has particularly delighted the producers and distributors of pornographic movies, a side of the industry which is flourishing. In fact, the mode for porno has been in full swing for some time, and business has never been better. Some of the better porno movies have left the "ghetto" of specialized theaters, even making it to the prestigious picture palaces along the Champs-Elysées, as well as to those cinemas in the Latin Quarter usually designated for art movies. This has been the case with *Emmanuelle*, which

Inspired by Emmanuelle Arsan's controversial novel, **Emmanuelle***, made by Just Jaeckin is already a genre prototype.*

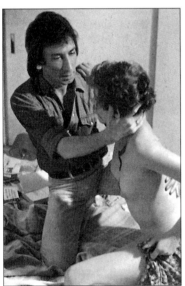

The first version of François Jouffa's **la Bonzesse** *was initially rejected by the censors. Its release has now been allowed.*

others, a lesbian archeologist and an elderly *roué*.

A couple of other recent movies, deemed soft-core, but from well respected *auteurs*, have followed in the wake of *Emmanuelle*. The latest film by the novelist Alain Robbe-Grillet, *Glissements progressifs du plaisir*, slides progressively further along the porn road than his previous ventures into erotic fantasy. And just released today is Walerian Borowczyk's *Immoral Tales*, reflecting the Polish director's fascination with the iconography of erotica and the emotions that lie beneath it. The film tells four stories, each situated in a different century. One involves Lucrezia Borgia's seduction of Pope Alexander VI, and another a virgin discovering masturbation.

is an unprecedented box-office triumph for this type of film since it was released two months ago. In addition, Sylvia Kristel, the 22-year-old Dutch actress in the title role, has become, in a matter of weeks, a real star of the screen. The phenomenal success of this soft-core picture can be attributed to the fact that the producers and the director, Just Jaeckin, chose a professional cast (including an actor of the quality of Alain Cuny), had a relatively large budget, and avoided any hard-core sex scenes. Jean-Louis Richard's screenplay deals with Emmanuelle, the bored wife of a French Embassy official in Bangkok, who is urged by her libertine husband to explore all the possibilities of sex. Thus, she finds herself in bed with, among

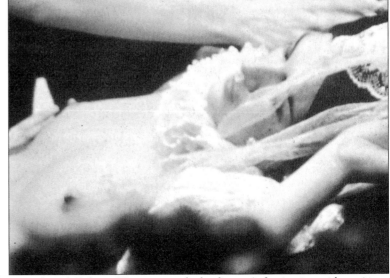

Immoral Tales*, directed by Walerian Borowczyk with Paloma Picasso, reveals the director's fascination with erotica.*

An orgy of blood and gore in Texas massacre

Philadelphia, 18 October
Director Tobe Hooper, who as a child gorged himself on films in his father's Texas cinema, serves up a bloody feast in *The Texas Chainsaw Massacre*. It's a grisly tale of travelers in rural America who fall into the clutches of a hellish inversion of the all-American family – three ghoulish brothers and their blood-sucking skeleton of a father. Like *Psycho*, the movie owes something to the real-life career of the "Wisconsin Ghoul", mass murderer Ed Gein, but it derives its considerable power from Hooper's assured camerawork and editing – the sensational title belies the fact that there is very little on-screen bloodletting – and an eerie *musique concrète* score which Hooper co-wrote with Wayne Bell. In part the film is a heavily ironic comment on the perversion of the "pioneer" ethic beloved of Americans: its deranged latter-day "frontiersmen" decorate their cabins with severed limbs and hunt humans rather than buffalo.

Marilyn Burns in Hooper's shocker about a murderous psychopathic family. The film was made for less than $200,000.

New York subway paralyzed with terror

New York, 2 October
At the best of times the New York subway is a hostile environment, but it becomes positively lethal in Joseph Sargent's pulsating thriller, *The Taking of Pelham One, Two, Three*. A gang led by ruthless Robert Shaw hijacks a subway train and holds its passengers hostage while demanding that a million dollars in cash be delivered within the hour. Can Walter Matthau's Transport Authority man thwart them? Peter Stone's cracking screenplay, adapted from John Godey's bestseller, swoops from black comedy to heart-stopping thrills while Sargent screws the tension up to breaking point.

*Robert Shaw in the subway in **The Taking of Pelham One, Two, Three**.*

Disaster becoming a new Hollywood genre

New York, 18 December
Movie companies have been rediscovering a genre which was popular in the late 30s, when such titles as *San Francisco* (1936) with its 1906 earthquake climax, *The Good Earth* with its plague of locusts, and *The Rains Came* (1939) rated highly with audiences. Now, able to take advantage of the latest advances in special effects, the Hollywood studios are once again promoting disasters in a big way. Universal intitiated the new cycle with the highly successful *Airport* in 1970, and Fox followed with *The Poseidon Adventure* in 1972. Now things have been really heating up with the release of *Airport 1975* and *Earthquake*, which introduces a new sensation to movie audiences – seats equipped to shake at key moments in the film so filmgoers can share the sensations experienced by the actors on the screen. Most recently we have been treated to *The Towering Inferno* in which a starry cast, that includes William Holden, Faye Dunaway and Fred Astaire, are trapped by fire in the penthouse restaurant at the top of the world's tallest building.

*Guillermin's **The Towering Inferno**.*

Chronicle of the Burning Years, *by Mohammed Lakhdar-Hamina*

*Bruno S. in Werner Herzog's **The Enigma of Kaspar Hauser**.*

*Anarchic comedian Lenny Bruce (Dustin Hoffman) in trouble in **Lenny**.*

*Richard Dreyfuss is waiter Duddy and Micheline Lanctot is chambermaid Yvette in Ted Kotcheff's **The Apprenticeship of Duddy Kravitz**.*

*David Drach, Marie-José Nat (both right) in Michel Drach's **les Violons du bal**.*

*Peter Boyle (l) and Gene Hackman in Mel Brooks' spoof, **Young Frankenstein**.*

*The avant-garde French theater director Ariane Mnouchkine's **1789**.*

Sean Connery in Boorman's **Zardoz**.

Brian De Palma's rock/pop remake,
Phantom of the Paradise.

Elliott Gould (left) and George Segal in Robert Altman's **California Split**.

Gena Rowlands is **A Woman Under the Influence** for spouse John Cassavetes.

Phase IV: Designer Saul Bass directed this sci-fi movie in the Arizona desert.

Jack Lemmon, Walter Matthau in Billy Wilder's remake of **The Front Page**.

Mrs. Hubbard (Lauren Bacall) explaining to Hercule Poirot (Albert Finney)
that a knife was found in her handbag in **Murder on the Orient Express**.

1975

★ ★

1974 Academy Awards, Dorothy Chandler Pavilion, 8 Apr.

Best Film:	*The Godfather Part II* (dir: Francis Ford Coppola)
Best Director:	Francis Ford Coppola
Best Actor:	Art Carney *(Harry and Tonto)*
Best Actress:	Ellen Burstyn *(Alice Doesn't Live Here Anymore)*
Best Supp. Actor:	Robert De Niro *(The Godfather Part II)*
Best Supp. Actress:	Ingrid Bergman *(Murder on the Orient Express)*

Paris, 1 January
Isabelle Adjani has left the Comédie-Française. After the success of *The Slap (la Gifle)*, the young actress is preparing to film *The Story of Adèle H. (l'Histoire d'Adèle H.)* with director François Truffaut.

Paris, 21 January
President Valéry Giscard d'Estaing, who was so moved by seeing Marcel Carné's *le Jour se lève (Daybreak)* (1939) on television, has invited the cast to lunch at his official residence, the Elysée palace. Actor Jean Gabin is the only one to have refused the invitation.

Los Angeles, 22 January
Superior Court Judge Norman R. Dowds today lifted a temporary restraining order against a segment of *Hearts and Minds*, a documentary produced by Bert Schneider and Peter Davis about the Vietnam War. Walt W. Rostow, national security advisor to President Lyndon B. Johnson, had tried to bar the use of an interview of himself, which he feels is damaging to his image.

Avoriaz, 26 January
At the closing ceremony of the third International Fantasy Film Festival, the main prize was awarded to the musical horror film, *Phantom of the Paradise*, a satirical rock opera from director Brian De Palma.

Paris, 29 January
Patrice Chéreau has released his first film *The Flesh of the Orchid (la Chair de l'orchidée)*, based on a James Hadley Chase novel, with Bruno Cremer, Simone Signoret, Edwige Feuillère and British actress Charlotte Rampling.

New York, 31 January
Lawyers for the Walt Disney Co. have filed a suit to have the "Mickey Mouse Club" song removed from the soundtrack of the pornographic film, *The Happy Hooker*. The music is played during an orgy scene.

Cairo, 3 February
Millions of fans took part in the funeral procession of Oum Kalsoum through the streets of Cairo today. The singer-actress, who is better known to her faithful following as the lady of Arab song and the star of the East, became famous through radio in the early 20s, and although she made relatively few films, those she did appear in were greatly appreciated by the public.

New York, 16 April
Variety has announced that Universal intends to run a TV advertising campaign with prime-time viewing spots for the release of *Jaws*. This method replaces the usual step-by-step approach. The studio feels that the high initial investment will prove economically worthwhile.

New York, 5 May
The Lincoln Center Film Society has paid tribute to Paul Newman and his wife Joanne Woodward for their contribution to the cinema.

Los Angeles, 25 May
The American Film Institute has organized a ceremony for the release of a new postage stamp honoring the memory of D.W. Griffith.

New York, 18 June
The American Legion has protested against, and is asking for a boycott of, the documentary about Vietnam *Introduction to the Enemy*. The film is co-directed by Haskell Wexler, Tom Hayden and Jane Fonda.

Hollywood, 7 July
Hollywood appears to have found a new gilt-edged hero to add to its long list of furry and feathered friends – a not-so-friendly, 25-foot-long killer shark. Peter Benchley's *Jaws* is helping to revive an otherwise gloomy year at the box office. According to Universal the film has grossed $25.7 million in box-office receipts around the country since its release on 21 June.

Moscow, 10 July
The absence of an American presence at the film festival here has been noticed. According to Jack Valenti, president of the MPAA, Hollywood's participation in the preceding years' festivals had not produced results worthy of further effort. The impact of American films on the Russian market remains insignificant.

Washington D.C., 13 August
D.W. Griffith's great film, *The Birth of a Nation*, has been declared out of copyright as a result of proceedings started by Epoch Productions against the Museum of Modern Art.

New York, 31 August
Benji, directed and scripted by newcomer Joe Camp, is an unexpected hit. The film has already grossed about $23 million and, judging by the long queues outside the Guild Theater in Manhattan where the picture is currently showing, it looks set to make a killing.

Hollywood, 2 September
John Milius has said that *Apocalypse Now* will be the most violent film ever produced. He has just completed the writing of the script.

Stockholm, 17 September
Ingmar Bergman has received an honory doctorate of philosophy from the University of Stockholm.

Rome, 27 September
Luchino Visconti, who has been in a wheelchair since a fall last April, has started shooting *The Innocent (l'Innocente)*, based on a novel by Gabriele D'Annunzio, with Giancarlo Giannini and Laura Antonelli.

Botswana, 10 October
Elizabeth Taylor has remarried Richard Burton. Their divorce was made final in June 1974.

Hollywood, 28 October
Actor Charlton Heston has been re-elected chairman of the American Film Institute. George Stevens Jr.'s position as head of this prestigious body has been renewed for another three years.

Hollywood, 3 November
Kathleen Nolan is the first woman to be elected president of the Screen Actors Guild.

Rome, 5 November
The Italian Communist Party has decided to handle all the funeral arrangements for Pier Paolo Pasolini as well as the commemorative service to be held at the Campo dei Fiori. The director was brutally murdered three days ago.

Paris, 21 November
The cinema sex magazine *l'Organe* has been banned.

Paris, 1 December
Joseph Losey has completed the first day of shooting of *Monsieur Klein*, starring Alain Delon.

New York, 15 December
Twentieth Century-Fox's board of directors has decided to go ahead with the production of *Star Wars*. George Lucas has been working on his original script since May 1974 and has finally convinced Alan Ladd Jr., the head of production for the studio, to back the project.

Hollywood, 25 December
Composer Bernard Herrmann has died. He was best known for his imposing film scores for directors Orson Welles and Alfred Hitchcock.

BIRTHS

Los Angeles, 22 February
Drew Barrymore

DEATHS

Los Angeles, 8 March
George Stevens

Los Angeles, 14 March
Susan Hayward

Los Angeles, 10 April
Marjorie Main

California, 13 April
Larry Parker

Los Angeles, 14 April
Fredric March

Los Angeles, 12 December
William Wellman

---

*The British director John Schlesinger, who turned a lethal eye on New York in **Midnight Cowboy**, dealt perceptively with Hollywood in this film version of Nathanael West's novel.*

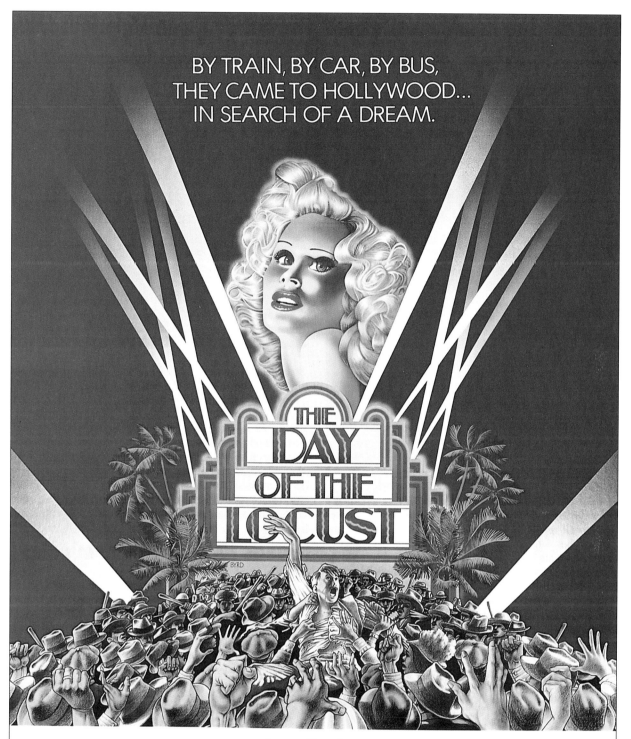

Danger in a seaside resort is good fun

Richard Dreyfuss, Roy Scheider and the terrifying denizen of the deep!

New York, 21 June
In *Jaws*, an adaptation from Peter Benchley's bestseller and directed by Steven Spielberg, a peaceful little New England holiday resort is getting ready to celebrate 4 July when a Great White shark claims its first two victims. When the mayor refuses to close the beaches and lose holi-day trade, local police chief Roy Scheider watches helplessly as the shark comes back for more. Enlisting the help of Richard Dreyfuss' breezy shark expert and Robert Shaw's Ahab-like shark hunter, the sea-fearing Scheider sails off to kill the monster. But the hunters soon become the hunted.

Kurosawa and a noble Siberian savage

Tokyo, 12 August
The distinguished Japanese director Akira Kurosawa has recovered from a 1971 suicide attempt to make *Derzu Uzala*, based on the journals of Vladimir Arseniev. Derzu Uzala is a young Russian scientist's guide on a topographical expedition in turn-of-the-century Siberia. In Max-im Munzuk's warm portrait, Uzala emerges as a wily expert in the art of survival, on several occasions saving his Russian employer from a sticky end. In one bravura set piece he constructs a shelter as a storm brews up, rendered magnificently on the 70mm screen with its six-track stereo sound.

Maxim Munzuk, hunter-guide Derzu Uzala, greets Yuri Solomin, the scientist.

'Picnic at Hanging Rock' is unnerving

Anne Lambert is Miranda in Peter Weir's striking Australian mystery story.

Sydney, 9 August
Director Peter Weir, who made his debut last year with *The Cars That Ate Paris*, has followed it with an atmospheric and unnerving mystery, *Picnic at Hanging Rock*. On a turn-of-the-century outing to a huge rock in the Australian outback, three schoolgirls and their teacher vanish. Their disappearance is never explained but it would seem that they have been claimed by the rock itself, a phallic force of nature. Weir skillfully moves from the recognizable world of the girls' school, thrumming with emergent sexuality, to a pagan environment in which "modern" values have no meaning.

Rocking with transvestites in Transylvania

London, 14 August
Richard O'Brien's stage hit, *The Rocky Horror Picture Show*, has been transferred on to the screen by writer-director Jim Sharman. A camp horror movie spoof larded with sex, transvestites and rock music, Richard O'Brien's monster of a musical is located somewhere be-tween Gay Liberation and Z-movie Gothick. Tim Curry reprises his stage role of Frank 'n' Furter, whose annual convention of transvestite Transylvanian aliens is interrupted by the arrival of "straight" couple Brad and Janet, played by Susan Sarandon and Barry Bostwick. Do you want to party, Brad?

Susan Sarandon plays Janet.

Riff-raff (Richard O'Brien) and pal.

Hollywood comes to elegant Deauville

*Ronee Blakely and Henry Gibson entertain in Robert Altman's **Nashville**.*

Sad, absorbing chronicle of desperation

John Cazale (left) with Al Pacino, the two ill-fated would-be bank robbers.

Deauville, 12 September
André Halimi and Lionel Chouchan are the driving force behind the first European festival of American film, which is being held in Deauville, the resort which provided the elegant backdrop to Claude Lelouch's *A Man and a Woman*. Henri Langlois is one of the sponsors of this festival, which declines to award prizes. At Deauville, films are shown but not judged. The program is comprised of seven categories, including works which have yet to be premiered, independent productions and films made for television. Two eagerly awaited films are Robert Altman's *Nashville*, a kaleidoscopic view of the home of American country music, and *Rollerball*, Norman Jewison's view of gladiatorial sport in a future dystopia.

New York, 21 September
Al Pacino is up against it in *Dog Day Afternoon*, directed by Sidney Lumet. He has a mountain of debts, an unhappy wife and a male lover who wants a sex-change operation. So he enlists the help of John Cazale to rob a Brooklyn bank. The heist goes horribly wrong and the two men wind up holding the staff and clients hostage while the incident snowballs into a city-wide ordeal. Pacino delivers a mesmeric performance as the loser who begins to relish the notoriety he wins while negotiating with the cops in the sticky heat of a New York summer. It is based on a real-life event (nothing surprises New Yorkers) and has been tautly scripted by Frank Pierson, drawing on an article by B.F. Kluge and Thomas Moore.

Pierre Blaise meets with fatal accident

France, 31 August
The young actor discovered by Louis Malle for the title role in *Lacombe Lucien*, has been killed in a car accident. He was born in 1955 in Moissac, and first worked as a woodcutter. Recently, there had been rumors in the press that he was Brigitte Bardot's new love. Sadly, *Lacombe Lucien*, in which he was so remarkable, remains his only film.

*While filming **Lacombe Lucien**.*

Isabelle Adjani plays out the passionate folly of Hugo's daughter

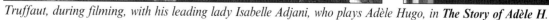

*Truffaut, during filming, with his leading lady Isabelle Adjani, who plays Adèle Hugo, in **The Story of Adèle H**.*

Paris, 8 October
François Truffaut has described his new film, *The Story of Adèle H*, as "a musical composition for one instrument." That instrument is the exquisite 19-year-old Isabelle Adjani as Victor Hugo's benighted daughter. Based on Adèle's diary, written in code and decoded in 1955, the film, shot partly in English, concentrates on Adjani in the throes of *amour fou*, as she follows a young English lieutenant from Guernsey to Nova Scotia and Barbados, despite his indifference to her.

▷

1976

★ ★

1975 Academy Awards, Dorothy Chandler Pavilion, 29 Mar.

Best Film:	*One Flew Over the Cuckoo's Nest* (dir: Milos Forman)
Best Director:	Milos Forman
Best Actor:	Jack Nicholson *(One Flew Over the Cuckoo's Nest)*
Best Actress:	Louise Fletcher *(One Flew Over the Cuckoo's Nest)*
Best Supp. Actress:	George Burns *(The Sunshine Boys)*
Best Supp. Actress:	Lee Grant *(Shampoo)*

Manila, 2 March
Francis Ford Coppola has arrived in the Philippines to shoot the location scenes for *Apocalypse Now.*

Paris, 2 March
Release of *The Best Way to Walk* (*la Meilleure façon de marcher*), the first full-length film directed by Claude Miller, who was formerly assistant to Jean-Luc Godard and François Truffaut.

Tennessee, 3 March
The trial involving the film *Deep Throat* has started in Memphis. Eleven people are being charged with "conspiring to distribute obscene material from one state to another". In several states the film has already been the object of 11 trials; in eight of them the film was exonerated from the obscenity accusations.

Paris, 17 March
Release of François Truffaut's latest picture, *l'Argent de poche (Small Change)*, with Virginie Thévenet, Jean-François Stévenin and numerous children and teenagers, among them the director's two teenage daughters, Eva and Laura Truffaut.

Westchester, 11 April
Frank Sinatra was photographed at a concert in the company of two notorious Mafiosi, Carlo Gambino and Paul Castellano.

Stockholm, 22 April
Ingmar Bergman announced today that due to tax problems he could no longer live in Sweden. He said that he had been harassed and humiliated by "prestige-seeking poker players" in the tax bureaucracy. He plans to continue his work abroad.

Salt Lake City, 27 April
A document purporting to be the will of Howard Hughes has been left by an unknown person at the Mormon Church's headquarters. One of Hughes' assistants has referred to it as "a very clever forgery."

Argentina, 27 May
The Argentinian film director Raymundo Gleyser has been arrested by the death squad.

Hollywood, 10 June
The American cinema magnate, Adolf Zukor, has died at the venerable age of 103. Zukor's life was a true rags-to-riches success story. Born in Hungary, he was selling rabbit skins in the streets of New York at the age of 16. By the time he was 30 he had started buying up penny arcades to transform into nickelodeons. The creator of Famous Players Pictures, he became head of Paramount in 1935.

California, 1 July
One of the most uniquely told stories of the American Bicentennial opens to the public today at the Smithsonian Institute. Filmed in IMAX, the world's largest film format, *To Fly*, the history of American aviation, is a visual and aural experience rather than an historical epic. It will be shown on a screen 75 feet wide and five stories high.

Berlin, 6 July
Robert Altman's *Buffalo Bill and the Indians* has carried off the main prize, the Golden Bear, at the Berlin Festival. Altman, who had in fact written an open letter to the head of the Festival asking that his film be ignored, refuses to acknowledge the version produced by Dino De Laurentiis for European distribution.

Paris, 16 July
Claude-Jean Philippe presented *le Roi des Champs-Elysées* during the Channel 2 program "Ciné-Club". The film, directed by Max Nosseck in 1934, was the only Buster Keaton film to be shot in France.

Karlovy-Vary, 20 July
The main prize at the 20th Festival was awarded to the Cuban director Humberto Solas for his *Cantata of Chile.*

Paris, 30 July
Simone Signoret has managed to finish her autobiography *La Nostalgie n'est plus ce qu'elle était (Nostalgia Is Not What It Used To Be)*, despite being very busy with the television series *Madame le juge.*

Los Angeles, 23 September
A preview is being held of *Marathon Man*, directed by John Schlesinger and starring Laurence Olivier and Dustin Hoffman.

Washington D.C., 6 October
Congress has brought in a new copyright law to replace that of 1909. It will take effect on 1 January 1978. Protection now lasts for the life of the author plus 50 years. In the case of films only the producer will be recognized as the author.

New York, 14 November
The most popular movie ever shown on American television is *Gone With the Wind.* The film, shown in two parts by NBC last week, was viewed on successive nights by 33.9 and 33.7 million householders.

Jerusalem, 29 October
Simone Signoret, Michèle Morgan, Kirk Douglas and Danny Kaye were part of an honorary committee for the first Jewish Film Festival which is taking place here.

Rome, 1 November
Release of the second part of Bernardo Bertolucci's epic *Novecento (1900).* The film traces the social evolution in the Italian provinces in the early 20th century. Robert De Niro and Gérard Depardieu star.

Los Angeles, 8 November
Premiere of Elia Kazan's *The Last Tycoon*, adapted from the unfinished novel by F. Scott Fitzgerald. Robert De Niro plays the title role, said to have been based, by Fitzgerald, on producer Irving Thalberg.

Los Angeles, 11 November
Universal and Walt Disney Pictures have commenced legal proceedings against the manufacturer and distributor of videotapes, Sony-Betamax, for breach of copyright laws.

New York, 15 November
Michael Eisner, who comes from the television industry, has been appointed head of Paramount.

New York, 30 November
The French film *Cousin, Cousine*, directed by Jean-Charles Tacchella, has been enthusiastically received here by both critics and the public.

Paris, 27 December
According to the results of a survey published by *l'Express* on the subject of film censorship, 65 percent of those questioned agree that some type of control is needed.

BIRTHS

West Hollywood, 16 April
Lukas Haas

DEATHS

England, 13 January
Margaret Leighton

Philadelphia, 23 January
Paul Robeson

England, 5 February
Roger Livesey

California, 11 February
Lee J. Cobb

Hollywood, 12 February
Sal Mineo

California, 13 March
Busby Berkeley

Rome, 17 March
Luchino Visconti

Hollywood, 28 March
Richard Arlen

London, 25 April
Carol Reed

Los Angeles, 2 August
Fritz Lang

London, 19 August
Alistair Sim

France, 15 November
Jean Gabin

Los Angeles, 28 November
Rosalind Russell

---

*Martin Scorsese's **Taxi Driver**, a dark and violent vision of New York's familiar 'mean streets', is a comment on the psychological after-effects of the Vietnam War. De Niro dazzles.*

Robert Fortier with Sissy Spacek in Robert Altman's enigmatic **Three Women**.

Outrageous: *wicked drag impersonator Craig Russell's Judy Garland.*

*René Ferracci's surreal French poster
reflects the tone of Buñuel's film.*

The war was over and
the world was falling in love again.

A love story is like a song. It's beautiful while it lasts.

LIZA MINNELLI   ROBERT DE NIRO
"NEW YORK, NEW YORK"

Liza Minnelli, sax player Robert De Niro in Scorsese's **New York, New York**.

Philippe Noiret and veteran Fred Astaire in Yves Boisset's **The Purple Taxi**.

Coline Serreau's **Pourquoi pas? (Why Not?)**: *Mario Gonzales (l), Samy Frey.*

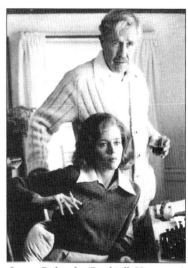

Left to right: Paul Le Mat, Candy Clark and Roberts Blossom in Jonathan Demme's **Handle With Care** *(aka* **Citizen's Band***).*

Bresson's **The Devil, Probably** *was the winner of the Berlin Jury Prize.*

Jason Robards (Dashiell Hammett), Jane Fonda (Lillian Hellman): **Julia***.*

Art Carney, the private investigator, in Robert Benton's **The Late Show***.*

Julie Christie in Donald Cammell's nasty sci-fi film, **Demon Seed***.*

Maximilian Schell and Klaus Löwitch in Sam Peckinpah's **Cross of Iron***.*

John Heard, Lindsay Crouse in Joan Micklin Silver's **Between the Lines***.*

1978

★ ★

1977 Academy Awards, Dorothy Chandler Pavilion, 3 Apr.

Best Film:	Annie Hall (dir: Woody Allen)
Best Director:	Woody Allen
Best Actor:	Richard Dreyfuss (The Goodbye Girl)
Best Actress:	Diane Keaton (Annie Hall)
Best Supp. Actor:	Jason Robards (Julia)
Best Supp. Actress:	Vanessa Redgrave (Julia)

Cannes, 7 January
The new director of the Cannes Film Festival, Gilles Jacob, has announced that the event will run for only 11 days this year. Hoteliers and shopkeepers are protesting.

Paris, 26 January
The X-rating of Francis Giacobetti's *Emmanuelle II* has been removed by a special court decision.

Peking, 30 January
Director Yuan Muzhi has died. He was an important personality during the 1930s and one of the leaders of the Popular Liberation Army's revolutionary cinema.

Prague, 1 February
Release of *Hra o jablko* (*The Apple Game*), by Vera Chytilova, made in 1976, with director Jiri Menzel in the lead role. It is Chytilova's first fiction film since 1969.

London, 9 February
Roman Polanski, recently convicted of corruption of a minor in the United States, has announced his intention to remain outside the U.S. He left California the day before the sentence was pronounced.

Calcutta, 12 February
Indian filmmaker Satyajit Ray is bemused by the lack of interest in his latest film in his native India. Despite his popularity abroad, Mr. Ray has been unable to find a distributor in India for *The Chess Player*. The distributors who had been planning to open the movie in Calcutta and several other major towns turned it down after a private showing. The film, starring British actor Richard Attenborough, was well received by the public and film critics at the London Film Festival last month.

Cairo, 26 February
The Egyptian Film Association has proclaimed Salah Abou Seif's film *The Death of the Water-bearer* (*As saqqa mat*) the best film for 1977.

Paris, 27 February
Actress Jean Seberg has published an open "Letter to drug addicts" in the daily paper, *Libération.*

Los Angeles, 2 March
The president of the MPAA, Jack Valenti, has denied press reports that there was a huge government investigation into alleged corruption in the motion picture industry. The reports of a Hollywood inquiry followed the recent upheaval at the Columbia studios, whose president, David Begelman, resigned after admitting to embezzling studio funds.

Lebanon, 15 March
The Palestinian filmmakers Ibrahim Mustapha Nasser and Abdel-Hafeth al Asmar have been killed while filming an Israeli military operation in the region.

Los Angeles, 7 April
The Ontario Film Classification Board has banned Louis Malle's film about a 12-year-old prostitute, *Pretty Baby.*

Switzerland, 17 May
Charlie Chaplin's coffin and body have been recovered in the town of Noville, only a few kilometers from the cemetery in Vevey where his tomb was robbed. It is believed that the criminals were hoping to extort money from the Chaplin family. No arrests have been made.

Bombay, 28 May
The kiss has come to the Hindi screen, shocking some and titillating others. Shashi Kapoor, India's answer to Robert Redford, kisses his co-star several times in a new film, *Love Sublime*, directed by his brother Raj. And although they are tame by Western standards, they are the first kisses on the Hindi screen for years. In the Indian cinema industry the film is seen as a landmark and as a sign of what the Government calls greater "creative freedom", after Indira Gandhi's authoritarian rule.

Los Angeles, 15 June
The Doheny Plaza theater, which had contracted to show the allegedly anti-Israel documentary by Vanessa Redgrave titled *The Palestinian*, was bombed at 4:26 a.m. today, causing an estimated $1,000 damage. Despite this the theater said it would show the film tomorrow night as scheduled. Two suspects have been arrested. Although Miss Redgrave has resolutely denied claims that she is anti-Semitic, she recently called for members of the British actors union to boycott Israel.

Copenhagen, 21 August
Release of *Honeymoon* (*Honning-mane*), by Bille August, with Claus Stranberg and Kirsten Olesen.

Hollywood, 17 September
Director Michael Cimino has had discussions with Stephen Bach at United Artists about his proposed new project, *The Johnson County War*, a Western.

Paris, 25 September
Director Eric Rohmer is shooting *Perceval le Gallois* (*Perceval*) in the Epinay studios, based on Chrétien de Troyes' epic poem, inspired by the Knights of the Round Table.

New York, 19 October
The body of actor Gig Young was found lying beside that of his bride of three weeks. He was clutching a revolver. Police think the actor killed his wife before turning the gun on himself. Young made over 50 films during his career, including his Academy Award-winning performance in Sydney Pollack's *They Shoot Horses, Don't They?*

Rio de Janeiro, 23 October
Considered as the best Brazilian film for the year at the Festival de Brasilia, *Tudo Bem* (*Everything is Fine*), directed by Arnaldo Jabor, is now on release.

Paris, 25 October
Release of Edouard Molinaro's *la Cage aux folles*, based on a play by Jean Poiret, with Michel Serrault and Ugo Tognazzi.

Biarritz, 15 November
Bernard Marie, the deputy mayor of Biarritz, has announced the creation of an annual Latin American and Spanish film festival here.

Paris, 22 November
Le Figaro magazine revealed in its latest issue that four giants of the American and English screen – Robert Mitchum, Richard Burton, Peter O'Toole and Richard Harris – all well-known to be heavy imbibers, have given up drinking.

France, 30 November
The Center of Research into Advertising has revealed that 55 percent of French people never go to the cinema. Audiences in the 15 to 20 age group (20 percent of the population) make up 52 percent of admissions.

Paris, 5 December
Opening of an exhibition at the George Pompidou Center of Soviet director Sergei Eisenstein's original sketches and drawings.

Paris, 26 December
Between December 17 and 25 this year, the three television channels programmed 28 movies. Some cinema professionals are uneasy about this profusion of films on TV.

DEATHS

California, 23 January
Jack Oakie

England, 27 January
Oscar Homolka

New York, 12 March
John Cazale

Los Angeles, 9 August
Jack L. Warner

Arizona, 26 August
Charles Boyer

Ireland, 28 August
Robert Shaw

Paris, 9 October
Jacques Brel

Los Angeles, 16 October
Dan Dailey

New York, 19 October
Gig Young

---

*Michael Cimino's **The Deer Hunter** is a significant movie about the Vietnam experience. In a brilliant cast, a relative newcomer named Meryl Streep made an impression.*

Sensitive, charming debut film wins Delluc

*Eléonore Klarwein (foreground left), Odile Michel (right) in **Peppermint Soda**.*

Paris, 14 January

The Louis Delluc Prize has been awarded to *Peppermint Soda* (*Diabolo menthe*), the first feature by Diane Kurys, a former actress with the Madeleine Renaud/Jean-Louis Barrault theater company. Kurys (born 1948) has drawn her screenplay from experiences of her own adolescence, with the action taking place in 1963, from the time of Kennedy's assassination. It revolves around Anne (Eléonore Klarwein) and Frédérique (Odile Michel), the teenage daughters of a divorced Jewish couple. They live with their mother, attend an authoritarian school, and spend their vacations with their father, with whom they are ill at ease. This gentle, observant and nostalgic debut movie, has attracted large audiences of young people since it opened in Paris a month ago.

A traumatic homecoming from Vietnam

Los Angeles, 15 February

Coming Home is very much Jane Fonda's project. She commissioned Nancy Dowd to write a story about the impact of the Vietnam War on people at home which would be implicitly critical of U.S. policy. Fonda plays an army wife married to Marine Corps action man Bruce Dern. While he is serving his tour of duty in Vietnam, she takes a job in a veteran's hospital where she meets an old high school classmate, Jon Voight, who is now paralyzed from the waist down. This condition does not prevent him from pleasuring her, however, and they embark on an affair which has a liberating effect on Fonda. When Dern returns from Vietnam, traumatized by his experiences there, she has to choose between the two men. Director Hal Ashby handles the love affair between Fonda and Voight with discretion, but the film slowly slithers into tearjerker territory while whole chunks of dialogue are lost in the din of a pounding rock soundtrack. For the moment the public have given this contemporary mixture of *Since You Went Away* and *Brief Encounter* a resounding thumbs down.

Jane Fonda and Jon Voight.

David Begelman affair, or Hollywoodgate

*Cliff Robertson (here in De Palma's **Obsession**), is at the center of the affair.*

New York, 6 April

David Begelman's departure from the presidency of the film and television division of Columbia Pictures is the culmination of an extraordinary series of events. It all began last year when actor Cliff Robertson discovered that he had been credited with a payment of $10,000 which he had never received. It turned out that a check for this amount had been forged and cashed by Begelman, who subsequently admitted to embezzling more than $60,000 from the studio. He was suspended on 30 September, 1977, then reinstated in December when the studio, who still regarded him as an important figure who had helped in its prosperity, hoped the furor had blown over. This, however, has proved to be wishful thinking, and casts an interesting light on the behavior of Hollywood studios and their executives.

Woody beats robots to the big awards

Los Angeles, 3 April

The 50th Academy Awards ceremony saw the odds-on favorite, George Lucas' innovative, effects-packed blockbuster *Star Wars*, ousted by the intimist New York Jewish comedy angst of Woody Allen. *Annie Hall* had Woody named Best Director of the Best Picture, and winning the Best Original Screenplay Oscar, while his co-star Diane Keaton was voted Best Actress for her performance in the title role. However, Best Actor was Richard Dreyfuss for his gleefully manic performance in Neil Simon's *The Goodbye Girl* as an egocentric off-Broadway actor. At only 29, Dreyfuss is the youngest winner of this award. For the second year in a row, Jason Robards was Best Supporting Actor, taking the Oscar this time for his performance as washed-up writer Dashiell Hammett in Fred Zinnemann's adaptation of Lillian Hellman's *Julia*. The best thing in the film was Vanessa Redgrave in the title role, the mystery woman saving Jews from the Nazis. It won her a deserved Best Supporting Actress Oscar and a chance to harangue the audience about Palestine.

Marsha Mason, Richard Dreyfuss.

UA is threatened by ruptures

New York, 19 April
Eleven years after the Transamerica Corporation took over United Artists, five of the film company's main executives – Arthur Krim, Robert Benjamin, Eric Pleskow, Mike Medavoy and William Bernstein – have resigned. They have already announced their plan to form a new company called Orion Pictures and make a distribution deal with Warner Bros, which will be providing substantial financial backing for the new studio. Krim and Benjamin were responsible for revitalizing UA in the 1950s and 60s and had headed the company for 26 years, during which time it won many Oscars and earned small but steady profits. Unfortunately, UA had a few bad years in the early 1970s which strained relations between Transamerica and the UA management. Though the company recovered and continued to do well, Krim and Benjamin were determined to regain their independence. The current Orion plan is the result of this determination.

Strange childhood in New Orleans brothel

*Life in the brothel: Keith Carradine and Brooke Shields in **Pretty Baby**.*

New York, 4 April
Twelve-year-old Brooke Shields, already a successful model, broke into films last year with *Alice, Sweet Alice*. Now, in Louis Malle's *Pretty Baby*, she is the star attraction in a New Orleans brothel in 1917. By any standards this is dangerous territory, but as Malle explains, "I'm always interested in exposing something, a theme, a character or a situation which seems to be unacceptable. Then I try to make it work." Malle has succeeded, and avoided sensationalism, by giving Shields a matter-of-fact approach, viewing the brothel as home and the workplace of her mother, Susan Sarandon.

Columbia troubled by Hollywoodgate

New York, 20 July
The ongoing controversy and publicity caused by the Begelman affair at Columbia during the past year, and related management problems, have now led to the firing of company President and Chief Executive Officer Alan Hirschfield. In fact, a difference of opinion as to how to deal with Begelman had opened up a rift between Hirschfield and Herbert Allen Jr., the most powerful member of the board of directors, whose company Allen & Co. had bought a controlling interest in the studio in 1973. In spite of the fact that Hirschfield had played a major role in the revival of the company, he was voted out of office by the board, with Chairman Leo Jaffe as the only one who opposed the move. In a masterful piece of understatement, the board's press release read, "It has recently become apparent that for Columbia to move forward to new levels of accomplishment, fresh leadership and greater management unity are required."

Now Travolta takes a trip to the Fifties

New York, 11 June
After drawing the crowds last year with his galvanic dancing in *Saturday Night Fever*, John Travolta has another smash with *Grease*. Based on the Broadway hit musical, it is a nostalgic trip back to the 50s, and stars Travolta and Olivia Newton-John as two kids at a rockin' 'n' rollin' high school. This takeoff of Beach Party movies pulsates with terrific numbers, including "Summer Nights" and "Look At Me, I'm Sandra Dee". The cast includes such veterans as Eve Arden, Joan Blondell and Sid Caesar, as well as stars of the period pastiched, Frankie Avalon and Edd "Kookie" Byrnes.

Crude, rude and comical college caper

New York, 28 July
Is this a new trend in the making? Writer Harold Ramis and director John Landis have concocted a new kind of college campus movie with *National Lampoon's Animal House*. Set sometime around the early 60s, the story – if story it can be called – concerns the antics of a bunch of vulgar newcomers at a college who set out to disturb the stuffed-shirt order of things by their outrageous behavior. The movie, with its crude gags and anarchic set pieces, taking in everything from sexual escapades to bad table manners, is so over-the-top that it becomes quite absorbing. Watch out for gross John Belushi.

*Olivia Newton-John and John Travolta, co-stars in Randal Kleiser's **Grease**.*

James Daughton (left) attacks John Belushi about his gross eating habits.

Harrowing ordeal in a Turkish prison relived

London, 10 August

After the "cute" violence of *Bugsy Malone*, director Alan Parker has turned to the real thing in *Midnight Express*. It's the story of the ordeal suffered by young American Billy Hayes, played by Brad Davis, while serving a sentence in Turkey for drug smuggling. The physical and emotional brutalization to which Davis is exposed has prompted accusations that Parker has painted a racist picture of the Turks, but the appalling state of the Turkish penal system represents only half of the picture's argument. The underlying theme tackles our deep-rooted fear of "otherness", which is an inescapable part of the human condition. Parker, himself a liberal-minded man, has defended himself vigorously against his critics.

The drugs that caused the trouble.

John Hurt (left) and Brad Davis, companions suffering in a Turkish prison.

Miraculous meeting of Ingmar and Ingrid

Stockholm, 8 October

Autumn Sonata is Ingrid Bergman's first Swedish film for almost 40 years, and it was her namesake Ingmar Bergman, who finally tempted her back to her native land. After some years in the kind of movies that hardly stretched her considerable talent, Ingrid has been handed one of her meatiest roles, in which she delivers a remarkable performance, displaying every aspect of her screen personality over the years – naivety, sophistication, gaiety and tragedy. Here, she plays Charlotte, a world-renowned concert pianist, who returns to Sweden to visit the two daughters she has not seen for many years, one married (Liv Ullmann) and the other severely handicapped (Lena Nyman). Charlotte has to face up to feelings of guilt for having put her career above her family, and the painful recognition that the past cannot be altered. The director, with a masterly use of close-up, and the flashback used as the subconscious, has created a work of Strindbergian intensity – a long night's journey into day.

The tragedy of an Australian half-caste

Melbourne, 21 August

The flowering of the Australian film industry, helped by constructive government funding, is continuing apace. The latest homegrown offering to open here, titled *The Chant of Jimmie Blacksmith*, received warm plaudits in competition at Cannes earlier in the year. Now, local audiences have the opportunity to see director Fred Schepisi's well-made, absorbing film, which deals with the plight of a half-caste aborigine. Jimmie Blacksmith, very movingly portrayed by non-actor Tommy Lewis, is caught in the trap of his mixed origins. Torn between the Christian teachings of his boyhood, and the ancient aboriginal lore, Jimmie decides to join the native life of the city. He finds himself living in a squalid shanty town, while his efforts to find work are increasingly characterized by humiliation and degradation, although he marries a white servant girl. The tale ends in tragedy and bloodshed, leaving audiences to face a disturbing indictment of our destruction of another race's culture and dignity.

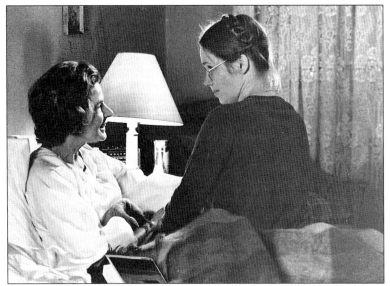

Mother and daughter share a rare moment of sympathy and understanding.

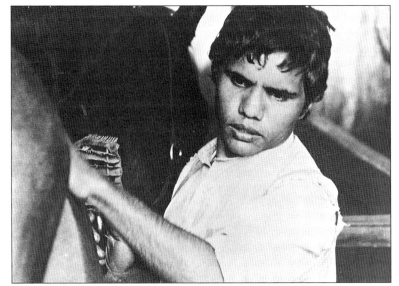

*Tommy Lewis stars in Fred Schepisi's **The Chant of Jimmie Blacksmith**.*

Seasonal shocker from John Carpenter

A frightened Jamie Lee Curtis.

Los Angeles, 27 October
In his latest film, *Halloween*, John Carpenter appears to have been afflicted with Psycho-itis. It's a horror film peppered with Hitchcockian shock cuts in which Jamie Lee Curtis (the daughter of *Psycho*'s Janet Leigh) is pursued by a mad killer who himself seems to be unkillable. While the Bernard Herrmann-like theme (composed by the director) cranks up the tension, Carpenter's camera prowls through the night, always hinting at something horrible about to burst in from the periphery of the Panavision screen. Such plot as there is concerns an insane killer who first struck as a child on Halloween and threatens to do so again 15 years later. There are plenty of shocks along the way, and film buffs will spot the sly in-jokes Carpenter has buried in the film.

Cimino and war-scarred American psyche

New York, 15 December
Michael Cimino's second feature (following *Thunderbolt and Lightfoot* four years ago) is the epically conceived *The Deer Hunter*, which attempts to address the effect of the Vietnam War on the American psyche. The three-hour film accurately captures the mood in America at the moment – the need to find some justification for the war. It focuses on the lives of three steelworkers – Robert De Niro, Christopher Walken and John Savage, before and after their Vietnam experiences. Using the camera as an observer, Cimino allows the narrative to unfold in an almost documentary style. In the first half, two long sequences introduce us to the characters: an elaborate wedding (practically a production number), and the deer-hunting expedition which foreshadows the horrors that await them in the jungles. In Vietnam, there is a gripping set piece when the friends are forced to play a game of Russian roulette by their Viet Cong captors, a scene which has been criticized for depicting the enemy as the incarnation of evil, without comment on the American tactics.

The Deer Hunter: *John Savage (left) and Robert De Niro at war in Vietnam.*

Superman flies high over humdrum world

*Clark Kent (Christopher Reeve) transformed into comic-book hero **Superman**.*

New York, 15 December
Joel Schuster and Jerome Siegel's comic-strip hero Superman made his screen debut in Sam Katzman's gimcrack 1948 serial. This time, at considerably greater expense, Christopher Reeve assumes the role of the Man of Steel in *Superman – The Movie*, directed by Richard Donner. Sidestepping the camp clichés celebrated by *Batman* 12 years ago, Donner and his screenwriting team tread a fine line between gently satirizing the original character and hymning his superhuman feats of strength. Christopher Reeve, an accomplished stage actor with an academic background, brings bags of ironic charm to the role of the self-effacing Clark Kent – dispensing a stream of earnest advice to Margot Kidder's Lois Lane – and dons his alter ego's red cape and blue tights with equal aplomb. His chiseled features and formidable physique, specially built up for the role, are the perfect expression of the fantasy hero lurking in the breast of every 98-pound weakling. Gene Hackman was reportedly paid $2 million to play Superman's eccentric enemy, Lex Luthor, but he looks far less happy in the role. Marlon Brando was paid even more, at least $2.5 million, to play Superman's father in the opening sequence when the infant Superman is dispatched to Earth from the exploding planet Krypton. It was worth every cent in publicity which, in the breathless build-up to *Superman*'s release, was summed up in the slogan, "You'll believe a man can fly!" *Superman*'s special effects ensure that you will.

Peter Falk, a spoof Bogart in Robert Moore's **The Cheap Detective**.

Tommy Chong (left), Cheech Marin in **Up in Smoke**, directed by Lou Adler.

Gérard Depardieu in Marco Ferreri's black comedy, **Bye Bye Monkey**.

Klaus Kinski as **Woyzeck** in Werner Herzog's version of Büchner's work.

On trial: Isabelle Huppert is Claude Chabrol's **Violette Nozière**.

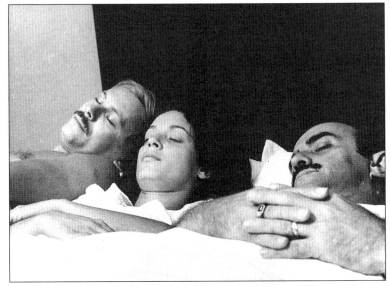

Dona Flor and her Two Husbands: Sonia Braga with José Wilker and Mauro Mendonca, directed by Bruno Barreto (Brazil).

The Herd (Sürü) was scripted by the imprisoned Turkish director Yilmaz Güney and made on his behalf by Zeki Okten.

Jill Clayburgh is Mazursky's **An Unmarried Woman**, Alan Bates her lover.

*Linda Manz in Terrence Malick's second film, the painterly **Days of Heaven**.*

*One of the year's successes, Michael Crichton's gripping, worrying **Coma**.*

*Nick Nolte and Tuesday Weld in the hard-hitting **Who'll Stop the Rain?** (aka **Dog Soldiers**), directed by Karel Reisz.*

*Gary Busey superb as tragic rock 'n' roll pioneer in **The Buddy Holly Story**.*

*John Cassavetes (l), Charles Durning in Brian De Palma's chiller, **The Fury**.*

*Amy Striker and Howard Duff in Robert Altman's merciless and hilarious satire on American middle-class mores, **A Wedding**.*

1979

★ ★

1978 Academy Awards, Dorothy Chandler Pavilion, 9 Apr.

Best Film:	*The Deer Hunter* (dir: Michael Cimino)
Best Director:	Michael Cimino
Best Actor:	Jon Voight *(Coming Home)*
Best Actress:	Jane Fonda *(Coming Home)*
Best Supp. Actor:	Christopher Walken *(The Deer Hunter)*
Best Supp. Actor:	Maggie Smith *(California Suite)*

New York, 10 January
The doyenne of Hollywood actresses, Katharine Hepburn, lives up to her reputation for bluntness. In a rare television interview for CBS, to be shown next Sunday, she lashes out at the current pervasiveness of pornography in films.

Los Angeles, 12 January
John Wayne, suffering from cancer, has undergone a serious operation in which most of his stomach had to be removed.

Rome, 23 January
Sophia Loren's husband, producer Carlo Ponti, has been charged by the Italian courts with illegal exportation of capital.

Paris, 24 January
Actress Jeanne Moreau has shown *Adolescente*, her second film as a director, with Simone Signoret and Francis Huster.

New York, 16 February
Following outbreaks of violence in several cinemas screening Walter Hill's *The Warriors*, Paramount has decided to cancel its advertising campaign and remake the trailers.

West Berlin, 22 February
The Soviet Union and other communist countries have withdrawn from the West Berlin Film Festival in protest against the showing of Michael Cimino's *The Deer Hunter*, a movie about the war in Vietnam.

Hollywood, 23 February
Despite sporadic outbursts of violence and vandalism at theaters showing *The Warriors,* a film about teenage gang violence in New York City, Paramount Pictures has now decided to continue advertising the film. However, the company said it would release exhibitors from their contractual obligations if they felt it posed a threat either to property or persons. The film grossed over $12 million in its first two weeks.

Hollywood, 9 April
After the Oscar ceremony, actress Jane Fonda declared that Michael Cimino's Oscar winner *The Deer Hunter* "was a racist film, which presented the official version of the war in Vietnam."

Ohio, 9 April
Bob Rafelson has started shooting *Brubaker.* The cameramen's union is up in arms about the signing of Bruno Nuytten, the French director of photography, as Haskell Wexler's replacement, and are demanding the withdrawal of his work permit.

New York, 20 April
Release of Woody Allen's *Manhattan.* Allen, Diane Keaton, Michael Murphy and Mariel Hemingway star. The luminous black-and-white photography is by Gordon Willis.

Montana, 28 April
Michael Cimino, on location with *Heaven's Gate*, is 10 days behind on his shooting schedule despite the fact that he has been here since the beginning of the month. He has apparently already spent $11 million of his budget.

Hollywood, 5 August
David Field, the joint head of United Artists production, has imposed a new budget of $27.5 million and a maximum of three hours viewing time on *Heaven's Gate.*

Colorado, 31 August
As part of the Telluride Festival, the uncut original version of Abel Gance's *Napoleon*, reconstructed by historian Kevin Brownlow, with its final scene projected onto a triple screen, was shown in the open air. The director, who was present at the screening, was given a standing ovation by the public.

New York, 30 September
Lauren Bacall has published a book about her private life and career titled *Lauren Bacall, by Myself.*

Los Angeles, 2 October
Universal and Disney Pictures have lost their court case against Sony-Betamax. The court has decided that the use of a video recorder for personal use does not constitute a breach of copyright laws.

New York, 5 October
Opening of Blake Edwards' film, *10,* and the revelation of the sexy Bo Derek, who co-stars with Dudley Moore and Julie Andrews. The film looks set to make Ravel's "Bolero" the hottest music of the moment. But Edwards, who wrote, produced and directed the comedy, is reportedly furious with Orion studios over the visual advertising they chose to promote the film. The poster in question, which the director classifies as "sexist and vulgar", shows Dudley Moore swinging from a chain around the neck of an extremely well-endowed girl.

South Carolina, 23 October
Monty Python's Life of Brian, has been short lived here in Columbia. Ecclesiastical outrage over the British comedy group's satirical movie has forced a cancelation after the first evening's showing. However, the withdrawal of the film is causing an even greater upheaval as citizen groups level charges of censorship and prior restraint at Senator Thurmond, the politician instrumental in the film's suspension.

New York, 7 November
Entertainer and singer Bette Midler has her first starring role on screen in Mark Rydell's *The Rose,* which is being released today. Alan Bates, Frederic Forrest and Harry Dean Stanton co-star.

Palm Springs, 22 December
Darryl Zanuck, the last of the big-name producers in the American movie industry, has died. Zanuck started his career as a gagman for Warner Bros. before becoming a scriptwriter and, by the end of the 20s, a producer. In 1933 he created his own company, 20th Century which merged with Fox two years later to become 20th Century-Fox. Zanuck reigned as absolute master of the company until 1956 when he decided to go independent. He returned to 20th Century-Fox as head of production in 1962 and saved the studio from ruin.

Hollywood, 22 December
Disney has announced plans for its first co-production. The film is *Popeye* and the co-producer Paramount.

Los Angeles, 23 December
When asked which French director they would most like to work with, 10 young actors out of 10 answered François Truffaut.

Hollywood, 31 December
The studios have announced a 5 percent increase in takings from U.S. releases this year. Richard Donner's *Superman* is well in the lead with $80 million in box-office receipts.

DEATHS

Los Angeles, 12 February
Jean Renoir

London, 24 March
Yvonne Mitchell

California, 26 May
George Brent

California, 29 May
Mary Pickford

New York, 2 June
Nicholas Ray

Los Angeles, 6 June
Jack Haley

Los Angeles, 11 June
John Wayne

Paris, 8 September
Jean Seberg

California, 26 September
John Cromwell

Capri, 27 September
Gracie Fields

California, 23 November
Merle Oberon

Paris, 26 November
Marcel L'Herbier

California, 25 December
Joan Blondell

Francis Ford Coppola broke new and terrifying ground with **Apocalypse Now.** *A major achievement, it cost a fortune (Brando was paid $1 million) and was dogged by disaster.*

Antoine Doinel takes a look at his past

*Jean-Pierre Léaud, Marie-France Pisier, Daniel Mesguish in **Love on the Run**.*

Paris, 24 January
François Truffaut's new film, *Love on the Run*, is the fifth in the series of the adventures of the director's alter ego Antoine Doinel alias Jean-Pierre Léaud. This picture is an affectionate backward look at the previous episodes, using some of the footage from them, the first being *The Four Hundred Blows* almost 20 years ago. Here, Doinel, at the age of 35, separated from his wife (Claude Jade) and young son, is involved with Sabine (Dorothée) until he meets Colette (Marie-France Pisier), a childhood sweetheart, now a lawyer. Although as lightweight as the other tales, the movie cannot hide the pain at the loss of youthful spontaneity and the difficulties of obtaining lasting love. This could be the last chapter.

Romy wins a second consecutive César

*Arlette Bonnard (left) and Romy Schneider in Claude Sautet's **A Simple Story**.*

Paris, 3 February
The Césars have been in existence for only four years, but already one star has been crowned best actress twice. Romy Schneider received her second César (after *l'Important c'est d'aimer*) for Claude Sautet's film *A Simple Story*, in which she plays a divorced woman with a teenage son, trying to come to terms with reaching 40. The best actor could also have been awarded the best actress prize, because it went to Michel Serrault's outrageously successful drag queen Alban in Edouard Molinaro's *la Cage aux folles*. *L'Argent des autres* was honored with Césars for both the best film and the best director (Christian de Chalonge), while the Italian Ermanno Olmi's *The Tree of Wooden Clogs* took the best foreign language film award.

Renoir, a French genius, dies far from his beloved Montmartre

Hollywood, 13 February
One of the truly great figures of the cinema, director and writer Jean Renoir has died at his home in Beverly Hills, aged 86. The second son of the Impressionist painter Auguste Renoir, the young Jean often modeled for his father and grew up within an artistic environment which profoundly influenced his attitude to the creative process. Throughout his life he preserved his creative independence, though he regarded the cinema very much as a collaborative art and was a quite talented director of actors. Renoir thus never became part of the French film industry, and fitted even less well into the Hollywood studio system when he arrived as a refugee from Occupied France in 1940. His great period as a director was during the 1930s, when he produced one remarkable film after another, ranging from drama (*la Chienne* 1931, *Toni* 1934, *le Crime de M. Lange* 1935) to thrillers (*la Nuit du carrefour* 1932) and comedy (*Boudu sauvé des eaux* 1932). But Renoir will be best remembered for his celebrated anti-war drama, *la Grande illusion* (1937) starring Jean Gabin and Erich von Stroheim, and for his great masterpiece *la Règle du jeu* (1939) which he scripted, directed and in which he starred. Despite his antipathy to the Hollywood system, he made five interesting films in the U.S. and went on to work in India, Italy, and back in his native France in the 50s. Sadly, he found it impossible to get financing for many of his projects and turned to writing in his later years.

*Renoir in his masterpiece **The Rules of the Game**, here with Carette (right).*

Alfred Hitchcock honored by the AFI

Hollywood, 7 March
The American Film Institute has presented director Alfred Hitchcock with its Life Achievement award. With the leading celebrities in Hollywood in attendance, the evening ceremony was held at the Beverly Hilton Hotel and recorded by CBS TV for broadcast later in the week. Many of the stars of Hitchcock's films, plus other associates, were there including Cary Grant, Jane Wyman and James Stewart, producer Sidney Bernstein and studio head Lew Wasserman, along with French director François Truffaut and Hitch's favorite female star of the 1940s, Ingrid Bergman, who served as the evening's MC. Unfortunately, it was impossible to disguise the fact that this was a sad occasion. Hitchcock and his wife, Alma, who had collaborated on many of his projects, are both in extremely poor health and, quite clearly, were unable fully to appreciate this event held in their honor.

The hippies of 'Hair' filmed by Forman

*The Czech Milos Forman filmed **Hair**, an archetypally American subject.*

Twyla Tharp was the choreographer.

New York, 14 March
After making films about adolescence in Czechoslovakia and *One Flew Over the Cuckoo's Nest*, a hymn to non-conformity, emigré Milos Forman was the logical choice to direct *Hair*, the movie version of hippiedom's hit 1967 stage musical. Although the Age of Aquarius is long over and the Flower People have withered and died, the film offers some vigorous dancing in the streets and parks of New York, some uninhibited playing from the young performers, and a touch of nostalgia for the over-25s. The episodic story follows a naive draftee (John Savage), who gets involved with a bunch of turned-on hippies at a "be-in" in Central Park.

Oscar pays homage to Vietnam this year

Los Angeles, 9 April
As Oscar enters its 51st year, films about Vietnam are honored with Michael Cimino's *The Deer Hunter* voted Best Picture and Cimino himself Best Director. Jon Voight and Jane Fonda, who co-star in *Coming Home*, won the Best Actor and Actress awards for their performances in that film. Christopher Walken was voted Best Supporting Actor for his harrowing performance in *The Deer Hunter* as the blue-collar boy from Pennsylvania undone by his experiences in Vietnam. Maggie Smith won her second Oscar, this time the Best Supporting Actress award, for her work in *California Suite* as, ironically, a Tinseltown actress nominated for an Oscar. The award for best foreign film went to *Préparez vos mouchoirs* (*Get Out Your Handkerchiefs*), directed by Bertrand Blier, while special awards were given to Laurence Olivier, director King Vidor and animator Walter Lantz, the man who created Woody Woodpecker.

Michael Caine and Maggie Smith.

'China Syndrome' comes horribly to life

Jane Fonda and Michael Douglas hot on the trail of the nuclear menace.

Pennsylvania, 28 March
The crisis which has gripped the nuclear power station at Three Mile Island has given a terrifying topicality to *The China Syndrome*, released two weeks ago. The title refers to a melt-down in a nuclear reactor triggering an uncontainable fire which, theoretically, could burn through to China. They say it couldn't happen but *The China Syndrome* entertains the possibility of a serious nuclear accident being hushed up. Jane Fonda plays the journalist on the trail of a hot story, and Michael Douglas, who also produces, is her intrepid cameraman. Jack Lemmon co-stars as the plant's chief engineer, undergoing his own emotional melt-down as disaster looms. James Bridges' intelligent direction focuses not only on the safety of nuclear power but also on the role and responsibilities of journalists.

Sober romanticism in 'The Brontë Sisters'

Paris, 9 May
André Téchiné has wanted to make *The Brontë Sisters* since 1972. Luckily, he waited until he could gather together three of the most talented young actresses in France to play the trio of celebrated Yorkshire authors: Isabelle Adjani (Emily), Marie-France Pisier (Charlotte) and Isabelle Huppert (Anne). The film, cut from three to less than two hours, centers around the sisters' somber relationship with Branwell (Pascal Greggory), their spoiled-genius brother, set in a careful re-creation of the period.

*l to r: Marie-France Pisier, Isabelle Huppert and Adjani are **The Brontë Sisters**.*

Germany and America share Golden Palm

Special Jury Prize winner **Siberiade**.

David Bennent (left) in Volker Schlöndorff's **The Tin Drum**.

Cannes, 24 May
Françoise Sagan and the other members of the jury at this year's Cannes Film Festival had difficulty in choosing between Volker Schlöndorff's *The Tin Drum* and Francis Ford Coppola's *Apocalypse Now*. Therefore they decided that the two films should share the Golden Palm. In a sense, the German and the American movies have something in common since both evoke black pages in their country's history – the rise of Nazism in Germany, and the misguided Vietnam adventure. *The Tin Drum*, based on Günther Grass' complex allegorical novel, is a disturbing look at German history through the relentless gaze of a weird child. The teenage Oskar stopped growing at the age of three by an act of will. Naturally, he is a concern to his parents, because he has tantrums, constantly bangs a toy tin drum, and has a scream that shatters glass. Oskar acts as a sort of conscience to the inhabitants of Danzig when the Nazis are in power and the war rages. The remarkable performance by 12-year-old David Bennent, son of actor Heinz Bennent, effectively brings the book's character to life. War is the principal subject of *Apocalypse Now*, a film which contains some extraordinary set pieces. Coppola has explained that he wanted "to give its audience a sense of the horror, the madness, the sensuousness and the moral dilemma of the Vietnam War." This the director has certainly achieved by camera and sound techniques that assault the senses.

'Alien' horror from British import Scott

Sigourney Weaver and a hideous space monster in Ridley Scott's **Alien**.

New York, 24 May
Constructed as skillfully as the commercials he used to make, Ridley Scott's *Alien* is located in the pulpy, phallic world of the surrealist artist H.R. Giger. Giger's visions of a disturbing biomechanical world owe much to the tales of necromancy written in the 19th century by H.P. Lovecraft. It is on a planet full of these strange shapes that the crew of the space cruiser *Nostromo* find the derelict spacecraft that contains the ultimately terrifying alien of the title. The alien hitches a ride with the *Nostromo* and, in a manner which recalls an old B-movie, *It! The Terror From Beyond Space*, begins to work its way through the crew, displaying a ferocious will to live and procreate at whatever cost to those around it. In the words of *Alien*'s advertising slogan, "In space no one can hear you scream!"

Hollywood mourns the death of its 'Duke'

Hollywood, 11 June
John Wayne has lost a long and painfully fought battle with cancer. Three years ago he made his last film, *The Shootist*, playing an aging gunfighter who is dying of the same affliction. Later he appeared in TV ads for cancer research funds, using the scene from *The Shootist* in which doctor James Stewart diagnoses the disease. Wayne had been a major star since 1939, when he played the Ringo Kid in *Stagecoach*, and grew into a monolith of survival. His approach to filmmaking was characteristically straightforward: "I play John Wayne in every picture regardless of the character, and I've been doing all right, haven't I?" But he has left a number of imperishable performances, notably as abrasive and solitary men, in *Red River*, *Rio Bravo* and, unforgettably, in *The Searchers*, where the character of Ethan Edwards is mapped so closely to Wayne's own gestures that he hardly seems to be acting at all.

In recent years the actor's right-wing views have been known to stir controversy, but his death and the brave manner of his departing have moved the film world.

John Wayne, defender of the faith.

Cannes pays homage to Miklos Jancso

Cannes, 24 May
Discovered on the Croisette in 1965 with his film *The Round-Up*, the Hungarian director Miklos Jancso has now been honored not only with a prize given to his complete oeuvre, but with the screening of many of his films during the Festival. These include *The Round-Up*, *The Confrontation* (1969), *Winter Sirocco* (1969), *Agnus Dei* (1970), *Red Psalm* (1971) and his latest production, *Hungarian Rhapsody*. The latter marks Jancso's return to his native land after making three less successful films in Italy. There are few directors so akin to a choreographer, his films being elaborate ballets, emblematically tracing the movements in the fight for socialism and Hungarian independence – ritual dances of life and death enacted on a bleak Hungarian plain where power constantly changes hands. The camera weaves in and out like an invisible observer, sometimes dancing with the people, at others tracking them down, shooting them. A tracking shot takes on new meaning in Jancso's films.

Coppola at the heart of darkness

Australia produces a star in Judy Davis

Melbourne, 17 August
Director Gillian Armstrong, the creator of several highly regarded short films, has made a sparkling feature debut with *My Brilliant Career*. Acclaimed at Cannes, and the winner of seven Australian awards, including best film and direction, it reveals Miss Armstrong's central concern with the rights of women to independence and free thought. Set in the late 19th century, the sense of period is beautifully evoked in the story of Sybylla, a headstrong young girl from a farming family who eschews the conventional life mapped out for her in order to become a writer. In this role, Judy Davis not only has presence, but also displays the kind of intelligent talent that gives notice of a star in the making. The supporting cast, especially Sam Neill, is excellent.

Martin Sheen finds himself plunged into a dark world of almost hallucinatory horror during the Vietnam War.

New York, 15 August
The making of *Apocalypse Now*, Francis Ford Coppola's latest film, was almost as apocalyptic as its subject. This work on the Vietnam War (loosely based on Joseph Conrad's *Heart of Darkness*) started shooting in March 1976 on location in the Philippines, where Coppola and his team had planned to work for 13 weeks. They finished 238 days later, having raised the budget from $12 million to $31 million. Much of this came out of Coppola's own pocket and from funding for which he, as an independent producer, could be held accountable. During the course of filming, the director faced many difficulties, including a typhoon that destroyed most of the huge and expensive sets. He also had problems with top-billed, top-salaried Marlon Brando, who appears as Colonel Walter E. Kurtz very far on into the two-and-a-half-hour movie. After a week, Harvey Keitel, in the key role of Captain Benjamin Willard on the quest for Kurtz, had to be replaced by Martin Sheen, who then suffered a heart attack, which held up much of the shooting until he had recovered. To make matters worse, a civil war broke out in the Philippines, depriving Coppola of the helicopters he needed. Such were the troubles and delays on the production that the press rechristened it "Apocalypse When?" After three nightmarish years, *Apocalypse Now* has finally reached our screens, but with two different endings – one with a bang, the other with a whimper – because Coppola himself was not sure how the film should conclude. The climax that was ditched from the one version, and reinstated in the other, is an assault on Kurtz's base by both American and Viet Cong forces, a sequence whose force justifies the movie's title.

Co-stars Judy Davis and Sam Neill.

Marlon Brando in the role of Colonel Kurtz, symbolic of a world gone mad.

In Krzysztof Kieslowski's *Camera Buff*, worker Jerzy Stuhr buys a home-movie camera to film his baby. However, he becomes the official filmmaker at the factory where he works and comes into conflict with his bosses.

The revitalization of the German cinema

Hamburg, 22 September

Not since the 1920s has the German cinema known as much feverish creative activity as it has in recent years. Heading the list of top directors are Rainer Werner Fassbinder, Werner Herzog, Wim Wenders and Volker Schlöndorff. The prolific Fassbinder has delivered two films this year, *The Third Generation*, about a group of terrorists, and *The Marriage of Maria Braun*, which retraces the history of postwar Germany through the portrait of a formidable woman, played by Hanna Schygulla, star of the young German cinema. Fifty-seven years after F.W. Murnau, Herzog has resuscitated the Dracula myth with *Nosferatu the Vampire*, in which Klaus Kinski, the director's favorite actor,

Director and young star (left) of **The Tin Drum***, a ferocious portrait of Germany under the stranglehold of the Nazis.*

hypnotically plays the title role. Wenders has moved into the world of *film noir* with *The American Friend*, adapted from the Patricia Highsmith thriller *Ripley's Game*. Shot partly in English, it stars Bruno Ganz and Dennis Hopper, with appearances by Hollywood directors Nicholas Ray and Sam Fuller. The international success of many of these films, especially Fassbinder's *The Marriage of Maria Braun* and Schlöndorff's *The Tin Drum*, has undoubtedly contributed to the rebirth of the German cinema. And a dozen West German directors, including Fassbinder, Schlöndorff, Edgar Reitz and Alexander Kluge, have contributed to the recent film *Germany in Autumn*, revealing the extent of the talent available.

Isabelle Adjani and Klaus Kinski in Herzog's version of **Nosferatu***.*

Dennis Hopper (left) and Bruno Ganz in Wim Wenders' **The American Friend***.*

Fassbinder's **The Marriage of Maria Braun***. On the right, Hanna Schygulla.*

The 'Declaration of Hamburg'

Hamburg, 22 September

"The German cinema of the 1980s will not submit to the decisions of commissions nor administrations, and its progress will not be determined by pressure groups," declared the 43 young German filmmakers who have gathered to assess the last few years of the industry. They have decided to take a united position in the face of the growing number of constraints put upon them by the powers-that-be. This declaration recalls the celebrated Oberhausen Manifesto of 1962 when a group of young filmmakers, working outside the commercial system, stormed the festival, criticizing "Papa's Kino" and promising to make good films at half the usual cost. Even more so than then, the directors' meeting in Hamburg has given proof of their talent and popularity, at home and abroad. To date, West Germany produces an average of 65 films a year, of which more than half derive from the so-called "Young German Cinema".

Jean Seberg falls victim to despair

Paris, 8 September
This evening, in a side street of the 16th arrondissement, the corpse of Jean Seberg was found in the back of a car. The American-born actress had disappeared from her home a week ago. Eleven days earlier, on returning from filming in Guyana, she attempted to commit suicide by throwing herself in front of a subway train. She succeeded on her second attempt with an overdose of sleeping pills. The 40-year-old Seberg shot to fame at the age of 17 playing the title role in Otto Preminger's *Saint Joan*. She later moved to France and for a while was married to the writer and film-maker Romain Gary.

*Seberg in Preminger's **Saint Joan**.*

Financial crisis over for Bergman

Stockholm, 29 November
It now looks likely that Ingmar Bergman, Sweden's leading director of films and theater, may be returning to his country after three-and-a-half years of self-imposed exile. The Swedish government is apparently taking steps to remedy the scandalous situation whereby Bergman, accused of owing back taxes, was treated quite disgracefully by the tax authorities. During his years in Munich, Bergman directed *The Serpent's Egg* (in English) as well as a British/Norwegian co-production *Autumn Sonata* (both 1978).

Polanski tackles English classic with 'Tess'

Paris, 31 October
Two years have passed since Roman Polanski skipped bail after being found guilty of having sex with a minor, and he remains a fugitive from American justice. His latest film, *Tess*, adapted from Thomas Hardy's Wessex novel *Tess of the D'Urbervilles*, has been filmed in France, since residency in Britain would have led to his extradition to the United States. It's a handsome production, starring the staggeringly beautiful Nastassja Kinski in the title role as the innocent country girl corrupted and discarded by polite society. The daughter of German character star Klaus Kinski, Nastassja made her film debut in 1975 with a small role as a juggler in Wim Wenders' *Wrong Movement*.

Nastassja Kinski is Hardy's heroine.

Losey's terrific excursion into filmed opera

Paris, 14 November
Joseph Losey's film adaptation of Mozart's *Don Giovanni* was the brainchild of Daniel Toscan du Plantier, a producer at Gaumont who wants to steer his company towards more cultural films. Losey, however, insisted that the film would not be merely a reproduction of a theatrical event, with static action and reduced decor. He, therefore, shot the opera in and around handsome Palladian villas in northern Italy, getting his singers to move through the settings as naturally as possible. For example, Don Ottavio's two arias have him being rowed along in a boat and walking over sleeping peasants. Then, during the "Catalogue" aria, a parade of nubile young women is displayed for Don Giovanni's delight. Losey and his co-scenarist, the well-named Frantz Salieri, have introduced a young man in black as a silent attendant on the libertine, and the climax has Giovanni tumbling into a glass-blower's vat rather than journeying to the depths of Hell. The work, conducted by Loren Maazel, is superbly sung by, among others, Ruggero Raimondi (Giovanni), Kiri Te Kanawa (Elvira), Edda Moser (Anna) and José Van Dam (Leporello).

Ruggero Raimondi sings Don Giovanni in Losey's film of Mozart's opera.

Soft-shoe shuffle of top executives

Hollywood, 18 December
The uncertainties of the movie business and the basic insecurity of the Hollywood studios lie behind the recent musical chairs played by many of the leading production executives during the past year. When, for example, a production chief is considered a "hot property", normal business considerations no longer apply. Thus, although it is not too clear to what extent David Begelman was responsible for the modest recovery at Columbia in the mid-1970s, the studio made every effort to keep him on even after he admitted he had embezzled money from the company. And now, a relatively short time since his departure from Columbia (in February 1978), he has been hired by MGM as their new studio head. Similarly, when Alan Hirschfield was dismissed by Columbia six months after Begelman, he soon found a new home as the boss of 20th Century-Fox, replacing Alan Ladd Jr. who had resigned in June 1979 along with his two vice presidents Gareth Wigan and Jay Kanter. As the team which had been most responsible for the revival of Fox during the 70s, they too were certain not to remain unemployed for long, and it was only a few months before they were able to announce the formation of a new independent production company. The Ladd Co., with financial backing from Warner Bros. as part of a deal to distribute their films, was obviously following in the footsteps of Arthur Krim and Robert Benjamin, who departed from United Artists to found Orion Pictures a year or so earlier.

All this activity, and the continual jockeying for position, reflects the film industry's recovery in general during the past couple of years – improved attendance and box office finally reversing the long postwar decline, and a rapid growth in the video and cable TV markets which is set to continue well into the forseeable future. The value to film production companies and owners of a backlog of old movies is obvious. This clearly looks like a new period of opportunity for the industry, and it is not surprising that there are many who wish to be a part of this growth and to reap the benefits. ▷

German Werner Herzog remakes F.W. Murnau's 1921 classic vampire tale.

*Dustin Hoffman plays mother to Justin Henry in **Kramer vs. Kramer**.*

*Barbara Harris, Alan Alda in the political drama **The Seduction of Joe Tynan**.*

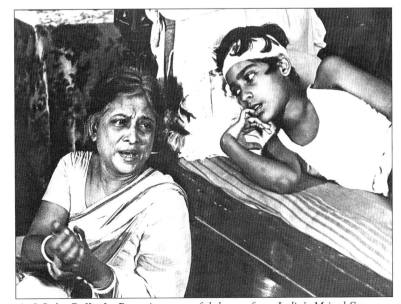

***And Quiet Rolls the Dawn** is a powerful drama from India's Mrinal Sen.*

*l to r: John Cleese, Michael Palin (Pontius Pilate), Graham Chapman in the irreverent **Monty Python's Life of Brian**, directed by Terry Jones.*

The last law in a world gone out of control. Pray that he's out there somewhere.

MAD MAX

INTERCEPTOR

Produced by BYRON KENNEDY · Directed by GEORGE MILLER · With MEL GIBSON · Music by BRIAN MAY
Written by JAMES McCAUSLAND and GEORGE MILLER

Australian George Miller's debut stars Mel Gibson as a leather-clad avenger.

Left to right: Jackie Earle Haley, Daniel Stern, Dennis Quaid and Dennis Christopher in **Breaking Away***, this year's sleeper hit.*

Miss Piggy, Kermit the Frog make their big-screen debut: **The Muppet Movie***.*

Flesh-eating zombies walk the earth in George A. Romero's suspense horror flick, **Dawn of the Dead***, follow-up to* **Night of the Living Dead***.*

Steve Martin is **The Jerk** *in Carl Reiner's movie.*

James Brolin, one of the victims of **The Amityville Horror***.*

The Arthurian legend retold.

Tedious script, amazing images.

*Dee Hepburn, Gordon John Sinclair in **Gregory's Girl** (Great Britain).*

*Oleg Tabakov is Nikita Mikhalkov's **Oblomov**, with Yuri Bogatyryov (r).*

*Wallace Shawn, André Gregory conversing in Malle's **My Dinner With André**.*

Reconstructed by Kevin Brownlow, Abel Gance's magnificent 1927 epic.

*Left to right: Jessica Harper, Bernadette Peters and Steve Martin in **Pennies From Heaven** from Dennis Potter's British TV success.*

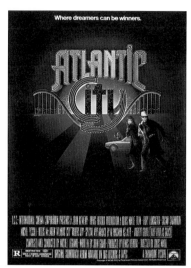

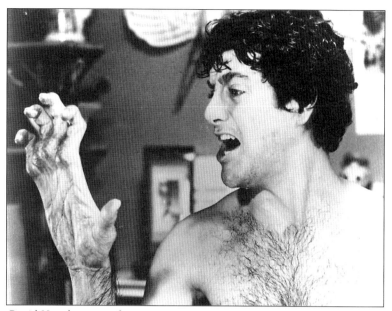

Louis Malle's superb evocation.

Forman made Doctorow's bestseller.

*David Naughton transforming into **An American Werewolf in London**.*

*A characteristically mind-blowing image from David Cronenberg's **Scanners**.*

Clash of the Titans, *directed by Desmond Davis, was a not too successful spectacle involving Greek mythology.*

*David Warner in Terry Gilliam's **Time Bandits**, a mix of violence and humor.*

1982

★ ★ ★ ★ ★ ★ ★ ★ **1982** ★

1981 Academy Awards, Dorothy Chandler Pavilion, 29 Mar.

Best Film:	*Chariots of Fire* (dir: Hugh Hudson)
Best Director:	Warren Beatty *(Reds)*
Best Actor:	Henry Fonda *(On Golden Pond)*
Best Actress:	Katharine Hepburn *(On Golden Pond)*
Best Supp. Actor:	John Gielgud *(Arthur)*
Best Supp. Actress:	Maureen Stapleton *(Reds)*

New York, 4 January
The National Society of Film Critics Awards ceremony last night (Louis Malle's *Atlantic City* took three of the major awards) was notable for the way critics called on Polish authorities to release Andrzej Wajda "and all other Polish film directors, producers, screenwriters, actors and craftsmen who are currently being detained for their political beliefs and associations."

Hollywood, 8 February
The filming of *Brainstorm*, which was interrupted last November by the death of its star, Natalie Wood, has started again. A new ending has been written for the film and Lloyd's of London have paid out $3 million so that the film can be completed.

New York, 18 February
Lee Strasberg, founder of the Actors Studio, died of a heart attack yesterday, just three days after his spirited chorus routine with former students Robert De Niro and Al Pacino at Radio City Music Hall's "Night of 100 Stars".

Paris, 24 February
Former scriptwriter Laurence Kasdan's first feature as director, *Body Heat*, opens here. A contemporary *film noir* with echoes of *Double Indemnity*, starring Kathleen Turner, it has made a substantial impression in America.

Berlin, 25 February
A homegrown film, Rainer Werner Fassbinder's *Veronika Voss*, has won the Golden Bear at the 32nd Film Festival here. The film, starring Rosel Zech as a has-been movie star, pays tribute to UFA.

Los Angeles, 4 March
Frank Capra was honored with the AFI's Life Achievement Award. Among the numerous stars of his films present for the occasion were James Stewart, Barbara Stanwyck, Claudette Colbert and Bette Davis.

Atlanta, 19 March
Columbia, the last of the majors from Hollywood's golden era to remain independent, has now been sold on the open market. The successful bidder is the Coca-Cola company, which is reported to have paid a cool $750 million for the prestigious film company.

Hollywood, 31 March
Carolco, the financing and foreign sales organization, has sold its first in-house production, *First Blood*, almost worldwide. The film, not as yet complete, has survived injuries to star Sylvester Stallone, the exit of Kirk Douglas over script disagreements, and the harsh Canadian weather. Carolco's partners blame the inflated $15 million budget on these mishaps.

Santa Fe, 27 April
Godfrey Reggio's *Koyaanisqatsi* stunned audiences last night at its Santa Fe Film Festival world premiere. The film, seven years in the making and shot across 14 states, features a minimalist musical score by Philip Glass. The title is a Hopi Indian expression meaning "life out of balance".

New York, 21 May
Release of *Annie*, John Huston's film version of the Broadway musical comedy inspired by Harold Gray's cartoon strip.

New York, 9 June
Steven Spielberg, an avid collector of cinema objects, has purchased "Rosebud", the child's sled belonging to Charles Foster Kane (Orson Welles) in the film *Citizen Kane*, for $60,500.

Hollywood, 30 June
Shooting starts today on *Psycho II*, to be directed by Anthony Perkins who will also reprise his role as the proprietor of the Bates Motel. Vera Miles, who was in the 1960 original, appears again.

Los Angeles, 8 July
Over 1,000 people are expected to turn out tonight at the Variety Arts Theater for the 6th Annual Erotic Film Awards. According to industry spokesman Dave Friedman, during 1981 over a million X-rated video-cassettes were sold in America.

Hollywood, 13 July
After 16 weeks of national release *Porky's* has become only the 27th film to top the $100 million mark.

Los Angeles, 12 August
The much loved stage and movie actor, Henry Fonda, has died after several months of illness. Fonda rose to international stardom in the mid-1930s and throughout his acting career was appreciated by the public and profession alike. He got the AFI Life Achievement Award in 1978 and won his only Oscar for *On Golden Pond* earlier this year.

Los Angeles, 16 August
Rouben Mamoulian was honored last night as the 13th recipient of the Directors Guild of America D.W. Griffith Award for a lifetime of outstanding contributions to motion pictures. On this occasion of the Golden Jubilee of his 1932 film, *Love Me Tonight*, the audience was treated to clips from many of his works, including *Queen Christina*.

London, 29 August
Ingrid Bergman has died. Her last film was Ingmar Bergman's *Autumn Sonata* in 1978.

Monaco, 14 September
Princess Grace of Monaco was killed in a tragic car accident today. The former actress Grace Kelly gave up her star status to marry Prince Rainier of Monaco in 1956.

Hollywood, 6 October
Fines totalling $62,375 were levied against five people or companies for 45 safety code violations in connection with the *Twilight Zone* helicopter tragedy last July. John Landis and his company Levitsky Prods. were fined $30,955 and Western Helicopter Inc. $20,965.

Tunis, 30 October
The major prize at the ninth cinema festival here has been awarded to the Malian film *The Wind* (*Finyé*), directed by Souleymane Cissé.

Los Angeles, 1 November
King Vidor has died at the age of 88. Vidor began directing with a two-reeler on car-racing, *The Tow*, in 1914, and made his final film (another short, *The Metaphor*) 66 years later in 1980. This makes his the longest directorial career on record.

London, 2 November
A new commercial television channel, Channel Four, dedicated to transmitting quality programs and catering to special interests, goes on the air today.

Los Angeles, 30 November
After her period as a political activist, Jane Fonda has taken up a less radical cause: the body beautiful. The star's fitness book, *My Method*, has already sold 700,000 copies in the U.S. and is now being published in Europe.

Hollywood, 31 December
Universal alone accounted for over 30 percent of all box-office takings during the year, thanks to the unprecedented success of Steven Spielberg's *E.T.*. During the year the major studios have produced only 50 films in the U.S., while the number of films made abroad was up 75 percent from 1981.

DEATHS

California, 11 February
Eleanor Powell

Los Angeles, 5 March
John Belushi

England, 26 April
Celia Johnson

Munich, 10 June
Rainer Werner Fassbinder

California, 29 June
Henry King

London, 12 June
Kenneth More

Paris, 5 November
Jacques Tati

This fairy-tale image captures the heart-warming theme of **E.T. The Extra-Terrestrial**. *Steven Spielberg's film deservedly won the hearts and minds of children of all ages.*

Richly international lineup at 35th Festival

Parsifal from Germany's Hans Jürgen Syberberg, shown outside competition.

Guney's **Yol***: sharing the Palm.*

Christine Boisson in Antonioni's film.

Cannes, 26 May

Because of the exceptional quality of this year's Festival entries, the jury, presided over by Italian stage director Giorgio Strehler, created a special award, the 35th Festival prize, as was done exactly 10 years ago for Cannes' 25th birthday. It was presented to Michelangelo Antonioni's film *Identification of a Woman*, his first in seven years, during which time he had been experimenting with video techniques. The great Italian director has returned here to familiar territory – the void at the heart of a relationship, and the diffi-

culty of loving someone fully in our times. The joint winners of the Golden Palm were both powerful denunciations of repressive regimes. *Missing*, Costa-Gavras' first American film, follows the tortuous quest of a father (Jack Lemmon, voted best actor) for his son who has been arrested by the military junta in Chile. The film chillingly captures the atmosphere of a police state, and the political message is unequivocal. *Yol* is even more remarkable in that it was shot in Turkey by Serif Gören from a detailed script written by Yilmaz Guney when he was in jail. The negative was smuggled out to Europe where Guney, following his escape from prison last year, edited it. *Yol*, "the road of life" being the nearest translation, follows the lives of five prisoners on a week's parole

to all corners of the country. It is acted with exceptional conviction, against vividly realized landscapes. And political repression, the 1956 Hungarian uprising, also forms the background to Karoly Makk's *Another Way*, featuring two brilliant actresses, one of whom (Jadwiga Jankowska-Cieslak) won the award. The Special Jury Prize went to a less contemporary but no less effective film. This was *Night of the Shooting Stars* (*La Notte di San Lorenzo*) by Paolo and Vittorio Taviani, which retells the events of August 1944 when a Tuscan town was threatened with destruction by the Nazis as the Americans advanced. It is full of bravura and inspiring sequences, as was the bizarre epic *Fitzcarraldo*, for which Werner Herzog won the best director award.

Terrific young cast makes a meal of 'Diner'

Baltimore, 14 May

Diner is a touching and funny portrait of a group of guys moving awkwardly out of their teens as the 60s are about to dawn. First-time director Barry Levinson has conjured up his own memories of hanging out with the gang at the eating place of the title in his native Baltimore. Each of the characters, played

brilliantly by relative newcomers, has a different problem to resolve. Daniel Stern, the only married man, finds he has nothing much to say to his wife, Ellen Barkin; Steve Guttenberg is afraid that the same thing will happen to him; Kevin Bacon is a dropout who drinks too much, and Mickey Rourke is under pressure to settle a gambling debt. Beguiling.

Daniel Stern, Mickey Rourke, Steve Guttenberg, Kevin Bacon, Timothy Daly.

Best actress Jadwiga Jankowska-Cieslak (left) and Grazyna Szapolowska.

Romy dies of a broken heart

Paris, 29 May
Romy Schneider has been found dead from a heart attack, brought about by an excess of alcohol and pills. Since the tragic death of her son David last July, Romy declared that she felt she was living on a sinking ship. "My life is over," she told the German magazine *Stern*. Nevertheless, she finished shooting a film dedicated to "David and his Father", and was hoping to return to the stage. Hounded by the tabloid press, she was forced to change her address several times before settling into an apartment with her new boyfriend Laurent Pétin. At 7:30 this morning, he found her dead on the sofa, a pen in her hand and an unfinished letter by her side.

Gossett gives a lesson to Gere

Hollywood, 28 July
Richard Gere has exchanged the designer suits he wore in *American Gigolo* for the crisp white uniform of *An Officer and a Gentleman*. He is the misfit in the middle of a grueling course at the Naval Officer Candidate School, who is challenged by tough black drill sergeant Louis Gossett Jr. to prove whether he's "a steer or a queer." Fortunately Debra Winger is on hand to put the issue beyond doubt in a romance which, in spite of swear words and steamy sex scenes, follows a tried and trusted Hollywood formula.

Richard Gere and Lou Gossett Jr.

Another magic message from space

Henry Thomas, the little boy, with his new friend, the gentle visitor from space magnificently created by Carlo Rambaldi.

New York, 13 June
Variety has already called Steven Spielberg's latest picture, *E.T. The Extra-Terrestrial*, "the best Disney film never made", and the movie is, indeed, a remarkable celebration of the childhood innocence dear to Walt Disney's heart. A fatherless 10-year-old boy, played by Henry Thomas, befriends a creature from another planet who has been stranded on Earth. Much of the movie is shot from hip height, the point of view of small children, and in the process the charming little alien becomes the secret companion of all our childhoods as Spielberg moves from terror through comedy and death to the exhilaration of the children's climactic magic BMX bike ride. This is Spielberg's most personal film, and it is all the more powerful for being filtered through his instinctive grasp of the power of myth. Smallness never diminishes anything in a Spielberg film, not least the small protagonists in *E.T.*

Ridley's replicants show a frightening future in 'Blade Runner'

Los Angeles, 25 June
After *Alien*, Ridley Scott has stayed in the world of science fiction with *Blade Runner*, adapted from the Philip K. Dick classic, *Do Androids Dream of Electric Sheep?*. An android might be programmed with sufficiently sophisticated human responses to convince him that he is, indeed, human. This possibility hovers in the background of *Blade Runner*, in which Harrison Ford plays the hardboiled bounty hunter on the track of a band of semi-human robot replicants in the trash-littered, steam-shrouded streets of Los Angeles' Chinatown in 2019. The replicants combine instinctive animal grace with balletically explosive violence directed against their human creators. Fighting to stay the hand of the executioner, these deadly creatures engage our sympathy more than their sub-Bogartian pursuer who, ironically, might himself be a highly specialized android. With superb production design by Lawrence G. Paull, special effects by Douglas Trumbull and an arresting performance by Dutch actor Rutger Hauer in the role of the blond and piercingly blue-eyed chief android, *Blade Runner* brilliantly combines the conventions of the private eye genre with a bleak vision of a 21st-century future. It's a world in which, as the film's publicity tells us, "no one gets out of life alive."

*Pris (Daryl Hannah) and Batty (Rutger Hauer), **Blade Runner**'s 'replicants'.*

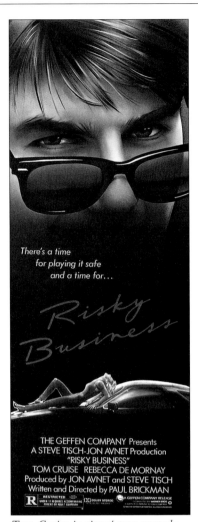

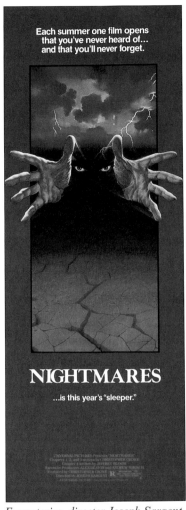

Nagisa Oshima's star David Bowie.

Tom Cruise in risqué teen comedy.

Jennifer Beals, a female Travolta!

Four stories, director Joseph Sargent.

Koyaanisqatsi: *non-narrative view of America with time-lapse photography.*

*Mia Farrow, Woody Allen in the latter's **Zelig**, about a human chameleon.*

*Peter Riegert (2nd right) and Burt Lancaster (r) in Bill Forsyth's **Local Hero**.*

*Isabelle Adjani is the deranged heroine of **One Deadly Summer** (France).*

*Vittorio Gassman, Geraldine Chaplin in Alain Resnais' **Life is a Bed of Roses**.*

This was a brave stab, but it doesn't match Lubitsch's 1942 masterpiece.

Psycho II: *Norman Bates and the old dark house are back after 22 years.*

*Linda Griffiths (left) and Jane Hallaren are lovers in John Sayles' **Lianna**.*

*Catherine Deneuve and David Bowie in vampire pic **The Hunger**.*

*Richard Farnsworth as a real-life robber in **The Grey Fox** (Canada).*

*Matthew Broderick and Ally Sheedy in John Badham's **War Games**: a school kid taps into the Pentagon computer, causing havoc.*

Off-beat, original mix of thriller, romance, and comment on movie-making.

Left to right: Richard Edson, Eszter Balint and John Lurie in **Stranger Than Paradise**, directed by Jim Jarmusch.

Martin Kove (l), trainer Pat Morita (r) and **The Karate Kid**, Ralph Macchio.

Greystoke: Christopher Lambert's Tarzan in England, with Ralph Richardson.

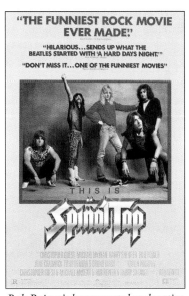

Rob Reiner's heavy metal rock satire.

Tom Hanks, Darryl Hannah starred.

Purple Rain: Prince makes a film.

Michael Palin in A Private Function.

Emilio Estevez (left) and Harry Dean Stanton in Alex Cox's Repo Man.

Redford as a big-league baseball star in an attractive Barry Levinson film.

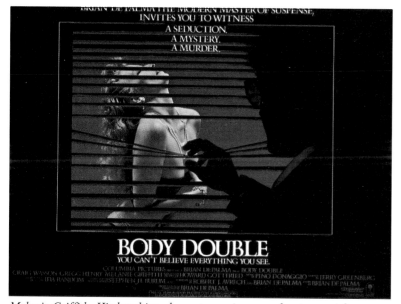
Melanie Griffith, Hitchcockian elements, semi-porn and extreme violence.

Ex-actor John Derek, Bo's husband, wrote and directed this unsavory piece.

★ ★

1984 Academy Awards, Dorothy Chandler Pavilion, 25 Mar.

Best Film:	*Amadeus* (dir: Milos Forman)
Best Director:	Milos Forman
Best Actor:	F. Murray Abraham *(Amadeus)*
Best Actress:	Sally Field *(Places in the Heart)*
Best Supp. Actor:	Haing S. Ngor *(The Killing Fields)*
Best Supp. Actress:	Peggy Ashcroft *(A Passage to India)*

Hollywood, 29 January
MGM-United Artists has just announced that *Yankee Doodle Dandy* (1942) is to be colored using a new process developed by Color System Technology. The studio is planning, initially, to have 20 black-and-white films colored.

Paris, 6 February
Emmanuelle, made by Just Jaeckin with Sylvia Kristel, has finished its long run. It had been showing at the Triomphe cinema on the Champs-Elysées since its release on 26 June 1974, beating the previous record held by *West Side Story*.

Hollywood, 7 March
Gene Kelly has been honored with the American Film Institute's Life Achievement Award.

London, 18 March
Launch of British Film Year with the presentation to the Queen of David Lean's screen adaptation of E.M. Forster's *A Passage to India*.

Hollywood, 25 March
The selection of *The Times of Harvey Milk* as Best Feature Documentary at this year's Academy Awards marks a significant shift in attitude from Academy voters. The portrait of San Francisco's murdered gay city supervisor, Harvey Milk, won against strong competion from Maximilian Schell's *Marlene* and the El Salvador chronicle, *In the Name of the People*.

Hollywood, 31 March
My Mother's Keeper, an autobiographical book by Bette Davis' daughter Barbara, has caused a scandal with its unsavory revelations about the great star.

Buenos Aires, 4 April
Luis Puenzo has released his much awaited film *The Official Story (La Historia Oficial)*, about middle-class life under the harsh dictatorship of the junta.

Paris, 15 May
Filmmaker Youssef Chahine is in Paris to present *Adieu Bonaparte*, the Franco-Egyptian co-production which he directed. The film, an official entry at Cannes, is about the life of an Egyptian family in Alexandria during Napoleon's occupation, and stars Michel Piccoli, Mohsen Mohieine, and Patrice Chéreau as the French Emperor.

France, 9 June
At this year's International Festival of Animated Pictures (JICA – Journée Internationales du Cinéma d'Animation) in Annecy, the jury, to everyone's amusement, awarded equal first prize to *Hell* (Soviet Union) and *Paradise* (Canada).

Paris, 8 July
Jean-Jacques Annaud announced that he plans to make a film version of Umberto Eco's prize-winning bestseller *The Name of the Rose*.

New York, 23 July
Woody Allen has signed a new contract with Orion Pictures. At his request it includes a clause forbidding the marketing of his films in South Africa because of that country's color *apartheid*.

France, 25 July
Actor Rock Hudson has been admitted to the American Hospital at Neuilly where he continues his battle against AIDS.

New York, 16 August
Singer Madonna and actor Sean Penn were married in a private ceremony here today.

New York, 27 August
The Warner Bros. production, *Pee Wee's Big Adventure*, was the top box-office draw in the New York area this past weekend. The episodic comedy, by first-time director Tim Burton, features the rather surreal Pee Wee Herman in a manic search for his stolen bicycle.

Venice, 7 September
At this year's Festival, French director Agnes Varda has carried off the Golden Lion for *Sans toit ni loi (Vagabonde)*, while the Silver Lion went to another woman director, Marion Hänsel, for *Dust*. The best actor award was won by Gérard Depardieu for his performance in Maurice Pialat's film *Police*. The jury's special prize was awarded to *Tangos, l'exile de Gardel*, directed by Fernando Solanas.

Los Angeles, 19 September
Elizabeth Taylor is organizing a gala evening to collect funds for the fight against AIDS.

New York, 7 October
Several thousand people took part in a demonstration in front of the Lincoln Center today. They were protesting, in response to an appeal by the Catholic League for Civil and Religious Rights, against the "blasphemous nature" of Jean-Luc Goddard's film *Hail Mary (Je vous salue Marie)*. The film is currently being shown as part of the 23rd New York Film Festival.

Hollywood, 15 October
Rupert Murdoch's relentless march towards media control in the U.S. is causing concern on Wall Street. His latest acquisition, 20th Century-Fox from Marvin Davis' holding company, cost him over $500 million. Last month Murdoch gave up his Australian citizenship and became an American in order to buy up five of Metromedia's television stations. The magnate has now announced the merger of Fox with the television stations to form Fox Inc.

New York, 16 October
Yul Brynner, who lost his fight against lung cancer last week, has left a last testament to the world – a short film "clip" begging all smokers to give up cigarettes.

Los Angeles, 13 December
Paramount's *Clue*, the first film to be based on a popular board game, is releasing today with four different endings on 1,006 screens. Along with Tim Curry, Madeline Khan and Christopher Lloyd, the film features Eileen Brennan. *Clue* heralds Brennan's return to the screen following a devastating run-in with a speeding Thunderbird in late 1982.

Los Angeles, 16 December
The "unreleasable" *Brazil* has won top honors at the Los Angeles Film Critics Association's annual vote. The controversial movie, which has been the center of a heated dispute between director Terry Gilliam and MCA president Sidney Sheinberg, almost scooped the pool by winning best picture, best director and best screenplay (Gilliam, Tom Stoppard, Charles McKeown).

New York, 31 December
According to a marketing company, in 1985 cinema attendance by the adolescent population dropped by 20 percent. On the other hand, this same group rents three times more films on video than previously.

DEATHS

England, 2 March
Michael Redgrave

California, 9 May
Edmond O'Brien

Connecticut, 16 May
Margaret Hamilton

New York, 8 August
Louise Brooks

Massachusetts, 28 August
Ruth Gordon

France, 30 September
Simone Signoret

Beverly Hills, 2 October
Rock Hudson

New York, 10 October
Yul Brynner

Hollywood, 10 October
Orson Welles

California, 1 November
Phil Silvers

California, 19 November
Stepin Fetchit

New York, 4 December
Anne Baxter

Witness is the first American movie made by the prize-winning Australian director Peter Weir. Set largely in an Amish community near Philadelphia, it has proved immensely successful.

Gung-ho flying saga 'Top Gun' is a sure-fire hit for Tom Cruise

Gruesome, effective remake of 'The Fly'

Los Angeles, 16 May
Like his brother Ridley, British director Tony Scott cut his cinematic teeth making television commercials. His mastery of the 30-second attention span-style has stood him in good stead in *Top Gun*, which he has turned into a two-hour recruiting advertisement for the U.S. Navy. At the Navy's elite aviation training school young tyros compete for glory in the air and on the ground. Ceaselessly smirking behind his Ray-Bans is pint-sized Tom Cruise, a gung-ho pilot and cardboard stud making a play for coolly leggy flying instructor Kelly McGillis. McGillis looms over Cruise in much the same way that tall leading ladies used to cast their shadow over Alan Ladd and, it has to be said, theirs is a pairing which generates absolutely no sexual chemistry. Scott seems more excited by the dogfights he stages like billion-dollar video games. What acting there is in the movie is accomplished by the boyish Anthony Edwards, cast as Cruise's sidekick, who emerges as the most personable and, therefore, ill-fated, of the clean-cut wannabes in this slickly contrived entertainment which, in Scott's hands, has become its own commercial.

Tom Cruise, flying ace in the making, with instructor and lover Kelly McGillis.

Director David Cronenberg examines Jeff Goldblum's amazing makeup.

Los Angeles, 15 August
One of the more engagingly dotty science fiction movies of the 1950s was *The Fly*, in which an unfortunate design defect in scientist Al Hedison's matter transmitter turned him into half-man, half-fly. Now David Cronenberg has remade this schlock classic, casting a frenetic Jeff Goldblum as Dr. Seth Brundle, whose teleportation experiments succeed only in fusing his genes with those of the insect of the title. The most literal-minded of horror and science fiction directors, Cronenberg piles one stomach-churning special effect on top of another as Goldblum's body is hideously distorted and his lingering humanity ebbs away. Cronenberg once observed that he could "conceive of a beauty contest for the inside of the human body where people would unzip themselves and show you the best spleen, the best heart, the best-looking viscera." *The Fly* is a truly visceral experience which the director sees as a metaphor for aging: "In time we all turn into monsters."

Brash Bette outwits the 'Ruthless People' in a mad comedy

Hollywood, 27 June
Big, bad, brassy Bette Midler is the world's most disagreeable kidnap victim in *Ruthless People*, directed by Jim Abrahams and David and Jerry Zucker, the team responsible for *Kentucky Fried Movie*, *Airplane* and *Top Secret*. She's been snatched by suburban couple Judge Reinhold and Helen Slater, whose fashion designs have been ripped off by Midler's slimy little husband Danny De Vito. The only problem is that De Vito, while bewailing the fate of his wife for the benefit of the cops, is quite happy to see his wife disappear – he was planning to murder her anyway. Meanwhile his mistress Anita Morris, suspecting that De Vito has contrived the kidnap himself, is hatching a plot to blackmail him with the help of her slow-witted boyfriend Bill Pullman. Amid all these shenanigans, the only people who fail the ruthlessness test at the first fence are health-conscious kidnappers Slater and Reinhold, who keep lowering the ransom price. All ends happily, if such a thing is possible with so many deeply unpleasant people stalking the screen. One suspects that the real purpose of the movie, apart from allowing Midler to holler her head off, is to send up Robert Redford's po-faced hit *Ordinary People*.

Helen Slater (left) with Bette Midler as the 'prisoner' she hopes to ransom.

Before his transformation into a fly.

How much do movie stars earn today?

London, 1 August

According to a long article in *Company* magazine last month, the most highly paid actor in the world is Sylvester Stallone. Based on the tremendous success of the *Rocky* films (which he wrote and, later, directed) and the two *Rambo*s (which he co-wrote), Stallone is the first star to break the $10-million barrier. He currently commands around $12 million per film, though this was topped by Brando, who got nearly $3.5 million for 12 days shooting on *Superman* (1978). Other highly paid stars are Dustin Hoffman, Warren Beatty and Robert Redford, all around the $5.5 to $6-million mark, followed by Paul Newman and Jack Nicholson between $4 and $5 million, and Eddie Murphy the one black star able to match this. The women have earned less than the men throughout the post-studio era, and only Streisand at about $5 million and Meryl Streep ($4 million) currently earn the real top bucks.

The Lido acknowledges Eric Rohmer's 'Comedies and Proverbs'

*Vincent Gauthier and Marie Rivière in Eric Rohmer's **The Green Ray**.*

'Round Midnight: Dexter Gordon.

Venice, 3 September

Once again the Mostra has cast its vote for a French film. The fifth chapter of Eric Rohmer's series of Comedies and Proverbs, *Summer (le Rayon vert)*, won this year's Golden Lion at the Film Festival. Unlike Rohmer's previous films, the dialogue of this comedy of manners was entirely improvised, creating both the tedium and fascination of real speech. Marie Rivière plays a Parisian secretary, alone during the long summer vacation, who takes herself off to various places but is bored and depressed everywhere.

The green ray of the French title is taken from the Jules Verne novel. It refers to the last magical ray of sunset, the green of which is supposed to make observers more aware of the feelings and perceptions of others. Eric Rohmer's films have much the same effect.

Unsavory subject given stylish treatment

London, 5 September

Busy, bustling Bob Hoskins gives his finest performance to date in Neil Jordan's dark drama *Mona Lisa*. He's superbly cast as the ex-con turned driver for beautiful, manipulative hooker Cathy Tyson. Hoskins is a hard nut with a soft heart who is finally betrayed by love and devotion. Jordan and screenwriter David Leland take Hoskins and the audience on a voyage of grim discovery through a London poisoned by vice and greed, where armies of child prostitutes and tramps camp near the homes of the rich. This moral collapse is personified in the slimy figure of Hoskins' boss, played by Michael Caine like Alfie's psychopathic twin brother.

Off-beat talents revealed in 'Down By Law'

New York, 19 September

The third feature from the independent writer-director Jim Jarmusch, whose laconic, observational style has more affinity with Europe than Hollywood, is an engaging bittersweet lark. A trio of incompatible no-hopers, played by musicians Tom Waits and John Lurie (who both contributed the soundtrack) and the Italian comic actor Roberto Benigni, share a jail cell in New Orleans, escape, and have bickering misadventures on the lam across Louisiana. Quirky and ironic, the movie is enhanced by its actors, particularly the hilarious Benigni in his English-language debut, and the arresting black-and-white cinematography of Germany's Robby Muller.

*Cathy Tyson and Bob Hoskins in Irish director Neil Jordan's **Mona Lisa**.*

l to r: Tom Waits, John Lurie and Roberto Benigni, three unlikely companions.

'Blue Velvet': the dark side of suburbia

*Sadistic pervert Dennis Hopper with Isabella Rossellini in **Blue Velvet**.*

Los Angeles, 19 September
Writer-director David Lynch has come up with an audacious shocker that proves itself a determinedly weird, disturbingly original and subversive take on middle America. In *Blue Velvet*, clean, sweet, small-town youngsters Kyle MacLachlan and Laura Dern get caught up in the mystery surrounding nightclub chanteuse Isabella Rossellini and discover, to their horror, what goes on behind neat picket fences. Rossellini is tormented by psychotic sadist, kidnapper and drug dealer Dennis Hopper, whose intense performance dominates and is appallingly riveting. The sexual violence and obscenities will offend those squeamish of eye and ear.

Runaway hit for bushwhacker Paul Hogan

*Paul Hogan as the appropriately nicknamed hero of **Crocodile Dundee**.*

New York, 26 September
Laid-back Australian TV comedian Paul Hogan has hit the jackpot with *Crocodile Dundee*, a vehicle tailor-made for his brand of amiable charm. He plays the adventurer of the title who shows American reporter Linda Koslowski around the outback before giving up wrestling the local animal life to tangle with the low life which infests her native Manhattan. Hogan's wry charm suggests that Dundee's legendary field-craft might hover on the fraudulent, but he certainly adapts quickly to life among the coke-snorting sophisticates of New York. Asked why he likes the Big Apple, he replies, "It's a real lunatic asylum. That's why I like it. I fit right in."

The short and horrible life of Sid Vicious

New York, 3 October
Explaining why he filmed the sordid tale of Sid Vicious and Nancy Spungen, director Alex Cox has said "Though a lot of people are put off by the idea of a love story between these two unsavory-seeming people, it *is* a love story..." In *Sid and Nancy*, Cox chronicles the downward spiral described by the Sex Pistols' singer and his junkie girlfriend, played by Gary Oldman and Chloe Webb. It's grim stuff, characterized by the moment when Nancy appears to Sid while he is watching *Night of the Living Dead* on TV.

'Fast' Eddie Felson, twenty-five years later

Los Angeles, 17 October
A quarter of a century after playing poolroom shark "Fast" Eddie Felson in *The Hustler*, Paul Newman reprises the role in Martin Scorsese's *The Color of Money*. Eddie is greying around the temples now and selling liquor for a living. But he returns to the world of high-stakes pool when he encounters a young version of himself in flashy cue man Tom Cruise, whom he decides to promote in another shot at the bigtime. Electrifying performances by both principals compensate for the film's anti-climactic conclusion.

Gary Oldman as Sid Vicious and Chloe Webb as girlfriend Nancy Spungen.

Paul Newman as the former pool champion with his young protégé Tom Cruise.

Debonair Cary Grant's long run is over

Still handsome in middle age.

New York, 30 November
Cary Grant, for 50 years a byword for suave good looks and the smoothest of screen talents, has died of a stroke while attending a film festival in Iowa. He was 82. His last film was the 1966 *Walk, Don't Run* but his seemingly ageless good looks never deserted him in a retirement enlivened by work as an executive for a perfume company. He was born Archibald Leach in Bristol, England, in 1904 and came to America as a teenage tumbler, making his screen debut in 1932 in *This is the Night*. The key to Grant's appeal was his ability to appear at once attractive and threatening, the animating force in films as disparate as *Only Angels Have Wings*, *Suspicion*, *His Girl Friday* and *Notorious*. There was a light and a dark side to Grant, as his fourth wife Dyan Cannon has attested. In his films, whenever one is dominant the other creeps into view. But the image that lingers is one of easy, self-deprecating sophistication and charm. When a journalist wired his agent "How old Cary Grant?", Grant himself replied, "Old Cary Grant fine. How you?"

Oliver Stone relives Vietnam experience

New York, 19 December
Platoon is the first movie about the war in Vietnam made by a veteran of that conflict. Director Oliver Stone, the son of a wealthy family, dropped out of Yale, volunteered for the infantry as a private and saw the war in Southeast Asia "from the lowest level", being twice wounded and decorated. In 1975, as Saigon was falling, Stone wrote a script about the war which has taken 11 years to bring to the screen. The movie reflects his own experience, with Charlie Sheen cast as a callow "grunt" (and Stone's alter ego) over whom two sergeants, nice Willem Dafoe and nasty Tom Berenger, fight a moral battle. Stone, who is a determined political liberal, entered films as a writer-director with the 1973 *Seizure*. He won an Oscar for the screenplay of *Midnight Express* and scored a success earlier this year with *Salvador*, a hard-hitting attack on U.S. policy in Central America.

*Charlie Sheen stars as the disillusioned rookie soldier in **Platoon**.*

Annaud films Eco's 'The Name of the Rose'

Christian Slater and Feodor Chaliapine Jr. in an affecting scene from the film.

Paris, 17 December
Jean-Jacques Annaud is not a director who goes for the easy option. After having made *Quest for Fire* (1981), the Stone-Age romance with an invented language, he has now tackled Umberto Eco's complex, metaphysical, medieval detective story, *The Name of the Rose*. Despite having had to reduce the plot for cinematic reasons, Annaud has almost carried off the impossible. Most impressive are the claustrophobic sets, especially the labyrinthine library, through which move Sean Connery as William of Baskerville, a Franciscan Sherlock Holmes, and Christian Slater as his teenage apprentice, trying to solve the mystery of a series of murders in a monastery. Connery has just the right mixture of humor and gravitas to make him an ideal guide. The monks, with F. Murray Abraham as a bald-pated, bearded inquisitor and Michel Lonsdale as an ambiguous abbott, are a wonderful collection of Breughelesque grotesques.

Tarkovsky, the Soviet perfectionist, is dead

Paris, 29 December
Andrei Tarkovsky, aged 54, has just died of cancer. The Russian director had been extremely ill for several months, and was thus unable to go to the Cannes Film Festival last May, where his final film, *The Sacrifice*, won the Special Jury Prize. This Franco-Swedish production, filmed on the island of Gotland in the Baltic Sea, was his second film after *Nostalgia* (1983), during his self-imposed exile from the USSR. His career in his own country had been a long struggle against the Soviet authorities, especially with their initial interdiction of *Andrei Rublev* (1966) and *Mirror* (1974). His two science fiction films, *Solaris* (1972) and *Stalker* (1979), somehow managed to escape their disapproval. Tarkovsky's perfectionism and rich pictorial sense was already evident in his first feature, *Ivan's Childhood*, in 1962. His seven films in 24 years are among the most intensely personal and visually powerful statements to have come out of Eastern Europe during the postwar era.

*During filming of **Mirror**.*

Christopher Lambert co-starred with Sean Connery in **Highlander**.

Writer-director-actor Spike Lee made his debut with **She's Gotta Have It**.

Adrian Lyne directed the sexy duo in this sensation-causing soft porn.

*François Cluzet in Bertrand Tavernier's evocative jazz film '**Round Midnight**.*

*Jeff Daniels and Melanie Griffith in Jonathan Demme's **Something Wild**.*

*Roland Joffe's **The Mission** was set in mid-18th-century South America.*

The first casualty of war is innocence.

This was a powerful return to the Vietnam War from ex-soldier Oliver Stone.

Juliette Binoche, Denis Lavant: Carax's **The Night is Young (Mauvais sang)**.

André Dussollier and Sabine Azema in **Melo**, directed by Alain Resnais.

Michael Mann's **Manhunter**: Brian Cox as cannibal Hannibal Lecter.

Macho wish-fulfillment with Chuck Norris in **Delta Force**.

Bernadette Lafont, Jean Poiret in Chabrol's 'tec thriller **Inspecteur Lavardin**.

1986 Academy Awards, Dorothy Chandler Pavilion, 31 Mar.

Best Film:	*Platoon* (dir: Oliver Stone)
Best Director:	Oliver Stone
Best Actor:	Paul Newman *(The Color of Money)*
Best Actress:	Marlee Matlin *(Children of a Lesser God)*
Best Supp. Actor:	Michael Caine *(Hannah and Her Sisters)*
Best Supp. Actress:	Dianne Wiest *(Hannah and Her Sisters)*

Paris, 18 January
Isabelle Adjani appeared as newsreader Bruno Masure's guest on the Channel Two news at 8 p.m. this evening. The appearance was planned to put an end to rumors that the star is dying of AIDS. Miss Adjani, who appeared to be in perfect health, said she had no idea how the rumor had started but that she was finding its persistence demoralizing.

New York, 19 January
Release of *Radio Days*, Woody Allen's nostalgic evocation of his childhood and the role played by the radio in American homes.

Hollywood, 18 February
Taxi's Emmy Award-winning actor Danny De Vito will make his directorial debut with a comedy for Orion Pictures, *Throw Momma From the Train*. Filming is scheduled to start in Los Angeles in April. De Vito will co-star with Billy Crystal.

California, 27 February
Hollywood has decided to hold a centenary celebration in its own honor. For those who are confused, in 1887 an estate agent named Harvey Henderson Wilcox registered a new land subdivision as Hollywood Ranch. It soon became the greatest dream-factory in the world.

Los Angeles, 20 March
Barry Levinson exposes the world of aluminum siding salesmen in the 50s with *Tin Men*. Danny De Vito and Richard Dreyfuss star.

Paris, 25 March
Release of *le Grand chemin*, by Jean-Loup Hubert, with Anémone and Richard Bohringer.

New York, 30 March
The Coen brothers, Joel and Ethan, have released their second feature *Raising Arizona*, starring Nicolas Cage. An offbeat satire, it confirms the promise of their debut feature *Blood Simple* (1985).

Hollywood, 10 April
At last nights's AFI Life Achievement Award dinner in her honor, Barbara Stanwyck's comment after being lauded for 90 minutes by many of Hollywood's top personalities was, "Honest to God, I *can't* walk on water!"

New York, 15 May
In *Gardens of Stone*, Francis Ford Coppola depicts the war in Vietnam indirectly, through the eyes of the men who take care of the military cemetery in Arlington.

Los Angeles, 1 June
A Los Angeles Superior Court jury has found director John Landis and four co-defendants not guilty of all charges related to the fatal 1982 helicopter accident. The judge declared the deaths of Vic Morrow and two child actors on the set of *The Twilight Zone* "an unforeseeable accident".

Paris, 18 June
Brigitte Bardot held an auction sale of her dresses, make-up case, guitar and other souvenirs to raise funds for her association for the prevention of cruelty to animals.

Washington D.C., 22 June
The U.S. Copyright Office's decision on Friday to register colorized versions of black-and-white films was a blow for the detractors of the process, and a boon to those in the colorization business who believe it opens up film classics to a new generation of viewers.

Los Angeles, 18 September
David Puttnam has announced he will resign his position as chairman of Columbia Pictures. The decision follows the Columbia-Tristar merger which formed Columbia Pictures Entertainment. The new company has appointed Victor A. Kaufman as its head, thus greatly reducing Puttnam's capacity as chairman and chief executive.

Washington D.C., 24 September
Bob Fosse collapsed with a heart attack a few minutes before he was due to go on stage in *Sweet Charity* last night. Fosse's highly acclaimed, semi-autobiographical film, *All That Jazz*, takes on a prophetic quality; its choreographer suffers a similar fate.

Los Angeles, 12 October
Barfly, the German director Barbet Schroeder's newly released American movie, evokes the twilit world of writer Charles Bukowski. Mickey Rourke and Faye Dunaway star as a pair of hopeless drinkers.

Los Angeles, 14 October
Lillian Gish is celebrating her 90th birthday today. Miss Gish, whose screen career began in 1912, made her last appearance to date in 1978 in Robert Altman's *A Wedding*.

New York, 31 October
The stock market crash has affected most film companies including the most successful. The major studios' shares have dropped by 20 percent.

Copenhagen, 15 December
According to statistics, a cinema closes in Denmark every two weeks.

New York, 20 December
Opening here of *The Dead*, the last film from director John Huston. It was completed just before his death last August.

New York, 23 December
Release of Oliver Stone's *Wall Street*. The film depicts the pitiless world of the stock market and high finance, with Michael Douglas as an unscrupulous dealer and mentor to rookie Charlie Sheen.

Copenhagen, 26 December
Release of *Pelle the Conqueror* (*Pelle Erobreren*), directed by Bille August, starring Pelle Hvengaard and Max Von Sydow.

France, 31 December
The latest survey of the number of cinemas has shown a drop of 346 from last year for a total of 4,808.

Hollywood, 31 December
Paramount has accounted for 20 percent of the total distribution takings for the year, thanks to three big films: *Beverly Hills Cop II*, *Fatal Attraction* and *The Untouchables*.

New York, 31 December
The total receipts from video sales and rentals in America has reached $7.4 billion: twice the total of box-office takings.

DEATHS

New York, 22 February
Andy Warhol

New York, 25 February
James Coco

Los Angeles, 2 March
Randolph Scott

Los Angeles, 3 March
Danny Kaye

Santa Barbara, 21 March
Robert Preston

New York, 14 May
Rita Hayworth

New York, 13 June
Geraldine Page

Los Angeles, 22 June
Fred Astaire

Texas, 1 August
Pola Negri

Rhode Island, 28 August
John Huston

Arizona, 29 August
Lee Marvin

Connecticut, 31 August
Joseph E. Levine

Beverly Hills, 13 September
Mervyn LeRoy

California, 25 September
Mary Astor

Spain, 2 October
Madeleine Carroll

France, 22 October
Lino Ventura

Los Angeles, 4 December
Rouben Mamoulian

---

*Bernardo Bertolucci's **The Last Emperor** is a magnificent spectacle which tells the poignant tale of the Emperor Pu Yi who ascended to the Dragon throne of China, aged three.*

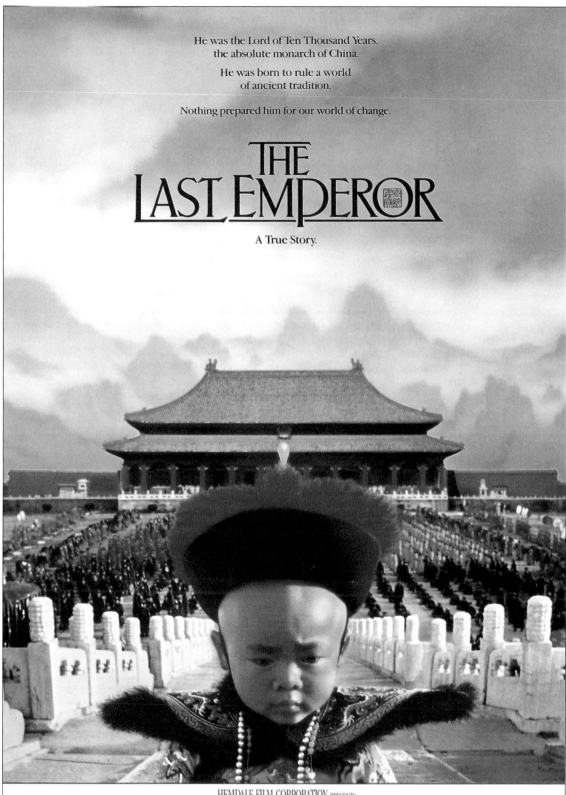

A cynical and observant conversation piece from French Canada

Paris, 4 February
The French-Canadian film director Denys Arcand has finally gained an international reputation with his fifth fiction feature, *The Decline of the American Empire*. It focuses on a group of Quebecois artists and intellectuals – four men and four women preparing a gourmet dinner in a country mansion. Their sexually segregated discussions range over the subjects of sexuality, fidelity, aging, success and failure. Later, at the dinner, the wide-ranging conversation takes a different turn when one of the women announces that she has slept with two of the men, including one whose wife is present. The film, on similar lines to John Sayles' *Return of the Secaucus Seven* (1979) and Lawrence Kasdan's *The Big Chill* (1983), is a cynical and observant conversation piece in which the protagonists' attitudes to sex serve to unmask their personalities, and their deeper political

The four women who match the men in their intellectual and sexual modernity.

concerns. From early on in his career, beginning with his full-length documentary *On est au coton* (1970), about abuses in the textile industry, Arcand has demonstrated that he is an astute chronicler of social and political life in Quebec. *The Decline of the American Empire* is informed with the same spirit, but with a sharper satirical edge.

American remake of French comedy

New York, 23 March
Coline Serreau's *Trois hommes et un couffin* (*Three Men and a Cradle*), one of the most popular French films for many years – it has attracted over 10 million spectators in France alone – is about to be remade by Hollywood, with the action transposed to the USA. It is to be directed by Leonard Nimoy, best known for his role as Spock in the *Star Trek* TV and film series, and not by Serreau as originally intended. She will be retained as screenwriter. The three carefree bachelors who have an abandoned baby thrust upon them are being portrayed by Tom Selleck, Steve Guttenberg and Ted Danson. The remake, called *Three Men and a Baby*, is being produced by Walt Disney's Touchstone company, with Jean-François Lepetit, the producer of the French film, as executive producer.

Gibson, Glover, a lethal box-office combo

Hollywood, 8 March
Once again Mel Gibson is cast as a man on the edge, this time playing strung-out cop Martin Riggs in *Lethal Weapon*, directed by Richard Donner. The weapon of the title is not a fearsome handgun of the type usually waved in the faces of hoods by Dirty Harry. It's Riggs himself, a veteran of the Special Forces in Vietnam who has been so traumatized by the death of his wife that he has become a pyschological time bomb, ready to explode at any moment. He teams up with middle-class black colleague Danny Glover to wreak spectacular justice on a gang of drug traffickers, led by maverick military man Mitchell Ryan and ex-Vietnam mercenary Gary Busey. This combination of cop thriller, buddy movie and vigilante picture enables Richard Donner to restage the Vietnam War – with heroin the issue at stake and, this time at least, the good guys coming out on top.

Oscars make reparation for Vietnam War

Los Angeles, 30 March
After a lull of seven years since *Apocalypse Now*, the last serious film to depict the Vietnam War, Oliver Stone's *Platoon* forcefully returned the war to the Hollywood agenda, and picked up Oscars for both Best Picture and Best Director in the process. Loosely autobiographical, Stone's screenplay follows raw recruit Charlie Sheen into the hell of Vietnam, where he witnesses the torture and killing of Vietnamese peasants by American soldiers who also suffer a dependency on drugs. The Best Actor award was given to Paul Newman, reprising his role as "Fast" Eddie Felson in *The Color of Money*, Martin Scorsese's sequel to the 25-year-old *The Hustler*. In contrast to Newman, who had astonishingly never won an Oscar before, the Best Actress winner was Marlee Matlin, a partially deaf actress making her screen debut as a deaf-mute in *Children of a Lesser God*.

Danny Glover and Mel Gibson as the two cops with a great relationship.

Marlee Matlin and William Hurt.

*Tom Berenger in **Platoon**.*

Rita Hayworth's suffering is over

New York, 15 May
Rita Hayworth died last night at the New York home of her daughter Yasmin. For a number of years she had been suffering from the incurable degenerative condition known as Alzheimer's disease. Born Margarita Carmen Cansino, Hayworth was a cousin of Ginger Rogers and began her career in her father's dance act while she was in her teens. She was signed by Fox, consigned to B-pictures and found her way to Columbia, where she became Rita Hayworth in the 1937 *Girls Can Play*. Her lustrous beauty blooming in the early war years, Hayworth quickly became a forces' favorite, unforgettably gliding across a moon-lit terrace with Fred Astaire in *You Were Never Lovelier*. She revealed her potent blend of casual eroticism in *Gilda*, vamping Glenn Ford while singing "Put The Blame On Mame", but her career never recovered from her marriage to Aly Khan in 1949 (her second husband had been Orson Welles). After the failure of her third and fourth (to Dick Haymes) marriages, fame, looks and confidence deserted her. Alcoholic breakdown overwhelmed her in the 70s, followed by Alzheimer's disease. In later years Hayworth said, "Every man I knew had fallen in love with Gilda and wakened with me."

Festival's special 40th anniversary prize goes to Federico Fellini

Gérard Depardieu and Sandrine Bonnaire in **Under Satan's Sun***.*

Cannes, 19 May
This year's prize-giving ceremony at the Cannes Film Festival was broadcast live throughout the world. A special 40th anniversary prize was presented to *Intervista*, Federico Fellini's affectionate tribute to the Cinecittà studios in Rome, where he made most of his movies. In contrast to the warm reception given to the maestro, Maurice Pialat was booed by a small section of the audience when he came up to accept the Golden Palm for *Under Satan's Sun*. True to his reputation, Pialat raised his fist at his detractors, and shouted, "If you don't like me, then

I can say I feel the same about you lot." This incident obscured the fact that this was the first French film to win the top prize since *A Man and a Woman* in 1966. Based on a novel by Georges Bernanos, *Under Satan's Sun*, an uncompromisingly bleak, claustrophobic and humorless film, was not destined to please the majority. Gérard Depardieu portrays a simple and devout priest who senses Satan everywhere, especially in the heart of a wild, young murderess (Sandrine Bonnaire). The German Wim Wenders was judged the best director for his fantasy *Wings of Desire*.

Best actor Marcello Mastroianni with Elena Sofonova in **Black Eyes***.*

Federico Fellini and Anita Ekberg.

Fred Astaire puts away his dancing shoes

Los Angeles, 22 June
Fred Astaire has passed away in his Hollywood home as gracefully and discreetly as he lived. Born Frederick Austerlitz on 10 May 1899, Astaire made his screen debut in 1933, following a disastrous early screen test which led a studio talent scout to conclude: "Can't act. Can't sing. Slightly bald. Can dance a little." In fact he was to become the most technically exacting and ambitious of screen dancers. With Ginger Rogers he made nine musicals that are the perfect expression of self-sufficient movement, where hard heels on glossy floors beat out a rhythm of bliss. He retained his breezy elegance and his professionalism to the end. He once said, "I suppose I made it look easy, but, gee whiz, did I work and worry."

Nobuko Miyamoto in the title role of *Tampopo*, **the widowed owner of a Japanese noodle shop. Juzo Itami's wonderful gastronomic comedy of table manners satirizes Japanese social behavior in a series of short scenes, most of which take place in the 'ramen', the Japanese term for the shop.**

With Ginger in **Top Hat***.*

Bizarre British comedy wins audiences

Withnail (Richard E. Grant, right) and his buddy (Paul McGann).

New York, 19 June
In *Withnail and I*, British writer-director Bruce Robinson takes us on an autobiographical return journey to the Sixties. It's the fall of 1969 and two out-of-work actors, Richard E. Grant's eponymous Withnail and Paul McGann's "I", abandon their grungy London flat for a trip to a country cottage owned by Withnail's homosexual Uncle Monty, played with gloriously corpulent relish by Richard Griffiths. After various wild and comic adventures they say goodbye to each other and to the Sixties themselves.

Futuristic violence from Paul Verhoeven

Los Angeles, 17 July
For his American debut with *Robocop*, Dutch director Paul Verhoeven has resurrected the Frankenstein myth in the form of the robot policeman of the title. This unstoppable composite is fashioned from the remains of mortally wounded patrolman Peter Weller and a grim carapace of computerized body armor. It's Robocop's duty to patrol the streets of a nightmarish Detroit of the near future where both police and criminals are controlled by Omni Consumer Products, the ultimate in rampant capitalism, which sees death simply as an opportunity to update its hardware. Things unravel violently when their latest example recalls his human past.

*Peter Weller is superb as the reconstructed **Robocop**, a reluctant killer.*

Enthusiastic welcome for 'Jean de Florette'

*Daniel Auteuil (left) and Yves Montand, both memorable in **Jean de Florette**.*

New York, 26 June
American audiences have given a warm welcome to *Jean de Florette*, the first of two pictures by Claude Berri based on Marcel Pagnol's 1963 novel. Faithful to Pagnol's vision, Berri has told a good yarn against gorgeous sun-bleached Provençal settings. The three male leads give towering performances: Daniel Auteuil, simple, comic and touching; Yves Montand, earthy, charming and cunning; and Gérard Depardieu, loving and tragic in the title role of the hunchback deprived of his land by the other two.

John Huston signs off with 'The Dead'

Rhode Island, 28 August
John Huston has died aged 81 of the emphysema that had plagued him for the last 10 years. His death has come just before his last film, *The Dead*, is to be shown at the Venice Film Festival. Huston's illness forced him to direct the picture from a wheelchair, while constantly using an oxygen mask. Nevertheless, he was seldom absent from the set, although the insurance company insisted that Karel Reisz stand by at all times to take over if necessary. *The Dead*, based on the James Joyce short story, stars the director's daughter Anjelica, and his son Tony wrote the script. "I won't retire until the last nail has been hammered into my coffin," Huston once said.

Huston's daughter Anjelica and Donal McCann in the director's final film.

Patrick Swayze takes over from Travolta

Agile heart-throb Patrick Swayze with dancing partner Jennifer Grey.

Hollywood, 21 August
Unheralded, a small-budget ($5 million) romance about a Jewish teen who gets lessons in life, love and dancing at a Catskills resort in the early 60s, is a wow. *Dirty Dancing* is a star-making showcase for hunky dancer-turned-actor Patrick Swayze, best known previously for television's *North and South*, now revealing himself as able to top Travolta. Jennifer Grey, daughter of Joel, charms as the awkward heroine and, if melodramatic clichés tend to take over from the comedy, Swayze's hot gyrations more than compensate.

Venice jury favors Malle, Olmi and Ivory

Raphael Fejto (left) is Jean Bonnet, Philippe Morier-Genoud (right) the master.

Venice, 6 September
Au revoir les enfants was based by Louis Malle on "the most dramatic experience of my childhood." Set at a French boys' boarding school during the Nazi occupation, this unsentimental but affectionate view of a boyhood spent in exceptional circumstances, deservedly won the Golden Lion at this year's festival. The Silver Lion was shared by James Ivory's *Maurice*, a view of the narrow attitude towards homosexuality in Edwardian England, and Ermanno Olmi's *Long Live the Lady!*, an allegory of greed.

Sparks ignite cop Quaid and DA Barkin

Los Angeles, 21 August
Set in New Orleans, *The Big Easy* is a flavorsome romantic thriller in which homicide detective Dennis Quaid locks horns with formidable lady DA Ellen Barkin. Competently directed by Jim McBride from a decent script, with stalwarts Ned Beatty and John Goodman among those lending local color, the film makes for smooth entertainment. But what makes it worthy of reportage is the combustible teaming of the two leads. Ellen Barkin in particular makes an impact as a woman repressed, uncompromising yet vulnerable. Playing uptight but undone by Dennis Quaid's easy charm, she and he give us one of the steamiest clothed sex scenes in memory.

'Hope and Glory' relives wartime London

London, 4 September
For *Hope and Glory*, the autobiographical wartime family saga written and directed by John Boorman, a meticulously detailed suburban street was built which was one of the largest outdoor film sets constructed in Britain since Hitchcock recreated the East End at Lime Grove for *Sabotage*. The film focuses on the early years of the war and follows the progress towards maturity of a young boy, played by Sebastian Rice-Edwards, and the experiences of his family as the Blitz brings disruption and excitement in equal measure. Rich performances and Boorman's sure feel for the deceptive intricacies of family life make *Hope and Glory* a hymn to England.

*Ellen Barkin and Dennis Quaid in a tender moment from **The Big Easy**.*

Sebastian Rice-Edwards and Geraldine Muir, children in the London Blitz.

Wenders whimsy is well-received

Paris, 16 September
Wim Wenders, winner of the best director prize at Cannes this year for *Wings of Desire*, is gratified by the film's success in Paris. The main strength of this whimsical tale of two angels descending on a modern and crumbling Berlin, is the masterful black-and-white photography of the great 75-year-old Henri Alekan.

A mad 'Fatal Attraction' stirs controversy

New York, 18 September
Adrian Lyne's *Fatal Attraction* from producers Sherry Lansing and Stanley Jaffe is causing a huge controversy. The story is unremarkable: successful executive Michael Douglas, happily married to Anne Archer, falls into the trap of a one-night stand with sophisticated Glenn Close when his wife is away. He thinks the terms are clear, but she clings on, gradually revealing herself as some kind of dangerous lunatic. It's a terrific melodrama, expertly put together, with steamy sex, tension, and goodies and baddies nicely delineated. However, a large body of opinion believes the Close character makes the film deeply suspect, and feminists are picketing. Others see it as a metaphor for AIDS and a warning against promiscuity. What *is* clear is that box-office tills will keep ringing.

Berenger watches over Mimi Rogers

New York, 9 October
In *Someone to Watch Over Me*, plainclothes man Tom Berenger must protect Park Avenue heiress Mimi Rogers from sinister death threats. He is a happily-married ordinary Joe, she's single and high society. They fall in love. Ridley Scott has shaped a stylish, unusual and gripping film from this premise.

Solveig Dommartin in Wenders' film.

Dan Gallagher (Douglas) comforts a distraught, suicidal Alex Forrest (Close).

Tom Berenger and Mimi Rogers.

Attenborough salutes Biko and Woods

New York, 6 November
Richard Attenborough brings his customary epic, *Gandhi*-style treatment to *Cry Freedom*. Kevin Kline is excellent as the crusading South African journalist Donald Woods, forced to flee after the death of his black activist friend Steve Biko (Denzel Washington). The movie plays like an old-fashioned escape adventure, missing its opportunities, but at least the anti-*apartheid* message is clear. It has been banned by the South African government.

Spielberg, Bertolucci share Chinese spoils

New York, 9 December
By coincidence, two recent films by leading directors have dealt with 20th-century China, although they are vastly different in subject and approach. Bernardo Bertolucci's *The Last Emperor* tells the life story of the last of the Manchu dynasty, covering nearly 60 years, while Steven Spielberg's *Empire of the Sun* concentrates on the period of the Japanese invasion in World War II, and the experiences of a young boy in a prisoner-of-war camp.

Twenty thousand mourners gather to hear the address at Steve Biko's funeral.

John Lone, the last emperor.

*Christian Bale in **Empire of the Sun**.*

Raucous young Emily Lloyd has star quality

An anarchic Emily Lloyd tormenting her father (Geoffrey Hutchings).

London, 2 December
Sixteen-year-old Emily Lloyd has already captivated audiences at the Cannes Film Festival with her performance in *Wish You Were Here* as a defiantly unruly and sexually precocious teenager ruffling the prim respectability of a seaside town in drab Fifties Britain. Now her clarion cry of "Up yer bum!" and determined public discussion of "willies" looks set to wow cinema audiences on both sides of the Atlantic. Based on Paul Bailey's biography of brothel-keeper Cynthia Payne and directed by David Leland, *Wish You Were Here* pokes pointed fun at the puritanical British bourgeoisie.

Moonbeams light Cher in 'Italian' comedy

Cher and Nicolas Cage are a pair of volatile, Italian-American lovers.

New York, 16 December
Director Norman Jewison has set out to make an old-fashioned fairy tale of love at first sight in the manner of Lubitsch or Capra. *Moonstruck* is set in the Italian section of New York and stars Cher as a widowed accountant who accepts a proposal of marriage from dull businessman Danny Aiello and then falls head over heels for his volatile baker brother Nicolas Cage. Cher's accent seems located more in Little Venice, California than Little Italy and the relentless emphasis on pasta and vino threaten to turn this romantic comedy into a compendium of clichés, but it charms nonetheless.

Fellini's touching reminiscences charm

Paris, 23 December
Conceived by Federico Fellini as a tribute to the 50th anniversary of the Cinecittà studios, *Intervista* is more of a self-homage from a director who has earned such a right. While in the process of making a film of Kafka's *Amerika*, the maestro, interviewed by a Japanese TV crew, reminisces about his first visit to the studio as a young reporter, lightly balancing illusion and reality. The director then takes the Japanese, and Marcello Mastroianni, on a nostalgic visit to Anita Ekberg's house in the country. Thus follows a moving reunion between the two stars of *La Dolce Vita*, changed by time, who watch a scene from the film together.

*Federico Fellini appears in his own mix of fact and fantasy, **Intervista**.*

Verbal pyrotechnics from Robin Williams

Chicago, 23 December
Stand-up comedian and TV's *Mork and Mindy* star Robin Williams, in his seventh feature film, *Good Morning, Vietnam*, now has a vehicle guaranteeing him a wider audience. Director Barry Levinson has turned to Vietnam for his subject but, this time, to satirize the buffoon-like stupidity of the top brass back in the comfort of their headquarters and, while not eschewing poignancy, to raise a barrel of laughs, largely provided by his star. Williams is (real-life) forces DJ Adrian Cronauer, and dazzles with his Danny Kaye-like and irreverent verbal pyrotechnics that win the devotion of the boys on the battlefield and provoke fury among their superiors.

Robin Williams as the irreverent radio disc jockey, Adrian Cronauer.

Army training and war: harsh view.

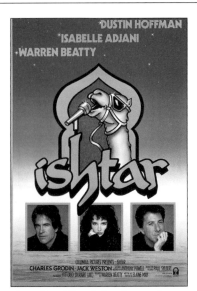

A multi-million-dollar floperoo!

Joan Cusack (standing), Holly Hunter and Albert Brooks in **Broadcast News**.

Julie Walters (left), John Shrapnel, Shirley Stelfox: **Personal Services.**

Lindsay Crouse in David Mamet's debut film, **House of Games**.

Biker-vampire Kiefer Sutherland threatens Jason Patric and Dianne Wiest.

Director Norman Jewison struck gold with this NY-based romantic comedy.

Steve Martin, a modern Cyrano de Bergerac, with Daryl Hannah in **Roxanne**.

David Hemblen, Gabrielle Rose in Atom Egoyan's **Family Viewing** *(Canada).*

Issiaka Kane, Aoua Sangare: Souleymane Cissé's **Yeelen (Brightness)** *(Mali).*

AL CAPONE.
He ruled Chicago
with absolute power.
No one could touch him.
No one could stop him.

Until Eliot Ness
and a small force of men
swore they'd bring
him down.

THE
UNTOUCHABLES

PARAMOUNT PICTURES PRESENTS AN ART LINSON PRODUCTION   A BRIAN DE PALMA FILM
THE UNTOUCHABLES   KEVIN COSTNER   CHARLES MARTIN SMITH   ANDY GARCIA
ROBERT DE NIRO as AL CAPONE and SEAN CONNERY as MALONE
Music by ENNIO MORRICONE   Visual Consultant PATRIZIA VON BRANDENSTEIN   Art Director WILLIAM A. ELLIOTT
Director of Photography STEPHEN H. BURUM, A.S.C.   Written by DAVID MAMET   Produced by ART LINSON   Directed by BRIAN DE PALMA
A PARAMOUNT PICTURE

Forest Whitaker as the legendary Charlie Parker in Clint Eastwood's **Bird**.

De Palma's bloody but stylish feature about FBI man Eliot Ness (Costner).

1988

★ ★ ★ ★ ★ ★ ★ ★ ★ **1988** ★

1987 Academy Awards, Shrine Auditorium, 11 April

Best Film:	*The Last Emperor* (dir: Bernardo Bertolucci)
Best Director:	Bernardo Bertolucci
Best Actor:	Michael Douglas *(Wall Street)*
Best Actress:	Cher *(Moonstruck)*
Best Supp. Actor:	Sean Connery *(The Untouchables)*
Best Supp. Actress:	Olympia Dukakis *(Moonstruck)*

Paris, 6 January
The Madeleine Renaud-Jean-Louis Barrault theater company is presenting a play written and directed by filmmaker Eric Rohmer.

Avoriaz, 24 January
The festival's main prize has been awarded to the American director Jack Sholder for *The Hidden*.

Paris, 7 February
Opening of the Paris Video Library. The public can now consult a databank of images on individual video screens. Films related to the capital will also be screened.

New York, 20 February
With *The Unbearable Lightness of Being*, Philip Kaufman has made an intelligent and faithful adaptation of Milan Kundera's novel. The film, which stars Daniel Day Lewis, Juliette Binoche, and Lena Olin, is now on release.

Berlin, 23 February
Chinese director Zhang Yimou's *Red Sorghum* has been awarded the Golden Bear at this year's festival.

France, 20 March
At this year's Women's Film Festival in Créteil there were over 100 films from 20 countries. A special tribute was paid to Agnes Varda, whose diptych on Jane Birkin was chosen to open and close the festival. Among festival highlights was a retrospective of nine of Dominique Sanda's films. Spectators were also able to see Anglo-American actress Ida Lupino's work as a director.

San Francisco, 19 March
A hypnotic documentary called *The Thin Blue Line* world premiered last night as part of the San Francisco Film Festival. The film, directed by Errol Morris, shows the bizarre aspects of a real-life murder case through the words of the actual participants – Randall Adams (convicted) and David Harris (suspect).

New York, 22 April
Crown publishers have just brought out a new book which they refer to as "a tour de force history of the American film industry." Titled *The Hollywood Story*, it was written by Joel Finler, an American movie historian currently living in London.

Paris, 7 June
Canal Plus has signed an agreement with cinema exhibitors restricting the screening of films before 11 p.m. (instead of 10 p.m. as previously).

Paris, 23 June
Producer Daniel Toscan du Plantier has been elected as the head of Unifrance Film, the industry organization which promotes French films.

Hollywood, 7 August
The scriptwriters' strike has come to an end after a five-month battle. Losses to the film studios are estimated at $150 million.

Los Angeles, 10 August
Francis Ford Coppola pays tribute to American business spirit and optimism with *Tucker: The Man and His Dream*. Jeff Bridges plays an independent car-builder determined to break the monopoly of the big Detroit firms in this film based on a true story.

London, 29 August
Release of Jonathan Demme's *Married to the Mob*, with Michelle Pfeiffer and Dean Stockwell. A comedy about the Mafia and its legendary bad taste.

London, 15 September
Prince Charles has opened England's new temple to the cinema, the Museum of the Moving Image (MOMI). The 3,000 square-meter museum is, like the National Film Theatre, situated under Waterloo Bridge. The MOMI offers visitors a chronological history of the cinema, illustrated by astonishing sets and machines.

Greece, 27 September
Under the aegis of the European Year of Cinema and Television, authors from the EEC have adopted the text of a European audio-visual charter. It is a real declaration of television and film authors' rights.

Los Angeles, 30 September
Bird is a departure for director Clint Eastwood. It is not a Western but a sober and sad film on the life of musician Charlie Parker (played by Forest Whitaker). Eastwood avoids the clichés so often encountered in jazz films.

Paris, 26 October
Jean-Jacques Annaud's latest film, *The Bear* (*l'Ours*), has drawn 3.5 million spectators in its first week of release here. The maker of *Quest for Fire* has told his charming and unusual tale from the bear's point of view using natural sounds and no dialogue.

New York, 29 October
Release of Woody Allen's *Another Woman*, starring Gena Rowlands, Mia Farrow and Gene Hackman, a somber drama reflecting the fears and regrets of a 50-year-old woman.

Marseilles, 31 October
Bertrand Blier has started shooting his new film, *Trop belle pour toi!* (*Too Beautiful for You*), starring Gérard Depardieu, Josiane Balasko and Carole Bouquet.

Paris, 19 November
Eric Serra's score for Luc Besson's *le Grand bleu* (*The Big Blue*) has won the prize for the best film music at the Victoires de la musique.

Berlin, 28 November
Over 300 million viewers watched last night's televised coverage of the first European Oscars from the Theatre des Westerns. Krzysztof Kieslowski's controversial entry *A Short Film About Killing* was voted Best Film. Wim Wenders won Best Director for *Wings of Desire*, while the Best Actor and Actress prizes went to Max von Sydow (*Pelle the Conqueror*) and Carmen Maura (*Women on the Verge of a Nervous Breakdown*). Louis Malle won the prize for Best Script for *Au revoir les enfants*. Ingmar Bergman was given a standing ovation as he received a special life achievement award.

Paris, 8 December
The Louis Delluc Prize has been awarded to Michel Deville's *la Lectrice*, starring Miou-Miou.

New York, 16 December
The New York Film Critics have voted Lawrence Kasdan's *Accidental Tourist* the best film of 1988.

Paris, 30 December
Le Monde has published an interview with Jean-Luc Godard which quotes him as saying, "The cinema is dead."

Hollywood, 31 December
Disney studios have reached almost 20 percent of all annual takings with three big successes: *Who Framed Roger Rabbit*, *Three Men and a Baby* and *Good Morning, Vietnam*.

Los Angeles, 31 December
Fifteen million videotapes of *E.T.* have been sold: a record number.

DEATHS

London, 7 January
Trevor Howard

Los Angeles, 7 March
Divine (Harris Glenn Milstead)

New York, 12 July
Joshua Logan

California, 5 August
Ralph Meeker

West Germany, 5 September
Gert Froebe

Spain, 20 September
Roy Kinnear

Hollywood, 1 October
Lucien Ballard

California, 31 October
John Houseman

Italy, 27 November
John Carradine

California, 27 December
Hal Ashby

Bruce Willis came to mega-stardom this year playing a cop who single-handedly outwits a gang of violent international thugs. John McTiernan directed with finesse.

Wild comedy-horror-fantasy directed by the imaginative Tim Burton.

*Charlotte Gainsbourg plays Claude Miller's **la Petite voleuse**.*

*Australia's Yahoo Serious directed, played and wrote **Young Einstein**.*

*Richard Donner updated Dickens with **Scrooged**, starring Bill Murray (above).*

*l to r: Freda Dowie, Dean Williams, Angela Walsh and Lorraine Ashbourne in Terence Davies' haunting **Distant Voices, Still Lives** (Great Britain).*

*From Britain's Peter Greenaway: **Drowning By Numbers**.*

Murphy an African prince in NYC.

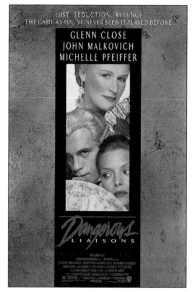

Stephen Frears' splendid version.

Strictly for Tom Cruise fans.

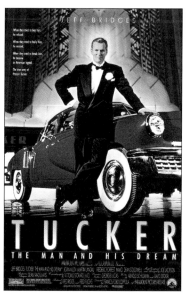

Coppola's homage to car pioneer.

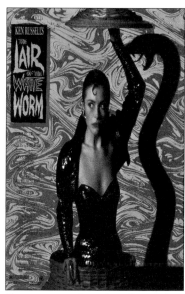

Grotesque, crude and unpleasant!

Isabelle Adjani as sculptress **Clamille Claudel**; Gérard Depardieu as Rodin.

River Phoenix and Martha Plimpton in Sidney Lumet's **Running on Empty**.

Dan Aykroyd and Kim Basinger in **My Stepmother is an Alien**.

Pierre Dux with Miou-Miou, **la Lectrice** of the title, in Michel Deville's film.

Lena Olin: **The Unbearable Lightness of Being** from Kundera's novel.

★ ★ ★ ★ ★ ★ ★ ★ ★ 1989 ★

1988 Academy Awards, Dorothy Chandler Pavilion, 29 Mar.

Best Film:	*Rain Man* (dir: Barry Levinson)
Best Director:	Barry Levinson
Best Actor:	Dustin Hoffman *(Rain Man)*
Best Actress:	Jodie Foster *(The Accused)*
Best Supp. Actor:	Kevin Kline *(A Fish Called Wanda)*
Best Supp. Actress:	Geena Davis *(The Accidental Tourist)*

Japan, 10 January
Akira Kurosawa has begun shooting *Dreams*, an American-Japanese co-production. The movie presents a series of vignettes, one of which is played by director Martin Scorsese.

New York, 30 January
Premiere of the new print of *Gone With the Wind*, with the color completely restored.

Hollywood, 16 February
Jane Fonda has divorced Tom Hayden after 16 years of marriage. He is said to be having an affair with Morgan Fairchild, the former star of the TV series *Flamingo Road*.

Texas, 1 March
Randall Dale Adams, the central figure in *The Thin Blue Line*, saw his conviction overturned today in the Texas Court of Criminal Appeals.

Paris, 2 March
Tom Cruise, who has been in France to promote *Rain Man*, has canceled all his engagements and returned to the U.S. after a short stay in the American Hospital at Neuilly with the flu.

New York, 6 March
The Museum of Modern Art is paying tribute to French producer Marin Karmitz, head of MK2, with the screening of 10 films produced by him, including *Une affaire de femmes*, by Claude Chabrol.

London, 18 March
Terry Gilliam's startlingly innovative update of *Adventures of Baron Munchhausen*, rumored to have cost an excessive $45 million, opens today in London.

Paris, 3 April
Elizabeth Taylor was at the Automobile Club to promote "Passion", her new perfume for men. Five hundred journalists from 35 countries attended the reception which was covered by Mondovision.

Hollywood, 18 April
First day's shooting of *The Two Jakes*, directed by and starring Jack Nicholson. The film, Nicholson's third as director, is a sequel to Roman Polanski's film, *Chinatown*.

Paris, 19 May
Brigitte Bardot has agreed to return to the screen but in a very different role. She is to host a program on Channel 1 called *SOS* in defense of her four-legged friends, a cause she has espoused for the last 15 years.

Paris, 7 June
Release of *Little Vera*, a Russian film by Vassily Pitchoul, starring Natalia Negoda. It is an outspoken portrait of disaffected youth which could not have been made before the new era of *glasnost*.

Aspen, 26 June
Melanie Griffith has married Don Johnson, hero of television's *Miami Vice*, for the second time.

New York, 6 July
Errol Morris is reportedly "hurt and upset" by the case being brought against him by Randall Adams, the man he helped to release from death row. Mr. Adams, who has received six-figure offers from publishers and film companies, is trying to regain the rights to his story.

Los Angeles, 7 July
The recent run of fatal helicopter accidents on movie sets abroad is worrying industry professionals. Some say the insurance companies used by producers bear a share of the responsibility. According to a spokesman from West Coast Helicopters, pilots involved in accidents were often not stunt-qualified.

Los Angeles, 10 July
Mel Blanc, the actor-voice specialist, has died. Blanc provided the voices for over 3,000 animated cartoons during his 60-year career, including Bugs Bunny and Daffy Duck.

London, 25 July
Actor Rex Harrison was knighted today at Buckingham Palace. Asked how he felt during the investiture he replied, "It was a marvelous moment kneeling there and getting tapped on the shoulder."

Hollywood, 31 July
Allegations that actor Rob Lowe made a pornographic home-movie with an underage girl have shocked fans of the man until now considered Hollywood's hottest property.

Prague, 23 August
Former child star Shirley Temple arrived in Prague today. She appears to have already won the hearts of Czechoslovakians, who gave her a warm welcome at a party held in her honor. Miss Temple is here as the United States ambassador to Czechoslovakia.

Cannes, 5 October
Director, former critic and a co-founder of *Cahiers du Cinéma*, Jacques Doniol-Valcroze has died of a heart attack.

New York, 16 October
Release of *Crimes and Misdemeanors* directed by Woody Allen, the most pessimistic and misanthropic of all his films to date.

Paris, 8 November
Pop singer Vanessa Paradis makes her screen debut in Jean-Claude Brisseau's *Noce blanche*.

Sarasota, 19 November
Audrey Hepburn has opened the first Festival of French Films to be held in the U.S. The directors and actors of many of the films are present to introduce their work to the public. The French industry is hoping this will open new doors (at present French films represent only one percent of the market here). A special homage was paid to René Clément and Jeanne Moreau.

Hollywood, 25 November
The most holy sanctuary of American culture – film production – has fallen to the Japanese giant Sony. The corporation has acquired Columbia Pictures for $3 billion. Producers Jon Peters and Peter Guber are to head the Japanese owned studio. The industry is reeling under the shock of this news.

Paris, 6 December
Valmont, the latest film from Milos Forman, has opened here. This is the second adaptation of Choderlos de Laclos' 18th-century epistolary novel this year; the first was Steven Frears' *Dangerous Liaisons*.

Los Angeles, 10 December
Fox's blacker-than-black comedy, *The War of the Roses*, took the top spot this week, out-grossing *National Lampoon's Christmas Vacation*.

New York, 20 December
Director Costa-Gavras has turned his attention to the issue of Nazism. His newly released film *Music Box* concerns a woman lawyer who, defending her own father against charges of Nazi war crimes, must confront a dark and disturbing past. Jessica Lange plays the role.

DEATHS

Los Angeles, 3 February
John Cassavetes

Paris, 29 March
Bernard Blier

Los Angeles, 26 April
Lucille Ball

Rome, 30 April
Sergio Leone

Los Angeles, 2 July
Franklin J. Schaffner

England, 11 July
Laurence Olivier

New York, 22 September
Irving Berlin

Paris, 6 October
Bette Davis

Los Angeles, 16 October
Cornel Wilde

California, 16 December
Lee Van Cleef

Madrid, 16 December
Silvana Mangano

---

*Phil Alden Robinson's **Field of Dreams** was the year's blockbuster hit. Iowa farmer Kevin Costner's involvement with the ghosts of the Chicago White Sox made baseball tops.*

786

Black South African ghetto could be Harlem

Thomas Mogotlane as 'Panic'.

London, 13 January
The cruel limitations placed on endeavor by South Africa's *apartheid* laws has resulted in a parochial and underdeveloped film industry. It is, therefore, quite an achievement for writer and director Oliver Schmitz (white) and writer-actor Thomas Mogotlane (black) to have made *Mapantsula* at all. Already seen at Cannes last year, it unveils a vivid picture of township life in Soweto. The main character, Panic (Mogotlane), an apolitical petty gangster, is finally forced to confront the political realities of the police state in which he lives. Low-budget but lively and revealing, the similarity in the habits and conditions of its underclass to that of Harlem is striking.

Almodóvar puts Spain on commercial map

Julieta Serrano (left), and Carmen Maura the woman on the verge...

Paris, 1 February
After having broken all box-office records in Spain, *Women on the Verge of a Nervous Breakdown* looks as though it might do the same in Paris and elsewhere. Although Pedro Almodóvar's previous picture, *Law of Desire*, did well last year, it was nothing compared to the impact of his seventh feature, which has really put Spain on the commercial map. The story focuses on Pepa (Carmen Maura), a volatile and attractive actress, pregnant by Ivan, her philandering lover who, like herself, dubs Hollywood movies. Unaware of her condition, he blithely abandons her via a farewell message on her answering machine.

As all her efforts to contact him fail, Pepa grows totally distraught and hysterical, setting fire to her bed, and flinging the telephone out the window. Yet she is still able to help other women with their men problems. A series of increasingly bizarre and manic events develop, among them the spiking of gazpacho with a heavy dose of barbiturates. Almodóvar, attempting to recapture the glossy and vulgar visual style of 20th Century-Fox movies of the 50s, has delivered a rapid farce without any diminution in his affection for the characters. All the performances are splendid, especially from the smoldering Maura, who is destined to be a big star.

Individualist Cassavetes dies of cancer

*Directing Gena Rowlands and Peter Falk in **A Woman Under the Influence**.*

Los Angeles, 3 February
John Cassavetes, aged 59, has just died of lung cancer. The son of a Greek-born businessman, Cassavetes made his name as an actor on TV in the 50s, playing private eye Johnny Staccato, an apt nickname for him as both actor and director. With money earned from acting, he directed his first film *Shadows* in 1960, shot in 16mm on location in New York with a crew of four and a script evolved from the actors' improvisations. It had a raw vitality and inspired other young filmmakers to make films outside the studio system. His next two pictures, *Too Late Blues* and *A Child is Waiting*, made within the system, were not happy experiences. From 1968 he was able to work in his own way with a group of technicians, actor-friends (Peter Falk, Ben Gazzara, Seymour Cassel) and his wife, Gena Rowlands. Like the jazz which often accompanies his films, they were made in an improvisational manner and the performers had a fairly free rein. Using *cinéma vérité* techniques with vast close-ups, the characters/actors are revealed to the camera/psychoanalyst, generally depicting menopausal (male and female) emotional crises. Cassavetes seemed to be aware that such a method did not always determine Truth, and acting itself became a theme, whether acting out one's social roles as in *Faces* (1968), or in the inability to identify any longer with the role of wife and mother in *A Woman Under the Influence* (1974), or in actual stage acting in *Opening Night* (1977). As an actor, he was best known for his role as Mia Farrow's husband in *Rosemary's Baby* (1968).

A recent photo of Cassavetes and his wife, the brilliantly gifted Gena Rowlands.

Babbitt wipes out Rabbit at the Oscars

Best Supporting: Geena Davis.

Hollywood, 29 March
Dustin Hoffman was judged Best Actor for his remarkable performance as the autistic Charlie Babbitt in *Rain Man*. In fact, *Rain Man*, which also won Best Picture, Best Director (Barry Levinson) and Best Original Screenplay Oscars, overwhelmed all other contenders, including the eye-boggling blend of live action and animation, *Who Framed Roger Rabbit*, which won for Film Editing, Sound and Visual Effects. The 26-year-old Jodie Foster, already a veteran of 20 films, carried off the Best Actress prize as the rape victim in *The Accused*, while Geena Davis was voted Best Supporting Actress for her comic role in *The Accidental Tourist*.

Baseball brings Costner another diamond

***Bull Durham**: with Susan Sarandon.*

Chicago, 21 April
Despite the popularity of his baseball sex comedy, *Bull Durham*, Kevin Costner's wisdom in making back-to-back baseball movies was questioned by industry skeptics. But the magical *Field of Dreams* is a vindication of the star's faith. Director Phil Alden Robinson's fine adaptation of *Shoeless Joe* by W.P. Kinsella is an enchanting, funny fable of reconciliation and faith that is sparked when an Iowa farmer, prompted by a ghostly voice, turns his cornfield into a baseball diamond to host heavenly players. The result of a cross-country journey of self-redemption makes for a male weepie that will have even tough guys groping for Kleenex.

Canada's film industry is 50 years old

Montreal, 2 May
For filmgoers, it is a day of celebration in Montreal, as well as in other parts of the country, because the National Film Board of Canada is 50 years old today. In 1939, to counteract the prevailing dominance of Hollywood and to coordinate all government film activity, the Board was set up under John Grierson, the British documentary producer. He brought over film experts from England, Joris Ivens from Holland, and the animator Norman McLaren from Scotland via New York, The NFBC then spearheaded Canada's role as a provider of war propaganda, especially in two series, *World in Action* and *Canada Carries On*, which were shown in many parts of the world. After the war the Board not only concentrated on educational films, but also had a profound effect in the long term on the Canadian cinema in general. Through its distribution system, people even in the remotest areas were able to see films. It also had an important influence on Canadian filmmakers,

*Canada now: **Jesus of Montreal**.*

most of whom have worked for the Board. In the early 60s, it became more involved with features, and gave increasing support to productions in French.

Indy looks for dad and finds Sean Connery

Hollywood, 24 June
Sean Connery is 59 and Harrison Ford is 47, but this hasn't stopped Connery from being cast as Indiana Jones' grizzled father in *Indiana Jones and the Last Crusade*, in which Indy once again tangles with a bunch of Nazis in a chase for the Holy Grail. The two stars strike sparks off each other in the third of Steven Spielberg's Indiana Jones adventures. Shot in Spain, Italy and Jordan and at Elstree Studios in Britain, the picture boasts a formidable array of sets and props, including no fewer than 7,000 rats and a replica World War I tank which cost over $150,000 to build. In the opening sequence the young Indy is played by the attractive young actor River Phoenix, who played Ford's unhappy son in *The Mosquito Coast*.

Baseball old-timer Burt Lancaster with loyal fan and dreamer Kevin Costner.

A difficult moment for Indiana Jones and his long-lost father, Sean Connery. ▷

Sex and deception compete with nostalgia

Trop belle pour toi!: Carole Bouquet.

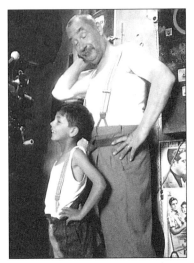

Noiret, Cascio: **Cinema Paradiso**.

Cannes, 23 May
The jury of this year's Cannes Film Festival, presided over by Wim Wenders, expressed eagerness to reward a work that would encourage confidence in the future of cinema. Thus, they had no hesitation in handing the Golden Palm to *sex, lies and videotape*, directed by first-time filmmaker, 26-year-old Steven Soderbergh. It was written in eight days, shot in a month and edited in four weeks, on the tiny budget – by Hollywood standards – of $1.2 million.

The result is a remarkably assured work, full of insight, humor and eroticism, which deals with the emotional life of four young people. Sharing the Special Jury Prize were Giuseppe Tornatore's *Cinema Paradiso*, about a touching friendship between a small boy and an old projectionist through an affection for the cinema, and *Trop belle pour toi!* (*Too Beautiful for You*), Bertrand Blier's perverse comedy in which a man with a beautiful wife falls for his plain and dowdy secretary.

Summer heat of Brooklyn sparks off Spike

New York, 30 June
Following his debut movie *She's Gotta Have It*, Spike Lee's latest, *Do the Right Thing*, is as hip, hot and accomplished a picture as is likely to be seen this year: an angry, funny, uncompromising commentary on the state of the nation seen as a slice of life in Brooklyn, where the residents of one block swirl in and out of Sal's (Danny Aiello) pizzeria that is the focal point of the street. The pace and the uneasy racial dynamics are shrewdly stepped up as the summer temperatures and tempers soar to a shocking climax, acknowledging that people, when pushed, choose sides. The talented Lee also plays the leading role.

Spike Lee in his own movie.

Robin Williams, a free-spirited teacher

New York, 2 June
It is three years since the Australian-born Peter Weir's last film, *The Mosquito Coast*, was greeted with less than enthusiasm. Now, 14 years after *Picnic at Hanging Rock*, he has come up with another school drama in *Dead Poets Society*. The movie is set in 1959 in Vermont, at a private boys' school whose repressive response to ideas and sensitivity is challenged by a new English master, who exhorts his students to "Seize the day" (*Carpe diem*). As the anti-conformist professor whose dedication to instilling a love of literature and poetry into over-privileged and previously uninterested boys leads to tragedy, Robin Williams brilliantly seizes his day, playing a dramatic role with passion and restraint.

James Spader, the video freak, and Andie MacDowell in **sex, lies and videotape**.

Rebel teacher Robin Williams at the head of the class in **Dead Poets' Society**.

Billy and Meg great as Harry and Sally

Sharing a sandwich during their long on-again off-again relationship.

New York, 12 July
In Rob Reiner's new comedy, bouncy blonde Meg Ryan is the "modern" girl who believes that she and Billy Crystal can be friends without being lovers. Crystal, on the other hand, believes that men and women can't enjoy a friendship without sex getting in the way. *When Harry Met Sally* is a variation on the time-honored Hollywood theme in which the leading man and woman spend the entire film finding an excuse not to fall in love before tumbling into each other's arms in the final reel. The stand-out scene in a likeable movie occurs in a deli where Ryan demonstrates beyond a doubt that it's possible to fake an orgasm of thermonuclear proportions.

Al Pacino returns, stronger than ever

Al Pacino as the New York detective involved with prime suspect Ellen Barkin.

New York, 15 September
After being wildly miscast as a fur trapper in the disastrous *Revolution*, Al Pacino withdrew from films. He consoled himself with stage work and, he now admits, heavy drinking. Now, four years on, he's back and in great form, playing the morose middle-aged cop cast adrift on a *Sea of Love* with explosively sexy murder suspect Ellen Barkin. The movie looks to be equally notable for establishing the immensely talented Barkin, who made her screen debut in the 1982 *Diner*, as a top-rank star. For his part, Pacino has told the press, "I'm coming back, out of hibernation. It's going to be interesting to see how the audiences accept me back."

De Palma follows Stone into Vietnam

Los Angeles, 18 August
Brian De Palma's *Casualties of War* intrudes into Oliver Stone territory. It does so with some power and in spectacular locations, but has probably come too late in the spate to be taken as seriously as its maker would want. Like the war on which it focuses, the picture is uncompromisingly horrible, as soldier Michael J. Fox attempts to protect a captive Vietnamese girl from his cronies who, incited by the near-psychopathic Sean Penn, are intent on rape. Despite the usual criticisms made against De Palma, he tells his terrible tale without a trace of salaciousness.

A protective Michael J. Fox ministers to Vietnamese Thuy Thu Le.

Baker boys get more than they bargain for

Los Angeles, 13 September
Gorgeous Michelle Pfeiffer, named one of the world's 10 most beautiful women by *Harper's*, scores a bull's-eye with *The Fabulous Baker Boys*. They are real-life brothers Jeff and Beau Bridges, here playing double piano in the lower echelons of the hotel and nightclub circuit. Deciding to hire a vocalist to revive their dying act, they land themselves with Suzie Diamond (Pfeiffer), former small-time whore with a great line in wisecracks, whose sexy presence plays havoc with the brothers' relationship. Pfeiffer, ably supported and singing in an attractively off-key voice, sets the screen alight.

Jack Baker (Jeff Bridges) and Susie Diamond (Pfeiffer), a steamy duo.

Woody Allen reveals a darker side of life

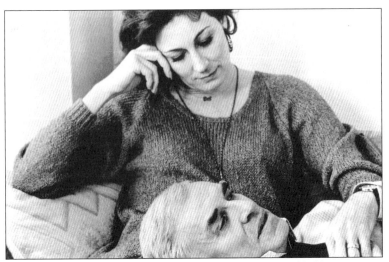

Anjelica Huston, the mistress, and Martin Landau, the troubled lover.

New York, 13 October
After two bleak dramas, *September* and *Another Woman*, both of which failed to appeal to the public or the critics, Woody Allen has come up with a more accessible but no less bleak film in *Crimes and Misdemeanors*. As the title suggests, the movie has Dostoevskian undertones with two stories running concurrently. One is serious, where adultery leads to murder; the other treats adultery in a more flippant manner. Though there is merely a tenuous link between them, Allen manages to keep them both in the air simulta-neously. The film is perhaps one of the director's most pessimistic statements, where evil remains unchallenged (in the form of the tortured figure of opthalmologist Martin Landau), and mediocrity triumphs (in the form of the smarmy egocentric TV personality, Alan Alda). The cast includes Woody himself in one of his most archetypal nebbish roles, Mia Farrow, whom he lusts after, Anjelica Huston (as Landau's mistress-victim) and Sam Waterston as a rabbi going blind, whose spiritual insight is contrasted with Landau's moral murkiness.

Tom Cruise proves himself a heavyweight

Disabled veteran Kovic (Cruise).

New York, 20 December
In Oliver Stone's *Born on the Fourth of July*, Tom Cruise has switched off his constant grin and disappeared beneath straggly hair and a mustache to play the wheelchair-bound Vietnam veteran Ron Kovic. Kovic, who was crippled in Vietnam, collaborated with Stone on the screenplay, which takes him from gung-ho patriot to anti-war activist. Cruise is superb as Kovic, banishing the sour taste left by his self-satisfied performance in the hawkish *Top Gun*. Stone claims, "It's the biggest film I've ever shot. It has about 170 speaking parts and covers about 30 years of life. It's about a boy coming of age in my generation, going to war and coming back, and what America was going through in that period... I wrote it 10 years ago, straight after *Platoon*... I never thought I'd get a chance to do it."

Branagh shoulders the mantle of Olivier

Young King Henry (Branagh) woos Catherine de Valois (Emma Thompson).

New York, 8 November
Kenneth Branagh, the Boy Wonder of English theater, steps into the seven league boots of Laurence Olivier to direct himself in the title role of Shakespeare's *Henry V*. To reclaim the play from its associations with Olivier's World War II film, he plays the victor of Agincourt as a calculating bully, and the battle itself is mounted as a mud-clogged slogging match reminiscent of World War I. It's a brave effort, but Branagh is no Olivier, and an element of strain clings to his assault on the play's great exhortatory passages before the siege of Harfleur and the moment of truth at Agincourt.

'Batman' busts 1989 box-office records

Hollywood, 31 December
The recent growth in movie attendance in the U.S. and the rise in average ticket prices – up from $4.11 last year to $4.45 – means that the total box-office receipts for 1989 have topped the $5 billion mark for the very first time. The biggest hit of the year was the Guber-Peters production of *Batman*. Released by Warner Bros. and shown simultaneously in 2,850 theaters in June, the picture, starring Michael Keaton, Jack Nicholson (as The Joker) and Kim Basinger, set several records in the first weeks of its opening, and continued strong throughout the peak summer months.

Michael Keaton as Batman.

Jack Nicholson is the Joker.

Box-Office Hits

It is perhaps unfortunate that the run of box-office hits from the major Hollywood producers during recent years have become all too predictable. Movies have long conformed to formula and genre, but, with the industry centenary approaching, technology increasingly drowns content. It has not always been that way. In fact, the list of hit movies during the first 50 years of the cinema is full of surprises, with the smaller and independent companies often outflanking the major studios. Since one and two-reelers were churned out by all the companies in vast numbers in the early years, the first big breakthrough at the box office came, not surprisingly, with the changeover to features during 1912-15. And here one can also chart the origins of the studios in the first big hits. For Adolph Zukor there was *Queen Elizabeth* (1912) starring Sarah Bernhardt; for Laemmle's Universal, *Traffic in Souls* the following year, Lasky and DeMille with *The Squaw Man* and Selig with *The Spoilers* (both 1914), and William Fox with his first Theda Bara movie, *A Fool There Was* in 1915. However, the most spectacularly successful film of all was D.W. Griffith's independently made *The Birth of a Nation*, widely shown all over the world with estimated grosses of $15-20 million. The next important cluster of popular successes is associated with the com-

l to r: Cher, Susan Sarandon, Michelle Pfeiffer were **The Witches of Eastwick** *(1987), directed by George Miller.*

ing of sound. Ironically, the top hit was not *The Jazz Singer* (1927), perhaps because there were not enough cinemas equipped to show it, but Warner Bros.' follow-up film with the same star, Al Jolson, *The Singing Fool* (1928), while musicals topped the bill the following year headed by MGM's *The Broadway Melody*, Warner's *Golddiggers of Broadway* and RKO's *Rio Rita*. In the same way that Warners, a small enterprising company, had stolen the box-office thunder from the large studios in the late 20s, so in the 30s did Disney, with *Snow White* easily the top hit of the decade, and Goldwyn in the 40s with *The Best Years of Our Lives*. And David O. Selznick's *Gone with the Wind*, first shown in December 1939, actually straddled the two decades as the most successful movie since *The Birth of a Nation*. In the 50s, the big companies' success in attracting audiences to the new, larger and wider screen movies is reflected in the hits headed by MGM's *Ben-Hur* (1959) filmed in Camera 65, and *The Ten Commandments* (1956) from Paramount in VistaVision. Others include *Around the World in 80 Days*

(1956) and *South Pacific* (1958) shot in Todd-AO, *The Robe* (1953) and *The Bridge on the River Kwai* (1957) in CinemaScope and *This is Cinerama* (1952). The surprise financial bonanza in the 60s came from two treacly films – *The Sound of Music* (1965) and *Love Story* (1970) – before a new generation of young directors arrived to take Hollywood by storm with rather stronger fare. First off the mark were Francis Ford Coppola with *The Godfather* (1972) and William Friedkin with *The French Connection* (1971) and *The Exorcist* in 1973. However, it was George Lucas and Steven Spielberg who soon established themselves as the most successful producer-director team in the history of Hollywood with *American Graffiti*, *Jaws*, *Close Encounters* and *Star Wars* in the 70s, through *E.T. the Extra-Terrestrial* and the *Indiana Jones* cycle in the 80s, up to *Jurassic Park* and *Schindler's List* in the 90s.

Charlton Heston (right) and Yul Brynner in **The Ten Commandments** *(1956), Cecil B. DeMille's hit remake of his 1923 epic success.*

★ ★ ★ ★ ★ ★ ★ ★ ★ 1990 ★

1989 Academy Awards, Dorothy Chandler Pavilion, 28 Mar.

Best Film:	*Driving Miss Daisy* (dir: Bruce Beresford)
Best Director:	Oliver Stone (*Born on the Fourth of July*)
Best Actor:	Daniel Day Lewis (*My Left Foot*)
Best Actress:	Jessica Tandy (*Driving Miss Daisy*)
Best Supp. Actor:	Denzel Washington (*Glory*)
Best Supp. Actress:	Brenda Fricker (*My Left Foot*)

London, 1 January
British actress Maggie Smith has been made a D.B.E. in the New Year's Honors List.

Paris, 20 January
Rain Man drew the highest number of paying customers ·to the box office in the Paris region during 1989, with 1,509,707 tickets sold.

Paris, 28 February
Release of *le Bal du gouverneur* (*The Governor's Ball*), which marks the directing debut of actress Marie-France Pisier. The talented Miss Pisier has adapted the film, shot mainly in New Caledonia, from her own novel.

France, 4 March
A preview of the versatile Serge Gainsbourg's film *Stan the Flasher*, has been shown on Canal Plus. The film is scheduled for release in three days' time.

Paris, 20 March
Brigitte Bardot's lawyer, Maître Gilles Dreyfus, has categorically denied rumors that his client is planning to play Elena Ceausescu, the wife of the powerful Romanian dictator, in a film.

Hollywood, 26 March
Thirty seconds of advertising space on television during the Oscars costs $3.5 million.

Los Angeles, 30 March
Teenage Mutant Ninja Turtles grossed a massive $25.4 million on its opening weekend in the U.S.

London, 2 April
Christies has sold 10 paintings of Alain Delon's for 2 million pounds.

Nantes, 9 April
Agnes Varda has started shooting a film about her husband Jacques Demy's childhood and adolescence in Nantes. The title of the film has as yet to be decided.

Switzerland, 23 April
Paulette Goddard, popular 40s star, has died. Among her four husbands were Charlie Chaplin, with whom she co-starred in *Modern Times*, and novelist Erich Maria Remarque. Managing to escape typecasting, she is also remembered in the title role of Renoir's *Diary of a Chambermaid* (1946).

Philadelphia, 25 April
Dexter Gordon, the famed jazz saxophonist who played the lead in Bertrand Tavernier's *'Round Midnight*, has died.

London, 2 May
Parkfield Picture's *The Krays*, an East End-thugland movie directed by Peter Medak, made a forceful first-week's entry in the capital with a box-office gross of 61,134 pounds.

Moscow, 6 June
The Confession (*l'Aveu*), an attack on Stalinism made by Costa-Gavras in 1970, is at last being shown in Moscow where, for obvious reasons, its release was withheld.

Paris, 20 June
Spanish director Pedro Almodóvar, who is in Paris to present his new film *Atame* (*Tie Me Up, Tie Me Down*) co-starring Victoria Abril and Antonio Banderas, is reportedly furious over the X-rating given to the movie by the MPAA and is seeking to have the film re-certified R.

Auckland, 10 July
New Zealand director Jane Campion has agreed to worldwide release of *An Angel at My Table*. At the outset, Miss Campion wanted to stop theatrical showings of her film, which was made as a three-part mini series for TV, as she felt it was unsuitable for cinema viewing. Favorable reactions from theatrical buyers in Cannes and the "most popular film" vote from audiences at the Sydney Film Festival are responsible for this change of heart.

Armenia, 21 July
Sergo Paradjanov, the innovative Russian director, has died. Paradjanov directed his first feature film *Andriesh* in 1955 but it was with *Shadows of our Forgotten Ancestors* (1964), which won over a dozen international awards, that he gained worldwide recognition. He earned further overseas acclaim in 1977 with the long withheld release of *Sayat Nova*. In 1974 he was imprisoned for five years for homosexuality and several trumped up charges. However, a campaign by European filmmakers led to an early release. Paradjanov made his final picture *Ashik Kerib* in 1988.

London, 10 August
Hong Kong director John Woo's melodramatic, ultra-violent thriller *The Killer* has opened at the ICA cinema today.

Hollywood, 22 August
Paramount's romantic thriller *Ghost* has overtaken the $100 million mark in only 39 days of domestic release and looks set to outdistance the summer's biggest blockbusters *Dick Tracy* and *Die Hard II*.

Sarasota, 15 November
The French Minister for Culture, Jack Lang, accompanied by Catherine Deneuve, Alain Delon and producer Daniel Toscan du Plantier, is in Florida to open the second Festival of French Films.

Moscow, 3 December
The Mir Cinema has reopened under the direction of Paris-Moscow-Media, a Franco-Soviet company. The renovated cinema, which seats 1,200, is intending to specialize in French films.

France, 10 December
The little district borough of Mériel in the Val d'Oise is creating a Jean Gabin Museum. A bust of the actor, donated by Jean Marais, is to be erected in the village square. It was here that Jean Moncorgé, the future Jean Gabin, spent the greater part of his childhood and adolescence.

Rome, 21 December
A recent poll shows that Italian arthouse attendances now account for almost 10 percent of all cinemagoers. Of Italy's 1,300 screens, 200 fit into the art-house category.

DEATHS

England, 8 January
Terry-Thomas

Los Angeles, 20 January
Barbara Stanwyck

London, 25 January
Ava Gardner

England, 19 February
Michael Powell

Maine, 5 March
Gary Merrill

Switzerland, 17 March
Capucine

New York, 15 April
Greta Garbo

Los Angeles, 16 May
Sammy Davis Jr.

New York, 16 May
Jim Henson

California, 18 May
Jill Ireland

New York, 2 June
Rex Harrison

London, 15 July
Margaret Lockwood

Hollywood, 4 September
Irene Dunne

New York, 14 October
Leonard Bernstein

Paris, 15 October
Delphine Seyrig

California, 20 October
Joel McCrea

France, 27 October
Jacques Demy

New York, 7 December
Joan Bennett

California, 8 December
Martin Ritt

Martin Scorsese's **GoodFellas**, *based on the memoirs of Henry Hill about his experiences with the Mafia, elevates the gangster movie genre to a new level of style and realism.*

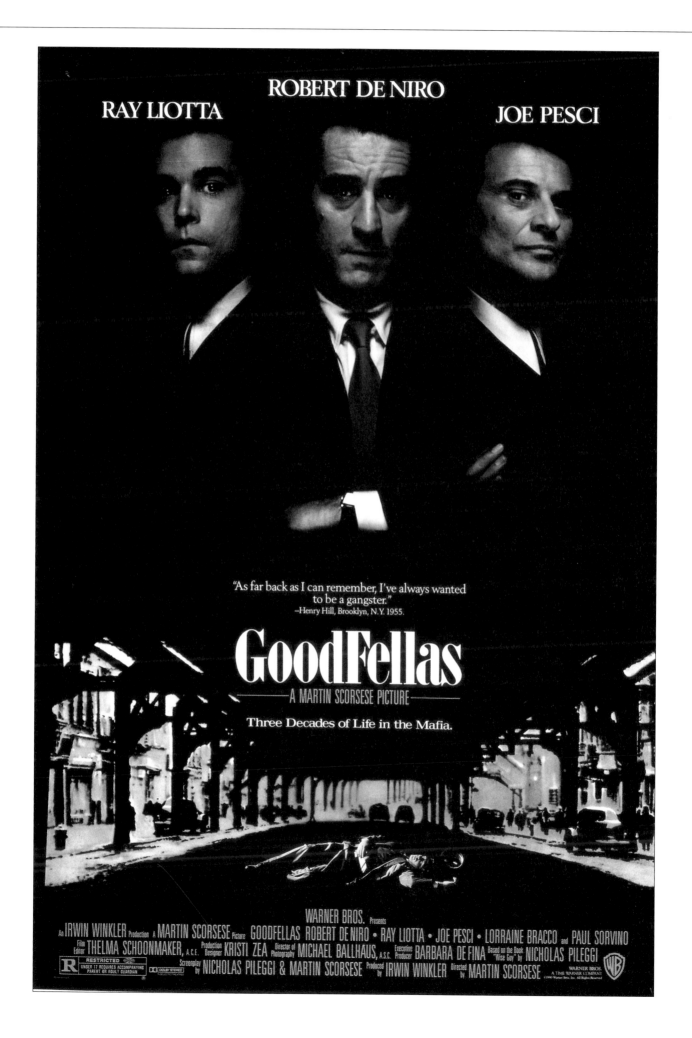

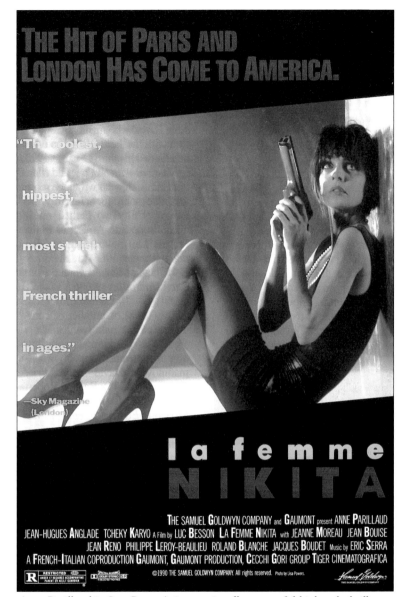

THE HIT OF PARIS AND LONDON HAS COME TO AMERICA.

"The coolest,

hippest,

most stylish

French thriller

in ages."

—Sky Magazine (London)

la femme NIKITA

THE SAMUEL GOLDWYN COMPANY and GAUMONT present ANNE PARILLAUD
JEAN-HUGUES ANGLADE TCHEKY KARYO A Film by LUC BESSON LA FEMME NIKITA with JEANNE MOREAU JEAN BOUISE
JEAN RENO PHILIPPE LEROY-BEAULIEU ROLAND BLANCHE JACQUES BOUDET Music by ERIC SERRA
A FRENCH-ITALIAN COPRODUCTION GAUMONT, GAUMONT PRODUCTION, CECCHI GORI GROUP TIGER CINEMATOGRAFICA

©1990 THE SAMUEL GOLDWYN COMPANY. All rights reserved. Photo by Lisa Powers.

Anne Parillaud in Luc Besson's internationally successful high-tech thriller.

*Gérard Depardieu, Andie MacDowell in Peter Weir's **Green Card**.*

*Kathryn Bigelow's tough thriller **Blue Steel** with cop Jamie Lee Curtis.*

*From Hong Kong's John Woo: Danny Lee (l), Chow Yun Fat in **The Killers**.*

*Dirk Bogarde, Jane Birkin, father and daughter in **These Foolish Things**.*

*Rebecca Smart in **Celia**, directed by Australian filmmaker Anne Turner.*

THE VIBRANT BLAIR BROWN WILL MELT YOUR HEART.

STRAPLESS

Popular English Playwright David Hare directed his own screenplay.

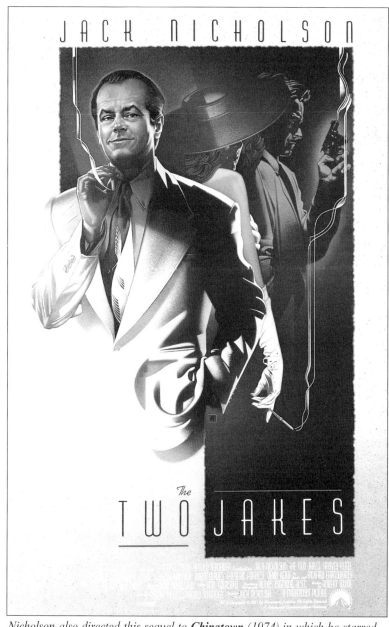

Nicholson also directed this sequel to **Chinatown** (1974) in which he starred.

Julia McNeal (l), Adrienne Shelly in Hal Hartley's **The Unbelievable Truth**.

Last Exit to Brooklyn: Tralala (Jennifer Jason Leigh) picks up a soldier.

Marco Hofschneider and Julie Delpy in Agnieszka Holland's **Europa, Europa**.

Let's Get Lost: trumpeter Chet Baker plays in a film based on his life.

Helen Mirren and Rupert Everett in **The Comfort of Strangers**.

★ ★ ★ ★ ★ ★ ★ ★ ★ **1991** ★

1990 Academy Awards, Dorothy Chandler Pavilion, 20 Mar.

Best Film:	Dances With Wolves (dir: Kevin Costner)
Best Director:	Kevin Costner
Best Actor:	Jeremy Irons (Reversal of Fortune)
Best Actress:	Kathy Bates (Misery)
Best Supp. Actor:	Joe Pesci (GoodFellas)
Best Supp. Actress:	Whoopi Goldberg (Ghost)

Hollywood, 4 January
The Academy of Motion Picture Arts and Sciences has announced that a record high of 37 countries have submitted entries for the foreign film Oscar this year.

New York, 6 January
The National Critics Association today voted Martin Scorsese as Best Director for *GoodFellas*, which was also judged Best Film. Jeremy Irons was Best Actor for his portrayal of Claus von Bulow in Warner Bros.' *Reversal of Fortune*, while the award for Best Actress went to Anjelica Huston for her performances in *The Witches* and *The Grifters*, which also won Best Supporting Actress for Annette Bening. Aki Kaurismäki's *Ariel* was voted Best Foreign Film.

Utah, 28 January
Todd Hayne's *Poison*, an unconventional three-part drama inspired by the writings of Jean Genet, overcame divided opinion at this year's Sundance Film Festival to win the Grand Jury Prize. Haynes first gained notoriety with his widely acclaimed film *Superstar: The Karen Carpenter Story*. The film, which employed Barbie and Ken dolls to dramatize the singer's tragic death in 1982 from anorexia nervosa, has since been withdrawn due to its illegal use of original Carpenters music.

New York, 30 January
According to the movie magazine *Premiere*, three couples paid the sum of $14,000 to have breakfast at Tiffany's with Audrey Hepburn, the allusion being to the 1961 film by Blake Edwards. The money will go to UNICEF for which Miss Hepburn is a roving ambassador and tireless fundraiser.

Burkino Faso, 2 February
The jury of the 12th Pan-African Film Festival in Ouagadougou, presided over by Malian director Souleymane Cissé, has awarded its main prize to *Tilai*, by Idrissa Ouedraogo.

New York, 7 March
Pauline Kael, the often controversial film critic, retires this month after 23 years as the regular critic for the *New Yorker*. Her last review appeared in the 11 February issue. Miss Kael, whose outspokenness caused a few difficult moments in her early days, was fired from McCalls in 1965 for calling *The Sound of Music* "The Sound of Money". Although considered a role model for a new generation of serious film critics, she could turn a phrase with the best of them. On Costner and *Dances With Wolves*, she quipped, "Costner has feathers in his hair and feathers in his head..."

Hollywood, 25 March
Popular actor and comedian Billy Crystal, this year's compere at the Oscars, threw the following at the Academy audience during the announcements: "We are very happy that there are no more American prisoners in the world... apart from those at Paramount."

Hollywood, 5 April
Ex-producer Julia Phillips, once one of Hollywood's brightest stars (she was the first woman producer to win a Best Picture Oscar) before her drug habit sent her on a downward spiral, is enjoying the sweet taste of revenge. Her autobiographical bestseller, already in its fourth printing after barely a month on the shelf, has been raising temperatures in Tinseltown with its biting disclosures of *le tout Hollywood*.

Paris, 17 April
Jean-Pierre Jeunet and Marc Caro, who have already directed numerous video clips and advertisements as well as the astonishing short film *le Bunker de la dernière rafale*, have released their first feature film *Delicatessen*. A strange story which mixes cannabalism with poetic realism, it stars Dominique Piñon and Jean-Claude Dreyfus and looks to be causing something of a sensation.

Paris, 22 April
A UNESCO report has revealed that American films are flooding African screens. In Egypt, for example, American films have captured 86 percent of the market.

Philippines, 22 May
Lino Brocka, the *bête noire* of the Marcos regime, has been killed in a car accident. His last film, *les Insoumis*, was presented as part of the official selection at the Festival of Cannes in 1989.

Toronto, 10 June
David Cronenberg has begun shooting *Naked Lunch*, adapted from William Burroughs' book about the sex and drugs culture. Until now it has been considered an impossible work to adapt for the screen.

Sarasota, 28 July
Popular actor Pee Wee Herman (Paul Rubens) was arrested here yesterday for indecent behavior in an adult movie theater. Pee Wee has been a phemonenon with children and adults alike since his wacky debut in *Pee Wee's Big Adventure* in 1985. He developed the cherry-lipped, loveable brat in shrunken grey suit and bow tie as a comedian with the Groundlings, a Los Angeles improvisational group, in 1979.

Hollywood, 12 August
Dustin Hoffman, who is at present making *Hook* with Steven Spielberg, has signed a three year contract with Columbia TriStar.

New York, 12 August
Jennie Livingston's acclaimed documentary about New York's Harlem drag balls, *Paris is Burning*, has come under harsh criticism from the Atlanta-based Christian Film and Television Commission, which seeks to promote "the moral, family-oriented, Judeo-Christian viewpoint". Prestige, the Miramax Films division distributing the film, has decided to counter the CFTC attack by handing out petitions over the weekend at the 26 theaters currently showing the film.

London, 30 August
Opening of Peter Greenaway's *Prospero's Books*, a loose adaptation of William Shakespeare's *The Tempest*. Michael Nyman has again composed the music for Greenaway.

Los Angeles, 6 October
Elizabeth Taylor has married for the eighth time. Her new husband, Larry Fortenski, is a builder whom she met while undergoing treatment for alcoholism. The wedding took place at Michael Jackson's ranch.

Los Angeles, 25 November
Anton Furst, the special effects designer who won an Academy Award for art direction on *Batman*, died yesterday. According to a Columbia spokesman he committed suicide. Furst developed and designed the holographic light show for the rock group The Who.

DEATHS

Paris, 2 March
Serge Gainsbourg

California, 27 March
Aldo Ray

London, 16 April
David Lean

California, 20 April
Don Siegel

Palm Springs, 1 May
Richard Thorpe

California, 19 June
Jean Arthur

California, 2 July
Lee Remick

Hollywood, 3 September
Frank Capra

Los Angeles, 13 September
Joe Pasternak

California, 5 November
Fred MacMurray

Texas, 6 November
Gene Tierney

France, 9 November
Yves Montand

Los Angeles, 14 November
Tony Richardson

Jodie Foster gives an extraordinary performance, matching that of Anthony Hopkins as Hannibal Lecter, in Jonathan Demme's screen version of the Thomas Harris novel.

'Truly, Madly, Deeply' a reply to 'Ghost'

*Juliet Stevenson and Alan Rickman 'reunited' in **Truly, Madly, Deeply**.*

Miscarriage of justice brilliantly filmed

The appalling moment when preparations are made to hang Derek Bentley.

London, 16 August
Already ecstatically received in the U.S., where it is being billed as the "thinking person's *Ghost*", the home-grown British, BBC-financed *Truly, Madly, Deeply* has its London release. Marking an accomplished feature debut by its writer-director, Anthony Minghella, the film's resemblance to *Ghost* begins and ends with the fact that the dead (of sudden but natural causes) lover of the grief-stricken girl he has left behind reappears in her life as a ghost. After that, despite much humor, the film is about coming to terms with pain and loss. It's charming, tender, tearjerking and, as cast and played (Juliet Stevenson and Alan Rickman star), truly, madly English.

London, 4 October
In the bleak postwar London of the early 50s, Derek Bentley, an 18-year-old youth of low IQ, subject to epilepsy, became friendly with 16-year-old Chris Craig, a delinquent on the fringes of the petty criminal underworld. The liaison led to an attempted robbery, in the course of which the boys were apprehended and Craig shot a policeman. Before he fired, Bentley, reportedly, shouted "Let him have it", meaning, give the gun to the cop. The jury found both boys guilty of murder, but recommended mercy for Bentley. However, since Craig was too young to hang, the recommendation was ignored and, despite repeated protests from the public and crusading members of parliament, Bentley went to the gallows. The attempts to clear Bentley still go on, and this unequivocal and appalling miscarriage of British justice is recounted in Peter Medak's *Let Him Have It*. A brilliant cast plays out the drama in a faultless period re-creation of the time and, if the film is harrowing, it is also thoroughly gripping and certainly to be applauded.

Jacques Rivette demonstrates the mystery of the creative process

Paris, 4 September
Just as Henri-Georges Clouzot once did with *The Picasso Mystery* (1956), in which he filmed the Spanish master in the process of painting, so Jacques Rivette, in his latest film *la Belle Noiseuse*, has attempted to capture the mystery of creation by observing an artist at work. Rivette has concentrated on a fictional painter, whom Michel Piccoli portrays with great conviction. The film reveals the ambivalent sado-masochistic relationship existing between Piccoli and his model, Emmanuelle Béart, and the manner in which nudity is used in painting, and by extension, on screen. The best scene is the meticulous preparation the artist goes through before brush touches canvas.

Jane Birkin and Michel Piccoli as the artist and his wife in Rivette's film.

Liz (Birkin) tries to understand.

Christopher Eccleston is Bentley.

France, U.S. and China divide lion's share

Gong Li, the arresting star of Zhang Yimou's **Raise the Red Lantern**.

Robin Williams (left) and Jeff Bridges in Terry Gilliam's **The Fisher King**.

An imposing visual moment from the Russian Nikita Mikhalkov's **Urga**.

Venice, 14 September
The televised award ceremony at the close of the 48th Venice Film Festival was held on a temporary platform set up in Saint Mark's Square, on which stood a huge plywood Golden Lion. The actual Golden Lion, made of gilded bronze, was awarded to the Russian director Nikita Mikhalkov for *Urga*, a visually stunning film from the USSR made mostly with French money. It is an enjoyably boisterous folk comedy set on the Mongolian Steppes, with a simple birth control message. The Silver Lion was shared by three pictures from different corners of the world: Philippe Garrel's poetic *J'entends plus la guitare* from France; Zhang Yimou's *Raise the Red Lantern*, a remarkable tale of female rivalry from China, and Terry Gilliam's haunting *The Fisher King* from the U.S. This last is set in contemporary New York, but adopts a medieval quest theme, with two down-and-outs (Jeff Bridges, Robin Williams) as a modern knight and his fool. Gus Van Sant's *My Own Private Idaho*, in which 20-year-old River Phoenix won the best actor prize for his poignant portrait of a lonely, narcoleptic gay hustler, is tenuously based on Shakespeare's *Henry IV* plays. Adding to the range of nations which left Venice with prizes was Great Britain, whose Tilda Swinton won the best actress award for her role as Queen Isabella in Derek Jarman's version of Christopher Marlowe's classical tragedy, *Edward II*.

Mike (River Phoenix, left) and Scott (Keanu Reeves): **My Own Private Idaho**.

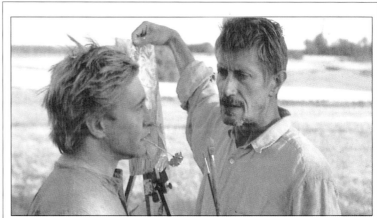

In his new film, *Van Gogh*, Maurice Pialat has scrupulously respected the truth of the great Dutch painter's final years. The ex-pop singer Jacques Dutronc (r) impresses, playing Van Gogh neither as saint nor visionary, but as a man with a secret pain that led him to paint but also to despair.

▷

Jean-Pierre Jeunet and Marc Caro's bizarre **Delicatessen** *was a surprise hit.*

Val Kilmer as musician Jim Morrison in Oliver Stone's **The Doors**.

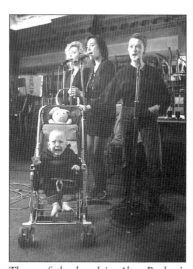

Three of the band in Alan Parker's **The Commitments** *(Ireland).*

David Cronenberg and William S. Burroughs invite you to lunch.

From the director of "Dead Ringers" and "The Fly".

NAKED LUNCH

Exterminate all rational thought.

Director David Cronenberg attempted the impossible and partly succeeded.

Dustin Hoffman as Spielberg's **Hook**, *which cost over $60 million to make.*

The Addams Family: *Morticia (Anjelica Huston), Fester (Christopher Lloyd).*

Outrageous star in a scene from **In Bed with Madonna** *(aka* **Truth or Dare***).*

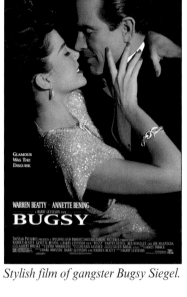

Stylish film of gangster Bugsy Siegel.

Midler showcased in nostalgia trip.

Danny DeVito as aggressive Larry the Liquidator in **Other People's Money***.*

Hugo Weaving, the blind photographer in **Proof***, a stunner from Australia.*

Trail-boss Jack Palance with townie Billy Crystal, one of three **City Slickers***.*

Elias Koteas in his role as **The Adjuster** *in Atom Egoyan's compelling film.*

'El Mariachi' shines sweetly at Sundance

Carlos Gallardo is the musician.

Utah, 31 January
Founded by Robert Redford's Sundance Institute in 1985 to showcase independent American Films, the Sundance Festival has consistently mined emerging talents, discovering films such as *Blood Simple* and *sex, lies and videotape*. One of this year's gems is *El Mariachi*, made South of the Border by 24-year-old Robert Rodriguez for a derisory $7,000. It's a remarkably assured and ingenious thriller of mistaken identity, in which a black-clad guitarist (Carlos Gallardo as the mariachi) in a small Mexican town is mistaken for an identically dressed hit man who carries weapons in a guitar case. The consequences make for a film that is full of panache and wit.

Would you really like your life over again?

New York, 12 February
A new and intriguing comedy directed by Harold Ramis, *Groundhog Day*, is about repeating the past. Bill Murray brilliantly takes the role of a cynical TV weatherman, sent for the fifth year running to the small town of Punxsutawney to cover the Groundhog ceremony held every February 2nd. He wakes up next morning to find it's February 2nd again, and he has to relive the day over and over, until forced to examine his attitudes and turn himself into a nicer person. In this he has help from Andie MacDowell as the romantic interest. This inventive and entertaining comedy-drama is reminiscent of Frank Capra's *It's a Wonderful Life*.

Phil (Bill Murray) with groundhog.

There's not much point in this 'Return'

Los Angeles, 19 March
Bridget Fonda stars as a killer druggie punk, transformed by a government agency program into a classy political assassin, Sound familiar? *The Assassin* is a virtual shot-by-shot remake of Luc Besson's *Nikita*, with a few Hollywood frills muting the stylish force of the original. Americanizing foreign hits is not new: in 1932 the French *Monsieur Topaz* was snapped up for John Barrymore, while *The Magnificent Seven* originates in Kurosawa's masterpiece, *Seven Samurai*. Now this approach – cheaper than developing an original idea – is becoming an epidemic since Disney's 1987 remake of *Trois hommes et un couffin* into the $250 million-grossing *Three Men and a Baby*. Others among many include *Cousins*, *Three Fugitives* and *The Woman in Red*. Italy's 1976 *Scent of a Woman* won Al Pacino his Oscar, while the classy *Sommersby* was fashioned from *The Return of Martin Guerre*. The trend shows no signs of slowing: Depardieu will reprise his French role in *My Father the Hero*, and *les Choix de la vie* becomes *Intersection* for Richard Gere and Sharon Stone.

The L.A. court rules against Kim Basinger

Kim Basinger leaving the court.

Los Angeles, 25 March
The law has ruled in favor of Carl Mazzocone and Main Line Pictures in their case against actress Kim Basinger. Miss Basinger backed out of *Boxing Helena* (directing debut of David Lynch's daughter, Jennifer), the tale of a man who severs the limbs of a beautiful woman in order to keep her to himself. Although sexy blonde Basinger, who was replaced by Sherilyn Fenn, argued that she had not signed a contract, the judge ordered her to pay a massive $8.9 million in damages for the loss of her advantageous presence.

*Jodie Foster and Richard Gere in the reasonably successful **Sommersby**.*

'Falling Down' provokes copy-cat unrest

Los Angeles, 3 April
With violence all too distressingly frequent here, the mindless shooting of at least six Asian grocers in the few weeks since *Falling Down* opened cannot be blamed on the film, but its reception has disquieted many. Michael Douglas, a stressed-out urban Everyman, snaps his spring and pitches into a Korean store owner, a fast food restaurant's staff, and anyone else who irritates him, using assorted weapons in a murderous spree that panders to the rage of self-pitying, middle-class white males who think themselves oppressed. The film takes a blackly comic stance on a screwed-up society, yet has provoked disturbing cheers of encouragement.

*Michael Douglas in **Falling Down**.*

Academy Award choices run the gamut

*Anthony Hopkins and Emma Thompson in James Ivory's **Howard's End**.*

Intelligent suspenser on Italian corruption

*A car is blown up by a bomb in this vivid sequence from **The Escort**.*

Hollywood, 30 March

Clint Eastwood, after 30 years in the movie business, has finally gained his first Oscar as Best Director for the Best Picture, *Unforgiven*. This "revisionist" Western is striking for its willingness to confront the effects of violence, and for the characters'

Best Supporting Actress Tomei.

realization of their own mortality. It took 25 years and eight nominations for Al Pacino to be honored with a Best Actor prize as the embittered blind ex-army colonel in *Scent of a Woman*. Pacino was completely convincing as a blind man, shifting seamlessly from comedy to pathos. The Best Actress award went to Emma Thompson for her nicely shaded performance as Margaret Schlegel in *Howard's End*, one of the most subtle and least showy winners in this category. The surprise of the evening was the Best Supporting Actress winner, the hardly known Marisa Tomei for her hilarious gum-chewing motor-mechanic in *My Cousin Vinny*. In contrast, the Best Supporting Actor recipient was veteran Gene Hackman, the brutal sheriff in *Unforgiven*.

Rome, 18 April

Ricky Tognazzi (son of actor-director Ugo) typifies a heartening return by a new generation of Italian filmmakers to social themes. *La Scorta* (*The Escort*), a fictional but grimly realistic political thriller, is derived from incidents in a brutal war on prosecutors by the Sicilian Mafia. The tale of four incorruptible young *carabinieri* assigned to protect a new judge (Carlo Cecchi) determined to root out corruption, is grippingly well-told, and an intelligent tribute to the bravery of decent men. It should travel well.

The Ken and Emma Shakespeare show

New York, 7 May

"This play is *youthful*," explained Kenneth Branagh, the director of the all-star *Much Ado About Nothing*. "There's a lot of sex in it. I felt it should be surrounded by nature and grapes and sweat and horses and just that kind of lusty, bawdy thing." Shot in the summer of 1992 in a 14th-century villa in the center of the Chianti wine region, this is a gorgeous, exuberant and sensuous movie, though it sometimes strives too strenuously to prove to a wide audience that "Shakespeare can be fun". Enjoying themselves thoroughly are Michael Keaton, Keanu Reeves, Denzel Washington, and Branagh as Benedick opposite his wife Emma Thompson as Beatrice.

Al Pacino and Gabrielle Anwar.

*Jaye Davidson in **The Crying Game**.*

*Benedick and Beatrice (Branagh, Thompson) in **Much Ado About Nothing**.*

The Adventures of Priscilla, Queen of the Desert: *Terence Stamp.*

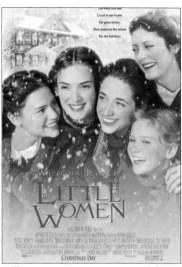

Gillian Armstrong's successful re-make of the much-loved classic.

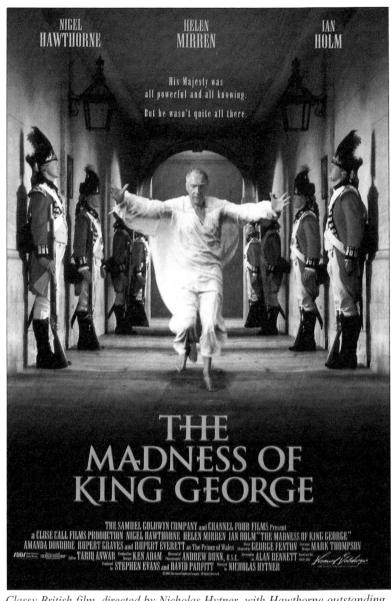

Classy British film, directed by Nicholas Hytner, with Hawthorne outstanding.

The Arnold Schwarzenegger-James Cameron team's **True Lies**.

Gary Oldman portrays a passionate Beethoven in **Immortal Beloved**.

Linda Fiorentino, a **noir** *'heroine' for the 90s, in* **The Last Seduction**.

Ace Ventura's Jim Carrey hit higher with **The Mask**, *Chuck Russell directed.*

Jack Nicholson and Michelle Pfeiffer in Mike Nichols' atmospheric **Wolf**.

A brilliant satire from Tarantino.

Poster provoked scandal in Europe.

Liam Neeson comes to the rescue of Jodie Foster's 'wild girl' in **Nell**.

Great cast in more from Grisham.

Paul Newman is **Nobody's Fool**.

The Shawshank Redemption: *Morgan Freeman (left), with Tim Robbins.*

Jorge Perugorria (r) as Diego, Vladimir Cruz as David, in the internationally successful Cuban movie **Strawberry and Chocolate**.

*The gorgeous Alicia Silverstone shops 'til she drops in **Clueless**.*

*Harvey Keitel in **Smoke**; the film had a sequel, **Blue in the Face**.*

***Chung King Express** was a garish love-letter to frenetic Hong Kong.*

*Bruce Willis gets physical in **Die Hard with a Vengeance**.*

*Pierce Brosnan is the latest incarnation of James Bond in **Goldeneye**.*

*Bittersweet story of life in suburban Australia in **Muriel's Wedding**.*

Ethan Hawke and Julie Delpy in the romantic travel movie **Before Sunrise**.

French drama – **The Horseman on the Roof**.

Mighty Aphrodite – the latest comic offering from Woody Allen.

Hal Hartley's stylish and ironic thriller **Amateur**.

In **Priest** a hypocritical closet gay cleric learns how to be human in a poor parish.

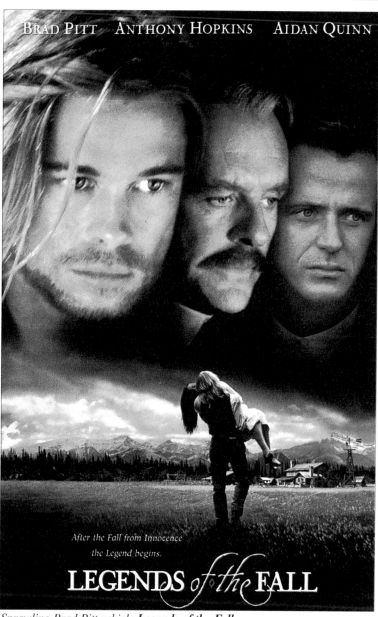

BRAD PITT   ANTHONY HOPKINS   AIDAN QUINN

After the Fall from Innocence
the Legend begins.

LEGENDS *of the* FALL

Sprawling Brad Pitt vehicle **Legends of the Fall**.

Nicole Kidman dazzled as the manipulative and ambitious bitch in **To Die For**. ▷

Special Effects: Tricks of the Trade

The origins of the many types of photographic tricks which can be accomplished with a movie camera can be traced back to the very beginnings of the cinema. Georges Méliès, the pioneering French director, stands out as the most imaginative and innovative creator of effects, which he used in his many fantasy films from 1897 to 1912, including *Voyage to the Moon* (1902), *20,000 Leagues Under the Sea* and *The Conquest of the Pole* (1912). From the days of Méliès onwards, the term 'special effects' is most often associated with fantasy, science fiction and horror on the screen. Yet remarkable effects have often been accomplished in other types of films ranging from the Buster Keaton comedy *Sherlock Jr.* (1924) to *The Wizard of Oz* (1939) and Woody Allen's *Zelig* (1982). And that great classic of the cinema, *Citizen Kane* (1941) makes far more extensive use of special effects photography (models, mattes, false perspectives) than was ever realized at the time of the film's first release. During the early years, special effects were most often achieved quite simply and cheaply *in* the movie camera by literally winding the film back and re-exposing it to get a dissolve, double exposure or split-screen effect, or in making use of models or miniatures. But by the 20s the growth of the large studios in the U.S. and Germany (notably UFA) led to major technical advances such as the development of the Schüfftan process, a sophisticated method of combin-

Meryl Streep, the victim of grotesque and brilliant special effects in Robert Zemeckis' **Death Becomes Her** *(1992).*

ing live action with models, which can be seen in Fritz Lang's *Metropolis* (1926). Back projection, mattes (background paintings on glass) and traveling mattes also came into use at that time. Special effects departments demonstrated their expertise in such films as MGM's *San Francisco* (1936) with its climactic earthquake, RKO's *King Kong* (1933), the horror cycle at Universal, and Korda's *Things to Come* (1936) and *The Thief of Bagdad* (1940) in Britain. But it was the 50s boom in sci-fi fantasy and hor-

ror which set the trend. There were some notable landmarks in the 60s such as *Fantastic Voyage* (1966) and *2001*, in which Kubrick pioneered the new computer technology. (His innovative use of front projection techniques was further developed in the later *Superman* movies.) But it was the spectacular success of such 'effects' pictures as *The Exorcist*, *Jaws*, *Close Encounters of the Third Kind* and, most notably, *Star Wars* in the 70s which led to ever larger budgets and greater technical resources. This change in emphasis

resulted in 'morphing' – the computerized creation of special effects – resulting in even more amazing images for such films as *Ghostbusters* (1984), *Who Framed Roger Rabbit* (1988, combining animation with live action), *The Abyss* (1989, underwater effects), *Terminator 2* (1991, simulated liquid metal transformations) and *Jurassic Park* (1993), which combined full-size dinosaur robotics with the latest in computer-generated imagery. By the mid-90s, effects were in danger of swamping other areas of creativity.

Terminator 2: Judgment Day (1991): *Schwarzenegger morphs into metal man.*

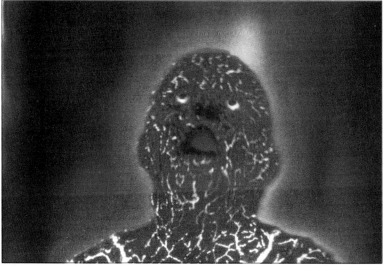

A bizarre, psychedelic image from Ken Russell's **Altered States** *(1980).*

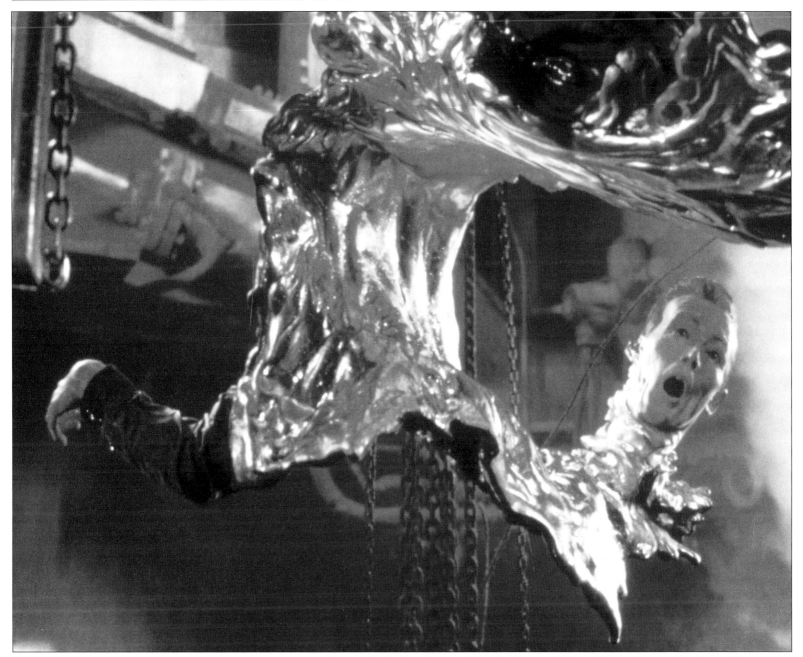

Terminator 2*: designers Dennis Murren, Stan Winstone, Gene Warren Jr., Robert Skotak. Made by Fantasy II Film Effects, Industrial Light and Magic.*

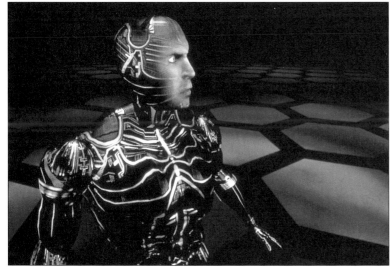

*Impressive simulations of 'virtual reality' enlivened **The Lawnmower Man**.*

*Steven Spielberg (left) and George Lucas, the **Indiana Jones** team at work.*

1995 Academy Awards, Shrine Auditorium, 26 March

Best Film:	*Braveheart* (dir: Mel Gibson)
Best Director:	Mel Gibson *(Braveheart)*
Best Actor:	Nicolas Cage *(Leaving Las Vegas)*
Best Actress:	Susan Sarandon *(Dead Man Walking)*
Best Supp. Actor:	Kevin Spacey *(The Usual Suspects)*
Best Supp. Actress:	Mira Sorvino *(Mighty Aphrodite)*

Dublin, 23 January
Ireland's recent film boom may be about to slow down as the tax shelter Section 35 is renewed today, but with a rule change that favors local low and middle-budget projects at the expense of big-budget Hollywood productions. The changes include a cap on spending that qualifies for tax relief. The Irish film industry has welcomed the move, which should attract a wider range of smaller films.

Los Angeles, 31 January
A little girl tries to buy a goldfish in an Iranian market: this unpromising synopsis for *The White Balloon* cannot do justice to a charming, uplifting film that is pleasing arthouse audiences. Last year's Cannes success is one of two niche hits from Iran. The other is *Gabbeh*, a French-Iranian production.

London, 1 February
The newly-formed London Film Commission has countered New York's recent ads in *Variety* listing ten good reasons to film in the city with a top ten list of its own. The New York list includes "homicides down 37%", "real bagels", "open all night" and "*Dave*" – an allusion to the David Letterman Show. London fired back with "no guns on our streets – homicide rates one tenth of New York", "real muffins", "we speak English" and "*Dave*" – a reference to the 1995 movie shot there. Both groups claim that the rivalry is tongue-in-cheek but with location filmmaking finally being appreciated as a potential money-spinner, other cities can be expected to join in.

Warsaw, 14 March
The Polish film director, Krysztof Kieslowski died of a heart attack yesterday, aged 54. He was the acclaimed director of *Dekalog* (for TV, some were remade as features), *Double Life of Veronique*, and the famous trilogy films, *Three Colours: Blue/Red/White*.

Cuba, 16 April
Tomás Gutiérrez Alea, Cuba's best-known director, has died of cancer. His breakthrough film was *Memories of Underdevelopment* (1972) set in 1962, the year of the Cuban missile crisis. It was based on the book *Inconsolable Memories* by Eduardo Desnoes. His comedy about Cuba's intolerance of homosexuals, *Strawberry and Chocolate*, was nominated for an Academy Award in 1995.

New York, 30 April
The latest film to get cult-movie status in the US is *Showgirls*. A flop on the big screen, it found a niche when it was released on video and New Yorkers took to throwing *Showgirls* parties. In February, *Sunset Boulevard* actress Betty Buckley screened *Showgirls* and invited guests to dress and behave appropriately. Since then, MGM has repackaged it as a 90s *Rocky Horror Picture Show*, aiming it at late-night audiences, and encouraging them to act out the lap dancing, cat-fighting and classic dialogue – "it's a Versase" (sic). Paul Verhoeven admitted "at least this appreciation is better than nothing".

London, 1 May
The first three months of 1996 saw the highest attendances since 1975, according to the Cinema Advertising Association. Over 36.5 million people were attracted into theatres by hits such as *Heat*, *Seven*, *Babe* and *Trainspotting*.

London, 31 May
John Hodge, the screenwriter in the trio who gave us *Shallow Grave* and *Trainspotting*, will resume his medical career after he finishes the script for their next project, *A Life Less Ordinary*.

Paris, 31 May
Gerard Depardieu has been made a *Chevalier de la Légion d'Honneur* (a knight of the Legion of Honor).

At the ceremony, President Jacques Chirac divulged that *Cyrano de Bergerac* is his favorite film.

Dublin, 1 June
Robert Rodriguez's *From Dusk til Dawn* will not see the light of day in Ireland, where it has become the latest film to be banned by chief censor Seamus Smith. The spoof vampire picture, starring Quentin Tarantino and *ER*'s George Clooney, is the seventh film since 1988 to find itself in trouble with strict Irish censors over explicit sex or violence, in the company of *Bad Lieutenant*, *Showgirls* and *Natural Born Killers*. Larry Clark's *Kids,* however, qualified for an 18 certificate, following two weeks of debate, and was screened at the Dublin Film Festival in March.

London, 15 June
Film distributors are taking advantage of Euro '96 fever in the UK (England is hosting the soccer championship) by releasing "chick movies". *How to Make an American Quilt*, *The Truth about Cats and Dogs*, *Moonlight and Valentino* and *Waiting to Exhale* have all been held back until late June and early July for their UK release as film companies hope that girlfriends and wives will take a break from soccer to go to the movies.

Los Angeles, 3 July
Cable Guy, directed by Ben Stiller (*Reality Bites*), has had a disappointing performance at the box office, considering Jim Carrey's $20 million dollar fee. The original script was toned down when Carrey signed up, leaving the film too dark for *Ace Ventura* fans and not dark enough for the initial target audience.

London, 9 November
David Cronenberg's film version of the J.G. Ballard novel *Crash*, which caused a stir at Cannes this year, has sparked an enormous censorship row at the London Film Festival. Councillors in Westminster, who govern what can and cannot be seen in the city's West End, are calling for the film to be banned. They urged the British Board of Film Classification not to issue a certificate to delay the film's release date. The councillors, many of whom have not seen the film, denounced its sexual content. Director Cronenberg is no stranger to controversy and is philosophical about the future of his film. His opinion is that *Crash* can be regarded as a black comedy and has been quoted as saying that his latest film isn't without humor and "I know I've got the right audience if they laugh".

London, 10 November
Some Mother's Son and *Nothing Personal* deal with issues concerning Northern Ireland now that *In the Name of the Father* has opened the way – *Name of the Father* scriptwriter Terry George has his directing debut with *Some Mother's Son*.

Los Angeles, 21 November
After alien invasions and hurricanes, there are currently two big studio films on volcanoes in production. *Dante's Peak* is Universal's offering, starring current James Bond actor Pierce Brosnan and Linda Hamilton (*Terminator 2*) in the leading roles, while rival Twentieth-Century Fox counters with *Volcano*. The films will have a head-to-head struggle as the distributors plan to release the films within a week of each other.

DEATHS

Los Angeles, 19 January
Don Simpson

Los Angeles, 24 April
David Cammell

Los Angeles, 25 April
Saul Bass

Switzerland, 11 June
Brigitte Helm

Beverly Hills, 27 June
Albert R. "Cubby" Broccoli

Barbados, 30 July
Claudette Colbert

Los Angeles, 25 December
Dean Martin

Mission: Impossible – *a much-hyped Tom Cruise vehicle that relies heavily on new expensive and elaborate special-effect sequences yet retains the original signature theme.*

Sundance Kids independent films performing well

Park City, 29 January
Robert Redford launched the Sundance Festival as a forum for the smaller independent films that Hollywood often neglects, but since the box-office success of *sex, lies and videotape* it has grown to become more of a feeding frenzy than a marketplace. Each year, increasing numbers of major distributors fight it out to find the next low-budget smash hit. This year saw even more films first viewed at the festival snapped up for widespread distribution after fierce bidding wars. The festival assigns minders to all filmmakers in competition to help them to play the publicity game and field the offers of seasoned Hollywood players. Studios are prepared to pay up to 20 times the original budget to secure a potential hit. With independent productions tipped to do well at this year's Academy Awards, there is a growing sense that the American independent sector is destined to become the new mainstream. Sundance purists are concerned that the original point of the festival is getting lost amid the hype, and that quantity is driving out quality, but

*Heather Matarazzo as the bullied schoolgirl in **Welcome to the Dollhouse**.*

so far, audiences and filmmakers alike can be thankful that the independent sector has found a conduit to mainstream release. The main beneficiaries this year include *Trees Lounge*, the Cassavettes-influenced directing debut of actor Steve Buscemi. Buscemi, up to now associated with stylized directors such as the Coen Brothers, has made a refreshingly unconvoluted character study of a womanizing, blue-collar barfly in Long Island. Cassevetes collaborator Seymour Cassel has a cameo and Chloe Sevigny (*Kids*) co-stars. Another success is the sweet but unsentimental girl buddy movie *Walking and Talking* by Nicole Holofcener, who is already being billed by the cognoscenti as a female Woody Allen. *Flirting with Disaster* is a movie about families from the director of *Spanking the Monkey,* David O'Russell. Todd Solondz's relentless account of the nightmare that is seventh grade in suburbia, *Welcome to the Dollhouse*, won the Grand Jury Prize for drama. Solondz, whose student short films at NYU Film School attracted studio interest in the 80s, had such a bad experience with his first script, *Fear, Anxiety and Depression*, that he had turned his back on the movie business and opted for a career in teaching until a friend offered to finance a low-budget feature. *Dollhouse*, which despite having a female protagonist draws partly on the director's own experiences, is bitingly funny, losing momentum only at the self-parodying closing section. Distribution rights for *The Spitfire Grill* were sold for a record $10 million, the highest figure yet for rights in a "low-budget" production.

Shakespeare adaptations just keep getting better

London, 15 February
The vogue for big-screen adaptations of Shakespeare's plays shows no sign of abating with an unprecedented ten films in the pipeline or post-production. Cynics attribute the latest love affair with the playwright to the fact that he is well out of copyright, and that most actors are eager to take on such prestigious and award-friendly material for a fraction of their normal fee – for example Keanu Reeves' recent stage *Hamlet* in Toronto. Low costs and the promise of awards do not explain, however, why the bard has captured the movie-goers' imagination. Are they, to paraphrase Quentin Tarantino, films for people who hate movies? Significantly it is predominately the fatalistic plays such as *Othello* that are getting the treatment. This suggests that they are catching a pre-millennium zeitgeist. Kenneth Branagh started the

Laurence Fishburne as Othello with Kenneth Branagh as the malicious Iago.

new round of Shakespeare blockbusters with his *Henry V* and a sumptuously sun-soaked Tuscan *Much Ado About Nothing*. His formula has been to use active camerawork to open out static stage settings, and to cast big stars that will appeal on both sides of the Atlantic, and this successful formula has been widely copied. Branagh previewed his four-hour long *Hamlet* in Cannes and not content with directing continues his acting career as a thoroughly convincing Iago opposite Laurence Fishburne in Oliver Parker's *Othello*. First-time director Parker quipped: "Shakespeare has been English for too long". Astonishingly, Fishburne is the first black actor to play the lead in *Othello* on film. (Orson Welles and Lawrence Olivier both blacked up in previous versions.) More adaptations are in the pipeline, with *Richard III* from Richard Loncraine and *Twelfth Night* from Trevor Nunn yet to come. As the best Shakespeare films of previous years have taken liberties with the original text, Baz (*Strictly Ballroom*) Luhrman's surreal *William Shakespeare's Romeo + Juliet*, set among rival gun-crazy white-trash and Latino gangs in a Mexican beach resort, should be interesting.

Mobsters gamble on in 'Casino'

Sharon Stone effervesces as Ginger.

London, 23 February
Martin Scorsese's three-hours-plus "urban Western" continues his fascination with the Mob. Robert De Niro puts in a polished performance as ultra-smooth mobster turned casino manager Ace Rothstein and Joe Pesci reprises his psychopath role from *GoodFellas*. Sharon Stone is a revelation as De Niro's sassy, glamorous, gold-digging wife Ginger. The triangle between the three characters, drawn together by a vision of Paradise in the desert and destroyed by their own greed is, as the final voiceover reveals, a comment on the death of the American Dream. The violence eclipses even that of *GoodFellas,* a particularly terrifying scene shows one of the mobsters having his head clamped into a vice. *Casino* is based on *GoodFellas* collaborator Nicholas Pileggi's book and features a smattering of moments of vintage Scorsese, among them its literally explosive opening, multilayered voiceovers and a meeting of the Mob bosses stylized so that they resemble the subjects of a Dutch Old Master. Occasional brilliant sequences are, however, punctuated with longeurs and marred by an overall structure that precludes any deep emotional involvement.

Mel Gibson and 'Braveheart' triumph

Los Angeles, 27 March
Mel Gibson's *Braveheart* took a clutch of five awards including Best Director and Best Film, as well as cinematography, sound effects editing and make-up. Nicolas Cage left with Best Actor for Lumiere's *Leaving Las Vegas*, and Susan Sarandon walked away with Best Actress for Working Title's *Dead Man Walking*. Kevin Spacey was Best Supporting Actor in Polygram/Spelling's *The Usual Suspects* and Mira Sorvino secured Best Supporting Actress for Miramax's *Mighty Aphrodite*. Chris McQuarrie beat favourite Randall Wallace's *Braveheart* to win Best Original Screenplay for *The Usual Suspects*. Emma Thompson's Best Adapted Screenplay for *Sense and Sensibility* gave the contender for Best Picture its sole prize from seven nominations. The fancied *Apollo 13* won only two of its nine nomination categories, editing and sound. *Babe* had to be satisfied

Winning actor-director Mel Gibson.

with Best Special Effects. Best Foreign Film was Marleen Gorris' *Antonia's Line*. *Superman* actor Christopher Reeve, now paralyzed from a tragic accident, made an impassioned plea for Hollywood to continue making films that deal with controversial issues.

More accolades for Aardman Animations

Long-suffering dog Gromit warily surveys his new house guest Shaun.

London, 3 April
Nick Park, a former student at the National Film and Television School and now a director of Aardman Animations picked up his third consecutive Oscar last month. Parks' most popular three-dimensional plasticine characters are Wallace, a 50-something Yorkshire inventor, and his silent but expressive dog, Gromit. There have been three amusing Wallace and Gromit stories. In the first film, *A Grand Day Out*, Wallace builds a rocket and visits the moon with Gromit to get cheese. During *The Wrong Trousers* Wallace constructs a pair of mechanical trousers which bizarrely lead to a crime wave. The latest 30-minute film, *A Close Shave,* was, at 13 months, by far the fastest-made production. In this third and possibly final tale Gromit endures a spell in prison as a falsely-accused sheep-rustler as Wallace fatefully falls in love.

Gilliam returns to dystopian fantasy

London, 15 May
Terry Gilliam's nightmare vision of the future, *Twelve Monkeys*, is loosely based on the classic French short *La Jeteé*. Bruce Willis reveals hitherto unseen depths in his acting range in a subtle interpretation of the violent yet fragile convict who, as the traveller from the future, is sent back to 1996 to prevent a plague that will wipe out most of the world's population. A further twist to the film's already complicated plot is that the whole disturbing story may only be taking place inside the mind of a madman. Gilliam's future world is even bleaker than in in his earlier feature *Brazil*. This brave new world is a grim place where the few survivors live underground, ruled by a group of blank-faced scientists who deprive them of sunlight and air. The film takes its name from the Army of the Twelve Monkeys, which is the name of an animal liberation group led by Brad Pitt. He plays an unstable fanatic, who was suspected of starting the plague. Superb computer-generated effects include a deserted Philadelphia where lions, bears and elephants roam free.

Bruce Willis and Madeline Stowe.

Terrifying futurescape.

Crazy Brad Pitt (left) with Willis.

All Cannes talking about 'Secrets and Lies'

Timothy Spall and Brenda Blethyn.

Emily Watson as Bess MacNeill.

Cannes, 20 May
British writer-director Mike Leigh saw off impressive competition, including Michael Winterbottom's *Jude* and the Coen Brothers' *Fargo* to win the Golden Palm for the British-French collaboration *Secrets and Lies*. This is Leigh's most humane work to date. Hortense, a young black woman, searches out her birth mother after the death of her adoptive parents. When she meets her white, working-class east-ender mother and family, walls of silence built up over years slowly crumble. Leigh's trademark strong cast and improvised script have yielded a more complex and understanding slice of life than usual. Brenda Blethyn gave an amusing yet moving portrayal as the mother in a film packed with brilliant performances and was a popular choice for Best Actress. Runner-up for the Golden Palm was *Breaking the Waves*, from Danish director Lars Von Trier. His emotional epic of love, degradation and redemption in 70s Scotland features a searing debut from newcomer Emily Watson as the naive heroine Bess MacNeill. At a festival with relatively few stars in attendance, the ubiquitous showbiz couple Liz Hurley and Hugh Grant cheered up the paparazzi by adding a spot of glamor as they anchored a yacht offshore to promote Grant's latest medic-drama offering, *Extreme Measures*. Danny Boyle, Andrew MacDonald and John Hodges' hard-hitting, yet funny version of the cult Edinburgh heroin novel by Irvine Welsh, *Trainspotting,* was shown out of competition but proved to be a big hit – and the post-screening party was the hot ticket in town. *Crash*, directed by David Cronenberg from the J.G. Ballard book of the same name, was awarded the Special Jury Prize by the committee but was booed at

*Cronenberg's controversial **Crash** was awarded the Special Jury Prize.*

its screening. A ten-minute preview show reel of Alan Parker's eagerly awaited *Evita*, starring Madonna as the charismatic Argentine first lady, gained an enthusiastic response from the audience.

'Richard III' – My kingdom for a tank

London, 2 May
By setting Shakespeare's Tudor propaganda play in an alternative 30s England in the grip of Fascism, Richard Loncraine has made his film, loosely based on his London stage play, a winner. The text has been pared of exposition, with no dialogue in the first ten minutes. Modernist monument Battersea Power Station stands in for the Tower of London and Ian McKellen delivers the famous "my kingdom for a horse" speech from an armored tank. Pitched as Shakespeare meets *Die Hard*, its other modern influences, from Bertold Brecht's *Resistible Rise of Arturo Ui* to Derek Jarman, make this the most original and cinematic Shakespeare adaptation since Kurosawa's *Ran*. McKellen plays King Richard as a sneering dictator, snob and child-killer. The strong supporting cast includes Kristin Scott Thomas as Lady Anne, with Americans Annette Bening and Robert Downey Jr. as nouveaux riches out of their depth in the court corruption and intrigue.

'Lone Star' – Sayles' Tex Mex Murder

Los Angeles, 12 June
John Sayles' thoughtful, engaging border-town drama *Lone Star* is turning into this year's must-see indie hit. When the local sheriff discovers a dead body in the desert, it turns out to be none other than that of the corrupt lawman his own father ran out of town forty years ago. In attempting to unravel a murder mystery, he uncovers instead the complex and overlapping histories of his townsfolk living on the Texas-Mexico border. The cleverly-edited seamless flashbacks are triggered by an ingenious tilting up of the camera. This simple device reinforces the idea that, to contradict the opening line of L.P. Hartley's novel *The Go-Between*, the past is not another country, but is all around us. Delightful, unclichéd and a brilliant account of how America's past still affects it in the present, Sayles has found a skilful way to examine the serious themes of small-town politics and race relations in a way that reaches out to a wider audience.

Ian McKellen resonates as the darkly sinister King Richard.

Kris Kristofferson plays the town's redneck sheriff.

Blockbusters hit Hollywood like a whirlwind

*A brief respite from the action in **ID4** with Will Smith (left) and Jeff Goldblum.*

Los Angeles, 11 July

Independence Day (*ID4*) became the fastest film to pass the $100 million mark, one week after its domestic release, ousting *Mission: Impossible* from the top slot. With *Twister* doing strong business too, US distributors are celebrating the best summer ever. The lack of romance has not affected takings.

Tom Cruise and Emmanuelle Béart do not get intimate in *Mission: Impossible*, *Twister*'s Bill Paxton and Helen Hunt are more obsessed with tornadoes than each other, while fighting off aliens leaves little time for love in *Independence Day*. Schwarznegger's *Eraser* is strictly platonic, as is the late Don Simpson's *The Rock*. An extensive teaser campaign and spectacular special effects propelled Roland Emmerich's *Independence Day* to the top, along with an earth-in-peril script complete with locust-like aliens who owe more to *The X-Files* than *ET*. The film has some astute gags (as the first signals arrive on Earth, REM's "It's the end of the world and I feel fine" plays on the radio), and audiences have cheered as the enemy totals the White House. Bill Pullman's nerdy president turned noble warrior is a sly pastiche of Clinton. Will Smith and Jeff Goldblum share a pacy twenty-minute sequence that has the impetus to turn the ensemble piece into a feel-good buddy movie. In Jan (*Speed*) de Bont's *Twister*, the chase is on as Bill Paxton and Helen Hunt pursue high-speed winds across the American midwest. Brian De Palma's *Mission: Impossible* bears scant resemblance to the 60s cult TV series that inspired it, apart from the theme tune. The double bluffs and double crosses in the espionage script are almost impossible to follow but the set pieces partly compensate.

The Rock is full of thrills and spills.

Another twister spins into action.

Choose life, choose a gritty look at drugs

Los Angeles, 1 August

Ever since cockney actor Michael Caine re-recorded 125 dialogue loops in *Get Carter*, for the US market, British releases hoping for box-office success have faced the dubbing dilemma. *Trainspotting* had little choice, since the action was in the heavy dialect of Scots drug users – Irvine Welsh's book featured a glossary for American readers. The makers opted to partially redub using the original cast. The Edinburgh accents were not softened, but the actors slowed down their speech, especially on the all-important "choose life..." monologues at the start and close. *Trainspotting* is now one of several independents doing brisk business.

Professor Murphy teaches critics a lesson

London, 27 September

Eddie Murphy's acting career has been given a much-needed boost in his remake of the 1963 Jerry Lewis classic hit comedy, *The Nutty Professor*. Murphy, who has been asking journalists not to refer to his return to form as a "comeback", had to spend a great deal of time in make-up to undertake his seven roles. He dons an enormous rubber bodysuit to play a shy, sweet 28-stone genetics professor who uses his secret "fat gene" to transform himself into lithe, loathsome lady-killer Buddy Love. Murphy energetically plays all of his seven roles during the film and during one scene he even plays an entire family seated around a dinner table.

Ewan McGregor on a temporary high after scoring another hit.

Eddie Murphy, convincing in his fat incarnation as genetics professor.

Oliver Stone's **Nixon** *starred Anthony Hopkins in the title role as president.*

Revenge is sweet for high school witches in **The Craft**.

Emma Thompson (right), whose sympathetic adaptation of Jane Austen's **Sense and Sensibility** *won her an Oscar.*

Action movie full of stunts **The Long Kiss Goodnight**, *starring Geena Davis and Samuel L. Jackson.*

Tempers are easily frayed in the sex triangle comedy drama from France **Gazon Maudit (French Twist)**.

In another Jane Austen film, American actress Gwyneth Paltrow convincingly plays the English nineteenth-century heroine in **Emma**.

Lavish literary decadence and redemption in **Restoration** England in a film resplendent with sumptuous sets and gorgeous costumes.

Ulysses' Gaze, a dreamlike political history of the Balkans.

A **Time to Kill** is yet another John Grisham book brought to the screen.

Demi Moore in a disappointing adaptation of Karl Hiaasen's **Striptease**.

A glorious Shakespearian romp – **Twelfth Night** in a directorial debut from Trevor Nunn with a strong British cast.

Re-releases strike back at the box-office

Return of the Rebel Alliance.

Los Angeles, 7 February
Star Wars shot to the number one slot in the US and grossed $35.9 million in the first weekend of its return to the big screen. The runaway success took distributors Twentieth-Century Fox by surprise. The company is planning another massive marketing offensive for *The Empire Strikes Back*, due back on 21 February, and *The Return of the Jedi* which returns on 7 March. *Star Wars* is now expected to take another $100 million, giving it the biggest all-time domestic box-office record, if the three installments don't clash with

each other for theatrical space. Hollywood studios will now be even more keen to sign up George Lucas for the long-discussed three *Star Wars* prequels. Distributor Fox is favorite, with DreamWorks SKG – part-owned by friend and collaborator Steven Spielberg – as a close second. Rumors of original cast members signing up are legion, as media interest escalates. Lucas intends to release the first new prequel in May 1999, with the next two to follow in 2001 and 2003. Lucas was not completely satisfied with the special effects of his spacebound trilogy when first released and has used enhanced technology to improve scenes and reinstate sequences which were not felt to work first time out – notably a meeting between Han Solo and Jabba the Hutt. The success of the re-release sees Hollywood gearing up for a spate of similar second outings for *ET* (ahead of its 20th anniversary in 2002), all three of Spielbergs' *Raiders* films, and Mike Nichols' *The Graduate*, coming

*Sequences of the **Star Wars** trilogy were filmed in the Tunisian desert.*

back for its 30th anniversary courtesy of boutique distributor Strand Releasing. On a smaller scale, the cult film *Withnail and I* also reversed conventional wisdom about re-releases being neither lucrative nor popular. It whipped up huge media interest and

respectable attendance figures last summer during its limited 10th anniversary re-release in the UK in a summer which saw a number of other classics, including Hitchcock's thriller *I Confess*, perform far better than expected at metropolitan box offices.

'Portrait of a Lady' lacks clarity

London, 28 February
Jane Campion's self-indulgent latest costume drama is too like *The Piano*, but it is still a beautifully shot study of a nineteenth-century woman trapped by the repressive mores of the time. *Portrait* is based on Henry James' psychological study of a freethinking American woman in Europe. Nicole Kidman

is superb as the lady of the title who turns down several marriage proposals before being trapped by Madame Merle (a cold Barbara Hershey) in a loveless match with manipulative, penniless artist Gilbert Osmond (John Malkovitz). Campion had promised the role to Nicole Kidman before the actress left Australia for Hollywood.

'Basquiat' seductive look at NY art world

New York, 20 February
Jeffrey Wright burns in the title role of this biopic of Jean-Michel Basquiat, the black graffiti artist who became the darling of the 80s New York art world and tragically died of a drug overdose at the age of 27. International pop star David Bowie plays an amusing cameo, competing with Jared Harris in last

year's *I Shot Andy Warhol* for the most pop-art portrayal of Warhol, and Courtney Love continues her transformation from rock chick to supporting actress playing a thinly-disguised Madonna. Hot 80s artist Julian Schnabel's direction is deliberately flashy to capture the youth market, and is reminiscent of cable music station MTV.

*Nicole Kidman excels as the Lady in **Portrait of a Lady**.*

Jeffrey Wright as the artist (l) and David Bowie (cl) as Andy Warhol.

Nine Academy Awards for 'The English Patient'

Independents win seven of the eight major awards

Cuba Gooding Jr. was awarded the Best Supporting Actor Oscar.

Los Angeles, 25 March

Billy Crystal was MC at the Oscars and started off what proved to be a well-compered ceremony with "welcome to Sundance on the Sea" and later quipped prophetically that "next to wheat and auto parts, the Oscar is now America's biggest export". Independent production *The English Patient* (Miramax) walked off with nine Academy Awards from its twelve nominations last night, including Best Director for Anthony Minghella and Best Film. Juliette Binoche secured the film's only acting award for Best Supporting Actress. She had not even prepared a speech, so sure was she that the favorite, Lauren Bacall, would win

for *The Mirror Has Two Faces*. The *English Patient* also took well-deserved technical garlands for cinematography, sound effects, editing, art direction, costume design and original dramatic score. This makes it the most successful British film ever, despite having American finance, an American producer, an English-Italian director and a source novel by Canadian Sri Lankan Michael Ondaatje. Producer Saul Zaentz also won the Irving Thalberg Award for an impressive career that includes *One Flew Over the Cuckoo's Nest* and *Amadeus*. Tristar's *Jerry Maguire* was the only studio film to take a major award – Best Supporting Actor for Cuba Gooding Jr. Working Title's *Fargo* won two awards, Best Actress for Frances McDormand's remarkable performance and Best Original Screenplay for the Coen Brothers. Hot favorite Geoffrey Rush won Best Actor for his sensitive role in *Shine*. It was a rare good year for women. Frances McDormand praised her fellow-nominees for Best Actress – Brenda Blethyn (*Secrets and Lies*), Emily Watson (*Breaking the Waves*), Diane Keaton (*Marvin's Room*) and Kristin Scott Thomas (*The English Patient*) and gave thanks that, for once, actresses had been offered decent roles. Britain's Rachel Portman made Oscar history by being the first woman to win Best

*Ralph Fiennes in **The English Patient**, the Oscar-winning film that proved that lower-budget co-production features can be dazzlingly successful.*

Composer for *Emma*. Czech film *Kolya* was Best Foreign Language Film, giving their film industry a much-needed boost. There was an overlap between Oscar contenders and the line-up at last May's acclaimed Cannes Festival. The fact that *Secrets and Lies* walked away empty-handed after five nominations indicates how strong the field was. The Academy responded to gripes about recent studio bias by opting for quality – a

move that, ironically, prompted ungracious carping in the American press about the paucity of "stars". On the night, despite being ignored in the nominations, Madonna sang *"You Must Love Me"* from *Evita* live. *Evita* won Best Song and David Helfgott performed on the piano. Frail-looking Muhammed Ali, the subject of the winning feature documentary *When We Were Kings*, got the biggest cheer of the evening.

Geoffrey Rush's non-stop portrayal of the brilliant but disturbed David Helfgott earned him a well-deserved Best Actor Oscar.

*For the cheerfully laconic, pregnant police officer in the Coen Brothers' **Fargo**, Frances MacDormand won the Best Actress Oscar.*

General Index

Film Index

In this index, dates are followed by page numbers in roman or italic. Those in italic refer to illustrated films with no text.

T

Picture Credits

Whilst every effort has been made to trace the Copyright of the photographs and illustrations used in this publication, there may be a possibility where an inadvertent error has been made in the picture credit. If this is the case, we apologise for the mistake and ask the copyright holder to contact the publisher so that it can be rectified.

The position of the pictures are indicated by letters: b=bottom, t=top, r=right, l=left, m=middle, x=middle left, y=middle right, sp=spread.

The following agency names have been abbreviated. Full names are:

BFI: BFI Stills, Posters and Design
Carson: The Carson Collection (Richard Allen)
Cinémathèque: Cinémathèque Française
Columbia: Columbia Pictures
Disney: The Walt Disney Company
Ent. Film Dist.: Entertainment Film Distributors
Finler: Joel Finler
Fox: 20th Century-Fox

Grant: Ronald Grant Archive
Kharbine: Kharbine-Tapabor
Kipa: Kipa-Interpress
Kobal: The Kobal Collection
Sipa: Sipa-Press
UA: United Artists
Warners: Warner Bros

1 – Finler, sp
12 – Fox, courtesy Kobal, sp
14 – RR/Cinémagence, tr, br – RR/Coll. Pierre Lherminier, mr
15 – All RR/Cinémagence
16 – RR/Cinémagence, bm – RR/Coll. Pierre Lherminier, tr
17 – RR/Cinémagence, br – RR/Coll. Larousse, tm – RR/Coll. Maurice Gianati, bl – RR/Coll. Pierre Lherminier, tr – RR/Kharbine, tl
18 – All RR/Coll. Maurice Gianati
19 – RR/Cinémagence, mr, bl – RR/Coll. Cinémathèque, br – RR/Coll. Pierre Lherminier, tm – RR/Kharbine, tl
20 – All RR/Cinémagence
21 – RR/Archives L'Avant-Scène, bl – RR/Cinémagence, tr
22 – RR/De Selva-Tapabor
23 – RR/Coll. Maurice Gianati, br
24 – Sygma/L'Illustration, br
25 – RR/Coll. Pierre Lherminier, mm – Sygma/L'Illustration, tl, bl, br
26 – RR/Cinémathèque, bl – RR/Cinémagence, mr – RR/Coll. André Marinie, tr
27 – All RR/Ciné-Plus
28 – RR/Cinémagence, mr
29 – RR/Coll. Maurice Gianati, br – Sygma/L'Illustration, tl, tm, tr
30 – RR/Cinémagence, br
31 – RR/Ciné-Plus, bl – RR/Coll. Cinémathèque, tr
32 – Archives du film/C.N.C., tr – RR/Cinémagence, bm
34 – Finler, bm
35 – RR/Cinémagence, sp
36 – RR/Ciné-Plus, tl, br – RR/Kharbine, bl
37 – RR/Cinémagence, tl – RR/Coll. Cinémathèque, r – RR/Coll. Pierre Lherminier, mm
38 – RR/Ciné-Plus, bm
39 – RR/Coll. Cinémathèque, sp
40 – BFI, tm – RR/Ciné-Plus, br
41 – BFI, bl – RR/Cinémagence, tl – RR/Coll. Cinémathèque, br
42 and 43 – All RR/Ciné-Plus
44 – RR/Cinémagence, br – RR/Cinémagence, tr
45 – RR/Ciné-Plus, bl – RR/Cinémagence, tr
46 – Finler, br
47 – RR/Cinémagence, sp
48 – BFI, bl – RR/Ciné-Plus, br – RR/Cinémagence, tr
49 – RR/Ciné-Plus, bl – RR/Cinémagence, tr – RR/DITE, br
50 – RR/Ciné-Plus
51 – RR/Cinémagence, sp

52 – RR/Ciné-Plus, bl – RR/Coll. Maurice Gianati, br – Finler, tr
53 – RR/Ciné-Plus, bl – RR/Cinémagence, br – RR/Coll. Maurice Gianati, tr
54 and 55 – All RR/Cinémagence
56 – Finler, tr
57 – RR/Ciné-Plus, tr – RR/Coll. Maurice Gianati, br
58 – Finler
59 – RR/Cinémagence, sp
60 – RR/Ciné-Plus, bl – RR/Cinémagence, br – RR/Roger Viollet, tm
61 – BFI, br – RR/Cinémagence, tl, tr
63 – RR/Cinémagence, sp
64 – BFI, br – RR/Ciné-Plus, ml, tr
65 – BFI, bm – RR/Cinémagence, ml, mr
67 – RR/Cinémagence, sp
68 – RR/Ciné-Plus, tr – RR/Coll. Maurice Gianati, bl, br
69 – RR/Cinémagence, br – RR/Coll. Maurice Gianati, tr
70 – RR/Ciné-Plus bl – RR/Cinémagence, br – Sygma/L'Illustration, tr
71 – RR/Cinémagence, br – RR/Coll. Pierre Lherminier, tr
73 – RR/Cinémagence, sp
74 – BFI, br – RR/Coll. Maurice Gianati, tl
75 – RR/Ciné-Plus, tm – RR/Cin´magence, br
75 – RR/Coll. Maurice Gianati, br – RR/Ciné-Plus, tm – RR/Cinémagence, br
76 – BFI, bl – RR/Coll. Chemel, ml – RR/Coll. Pierre Lherminier, tr, br
77 – BFI, tl, bl – RR/Coll. Cinémathèque, br – RR/Coll. Maurice Gianati, tr
78 and 79 – All Finler
81 – BFI, sp
82 – RR/Archives Gaumont, mm – Finler, br
83 – RR/Ciné-Plus, tl – RR/Cinémagence, tr – RR/Coll. Cinémathèque, mr – Finler, bl
84 – BFI, bl – RR/Coll. Pierre Lherminier, tr – Finler, bl
85 – RR/Archives Gaumont, br – RR/Ciné-Plus, mr – RR/Cinémagence, bl – Finler, tl
87 – Finler, sp
88 – Finler, br – Vitagraph, courtesy Kobal, tr
89 – RR/Ciné-Plus, tr – RR/Cinémagence, br – Sipa, ml
90 – All RR/Ciné-Plus
91 – RR/Archives Gaumont, tr – RR/Cinémagence, bm
93 – RR/Ciné-Images, sp
94 – All RR/Cinémagence
95 – RR/Coll. Pierre Lherminier, tm – Finler, bl
96 – All RR/Coll. Pierre Lherminier
97 – RR/Archives Gaumont, ml – RR/Cinémagence, tr, sr
99 – Finler, sp

100 – RR/Coll. Maurice Gianati, br – RR/Coll. Pierre Lherminier, tr – Finler bl
101 – RR/Archives Gaumont, tm – RR/Ciné-Plus, bl – Finler, br
102 – BFI, tr – RR/Ciné-Plus, bl – Finler, br
103 – BFI, tr – RR/Coll. Pierre Lherminier, bl
105 – Finler, sp
106 – BFI, tl – RR/Cinémagence, ml – RR/Coll. Pierre Lherminier, mr
107 – RR/Ciné-Plus, tr – RR/Det Danske Filmmuseum, bl
108 – BFI, tl – Finler, tr, br
109 – BFI, bm – RR/Ciné-Plus, tm
111 – RR/Ciné-Plus, sp
112 – All BFI
113 – All RR/Ciné-Plus
114 – RR/Ciné-Plus, tr, bm – Finler, ml
115 – RR/Ciné-Plus, tr – RR/Cinémagence, tm – RR/Coll. André Bernard, tl – Paramount, courtesy Kobal, bl
117 – Carson, sp
118 – All RR/Ciné-Plus
119 – Bubbles Inc., 1994, bl – RR/Archives Gaumont, tr br
120 – RR/Ciné-Plus, br, tl – RR/Cinémagence, tr
121 – Bubbles Inc., 1994, bl – RR/Ciné-Plus, br – RR/Coll. Pierre Lherminier, tm
123 – Finler, sp
124 – RR/Ciné-Plus, tr, br – RR/Coll. Cinémathèque, bl
125 – Bubbles Inc., 1994, br – RR/Archives Gaumont, tm, ml
126 – RR/Cinémagence, bl, bm – Finler, tl, tm, br
127 – RR/Ciné-Plus, tl – Finler, br
129 – Finler, sp
130 – RR/Cinémagence, tr -Finler, tl – Sipa, br
131 – BFI, br, bm – RR/Ciné-Plus, tl, tm
132 – BFI, tr – RR/Coll. Pierre Lherminier, mr – RR/Gosfilmofond, bl – Universal, courtesy Kobal, tl
133 – BFI, tl, tm – RR/Coll. Pierre Lherminier, br – Finler, bl
135 – Finler, sp
136 – RR/Ciné-Plus, bl -Finler, tr
137 – RR/Ciné-Plus, br – RR/Cinémagence, bm – Finler, tl
138 – RR/Ciné-Plus, bm -RR/Coll. Cinémathèque, bl – Finler, tm
139 – BFI, bm – RR/Ciné-Plus, tr – Finler, tl
140 – RR/Ciné-Images, ml, tm, tr, bl, br – Carson, tl, mr, bm
141 – RR/Ciné-Images, br – Carson, tl, ml, tm, tr, mr, bl, bx, by
142 and 143 – All Finler
145 – RR/Ciné-Plus, sp

146 – RR/Coll. Cinémathèque, tl – RR/Coll. Pierre Lherminier, bm – Finler, tr
147 – BFI, tm – RR/Ciné-Plus, br – Sygma/L'Illustration, bm
148 – BFI, tl, bm – RR/Cinémagence, mr – RR/Coll. Larousse, tr
149 – BFI, br – Bubbles Inc., 1994, bl – RR/Ciné-Plus, mr – Finler, ml
151 – RR/Ciné-Plus, sp
152 – BFI, bl – Bubbles Inc., 1994 tl, tm – RR/Cinémagence, tr – Sipa, bm
153 – RR/Ciné-Plus, tl – RR/Coll. Pierre Lherminier, bl – Sygma/L'Illustration, tr
154 – RR/Coll. Cinémathèque, tr – Finler, ml, bm
155 – RR/DITE, bl – Finler, tm, tr
157 – Finler, sp
158 – RR/Coll. Pierre Lherminier, tl – RR/Kharbine, mr
159 – RR/Cinémagence, tl – RR/Coll. Pierre Lherminier, br – Finler, mr
160 – RR/Archives Gaumont, tr – RR/Ciné-Plus, bl, br – Finler, tl
161 – BFI, bm – RR/Ciné-Plus, br – Finler, tl
163 – RR/Cinémagence, sp
164 – BFI, br – RR/Coll. Cinémathèque, tm – Finler, bl
165 – All Finler
166 – Bubbles, Inc., 1994, tr – RR/Cinémagence, bl – RR/Coll. Cinémathèque, tl – Finler, br
167 – RR/Coll. Pierre Lherminier, tl – Finler, mr, bm – Sygma/L'Illustration, tm
169 – Finler, sp
170 – RR/Coll. Cinémathèque, tm – Finler, bm
171 – Finler, tl, br – Kobal, bl
172 – RR/Cinémagence, ml – RR/Coll. Cinémathèque, bm – Finler, mr
173 – BFI, tr, br – Finler, bl
175 – Carson
176 – RR/Ciné-Plus, mr – RR/Cinémagence, bm – Finler, tl, tm
177 – All RR/Cinémagence
178 – Bubbles Inc., 1994, tm, mm, bl – Finler, br
179 – BFI, tr – RR/Ciné-Plus, bl – Finler, tl, br
181 – Carson, sp
182 – RR/Cinémagence, tr – RR/Coll. Cinémathèque, tl – Kobal, br
183 – RR/Ciné-Plus, bm – Finler, tr
184 – RR/Cinémagence, mr – RR/Coll. Pierre Lherminier, tr, bm – Finler, tl, br
185 – RR/Coll. Pierre Lherminier, bm – Finler, tl, tr, br
187 – RR/Cinémagence, sp

188 – RR/Cinémagence, tr, bl, br – RR/Coll. Cinémagence, mm – RR/De Selva-Tapabor, tm
189 – RR/Cinémagence, mr – Finler, tl, bm
190 – RR/Ciné-Plus, tl – RR/Cinémagence, tr, bm – RR/Coll. Cinémathèque, tm – Finler, mm
191 – BFI, tl – Bubbles Inc., 1994, bm – RR/Coll. Pierre Lherminier, bl
192 – RR/Cinémagence, tm, tr – Finler, bl
193 – RR/Cinémagence, tl, br – Finler, bl
195 – Finler, sp
196 – Bubbles Inc., 1994, ty, tr – RR/Cinémagence, bm, bm, bl
197 – RR/Kharbine, br – Finler, tl, tr
198 – RR/Cinémagence, tr, mm – RR/Kharbine, mr – Finler, tl
199 – BFI, mm – Finler, tr, bm
201 – Carson, sp
202 – RR/Cinémagence, tl – RR/Gosfilmofond, bm – Finler, tm tr
203 – RR/Archives L'Avant-Scène, tm – RR/Cinémagence, bl, bm – Finler, mr
204 – RR/Cinémagence, tl, tr, mm – Finler, tm – Photo X/RR, bm
205 – RR/Cinémagence, tr – RR/DITE, bm – TM ©, L. Harmon Pict Corp, ml
206 – BFI, tr – Finler, tl, bl
207 – Finler, bm – Keystone, tl
208 – RR/Ciné-Images, ml – Carson, tl, tm, tr, mr, bl, bx, by, br
209 – RR/Ciné-Images, bl, bm – Carson, tl, ml, bm, tl, mr, br
210 – BFI, tr – RR/Cinémagence, tl, tx, ty, ml, mx, mr, by – Finler, my, bl, bx, br
211 – Jacques Legrand SA, tl – Finler, tr, bl – Sygma/L'Illustration, br
212 and 213 – All Finler
215 – RR/Cinémagence
216 – RR/Archives L'Avant-Scène, bl – RR/Ciné-Plus, tl – RR/Cinémagence, mr
217 – BFI, bl – RR/Cinémagence, tr – Finler, tl, br
218 – RR/Ciné-Plus, tr, br, bm – RR/Cinémagence, bl – Finler, tl
219 – RR/Ciné-Plus, br – RR/Cinémagence, br -Finler, tl, tr
220 – RR/Ciné-Plus, tm, bl, bm – RR/Cinémagence, br – Turner Entertainment, tr
221 – RR/Ciné-Plus, tr, br – RR/Cinémagence, bm – RR/Kharbine, bl
222 and 223 – All Carson
225 – Finler, sp
226 – RR/Cinémagence, tm, tr, br – RR/Kharbine, tl, bl

227 – RR/Cinémagence, bm, bl – Finler, tl, tm – Keystone, mr
228 – RR/Ciné-Plus, br – RR/Cinémagence, tl, bl – Finler, tr
229 – RR/Ciné-Plus, ml, tr, bm - RR/Cinémagence, tm, br
230 – RR/Ciné-Images, tm, tr – Carson, tl, bl, bm, br
231 – RR/Ciné-Images, br – Carson, tl, tm, tr, bl, bm
233 – Disney, sp
234 – RR/Ciné-Plus, ml – RR/Cinémagence, mr – Finler, br, bl
235 – BFI, br – RR/Cinémagence, tl – Finler, bl, tr
236 – RR/Ciné-Plus, tl, br – RR/Cinémagence, tm, bl, tr
237 – BFI, bm – RR/Ciné-Images, tl – Finler, tr
238 – All Carson
239 – RR/Ciné-Images, tl, br, LX, LY – Carson, bl, bm, tr
241 – Carson, sp
242 – RR/Cinémagence, tm – RR/Coll. Pierre Lherminier, bl – Finler, br
243 – RR/Cinémagence, tl, tm, bm – Finler, br
244 – RR/Archives Gaumont, tl – RR/Ciné-Plus, bm – RR/Cinémagence, br – RR/Coll. Pierre Lherminier, tm
245 – RR/Ciné-Images, tl – RR/Cinémagence, tr – Finler, bm
246 – All RR/Cinémagence
247 – RR/Ciné-Images, bl – RR/Ciné-Plus, bm, br – Finler, tl, mr
248 – RR/Ciné-Images, tr – Carson, tl, ml, tm, mr, bl, bx, by, br
249 – RR/Ciné-Images, bm, br – Carson, tl, tm, tr, bl
251 – Carson, sp
252 – RR/Ciné-Plus, tm, bl – RR/Cinémagence, tr – Sygma/L'Illustration, bm
RR/Cinémagence, tr -= Sygma, L'Illustration, bm
253 – RR/Cinémagence, tm, mm – RR/Coll. Cinémathèque, tl – Finler, bm – Keystone, mr
254 – RR/Ciné-Images, bm – RR/Coll. Pierre Lherminier, br – Finler, tl, tr
255 – RR/Cinémagence, br – Finler, tl, bl, tr
256 – RR/Ciné-Images, ml – Carson, tl, tm, tr, mr, bl, bx, by, br
257 – RR/Ciné-Images, tl, ml – Carson, tr, bl, bx, by
259 – Carson, sp
260 – RR/Cinémagence, bl, bm – RR/Coll. Larousse, tl – Finler, tr, mm
261 – BFI, bl – RR/Cinémagence, tm, br – Finler, tl
262 – RR/Cinémagence, bm, br – Finler, tr, tl, tm, bm, bl
263 – BFI, bl – Finler, tm, br, tr
264 – RR/Ciné-Images, tr, mr, bl, bx – Carson, tl, by, br
265 – RR/Ciné-Images, ml – Carson, tl, tm, tr, mr, bl, bx, by, br
267 – Carson, sp
268 – Bubbles Inc., 1994, tm, tr – RR/Ciné-Plus, bm – RR/Cinémagence, ml
269 – RR/Cinémagence, tl, bl – Finler, tm, tr, br
270 – RR/Ciné-Plus, tl – RR/Cinémagence, tm – Finler, tr, bm
271 – RR/Cinémagence, bm, br – RR/Kharbine, tl, tr
272 – RR/Cinémagence, br – RR/Coll. Pierre Lherminier, bl – Finler, tl, tr
273 – RR/Ciné-Plus, tl – RR/Kharbine, tm – Finler, mr – TM ©,L. Harmon Pict Corp, bl, bm
274 – RR/Ciné-Images, tr, bl, bm, br – Carson, tl, mr
275 – All Carson
277 – Finler, sp
278 – RR/Cinémagence, br – RR/Coll. André Marinie, tr – RR/Coll. Pierre Lherminier, bm – Finler, tl, bl
279 – RR/Cinémagence, br – RR/Kharbine, tl – Finler, bl
280 – All RR/Cinémagence
281 – RR/Ciné-Plus, tr – RR/Cinémagence, tl, bm, bl, br
282 – RR/Ciné-Plus, bm, br – RR/Cinémagence, tl, tr
283 – Finler, tr, tl, tm, bl – Disney, bm, br
284 – All Carson
285 – RR/Ciné-Images, tl, ml, bl – Carson, tr, mm, bm, br
287 – Carson, sp
288 – RR/Ciné-Plus, br – RR/Kharbine, tr - Kobal, bl
289 – All RR/Cinémagence
290 – Finler, bm – Keystone, tr – Roger Corbeau, tl
291 – RR/Ciné-Plus, tl, mr – RR/Cinémagence, tm, ml, bm
292 – RR/Ciné-Plus, tr – Finler, br – Roger Corbeau, tl
293 – RR/Ciné-Plus, bl – RR/Cinémagence, bm – Finler, tl – Les Films du Carosse, tr
294 – RR/Ciné-Images, br, tl, ml – Carson, tr, bl, bm
295 – RR/Ciné-Images, mr, tm – Carson, tr, bm, br, tl, bl
297 – Carson, sp
298 – RR/Ciné-Plus, tl – RR/Cinémagence, tm, bl, bm – Finler, tr
299 – RR/Cinémagence, tl, bm – PH X/RR, br – Warners, courtesy Kobal, tr
300 – RR/Ciné-Plus, bl – RR/Cinémagence, tl, tm – Paramount, courtesy Kobal, br
301 – BFI, bm – Finler, tm
302 – BFI, br – Finler, bl, tl – Sygma/L'Illustration, tr
303 – RR/Ciné-Plus, tr, ml, br – RR/Kipa, tl
304 – RR/Ciné-Images, ml, bl – Carson, tl, tm, tr, bm, br
305 – RR/Ciné-Images, mr – Edgar Rice Burroughs 1994, tr – Carson, tl, bm, bl, bx, by, br
306 and 307 – All Finler
309 – Bubbles Inc., 1994, sp
310 – RR/Ciné-Images, tl – RR/Cinémagence, tm, br – Finler, bl
311 – RR/Cinémagence, tl – Finler, tr, bm
312 – Bubbles Inc., 1994, tm, br – RR/Cinémagence, bl – Finler, tr
313 – RR/Ciné-Images, bl – Finler, br – Disney, tm, tr
314 – RR/Ciné-Images, bl – Carson, tl, tm, tr, br
315 – RR/Ciné-Images, ml, mr, bm – Carson, tl, tm, tr, bl, br
317 – RR/Cinémagence, sp
318 – RR/Cinémagence, tr – Finler, bl, br
319 – BFI, bl – Finler, tl, tr – Warners, courtesy Kobal, br
320 – RR/Ciné-Images, tr – RR/Ciné-Plus, bl – RR/Cinémagence, br – RKO/Samuel Goldwyn, courtesy Kobal, tl
321 – RR/Ciné-Plus, br – RR/Cinémagence, tl, bl – Finler, tr
322 – RR/Ciné-Images, ml – MGM, courtesy/Kobal, br – Carson, tr, bl, bm, tl, tm
323 – RR/Ciné-Images, tl, ml – Carson, tr, by, br, bl, bx
325 – Carson, sp
326 – All Finler
327 – RR/Ciné-Plus, tl – RR/Cinémagence, bm – Finler, tr
328 – RR/Cinémagence, tl, tr – Finler, br – Warners, courtesy Kobal, bl
329 – BFI, tl, br – RR/Cinémagence, tr – Finler, ml
330 – RR/Ciné-Images, br, tl, tm, ml – Carson, tr, bl, bm
331 – RR/Ciné-Images, ml – Carson, tr, bl, bm, br, tl, tm
333 – Carson, sp
334 – RR/Cinémagence, br – Finler, tm, bl
335 – RR/Cinémagence, bm, br – Finler, tr – Carson, tl
336 – RR/Cinémagence, br – RR/Kharbine, tr – Finler, tl, ml
337 – BFI, bl – RR/Ciné-Plus, br – Finler, tl, tm
338 – Finler, bl – Carson, tl, br, tm, tr
339 – RR/Ciné-Images, tl – Carson, tr, bm, br, bl, tm
341 – Grant, sp
342 – BFI, bl – RR/Ciné-Plus, tl – RR/Cinémagence, tr – Finler, br
343 – BFI, tl, tr – RR/Cinémagence, bm
344 – BFI, tl – RR/Archives l'Avant-Scène, br – RR/Ciné-Plus, bm – RR/Coll. Larousse, tr – Finler, bl
345 – All Finler
346 – RR/Ciné-Images, tl, tr, mr, bl, br – Carson, ml, tm
347 – RR/Ciné-Images, mr, bl – Finler, br – Carson, tl, ml, tm, tr, bm
349 – RR/Ciné-Images, sp
350 – RR/Ciné-Plus, tm – Keystone, bl, br
351 – RR/Cinémagence, tl, br – Finler, tr, bl
352 – BFI, tl – RR/Cinémagence, tr, bl – Finler, br
353 – All Finler
354 – RR/Ciné-Images, ml, bl – Finler, br – Carson, tl, tm, tr, mr, bm
355 – RR/Ciné-Images, ml, bl – Finler, tl, br – Carson, tr
357 – Carson, sp
358 – BFI, tr – RR/Cinémagence, bm – Finler, tl
359 – BFI, bl, br – Finler, tm
360 – RR/Aero/Sipa Press, tl, tm – RR/Ciné-Plus, bl – RR/Cinémagence, br
361 – Denis Huisman, tm, tr – RR/Cinémagence, bl – RR/Kharbine, br – Roger Corbeau, mm
362 – RR/Ciné-Plus, bl – RR/Cinémagence, tl – RR/Cinémathèque de Prague, mr – RR/Sygma/L'Illustration, ml – Finler, br
363 – RR/Cinémagence, bm – Finler, tl, tr
364 – RR/Ciné-Images, bl, ml, tl, bm, br – Carson, tr
365 – RR/Ciné-Images, by, br, tm, ml, bl – Carson, tr, tl, bx
367 – Bubbles Inc., 1994, sp
368 – BFI, tl – Finler, tr, bm
369 – RR/Ciné-Plus, tr – RR/Cinémagence, tl, bl – Finler, bm
370 – RR/Cinémagence, tl, ml, br – Finler, tr – Sygma/L'Illustration, bl
371 – RR/Coll. André Marinie, mr – Finler, tm, bl
372 – BFI, tl – RR/Ciné-Plus, br, bl, bm – RR/Cinémagence, tr
373 – BFI, br – Finler, tm, bl
374 – RR/Ciné-Images, tr, br, bl – Finler, tl – Carson, ml, mm
375 – RR/Ciné-Images, by, br, ml, bm, tl, tm - Carson, tr, bm, tm
377 – RR/Ciné-Images, sp
378 – BFI, tr – RR/Ciné-Plus, tl – Photo RR/Ciné-Images, bm
379 – BFI, tl, br – RR/Cinémagence, bl – Finler, tr
380 – RR/Cinémagence, bl – RR/Kharbine, br – Finler, tl, tr
381 – RR/Cinémagence, mr – Finler, tl, bm
382 – RR/Ciné-Images, tr, bm, br, mt, mb – Finler, bl – Carson, tl, mm
383 – RR/Ciné-Images, tr, mr – Finler, bl, tm – Carson, tl, bm, br
385 – RR/Ciné-Images, sp
386 – RR/Cinémagence, tm, mr – Finler, bl, br
387 – BFI, mm – RR/Cinémagence, tr – Finler, tl, bl, br
388 – RR/Cinémagence, tr – Finler, tl, br – Novosti, bl
389 – RR/Cinémagence, ml, tr – RR/Kharbine, bl – Traverso, tl
390 – RR/Cinémagence, bl – Finler, tl, tr
391 – All Finler
392 – All RR/Ciné-Images
393 – RR/Ciné-Images, bl – Finler, tl – Carson, tr, bm, br, mm, ml
394 – Finler, mm
395 – Universal, courtesy Kobal, mm
397 – Carson, sp
398 – RR/Cinémagence, tl, bl – Finler, tr br
399 – BFI, bl – RR/Cinémagence, tr, mr – RR/Kharbine, br – Finler, tl
400 – BFI, tl – RR/Ciné-Plus, br, bl – RR/Kipa, bm – Finler, tr
401 – All Finler
402 – BFI, bm – RR/Kharbine, tl – Photofest, tr
403 – RR/Kharbine, tl, bm – Finler, tr
404 – RR/Ciné-Images, bl, tr, ml, mr – Carson, tl, bm, br
405 – RR/Ciné-Images, tm, mr – Carson, tr, tl, bm, br – Roger Corbeau, bl
407 – Carson, sp
408 – RR/Ciné-Images, tl – Finler, bl, br – Roger Corbeau, tm
409 – RR/Ciné-Plus, tl – Finler, bm – Photofest, tr
410 – BFI, tr – RR/Kharbine, tl – Finler, br, bl
411 – BFI, br – RR/Kharbine, bl – MGM, courtesy Kobal, tl, tr
412 – RR/Ciné-Images, bl, tm, tr, mr – Finler, br – Carson, bm
413 – RR/Ciné-Images, tm, tr, mr, bm, br – Estate of Marilyn Monroe, 1994, bl – Carson, tl
415 – Carson, sp
416 – BFI, bm – RR/Ciné-Plus, tr – Finler, tl – Léo Mirkine, tm
417 – Finler, br – MGM, courtesy Kobal, tl, tr
418 – 20th Century Fox, courtesy Kobal, tl – Franco Civirani, br – Robert Tomatis, bl – Stanley Kramer/UA, courtesy Kobal, tr
419 – BFI, bl, br – Bubbles Inc., 1994, tr, tl
420 – Finler, bl, tm – Carson, tl, br, tr
421 – RR/Ciné-Images, tr – R. Forster/R. Poutrel, bl – Carson, tl, br
423 – RR/Ciné-Plus, sp
424 – André Dino, bm – RR/Ciné-Plus, tr – Finler, tl
425 – BFI, tl – RR/Kharbine, tr – Finler, bl, br
426 – RR/Ciné-Plus, mm – RR/Coll. Larousse, bl, br – Keystone, tr – Lucienne Chevert, tl
427 – RR/Ciné-Plus, br – Finler, tm, bl
428 – RR/Ciné-Plus, tl – Finler, br – Photofest, bl
429 – Finler, tl, tr, mm – Sipa, br – Warners, courtesy Kobal, bl
430 – RR/Ciné-Images, tr, br – Finler, bl, mr – Carson, tl
431 – RR/Ciné-Images, br, ml – Carson, tr, tl, tm, bl, bm
433 – Carson, sp
434 – Finler, tr, bm – Marcel Bouguereau, tl
435 – BFI, tr – RR/Ciné-Plus, bm – RR/Cinémagence, tl – Finler, br
436 – RR/Ciné-Images, bl – RR/Cinémagence, tl – RR/Coll. Larousse, tr – RR/Kharbine, br
437 – RR/Ciné-Plus, bl, tm – Paramount, courtesy Kobal, br
438 – Cyril Stanburough, bm – RR/Ciné-Images, mm, tr, mr, ml, bl – Carson, tl, br
439 – Estate of Marilyn Monroe, 1994, bl – Finler, br – Carson, tl, tm, tr
441 – Carson, sp
442 – BFI, bl – Finler, tr, br – L. Mirkine/R. Joffres, tl
443 – Finler, bl, br – Raymond Bègue, tl – Serge Beauvarlet, tr
444 – RR/Kharbine, br – Estate of Marilyn Monroe, 1994, tl – Popperphoto, bl
445 – RR/Cinémagence, tl, bl – RR/DITE, tr – RR/Sunset/Kipa, br
446 – BFI, br – Finler, bl – MGM/Samuel Goldwyn, courtesy Kobal, tl
447 – Estate of Marilyn Monroe, 1994, bl - Raymond Voinquel, tr
448 – RR/Ciné-Images, bl, tm, tr, mr – Carson, tl
449 – RR/Ciné-Images, tr, bm, br – Finler, bl – Carson, tl, tm, ml, mm
451 – Carson, sp
452 – All Finler
453 – RR/Ciné-Plus, bl – RR/Kipa, ml – Finler, tr
454 – Fox, courtesy Kobal, bl – Finler, tr – MGM, courtesy Kobal, br – Warners, courtesy Kobal, tl
455 – Emmanuel Lowenthal, bm – Finler, tr, ml
456 – BFI, br – RR/Kipa, tm – Finler, ml, bl
457 – RR/Ciné-Plus, tl, br – Emmanuel Lowenthal, bl – Léo Mirkine, tr
458 – RR/Ciné-Images, tl, bl, mr – Léo Mirkine, mm – Carson, tm, tr, br
459 – BFI, mr – RR/Ciné-Images, bl – Carson, tl, tm, tr, bm, br
461 – Carson, sp
462 – RR/Cinémagence, mr – Keystone, bl - PH X/RR, tl
463 – BFI, tr – RR/Cinémagence, tl – Finler, bl – UA, courtesy Kobal, br
464 – BFI, br – RR/Cinémagence, tm – Finler, bl
465 – Fox, courtesy Kobal, mr – BFI, tl, bl
466 – BFI, bl – RR/Cinémagence, tm, tr – RR/Kharbine, tl – Finler, br
467 – BFI, br – RR/Ciné-Plus, tl – Finler, bl
468 – All Carson
469 – RR/Ciné-Images, mr – Finler, bl – Carson, tl, tm, tr, mm – Roger Corbeau, br
471 – Carson
472 – BFI, br – RR/Cinémagence, bl – Jean-Louis Castelli, tl, tm
473 – Henri Thibault, tr, tm – Finler, br – MGM, courtesy Kobal, M, bm
474 – André Dino, bl – RR/Cinémagence, tl, mr
475 – RR/Cinémagence, bm, tr – Paramount, courtesy Kobal, tl
476 – Finler, bl – Walter Limot, tl, tm, br
477 – Finler, bm – Vincent Russel, tl, tm
478 – RR/Ciné-Images, tl, bl, bm, br, tr – Carson, mr
479 – RR/Ciné-Images, tl – Finler, br – Carson, tr, ml, bl, bx, by
481 – Carson, sp
482 – Finler, tr, bm – Roger Corbeau, tl
483 – André Dino, bl – Finler, tm – PH X/RR, br
484 – André Dino, tm, tr – RR/Cinémagence, bl, bm – RR/Kipa, ml
485 – BFI, bl – Finler, tl, tr, br
486 – BFI, br – RR/Sunset/Kipa, tl – Finler, tr, bl
487 – RR/Cinémagence, tr – Finler, br, bl
488 and 489 – All Finler
490 – RR/Ciné-Images, tl, bl, tr – Finler, mr – Carson, bm, br
491 – BFI, bl – RR/Ciné-Images, bm, br – Estate of Marilyn Monroe, 1994, tr – Carson, tl
492 and 493 – All UA, courtesy Kobal
495 – Carson, sp
496 – RR/Cinémagence, tl – Henri Thibault, tr – Production Georges De Beauregard, bm – Raymond Cauchetier, br
497 – BFI, bm – RR/Cinémagence, tl – Finler, tr, mr
498 – RR/Cinémagence, tm – Finler, tl, bm
499 – Finler, tl, tr – Paramount, courtesy Kobal, bm
500 – Jean-Louis Castelli, br – Finler, ml, tr – UA, courtesy Kobal, bl
501 – Estate of Marilyn Monroe, 1994, tl, tm – Finler, bl, br
502 – RR/Ciné-Images, mm, bl – Finler, tm, tr – Carson, tl, br – Universal, courtesy Kobal mr
503 – RR/Ciné-Images, mm, mr – Finler, tr - Paramount, courtesy Kobal, bl – Carson, tl, br
505 – Carson, sp
506 – RR/Ciné-Plus, bl – Estate of Marilyn Monroe, 1994, tl – Finler, tr – Carson, br
507 – RR/Cinémagence, tr, bl, br – PH X/RR, tl
508 – All Finler
509 – BFI, tl, tr – Warners, courtesy Kobal, bm
510 – BFI, bm – RR/Cinémagence, tl, mr
511 – RR/Cinémagence, tl, bm – Finler, tr
512 – R/Ciné-Images, tl, tm, tr, bm, br – Production Georges De Beauregard, bl – Carson, mr
513 – RR/Ciné-Images, br, bl – Finler, ml - Carson, tr, tl, tm
515 – Carson, sp
516 – RR/Cinémagence, bl – Les Films du Carosse, tl – Les Films du Carosse/SEDIF, courtesy Kobal, tm – Production Georges De Beauregard, br
517, BFI, tl – RR/Coll. Pierre Lherminier, br – Finler, bl – Grant, tr
518 – BFI, bl – RR/Cinémagence, tr, br – RR/Kipa, tl
519 – Fox, courtesy Kobal, ml – Keystone, tr, mr
520 – RR/Cinémagence, tm, tr, br – RR/Kharbine, bl
521 – All Finler
522 – RR/Cinémagence, br, bl – RR/Kharbine, tr – Finler, tl
523 – BFI, bl – Finler, tl, tr
524 – RR/Ciné-Images, bl – Finler, br, tr, mr – Carson, tl – Grant, bm
525 – RR/Ciné-Images, bl, br, tm – Carson, tl, mr, tr
527 – Carson, sp
528 – RR/Cinémagence, tr, mr – Finler, tl – Production Georges De Beauregard, bl
529 – RR/Cinémagence, tl – RR/Kipa, tr – PH X/RR, ml – Photo RR/Ciné-Images, br
530 – RR/Kharbine, br – RR/Kipa, tr – Kobal, bl – Photo RR/Ciné-Images, tl
531 – BFI, br – RR/Cinémagence, bl – Finler, tm
532 – Finler, tl – Grant, tr – UA, courtesy Kobal, bm
533 – Finler, tl, bm – Photo RR/Cinémagence, tr
534 – RR/Ciné-Images, tl, ml, mr, br – MGM, courtesy Kobal, bm – Carson, tr, bl
535 – RR/Ciné-Images, tr, mr – Finler, bm – Carson, tl, br, bl
537 – Carson, sp
538 – RR/Cinémagence, tl – Jean-Louis Castelli, bm – Finler, tr
539 – RR/Ciné-Plus, tl – RR/Kharbine, bl – Les Films du Carosse, mr
540 – BFI, bl – RR/Cinémagence, tr, br – RR/Kharbine, tl
541 – RR/Cinémagence, tr – Finler, tm – Disney, bm
542 – RR/Cinémagence, tr – RR/Kipa, br – Warners, courtesy Kobal, tl, bl
543 – RR/Cinémagence, tl – RR/Kipa, tr, br – Finler, bl
544 – RR/Ciné-Images, tr, bl, bm, mm, br – Carson, tl, mr
545 – RR/Ciné-Images, br, tl – RR/Kipa, mm – Finler, bl – Carson, tr, ml

Picture Credits

547 – Carson, sp
548 – Claude Schwartz, mr – RR/Cinémagence, tl, tr – Finler, bm
549 – BFI, bl, tr – Finler, tl, br
550 – BFI, tr – RR/Ciné-Plus, ml – RR/Cinémagence, tl – Finler, bl, br
551 – RR/Cinémagence, bl – Georges Pierre, tr – Finler, br
552 – RR/Ciné-Images, bl, br, mr, tm – RR/Kipa, tr – Carson, tl
553 – RR/Kipa, tm – Finler, br, bl, tl – Carson, tr, mm, ml
555 – Carson, sp
556 – BFI, tr – RR/Kipa, br – Finler, ml
557 – BFI, tm – Pierre Zucca, bm
558 – RR/Ciné-Plus, br – RR/Cinémagence, tl, tm – Finler, bl
559 – RR/Cinémagence, br – RR/Kharbine, tr – Les Films du Carosse, tl, ml
560 – RR/Cinémagence, tr, mm, bm – RR/Kharbine, br
561 – RR/Cinémagence, bl, mr – RR/Coll. Abbas Fahdel, br – RR/Kipa, mm
562 – BFI, tr – RR/Ciné-Images, mm, bl – Finler, br – Carson, tl, tm, mr
563 – BFI, mm, br – RR/Ciné-Images, bl – Finler, tr – Carson, tl, tm, mr
565 – Carson, sp
566 – RR/Ciné-Plus, tl – Les Films du Losange, br
567 – BFI, br – RR/Ciné-Plus, tr – RR/Cinémagence, tl – Finler, bl
568 – RR/Kharbine, tr – RR/Kipa, tm – Finler, bm
569 – RR/Ciné-Plus, bm, br – Finler, tr – Warners/Seven Arts, courtesy Kobal, tl
570 – BFI, tr, bl – RR/Cinémagence, tl – Warners, courtesy Kobal, br
571 – RR/Archives Gaumont, tr – RR/Cinémagence, br, bl – Finler, tl
572 – RR/Ciné-Images, tl, mr, br – Finler, bm – Carson, bl
573 – Columbia, courtesy Kobal, ml – RR/Ciné-Images, tr – Finler, tl, bl – Carson, br
575 – Carson, sp
576 – Fox, courtesy Kobal, tm – BFI, ml – Finler, br
577 – All RR/Ciné-Plus
578 – BFI, tl, bl – Sygma, tr – U. Josephsson, Cahier du Cinéma, br
579 – RR/Christophe L., tr – RR/Sunset/Kipa, bm -Sygma, tl
580 – RR/Cinémagence, tr – RR/Kipa, bl – Finler, br – UA, courtesy Kobal, tl
581 – BFI, bl – Kobal, mr – Carson, br – Warners, courtesy Kobal, tl
582 – Columbia, courtesy Kobal, bl – RR/Ciné-Images, tr – Finler, br – Carson, tl, mm, mr
583 – RR/Ciné-Images, bl, br, mm, mr, tr – Carson, tl
585 – Carson, sp
586 – RR/Cinémagence, bl – Finler, br – Paramount, courtesy Kobal, tl, tr
587 – RR/Cinémagence, tr, mr – RR/Kipa, tl – Finler, bm
588 – RR/Ciné-Images, tl – RR/Kipa, tr – Pegaso-Italnoleggio-Praesidens-Eichberg, courtesy Kobal, bl, bm – Warners/Seven Arts, courtesy Kobal, br
589 – RR/Ciné-Plus, bl – RR/Cinémagence, br – Finler, tm, tr – MGM, courtesy Kobal, tl
590 – Fox, courtesy Kobal, tl – Finler, mr, bl – Grant, bm
591 – RR/Ciné-Plus, tl – RR/Cinémagence, tm – Finler, br
592 – RR/Ciné-Images, tr, mr, bl, br – Finler, tl – Carson, ml, mm
593 – RR/Ciné-Images, tr, mr, ml – Finler, br, bl – Carson, tl
594 – Warners, courtesy Kobal, mm
595 – Finler, mm
597 – Carson, sp
598 – RR/Ciné-Plus, bm – RR/Cinémagence, tl, tr, bl – Georges Pierre/Sygma, tm
599 – Finler, bl, br – Pierre Zucca, tl, tm
600 – RR/Ciné-Plus, tl – RR/Kipa, br – Finler, tr, mr, bl
601 – RR/Kipa, tl, tm – Finler, bl, mr
602 – Fox, courtesy Kobal, bl – RR/Coll. Abbas Fahdel, br – Finler, tr – Paramount/Filmways, courtesy Kobal, tl
603 – RR/Cinémagence, bl – RR/Kipa, tl – Finler, tr, br
604 – BFI, bl – RR/Ciné-Images, tl, mr – Finler, ml, tm, tr, br
605 – RR/Ciné-Images, br – Carson, tr, tl, tm – Grant, bl
607 – Carson, sp
608 – RR/Cinémagence, ml, mr – Finler, tl, tr
609 – RR/Cinémagence, tm – RR/Kipa, br – Warners, courtesy Kobal, bl
610 – All Finler
611 – Avco Embassy, courtesy Kobal, tl – Finler, tr, bl, br
612 – BFI, bl – RR/Cinémagence, tl – Etienne George, tr – Finler, br
613 – RR/Cinémagence, bl – Finler, tl, br – Paramount, courtesy Kobal, tr
614 – RR/Ciné-Images, br – Finler, bl, tr, mr – Carson, tl
615 – RR/Ciné-Images, mr, ml, mm, bl – Etienne George/Sygma, tr – Carson, tl, br
617 – Carson, sp
618 – BFI, br – RR/Cinémagence, tm – Finler, bl
619 – RR/Cinémagence, tm, tr, bl – RR/Kharbine, bm
620 – Bubbles Inc., 1994, tm – RR/Cinémagence, mm, br – RR/Kipa, ml
621 – BFI, br – RR/Kharbine, tr – Finler, tl, bl
622 – RR/Ciné-Images, bl, ml, my – RR/Kipa, tr – Finler, br, mx, tl – Carson, mr
623 – RR/Ciné-Images, bl, tl, tr, mm – Finler, ml, mr, br
625 – Carson, sp
626 – RR/Ciné-Plus, tl, bm – RR/Kipa, tr
627 – RR/Ciné-Plus, ml – RR/Cinémagence, tm – RR/Kipa, tr – Finler, br
628 – RR/Cinémagence, tr – RR/Kipa, tl, mm – Keystone, br – Topor, bl
629 – RR/Kipa, bl – Finler, tl – Pierre Zucca, tr, br
630 – RR/Cinémagence, br – Finler, ml, tr, tl
631 – RR/Ciné-Plus, tl – RR/Kipa, bl – Finler, tm, tr, br
632 – Concord/Warners, courtesy Kobal, mr – RR/Ciné-Images, br – RR/Kipa, bl – Finler, tl, tm, tr – Topor, ml
633 – BFI, ml – RR/Ciné-Images, tm, tr, mr, br, bl – Finler, tl
635 – Carson, sp
636 – Etienne George, tl – Finler, tr, br – Pierre Zucca, bl
637 – RR/Ciné-Plus, tl, tm – RR/Kipa, br – Julian Wasser/Gamma, bm – Warners, courtesy Kobal, bl
638 – RR/Ciné-Plus, bl, br – RR/Cinémagence, tl, tr
639 – RR/Cinémagence, bl – RR/Coll. Abbas Fahdel, br – Finler, tl, tr
640 – RR/Ciné-Plus, ml, mm, bm – RR/Cinémagence, tr – RR/Kipa, tl, br
641 – RR/Cinémagence, br – Finler, tr, bl
642 – RR/Ciné-Images, tl, br, bl, mr – Finler, ml, tr – Pierre Zucca, tm
643 – RR/Ciné-Images, tm, tr, bl, ml – Finler, br, mr, tl
645 -Carson, sp
646 – RR/Cinémagence, tr, br – Finler, tl, bl
647 – RR/Cinémagence, br – RR/Kipa, ml, bl – Finler, tm
648 – BFI, bl – Finler, tl, tr, bm, br
649 – RR/Cinémagence, tl – Finler, tr – Les Films du Carosse, bm, br
650 – RR/Ciné-Plus, bl – RR/Cinémagence, tm, br – Georges Pierre/Sygma, bm – Sygma, tr
651 – RR/Cinémagence, bm, br – Finler, tl, tr, bl
652 – RR/Ciné-Images, ml, bl, bm, br, tl – Finler, tr, mr
653 – RR/Ciné-Images, mr, bl, br, tl – Finler ml, mm, tm, tr
655 – Carson, sp
656 – RR/Archives Gaumont, tm, tr – RR/Cinémagence, bl – Finler, br
657 – Claude Schwartz, br – RR/Cinémagence, ml – Georges Pierre/Sygma, tl – Finler, tr
658 – RR/Ciné-Images, tl – RR/Cinémagence, tr, bl
659 – RR/Cinémagence, tl – Finler, tr, bm
660 – James Andanson/Sygma, tr – Finler, tl, bl, br
661 – RR/Ciné-Plus, br – RR/Cinémagence, bl, tr – Carson, tl
662 – BFI, tl – RR/Ciné-Images, mr, ml, bl – RR/Kipa, tr – Finler, tm, br – Carson, mm
663 – RR/Ciné-Images, tr, ml, bl, br – Finler, tm, mr, tl
665 – Carson, sp
666 – RR/Cinémagence, bl – RR/Kipa, tl, tr
667 – RR/Cinémagence, tr – RR/Kipa, tl, bm
668 – RR/Kipa, br – Finler, tl, tm, bl
669 – RR/Ciné-Plus, tr – RR/Kipa, tl – Sunshine/Sipa-Press, bm
670 – All Finler
671 – D. Hennings/Sygma, bm – James Andanson/Sygma, br – Finler, tr, bl
672 – RR/Ciné-Images, br, mm – RR/Kipa, bl – Finler, ml, tl – Carson, tr
673 – BFI, br, tl – RR/Ciné-Images, bl, tm – RR/Kipa, mr – Eva Sereny/Sygma, tr – Finler, ml
675 – Carson, sp
676 – RR/Ciné-Plus, tl – RR/Cinémagence, tr – Finler, br – UA, courtesy Kobal, bl
677 – RR/Kipa, bl – Finler, tm – Universal, courtesy Kobal, br
678 – Finler, tm, bl, br – Grant, tr
679 – RR/Ciné-Plus, bl – Falcon International, courtesy Kobal, tl – Finler, tr
680 – RR/Kipa, tr, ml – Finler, tl, tm, mr, bl, br – Roger Corbeau, mm
681 – RR/Ciné-Images, tr, br – Finler, tl, ml, mr, bl
683 – Carson, sp
684 – RR/Kipa, tl, tr – Finler, bm
685 – Finler, tr, bl – Moune Jamet/Sygma, br – T. Korody/Sygma, tl, ml
686 – RR/Ciné-Plus, tr, br – RR/Cinémagence, tl – RR/Kipa, ml, tm
687 – RR/Kipa, tl, bl – Finler, br – N.S.W. Film Corp., courtesy Kobal, mr
688 – RR/Cinémagence, tm, mr, bl, bm – RR/Kipa, tr – Eva Sereny/Sygma, ml
689 – C. Simonpietri/Sygma, tr – RR/Archives Gaumont, bm – Finler, ml
690 – Finler, br – Lacombe/Sygma, bl – Schapiro/Sygma, tl – UA, courtesy Kobal, tr
691 – Finler, mm
692 – Finler, bl, br, tr, mr – Carson, tl
693 – BFI, tr – Finler, bl, bm, br, mr – Carson, tl
694 – Fox, courtesy Kobal, mm
695 – RENN/Films AZ/RAIZ/AMLF, courtesy Kobal, mm
697 – Carson, sp
698 – All Finler
699 – Deborah Beer/Sygma, tl – RR/Cinémagence, tr – RR/Kipa, bl – Sygma, mr, br
700 – RR/Ciné-Plus, br – RR/Kipa, tl, bl, bm, tr
701 – C. Simonpietri/Sygma, bl – Finler, tl, br
702 – RR/Kipa, br – Finler, tm, tr, bl
703 – RR/Cinémagence, br – Finler, tl, tr – L. De Raemy/Sygma, bl
704 – BFI, bl – RR/Archives Gaumont, bm – RR/Kipa, tl, br – Paul Grimault, ml – Carson, tr
705 – courtesy CIBY, ml – Finler, tl, mm, br – Carson, tr, bl, bm
707 – Carson, sp
708 – Dominique Le Strat, br – RR/Cinémagence, tr – RR/Kipa, tm – Morgan Renard/Sygma, bl
709 – RR/Cinémagence, tl, tr, bm – Finler, bl – John Bryson/Sygma, br
710 – RR/Kipa, ml – G. Ranciman/Sygma, tm – Sygma/Lucas Production, br
711 – All Finler
712 – Finler, tl, bl, bm – Paramount, courtesy Kobal, tr
713 – J.P. Naffony/Sygma, br – Finler, tr – Carson, bl
714 – RR/Ciné-Images, tx, tl – Finler, bl, ty, tr, ml – Carson, br
715 – RR/Ciné-Images, bl – Finler, br, ml, tr – K. Heyman/Sygma, tm – Carson, tl
717 – Carson, sp
718 – Dominique Le Strat, br – RR/Kipa, tl, tm – Finler, bl
719 – RR/Kipa, tr, ml – Finler, bm, br
720 – RR/Kipa, tm, tr – Finler, bl, br – Sygma, tl
721 – RR/Ciné-Plus, tm – Finler, bl, br – Sygma, tr
722 – RR/Kipa, ml – Finler, tr, bl, br
723 – RR/Kipa, tr – Finler, tl, br, bl
724 – BFI, bl – RR/Ciné-Images, mm – RR/Kipa, tr, mr – Finler, br – Carson, tl
725 – BFI, mr – R/Kipa, tr – Finler, bl, bm – Carson, tl, br
727 – Carson, sp
728 – G. Schachmes/Sygma, tr – Finler, tl – Sygma, bl, br
729 – Etienne George/Sygma, bl – Finler, tl, tm, br
730 – RR/Kipa, tl, tm – Finler, bm – Carson, tr
731 – BFI, br – RR/Kipa, tr, bl – Sygma, tl
732 and 733 – All Finler
734 – BFI, ml – RR/Ciné-Images, mr – RR/Kipa, br – Finler, bl – Carson, tl, tx, ty, tr
735 – BFI, mr – RR/Ciné-Images, bl – RR/Kipa, tl, br – Finler, bm, ml – Carson, tr
737 – Carson, sp
738 – Georges Pierre/Sygma, bm – Finler, tl – William Karel/Sygma, tr
739 – RR/Cinémagence, tm – RR/Kipa, tl – Finler, bl, br – Jonathan Levine/Sygma, tr
740 – RR/Kipa, bl – Finler, tl, tr, br
741 – Etienne George/Sygma, bl – John Bryson/Sygma, mm – Sygma, tm, br
742 – Finler, ml, tr, bl – Les Films du Carosse, br
743 – All Finler
744 – RR/Ciné-Images, tr – Finler, bl, mr – Carson, tl, bm, br
745 – Finler, tl, tm, ml – Carson, tr, br, bl
747 – Carson, sp
748 – 20th Century-Fox Film, bl – Finler, tl, tr – Paramount, courtesy Kobal, ml
749 – Etienne George/Sygma, bm – Finler, tr – Orion, courtesy Kobal, tl – TriStar, courtesy Kobal, tm – William Karel/Sygma, bl
750 – RR/Kipa, bl, ml – Finler, tr – Mafilm/Mokep/ZDF, courtesy Kobal, tl
751 – Finler, bl, bm – Matsumo/Sygma, tm – Warners, courtesy Kobal, br
752 – Amblin/Universal, courtesy Kobal, bl – Finler, tl, tr, br
753 – Finler, tl, tm, tr – Svensk Filmindistri/AB Filmteknik, courtesy Kobal, br – Working Title/Channel 4, courtesy Kobal, bl
754 – Andy Schwartz/Sygma, ml – BFI, mr – RR/Ciné-Images, tl – RR/Kipa, tm, bl – Finler, tr, br
755 – RR/Ciné-Images, tr – Finler, bm, tl, mr, ml – Carson, br, bl
757 – Carson, sp
758 – Fabian Cevalo/Sygma, tl, tm – Finler, mr, bl – Merchant-Ivory/Goldcrest, courtesy Kobal, br
759 – Fox, courtesy Kobal, tl – Island Alive, courtesy Kobal, tr – J. Jacques Beineix/Gaumont, bm, br – Finler, tm
760 – All Finler
761 – Island Films, courtesy Kobal, br – Jérôme Minet/Kipa, tr – Finler, bl – Les Films du Losange, tm
762 – De Laurentiis, courtesy Kobal, tl – Finler, bl, tr, br
763 – RR/Cinémagence, br – Finler, tl, bl – Richard Melloul/Sygma, tr
764 – David James/Sygma, tm – RR/Ciné-Images, tr – RR/Kipa, br – Jérôme Minet/Kipa, mr – Finler, bl – Carson, tl
765 – Bernard Fau/Sipa Press, tr – Cannon, courtesy Kobal, bm – De Laurentiis, courtesy Kobal, bl – RR/Kipa, br – Etienne George/Sygma, mr – Carson, tl
767 – Carson, sp
768 – RR/Kipa, tm, bm, br – Finler, bl
769 – BFI, bl – RR/Kipa, tr – E. Lari/Sygma, mr – Finler, br – S. Legrand/Kipa, tm
770 – RR/Kipa, br – Finler, tl, bl – RENN/Films AZ/RAIZ/AMLF, courtesy Kobal, tr
771 – Columbia, courtesy Kobal, bl – Jeanne L. Bulliard/Sygma, tr – Finler, br – Vestron, courtesy Kobal, tl
772 – Columbia, courtesy Kobal, mr – RR/Kipa, ml – Fabian/Sygma, bm – Finler, mm, bl, br
773 – RR/Kipa, bl – Finler, tl, tr, br
774 – Fox, courtesy Kobal, tr – Finler, ml, mm – Carson, br, tl, tm, bl
775 – RR/Kipa, ml – Finler, tr, tl – Marcia Reed/Sygma, bl – Carson, br
777 – Carson, sp
778 – Finler, tr – Moune Jamet/Sygma, tl – Sygma, bm, br, bl
779 – RR/Ciné-Images, br – Finler, bl – Patrick Camboulive, tm
780 – Fox, courtesy Kobal, br – BFI, tr – RR/Kipa, mr – Finler, tl, ml, bl
781 – Fox, courtesy Kobal, tl – RR/Ciné-Images, tr – Finler, bl – Paramount, courtesy Kobal, mr
782 – Benoît Barbier/Sygma bl – Finler, tr – Orion, courtesy Kobal, br – Sygma, tl
783 – RR/Kipa, br – Finler, bl – UA, courtesy Kobal, tl – Warners, courtesy Kobal, tr
784 – BFI, bl – RR/Ciné-Images, tr, bm – Finler, mr – Carson, tl, br – Valérie Blier/Sygma, tm
785 – RR/Kipa, bl, bm, ml – Carson, tl, tx, ty, tr – Sygma, br – Warners, courtesy Kobal, mr
787 – Carson, sp
788 – El Desea/Lauren, courtesy Kobal, ml – Finler, tl, tr, br
789 – RR/Kipa, tr – Gordon/Universal, courtesy Kobal, bl – Lucasfilm Ltd/Paramount, courtesy Kobal, br – Orion, courtesy Kobal, ml – Warners, courtesy Kobal, tl
790 – RR/Kipa, tm, br – Finler, tr – Outlaw, courtesy Kobal, bl – Valérie Blier/Sygma, tl
791 – Finler, tl, tr, br – Columbia TriStar, courtesy Kobal, bl
792 – Finler, tl, bl, bm – Muray Close/Sygma, br – Renaissance Films/BBC/Curzon Films, courtesy Kobal, tr
793 – Finler, bl – Kobal, tr
794 – David Doyle, bl – Finler, br, tl, tm, ml – Carson, tr
795 – Cinemarque-New World, courtesy Kobal, bl – courtesy Mainline Pictures, tr – Finler, tm, tl, mr, ml – Richard Melloul/Sygma, br
796 – Finler, mr – Paramount, courtesy Kobal, mm
797 – First Independent, mm
799 – Carson, sp
800 – Jeanne L. Bulliard/Sygma, bl – Paramount, courtesy Kobal, mm – Warners, courtesy Kobal, br
801 – Artificial Eye, br – Benoît Barbier/Sygma, bm – Finler, tl – Patrick Camboulive/Sygma, bl – Touchstone/Warners, courtesy Kobal, tr
802 – RR/Kipa, tm – Finler, bl, br – MO/Kipa, tl
803 – Carolco/TriStar, courtesy Kobal, bl – Finler, br – Nikolai Ejevski, tm – Sygma, tr
804 – Columbia, courtesy Kobal, br – Hollywood Pictures/Amblin, courtesy Kobal, bl – Finler, tr – Warners, courtesy Kobal, tl
805 – RR/Ciné-Images, br – Jérôme Prébois/Sygma, bl – Paramount, courtesy Kobal, tl
806 – RR/Kipa, bm – Finler, tm, bl, br – Orion, courtesy Kobal, tr
807 – Finler, mm
808 – David Doyle, bl – Electric Pictures, bm – Film workshop, courtesy Kobal, tr – Finler, tm – Carson, tl, br – Vestron/MGM/UA, courtesy Kobal, mr
809 – courtesy Electric Pictures, tr – courtesy Mainline Pictures, bm – RR/Kipa, bl – Erre Prods/Sovereign Pictures/Reteitalia, courtesy Kobal, bl – Finler, mr – Carson, tl
811 – Carson, sp
812 – Cineplex Odeon, courtesy Kobal, bl – RR/Kipa, tl – Finler, br – Paramount, courtesy Kobal, tr
813 – RR/Kipa, tl – E.D.R. Pressman/Shochiku Fuji/Sovereign Pictures, courtesy Kobal, mm – James Andanson/Sygma, br – P. Ramey/Sygma, bl – Carson, tr
814 – CEH, br – David Doyle, bl – RR/Kipa, tr – Finler, tl
815 – CEH, br – RR/Kipa, tr – Reitalia/Scena Film, courtesy Kobal, bl – Warners, courtesy Kobal, tl
816 – BBC Films, courtesy Kobal, tl – Moune Jamet/Sygma, bl, bm – Vivid/Canal Plus/British Screen, courtesy Kobal, tr, br
817 – CEH, tr – Electric Pictures, tl – Finler, bl – Luc Roux/Sygma, br – Sygma, ml
818 – Benoît Barbier/Sygma, tl – J. Jacques Beineix/Sygma, bl – Disney, tr, br
819 – Columbia, courtesy Kobal, bl – Finler, br – Universal, courtesy Kobal, tl – Warners, courtesy Kobal, tr
820 – CEH, bl – David Doyle, br, ml – RR/Kipa, tl – Finler, mm – Carson, tr
821 – BFI, bl – courtesy Artificial Eye, mr – De Laurentiis/Propaganda/Boy Toy, courtesy Kobal, tl – Finler, br – Carson, tr, tm – Warners, courtesy Kobal, ml
823 – Photofest, sp
824 – CEH, tr – David Doyle, br – RR/Kipa, bl -Lux Roux/Sygma, tl
825 – David Doyle, tl – RR/Kipa, tr – Jean Marie Leroy/Sygma, mm – Patrick Chauvel/Sygma, bm
826 – Finler, bl – Sygma, tl – TriStar, courtesy Kobal, tr – Warners, courtesy Kobal, br
827 – 20th Century-Fox/Morgan Creek, courtesy Kobal, bl – CEH, tm, br

828 – Artificial Eye, bl – CEH, tr, tl – Finler, br

829 – Carolco/Canal Plus/RCS Video, courtesy Kobal, by, br – CEH, tr – Electric Pictures, bl – Finler, bx – Disney, tl

830 – courtesy Metro Tartan Pictures, mr – Finler, bl – Paramount, courtesy Kobal, br – Carson, tl, tm, tr

831 – CEH, ml, bl – courtesy Artificial Eye, tr – courtesy Electric Pictures, mr – David Doyle, tm – Carson, tl – Warners, br

833 – Carson, sp

834 – CEH, br – Finler, tr – Los Hooligans/Columbia, courtesy Kobal, tl – Sipa, mm – Warners/Regency/Canal Plus, courtesy Kobal, bl

835 – Fox, courtesy Kobal, ml – CEH, tl, bm, bl – courtesy Ent. Film Dist., br – courtesy Metro Tartan Pictures, tr

836 – Artificial Eye, tr – CEH, br, bl – Ent. Film Dist., tm – Film 4 Int/British Screen/Thin Man Prods, courtesy Kobal, tl

837 – Arau/Cinevista/Aviacsa, courtesy Kobal, tl – Buena Vista/Hollywood, courtesy Kobal, br – CEH, tr, br

838 – Artificial Eye, tl, tm – CEH, bl, bm – RR/Sygma-Finler, tr, br

839 – courtesy Artificial Eye, br – courtesy Electric Pictures, bl – Finler, tl – Silver Pix/Warners, courtesy Kobal, tr

840 – Merchant-Ivory/Columbia, courtesy Kobal, bm – Sipa, tl, tx, ty, tr

841 – courtesy © TriStar Pictures, bl – courtesy © Touchstone Pictures, br – David Doyle, tl, tr

842 – courtesy First Independent Films, tr – courtesy ICA Projects, br – Finler, bl, mr – Metro Tartan Pictures, tm – Carson, tl

843 – CEH, tm – Anita Weber/Sipa Press, tr – courtesy Arrow Films, bm – courtesy First Independent Films, mr – courtesy ICA Projects, br – Finler, bl – Carson, tl

845 – Carson, sp

846 – CEH, tl – Columbia, courtesy Kobal, bl – Sipa, br – Universal, courtesy Kobal, tr

847 – CEH, tr, tl – David Doyle, tm – Finler, bl – Photofest, br

848 – Artificial Eye, bm – Ent. Film Dist., tl, tr – Photofest, bl, br

849 – CEH, tm, bm – courtesy © CIBY, tl – Finler, bl – Photofest, mr

850 – Disney, tl – courtesy © Hollywood pictures, tr – courtesy Polygram Filmed Entertainment (UK), tl – Photofest, bl, bm, br

851 – Universal, courtesy Kobal, ml – courtesy Polygram Filmed Entertainment (UK), tl – Sygma, bl – © Miramax, courtesy McDonald & Rutter, tr

852 – courtesy Polygram Filmed Entertainment (UK), tl – Ent. Film Dist., br – Photofest, ml – Carson, tm, tr – courtesy Ent. Film Dist., mr – courtesy Metro Tartan Pictures, bl

853 – courtesy © Columbia, tl – Carson, tm, tr, mm – Photofest, mr, bl –

courtesy Metro Tartan Pictures, br – courtesy Polygram Filmed Entertainment, ml

855 – Carson, sp

856 – courtesy McDonald & Rutter, bl – Geffen Pictures, courtesy Kobal, tm – Sipa Press, tr – courtesy © TriStar Pictures, br

857 – courtesy © First Independent Films, t – Photofest, br – © Columbia Pictures, courtesy Kobal, bl

858 – courtesy Kobal, tl – courtesy McDonald & Rutter, bm – courtesy Electric Pictures, br – courtesy Gala Film Distributors, bl – © Miramax Films, tr

859 – © Universal, courtesy Kobal, tl – © Artificial Eye, courtesy Kobal, tr – © Paramount Pictures, courtesy Kobal, bl – Kobal, br

860 – © Paramount Pictures, courtesy Kobal, tl – Tom Collins/UA, courtesy Kobal, mr – Parallax, courtesy Kobal, bl – Universal, courtesy Kobal, br

861 – Corbis/Everett, tl – Polygram/Pictorial Press, tr – U/A, courtesy Kobal, bl – courtesy Kobal, br

862 – © Paramount, courtesy Kobal, tr – Lorey Sebastian/© Miramax, courtesy Kobal, tx – JetTone, courtesy Kobal, br – courtesy Kobal, bl – CIBY 2000, courtesy Kobal, br – © Cinergi/Buena Vista, courtesy Kobal, y

863 – © Castle Rock Entertainment, courtesy Kobal, tl – courtesy Moviestore Collection, tr – Corbis/Everett, x –

Brian Hamill/© Miramax, courtesy Kobal, x – Zenitl, courtesy Kobal, x – BBC/Electric/Polygram, courtesy Kobal, bl – Rank, courtesy Kobal, bl – Rank, courtesy Kobal, br

864 – Carolco, courtesy Kobal, bl – Universal, courtesy Kobal, tr – Warners, courtesy Kobal, br

865 – Carolco, courtesy Kobal, t – First Independent, bl – Finler, br

867 – Courtesy Kobal, sp

868 – Courtesy Artificial Eye, t – Rolf Konow/Castle Rock Ent., courtesy Kobal, bm

869 – © Phillip Caruso/Universal, courtesy Kobal, tl– Paramount, courtesy Kobal, tr – courtesy Arthur Sheriff PR, bl – Polygram, courtesy Foresight, x, mx, br

870 – CIBY 2000, courtesy Kobal, tl – Zentropa, courtesy Kobal, x – Mayfair courtesy Kobal, bl – Fox, courtesy Kobal tr – Alan Pappe, Castle Rock Ent., courtesy Kobal, br

871 – Claudette Barius, Fox, courtesy Kobal, tl – WB/Amblin, courtesy Kobal, y Hollywood Pictures, courtesy Kobal, tr – Polygram/Pictorial, bl – Universal, courtesy Kobal, bl

872 – Andy Schwartz, Paramount, courtesy Kobal, m – Hollywood Pictures, courtesy Kobal, tr – Sidney Baldwin, WB/Monarchy, courtesy Kobal, bl – Sophie Baker, Miramax/Film Four, courtesy Kobal, br

873 – Geffen/WB, courtesy Kobal, tl – courtesy Yemeyah Communications, Michael Tackett, Polygram, bl – Kobal, tr – Profegi/Cipra/CCM, courtesy Kobal, br

874 – Illusion/Cinergi, courtesy Kobal, tl – Columbia/Tristar, courtesy Kobal, tr – New Line, courtesy Kobal, bl – Columbia/Tristar, courtesy Kobal, x – Corbis/Everett, br

874 – David Appleby, Miramax, courtesy Kobal, tl – David Appleby, Miramax, courtesy Kobal, tr – Artificial Eye, courtesy Kobal, x – Monarchy/Regency Ent., courtesy Kobal, y – Kobal, bl – Alex Bailey/Fine Line, courtesy Kobal, br

877 – Courtesy Buena Vista, sp

878 – Momemtum Films, courtesy Kobal, tl, tr – Touchstone Pictures, courtesy imagenet, bl – Columbia/Tristar, courtesy McDonald & Rutter, br

879 – Barry Wechter, Miramax, courtesy Kobal, tl – Phil Bray, Miramax, courtesy Corbett and Keene, tr – Brennan Linsley, Polygram, courtesy McDonald & Rutter, bl – Eva Sereny, LucasFilm, courtesy Kobal, br

000 – LucasFilm/Fox, courtesy Kobal, tl, tl – Polygram, courtesy McDonald & Rutter, bl – Guild Pathé Cinema, courtesy McDonald & Rutter, br

881 – Columbia/Tristar, courtesy Kobal, tl – Phil Bray, Miramax, courtesy Corbett and Keene, tr – Momentum, courtesy Kobal, bl – courtesy Yemeyah Communications, Michael Tackett, Polygram, br

Jacket Credits: FC = Front Cover; BC = Back Cover; S = Spine

All Action: *The English Patient* 1996; Miramax; FC cl.

Joel Finler Collection: *Gentlemen Prefer Blondes* 1947; 20th Century Fox; FC bc. *Superman* 1978; Warner Brothers; FC c.

Kobal Collection: *Dirty Harry* 1971; Warner Brothers/Malpaso; BC cl. *Doctor No* 1962; United Artists/Eon; FC br. *Gone With The Wind* 1939; Selznick/MGM; BC cr, S t. *Guys And Dolls* 1955; MGM; FC bl. *Independence Day* 1996; 20th Century Fox; BC bl. *The Kid* 1921; First National/Charles Chaplin;FC c. *King Kong* 1933; RKO; BC tl. *The Mask* 1994; New Line/Dark Horse; BC br. *Pulp Fiction* 1994; Miramax/Buena Vista; BC tr. *The Searchers* 1956; Warner Brothers; FC cb. *Speed* 1994; 20th Century Fox; FC bl.

Pictorial Press: *My Fair Lady* 1964; CBS/Warner Brothers; FC br.